Rhetorical Dimensions in Media
A Critical Casebook
Revised Printing

Edited by

Martin J. Medhurst
University of California, Davis

Thomas W. Benson
The Pennsylvania State University

**KENDALL/HUNT
PUBLISHING COMPANY**
Dubuque, Iowa

B   404067   02

TO KENNETH BURKE

"The main ideal of criticism, as I conceive it, is to use all that is there to use."

The Philosophy of Literary Form (1941)

Contents

Preface

Rhetorical studies have been an important part of humanity's education since before the time of Plato and Aristotle. To the ancient Greeks and Romans, rhetoric was a vitally important subject for study and contemplation because it formed the basis for mankind's ability to live in society. With rhetoric—*the attempt by one person or group to influence another through strategically selected and stylized speech*—a society could perpetuate itself, debate its internal problems, and decide which norms and values it would follow without resorting to violence. Persuasive speech was seen as a mechanism by which people could reason together, present their ideas for discussion, and seek to win the assent of those responsible for making social, cultural, and political decisions.

Today rhetorical studies are no less important. Human speech is still the primary mechanism by which people in society seek to influence one another. The politician, evangelist, educator, attorney, and businessperson all have audiences to which they address speech designed to elicit a certain sort of response. Even in everyday conversation all of us—sometimes consciously, sometimes unconsciously—structure the messages we deliver to achieve a particular effect. The study of how people chose *what to say* in a given situation, *how to arrange or order* their thoughts, *select the specific terminology* to employ, and decide precisely *how they are going to deliver their message* is the central focus of rhetorical studies.

As long as face-to-face human speech was the primary way to convey complex messages, the domain of rhetoric was generally limited to speech and writing. The orator or writer learned how to discover ideas, how best to arrange them to achieve a particular effect on the hearer, how to clothe the discourse in the appropriate language, and how to use the voice and gestures to convey the message to the audience. The platform oration became the staple of oral persuasion for over 2300 years—from the Greek city-states where democracy was born to 20th century America where it continues to thrive.

But the 20th century has brought many changes in communication. No longer is platform oratory the primary means of exchanging important information. Today we are bombarded by messages from radio, television, film, newspapers, magazines, and a host of other media which bring with them a "rhetoric" all their own. Just as the linguistic capacities of the ancient rhetoricians determined, to a large degree, how their discourses were formed, so today the capacities of the different media present rhetorical opportunities and choices, some unique to themselves, and some shared with public speech and other media\ It is important that we learn more about these new "languages" as some have called them, if we are to be able fully to understand and appreciate the messages they bring.

This collection of critical essays is an attempt to help students learn more about how the languages of media function. Ten different media are explored: television, radio, film, graphic art, public letters, music, popular magazines, literature, political action, and architecture. Each has some characteristics in common, yet each is different with respect to how rhetorical appeals are structured and presented to the audience. [The authors represented in this volume each explore a particular artifact—a television program, film, novel—for the purpose of suggesting not only how one might better understand the persuasive appeal of that one work, but also how other works of the same type might be evaluated.]

The introductory essay which follows is an attempt to place rhetorical criticism of media artifacts into the larger debate over the nature, scope, and functions of rhetoric and poetic. By examining the theoretical positions which rhetorical critics have held during the twentieth century, the reader will be better able to appreciate and evaluate the contributions made by each of the authors represented in this anthology. As the only collection of its type, *Rhetorical Dimensions in Media: A Critical Casebook* owes much to its theoretical and generic predecessors, including Edward P. J. Corbett's *Rhetorical Analyses of Literary Works;* Richard L. Johannesen's *Contemporary Theories of Rhetoric: Selected Readings;* Douglas Ehninger's *Contemporary Rhetoric: A Reader's Coursebook;* Bernard L. Brock and Robert L. Scott's *Methods of Rhetorical Criticism;* and G. P. Mohrmann, Charles J. Stewart, and Donovan J. Och's *Explorations in Rhetorical Criticism.* These and other important works are listed in the bibliography which concludes this collection.

The practice of rhetorical criticism is essential in today's mediated world. It is important to understand how an orator can manipulate language to influence an audience. It is even more important to begin reflecting on how individual media, apart from the content they convey, can function as instruments of persuasion. As we start to understand the complex interactions of medium with content, we take one more step toward the preservation of the democratic form of government which gave birth to rhetoric and which is still sustained by it.

Introduction

Rhetorical Studies in a Media Age

Martin J. Medhurst
Thomas W. Benson

Rhetoric is one of the most important inventions of Western culture. The practice of public discourse has been an essential feature in shaping our history. And rhetoric as the theory of that discourse has been a central element in the history of ideas. At times in that long history, the idea of rhetoric as an aspect of human knowledge has been confined to the theory and practice of public speaking. At other times, rhetoric has been expanded to encompass any purposive or effective communication, and any theory or criticism that tried to account for such communication.

We live in an age when more and more human beings spend more and more of their time processing information: sending and receiving messages. This volume is a collection of the best recent critical writing on non-oratorical communication from a rhetorical perspective.

In this introductory chapter we would like to sketch the major issues of the debate that, until quite recently, has retarded the rhetorical criticism of the media. We provide this background as a guide to understanding where this anthology stands in the evolution of rhetorical thought and as a conceptual primer for readers interested in the twentieth-century debate about the relations between rhetoric and poetic.

In 1969 Edward P. J. Corbett edited an anthology titled *Rhetorical Analyses of Literary Works.* In an introductory essay Corbett argued that the art of rhetoric—defined as the art of persuasive oratory—provided a unique perspective for the analysis and criticism of works generally thought to be essentially poetic in nature. These poetical works—literature in the broadest sense of the term—had, for most of the past two centuries, been largely neglected by rhetorical critics. Rhetorical scholars had confined their interest to oratory, and literary scholars had either avoided rhetoric altogether; had limited its domain to matters of style; or were largely ignorant of the tradition which, from the time of Aristotle until the middle of the eighteenth century, had provided the dominant conceptual schema for both artists and critics of literature.

Corbett's purpose in publishing his anthology was to demonstrate that rhetorical criticism that mode of criticism that "regards the work not so much as an object of aesthetic contemplation but as an artistically structured instrument for communication," is indeed capable of illuminating literary texts in new and insightful ways. That such an anthology was needed in the middle of the twentieth century says much about the historical movement away from rhetoric as a means for ordering literary values as well as the movement away from literature as an instrument for communicating ideas, values, and beliefs to an audience.

It was the concern for the audience for the receivers, consumers, and processors of communication, that had distinguished rhetorical theory and criticism since the days of Plato and Aristotle. It was not enough, according to the rhetorical tradition, to focus solely on the work of art, be it an oration, a poem, painting, or play. Neither was it sufficient to place primary emphasis on the artist or creator, be he orator, playwright, sculptor, or poet. Even the most ancient of critical theories which held that art was to be an imitation of nature, that its subject was the universe and its purpose to reflect in some ideal form the reality of that universe, was not sufficient for the rhetorician. It was not that the work of art itself was unimportant, or the creator uninteresting, or the universe an unfit subject. Not at all. Rhetorical theorists affirmed, in part, all of these approaches while they insisted on including one more element: the audience.

If the work of art was viewed primarily as "a means to an end, an instrument for getting something done,"[2] then clearly the audience had to be considered the essential element in the rhetorical process. There could be no communication, no persuasion, no end or goal toward which the discourse moved unless there was an audience to influence. If art was a form of communication that had "designs on an audience,"[3] then it was only in terms of that audience and its response to the work that judgment could be made as to the success or failure of the communicative effort. The rhetorical critic thus insisted, at least in theory, on examining all of the components of the artistic and communicative process—author, message, subject, context, and audience.

Corbett is right, therefore, when he asserts that "a critic becomes 'rhetorical' when he tries to show that the choices from among the various options were made in reference to subject-matter or genre or occasion or purpose or author or audience—or some combination of these."[4]/A rhetorical critic is interested in why an artist chose to deal with certain topics (and not others); why the artistic elements chosen were structured as they were (and not some other way); why certain characteristics of the medium, be it clay, celluloid, proscenium, or pigments are emphasized (and others are not emphasized); what purpose, among all those possible, seems to be governing these choices; and to what audience the work addresses itself with what potential effect. Thus Corbett concludes that "the term *choices* gets us to the heart of rhetoric in general and of rhetorical criticism in particular."[5]

However, we must remember that rhetoric was originally conceived as the art of persuasive *oratory,* not of persuasive art. The realm of art was poetics, not rhetoric. That was why Aristotle wrote two separate works—the *Rhetoric* and the *Poetics*—claim some scholars, because he conceived of art as something categorically separate from oratory, as something different from communication with an audience. Starting with this distinction, it seemed reasonable for these scholars to conclude that the tenets of rhetoric were off limits for poetic artifacts and that rhetorical criticism should therefore be limited to analysis of speeches or, at the widest stretch, argumentative prose. It was partially as a response to this position that Corbett assembled his *Rhetorical Analyses of Literary Works,* to demonstrate that a small but significant band of scholars, working against the mainstream, had applied rhetorical methods to literary works with remarkably informative results. To understand more fully why *Rhetorical Dimensions in Media* will appear to some to overextend rhetorical criticism, we need to outline the major positions of those who hold to a strict demarcation between rhetoric and poetic, between rhetorical criticism and literary criticism.

From the beginnings of criticism, there have been competing theories of the nature, purpose, and evaluation of artistic works. The noted literary scholar M. H. Abrams identifies four approaches that have dominated the history of literary criticism: the mimetic or imitative, the expressive, the objective, and the pragmatic or rhetorical.[6] Today many literary scholars identify themselves with the mimetic, expressive, and objective perspectives. Fewer literary scholars, on the other hand, identify themselves with the pragmatic or rhetorical perspective even though this approach has, historically, "been the principle aesthetic attitude of the Western world."[7] Not only do most literary professionals avoid the rhetorical approach, but a large and influential group of rhetoricians—teachers of speech and oratory—either oppose any overlapping of rhetoric and poetic, or wish to restrict rhetorical analysis of artistic works to certain, very limited, kinds or classes of artifacts. To understand their reasoning, how it developed, and where it allows room for disagreement, is to understand a large part of our purpose for bringing this collection into being.

Perhaps the best way to describe twentieth-century rhetorical thought on the relationships between rhetoric and poetic is to create some admittedly artificial categories, but categories that will help to clarify some dominant strains of thought and some reasons for our selection of certain essays for inclusion in this anthology. For purposes of description and identification it is useful to think of three schools of thought concerning the rhetoric-poetic relationship. The first school holds that rhetoric and poetic are two separate and distinct arts, and advances specific criteria upon which to maintain this distinction. The second school is composed of a wide range of thinkers who, while maintaining a theoretical distinction between rhetoric and poetic, nevertheless recognize that there are certain rhetorical *dimensions* in works that are essentially poetic in nature. This second school comes in two basic varieties: those who wish to limit analysis of the rhetorical dimensions of the arts to particular kinds of works, usually satire, irony, didactic poems, or other forms of "literature" in which rhetorical structure or intention is both obvious and essential to any adequate reading; and, on the other hand, those who recognize and celebrate rhetorical dimensions in all types of artistic productions. The third school is composed of those who hold either that there is no substantive theoretical distinction between rhetoric and poetry or, if there is such a distinction, it is so complex and unwieldy (or so narrow and categorical) that it has become an impediment rather than a tool for critical activity. Most members of this school tend to see rhetoric as an inherent and inseparable part of all creative activity, and therefore instead of trying to end the debate with a fixed and categorical statement of the relations between rhetoric and poetic, they concentrate on how rhetoric and poetic interact to produce or invite a certain sort of response in the audience.

Let us examine a group of representative spokesmen for each position, to see the outlines of each position more clearly, and to understand the implications of each position for the practice of rhetorical criticism. School number one is best represented in the writings of three of this century's outstanding scholars of rhetoric and literature: Charles Sears Baldwin, Herbert A. Wichelns, and Wilbur Samuel Howell.

School Number One: Firm Distinctions

In his *Ancient Rhetoric and Poetic,* Charles Sears Baldwin presents a standard recital of the differences traditionally asserted to exist between rhetoric and poetic:

> Rhetoric meant to the ancient world the art of instructing and moving men in their affairs; poetic the art of sharpening and expanding their vision. . . . The one is composition of ideas; the other, composition of images. In the one field life is discussed; in the other it is presented. The type of one is a public address, moving us to assent and action; the type of the other is a play, showing us in action moving to an end of character. The one argues and urges; the other represents.[8]

Baldwin's perspective, published in 1924, was echoed and extended the following year by Herbert A. Wichelns, the father of modern rhetorical criticism, when he wrote that "poetry always is free to fulfill its own law, but the writer of rhetorical discourse is, in a sense, perpetually in bondage to the occasion and the audience; and in that fact we find the line of cleavage between rhetoric and poetic."[9] In contrast to rhetorical criticism, wrote Wichelns, literary criticism was distinguished by "its concern with permanent values; because it takes no account of special purpose nor of immediate effect; because it views a literary work as the voice of a human spirit addressing itself to men of all ages and times; because the critic speaks as the spectator of all time and all existence."[10]

xii

The perspective articulated by Baldwin and Wichelns held sway among rhetorical scholars until well into the 1950s. Indeed, the cleavage between the two arts was strengthened from time to time by the introduction of new arguments supporting their separation. Wilbur Samuel Howell provided one such argument when he asserted that "the words which make up the rhetorical utterance lead the reader to states of reality, whereas the words making up the poetical utterance lead the reader to things which stand by deputy for states of reality. These things which stand by deputy for states of reality are . . . the poet's symbols."[11]

Standing on the shoulders of Baldwin and Wichelns, Howell could conclude, "It would therefore appear that rhetoric and poetry, as the two chief modes of communication and persuasion, diverge from each other because the one uses words to illuminate factual matters, and the other uses words to illuminate things that in turn illuminate factual matters."[12]

Those who most actively defend firm distinctions between rhetoric and poetic do so when writing in a theoretical vein—the distinctions are often harder to maintain when confronting an actual body of discourse. In the making of distinctions, theorists have relied upon various elements in the symbolic process: subject matter and its representation, the form of the symbolic act, the purposes of the poet or orator, the expectations and situations of audiences, and the question of effect. Further, we should note that some of the theoretical distinctions have been allowed to harden beyond their initial intentions. Wichelns, for example, writing in 1925, was not so much trying to prevent something as to start something: he understood that he was helping to rediscover rhetoric as pragmatic discourse, and that public address needed to be criticized in terms of its purposes, rather than as an aspect of the orator's biography or as a lesser form of literature.

Wichelns' vigorous call for a new form of criticism had impressive results, but he did not, himself, remain satisfied with easy and fixed distinctions. In a later essay on Ralph Waldo Emerson, Wichelns perceptively and sympathetically remarks on Emerson's painful attempt to recreate himself as the orator he thought he should be:

[Emerson] needed a decade or more to determine the nature and proper use of his gift of expression and to find his right relation to his audience.

For one of Emerson's temperament and constitution, the right relation to his audience was not easy to find. He had great admiration for the civic leader and great respect for the power of persuasion. His ideal speaker was a man thoroughly at home in the community, on easy terms with its members, leading and commanding them by force of personality, strength of mind, and power of statement. Nor was the ideal speaker far removed in thought from those he led. Yet Emerson himself was reserved and awkward in social contacts, unhappy in forced intimacy with his fellows, hesitant in speech. His early struggle with tuberculosis had left him with reduced energy and low vitality. The course of his thought had deprived him of common ground with any large section of his fellow citizens. Hence, seeking outlet for his undoubted gift for expression, he was gradually but inevitably driven to deny his own ideal. . . . Presently he was to release himself

. . . from that intellectual accountability to his peers which every writer and speaker—on the higher levels at least—customarily acknowledges. As we review his changing conception of his own function—and his performance—we shall see that Emerson in the end found his true calling and his right relation to his hearers by making himself thoroughly independent of them.[13]

Just as Wichelns describes Emerson driven, in the press of actuality, to differ from his abstract ideal of the orator, so we find Wichelns, in the actual performance of rhetorical criticism, refusing to be bound by the strictures of his own earlier theoretical and methodological statement. When faced with the complexity of Emerson, Wichelns modified his earlier position with a characteristic boldness and generosity of view—Wichelns refused to take the course that might have been suggested by his earlier essay, and accuse Emerson of being more poet than orator. The ideal is used as a point of departure, but it is not allowed to blind the critic to the demands of circumstance.

Although Wichelns' published works are few, he had an enormous influence through his writings and as a teacher and advisor. His "Literary Criticism of Oratory" is often cited as having stimulated a rebirth of rhetorical criticism or as having artificially narrowed the ground for such criticism to the effects-oriented study of public speaking. But, equally important, Wichelns was the mentor of two early works that helped to announce a wider field for rhetorical criticism: Edwin Black's *Rhetorical Criticism: A Study in Method,* which articulated the objections of a generation of critics to the "neo-Aristotelian" focus on effects in rhetorical criticism, and James Wood's early application of rhetorical theory to film. Both of these works were doctoral dissertations directed by Wichelns.[14]

School Number Two: Rhetorical Dimensions

The second school of thought concerning the rhetoric-poetic relationship is distinguished by one basic assumption that differentiates it from school number one, namely, that the line separating rhetoric and poetic is not nearly so distinct as Baldwin, Wichelns, and Howell have usually been read as suggesting; but that there are, in practice, *rhetorical dimensions* in many works that fall under traditional literary categories and genres.

This second school is, itself, divided into two camps. One group, represented by such scholars as Donald C. Bryant and Carroll C. Arnold, holds that examination of rhetorical dimensions of poetic works may be appropriate in *some* situations or in the analysis of *some* genres. A second group, represented by Edward P. J. Corbett and Thomas O. Sloan, also subscribes to the rhetorical dimensions approach, but does not seek to limit its application either to particular types of literature or to written or oral modes only. The distinction between the two camps within this school is, therefore, more a matter of scope, applicability, and utility rather than any deep theoretical disjunction. Group one is conservative in its application of the rhetorical dimensions perspective; group two is more liberal.

Donald C. Bryant is a pivotal figure in twentieth-century thinking about rhetoric and poetic not only because of his stature as theorist and critic, but also because he provides the bridge from school one to school two. Like Baldwin, Wichelns, and Howell, Bryant holds to a theoretical distinction between rhetoric and poetic, and to a practical distinction between literary criticism and rhetorical criticism. Echoing his intellectual forebears, Bryant points to the distinction "between the treatment of artifacts as significant primarily for what they *are* and the treatment of them as primarily significant for what they *do*."[15] The use of the term "primarily" is what saves Bryant from standing wholly with school number one. Unlike the representatives of firm distinctions, Bryant argues that "rhetorical dimensions in the theory and criticism of poetry have been evident almost from the beginning of the formulation of the art."[16] Instead of denying any overlap between the rhetorical and poetic realms, Bryant seeks to define in a precise manner the nature, scope, and function of this area of overlap.

Bryant's use of the term "primarily" gives a clue as to what he believes the nature and scope of the rhetorical dimensions approach to literature should be. In short, it should be limited to works that manifest an obvious persuasive intent (such as a propaganda novel or political tract), or whose literary techniques can be most conveniently explained through reference to traditional rhetorical concepts (such as satire, irony, hyperbole, and so on). Bryant writes:

> As the province of literary criticism is the poetic—the fictive and imaginative, the beautiful, the enduring in poems and prose, the eloquence of public affairs and the pulpit—so rhetorical criticism treats of the illuminative and suasory in speeches and speaking, in pamphlets and pamphleteering, in controversy and debate, in editorials and editorializing, in *Grapes of Wrath* and *Mother Courage* and the vehicles and media to which they belong.[17]

Those who advocate firm distinctions between rhetoric and poetic typically argue that the two genres are distinct and that criticism of them should be equally distinct: the one concerned with the effects of oral persuasion, the other with written (or performed) aesthetic compositions. Bryant seeks to extend the legitimate scope of rhetorical criticism to include any works of *language* that are essentially or importantly *persuasive*. But he is unwilling to extend rhetorical criticism beyond language and persuasion. Bryant writes, "I do not find it fruitful, even if plausible, to enlarge the rhetorical to comprehend all symbolic interaction, by whatever vehicle communicated. Nor do I find it fruitful or plausible to extend the rhetorical dimensions to encompass all kinds of study of all kinds and vehicles of symbolic interaction."[18]

Another group of rhetorical critics and theorists is willing to accept the limitation of rhetoric to persuasion, but refuses to accept the limitation to language. A major announcement of this position occurred as the result of a series of conferences sponsored by the Speech Communication Association and the National Endowment for the Humanities in 1969–1970. One group of conferees, meeting under the chairmanship of Thomas O. Sloan, argued that "any critic, regardless of the subject of his inquiry, becomes a rhetorical critic when his work centers on suasory appeal or persuasive effects, their source, nature, operation, and consequences."[19] In its report, the Committee on Criticism sought to expand the boundaries of rhetorical inquiry beyond language, and to invite scholars from other disciplines into rhetorical criticism. No longer was rhetorical criticism to be limited to speech, or even to language, but the focus would continue to be on persuasion—intentional or unintentional. The final report advised:

> The effort should be made to expand the scope of rhetorical criticism to include subjects which have not traditionally fallen within the critic's purview: the non-discursive as well as the discursive, the non-verbal as well as the verbal, the event or transaction which is unintentionally as well as intentionally suasive. The rhetorical critic has the freedom to pursue his study of subjects with suasory potential or persuasive effects in whatever setting he may find them, ranging from rock music and put-ons, to architecture and public forums, to ballet and international politics. Though the subjects of his investigations should be expanded, his identity need not be lost.[20]

School Number Three: Rhetoric As Inherent and Intrinsic

A third position on the scope of rhetorical criticism takes a still broader view. Such critics as Kenneth Burke and Wayne Booth argue that all symbolic behavior is inherently rhetorical insofar as it is designed to communicate, and that the rhetorical critic's job is to understand the communicative potential of symbolic forms.

Wayne Booth, for example, has argued that the rhetoric of fiction is not confined to works that are didactic or propagandistic, nor to those aspects of a work in which the author directly indicates how the reader should be thinking and feeling, but extends to all fiction as it is designed to communicate to readers. He states:

> Though some characters and events may speak by themselves their artistic message to the reader, and thus carry in a weak form their own rhetoric, none will do so with proper clarity and force until the author brings all his powers to bear on the problem of making the reader see what they really are. The author cannot choose whether to use rhetorical heightening. His only choice is of the kind of rhetoric he will use.[21]

For Booth, fiction is inevitably rhetorical, and works through every choice the author makes about the design of the work, guiding a reader who is constantly relying on the text for guidance in how to experience the text.

For Kenneth Burke, too, rhetoric is an inherent part of the poetic (or any communicative) process. Like Booth, Burke sees the author as a rhetorician who selects and "weights" certain portions of the poetic structure to invite a particular interpretation by the reader. Burke is interested in the "forms" an author employs to arouse in the reader certain expectations. He defines form as "the arousing and fulfillment of desires."[22] A work has form, says Burke, "in so far as one part of it leads a reader to anticipate another part, to be gratified by the sequence."[23]

Burke calls his approach "pragmatic" inasmuch as it "assumes that a poem's structure is to be described most accurately by thinking always of the poem's function. It assumes that the poem is designed to 'do something' for the poet and his readers, and that we can make the most relevant observations about its design by considering the poem as an embodiment of this act."[24] To get at poetic structure and its possible functioning for an audience, Burke suggests that the critic look for "associational clusters" of "what goes with what" in a work.[25] In other works, Burke developed his ideas of symbolic action into a remarkable instrument of critical inquiry. His philosophy of dramatism, with its elaborate account of the structure of human motivation, and his concept of identification have set the foundation for an expanded rhetorical criticism.[26]

Burke and Booth confine most of their critical activities to "literature" in the narrow sense of that term: poems, plays, novels, and the like. Yet both agree that rhetoric pervades all artistic creations and Burke quite clearly argues that all human action is rhetorical. Both encourage the critic to apply rhetorical theory and criticism to the creation and understanding of all sorts of non-oratorical forms: film, television, architecture, painting, dance, radio, or whatever.

Booth writes of the need for rhetorical analysis of popular art forms:

> If all good art has no rhetorical dimension, as so many have argued, then the 'rhetoric' is left to those who will use it for the devil's purposes. . . . How much better it would be if we could develop a way of understanding how great literature and drama does in fact work rhetorically to build and strengthen communities. Reading *War and Peace* or seeing *King Lear* does change the mind, just as reading *Justine* or taking a daily dose of tv fare changes minds. A movie like *The Graduate* both depends on commonplaces shared much more widely than our slogans of fragmentation and alienation would allow for, and strengthens the sharing of those commonplaces; like *The Midnight Cowboy* or *Easy Rider,* it can be said to make a public as well as finding one already made. All of them work very hard to *appear* nonrhetorical; there are no speeches by anyone defending the graduate's or the cowboy's values against the 'adult' world that both movies reject so vigorously. But the selection from all possible worlds is such that only the most hard-bitten or critical-minded viewer under forty is likely to resist sympathy for the outcasts and total contempt for the hypocritical aging knaves and fools that surround them. If sheer quantity and strength of pressure on our lives is the measure, the rhetoric of such works, though less obvious, is more in need of study than the open aggressive rhetoric of groups like *The Living Theatre.*[27]

The three "schools" we have outlined on the issue of rhetoric vs. poetic have somewhat indistinct boundaries. Each school has theoretical and critical advantages and disadvantages. At times the differences between the schools are substantive, at times merely a matter of differences of perspective, usage, academic habit, or definition of terms. And it might be that "schools" is in itself a misleading term: the schools really represent *positions* on the issue of the relations of rhetoric and poetic, and, in practice, theorists and critics move from one "school" to another, as we have shown in the case of Herbert Wichelns. And it is right that they should do so: a diehard loyalty to any theoretical position can inhibit clear thinking.

Our own position on rhetorical criticism and its relation to poetic and other forms is eclectic. In general, critical practice should be judged by the insights and understandings it affords the reader, not by any *a priori* assertion of territorial rights. Like Burke, we are "more interested in bringing the full resources of Poetics and *Rhetorica docens* to bear upon the study of a text than in trying to draw a *strict* line of demarcation between Rhetoric and Poetics."[28]

Still, those who hold to firm distinctions between rhetoric and poetic cannot be dismissed as arbitrary or irrelevant. For example, Wichelns was writing at a time, in 1925, when American universities were re-discovering the rhetorical tradition and attempting to develop standards for judging and teaching the practice of public address. Public address was deemed to be an essential aspect of democratic citizenship, and it needed, at the time, to be rescued from a point of view that looked upon public speaking as a "literary" exercise or an aspect of a speaker's biography. Wichelns and others were right to insist that public speaking be responsibly argumentative and concerned with immediate results. As a new and threatened discipline in American higher education, the revived rhetoric followed the classic pattern: it tried to define itself by distinguishing itself from other closely related branches of knowledge (literature, psychology, politics).

And if public speaking needed to be rescued from being reduced to poetry, it seemed clear to many critics that poetry needed to be protected from being reduced to rhetoric, if such a reduction meant seeing poetry as an anesthetized, thematic, didactic vehicle of social criticism. There is much to be said for the view of those who insist on firm distinctions. Society benefits from using public speaking (and other forms of linguistic discourse) to argue public policy and artists and their readers benefit from a liberated release from daily realities and immediate effects into a space where beauty and vision are possible.

Those who soften the firm distinction between rhetoric and poetic by discovering rhetorical dimensions in artistic works point the way to a more flexible critical response. But in trying to restrict critical analysis to certain types of texts or to define rhetoric as a unitary and entirely separate domain, many of the "rhetorical dimensions" arguments seem untenable. Donald C. Bryant, perhaps the most eloquent spokesman for the rhetorical dimensions approach, has emphasized the distinction "between the treatment of artifacts as significant primarily for what they *are* and the treatment of them as primarily significant for what they *do*."[29] Bryant's distinction here is a traditional one, but it seems to us that it is not so much that poetry *is* and rhetoric *does,* but that perhaps rhetoric and poetry both are and do—even when they are and do different things. Indeed, for many critics, criticism is rhetorical when it examines how a poem's form leads a reader to a certain state of thoughts and feelings: what the poem is leads to what it does.[30]

It may appear from the discussion so far that, because of our difficulties with the positions of the firm distinctionists and the rhetorical dimensionists we align ourselves with the third school. To a large degree this is the case, but with some reservations. Rhetorical studies have traditionally been concerned with public discourse, and with the argumentative and ethical dimensions of that discourse. In our view, it would be a disservice to our culture to merge all former distinctions in such a way as to see all symbolic action as both functionally and essentially monolithic. Rhetoric needs to retain a critical stance that encompasses something more than the study of techniques, more than a list of persuasive devices, more than eloquence or propaganda. One of the roles of rhetoric in our society is to help us envision and realize a cultural ideal that holds speakers responsible for their words and deeds, demands evidence in support of argument, and provides forums for argumentation to occur. Whenever we use rhetoric in a broader sense than that foreseen by its classical inventors, as school three urges us to do, we do so at the risk of losing sight of rhetoric not simply as a technique but also as a vision of society.[31] Most of the essays in this collection, even those with the broadest definition of rhetoric, reflect awareness of the ethical dimensions of rhetorical studies.

School Three presents another, related, problem. If we see rhetoric as inherent, inevitable, and universal, we are in danger of claiming that all communication is nothing but rhetorical. In which case, rhetoric means so much that it may not mean anything at all. On the one hand, an absolutism of fixed distinctions between rhetoric and poetic. On the other hand, an absolutism of rhetoric as universal. Between these absolutes, rhetorical critics are using aspects of the rhetorical tradition to extend our understanding of symbolic actions in all media.

Rhetoric and Media

We have organized this anthology by focussing on ten media and genres. The principles we have used for selecting these media and genres are simple. First, we recognized that television, film, and radio are the most pervasive media types. Even though rhetorical studies of these three media have been few, we believe the essays offered here provide a good starting point for further theoretical and critical refinement. Second, we chose chapters on public letters and literature because both have long rhetorical histories stretching back into antiquity and because, of all the non-oratorical genres, literature has been the most frequent subject for rhetorical criticism. Third, we filled out our sketch of the scope of rhetorical criticism by including essays on graphic art, music, popular magazines, political action, and architecture. Even this list, however, is not exhaustive: we have had to leave some things out. Among the omissions we most regret are essays on interpersonal communication, photography, painting, and fashion.[32]

Within each medium and genre some difficult decisions had to be made concerning which essays, out of all those possible, should be included. Our first principle in all cases was perceived quality of analysis and ability to demonstrate one or more ways of conducting a rhetorical critique. A second principle upon which we operated was a desire to be inclusive rather than exclusive: that is, we wished to include examples of rhetorical criticism from fields and publications beyond speech and communication studies. Rhetorical criticism is applicable to many disciplines, including literature, semiotics, theology, popular culture, and studies of various forms of visual communication. Each of these areas is included in this anthology as an indication of the possibilities for cross-fertilization between rhetorical studies and all disciplines concerned with symbolic forms. Implicit in this view, of course, is that theory can be generated from critical practice. We believe it can and that these essays raise many important questions of a theoretical, as well as critical, nature. An additional criterion of selection has been recency: we have included studies published for the most part within the past ten years, so as to capture a sense of the current range and strength of the enterprise. Earlier studies have been important, of course, and are cited where appropriate in the critical essays we have included, and in the bibliography that concludes this volume.

Because of our inclusive, pluralistic approach, the reader should be alerted to some features that might, at first, seem troublesome. Chief among these is the use of the term "rhetoric" or "rhetorical criticism" by our contributors. Put bluntly, the reader will find that some authors (1) do not use "rhetoric" or "rhetorical criticism" at all; (2) use the term "rhetoric" in more than one sense within the same essay; or (3) use a definition of "rhetoric" that is different from the one used by others writing about the same genre or medium. If we were interested in theoretical consistency this would be a problem. What we are interested in, however, is critical practice—the ability to explicate a text and bring to the reader new insights and understandings about how a particular text functions as rhetoric—as a symbolic form whose structure and context lead the audience to think, feel, believe, understand, or act in an arguably predictable way.

What do our authors mean by "rhetoric?" In recent attempts to expand the usage of "rhetoric" beyond public speaking, nine senses of the term seem to emerge.

1. Rhetoric as intentional persuasion.
2. Rhetoric as the social values and effects of symbolic forms, whether intentional or not.
3. Rhetoric as the techniques by which nondidactic arts communicate to audiences.

4. Rhetoric as the persuasion addressed by one character to another within a dramatic or narrative work.
5. Rhetoric as the body of principles and techniques of rhetorical theory—the traditional resources of invention, disposition, style, memory, and delivery as they are discovered in texts.
6. Rhetoric as the study of genres or types.
7. Implicit rhetorical theory: rhetoric as the theories about human symbolic interaction implied by the authors of symbolic forms.
8. Rhetoric as an ideal for the conduct of human communication.
9. Rhetoric as the study of what gives effectiveness to form; the pragmatics of human communication.[33]

These nine senses or definitions of rhetoric are not, of course, mutually exclusive. Some of the more expansive definitions, such as number nine, encompass or incorporate others that are drawn more narrowly. We offer these senses as a clue for readers of the essays that follow, as a way of seeing how a particular author may be defining rhetoric. The senses may also be useful as topical starting-points for readers who wish to undertake rhetorical criticism themselves. The criterion for evaluating a particular usage of "rhetoric" should, in our view, be the author's success in bringing the resources and perspectives of rhetoric to bear upon the analysis and criticism of the text under study.

Each essay is introduced with a short series of observations and questions. These questions are meant to raise important theoretical, methodological, and analytical concerns that may or may not have been raised in the essay itself. It is our position that the function of criticism is not only to argue for particular positions but also to raise questions—and not to make further analysis or criticism unnecessary. Our brief introductions are intended as probes inviting students to question as they read.

The concluding bibliography on the theory, methods, and practice of rhetorical criticism is limited primarily to the genres represented in the text itself. We do not mean to imply by this selection that other genres are not worthy of exploration. Clearly they are. But one must begin somewhere, and for purposes of introducing students to the criticism of non-oratorical forms we believe this selection covers the most useful starting points. The bibliography represents critical work done in the rhetorical tradition from 1945 to the present—with a few glances at earlier work. Even in the literature since 1945 we have found it necessary to be selective rather than comprehensive. Disciplines surveyed include speech communication, popular culture, literary criticism, semiotics, English, mass communication, and American studies. In choosing which books and articles to include in the bibliography we have, again, sought to be theoretically and methodologically inclusive, listing works falling under all nine senses of rhetoric.

The revival of rhetoric continues. Rhetorical criticism provides a way of connecting ancient traditions with modern actions; of connecting academics, artists, and audiences in an ongoing forum; of connecting abstract theories of symbolic form to the realities of judgment and passion that become entangled in human speech, art, and action. In the face of a burgeoning diversity and enthusiastic forward movement in many related branches of knowledge, we present this collection as a celebration of the contributions of rhetoric to an understanding of culture.

Notes

1. Edward P. J. Corbett, ed., *Rhetorical Analyses of Literary Works* (New York: Oxford University Press, 1969), p. xxii.
2. M. H. Abrams, *The Mirror and the Lamp: Romantic Theory and the Critical Tradition* (New York: W. W. Norton and Co., 1953), p. 15.
3. Corbett, p. xxii.
4. Corbett, p. xxvi.
5. Corbett, p. xxvi.
6. Abrams, pp. 6–29.
7. Abrams, p. 21.
8. Charles Sears Baldwin, *Ancient Rhetoric and Poetic* (1924; rpt. Gloucester, Mass.: Peter Smith, 1959), p. 134.
9. Herbert A. Wichelns, "The Literary Criticism of Oratory," [1925; reprinted in] *Methods of Rhetorical Criticism: A Twentieth Century Perspective,* ed. Bernard L. Brock and Robert L. Scott, 2nd ed. (Detroit: Wayne State University Press, 1980), p. 69.
10. Wichelns, p. 70.
11. Wilbur Samuel Howell, "Literature As an Enterprise in Communication," in *Contemporary Rhetoric: A Reader's Coursebook,* ed. Douglas Ehninger (Glenview: Scott, Foresman and Co., 1972), p. 102.
12. Howell, p. 106.
13. Herbert A. Wichelns, "Ralph Waldo Emerson," in *A History and Criticism of American Public Address,* Vol. II, William Norwood Brigance, ed. (1943; rpt. New York: Russell & Russell, 1960), pp. 501–502.
14. Edwin Black, *Rhetorical Criticism: A Study in Method* (New York: Macmillan, 1965); James A. Wood, "An Application of Rhetorical Theory to Filmic Persuasion," Diss. Cornell University, 1967.
15. Donald C. Bryant, *Rhetorical Dimensions in Criticism* (Baton Rouge: Louisiana State University Press, 1973), p. 25. For further development of this view see Donald C. Bryant, ed., *Papers in Rhetoric and Poetic* (Iowa City: University of Iowa Press, 1965), especially chapters 1, 4, and 5.
16. Bryant, *Rhetorical Dimensions,* p. 31.
17. Bryant, *Rhetorical Dimensions,* p. 34.
18. Bryant, *Rhetorical Dimensions,* p. 40.
19. Thomas O. Sloan, Richard B. Gregg, Thomas R. Nilsen, Irving J. Rein, Herbert W. Simons, Hermann G. Stelzner, Donald W. Zacharias, "Report of the Committee on the Advancement and Refinement of Rhetorical Criticism," in *The Prospect of Rhetoric,* ed. Lloyd F. Bitzer and Edwin Black (Englewood Cliffs: Prentice-Hall, 1971), p. 221.
20. Sloan, et al, p. 22.
21. Wayne C. Booth, *The Rhetoric of Fiction* (Chicago: University of Chicago Press, 1961), p. 116.

22. Kenneth Burke, *Counter-Statement* (1931; rpt. Berkeley: University of California Press, 1968), p. 124.
23. Burke, *Counter-Statement,* p. 124.
24. Kenneth Burke, *The Philosophy of Literary Form: Studies in Symbolic Action,* 3rd ed. (1941; rpt. Berkeley: University of California Press, 1973), p. 89.
25. Burke, *Philosophy of Literary Form,* p. 77.
26. In addition to the other works cited here, see Kenneth Burke, *A Grammar of Motives* (1945; rpt. Berkeley: University of California Press, 1969); and *A Rhetoric of Motives* (1950; rpt. Berkeley: University of California Press, 1969).
27. Booth, "The Scope of Rhetoric Today," in *The Prospect of Rhetoric,* p. 102.
28. Burke, *Language as a Symbolic Action* (Berkeley: University of California Press, 1966), p. 307.
29. Bryant, *Rhetorical Dimensions,* p. 25.
30. There have been times in the history of critical theory when the art of poetry was interested in poetry both as form and as communication. But when poetic theory abandoned its interest in communication, preferring to see poetry as pure form or as self-expression, some rhetorical critics came forward to fill the gap, and both they and their opponents called the resulting criticism rhetorical.
31. Cf. Thomas W. Benson, "*Joe:* An Essay in the Rhetorical Criticism of Film," *Journal of Popular Culture,* 8 (Winter 1974), p. 610.
32. For studies on these and other media and genres, consult the bibliography at the end of this volume.
33. For a more complete explanation of these senses, see Thomas W. Benson, "The Senses of Rhetoric: A Topical System for Critics," *Central States Speech Journal,* 29 (1978), 237–250.

1

Rhetoric of Television

When Vladmir Zworkin completed the first iconoscope—the technological basis for modern television—few people could foresee the social changes that would be wrought by its introduction. The year was 1923 and it would be more than a decade before electronic television was perfected and another decade yet before individual sets were mass marketed. Television as we know it today, as a means of mass communication, had to await the end of World War II, but even in its formative years it presented artistic and propagandistic possibilities far beyond those of any previous medium.

Like film, television could capture the dynamics of sight, sound, and motion, alter space/time relationships and employ narrative conventions to create "reality." Like radio, it could transcend geographical boundaries, deliver the same message to millions of listeners or viewers simultaneously, and create a sense of personal involvement. Most important, unlike its predecessors, television was, from the outset, a medium of intimacy. It entered into the home, became part of the environment, and soon began to fulfill roles ranging from babysitter to entertainer to vehicle for social indoctrination and education.

Though television has fulfilled all these functions for nearly forty years, it has been only within the past ten to fifteen years that scholars from the humanities—English, literature, rhetoric, philosophy, and so forth—have recognized its importance to the liberally-educated person and sought to understand and evaluate its influence. Though early critics such as Gilbert Seldes and Robert Lewis Shayon were quick to recognize the artistic and dramatic possibilities of the medium, and social scientists were among the first to speculate about television's potential effects on viewers, academic humanists have only recently begun to develop critical vocabularies for the analysis and evaluation of televised material.

In this section several academic humanists attempt to develop vocabularies for the criticism of television fare, and to apply those vocabularies to individual "texts" in an effort to demonstrate their utility as analytical tools. Gronbeck offers a three-pronged analysis of the late domestic series, *Family* (1976–1980). Schrag, Hudson, and Bernabo examine another generic staple of prime-time television, the situation comedy. They investigate similarities across four programs: *M*A*S*H, Lou Grant, Taxi,* and *Barney Miller.* Finally, Barton and Gregg explore the formal dimensions of television news by examining the treatment of a particular story as it developed, evolved, and receded.

1

Though all of these essays seek to explicate one or more rhetorical dimensions of television programming, they do so in distinctly different ways. Gronbeck conducts a microscopic examination of one episode from the 1978–79 season of *Family*. Schrag, Hudson, and Bernabo, on the other hand, operate on a macroscopic level as they analyze four programs across an entire season. Barton and Gregg, though conducting their investigation on the microscopic level, nevertheless extend the analysis over a one week period from the inception of a news story to its "fall" from the headlines. But the differences are more than those of programmatic scope and analytical depth. Each of these essays is undertaken for a different purpose and is conducted using different procedures.

Gronbeck's purpose seems to be to demonstrate the interpenetration of the artistic, social, and ideological dimensions of television programming. He wants the reader to come away with a heightened appreciation of how television programs "embody" messages and the various sorts of codes that are used to cue audience engagement with those messages. Schrag, Hudson, and Bernabo have a different substantive purpose: to establish the existence of a hitherto unrecognized program type that manifests a unique vision of social relations. They want to argue that this vision—the "new humane collectivity"—is a model both for improved television programming and for understanding how people *ought* to interact in the real world. The purpose animating the Barton and Gregg essay is, like Gronbeck's, to account for the sort of invitation that is issued to the viewer through the strategic use of technical, stylistic, and narrative conventions. But, unlike Gronbeck, Barton and Gregg are more interested in the rhetorical forms *as forms* than in the particular messages, implicit or explicit, conveyed by those forms. Barton and Gregg focus reader attention on *how* meaning is created through the interactions of conventional and organic form. Theirs is a processual, developmental perspective.

If these essays are undertaken for different analytical purposes, then it might seem natural that the methods of investigation should differ as well. They do. Gronbeck records dialogue and notes the use of aesthetic elements such as sound, lighting, and motion. He examines specific portions of the episode— the opening credits, the initial scene, and a series of related scenes that deal with the theme of motherliness. Gronbeck then uses his examination of these scenes to construct propositions which, though not articulated by the characters, are nevertheless necessary premises for making "sense" of the action. Having deduced these propositions, Gronbeck then speculates about how the artistic, social, and ideological levels of meaningfulness interact with and reinforce one another.

Schrag, Hudson, and Bernabo proceed in a much different fashion. Whereas Gronbeck selects *Family* for analysis specifically because it is mundane and therefore representative of its genre, Schrag and his associates implicitly argue that there is "good" programming and "bad" and that it is the former rather than the latter that merits investigation. To determine what constituted "significant" programming the authors constructed a list of their personal favorites, videotaped an entire season's run of those shows, then examined four of them to search for an emerging rhetorical vision. They claim to have found such a vision in the ideal of a new humane collectivity.

Barton and Gregg take cues from the methods employed by both previous essays when they select a "major event" for their analysis of television news and when they limit their examination to the "most prominent meaning structures." Like Gronbeck, they are sensitive to the interaction of the artistic with the social. Like Schrag, Hudson, and Bernabo, they search for patterns that seem to suggest ways in which viewers are to understand what is being shown. By examining the interaction of conventional and organic forms, Barton and Gregg are able to identify two patterns that seem to account for a large portion of television news rhetoric. To what extent, however, are the forms and processes described by Barton and Gregg alleged to be motivated by television as a medium, by news as a genre, or by other forces?

Each of these essays examines a different genre, with different goals, and with different analytic methods. These differences suggest, in themselves, some important questions that the critic needs to consider. First, if television offers many different types or genres of programming, how is the critic to choose which to analyze? Does the critic examine the program that is the most popular, the most artistically creative, the most socially significant, or the program that is most personally satisfying? How, in other words, might a critic justify the genre to be studied? Second, having chosen a type of program to study, how does the critic know how many episodes must be examined? Gronbeck examines only one episode but refers the reader to other episodes of the same program and to other programs within the same genre. Schrag, Hudson, and Bernabo, on the other hand, examine all the episodes of *M*A*S*H, Barney Miller, Taxi,* and *Lou Grant* over an entire season. How did they make these choices? How generalizable are the conclusions from these two essays? Third, what are the acceptable reasons for studying *any* television program? The authors represented in this section give three different reasons for undertaking their studies. Can you think of any other reasons why one might want to analyze television programming? Are there some important questions that rhetorical criticism cannot answer effectively? If so, what sort of methods might a critic employ to answer such questions?

Audience Engagement in "Family"

Bruce E. Gronbeck

The criticism of television, recently, has taken a decidedly sociocultural turn. The "elitist" social critics of the '50s were in the business of serving up anti-television tirades, and the "popularist" critics of the '60s celebrated the medium along with other artifacts of the mass society. Today's sociocultural television critics, however, for the most part, have more analytical and more discourse-centered purposes.[1]

The phrase "sociocultural criticism" is wonderfully elastic; many a critical crime can be committed in its name. In another essay I was concerned with articulating the kinds of communicative relationships existing between the "authors" of television programs—network executives, producers, writers, directors, actors—and viewers of those programs.[2] Essentially, I argued that authors and viewers can communicate—can share "meanings"—because both groups bring to TV shows common formal and substantive codes. Because authors ("tellers") and viewers ("told-tos") have been acculturated more or less similarly, they have access roughly to the same codes or languages and to the same stocks of knowledge (generalized beliefs, attitudes, values, presuppositions, and myths).

In this essay, we will be focusing on two[3] kinds of culturally shared codes: (1) artistic signs or symbols which assign meanings to such poetic conventions as different kinds of theme music, lighting techniques, types of camera shots, use of narrators, editing styles, and the like; and (2) social codes which represent a society's "rules for living," of "proper" relationships between parents and children, friends and strangers, institutions and individuals, and one institution with others. We will explore some important—perhaps crucial—relationships between the artistic and social arenas of knowledge and meaningfulness. I will argue that viewers' knowledges of artistic conventions and sociocultural truisms *interpenetrate* each other, with their knowledge of artistic conventions affecting the ways they interpret and the degree to which they accept as utilitarian television's social messages. Focusing on such interpretation, I am convinced, sheds light on an issue central these days to television criticism—the ideological force of television programs. Once we have examined a television program, we will discuss more fully notions of "ideology," "masking," and "hegemony."[4]

In this essay I wish to analyze an episode from the 1976–1980 program, *Family*. It is a near-ideal program for my purposes. First, it was lauded as an artistic achievement in its time; not only did critics find it sensitive, but three

4

of its four leads—Sada Thompson, Gary Frank, and Kristy McNichol—received Emmys for their preformances.[5] Second, it centers on the primal American family, and hence is comparatively easy to analyze on the second level of poetic meaningfulness, the social level. I have selected *Family,* therefore, because it permits me to offer a kind of paradigmatic case study of (1) the relationships between the poetic and sociocultural "content" of television programs, and (2) the ideological uptake or force of an ordinary type of television program, a family drama.

More specifically, I will examine the opening episode of the 1978–79 season, the one in which step-child Annie Cooper is introduced into the group. First, I will describe the episode, and then, in a series of replays, discuss some of the mechanisms by which the artistic and sociocultural cues-to-meaning engage the viewer. Such description and analysis will allow me to offer speculative statements on "audience engagement" as a televisual phenomenon— on art, society, and ideological force.

last clause?

An Episode of "Family," September 21, 1978

To describe an episode of an hour-long TV drama is difficult in a short space. I therefore have included Figure 1 with a partial description of scenes relevant to this paper. The episode is a twenty-five segment dramatic show,[6] divided into opening Titles, Acts I, II, III, IV, and Epilogue, running something over forty-eight minutes, with commercial breaks between each of the six main units.

The story itself deals with the introduction of Annie Cooper into the Lawrence household. Eleven-year-old Annie's parents had been killed in an auto accident six months earlier, and she had been living since that time with her father's sister, who at the opening of the show decides that parenting and a career do not mix. The aunt therefore asks the Lawrences to honor a letter-of-agreement they had signed nine years earlier, a letter declaring they would care for Annie should anything happen to her parents. The show itself concentrates upon the various moves made to accommodate the stepchild by family members—the mother (Kate), the father (Doug), the almost-sixteen-year-old daughter (Buddy), the twenty-year-old stay-at-home son (Willie), and the divorced-though-soon-to-be-remarried daughter (Nancy, aged thirty).

Annie is a hardened, smart-mouthed, precocious child; she staves off all advances by family members, working hard to alienate one person after the other. By mid-act IV, all of the children have written her off, and the parents, too, have serious doubts. But finally, just as mother Kate is packing Annie's possessions to return her to her aunt, a confrontation occurs, Annie breaks down, sobbing over her dead parents, and a new union is created. And thus has been enacted an American family melodrama.

5

Three additional details are important for our understanding of how *Family* works: the function of a familial metaphor, the theme of new beginnings, and the centrality of the mother figure. The dominant metaphor for familial integration is an annual family portrait. The show opens with Kate reminding Doug that the portrait will be taken the following weekend, and it closes with a sitting. Second, apropos to the first episode of a new season, it also stresses new beginnings. Reviews of each character's life since the previous season stress individual changes in circumstances. Thus, the permanence of photograph and family is contrasted with individual and collective evolution even from the opening scenes. And, third, this particular episode, like almost every preceding installment, is centered on the mother—Kate Lawrence. There has never been any doubt in regular viewers' minds that we are witnessing a matriarchy—a point which will be essential to some later speculations. Father does not know best in *Family;* mother does.[7]

Levels of Meaningfulness in 'Family'

If television drama can be said to exist on multiple levels of meaningfulness, then we ought to be able to chart a show level by level or arena by arena; and, too, we should be able to suggest the "markers" or symbolic cues which signal the kinds of knowledge viewers need to possess in order to understand it.[8] As indicated earlier, I will explore this show's functioning on the aesthetic and sociocultural levels.

The Aesthetic Level

Considering this show as a piece of performed art, a series of artists—Sada Thompson as Kate, James Broderick as Doug, Kristy McNichol as Buddy, Gary Frank as Willie, Meredith Baxter-Birney as Nancy, and Quinn Cummings as Annie—are acting out by-now familiar roles. Regular viewers might have read some of the many columns and articles featuring these artists, ABC's strategies in scheduling the show, director Mike Nichols' demands for quality production, and producers Aaron Spelling and Leonard Goldberg's commitments to serious television drama through this vehicle.[9] Those viewers, too, perhaps knew the show's irregular history. It first appeared March 9, 1976, as a late-season replacement for *Marcus Welby, M.D.* It did not do especially well, and therefore had another shortened season in 1977–78. Yet, that season earned it critical acclaim and Emmys, so in 1978–79 ABC pushed it into a competitive Thursday evening time slot, against CBS's popular *Barnaby Jones,* which had finished in the Top 25 during 1977–78. *Family's* reputation as a clean, thoughtful, lush, high-quality drama, ABC assumed, could attract an up-scale audience which already was watching other "high quality" shows— *The Waltons* on CBS (8–9 p.m.) and *Quincey, M.E.* on NBC (9–10 p.m.)— broadcast on Thursdays.

The initial episode of 1978–79, called "Starting Over," has all the earmarks of TV's aesthetically pleasing dramas: musical bridges, smooth editing, integrated and elevated dialogue, and classic plot construction. The musical background is used as a bridge between all but five scenes; and in those cases where it is not used, the scenes are presumably contiguous, and hence it is not really needed. Further, the music is slow and melodic, almost mournful, and dominated by guitars, violins, cellos, flutes, and French horns; it glues scenes together unobtrusively. And finally, the music is faded in—often thirty or more seconds before the end of a scene—and carried well into the next scene, reinforcing the viewers' sense of overall seamlessness or continuousness.

The editing harmonizes with the music. Individual scenes run as long as five-and-a-half minutes—almost unheard of in these days of fast and action-centered editing. Dissolves are employed for all but six changes between scenes, again adding to the illusion of flow and sweep. Dialogic bridges accomplish much the same thing. So, a reference to Willie ends Act I, scene i, and then Act I, scene ii is set in his bedroom; a phone rings in Act I, scene iii, and Act I, scene iv is the conversation; that phone conversation is concluded with an address of a law office, which then is the setting for Act I, scene v; and so on, through most of the show. Further, the editing is never quick-paced. All shots are at least two seconds long, and the vast majority are much longer. And, as well, the show is dominated by pictures of talking characters, almost always shot close-up and against static backgrounds. Overall, therefore, the lengths of scenes and shots, the music,[10] the camera work, and the editing all contribute in *Family* to a sense of seriousness, character-centeredness, flow—even leisurely exploration of human problems and their solutions.

To these physical features of the program we must add the dialogue and plot structure. While much of the conversation between characters is mundane, reflecting the program's attempt to present us with a slice-of-life, even eleven-year-olds and sixteen-year-olds talk in metaphor, and the adults utter psychological/social truths befitting social psychologists and philosophers—in phraseology often belying their station and situation. Further, the plot is well-made. Though this particular episode (as one would expect from a television show structured around quarter-hour commercial breaks) is constructed in four acts and an epilogue instead of the three or five acts of classic drama, it works structurally in classic ways, with a problem arising in Act I, complications developing in Act II, crises reaching destructive heights before a resolution in Acts III and IV, and a confirmation of the solution appearing in the Epilogue.

So, in all, the quality of characterizations, the physical aspects of production, the dialogue, and the plot formation all conspire to create an aesthetically interesting, smooth, and certainly pleasing show. In the fall of 1978, few series could boast of such high production values.

The Social Level

While the writing, acting, dominating use of single-shots, editing, scripting, and visual-aural bridging all interact to heighten the viewers' televisual experience when watching *Family,* the subject-matter itself comes off as standard family fare on the sociocultural level of meaningfulness. That is, while the artistic conventions of "high quality" or aesthetically sophisticated visual artforms are invoked, the actual "content" is, simply, mundane; the problems and the achievements of "everyday life" in an "ordinary" family are examined and commented upon in almost all episodes. To be sure, this particular episode, "Starting Over," deals with an unusual event—the introduction of a new family member—yet the treatment of that incident calls for little that is extraordinary from the other family members.

"Day in the Life"

Ideally, to demonstrate the everydayness of the "content" of this episode, we should analyze the entire show, scene by scene; space does not permit that. Instead, to get at its sociocultural dynamics, I will offer three exemplary analyses—one of the opening credits, one of a single scene, and one of a social theme (motherliness) which is developed across many scenes. Examining the opening credits will allow me to discuss the ways in which viewers are initially engaged by the program—the ways in which specific expectations are aroused and a particularized "symbolic environment" is created. Looking at a single scene (in this case, Act I, scene i) closely should demonstrate the kinds of "social knowledge"—the kinds of generalized beliefs, values, and attitudes about a culture—viewers are expected to bring to bear in their effort to find the program meaningful. And, tracing a single theme—motherliness, because it so dominates the program—will give us, ultimately, clues to the predominating ideology of *Family.* Furthermore, I hope in these three sample analyses to demonstrate the variety of methodological tacks one can, even must, take in doing a close textual analysis of sociocultural meanings inhering in televised family drama.

The Opening Credits. The stress on social roles and relationships starts right from the beginning of the show, in the opening credits. Against the show's melodic, sprightly-but-muted theme song, the titles open with an establishing shot high in the trees, with the shot moving down to a driveway framed by corner posts leading to an upper-middleclass home, surrounded by lush shade trees and shrubbery. We know that we are supposed to be in Pasadena, but the feeling is more midwestern than Californian. The title, *"Family,"* rises. In much of television, family names are used for titles—*The Adventures of Ozzie and Harriet, The Donna Reed Show, Life with Riley, The Jimmy Stewart Show, The Partridge Family, The Brady Bunch, The Waltons.* This show, its title suggests, belongs to the more generic character-centered and theme-centered, rather than star-centered, shows which began in 1949 with *Mama* and ran through *Make Room for Daddy* (until it was corrupted into *The Danny*

Thomas Show); Father Knows Best; Family's mid–70s counterpart, *Eight is Enough;* the short-lived 1979 show *A New Kind of Family;* and the Carol Lawrence comedy, *Mama's Family,* which opened in 1982.

From the title we cut to the front door, from which Kate emerges, *leaving* her domicile, with textbooks in arms and slightly raised eyebrows. She is frozen there, as the picture turns from clear to a linen-like photographic finish. We cut to the foyer, showing us Doug *entering* the home, obviously after a day's work, for he picks up the mail while still dressed in his lawyerish dark blue three-piece suit and muted red tie. His face likewise goes to a linen finish. Next, we cut to the sideyard shrubbery, where Willie is taking a picture of something just below the camera. We freeze on the studied look he is giving to his subject, again in linen. Then comes Buddy, running downstairs; she looks off camera right, smiles broadly, even warmly, and is frozen in a linen finish. We cut to Annie, swinging in the backyard; she, too, is frozen in a linen finish. Finally, there is Nancy, walking from the kitchen area to the foyer, dressed in the adult blouse-and-skirt of the thirty-year-old she nearly is, with the look of meeting someone new or loved off to camera right.

As the camera freezes her in linen finish, it pulls back to reveal the freeze-shots of all six main characters arranged in portrait fashion over a picture of the house and frontyard. Thus, the opening credits finish in a composite. Kate's picture is at the apex of the triangle, signaling the matriarchy we are about to enter; on the middle row are Willie, Doug, and Buddy as the principals; and the bottom row features Annie and Nancy, those characters furthest from the center of wisdom and action. Finally, the title *Family* appears again, this time in the lower lefthand corner, discreetly out of the way.

Even in the opening titles, therefore, we find cues to the predominating themes of the show. The family's namelessness makes a more or less generic statement about its thrust—its focus upon essences. The stress on portraiture not only foreshadows a dominating metaphor for this particular episode, but, in freezing individuals and relationships, reminds viewers of the tension between permanence and change—the permanence of familial values in the face of changing social circumstances—which inevitably becomes the central engine for all plots in this show. And, the audience's exposure to Kate as the primary character, to her positioning at the apex of the composite picture, and her movement out of the house (as opposed to Doug's movement into it) highlight domain: The home *is* mother's, without a doubt.

I stress here the analysis of opening credits because they are vehicles for drawing viewers into the symbolic environment. They set a mood, foreground themes which will come to be played in many an episode, and even contain for each character iconic details that stand for a portion of his or her makeup and tendencies. The opening credits, in a sense, are formal signs which, in Kenneth Burke's words, create "an appetite in the mind of the auditor [viewer]." "If," Burke says, "the poet . . . writes in such a way that we desire to observe [the action], and then, if he places that [action] before us—that is

9

form."[11] That so-called appetite could not be created had we not foreknowledge of such artistic conventions as patterned camera movement, freezes, "linen" finishes, and musical modes.

The other portion of the viewer's foreknowledge comes from "life"—from socialization into American culture. At least in the dominating upper-middleclass stratum, fathers work by day, and come home in the evening, especially if they belong to the professional class; Doug's opening actions, therefore, are perfectly intelligible to "up-scale" viewers. Twenty-year-olds occasionally withdraw, searching for means of self-fulfillment and self-expression; no wonder Willie is out of the house, capturing life and himself in photographs. Mothers can rule the roost, although "modern" mothers in the mid-'70s also venture out, often to school; and so on, with each character's initial actions. Now of course the meanings we assign to first impressions are notoriously susceptible to error. Viewers must confirm these impressions by examining later behaviors, later expressions of self, later interactions. But that, really, is the point of Burke's theory of form; form is an anticipatory mechanism. It creates and then, if the work is well-made, it satisfies appetite—the first impressions we form on the basis of our previous knowledge of such forms.

I have belabored the analysis of the opening credits in order to suggest the range of iconic and symbolic cues viewers have arrayed even in "mere" titles (in but one minute, ten seconds of TV), and to argue that both form and content depend for their communicability upon foreknowledge brought by viewers to the event.[12] Any messages "communicated" by television series lie not so much "in" the program or "in" the intent of the producers, directors, writers, actors, and editors. Rather, the messages lie in the culture and codes which are shared by all these people—and their viewers. The program itself is but a series of cues that creates viewer expectations—that "engages" an audience formally and substantively—and then, if the program is well-executed, satisfies and confirms those expectations. Different groups of viewers, of course, will be engaged on different levels or in different arenas-of-meaning, depending upon their sophistication, experiences, and the like. No matter what the ultimate degree of meaningfulness shared by TV "authors" and any particular "reader," communication, in television as elsewhere, simply could not occur were it not for the presence of shared stocks of knowledge—knowledges of things, of cultureways, of signs and their related signifieds—which can be called up symbolically or iconically.

The Opening Scene. Let us examine a regular scene now, to notice ways in which viewers' presumed knowledge of their culture is related to ordinary family conversation. In Act I, scene i, we witness a morning exchange between Doug and Kate dealing with what Doug should wear for the upcoming family portrait. After some witty dialogue about husband-wife relationships, we come to the closing lines of the scene:

Doug: "Why are you so hell-bent on getting another family portrait? We've got zillions of family portraits around here."

10

Kate: "I know. A feeling of imminent change, I suppose . . . Nancy and Jeff getting married again, Buddy turning sixteen next week, and Willie, oh, my heart, Willie. . . ."

Doug: "Willie will be fine. He's going to be the next king of the TV game shows." (Cut to Act I, scene ii, in Willie's bedroom.)

These lines, by themselves, are manifestly bare, yet they potentially trigger latent meanings in American viewers. Previous viewers can use this brief narration to remember (1) Kate as the force of the family (for it is she, as usual, who has initiated the family activity), (2) Doug as a reflective husband who seldom initiates but always reassures and responds, and who even comes close to trivializing the subject of the conversation, (3) the divorce of Nancy and Jeff, (4) the stormy transition Buddy has been going through from early tomboyish puberty to the pre-adult state of late teens, and (5) Willie's search for a post-high-school life of work and love. Even the occasional or new viewer of *Family* has been given a light-but-important load of background information, and has heard a line key to the central theme of the show—"A feeling of imminent change, I suppose. . . ." When that new viewer is attempting to make sense out of the array of characters introduced in the opening credits and referred to in this dialogue, he or she can draw from a stock of general American social stereotypes: Mothers, Americans have presumed (rightly or wrongly), are the creators of familial bonds, and hence are the family members who worry about such iconic tokens of permanence as portraits. Divorce is a jarring rupture that can be healed through talk, love, and even remarriage. Sixteen, "Sweet sixteen and never been kissed," is a transitional age and hence productive of doubt, conflict, but yet growth. Work is a route into a mature, adult world, although if Willie is connecting himself with such an abnormal job as TV game show worker, he probably is still in search of himself.

This range of meanings, cued by but a snippet of dialogue, represents a series of conjectures drawn from social stereotypes and other bits of social wisdom floating through the collective consciousness of Americans. Such meanings are not "in" the show; rather, they represent statements that allow a viewer to rationalize what has been seen and heard. Without such beliefs and attitudes, viewers probably would find Act I, scene i, *meaningless*. Note, too, of course, that such statements probably are but tentatively advanced by viewers; like the meanings we found in the opening credits, these, too, must be verified by examining later behaviors and statements of the characters— and sociocultural character types—involved in this symbolic-social universe. Early in a show, especially, such rationalizing statements are mere hypotheses, selected from viewers' knowledge of their culture and its social rules; only if confirmed *within the universe of the artifact*—within the aesthetic world being "performed" by the actors—will they be forged into a coherent meaning-structure. Viewers come to "understand" an episode and a series only through the interaction of their stock of social knowledge with characterizations offered in that episode and series. We will return to this extremely important point later.

The Attributes of Motherliness. To discover the sorts of meaning-structures I have been discussing, we need to look for a particular theme which gets developed across several scenes of a show. Because, as already noted, "matriarchy" lies at the base of *Family,* let us look at some of the dialogue which contributes to the show's vision of motherliness. Following are pieces of dialogue, scattered through this particular episode, relevant to viewers' reconstructions of the attributes of motherliness:

From Act I, scene iii: Kate and Nancy are getting ready for the day, before knowing about Annie. Nancy notes that she will spend part of her day just "doing some shopping." Kate responds, wishing she could be in Nancy's shoes. Then:

Nancy: "You've been in my shoes for almost thirty years."

Kate: "No round numbers, please."

Nancy: "Well, it's true."

Kate: "But there's light at the end of the tunnel. Buddy's pretty well shifting for herself these days." (Phone rings in the house.) "Oh nertz!"

Nancy: "Let it ring."

Kate: "I can't—it might be Buddy."

Nancy: "I thought you said she could shift for herself."

Kate: "I lied."

From Act I, scene v: Once Doug and Kate arrive at Al Krantz' law office, he explains Annie's situation. Annie's aunt Sophie, after some small talk about Annie's reaction to her parents' deaths, begins to recite difficulties she has had in coping with a child in her home:

Sophie: "It's impossible. I'm a woman who has always had a career. I own a number of dress shops in California, Arizona, Nevada, and when my brother and Grace were killed, I thought I would be able to find ways to look after Andrea and go on with my work. But, I want to bow out."

Kate: "Bow out?" (The line is said slowly, Kate's face betrays incredulity, and the camera tightens its shot on her.)

A few lines later, after Al Krantz hands the Lawrences the note they signed and reminds them of their signing, Kate resumes:

Kate: "Friends often do that [i.e. sign notes of guardianship]."

Sophie: "I'm asking you to honor the terms of that agreement. Being a parent is a full-time job—a job for which, I discovered somewhat belatedly, I have but minimal talent. So, for Andrea's own good, and, frankly, for mine, please." (Music comes up, dissolve out of this scene and into the next one.)

12

From Act I, scene iv: In the next scene, Kate and Doug are in bed at night, Kate up on an elbow, Doug apparently sleeping. She turns on the light, and starts talking:

Kate: "Doug, I don't think I can do it." (She pauses, Doug slowly realizes he is being addressed, and finally rolls to face her.)

Doug: "Andrea?"

Kate: "I'm running scared." (pause)

Doug: "Well, I know it's going to be easier for me—the whole burden will be on you. But, we'll all be there—especially me. That help?"

Kate: "A little." (pause) "Besides, Andrea's going to need mothering desperately—she deserves someone who can give it to her, full out. Just don't think I have enough left. I know I don't."

Doug: "And I know that any child that needs love and comes within fifty yards of you will get it." (Soft, fluty music comes up, Kate turns off the light, Doug rolls over. Kate is still on her elbow.)

Kate: "She was an awfully sweet baby. . . ."

Doug: "Aha! There you go. It's started already." (The music swells, dissolve to next scene.)

From Act II, scene iv: It is after supper during Annie's first full day. Kate has indicated her tiredness, calling for a volunteer to help. As Doug is the only other person in the room, he says he will. Then:

Kate: "Try *Wind in the Willows*."

Doug: "*Wind in the Willows*?"

Kate: How quickly they forget. That was guaranteed cuddle-up material when Buddy was in this age—I think there's a copy in the library."

From Act II, scene vii: Doug knocks, enters Annie's room, to find her seated on the window shelf. He says:

Doug: "I found this book. It was a favorite of Buddy's when she was your age. She used to snuggle up in bed, and then I'd sit down next to her and read to her. I miss that. How do you feel about being read to?" (No response. After he starts to read, Annie recognizes the work, says she "outgrew it," and shortly thereafter, Doug leaves. Annie proceeds to recite it from memory as the scene dissolves.)

From Act IV, scene iii: Annie has been found in Willie's car. Annie and Willie return home after their talk (see Figure 1), Willie goes to Nancy's, and Annie says "good night," heading upstairs. The parents are left:

Doug: "Go get her, Kate."

Kate: "I don't think I know how."

Doug: "You always have."

13

Kate: "Couldn't I put it off until tomorrow?"

Doug: "Could you?"

Kate: "I suppose not. I could stall a little. . . ."

Doug: "Finish your drink."

Kate: "We who are about to take the kid by the horns, salute you." (She quaffs her drink, hands the glass to Doug, turns smartly on her heel, and heads upstairs with a firm step. Cut, no music.)

From Act IV, scene iv: Kate marches into Annie's room, not knocking. She excuses herself verbally for that inconsideration, but her demeanor and manner make it clear she is not asking for forgiveness at all. She says:

Kate: "You and I have some talking to do, Annie. Better put the cards aside. . . ." (Annie, for the third time in the show, has been playing Solitaire, an obvious metaphor for solitude.) ". . . so I can put mine on the table." (Annie refuses, continuing her one-person card game.) "Ok, then." (She goes to the closet for a suitcase, and starts emptying drawers into it. When Annie asks if she must go back to her aunt, Kate affirms it, referring to the terms of the agreement between the Lawrences and the Coopers. Then:)

Kate: "And, it was agreed on, if anything ever happened. . . ."

Annie: "I guess they made the wrong decision."

Kate: "They who?"

Annie: "They . . . it wasn't the right decision."

Kate: "They *who,* Annie?"

Annie: "My mother and father!"

Kate: "That's a relief. You know, in the whole time you've been here, that's the first time you've ever mentioned your parents."

Annie: "There's nothing to say, so why bring them up?"

Kate: "Nothing? You sure?"

Annie: "Quite sure. . . ." (Annie is ready to march out the door. Kate looks defeated, but comments on the fact that, sooner or later, Annie will have to quit running. Then:)

Annie: "I wasn't running anywhere [in reference to her hiding in Willie's car]—I needed a place to think!"

Kate: "All right, but you are running, Annie. I think you have been, ever since the accident happened. I wish you could try to stand still, and face it. You think if you do, you won't ever recover; that you'll just fly apart into hundreds of bits and pieces. . . ."

Annie: "I don't think that!"

Kate: (Unconvinced) "You know, no matter how hard you run, eventually it's going to catch up with you—the anger you feel, the terrible desolation."

Annie: "Actually, I think my aunt's will be a lot better."

Kate: "You know, having you here is like seeing your mother again. . . ." (At this point, Kate launches an extended narrative about the Lawrences' separation from the Coopers, and then, going back farther, about Kate's relationship with Grace Cooper—their friendship in college, a parrot Grace purchased, the circumstances under which the Coopers met, the Coopers' desire for a child, Annie's birth. Annie seems to be leaving now that the suitcase is packed. Kate intercedes:) "Don't forget Sam [Annie's stuffed dog]. Your mother bought him before you were born—I was with her the day she picked him out." (Long take of the back of Annie's head as she stands in the doorway with Sam. Her head tilts back slightly, tensely, as she slowly turns to reveal tears and anguish.)

Annie: "Why did they have to die?" (Walking toward Kate, seated on the bed.) "Why they? Why?" (Hurrying to Kate, sagging into her arms.) "Why they? Why die?" (These lines are almost unintelligibly muffled in Kate's neck.)

Kate (holding her tightly): "I don't know, honey, I don't know. . . . Oh, Annie, please stay with us. I'll hold you together."

Annie: "Can you?"

Kate: "I'll try. . . ." (Scene fades to black as the camera pulls back slowly, leaving them in a madonna-and-child-like pose.)

Much of this dialogue, befitting a slice-of-life televised family drama, is cliche-ridden, pathetic, even bathetic, in the way it has been visualized and spoken. Its statements about motherliness are but partially "said"; complete messages are not developed, explicated, or even directly endorsed often. Yet, taking in hand the great box of conventional wisdom packed away in sensitive American viewers' social memories, and realizing that these scenes are related to each other *mimetically* (for what has been acted out in one scene is verisimilar to what has been acted out in the others), then we can say that these pieces of dialogue and action *enthymematically* make sense.

The notion of "mimesis" or "imitation" has a full and complicated history since ancient times. Generally, we can say that the classical doctrine of "mimesis" had two dimensions: (1) Primarily, the word referred to the degree to which "art" imitated or was verisimilar to "life." This notion is drawn primarily from Aristotle's famous definition of "tragedy" (*Poetics,* 1449b). (2) Secondarily, the word referred essentially to artistic, internal verisimilitude, that is, the degree to which actions taken by characters in one portion of an artistic work are consistent with those they take in other portions of that work. It is in this second sense that I am using the word "mimetically" in this essay.[13]

Again, Aristotle is our primary classical source on the notion of "enthymeme." Roughly speaking, an "enthymeme" is an argument—one much like a syllogism—one of whose premises or assumptions (normally unstated) is held to be true by an audience. Indeed, an "enthymeme" often is termed a "rhetorical syllogism," in that it (1) operates rationally like a syllogism, yet (2) in its technical informality is easily adapted to rhetorical situations.[14]

The central argument I am making, then, can be restated in this manner: Viewers draw upon their social experience and other kinds of knowledge to make sense of—to interpret—what they see in TV fictional programs. More technically, their experience/knowledge serves as kinds of "major premises," the manifest content of the program serves more or less as "minor premises," and the "meaning" they assign to those scenes—based on what they see as rational connections between their experience/knowledge and the manifest content of a series—becomes the "conclusion" drawn. For example, proposition 7 below states "Children who have problems can be reached through narrative recitations drawn from their own lives." Audience members who accept that presupposition will connect it to, in "Starting Over," Doug's reference to what Buddy liked as a child (a negative tactic that does not work because the narrative is being drawn from someone else's life), Buddy's and Willie's attempts to get Annie to "act" like a sibling (a negative tactic that does not work because action and not story-telling is proposed), and, of course, Kate's long recitation of Annie's own history (a positive tactic that does work because it is drawn from Annie's own background and because the narrative unites Annie's life with the Lawrences' lives). The "conclusion" to be drawn from this "unit of reasoning" is "So if you want to break through children's defenses, tell them stories about themselves." In other words, through the dramatic action, a presupposition is given illustration in the artifact, and a hortatory conclusion—a directive on how to live one's life—is implied and reinforced.

Such conclusions, *during the process of viewing,* are but tentative: viewers, after all, cannot really "know" the message as it is unfolding. While viewing, however, they do have recourse to their own memory. If they are long-time viewers of a program, they can remember previous episodes, and even within a single program they can remember previous segments, comparing both previous episodes and previous scenes with what they are now watching. They can make mimetic comparisons between what they are now watching and characters' behaviors and seeming motivations in previous episodes and scenes; in that way, they can, in a sense, "certify" their interpretation of the scene they are now watching. Overall, therefore, the idea of "enthymematic reasoning" may help us explain the ways in which viewers bring their experience and knowledge to bear on televisual artifacts (especially those, such as *Family,* which are set in the "everyday" or "mundane" world) so as to interpret or "understand" those artifacts. And, the idea of "mimetic comparisons" helps explain the role of memory in the certification process.[15] Following are ten propositions which serve as "major premises" rationalizing positions taken and statements made in the dialogue we have reviewed:

1. Mothers' leadership obligations continue until children have left home; once a mother, always a mother. Even when specific leadership needs are satisfied, it is a lifelong role which never can be completely relinquished. (Act I, scene iii; Act I, scene vi; Act IV, scene iii.)
2. Women must make careful decisions between homelife and careers, for they do not mix easily. In making such decisions, mothers must consider first the needs of children. (Act I, scene v, twice.)
3. Mothering is a social role which does not come wholly naturally, but rather demands the acquisition of specific skills. Hence, motherhood is an occupation as well as an avocation. (Act I, scene v.)
4. Fathers can help in the running of families, but mothers maintain the central burden. (Act I, scene vi; Act II, scene vi; Act IV, scene iii.)
5. Mothering is a complex activity, and hence even good mothers experience self-doubt; they must have the courage to face moments of crisis. (Act I, scene vi; Act IV, scene iii.)
6. Mothers' familial memories are longer than fathers' memories. And, that is one of the reasons for their familial dominance—they are families' cultural repositories. (Act II, scene vi.) *interenty*
7. Children who have problems can be reached through narrative recitations drawn from their own lives. Attempts to reach them with mere exhortation, narratives drawn from other people's lives, or mere collective activity are likely to fail. (Act II, scene vii, e.g., is a negative example; Act IV, scene iv, e.g., is a positive example; Annie's interactions with most other characters throughout the episode are relevant as well.)
8. Mothers know that the key to solving childrens' problems is exploration of their emotional lives, their hidden hopes and fears. Mothers know how to break through emotional barriers, even when others cannot. (Act IV, scene iv, especially.)
9. Mothers, like everyone else, may err and have weaknesses, but they persevere in their missions—holding families together and ensuring the social-emotional development of family members. (Act IV, scene iii; Act IV, scene iv.)
10. Ultimately, families—especially matriarchal families—are the sources of all problem-solving and succorance in life. (Act I, scene v; Act IV, scene iv.)[16] *imp*

What we have in these ten propositions, as I said, are pieces of conventional wisdom which rationalize the dialogues we have reviewed. These are the propositions which function as "major premises" for the "arguments" relative to motherliness implicit in the "Starting Over" episode of *Family*. Two additional points about these propositions should be made:

First, these propositions have been *cued* in a number of different ways, via several different codes. Temporally, changes in tempo and the introduction of pauses have been used to signal "important" statements. Visually, camera movements have been used to bracket key segments of scenes. Aurally, musical accompaniment has been selected to reinforce the emotional tenor of verbal statements, and actors' vocal patterns likewise provide aural emphases. Iconically, the interrupting (even disrupting) phone, the portrait, the game of Solitaire/solitude, the drink, the suitcase, and the stuffed animal—especially the stuffed animal as an icon which has existed longer than Annie and which unites Annie with both the Coopers and the Lawrences because Kate helped purchase it—add resonance to the snatches of dialogue with which they are surrounded. And, dialogically, of course, the presence of statements concerning social roles is signaled in a variety of ways: (1) Doug uses the imperative mood (as in "Go get her, Kate"), while Kate tends to rely on first-person singular statements (as in all of her "I will" and "I don't think" statements). (2) Doug tends to offer short, single-sentence comments, while Kate tends to talk in longer and more explanatory "paragraphs" (see the above dialogue). (3) Kate, in talking with others, tends to rely on reflective questions ("Bow out?" "Nothing?" "You sure?"); other characters, as exemplified in Figure 1, concentrate generally on describing themselves. Dialogically, in other words, the explicit "content" of statements is surrounded by a series of linguistic markers—sentence moods, personal voice, verbal redundancy and fullness, other-reflexive and self-reflexive constructions vs. non-reflexive constructions—which help viewers isolate the interpersonal "meanings" lying behind those explicit contents.

A second point should be made as well: As one inspects the ten propositions, it becomes relatively easy to fit them together into a coherent social ideology, a matriarchal vision of social life. The motherly role and its attendant relationships with other familial roles can be thought of as ideological, first, on the linguistic or codic level of statement. As we have just seen, many of the propositions are phrased as descriptive generalizations, yet contain strongly loaded value-concepts—such as "obligations," "must consider first," "occupation" and "avocation," "central burden," "self-doubt," "courage," "social-emotional development," and the like. It is such valuative loading of propositions which makes them ideological, in Bergmann's linguistic sense of that word.[17] Not only do these propositions seem "descriptive" while carrying valuative baggage, but, as well, there is even a masking of exhortation and evaluation created by the artistic qualities of the show. Part of that masking derives from the sense of smoothness, luxuriousness, and seamlessness created by director Mike Nichols and other members of the production crew; televisually, the episode is so smooth and continuous that it is lulling. Nothing is overemphasized in the show; hence, it is unlikely that the viewer looking for "easy viewing" and "entertainment" will examine the show's propositions critically. The cinematic artistry and the social themes interpenetrate each other, in such a way that the themes become, in a sense, legitimated by the high-quality production of the show.

Further, the series *Family* has ideological force for another reason—sheer repetition. In almost all episodes through its history, the series featured the matriarchal principle; in almost all episodes, Kate was the primary force, the problem-solver. Through *Family's* run, the mother-type transacted social business with the father-type and the children-types, all the while exhibiting control yet compassion, wariness yet warmth, and hence authoritativeness yet extreme attractiveness. This point, I think, would stand out even more clearly had we the space to contrast the show's depiction of "motherliness" with its rendering of "fatherliness" and "childrenness." (Readers perhaps can sense the episode's visions of fatherliness and childrenness by examining the segments of dialogue reviewed in Figure 1.)

Overall, *Family's* artistic qualities combine with its repeated depiction of Kate's success with social-level transactions to give the ten ideological propositions a good deal of force. The ideology could be construed even as pernicious—to people offended by its matriarchal vision—because it comes off as simultaneously artistically natural and socially pragmatic or successful.

Act/Scene (Length)	Dialogue Related to Motherliness
Opening Titles (1:10)	(See the text for a description.)
Act I/sc. i (1:25)	Morning in Doug and Kate's bedroom. Kate is picking out clothes for the upcoming portrait; husband-wife banter. Then:
	Doug: "Why are you so hell-bent on getting another family portrait—we've got zillions of family portraits around here."
	Kate: "I know. A feeling of imminent change, I suppose . . . Nancy and Jeff getting married again, Buddy turning sixteen next week, and Willie, oh, my heart, Willie. . . ."
	Doug: "Willie will be fine. He's going to be the new king of the TV game shows."
Act I/sc. ii (:54)	Exchange between Buddy and Willie in his room; sibling banter showing their open and warm relationship.
Act I/sc. iii (:41)	Outdoor conversation between Kate and Nancy as they start their days; reference to Nancy's freedom to shop, with Kate wishing she could be in Nancy's shoes. Then:
	Nancy: "You've been in my shoes for almost 30 years."
	Kate: "No round numbers, please."
	Nancy: "Well, it's true."
	Kate: "But there's light at the end of the tunnel. Buddy's pretty well shifting for herself these days." [phone in house] Oh nertz!"
	Nancy: "Let it ring."
	Kate: "I can't—it might be Buddy."
	Nancy: "I thought you said she could shift for herself."
	Kate: "I lied."

Figure 1. The story of "Starting Over," *Family* episode (9/21/78); and dialogue analyzed in this paper.

Figure 1—*Continued*

Act I/sc. iv (:45)	Phone call from Doug; a lawyer Al Krantz wants the Lawrences to come to a meeting that afternoon; uncomplimentary references to lawyers (Doug's occupation); address for meeting.
Act I/sc. v (3:27)	Krantz' office; introduction of Sophie Sullivan, sister of Ralph Cooper, aunt of Andrea (Annie); narration on death of parents, polite conversation about Annie. Then:

Sophie: "It's impossible. I'm a woman who has always had a career. I own a number of dress shops in California, Arizona, Nevada, and when my brother and Grace were killed, I thought I would be able to find ways to look after Andrea and go on with my work. But I want to bow out."

Kate: "Bow out?" [Review of Lawrences' note of agreement; then:]

Sophie: "I'm asking you to honor the terms of that agreement." [silence] "Being a parent is a full-time job—a job for which, I discovered somewhat belatedly, I have but minimal talent. So, for Andrea's good, and, frankly, for mine, please."

Act I/sc. vi (2:00)	Darkened bedroom of Kate and Doug; Kate on elbow, Doug apparently asleep; Kate turns on light—

Kate: "Doug, I don't think I can do it." [Doug slowly wakens]

Doug: "Andrea?"

Kate: "I'm running scared." [pause]

Doug: "Well, I know it's going to be easier for me—the burden will be on you. But, we'll all be here—especially me. That help?" [pause]

Kate: "A little." [pause] "Besides, Andrea's going to need mothering desperately—she deserves someone who can give it to her, full out. Just don't think I have enough left. I know I haven't."

Doug: "And I know that any child that needs love and comes [music starts] within fifty yards of you will get it." [Doug rolls over. Kate turns out light, still on elbow.]

Kate: "She was an awfully sweet baby."

Doug: "Aha! There you go. It's started already."

Act I/sc. vii (1:56)	Next day, in Lawrence living room; Kate, Nancy, and Buddy fidgeting over arrival; Willie comes; finally Doug and Annie arrive; banter and introductions, with Annie snapping out her lines and reactions. A final "Oh boy . . ." from Kate.

[ACT I = 10:08 min.]

Act II/sc. i (2:26)	Kitchen scene, next morning; greeting of Annie, who has not slept; suggestions from everyone about what they can do with her; all ignored or rejected; all leave; Annie starts on a crossword puzzle, a solitary activity.

Figure 1—*Continued*

Act II/sc. ii	Kate and Doug outside as he's getting ready to leave; dialogue about whether to pursue the portrait; left up-in-the-air.
Act II/sc. iii (1:13)	Annie and Kate in the kitchen; discussion of tasks, school, desires, freedom of this day; discussion of what Annie should call Kate; little reaction; Annie goes upstairs with puzzle.
Act II/sc. iv (2:08)	Annie walks into Willie's room, with puzzle, where he's working on his game show; he impresses with his knowledge of trivia; when he suggests a personal outing to play pinball, Annie freezes over and leaves.
Act II/sc. v (2:02)	Scene in Nancy's guest house, with Timmy (Nancy's child), Nancy, and Buddy; questions about how Buddy is getting along with Annie—noncommital answers, reference to how hard Annie is on Kate; enter Annie, who is introduced by Nancy to Timmy as "your new aunt"; Annie freezes; Timmy, Nancy, and Buddy go to the backyard swing, with Annie watching forlornly.
Act II/sc. vi (1:12)	Kate and Doug cleaning up after supper; review of supper and Annie's coldness; call for volunteer to take over by Kate; then:

> *Kate:* "Try *Wind in the Willows.*"
> *Doug:* *"Wind in the Willows?"*
> *Kate:* "How quickly they forget. That was guaranteed cuddle-up material when Buddy was in this age—I think there's a copy in the library."

Act II/sc. vii (3:04)	Annie's bedroom, where she sits curled up in a near-fetal position in the window shelf, clutching Sam, a stuffed dog; Doug knocks, enters, greets her, and then:

> *Doug:* "I found this book. It was a favorite of Buddy's when she was about your age. She used to snuggle up in bed, and then I'd sit down next to her and read to her. I miss that. How do you feel about being read to?" [silence; Doug reads; Annie recognizes the story, saying "They . . . I used to read"; says she outgrew it; Doug leaves, giving the book to Annie; Annie recites it from memory when alone, looking forlornly out the window.]

[ACT II = 14:32 min.]

Act III/sc. i (1:31)	Backyard the next day, with Annie swinging Timmy happily; Kate watches hopefully; then Timmy must leave for pediatric appointment, and Annie refuses the invitation to go along.
Act III/sc. ii (:56)	In Annie's bedroom, where she's playing Solitaire; Buddy enters, offers to take her skateboarding; rebuff, with "By definition, Solitaire means one" and with references to her lack of athletic ability; Buddy wheels out; Annie looks dissatisfied.

Figure 1—*Continued*

Act III/sc. iii (1:32)	Driveway scene between Buddy and Kate; Buddy vents her negative feelings, encouraged to express them by Kate ("Second thoughts about the advantages of a younger sister? Nothing you say will be held against you").
Act III/sc. iv (4:37)	Living room, with Annie playing the piano; conversation about possible piano lessons when Kate arrives; Kate leaves to make them tea, Willie enters; phonecall; photographer wants to know how many in picture; Willie says seven; Annie screams "Six! Six! Six!"; Willie corrects the message, leaves in disgust; Kate returns as Willie leaves, tries to talk with Annie about family; Annie is silent, then under the pressure leaves, with Kate calling after her "Annie? Annie! Damn!!!"; it continues outside; as Doug drives up, Annie hides in Willie's car; Doug and Kate worry together about where she is.
Act III/sc. v (:45)	Willie, now that it's dark and suppertime, comes out of Nancy's to go get Chinese food; gets in car with Annie hiding in the back, and starts uptown.

[ACT III = 9:21 mins.]

Act IV/sc. i (1:57)	Willie driving in downtown nighttime traffic; Annie finally sits up talks, startles Willie; he pulls to the curb, says she doesn't have to go home yet if she calls; she asks him to do it for her, to which he replies wryly, "A chink in the armor, huh?"
Act IV/sc. ii (1:59)	Willie drives Annie to a park, so they can talk; oddly, the park is a passion pit, and they're soon surrounded with necking young couples; against this background of shallow passion Willie and Annie discuss feelings, with Annie insisting that "old feelings can [never] be recaptured"; Willie counters, "You're right; however, if people want to, they can put aside old feelings and let new ones grow"; Annie is silent, they leave.
Act IV/sc. iii (1:29)	Back to livingroom, with Willie leaving; Annie apologizes for worrying them, and leaves. Then: *Doug:* "Go get her, Kate." *Kate:* "I don't think I know how." *Doug:* "You always have." *Kate:* "Couldn't I put it off until tomorrow?" *Doug:* "Could you?" *Kate:* "I suppose not. I could stall a little." *Doug:* "Finish your drink." *Kate:* "We who are about to take the kid by the horns, salute you."

Figure 1—*Continued*

Act IV/sc. iv
(5:38)

Almost half of this scene (2:46) is spent in initial maneuvering, before the long narrative. Kate enters without knocking, apologizing for not knocking (but making it clear in her demeanor that she meant to enter abruptly):

Kate: "You and I have some talking to do, Annie. Better put the cards aside, so I can put mine on the table." Annie avoids contact, so Kate starts packing; Annie wonders if she has to go back to her aunt's, Kate affirms that; the Cooper-Lawrence agreement is talked about, then:

Kate: "And it was agreed on, if anything ever happened. . . ."

Annie: "I guess they made the wrong decision."

Kate: "They who?"

Annie: "They . . . it wasn't the right decision."

Kate: "They *who,* Annie?"

Annie: "My mother and father!"

Kate: "That's a relief. You know, in the whole time you've been here, that's the first time you've ever mentioned your parents."

Annie: "There's nothing to say, so why bring them up?"

Kate: "Nothing? You sure?"

Annie: "Quite sure."

[Annie goes back on the offense, jeering Kate for expecting to make her cry with the threat of leaving; Kate accuses her of running away; then:]

Annie: "Wasn't running anywhere—I needed a place to think!"

Kate: "All right, but you are running, Annie. I think you have been ever since the accident happened. I wish you could try to stand still, and face it. You think if you do, you won't ever recover, that you'll just fly apart into hundreds of bits and pieces."

Annie: "I don't think that!"

Kate: "You know, no matter how hard you run, eventually it's going to catch up with you—the anger you feel, the terrible desolation."

Annie: "Actually, I think my aunt's will be a lot better."

Kate: "You know, having you here is like seeing your mother again . . . [long narrative about Lawrences and Coopers, the way Annie's parents met, a parrot, Annie's birth, etc.; Annie still tries to leave with suitcase, then:]

Kate: "Don't forget Sam. Your mother bought him before you were born—I was with her the day she picked him out."

Annie: "Why did they have to die? Why they? Why? Why they? Why die?"

Figure 1—*Continued*

> *Kate:* "I don't know, honey, I don't know. Oh Annie, please stay with us. I'll hold you together."
> *Annie:* "Can you?"
> *Kate:* "I'll try."

[ACT IV = 11:03 mins.]

Epilogue (2:07)   Photographic session; nothing's right until Sam is included.

Final Speculations

Some larger implications concerning ideology, art, and society should be stated, although their development would require a more complete historical review than I can provide here. The first one is this: Not only does *Family* exhibit ideological characteristics on the linguistic and artistic levels of comprehension, but further, the show's ideological force can be assessed more holistically, by noting its relationships to other television programs airing in America both previous to and simultaneously with it.

More specifically, I think it can be argued that the show functioned sociopolitically as a kind of rearguard conceptualization of American society in the '70s. In *Julia*, a Black nurse and single parent had managed to combine career and motherliness successfully; Mary Tyler Moore had been told weekly that she would "make it after all" professionally and humanely; *Maude* triumphed with toughness yet warmth both in family and in professional settings; *Rhoda's* worklife compensated for her difficult family life with mother and husband; *Alice* was making a go of it in Phoenix; and Bonnie Franklin as another single mother was likewise surviving *One Day At A Time.* Further, the '70s also was the decade of professionals more generally, especially doctors, lawyers, detectives, police men and women, and even heroic medical examiners and newspaper people. In almost all of TV's top-rated shows—which tended to be the profession-centered vehicles—society's problems were put in the laps of people outside one's family. Doctors, lawyers, and the others were expected to serve not only institutional needs but also to solve individuals' psychological and social-psychological problems.[18] *Family* was swimming against two currents—the trend in female characterizations and lifestyles as well as the trend toward the professionalization of problem-solving.

Family, therefore, stood as a bulwark. It did not stand alone, of course, for on its ideological side were *Little House on the Prairie, The Waltons,* occasionally *One Day At A Time* and *Alice,* and even such blockbuster specials as *Roots*—shows ideologically akin, even though some were matriarchal, and others, patriarchal. Generally, though, the matriarchal vision pervaded but a handful of TV programs in the '70s, especially the late '70s. The age, after all, was one of equal opportunity and affirmative action, the Equal Rights Amendment controversy, an exploding divorce rate, single parenthood, zero population growth, and dress-for-success female professionalism. *Family's* ideological tune was played in loud counterpoint to the society in which it was presented. Its social vision flew in the face of literal social facts—especially the social facts we associate with its locale, the urban sprawl of metropolitan Los Angeles.

This is not to say, however, that its vision was anachronistic in the same way the visions of the 19th-century Ingalls family or the Depression-Era Walton family were in *Little House on the Prairie* and *The Waltons*. Their anachronistic symbolic environment gave those shows a more mythic than mundane sociocultural air.[19] The family of *Family* lived in the here-and-now. The show's stress upon open expressiveness, psychological exploration of problems, and such topical themes as divorce, pre-marital sex, marriage, love, dying, unemployment, intergenerational conflict, and individual maturation—that is, its stress upon permanence in the face of change—made its vision contemporary. The episode we have examined, "Starting Over," certainly illustrates the show's concerns for contemporaneity and, more important, permanence and change: We have had cued references to adoption/guardianship, divorce and marriage, careers and personal development, teenage maturation, single parenthood. Further, the question of permanence vs. change has been seen in the dominating metaphor of the family portrait; Buddy's and Willie's shifting statuses; Nancy's decision to remarry even while living at home (and, it should be noted, she and Jeff lived on the family property even when married before); and Sam, the stuffed dog, as a symbol of continuity and inter-familial linkage.

Indeed, a good deal of *Family's* perniciousness—if that is the right word— arose from its contemporaneity. Its vision therefore was socially or culturally combative and challenging to other visions of life in America; and, because of its high production or artistic values, that vision was all the more alluring. *Family's* matriarchal vision of modern life was, in fact, presented as a viable alternative to the American lifestyles and sociocultural trends of the '70s. Enticing us into its version of the New Momism via soft flutes and guitars, beautifully shot scenes, well-performed characterizations, and yet contemporary social themes, *Family* ultimately had what we might be tempted to call an *ideologically subversive message* concealed within its simplicity, grace, and warmth. Kate may have sworn and tippled, yet those "vices" only made her more human and were more than compensated for by her overpowering interpersonal virtues. The show was built around her humanness and humanity. It was a call back, not to the lifestyle of earlier eras, but to a much more primal conceptualization of family—and especially motherliness—as the ultimate pivot of all social existence.

But there is a second level at which ideology operates, beyond these considerations of the relationships between lived and symbolically experienced social reality. While I have suggested along the way some of the dynamics of audience engagement—some of the specific artistic and sociocultural techniques which engage viewers' experiences and knowledge—we need to pursue these matters even more broadly.

British TV critic Mick Eaton concluded his far-ranging analysis of situation comedy by noting that family-centered shows "[hold] us there by a celebration of our own subject position as television viewer."[20] Going even beyond Eaton, one can argue that "we are what we view," when it comes to family shows especially, in two senses: In one sense, we are what we view because most of us select for consumption TV fare which reflects our own beliefs and values, or, conversely, which projects our hopes and dreams onto the characters who populate TV shows.[21] Indeed, the whole controversy between the networks and the FCC regarding "Family Viewing Hours" in 1975 was rooted in precisely that assumption—that television, in its reflective-projective operations, morally has an obligation to present "wholesome" American beliefs, attitudes, and values during times when our objects-of-socialization, children, are up and around because TV is a *vehicle* for social education and an object of imitation. If our culture did not take as axiomatic that we are what we view, the Family Viewing Hours dicta never would have been acceded to, given their questionable legal foundations.

In addition, though, I would argue that "we are what we view" in a much more important, epistemological sense. Our very conceptions of "self"—of who we are, how we live and ought to live, why we are who we are—are derived, as George Herbert Mead argued brilliantly some fifty years ago,[22] from our interactions with "significant others," with cultural representatives such as friends, acquaintances, institutional personnel. Given their ubiquity and general attractiveness (and hence presumed power), television programs are "significant others" in our lives. Television, to the average American, is fully integrated into the rest of life experience, and hence is a primary source for an individual's conception of life and the rules-for-living. As Todd Gitlin argues:

> The forms of mass-cultural production [including television] do not spring up or operate independently of the rest of social life. Commercial culture does not *manufacture* ideology: it *relays* and *reproduces* and *processes* and *packages* and *focuses* ideology that is constantly arising both from social elites . . . and groups . . . and movements . . . and media . . . practices.[23]

More specifically, then: The stocks of knowledge and norms which each of us has acquired through injunctions from institutions (church, state, exhortative media operations), interactions with peers, and introspective musings about Self and others are the sources for judgments about meaningfulness and meaninglessness, propriety and impropriety, truth and falsehood. Viewers and producers alike draw from the same cultural resources. Televised narrative programs, therefore, do not so much "send"—or even "project," as Loevinger

26

would have it—messages as "embody" them. Like other mass media, television programs, for the most part, can but arrange and rearrange the data of socially shared knowledge and the elements in pre-existing codes in the hope of offering a configuration of cues or signs which allow the teller's stocks of knowledge and visions of life to be reproduced in the audience's (the "told-to's") mind. The phrase "in the hope of" is important here, for of course successful reproduction of meaning-structures in other people's minds is dependent upon those individuals' sophistication in cue or sign interpretation, their ranges of actual and vicarious experiences (including previous TV viewing), their attentiveness, and so on. Television's communicativeness always depends upon the degree to which knowledge and experience are shared by the teller and the told-to, and hence always is a differential phenomenon.

Because viewing experiences *are* different, and because network television, especially, is a commercial enterprise which depends for its livelihood upon sizable audiences, TV, as we all know, has pitched its messages to some of the "lowest common denominators" in society. It has traded on entertainment values and familiarity more than explicitly informational values and novelty in its search for the audiences it can sell to advertisers. American television generally, therefore, has featured blood-and-guts, sex, comedy, and family in its dramatic and comedic series, for they are the raw materials of life in the *communitas.* Television programming, as Gitlin intimated in the above quotation, simply *must* relay, reproduce, process, package, and focus upon predominating ideologies, preserving or conserving the "normal" ways of doing things in the culture. Such a perserving or conserving impulse certainly explains, ultimately, why ABC was willing to invest in *Family,* even in the face of the comparatively rapid social-political changes of the '70s. That impulse, as well, explains why viewers were willing to watch it, for it provided audiences with the "old" and "familiar" matriarchal vision; in watching that vision unfold itself week after week, in implicit ideological contradiction to the "new" visions of other series, viewers in fact were participating in a great ideological conflict or dialectic. Collectively, we were being "given back" an older life which we then were able, if we desired, to compare with the newer visions.

In other words, "we are what we view," yes, but the viewing we do, normally, contains myriad visions of social life, visions sometimes complementing, sometimes competing with, each other. *All* such visions, usually, dwell together in a culture, in both positive and negative relationships with each other. All of us, as viewers (especially in our more contemplative moments), can "understand" those visions—even the contradictory ones. (If we cannot, then, like some members of the Moral Majority, we attempt to drive the "evil" visions from television.) Our culture's ideological universe seldom is monolithic; and hence its very diversity makes room for the kinds of social dialectic which characterized *Family's* relationship to other popular programs in the late '70s.

If the foregoing analysis is generally accurate, then we can conclude that popular art, society, and ideology live in complex yet harmonious relationships, in which social practices and beliefs about those practices reinforce each other, and hence serve to legitimate each other. We do "what we say we should do," and our very doing it demands that "what we say we should do" be accepted as all the more "right." And so, social arrangements and their ideological underpinnings provide the material, the translatable codes, and the means of understanding that material and of interpreting those codes of art— including televisual art. More particularly, because social arrangements are varied and because ideology is multi-vocal, popular art even may be a necessary vehicle for cultural discussion and dialogue, because symbolic universes—of the sort depicted especially (but not only) in popular narrative artifacts—allow lifestyles to be examined "safely," in a detached or "semi-real" manner. Fictive television programs provide a utilitarian symbolic space for examining, perhaps paradoxically, real-world arrangements, behaviors, and rules-for-living. Art, society, and ideology thus live in harmony.[24] And thus is popular art fully integrated into, and perhaps even demanded by, collectivities. Indeed, it becomes impossible for most of us to specify where "popular art" ends and "real life" begins, so tightly are they bonded together.

Third, such social dialectics almost "naturally" find a welcoming home in family-centered shows, if only because familial roles and relationships form the microcosm of all human life. Most of us have been born into, raised by, and succored within family. The individual's mind finds its primary existence—almost inevitably—in family and family-like structures[25] in which verbal-social-physical behavior is comfortably explored, routinized, and ultimately legitimated or confirmed. Family dramas are the dramas, indeed, of Self. Family shows, as Eaton says, give us ourselves back.

The 1976–80 show *Family,* despite its implied challenge of the feminized social facts of its era as well as the popular profession-centered ideology purveyed in other Top 25 series, nevertheless reflected our expectations of what a "good," a "comfortable" American family ought to be like. It struck near-primordial chords in its portrayal of the social womb. In *Family,* "we are what we view" because our collective stocks of knowledge and experiences contained a few—almost forgotten, to some—propositions which could rationalize and legitimate the show's messages, and because as individuals we all could confirm our hope for self-durability in the face of change within its symbolic environment.

Notes

1. The thinking of many of the so-called "elitist critics"—those proceeding from the assumption that "high culture," the culture of art and creative excellence, should be the standard of worth of all human artifacts—can be found in the records of the Taitment Conference: Norman Jacoby, ed., *Culture for the Millions?* (Boston: Beacon Press, 1962). The inspiration for those who wished to celebrate rather than

Macro/micro dialectics

28

denigrate items of mass culture, probably, was Marshall McLuhan, especially after the publication of his *Understanding Media: The Extensions of Man* (New York: McGraw-Hill, 1964).

It is extremely difficult to trace clearly the gradual emergence of sociocultural perspectives on television programming. Any history of sociocultural studies of television must include works coming from several intellectual traditions: the neo-Marxist work from England; structuralist study of myth and society by the likes of Roland Barthes and Claude Lévi-Strauss; anthropological examinations of myths, rituals, and routines, as in the work of Victor Turner; the work on material culture, American style, offered by Ray Browne, Russel Nye, and other founders of the Popular Culture Association; the political symbolists, typified by Murray Edelman, who have examined the symbolic relationships between leaders and the led; and even some psychoanalytic scholars, following Jung into exploration of ways in which the Collective Unconscious is expressed. I document these trends in Bruce E. Gronbeck, *Television Criticism* (Chicago: SRA, 1984), Units 4 and 5.

2. Bruce E. Gronbeck, "Narrative, Enactment, and Television Programming," *Southern Speech Communication Journal,* 48 (Spring 1983), 229–243.

3. In "Narrative . . . ," I discussed three levels of knowledge—the artistic, the social, and the mythic. I will not examine mythic knowledge here, however, to save space and to hold our focus on ideology. Readers are encouraged to examine mythic analyses of TV, however. See Arthur Asa Berger, "Kung Fu: The Resolution of the Dialectic," in *Television: The Critical View,* ed. Horace Newcomb (New York: Oxford University Press, 1976), pp. 105–112. (Originally published in his *The TV-Guided American* [New York: Walker & Co., 1975].) See also Anne Roiphe, "Ma and Pa and John-Boy in Mythic America: The Waltons," and Curtis L. McCray, "Kaptain Kronkite: The Myth of the Eternal Frame," both in Newcomb's *Television: The Critical View,* 2nd ed. (New York: Oxford University Press, 1979), pp. 8–17, 319–333. For a more general discussion of mythic criticism, see Robert R. Smith, *Beyond the Wasteland: The Criticism of Broadcasting,* 2nd ed. (Annandale, Va.: Speech Communication Association, 1980), pp. 17–27.

4. While notions of "ideology" and "ideological force" are being developed in almost all humanistic, artistic, social-scientific, and natural-scientific disciplines, they have become particularly important to students of mass media; mass media, after all, are in an important sense "mass," affective or even infective of great numbers of people. Mass communication scholars interested in relationships between television programs and ideology have been influenced by the work of several British scholars emanating from Cambridge University (under the guidance of Raymond Williams) and, until Stuart Hall moved to the British Open University, from the Birmingham University Centre for Contemporary Studies. Basic works exploring television and ideology include: Raymond Williams, *Television: Technology and Cultural Form* (New York: Schocken Books, 1974); his "Cultural Theory: Hegemony," in his *Marxism and Literature* (Oxford: Oxford University Press, 1977), pp. 108–114; Todd Gitlin, "Prime Time Ideology: The Hegemonic Process in Television Entertainment," *Social Problems,* 26, No. 3 (1979), 251–266; essays in Stuart Hall, ed., *Culture, Media, Language: Working Papers in Cultural Studies, 1972–79* (London: Hutchinson and Co., 1980); essays in Tony Bennett et al., *Popular Television and Film* (London: BFI Publishing, 1981); and John Fiske and John Hartley, *Reading Television* (London: Methuen, 1978).

5. In 1977, Gary Frank was named best supporting actor, and Kristy McNichol, best supporting actress. In 1978, Sada Thompson received an Emmy as best lead actress. The show likewise won technical awards.

6. By "segment" I refer to a sequence of continuous and contiguous actions which are separable from other such actions by cuts, fades, etc. I prefer to use both continuousness and contiguity as criteria because it saves us some problems in defining "scene." E.g., Act I, scene iii, and Act I, scene iv, are strongly related—it presumably only would have taken Kate a few seconds to walk into the house and answer the phone. Yet, they serve quite different purposes in the show, and hence should be analyzed separately. The same can be said about Act IV, scenes iii and iv. (See Figure 1.)

7. The matriarchal family drama has had a long history in television, going back to CBS's *Mama* (1949–56), a show based on Kathryn Forbes' semi-autobiographical book *Mama's Bank Account,* a true-to-life account of a Norwegian-American family. So, while patriarchal family series have tended to dominate TV, the matriarchal family has been seen since TV's beginnings. Those wishing descriptions of TV shows on American television since 1946 should consult a work such as Tim Brooks and Earle Marsh, *The Complete Directory to Prime Time Network TV Shows 1946-Present,* rev. ed. (New York: Ballantine Books, [1981]).

8. I discuss briefly the linguistic notion of "markers" in Gronbeck, "Narrative . . . ," pp. 239–241.

9. *Family* was launched by ABC during the golden years of Fred Silverman's reign over programming. While with ABC, he earned his reputation as a man willing to experiment with scheduling, with format, and with quasi-independent production teams, among other things. And, it should be emphasized, the show *Family* represented many risks: Sada Thompson came to television as a Shakespearean actress unknown to viewers; Meredith Baxter-Birney was the only established television "star" among regular cast members; Mike Nichols had no television reputation as a director, and while lauded as a stage and film director, his slow and demanding style might have been disastrous in the fast-moving world of television production; and finally, the show represented a great scheduling risk, as it replaced the once-popular but now fading *Marcus Welby, M.D.*

10. The critical arts of analyzing television background music are not so advanced as they could be, and I apologize for the crudeness of this analysis. It is based, however, in part on some critical impulses found in Alan P. Merriam, "Music as Symbolic Behavior," in *The Rhetoric of Nonverbal Communication,* ed. Haig A. Bosmajian (Glenview, Il.: Scott, Foresman and Co., 1971), pp. 85–92. (Reprinted from Merriam's book, *The Anthropology of Music* [Evanston, Il.: Northwestern University Press, 1964].)

11. Kenneth Burke, *Counter-Statement* (1931; rpt. Los Altos, Ca.: Hermes Publications, 1953), p. 31.

12. And, it must be emphasized, different groups of viewers bring different stocks of knowledge to any given show. TV professionals, for example, with their knowledge of production techniques, might be particularly interested in the shooting and editing of the credits. Childless couples conceivably might miss some of the cues relating to adolescent children. Younger children coming from highly patriarchal families might not notice or understand the dominance of mother, and so on. Indeed, any conventional, narrative television program is "read" or interpreted in different ways by various groups of viewers, depending upon degrees of technical sophistication, life experiences, and particular interests. Therefore, I would argue, there is no "right" or "wrong" interpretation of a television program, but rather many ways of "making sense" of that program; the "cues to meaning" are many and variegated, given the richness of human symbol systems, and thus so are justifiable "readings."

30

Hence, I disagree with Fiske and Hartley's tendency to assume a dominant or "ideal" reading of a program (see Fiske and Hartley, e.g. p. 188). I agree, on this point, with a critique of their position on dominant readings offered in Janet Woollacott, "Messages and Meanings," in *Culture, Society, and the Media,* ed. Michael Gurevitch et al. (London: Methuen, 1982), esp. pp. 102–103.

13. For a fuller discussion of *mimesis,* see Richard McKeon, "Literary Criticism and the Concept of Imitation in Antiquity," *Critics and Criticism: Ancient and Modern,* ed. and intro. R. S. Crane. (Chicago: University of Chicago Press, 1952), pp. 147–176. Aristotle's doctrine of *mimesis* can be reviewed in Aristotle, *Poetics,* trans. Ingram Bywater, The Modern Library (New York: Random House, 1954), pp. 230–245.

14. See Aristotle, *Rhetoric,* 1356b. For one of the fuller reviews of scholarship on enthymemes, see Lloyd F. Bitzer, "Aristotle's Enthymeme Revisited," *Quarterly Journal of Speech,* 45 (December 1959), 399–408. Aristotle's basic discussion of enthymemes can be found in Aristotle, *Rhetoric,* trans. W. Rhys Roberts, The Modern Library (New York: Random House, 1954), pp. 26–31.

15. For a fuller discussion of the role of memory in the interpretation of discourse, see Eugene Vance, "Roland and the Poetics of Memory," *Textual Strategies: Perspectives in Post-Structural Criticism,* ed. and intro. Josué V. Harari (Ithaca: Cornell University Press, 1979), pp. 374–403.

16. Actually, in this particular episode, there is very little evidence for this most important proposition. The only evidence provided here is (1) Al Krantz' professional inability to offer any constructive advice during the meeting between Sophie and the Lawrences, and (2) Kate's motherly ability to break through Annie's defenses when others cannot. That is precious little evidence. But, a regular viewer would have seen, time and again, the same pattern: In *Family,* outside professionals never solve problems. Even during Nancy's counseling when she was considering an abortion and when she was contemplating divorce, those counselors did not help her make decisions—only family members did. And, when Kate was struggling with school and its demands upon her time and energy, her professor was of no help; only Doug and the kids were. Overall, it can be safely asserted, I think, that the entire genre of "family television dramas" is premised on the assumption that families are the ultimate source of problem-solving and succorance. Similar arguments are made by Horace Newcomb, *TV, The Most Popular Art,* Anchor Books (Garden City, N.Y.: Anchor Press/Doubleday, 1974), Chap. 2, and by Mick Eaton, "Television Situation Comedy," in Bennett et al., pp. 26–52. See especially Eaton's distinction between "home" as the "inside" and "work" as the "outside" world in his analysis of the BBC program, *Going Straight.*

17. Because I here am concentrating upon languages or codes, I am relying upon a linguistic-centered definition of "ideology," that offered by Gustav Bergmann in "Ideology," *Ethics,* 61 (April 1951), 205–218. In general, a linguistic definition of "ideology" focuses on individual statements, and the degree to which values and evaluative standards are "masquerading" as facts. So, a statement such as "John is a man" is a factual statement; one such as "John is a good man" is an evaluative statement, because the judgment is made explicitly; and, one such as "John is a true-blue American" is ideological because it not only describes him (as an American) but implies—but does not state—a positive value (in the phrase "true-blue"). I will use an essentially linguistic definition of "ideology" right now so that we can examine individual statements or propositions; later, though, I will move to a broader definition, one stressing entire systems of cultural behavior and modes-of-thought (a la Williams, Fiske and Hartley, and Gitlin).

18. The distinction between "family" and "professionals" as problem-solvers is stressed in Newcomb, *TV, The Most Popular Art,* Chaps. 2, 4, and 5.

31

19. On anachronism, myth, and social commentary, see Roiphe.

20. Eaton, p. 52. (Originally published in *Screen,* 19, no. 2 [Spring 1968].)

21. The reflection-projection thesis is developed in Lee Loevinger, "The Ambiguous Mirror: The Reflective-Projective Theory of Broadcasting and Mass Communications," in *Mass Media: Forces in Our Society,* ed. Francis and Ludmila Voelker (San Francisco: Harcourt Brace Jovanovich, Inc., 1978), pp. 424–440. (Originally published in *Journal of Broadcasting,* 12, no. 1 [Spring 1968].)

22. George Herbert Mead, *Mind, Self, and Society* (Chicago: University of Chicago Press, 1934).

23. Gitlin, p. 264.

24. The relationship is generally harmonious, even symbiotic, although it is nevertheless complex. A rewarding though difficult exploration of that relationship can be found in Stephen Neale, "Genre and Cinema," in Bennett et al., pp. 6–25. (Reprinted from his book, *Genre* [London: British Film Institute, 1980].) Some neo-Marxist scholars have used the term "hegemony" to discuss these complex relationships. "Hegemony" is a concept added only relatively recently to the vocabulary of scholars interested in sociocultural analysis and ideology. Perhaps one of the most straightforward definitions of it is offered by Gitlin (p. 251): "bourgeois domination of the thought, the common sense, the life-ways and everyday assumptions of the working class . . . routine structures of everyday thought." Hegemonic relationships, therefore, are rationalized and generally accepted (1) patterns of social relationships within a culture, which (2) dictate the ways groups interact and also (3) justify those interaction patterns. To people living in different groups and raised in the culture, those relationships seem "natural"; "things are simply done that way in this society" is a statement probably signaling a hegemonic relationship. Marxists such as Gitlin, of course, wish to stress that hegemonic relationships are power relationships, representative of the means by which one class dominates another. We need not, however, from my viewpoint, stress class structure analysis when using the concept.

25. With the general decline of "family" series has come a concomitant increase in "family-like" structures, in so-called "surrogate families" which operate in many of television's symbolic environments. See Carol Traynor Williams, "It's Not So Much, 'You've Come a Long Way, Baby'—As 'You're Gonna Make It After All,' " in Newcomb, *TV: The Critical View,* 2nd ed., pp. 64–73; and, Robert L. Schrag, Richard A. Hudson, and Lawrance M. Bernabo, "Television's New Humane Collectivity," *Western Journal of Speech Communication,* 45 (Winter 1981), 1–12.

Middle East Conflict as a TV News Scenario: A Formal Analysis

Richard L. Barton and Richard B. Gregg

There is a commonly held assumption in the area of television newscast analysis that televised news reporting interposes itself between the "hard reality" of events being reported and the newscast audiences in a way that transforms the nature of those events. Roeh (11, p. 87) puts it this way: "Although U.S. media operate under the 'objective rhetorical' prescription of 'letting the facts speak for themselves,' the 'facts' are subject to many crucial alternative means of presentation through language and images." In a similar vein, Smith (12, p. 141) states that "television [news] involves the instantaneous mingling of theatre with the dissemination of actuality. The two faces of television are inseparable."

Studies employing the methods of content analysis to examine the nature of news reporting are satisfying in some respects but disappointing in others. Patterson's summary of content analysis research on TV news is cogent:

> Most content research on television news is ad hoc. Frequently, content analysis is confined to providing simple descriptions of the most easily observable dimensions of news coverage—for instance, estimating the amount of airtime given to certain issues, interests, or institutions. At the same time, research has often been a direct response to public debate on an issue, such as the series of studies that followed Spiro Agnew's charge of liberal bias in network news coverage. When timely and accurate, such work performs a valuable service by informing public debate; but much of this research is innocent of any theoretical notions and has little relevance beyond television's handling of a particular topic at a particular time (10).

Some departures from the content analysis approach have stressed the impact of certain conventions of newsgathering and production on the ways in which television presents the news. From the work of Epstein and others, for example (3; 13; 14, especially pp. 189–196), we have learned that reporting emphasizing movement or activity is preferred over passive stories; that whenever possible, conflict between persons or viewpoints is to be featured; and that television newscasting tends to highlight immediate events and to disregard the "soft" context or historical content of the events.

Another failing of content analysis studies that has been identified (see, e.g., 2, 9) is that they do not adequately account for features that might be broadly considered as "formal." Williams (15, p. 44) has recommended the study of the form of television fare in its own right. He argues that while television forms are in part derived from earlier forms (newspaper, public meetings, the cinema), the medium of television also includes "innovating forms which are not in any obvious way derivative."

Historically, form has been considered within one of two general conceptual frameworks. First, there is what might be called conventional or technical form, which refers to artificial presentational or shaping devices that are imposed upon content to give it the quality of discreteness. Second, there are essential formative principles that are intrinsic to the content and grow organically within it to imbue it with unique characteristics of formed meaning.

Aspects of conventional form can be easily identified and studied in television news. They are the result of the kind of technology employed and the production decisions made with regard to how certain stories are to be presented. Thus, we can refer to shot composition, video mix, dramatistic format, the personalizing of issues, and the juxtaposition of news stories. The components of organic form are more difficult to delineate.

The distinction between conventional and organic form was clearly stated by Samuel Taylor Coleridge over a century ago:

> The form is mechanic, when on any given material we impress a predetermined form, not necessarily arising out of the properties of the material; as when to a mass of wet clay we give whatever shape we wish it to retain when hardened. The organic form, on the other hand, is innate; it shapes as it develops itself from within and the fullness of its development is one and the same with the perfection of its outward form. Such as the life is, such is the form (1, p. 186).

Particularly suggestive is Coleridge's notion that the full realization of organic form culminates in its perfection as outward form. In other words, if one is to account for the way form is manifest in its most complete sense, that is, the sense in which it is apprehended, comprehended, and appreciated, then one must examine the interaction of conventional and organic form. For any final product of human endeavor is a holistic presentation, comprised of materials never wholly raw because of the nature of human perception, materials that are further organized through limiting and shaping procedures guided by artistic or technical procedures. It may be, then, that "form" in television newscasting has not yet been adequately accounted for because the *distinction* between conventional and organic form, rather than their *intermingling,* has guided the explication.

The analysis that follows attempts to isolate
and examine patterns of meaning that may be
created or evoked by the interaction of conventional
and organic form in television newscasting.

We limited our analysis to news coverage of one major event with long-term international political implications—the March 1978 Israeli invasion of Lebanon in retaliation for a Palestine Liberation Organization (P.L.O.) terrorist attack in Tel Aviv. Our discussion will be microscopic rather than macroscopic; that is, we will not attempt to account for all of the nuances of meaning in a complete newscast. Rather, we will attempt to isolate and closely scrutinize several of the most prominent meaning structures that are formed by the interaction of conventional and organic form.

The episode that triggered the Israeli action occurred on Sunday, March 12, 1978, when 13 Palestinian terrorists landed by boat near Tel Aviv. They seized and commandeered a bus and were surrounded by Israeli police; in the ensuing gun battle, 36 Israelis were killed and 70 wounded; 9 terrorist raiders were killed by the police. Al Fatah, the largest guerrilla group in the P.L.O., claimed responsibility for the attack. Israeli Defense Minister Ezer Weizman characterized the raid as the worst to occur in Israel in thirty years. Prime Minister Menachem Begin immediately suggested that Israel would stage a military reprisal.

In the week that followed the March 12 incident, CBS Evening News devoted 28 minutes to covering the events whose story lines are summarized below:

Monday, March 13—Sunday's P.L.O. guerrilla attack is reviewed and the likelihood of Israeli military reprisals is investigated.

Tuesday, March 14—The Israeli retaliatory attack is reported. It is clear that this is one of the largest retaliatory attacks Israel has ever staged, surpassing even the one that followed the Munich Olympic atrocity in 1972. There is concern about how 30,000 Syrian troops stationed in Lebanon at the request of the Lebanese government will react to this invasion. Egypt's Anwar Sadat publicly condemns the P.L.O.

Wednesday, March 15—Seventeen hours after the retaliation began, the Israelis announce that the main part of the operation is over; they have secured a six-mile-deep corridor extending from the Mediterranean to the mountains. Prime Minister Begin announces that Israel will continue to occupy the area until arrangements are made to guarantee security there. The Israeli forces are joined by Christian forces in Lebanon who are sympathetic to their anti-P.L.O. fighting. There is speculation that this will be a long stay for the Israeli troops.

Thursday, March 16—The United States calls for the Israeli withdrawal from Southern Lebanon, suggesting that a peace-keeping force, possibly under United Nations auspices, be organized. Meanwhile, combat between Israelis and Palestinian guerrillas continues as the Israelis try to hold the six-mile-wide, 372 square mile area that is now referred to as the "buffer zone." Egyptian President Sadat publicly condemns the Israeli invasion.

Friday, March 17—Israeli soldiers continue to raid villages in the six-mile corridor. Palestinian refugees flee the area using any means of transportation available. The U.N. Security Council begins meeting at the request of both Lebanon and Israel to consider the crisis. The Lebanese Christian troops sympathetic to the Israeli cause and the Syrian troops in Lebanon are considered by the U.S. State Department as possible policing forces for the six-mile corridor.

Overall, the CBS Evening News "package" of the story contained elements that stress immediacy, journalistic expertise regarding the subject, and control over information and its flow.

A sequence of reports is introduced under the apparent control of the authoritative anchorperson. Each field report is under the production jurisdiction of the field producer and "our man/woman" correspondent. Communicator credibility and an aura of stability are maintained through the elimination of contradictory information. The news items are ordered so that the more dramatic international events involving well-known political figures have priority. National items follow, and the newscast concludes with folksy, often humorous human interest stories.

Our preliminary analysis of the CBS Israeli invasion story from videotape suggested that the interaction of conventional and organic form resulted in two major patterns. *Prediction* refers to the tendency for newscasters to anticipate and predict events, then describe them selectively in terms of news sounds and images. *Affirmation of network authority* is the selection, arrangement, and presentation of news items in a way that establishes and aggressively maintains the authority of the network as news source.

Of the three major themes repeated in this story during the week, two take the form of predictions (the likelihood of Israeli retaliation and the length of the Israeli military presence in Lebanon after the retaliatory strike) and are the focus of our explication. The pattern of affirming network news authoritativeness intertwines throughout the weeks' patterns of prediction as the news unfolds. The two patterns are, in fact, mutually supportive. The third major theme, a preoccupation with the influence of the military confrontation on the Begin-Carter talks that were originally scheduled for Tuesday, March 14, 1978, is not included in our discussion.

The first episode can be divided into three segments (see Figure 1). Each is a separately produced unit, but all are edited together and presented as a whole. A number of predictable journalistic television production conventions are used. Synchronous sound (as distinguished from reporter's commentary) is typically the first sound heard. It is faded under at the beginning of the reporter's commentary, faded up for on-location emphasis at certain points during the commentary, and brought up at the conclusion of the commentary to end the episode. Synchronous sound, then, highlights and brackets the episode and each of the segments within it.

36

Audio (spoken commentary)	Audio (synchronous sound)	Video

Segment 1
Monday, March 13, 1978

(Bowen) 1. Speaking before a hushed and somber Israeli Parliament today, Prime Minister Begin strongly hinted at reprisals for the weekend terrorist raid which killed 36 Israelis and wounded more than twice that number.	Sound of Begin's words, faded under as Bowen starts his commentary, continues under commentary throughout this segment.	Long shot of Israeli Parliament in session.
2. The prevention of similar attacks is only possible, the Prime Minister said, by destroying the murderers and their bases, adding, "we shall cut off the arm of evil."		
3. Mr. Begin called on Western nations to close down P.L.O. offices in their countries and he harshly condemned the Soviet Union for supplying weapons to the terrorists.		Pan left and zoom in on close-up of Begin speaking. Series of cuts to show Parliament members listening to Begin, including Moyshe Dayan and other internationally known figures.
4. It was the second straight day that the Prime Minister hinted at retaliation.		

Segment 2
Monday, March 13, 1978

(Bowen) 5. The question has never really been *if* Israel will stage a reprisal strike across the frontier into Lebanon but *when*.		Cut to shot of Bowen at Israeli-Lebanon border fence holding microphone. Zoom in on Bowen. Cut to official Israeli censored footage of armored vehicle maneuvers and smiling soldiers.
6. Still, serious concerns exist; with Prime Minister Begin's U.S. visit set for next week, there is Washington reaction to consider and Israeli government officials have not forgotten the severe criticism that followed last November's reprisal raid into Lebanon which claimed many civilian victims.	Sounds of military vehicles and random, unintelligible voices of soldiers.	

Segment 3
Monday, March 13, 1978

(Bowen) 7. In Tel Aviv today a police spokesman released new information on the terrorists.		Daytime—a medium close-up of houses, apartments. Quick zoom out reveals
8. He said two of them drowned on their way to Israel when a rubber boat they were in capsized.		
9. Eleven terrorists made it ashore to a kibbutz north of Tel Aviv, when actually their target was the city itself.		shot of body of water in front of these dwellings with mountains behind. Cut to shot showing a road next to water; pan left to road as subjective camera takes perspective of auto driver moving quickly along this road.
10. But their rampage resulted in the worst terrorist incident ever in Israel.	Sounds of solders, confusion, and fire burning debris.	Cut to long shot of burning bus at nighttime. Cut to medium close-up of burning bus.
11. Nine of the terrorists were killed, including a woman, and two were captured.		Cut to medium close-up of Israeli soldiers searching, then dragging away the dead body of a suspected terrorist.
12. For a while it was thought that some of the terrorists managed to escape and this set off the largest manhunt in Israeli history.		Cut to medium long shot of soldiers in front of a building. Zoom in to show two of them. Cut to shot of running soldier.
13. But the report proved false.		Cut to long shot of soldiers in field; zoom in.

Figure 1. Summary of CBS news coverage of "the retaliation" prediction.

37

Figure 1—*Continued*

14. Meanwhile, near Haifa, more Israeli victims of the attack were buried today.	Sound of voices, crying at burial site.	Cut to soldiers carrying coffins draped with Israeli flags.
15. The people are still in a state of shock and outrage.		Cut to extreme close-up of mourning women's faces, cut to close-up of child's face. Cut to medium shot of man shoveling dirt onto grave.
16. Judging from their mood and the remarks of the Prime Minister, just about everyone would be startled if retaliation is not swift and punishing.		Cut to medium close-up of Israeli soldier's face as he looks toward grave. Pan right to include a second soldier's face.
17. Jerry Bowen, CBS News, along the Israeli-Lebanese border.	Sounds at burial site up, then faded out.	Cut to wreath being placed on grave. Tilt up to mother and child embracing at the head of the grave.

The visual formula for each segment within this episode follows a similar pattern. An establishing orientation shot (a long shot or a shot that shows the reporter's geographic location, often accompanied by a superimposed title in the upper left-hand corner, e.g., reporter's name, CBS News, Lebanon-Israeli border) is followed by a series of main-action shots, with zooms and pans mixed in to reveal the physical surroundings in which the main action is occurring. An episode typically concludes with a long shot of the reporter against an identifiable background. The tempo at which these shots are edited and their placement relative to the audio track are functions of what materials are available and the editor's judgment. The editing tempos of the three segments of this episode vary greatly. The reconstructed terrorist landing (lines 7–13 of Figure 1) involves rapid cutting between its very dramatic shots. In contrast, the official Israeli footage of troop maneuvers is a series of undramatic shots placed together with seeming casualness.

The uses of these conventional production techniques accomplish a number of predictable effects.

The authenticity of the news report is enhanced by the presence of reporters who are "on the scene." This feeds an unstated presumption that those news sources which are able to maintain foreign correspondents are more likely to get the benefit of direct, firsthand data. Scenes from the news location enhance this sense of authority. Further, the variety of visual and auditory messages helps gain and maintain the attention and interest of the television viewer.

The opening scene of the episode is a direct shot of Prime Minister Begin addressing the Israeli Parliament. The audio focus of this segment is not on Begin, however, but on the reporter, who quotes only one phrase from Begin's statement. This phrase serves to support the major claim of the reporter's comments, which takes the form of a prediction; the Israelis will retaliate for the terrorist raid. The reporter refers to the claim at the beginning and end of his commentary by observing that Begin was "hinting" at reprisal in his speech, and then noting that the Prime Minister had so "hinted" for two straight days. During the middle portion of his commentary, however, the reporter's paraphrase and direct quotation of Begin's remarks seem much stronger than a hint. With the direct switch to the visual shot of the reporter standing on the Israeli-Lebanese border at the beginning of the second segment, the nature of the hint is further qualified. It is not a matter of whether there will be a reprisal, says the reporter, only a question of when it will occur.

This form of prediction is one that the CBS news crew uses throughout the week. The claim is first supported with film of Begin actually making his statement. It is further corroborated by the visual presence of the news reporter on the scene. But the most intriguing support comes from the showing of official Israeli film of an armed vehicle with soldiers inside. We do not know when the film was taken, or where the vehicle was filmed. But in the full context of the news report, these matters are not important. The film supports a perception of the Israeli army as well equipped, well trained, on the alert, and ready to respond to a threat instantaneously. The uncertainty and drama of the prediction of the reprisal are enhanced by the fact that military action will not require a prolonged period of planning; it can occur at once. Furthermore, the Israeli soldiers in the field are relaxed and smiling even though fully armed for war; their whole countenance exudes confidence. This impression of Israeli preparedness and competence will be confirmed, along with the prediction of reprisal itself, with the Tuesday evening news report of the Israeli invasion of Lebanon.

The third segment of the episode, ostensibly focused on the immediate past, actually bears on the predictive claim. This segment recounts the terrorist raid in Tel Aviv which occurred the previous day. The reporter's narrative account is vividly descriptive. We hear how terrorists got where they were, how many terrorists were killed and captured, and what the Israelis felt and did. We first see the general physical location of the event, and then are drawn into the scene as quasi-observers when the camera moves along the road traveled by the commandeered bus. The scene becomes more dramatic as we see several nighttime shots of the bus burning, of Israeli soldiers removing bodies, and of soldiers presumably searching for the terrorists. The accompanying audio carries sounds of confusion, of soldiers' voices, and of fire.

The last portion of the segment evokes emotional identification by focusing on the sorrow that comes with death. We see Israeli soldiers carrying coffins, a grave being filled, the placing of a wreath; most poignant are the close-up faces of women and children etched in shock and grief.

The combined impact of these scenes, from the initial location shots to the final scenes of the dead and the mourning, adds up to more than a pictorial narrative. They may be seen to constitute an emotional justification for the predicted reprisal. Structurally, this pattern of prediction recalls an element of ballad form known as incremental repetition: the repetition of lines in such a way that their meaning is enhanced either by their appearing in changed contexts or by minor successive changes to the lines themselves (4, pp. 269–270). In this case, the form of prediction moves from legitimation via Prime Minister Begin's comments and presence, through place authentication by displaying the geographical setting (the border) of the predicted retaliation, to an emotional identification with the retaliators (Israeli soldiers and families who are burying their dead). This is a complex synthesis, not a typical hard news convention. It is a detailed construction by the film editors in collaboration with the reporter.

The predictive pattern or format of news presentation can create several ensuing patterns of expectation, which interact. There is first a continual emphasis on the future. Those events reported on a given day's news receive contextual importance not so much from events that preceded them but from the events that will follow and are foreshadowed by immediate happenings. Second, a framework of receptivity is created for viewers, which encourages interpretation of events to come in ways that will link them to the immediate events, whether or not such linkage is justified. In other words, there may be a tendency for viewers to perceive fairly direct causal linkages between events when only associational linkages are warranted or associational linkages when events are only coincidentally joined. Third, if immediate predictions and projections receive early confirmation, or are in some manner imbued with confirmation from past events, an aura of authoritativeness can redound throughout the forms of future prediction.

> *These coalescing nuances of meaning, created by the interplay of conventional and organic forms in the CBS newscast, created further patterns of nuance regarding events in the Middle East, which turned out to be misleading.*

Two other patterns of news prediction continued with some regularity throughout the week. These predictive patterns first occur on the Tuesday evening newscast, immediately following the announcement that the Israeli retaliation is underway, and a brief description of that retaliation is provided (see lines 1–2 of Figure 2) by a CBS reporter, standing in what appears to be a conference room in which the seal of the State Department is fully visible.

The newscast audience is invited to make an inference regarding authoritativeness, and hence factuality. In a literal sense, when the reporter says, "there are two major concerns here in Washington tonight," we cannot identify with certainty who holds or expresses those views. That the concerns may be only those of the newscasters themselves is probably not seriously considered, because we generally expect reporters to gather their data from other news sources, and because of the visual, "on the scene" presentation of the reporter himself. The interpretation encouraged by such presentation is that we are hearing the "official" concerns of the administration in general or of the high command in the State Department in particular. This interpretation is further enhanced by the visual shots, which appear to focus on State Department personnel as the reporter talks.

40

Let us first examine the suggestion that the Israeli military occupation of Lebanon may be a long one. On Wednesday evening's newscast, anchorman Walter Cronkite, sitting at his desk with a chroma-keyed map of the contested area over his shoulder, paraphrases a statement from Israel's prime minister: "And Prime Minister Begin said Israel will continue to occupy the area until arrangements are made to guarantee security there, an indication it could be a long stay for Israeli troops" (line 3 of Figure 2).

Audio (spoken commentary)	Audio (synchronous sound)	Video
	Tuesday, March 14, 1978	
(Kalb) 1. There are two major concerns here in Washington tonight.	There is no synchronous sound other than Kalb's voice.	The visual form for all of Kalb's State Department reports follows the same basic pattern: an establishing medium shot of Kalb within a State Department meeting room, in which the State Department seal is fully visible. The camera slowly zooms into a medium close-up, stays on that shot for the bulk of the report and slowly zooms out to the original shot during his concluding words; occasional cuts to filmed coverage of State Department officials are included in Kalb's report.
2. First that the Israelis may stay in Lebanon for a period of time until they have accomplished their mission, and second that the Syrian army, based in Lebanon north of the Litani River, might join with the P.L.O. in battle against Israel which would considerably widen the scope of this entire operation.		
	Wednesday, March 15, 1978	
(Cronkite) 3. And Prime Minister Begin said Israel will continue to occupy the area until arrangements are made to guarantee security there, an indication it could be a long stay for Israeli troops.	There is no synchronous sound other than Cronkite's voice.	Standard studio set medium close-up of Cronkite with chroma-key map over his shoulder, with graphic elements such as the word "corridor" superimposed onto the map as he speaks.
(Bowen) 4. The Israelis say they don't want to occupy Lebanon but they couple that with the stated desire to establish a safe corridor extending six miles across the frontier which raises the question of how long the Israelis will stay before they feel it's safe enough to leave.	There is no synchronous sound other than Bowen's voice.	Long shot of border fence with Bowen in left foreground holding the microphone (continues throughout the piece).
5. If the recent history of the area is any indication, the Israeli stay may not be brief.		
6. The administration fears there is no effective military force acceptable to Israel that can patrol Southern Lebanon and keep Palestinian terrorists out.	There is no synchronous sound other than Kalb's voice.	Same as for lines 1–2, with the addition of a chroma-keyed map of the battle area over Kalb's left shoulder.
7. That suggests the possibility of a small but long-term Israeli presence in the area.		
	Thursday, March 16, 1978	
(Bowen) 8. But there is a growing feeling Israel may become mired down in a land it does not want to occupy.	Synchronous sound of soldiers and vehicles.	Shot of tanks and army personnel. Camera pans by from moving vehicle while soldiers wave to camera.
	Friday, March 17, 1978	
(Fenton) 9. The Israeli army is prepared for a long stay; many Israeli officials doubt the U.N. will be willing to assume an antiterrorist role.	Background sounds of soldiers' activity.	Israeli censored footage of smiling, relaxing soldiers. Zoom out; cut to soldiers playing harmonica. Cut to camp. Medium long shot of Fenton standing in front of the relaxing Israeli soldiers.

Figure 2. Summary of CBS news coverage of the Israeli occupation.

Figure 2—*Continued*

10. The evidence that the Israelis are prepared to stay in Lebanon for a long time and are likely to do so will complicate Prime Minister Begin's talks with President Carter next week, talks which promised to be difficult even before the Israeli incursion.
    (Tennel)

11. Most of those who are fleeing Southern Lebanon now are convinced that there's going to be another attack and that the Israeli army is going to move even further north than it already has.
    conclusion: (Kalb)

    Street sounds.

    Cut to medium close-up of Tennel on street where people are loading.

12. . . . Secretary Vance is under no illusion that the Israelis are going to leave until some arrangement is devised to keep the area relatively free of Palestinian terrorists.

    (The earlier description of reference lines 1–2 applies here.)

There is abundant evidence, of course, that the persona of Cronkite lends authoritativeness to whatever claims he makes. Thus, his considerable prestige is added to the authority already evoked by the previous day's "on the scene" reporter. But there is more at work here. Begin's brief dramatic statement about cutting off "the arm of evil" on Monday's newscast (line 2, Figure 1) had become central to the predictive pattern concerning the impending reprisal. His statement was a certain harbinger because the facts of the Israeli incursion provided verification. When Cronkite on Tuesday informs us of another of Begin's statements concerning the future, it seems likely that Begin's Monday evening authoritativeness will carry over. What could easily go unrecognized here is that the phrase "an indication it could be a long stay for Israeli troops" is an inference drawn by Cronkite, not by Begin. The general effect of this episode is to enhance the force of the predictive speculation that Israel will remain in Lebanon for an extended period of time.

In a following episode on the same evening's newscast this pattern of forecasting is repeated in a way that moves beyond the kind of inference invited by Cronkite's statement. Lines 4 and 5 of Figure 2 may lead the viewer to infer that there is a continual accumulation of evidence which lends to the further credence of the prediction. But, once again, the general expectancies regarding authoritativeness and the predictive presentational pattern may prevent the full realization that the reporter, by inserting the article "but" into his comments, has presented the paraphrases of two Israeli statements as being antithetical, and in such a way that their juxtaposition corroborates the continuing prediction. Then, in the latter part of the reporter's comments, he interjects the phrase "if the recent history of the area is any indication" without any further explanation. While this reference is vague, within the overall

42

interpretative pattern that has been established and which is continually refurbished in the newscasts, it further enhances the predictive claim. And before the episode is over, yet another reporter, back "on location" at the State Department, refers once again to the administration's fear of "a small but long-term Israeli presence in the area" (line 7, Figure 2).

On Thursday evening's newscast, an episode occurs that continues the predictive form in a most interesting way (see line 8, Figure 2). First, the reporter's comments seem to change the nature of concern for Israeli occupation in an abrupt fashion, but at the same time, the video and audio portions of the episode appear to contradict the reporter's comments, continuing to fill out the predictive pattern already established. The reporter says, "But there is a growing feeling Israel may become mired down in a land it does not want to occupy." Up to this point in the week's newscasts, the whole thrust of the predictive episodes regarding the length of the Israeli stay in Lebanon had featured Israeli intention and will, as reflected in Prime Minister Begin's tone of voice and solemn appearance, and in reporters' interpretations of Begin's statements of Israeli intentions. Several times prior to Thursday, we had been told that Israel would maintain a military presence in Lebanon until a safe corridor across the border was secured and guaranteed. By inference, the fears of the U.S. government seemed connected to Israeli determination. Now, suddenly, a new reason for the Israeli stay in Lebanon is introduced; it has nothing to do with intention or determination, but rather with the possibility of military overextension and a resulting inability to achieve military extrication.

This would seem to invite a change in our perceptions of events taking place in the Middle East. But we would suggest that such change is of no lasting import, for three reasons. First, this is the first time Israeli military inadequacy is mentioned, and the reference to it goes against the flow of reporting, both oral and visual, which has underlined Israeli competence and determination all week. Second, no similar references occur again in news reporting of this event, and the sources for the references are not documented. Third, the concurrent visual dialogue works to deny the reporter's comments. While the reporter talks, we see shots of Israeli tanks and personnel moving casually but steadily across the Lebanese countryside. A camera pans by a moving vehicle while Israeli soldiers, looking relaxed and confident, wave to it. The camera then zooms out and cuts to a relaxed camp scene where soldiers are pictured in repose, listening to the harmonica music played by one of their comrades. Hence the force of the predictive pattern of meaning formed in earlier newscasts, in conjunction with the visual dialogue of this episode, will work to override the abrupt change of perspective introduced by the reporter, so that the original predictive pattern remains intact.[1]

We have not been concerned here with accounting for the actual intentions of the news production team (executives, producers, reporters, editors, or technical personnel). Nor has our concern been one of enumerating the motifs or interrelated themes and images of the episodic forms which make up the newscasts, either in the conventional or organic state. Rather, we have tried to locate those patterns of meaning that emerge from the continuous interaction of conventional and organic forms in the newscasts. And as we found them, we asked not only about their meaning "for now," but also about their ongoing and future possibilities for the continual constraint of meaning. This helped reveal not only the primacy of the predictive form that shaped the meaning of one important facet of the story, but the way in which the expectancies created by that pattern operated to create linkages, fill in gaps, and suggest interpretative nuances for related news items as they occurred throughout the week.

Throughout the week's reporting, we saw the intermingling of the form of prediction with patterns that enhanced the authoritativeness of the network news in such a way that one form tended to provide confirmation for the other. There are the shaping words of an authoritative anchorperson. There are the further shaping words of on-location reporters. There is the occurrence of an event, the retaliation, which occurs early in the week and confirms and reinforces the predictive authoritativeness of the reporters. Throughout there are the selected supporting visual scenes, or scenes which could be interpreted in supportive ways. The result was the shaping of a coherent unit, with the potential to satisfy the expectancies it continually created.

At least five patterns of meaning can be seen to have developed and sustained the prevailing patterns of prediction and affirmation of authority in the CBS news coverage of the 1978 Israeli incursion into Lebanon:

1. The repetition of limited themes and modes.
2. The exclusion of details, ambiguity, and complexity relating to the event.
3. The distortion of the dimension of time, including the stripping away of the historical context relating to the event.
4. The substitution of a variety of visual settings in the place of journalistic balance based on the presentation of comment by participants themselves.
5. The use of selective language, such as labels, which supports the network's "angle" and narrative style.

Ironically, one major predictive pattern developed consistently throughout the week—that the Israeli occupation of Lebanon would be an extended one—proved to be specious. On April 12, Israeli troops began withdrawing from the occupied area, and by the end of the month the majority were gone. In the case examined here, then, it is evident that the shaping of the televised news flow created mistaken expectancies on the part of the viewing audience and misrepresented the intentions of some of the parties directly involved.

More important, from an analytical standpoint, perhaps we have found a useful way to explicate television newscast form. Because of the partial regularities of events, the conservative nature of the human minds which structure meanings, and the techniques and conventions of televised news production,

44

we would expect resulting regularities of meaning patterns in television news-casting. But such regularities need to be teased from actual newscasts rather than imposed upon them.

Notes

1. Among the number of seemingly minor items that lent further credence to the structure, one is particularly illustrative. By the fourth day of newscasting, various members of the CBS news crew were rather consistently using the term "buffer zone" to refer to the land in Lebanon occupied by Israeli troops. Cronkite began the Friday evening newscast by referring to a full-screen map which graphically pictured the "buffer zone" area. "Buffer zone" is a term with the potential to evoke connotations of permanence and stability, of carefully constructed and strategi-cally located fortifications, of steady and recurrent patrols of troops garrisoned in fully provisioned encampment. These are connotations that give further support to the notion that the Israelis intended an occupation of some duration. It is in-teresting to note that, as reported in the *New York Times,* the term "buffer zone" was used pejoratively against the Israelis by P.L.O. leader Mustafa Saad, who insisted that Israeli spokesmen were covering up their true intentions (8). Israeli leaders just as insistently refused to use the term (5, 7). The *Time's* coverage also includes direct denials by Israeli spokesmen that Israel intended a long occupation (e.g., 6).

References

1. Coleridge, Samuel Taylor. *Coleridge's Literary Criticism.* Introduction by J. W. Mackail. London: Oxford University Press, 1908.
2. Culbert, David. "Historians and the Visual Analysis of Television News." In Wil-liam Adams and Fay Schreibman (Eds.) *Television Network News: Issues in Con-tent Analysis.* Washington, D.C.: George Washington University, 1978.
3. Epstein, Edward. *News from Nowhere.* New York: Random House, 1973.
4. Holman, C. Hugh (Ed.) *A Handbook to Literature* (3d ed.). New York: Odyssey Press, 1972.
5. "Israelis Seize a 'Security Belt.' " *New York Times,* March 16, 1978.
6. "A Limited Action." *New York Times,* March 15, 1978.
7. "Major Fighting Ends." *New York Times,* March 16, 1978.
8. "Palestinians Fleeing the Israelis Crowd into Saide; Lebanese Port City Fears it Will be Next Target." *New York Times,* March 17, 1978.
9. Paletz, David and Roberta E. Pearson. "The Way You Look Tonight: A Critique of Television News Criticism." In William Adams and Fay Schreibman (Eds.) *Television Network News: Issues in Content Analysis.* Washington, D.C.: George Washington University, 1978, pp. 78–79.
10. Patterson, Thomas. "Assessing Television Newscasts: Future Directions in Con-tent Analysis." In William Adams and Fay Schreibman (Eds.) *Television Network News: Issues in Content Analysis.* Washington, D.C.: George Washington Uni-versity, 1978, pp. 177–196.
11. Roeh, Itzhak. "Israel in Lebanon: Language and Images of Story Telling." In Wil-liam Adams (Ed.) *Television Coverage of the Middle East.* Norwood, N.J.: Ablex, 1982.
12. Smith, Anthony. *The Shadow in the Cave.* London: Quartet Books, 1976.

13. Sperry, Sharon Lynn. "Television News as Narrative." In Richard Adler and Douglass Cater (Eds.) *Television as a Cultural Force*. New York: Praeger, 1976, pp. 129–146.
14. Wicker, Tom. *On Press*. New York: Berkeley, 1978.
15. Williams, Raymond. *Technology and Cultural Form*. New York: Schocken, 1974.

Television's New Humane Collectivity

Robert L. Schrag
Richard A. Hudson
Lawrance M. Bernabo

A world seen by many as overpopulated with cops, thugs, hitmen, and hucksters may seem a strange place in which to posit an emergent rhetorical vision of a new humane collectivity, yet far stranger things are accepted with varying degrees of certainty from television's glowing screen, e.g., human beings hitting golf balls around on the surface of the moon, a President of the United States resigning his office, the crowning of a $1.98 Beauty Queen, and the landing of an alien from the planet Ork in Boulder, Colorado. The notion of significant rhetorical visions emerging from primetime television should not be rejected simply because the environment might seem too prosaic.

Brown advanced the idea that primetime television programs create an environment of shared ideas where effect hinges on the content of the programs.[1] While his analysis tended strongly toward the pessimistic, he did allow that *M*A*S*H* represented a program type which contained elements "compatible with the requirements for a new encompassing rhetorical vision; they are collectivity- and urban-centered at the same time that they show the uniqueness of the individual participants."[2] This vision is now extant: *M*A*S*H* and several conceptually related programs form a television environment in which the rhetorical vision of a new humane collectivity can be seen, a vision which portrays a humane, sympathetic awareness of group and person as the basis for a meaningful and rewarding existence.

A rhetorical vision is a unique perception of an ideal state, a dream of how things can or should be, a vision which can be sustained regardless of whether or not the ideal state is attained. For example, when politicians campaign for office the contextual elements of the platform become a vision of how government *can* best be managed and not necessarily how government *will* be managed.

The concept of rhetorical vision first drew attention from rhetorical critics in 1972 when Bormann introduced fantasy theme analysis to the communication field.[3] He based his theory on Bales' small group research in which the tendency of groups to find themselves caught up in "fantasies" concerning material and issues the group viewed as valuable was noted.[4] Information introduced into the group relevant to a shared vision caused group members to become excited, increase their interaction and introduce "fantasy types."[5]

From *The Western Journal of Speech Communication*, 45, 1981. Reprinted with permission of the journal and the authors.

Fantasy activity, however, is not specific to group interaction but may be introduced through any face-to-face, public, and mass communication rhetorical act.

Fantasy theme analysis provides a valuable tool for studying a variety of subjects, including political campaigns,[6] social movements,[7] public speeches,[8] advertising campaigns,[9] political conventions,[10] political debates,[11] wars and riots,[12] magazines,[13] comic strips,[14] and firefighters.[15] The flexibility of the method stems from its ability to encompass the most complex rhetorical acts. As Bormann describes it, within the rhetorical vision there abound fantasy themes, heroes and villains, outsiders and insiders, and each works to shape the vision. By examining the various elements of the vision the critic is able to view the birth, development, climax, and eventual decay of the rhetorical drama.

Fantasy themes are messages, actions, thoughts, ideas, and symbols which directly affect the vision by supporting or negating it. Group members—whether in a dyad, small group, organization, or society—are usually attracted to the larger vision through a personal identification with one or more of the vision's composite fantasy themes.

Heroes and villains are identifying factors for group members. Heroes are those people or events which represent the ideal for the group, a person, or thing elevated to a higher status because it is symbolic of the vision. For example, Christians view Christ as the ultimate hero while at the other end of the spectrum the American Nazis would view Hitler as their ultimate hero. Whereas the hero is symbolic of everything the group feels is worthy, the villain allows group members to more clearly establish what they value by personifying that which they do not value. Hence, Christianity has its devil and the American Nazis have the Jews, the Blacks, the Catholics, and so on. By identifying the heroes and villains espoused by a group a critic may begin to understand its ultimate goals.

Insiders and outsiders assist in defining the vision by revealing what type of person shares the vision and what type does not. Analysis helps determine how support is sustained for the vision, how insiders identify with each other, how people within the group treat those outside, and what function the outsider assumes in relationship to the vision. Acceptance and rejection of the vision often falls along a continuum whose endpoints are fervent support and fervent opposition. Analysis of insiders and outsiders helps define points between these extremes.

Beyond the examination of these components the critic has other responsibilities, foremost of which is the identification of the rhetorical vision. Also, since the vision develops over time, its history needs to be traced. Finally, the vision must be compared with reality. Although the vision creates a social reality for the group, there may be wide discrepancies between the group's social reality and the material reality of the surrounding society.

Although at least twenty studies used fantasy theme analysis to investigate their subject matter, little attention has been paid to that form of communication that most beguiles the American public: television's primetime programming.[16] The application of this methodology to primetime television environments could benefit both the rhetorical critic and the media scholar. Yet before it may be used effectively several problems of definition need to be addressed. Specifically, definitions need to be operationalized for (1) television environment, (2) group, and (3) "visionary."

why?

What defines a *television environment?* The spectrum of potential responses is large: at one end fall the cosmic ruminations of Marshall McLuhan hovering around the twin mantras of "medium" and "message";[17] toward the middle of the spectrum lies the presentational genre framework documented by Newcomb which groups programs according to formulaic elements within the various programs;[18] and at the other end of the spectrum is the totally personalized concept that each individual's television environment contains all (and only) those programs which he or she watches. Each of these positions was rejected as a definition of television environment for the present investigation. First, McLuhan's denial of the importance of content made it an untenable point from which to examine the construction of television environments whose content affects the viewer's structure of reality.[19] Second, the midpoint reflected by Newcomb was rejected because it seemed highly unlikely that an individual's television environment was made up of any one genre and because at least one research study indicated that the elements which Newcomb defined as the distinguishing ones of the various genre were not perceived by audience members as existing within those genre.[20] Third, the final perspective was rejected because generalizations would be impossible given the assumption of unique and idiosyncratic television environments.

With both ends and the middle of the spectrum rejected, a point somewhere between "Newcomb" and "total individuality" appeared to be the best choice. While "total individuality" might have led to the most accurate analysis, it would nevertheless have been a defensible approach only if a number of very similar television environments existed and affected viewers who shared those environments in similar ways. The design and execution of the study that could provide that information, while fascinating, was beyond the scope of the present project. It was decided that the researchers would create the television environment that represented the most significant portion of their own *shared* television environment. Since the focus of the study was the examination of rhetorical visions in primetime programming, that was the area of programming to which the investigation was restricted. The environment was created by a video version of the "book-on-a-desert-island" game in which a subject chooses the one book he or she would take to a desert island on which he or she would spend the rest of his or her life. The premise was the same except that selection was limited to primetime television programs and not books. The rules of the game were as follows: admitting that one television program did not equal one book, each subject was allowed to select two programs each

?

of which the subject enjoyed and "learned something significant from."[21] The initial list created from the results of the game included *M*A*S*H, Lou Grant, Barney Miller, The Rockford Files, Taxi,* and *The White Shadow. The White Shadow* and *The Rockford Files* were eliminated after viewing episodes of the 1978–1979 season because it was observed that while the programs were entertaining no significant messages were evident.[22]

Having defined television environment, the concept of *group* also demanded clarification. The work of Bormann and Bales centered around the group and how fantasies generated in groups chained out into the larger society.[23] However, television programs and the groups contained within those programs exist in an artificially divided society. The vision of a television series group, for example the people of the 4077th M.A.S.H. unit, cannot chain out to the city room staff on *Lou Grant.* Yet, if conceptually related, some method of grouping these programs for the purpose of critical analysis is necessary. For the purposes of this investigation the word *collectivity* was used to indicate the group of people who are the *combined residents* from various programs which reflect the vision. This allowed the term *group* to be used in its more traditional sense, i.e., the group *within* a program which shares a vision.

Finally, a related term, *visionary,* needed to be defined. This term was also made necessary by the artificial delineations of the world of television. In the larger society the exemplary behavior of a hero is apparent to the world. In the world of television dramas a hero acts within the isolation of the series. Yet, within the constraints of the individual series characters may be seen who exemplify the vision of the entire collectivity. The term *visionary* was selected to define such collectivity-wide heroes. This allowed the term *hero* to be used for traditional application in series specific analysis.

The Fantasy Themes

The vision of the collectivity does not spring full-blown from any one show, but is rather a mosaic which gradually emerges from an interaction with all four series. The vision can best be understood by examining each of its dominant fantasy themes. The first theme of the vision, *realization of significant others,* centers on the notion that the individual is strengthened by forming alliances with compassionate others. The second theme of the vision, *alliance in action,* examines the compassionate alliance as it is tested for occupational viability and for an ability to make manifest the best in all its members. The third theme of the vision, *membership into personhood,* highlights the emergence of the revitalized individual who, while continuing to expand and explore the potentialities of the allied group, also seeks to expand his or her individual horizons and capabilities.

The relationship of each individual program group to the vision of the collectivity is holographic. When the plate upon which a hologram has been recorded is broken, each piece of the plate, no matter how small, reproduces the entire image. So it is with the groups within the collectivity. Each program, in the course of a season, addresses all three of the vision's dominant fantasy themes. Yet each program seems to pay special attention to particular themes within the vision. The first theme—realization of significant others—is the least evolved portion of the vision. *Taxi,* which debuted on September 12, 1978, most clearly reflects this theme. The second theme of the vision—alliance in action—is more complex and is the major concern of *Lou Grant,* which debuted on September 20, 1977,[24] and *Barney Miller,* which debuted on January 23, 1975. The final and most complex theme of the vision—membership into personhood—finds its best articulator in the oldest program, *M*A*S*H,* which first aired on September 17, 1972. The twin evolution, philosophical and chronological, of the rhetorical vision's composite fantasy themes and the collectivity's composite groups can be seen by examining specific episodes from the 1978–79 season.

The first theme, realization of significant others, is the central theme of *Taxi.* The most common strategy to portray this theme places one character in the position of having to ask another member of the group for help. The asker often feels that his or her demands are unreasonable and is amazed when the other character comes to his or her aid. This experience causes characters to realize that others in the group are significant people in their lives. The October 24, 1978 episode is a case in point. Louie, the abrasive dispatcher, desperately wants to go to his twenty-year high school reunion as an affluent, debonair, tall, handsome ladies man who will sweep off with the fickle beauty who broke his heart years ago. Louie is none of those things, yet when he reluctantly shares his desires with the group, Bobby, an aspiring actor, volunteers to go to the reunion and impersonate him. He successfully impersonates Louie and as a result becomes a significant other in Louie's eyes. Similarly, in the February 15, 1979 episode Bobby quits the group in order to take a job acting in a soap opera. Louie tells him he will come crawling back "just like all the others." Bobby tears up his cabby's license, sprinkles the pieces on Louie's head, and walks out. In a few weeks Bobby "dies" on the soap opera and faces the ordeal of crawling back. Alex, the father figure and usual hero of the group, asks Louie to take it easy on Bobby when he comes back. Louie goes through a tirade about what he should do to Bobby, but when Bobby walks in Louie treats him kindly. Hence, Louie becomes a significant other in the eyes of the group. Finally, in the November 14, 1978 episode, John, a cabby/college student, and his new bride find themselves in a financial squeeze which will force one of them to leave school. Alex could lend them the money that would allow them both to continue in school, but is concerned about how that would affect their friendship with him. John tells his wife he would never ask Alex for money, yet as the financial pressure puts more and more stress upon the young marriage John's resolve weakens. He finally goes to Alex and asks to borrow the money. Alex agrees and in doing so becomes a significant other in the eyes of John and his wife.

51

The second theme, alliance in action, is the central concern of many episodes of both *Barney Miller* and *Lou Grant*. In *Barney Miller* one dominant scenario is to bring outsiders into the group where they can explore their problems in a noncondemning, supportive atmosphere. The end result is not the inclusion of the outsider in the group, but rather a conversion of the outsider to the vision of the collectivity. For example, in the September 21, 1978 episode a woman shows up at the station house to report that her missing father—missing for the twenty-eight years since her birth—has been traced by her to a health club nearby. The man arrives to complain that Ms. Schnabel (the woman who believes he is her father) has been harassing him and to request a court order preventing further attacks upon his privacy. The paperwork is set in motion, but the interactions that occur within the nurturing environment of the group result in the man offering his "daughter" a ride home, and asking her to drop him a card on Father's Day. The two have not become members of the group but they have become converts to the humane, sympathetic vision of the collectivity. Similarly, the March 15, 1979 episode brings into the station house a medical doctor from Johns Hopkins University and the Jamaican woman he swears put a curse on him. The initial antagonism between the two relaxes in the supportive climate of the group and they eventually depart not as friends, but with a new found mutual respect for each other and for the vision of the collectivity.

While occasionally employing the *Barney Miller* strategy of bringing outsiders into the group in order to convert them to the vision of the collectivity, *Lou Grant* more often sends group members out into the community. Once involved in the community the group member draws support and assistance from the group. This strategy was particularly evident in the February 26, 1979 episode which dealt with the plight of the elderly. Lou, city room editor of the Los Angeles *Tribune,* becomes involved with a very "young" older man whose confidence is severely shaken when he is mugged. Billie, the young female reporter, is working on an exposé of a nursing home where an elderly patient she had befriended was left unattended in a barren room. Rossi, the hard-nosed newshawk, is working on a feature dealing with some of the more positive aspects of health care and social services for the elderly. These interactions in the community glean mixed results: Billie's friend dies; Lou's friend finds new employment and confidence; and Rossi gets over being uncomfortable around "old people." This episode is typical of *Lou Grant's* subtle variations on the alliance in action theme. The actions of the group may not always result in bringing people into the group, nor in the conversion of outsiders to the vision of the collectivity; rather, the action of the alliance always confirms the validity and the necessity of the vision of the collectivity as the guiding principles for the group. This can also be seen in the October 16, 1978 episode in which Billie, while investigating the murder of a prostitute, encourages another hooker who is studying for her real estate broker's license. While the hooker ultimately fails in her attempt to leave the life of prostitution, Billie has learned to view another segment of society with greater compassion and in sharing that perception with the group deepens the group's commitment to the vision.

The third fantasy theme, membership into personhood, is most manifest in *M*A*S*H* where the individuals may be seen stretching the group's boundaries, exploring attitudes and beliefs within themselves which allow for the continued growth and evolution of both the group and the vision of the collectivity. In the January 1, 1979 episode B. J., one of the doctors, becomes deeply involved with a Korean family. B.J.'s loneliness for his own family and his feelings of guilt about not being home to care for them lead him to drive himself to the brink of collapse in his attempt to care for his "adopted" Korean family. At the end of the program he roars up in a jeep to tell his Korean family that he has located their lost son and has arranged to have him transferred closer to home. B.J. finds the village deserted; his "family" has gone further up into the hills to escape the fighting. Even though he is bitterly disappointed, he admits to Hawkeye, another surgeon, that he will probably do it again. He realizes that his attempts to "atone" for his absence from his own family may be irrational, but he also realizes that those attempts do no harm and in fact are quite supportive of the vision of the collectivity. Winchester, a surgeon whose competence is dwarfed only by his ego, went through a similar process of self-realization in the November 6, 1978 episode. A patient dies on the operating table and Winchester revives him with heart massage. The ensuing publicity brings a reporter from *Stars and Stripes* to do a story about Winchester. Winchester, being interviewed in the operating room, makes a potentially fatal surgical error which is later caught and corrected by Hawkeye. After discovering his error, he makes the reporter tear up the glowing story and the episode ends with the vision supported and Winchester more in tune with it.

While there is evidence that each show favors a specific theme, all three themes, as well as the vision, are reflected in each program. This is perhaps most easily seen through the eyes of the visionaries who appear in all the programs. In the episode of *Taxi* which dealt with Bobby's soap opera job, Alex functions in the dual role of hero and visionary. He is a hero in that he intercedes for Bobby and he becomes a visionary when he admonishes Louie: "It's not hard to humiliate people, it's not hard to make people feel rotten about their lives; the difficult thing is to make people feel good about their lives." As a visionary Alex gives voice to the vision.

Visionaries are not always heroes nor even members of the group. The September 14, 1978 episode of *Barney Miller* provides an example of such a visionary. Marsha, a prostitute new to the neighborhood who has just been arrested, proceeds to make pleasant conversation and helpful suggestions to the men at the station house as she and her client are being booked. Unable to cope with this, Wojehowiez, the arresting officer, asks her if she realizes that being arrested is not supposed to be fun. Her response defines her as a visionary: "Look, there is nothing I can do about it, right? So why shouldn't I just make the best of the situation and enjoy the people around me?" A visionary is anyone who through word or action manifests the encompassing vision of the collectivity. Like the vision itself, the visionaries wind throughout all of the programs of the environment pulling the three major fantasy themes into a collective vision.

The Rhetorical Vision

Analysis of the manifest content of *Taxi, Barney Miller, Lou Grant* and *M*A*S*H* reveals three predominant fantasy themes: the realization of significant others, the alliance in action, and membership into personhood. From these three themes emerges a rhetorical vision which focuses on a meaningful and rewarding existence based on humane, sympathetic awareness of and concern for the group, the individuals who comprise the group, and the society which surrounds it.

This emergent vision—*the new humane collectivity*—could well signal the advent of a new positive social statement on the part of entertainment oriented television programming. It confronts the realistic concerns of our society, presents reality-based models for problem solving, and advocates a refreshing brand of personal and social optimism. But, just as certain definitions were necessary to establish the vision, further definitions are now required to give it final focus.

What is "new" in the new humane collectivity? Initially, and most simplistically, the vision is new in a chronological sense. Although M*A*S*H began in September of 1972, the program did not begin to reflect the more complex aspects of the vision until the 1977–78 season (largely because specific characters prior to 1977 prevented the evolution of the program to the point where it could become reflective of the vision). For example, the first and most rudimentary theme within the vision is the realization of significant others. This demands some depth of character development in all characters within the group; indeed, it is this depth of character which allows the group to form. Pre-1977, Margaret Houlihan and Frank Burns were never given enough depth to allow their inclusion in a group of significant others. Even *Taxi's* Louie, a character often at odds with the rest of the group, has sufficient depth to allow him to accept significant others in his life and to become a significant other to other members of the group. Until Frank Burns left *M*A*S*H* at the beginning of the 1977 season, the show was prevented from evolving to the stage necessary to begin reflecting the vision. The youngest group of the collectivity, *Taxi,* did not make its debut until fall of 1978. Hence, the vision is "new" in that it has not existed in this particular form for very long.

There is a more significant aspect to the "new" in the new humane collectivity: it advocates a vision that has been largely absent in form and content from primetime television. It is the uniqueness of form that most strongly supports the notion that this is a new vision for television. The content of the programs, the themes dealing with the value of friendship, strength in unity, and the necessity for personal growth, has been presented in other, older television programs. *Playhouse 90,* which ran from October, 1956 until January, 1960,[25] aired many dramatic pieces which spoke to these issues. There are, however, significant differences between *Playhouse 90* and the programs of the new humane collectivity. For example, *Playhouse 90* presented a different 90-minute drama each week; this restricted character development. More importantly, audience members interacted with any group of characters only once. The shows of the collectivity allow audience members to return to the same characters week after week, year after year. Characters grow and evolve as the audience comes to "know" them, even to trust them.

Another of the significant differences between the programs of the collectivity and its thematically related predecessors can be seen in the Nielsen ratings. *Playhouse 90* never made the list of the top 25 programs during its broadcast history, whereas the programs of the collectivity are rarely out of the top 20.[26] The programs of the collectivity have brought to fruition one of the lingering dreams of television: they combine significant social statements with good, popular entertainment.

Undoubtedly, the newest aspect of the new humane collectivity is that it is both *humane* and *collectivity centered.* Humane, as used here, is intended to include and go beyond the simple dictionary definition, "characterized by tenderness and compassion for the suffering or distressed."[27] Use of the term here stems more directly from an idea voiced by Hegel in his essay on art: "fine art is frequently the key—with many nations there is no other—to the understanding of their wisdom."[28] The vision is humane in that it reflects and advocates those ideas which are traditionally considered laudable in American society, while simultaneously demonstrating the benefit of another more contemporary concept: the value of the emotional collective. The net effect of this process is the creation of an artistic model for a wiser society, one dominated by tenderness and compassion.

Furay, in his work *The Grass-Roots Mind in America,* contends that an in-depth examination of America's popular culture reveals three dominant idea clusters: optimism as a basic assumption of life; legitimacy of traditional American values; and an emphasis upon individualism.[29] All three of these idea clusters are touched by the vision. The first theme of the vision, the realization of significant others, depends on an optimistic view of life. To open up emotionally to another individual in the hope that he or she will assist you is an act of faith that can occur only when the optimistic belief that others will help overcomes the pessimistic fear that they will harm.

The legitimacy of traditional values is perhaps most obvious in the alliance in action theme. In this theme the traditional values of puritan and pioneer morality, achievement and success, efficiency, practicality, and pragmatism are all in evidence.[30] Other traditional values such as sociality, humor, ethical equality, generosity, and considerateness, find comfortable homes within the vision of the new humane collectivity.[31]

Furay's third idea cluster, emphasis upon the individual, receives rather interesting treatment from the vision. The third and most complex theme within the vision, membership into personhood, centers on the notion of the individual. Yet the vision and the theme demand that the individual continue to function in relationship to the group. It is the security and support of the group that allows the individual to examine the boundaries of his or her personhood; it is expected that the insight gained in those forays into personhood will be shared with the group, so that it too can grow—an idea which leads directly to the last component to the vision, the collectivity.

The idea of the collectivity is perhaps the most unique facet of the vision. It directly confronts the most cherished ideals of the "me" generation by saying lives are spent dependent in one way or another upon other people and groups, that cooperation is an option in human interaction, that the greatest happiness, the most serious challenge, and the fullest understanding come in the company of others.

Real world people who hope to share this telemediated vision must shoulder certain obligations. They must first abandon the grand isolation of the you-are-a-child-of-the-universe mystique. They must summon up the courage and optimism to allow significant others into their world. They must strive to put their best into the tasks confronting the group while at the same time strive to bring out the best in the other group members. If they accomplish these things they have helped to create an environment that is warm, secure, and still challenging. But the vision demands still more: even while a member of this group, the individual must remain unique and share that uniqueness with the group.

The demands of the vision seem harsh on occasion—*M*A*S*H* frequently makes that clear—but the rewards of the life presented through the eyes of the vision are also great: friendship, love, happiness, and a sense of personal and social accomplishment. They are rewards that apparently are striking a harmonious chord with millions of television audience members.

Notes

1. William R. Brown, "The Prime-Time Television Environment and Emerging Rhetorical Visions," *Quarterly Journal of Speech,* 62 (1976), 389.
2. Ibid., 398.
3. Ernest G. Bormann, "Fantasy and Rhetorical Vision: The Rhetorical Criticism of Social Reality," *Quarterly Journal of Speech,* 58 (1972), 396–407.
4. Cf. Robert F. Bales, *Personality and Interpersonal Relations* (New York: Holt, Rinehart and Winston, 1970).
5. "Fantasy types" are words, phrases, actions, and ideas which excite the group and form the basis for fantasy themes. Ernest G. Bormann and Nancy C. Bormann, *Speech Communication: A Comprehensive Approach,* 2nd ed. (New York: Harper and Row, 1977), pp. 309–310.

6. Ernest G. Bormann, "The Eagleton Affair: A Fantasy Theme Analysis," *Quarterly Journal of Speech,* 59 (1973), 143–159; Charles Richard Bantz, "The Rhetorical Vision of the ABC Evening News: Campaign '72," thesis University of Minnesota 1973; William Daniel Semlak, "A Rhetorical Analysis of George S. McGovern's Campaign for the 1972 Democratic Presidential Election," diss. University of Minnesota 1973; David R. Beisel, "Towards a Psychohistory of Jimmy Carter," *Journal of Psychohistory,* 5 (1977), 201–238; John F. Cragan and Donald C. Shields, "Foreign Policy Communication Dramas: How Mediated Rhetoric Played in Peoria in Campaign '76," *Quarterly Journal of Speech,* 63 (1977), 274–289; John J. Hartman, "Carter and the Utopian Group Fantasy," *Journal of Psychohistory,* 5 (1977), 239–258; David L. Rarick, Mary B. Duncan, David G. Lee, and Laurinda W. Porter, "The Carter Persona: An Empirical Analysis of the Rhetorical Visions of Campaign '76," *Quarterly Journal of Speech,* 63 (1977), 258–273; Ernest G. Bormann, Jolene Koester and Janet Bennett, "Political Cartoons and Salient Rhetorical Fantasies: An Empirical Analysis of the '76 Presidential Campaign," *Communication Monographs,* 45 (1978), 317–329.
7. Carl W. Hensley, "Rhetorical Vision and the Persuasion of a Historical Movement: The Disciples of Christ in the Nineteenth Century American Culture," *Quarterly Journal of Speech,* 61 (1975), 244–257; Sonja Kay Foss, "A Fantasy Theme Analysis of the Rhetoric of the Debate on the Equal Rights Amendment, 1970–1976: Toward a Theory of the Rhetoric of Movements," diss. Northwestern University 1976; Richard J. Illka, "Rhetorical Dramatization in the Development of American Communism," *Quarterly Journal of Speech,* 63 (1977), 413–427.
8. Bill Henderson, "An Evaluation of the October, 1972 Rhetorical Strategy of the White House When It Chose to Attack the Washington *Post* Coverage of Watergate: A Fantasy Theme Analysis of the Rhetorical Situation," diss. University of Minnesota 1975; Charles J. O'Fahey, "Reflections on the St. Patrick Day Orations of John Ireland," *Ethnicity,* 2 (1975), 244–257; Barbara Larson, *Prologue to Revolution: The War Sermons of the Reverend Samuel Davies* (Falls Church, Virginia: Speech Communication Association, Bicentennial Monograph Series, 1976).
9. Steven N. Barton and John O'Leary, "The Rhetoric of Rural Physician Procurement Campaigns: An Application of Tavistock," *Quarterly Journal of Speech,* 60 (1974), 144–154.
10. John Richard Breitlow, "Rhetorical Fantasy at the Virginia Convention of 1788," diss. University of Minnesota 1972; Gordon Alan Zimmerman, "A Comparative Rhetorical Analysis of the Nevada Constitutional Convention of 1864," diss. University of Minnesota 1973.
11. James Donnell Brown, "Rhetorical Fantasy in the Webster-Calhoun Debate on the Revenue Collection Bill of 1833," diss. University of Minnesota 1977.
12. John Francis Cragan, "The Cold War Rhetorical Vision 1946–1972," diss. University of Minnesota 1972; Kurt W. Ritter, "Confrontation as Moral Drama: The Boston Massacre in Rhetorical Perspective," *Southern Speech Communication Journal,* 42 (1977), 114–136.
13. Virginia Kidd, "Happily Ever After and Other Relationship Styles: Advice on Interpersonal Relations in Popular Magazines, 1951–1973." *Quarterly Journal of Speech,* 61 (1975), 31–39.
14. Kathleen J. Turner, "Comic Strips: A Rhetorical Perspective," *Central States Speech Journal,* 28 (1977), 24–35.
15. Donald C. Shields, "Fire Fighters' Self-Image, Projected Image and Public Image," *Fire Command,* 41 (1974), 26–28.
16. Robert L. Schrag, "Mork and Mindy: A New Vision for American Youth," *Exetasis,* 4 (1979), 27–36.

17. Marshall McLuhan and Quentin Fiore, *The Medium is the Message: An Inventory of Effects* (New York: Bantam Books, 1967).
18. Horace Newcomb, *TV: The Most Popular Art* (Garden City, New York: Anchor Books, 1974).
19. Howard L. Gossage, "The New World of Marshall McLuhan," in *McLuhan: Hot and Cool,* ed. Gerald F. Stern (New York: The New American Library, 1969), p. 23.
20. Robert L. Schrag, "Newcomb and Beyond: An Examination of Contemporary Television Comedy," Speech Communication Association Convention, San Antonio, Texas, November 1979.
21. Brown created the environments for his study by simply stating they existed, e.g., he discusses "value shows" without clarifying what they are (Brown, p. 389). Newcomb groups programs because they appear (to him) to share a concept or a structural element, not because they share an audience that finds them significant. The method employed in this study draws support from Warshow, who said, "A critic may extend his frame of reference as far as it will bear extension, but it seems to me almost self-evident that he should start with the simple acknowledgement of his own relation to the object he criticizes; at the center of all truly successful criticism there is always a man reading a book, a man looking at a picture, a man watching a movie." (Robert Warshow, *The Immediate Experience* [Garden City, New York: Anchor Books, 1964], p. xxv.) The process used in this study centers on a person watching television, but moves beyond that by establishing the fact that the programs in this environment share a common interested audience.
22. All episodes of these programs for the 1978–79 season were taped, analyzed for the purpose of the study, and erased. In retrospect, dropping *The Rockford Files* from the environment still seems justified; however, an argument could be made that *The White Shadow* should have been retained (although support for this argument would come primarily from the 1979–80 season rather than the 1978–79 season used in this study).
23. Bales, Bormann; "Fantasy and Rhetorical Vision."
24. *Lou Grant* as a program debuted on this date, but Lou Grant as a character debuted on September 15, 1970 on the *Mary Tyler Moore Show.*
25. Tim Brooks and Earle Marsh, *The Complete Directory for Primetime Network TV Shows, 1946-Present* (New York: Ballantine Books, 1979), pp. 498–499.
26. Ibid., pp. 802–810.
27. *The American College Dictionary* (New York: Random House, 1969), p. 588.
28. G. W. F. Hegel, *On Art, Religion, Philosophy* (New York: Harper and Row, 1970), p. 29.
29. Conal Furay, *The Grass-Roots Mind in America: The American Sense of Absolutes* (New York: New Viewpoints, 1977), pp. 27–50.
30. Edward D. Steele and W. Charles Redding, "The American Value System: Premise for Persuasion," *Western Speech,* 26 (1962), 83–91.
31. Ibid.

2
Rhetoric of Film

Since the days of D.W. Griffith, filmmakers have understood the power inherent in recording physical reality, structuring that reality through framing, image composition, editing, and various narrative conventions, and moving the spectator to an attitude toward the events depicted. The ends of such early filmic rhetoric ranged from pure entertainment (*The Adventures of Dollie,* 1908), to social criticism (*A Corner in Wheat,* 1909), to moral instruction (*What Drink Did,* 1909), to blatant propaganda (*The Birth of a Nation,* 1915), to a vision of human relations (*Intolerance,* 1916)—and all this from the heart and mind of one artist, the first practitioner of a complex film language, David Wark Griffith.

For the past seventy years other filmmakers—Sergei Eisenstein, Fritz Lang, Alfred Hitchcock, John Ford, Jean Renoir, François Truffaut and others—have extended the language of cinema and its techniques for conveying a message to an audience. The essays in this section are attempts to understand and explain the language-like capacities of film, particularly the grammatical, syntactical, and rhetorical dimensions which relate film form to audience interpretation and influence.

The authors of these three essays approach the critical task from different perspectives, with different assumptions and different interpretive constructs. Rushing and Frentz employ a form of model criticism to reveal psychological and ritual patterns structuring the persuasive message of *The Deer Hunter.* They derive their model from two sources extrinsic to the film itself, then use the insights provided by this extrinsic model to discuss the form of the film.

Benson also introduces a psychological model into his critique of the documentary film, *High School.* But, unlike Rushing and Frentz, Benson seems to derive his model—the double bind—from within the film itself and then to relate the concept back to its psychological origins. Whereas Rushing and Frentz employ an *external* model, Benson discovers an *internal* model or principle which helps to explain the rhetorical potential of the film.

Medhurst employs no model, but develops the extended metaphor of "marking time" which he uses to structure his argument that *Hiroshima, Mon Amour* is a film about humanity's attempts to know reality and communicate truth. The metaphor has both a figurative and literal sense, and seems to be used in both senses throughout the essay.

59

Not only are the interpretive constructs different in each of these essays, but the authors seem to derive their constructs in different ways as well. How did the critics discover or decide on their models or metaphors for encompassing these films? Where did they originate? Are they appropriate for explaining the rhetorical potency of the artifact? How successful is the analytic method in relating filmic form to audience interpretation?

Rushing and Frentz first lay out their model, apply the model to the film, then step back and discuss the implications of the model for the practice of rhetorical criticism. Benson begins by explicating the opening sequence of the film, stops to note the double bind pattern being developed, then proceeds systematically in a linear fashion from one sequence to the next until the end of the film. Medhurst starts by laying out the sequential pattern of the narrative, but claims that it is not helpful in understanding the film's message. He then breaks the filmic text into visual motifs and discusses groups of similar imagery without regard for the sequence in which they occur in the film. Is any one of these methods of proceeding better than the others? If so, what criteria should be used to determine better or worse methods for analyzing a text? Is there such a thing as the one best method of proceeding, or is each film unique, requiring a method of analysis all its own?

Perhaps one way to begin exploring these questions is to look at how each of these authors makes arguments. If criticism is an exercise in forensic reasoning, as Lawrence Rosenfield claims, then exploring how the movement is made from data to conclusions might prove helpful. What do the authors consider to be the primary data for their analysis? From where do they start?

Rushing and Frentz seem to look for various sorts of rituals. The rituals become the data from which arguments about the film's meaning are constructed. If a portion of the film is not part of one of the rituals described, then are the authors allowed to disregard it as superfluous to the analysis? How does one determine which data are admitted and which deleted?

Whereas Rushing and Frentz focus on large ritual patterns that recur throughout the film, Benson looks at smaller units of data such as specific lines of dialogue or the interaction between words and images. He places particular emphasis on verbal word play and uses the speeches delivered by characters within the film to form arguments about the invitation being offered to the audience. Does it make any difference if the verbal strategies or visual puns described by Benson were intentionally or unintentionally included by the filmmaker? How much of Benson's interpretation is dependent on the issue of intentionality? Would it make any difference to our judgment of the critic's art if the filmmaker were to deny any intention of having interwoven double binds into the text? Does Benson's critical effort stand or fall with the director's purpose and intent?

Medhurst, like Benson, looks to specific lines and images as data for arguments, but seems to place much heavier emphasis on the visual dimensions. He might even be read as implying that persuasion occurs primarily through the visual imagery rather than through dialogue, narration, or character development. Whereas Rushing and Frentz look to large patterns of ritual and Benson to action within and between sequences to generate critical data, Medhurst looks to specific movements, actions, and gestures within individual scenes for his critical building blocks.

One question the critical reader will want to ask concerns the level of generality at which data is generated. Is it legitimate or helpful to look at such minute dimensions of image construction as those isolated by Medhurst? Would any audience ever understand the logic of such details and their composition? All of these are questions about the critic's beginning data, where they originate and how they are used to form arguments.

Still to be answered are questions about the inferences the critics make between the data they introduce and the conclusions they reach. How are their conclusions warranted? What is the evidence upon which the conclusion is based? And are there other possible conclusions that are equally (or more) plausible given the data presented?

"The Deer Hunter":
Rhetoric of the Warrior

Janice Hocker Rushing and Thomas S. Frentz

"The Deer Hunter," winner of five Academy Awards, was one of the most controversial films of 1978. The film was celebrated for its "power,"[1] its "range and . . . breadth of experience," its "authenticity,"[2] and its "fiercely loving embrace of life in a death-ridden time."[3] Representative of this laudatory perspective is Kroll's statement: " 'The Deer Hunter' dares to say that things have come down to life vs. death, and it's time that someone said this big and strong and without fear"[4] But "The Deer Hunter" was also deprecated because of its limited view of the Vietnam War,[5] its "romantic adolescent boy's view of friendship,"[6] and its reflection of the director's ignorance and perversity "to the point of being megalomaniacal."[7] Epitomizing this stance is Terkel's reaction: "Not since *The Birth of a Nation* has a non-Caucasian people been portrayed in so barbaric a fashion. . . . The difference between *The Birth of a Nation* and *The Deer Hunter* is the difference between D. W. Griffith and Michael Cimino. One was a genius who happened to be a racist. The other is simply a cheapshot artist."[8]

What interests us in these criticisms is a particular pattern in the way these critics interpreted the film. Those who praised it saw it as an artistic event and its message as a metaphor transcending the immediate subject matter. Those who condemned it viewed it as a social-political statement, a literal representation of the true meaning of the Vietnam War and the United States' participation in it. Our position is that "The Deer Hunter" is an important aesthetic-rhetorical artifact. Its message concerns the psychological pattern of change that men experience in war and how this change affects their future societal growth. This change is determined by the attitudes toward and participation in culturally sanctified rituals. The theme that unifies the film's message is universal, and the persuasive power of its expression in "The Deer Hunter" justifies our claim of the film's high artistic achievement. In support of these claims, we propose a "Psychological/Ritual Model," which we use to analyze the film. From that analysis, we suggest implications of both the model and the film for future studies in rhetorical criticism.

Before presenting the theoretical framework, we need to clarify our notion of "model criticism," because it differs from some other typical conceptions and usages of the method. Our use of the model method of criticism is most in line with what Brockriede terms "explanation," an attempt to account for how an aspect of a rhetorical experience works by relating it to a theoretical

From *The Quarterly Journal of Speech,* Volume 66, 1980. Reprinted with permission of the Speech Communication Association and the authors.

system more general than itself. Motivated to solve some problem or problems in a rhetorical event that cannot be explained by referring to internal relations within the work itself, the critic proceeds inductively rather than deductively, selecting appropriate concepts and categories while in the process of studying the event.[9] These concepts may occur to the critics only as they approach the particular event, or the concepts may be part of a larger theoretical system extrinsic to the critical object; at times, the theory will not have been originally created to solve problems in criticism (e.g., Freudian criticism). A model may consist of a single theoretical framework (e.g., Burke's dramatistic theory) or a synthesis of more than one perspective (e.g., Jung's psychology and Eliade's perspective on ritual, as in this project).

As a model unfolds, it typically points to new problems in the work at the same time it aids the critic in answering the initial questions. These new questions necessitate modification and extension of the model. That is, the model and the critical explanation grow together symbiotically. As Brockriede puts it, the explaining critic "makes an *active* use of both partners [data from the experience and the general concept or category system] and creates an *active* interaction between them. The explanation is a product of inferences that grow out of that interaction."[10] In turn, the expanded model may illuminate other messages manifesting general issues similar to those of the artifact that originally gave rise to the model, and these new messages will again modify the model. Thus, the model will generalize *to,* but *not beyond,* similar critical objects.

Psychological/Ritual Model

The present model has three components. First, it depends on an interpretation of the human psyche. Second, it advances a view of the form and function of initiation rituals. Third, it identifies types and patterns of psychological change that are linked to specific attitudes toward rituals.

The Psyche

Our interpretation of the human psyche is based on the works of Carl Jung, especially that part which concerns the unconscious and dreams.[11] The relevance of this interpretation to "The Deer Hunter" is indicated by a statement made by Cimino in defending the film against those who decried its lack of realism. "The Deer Hunter," he said, is "surrealistic, a dreamscape."[12] The psyche, according to Jung, is a self-regulating system that seeks "balance" between its two parts: the conscious and the unconscious.[13] The archetypal part of the self that is observable to other people is one's *persona,* a sort of "dressing" for the ego—the conscious, intentional part of the person. The persona is unconsciously formed and appears commonly in dreams. In Jung's view, the persona, as its name implies, is a mask that *"feigns individuality,* making others and oneself believe that one is individual . . . it is a compromise between individual and society as to what a man should appear to be."[14] As such, the persona presents the self to society in accordance with socially approved roles.

63

The reverse of the respectable persona is what Jung calls the archetype of the *shadow,* "the dark, other self which exists in each one of us: it is the dreadful and evil person that we might have been if we had not been so careful to put aside all the tendencies within us of which we do not approve."[15] Paradoxically, the shadow is potentially a source of strength and power.[16] Its power is positive only if the shadow is recognized and accepted by the individual; Jung regards confrontation with one's shadow as the essential prerequisite to self-recognition and change. Such confrontation requires "a considerable expenditure of moral resolution."[17] Typically unconscious to the individual, the shadow appears in waking life as negative projections onto other people.

The fundamental archetype lying at the center of all the others Jung calls "the Self." It is "the archetype of wholeness," because it represents the entire psyche, conscious and unconscious, and Jung says that when active it expresses itself in symbols usually connected with the idea of the deity.[18] When a person deliberately takes on the goal of unifying various parts of the psyche, or searches for the Self, that person is said to be seeking "individuation," the process of becoming undivided.[19]

Ritual

In large measure, "The Deer Hunter" derives its power from its portrayal of myth and ritual. Their use is fundamental to the psychological development of the film's main characters. Myth and ritual are critical to self and social definition; they permeate all aspects of life, whether in their presence or absence. Myths give archetypal form to widely shared values, providing principles for conduct, while rituals provide expression of the human desire to imitate the gods—or heroes, who become what they are by imitation of the gods and represent the hopes and aspirations of their people.[20]

The ritual most germane to "The Deer Hunter," one common to all cultures, is male initiation into adulthood. "Initiation," writes Eliade, "is equivalent to a second birth. It is through the agency of initiation that the adolescent becomes both a socially responsible and culturally awakened being."[21] The ritual takes two forms. Partial rituals concern the conscious self because they reaffirm culturally specific values, and, if successfully experienced, lead to a strengthened persona. Holistic rituals involve the total person in a radical rebirth. Archaic cultures, for instance, required men to participate in ordeals of torture, suffering, or military combat, risking at least a symbolic death.[22] The purpose of such rituals was to cause the initiate to go back to the origins of Earth and life, to confront the gods and to face his unconscious being.

War is a holistic ritual. In combat, the warrior faces his own shadow figure. The "enemy is a monster . . . in killing him one is protecting the only truly valuable order of human life on earth, which is that, of course, of one's own people."[23] Thus, war is more than deer hunting; it is man hunting. One's own life is at stake. If warriors approach this risk as a sacred act, those who survive triumph, become men and honored members of society. If they approach war profanely, "the combatants are no longer aware of the deeper significance of their 'ordeals' and hence scarcely benefit by their initiatory meaning."[24] War becomes, then, a senseless act of killing and dying, devoid of mythic import.

A warrior's confrontation with an enemy as intelligent and capable as he forces the surfacing of his own shadow; his persona must contend with its antithesis, both in the enemy and himself, under life and death circumstances. Only the man with a strong persona is likely to survive psychologically a sacred war experience.[25]

Changes in Psyche

Jung maintains that recognition of the "morally inferior" part of one's self creates disequilibrium, demands that the "deficit" be redressed, and requires its assimilation into consciousness—the result being an altered personality.[26] Four ways are posited by which this process may occur and be revealed in postwar behavior.[27] Three of these paths would most typically be followed by a person with a *weak* warrior persona. First, the person might credulously *accept* the unconscious, becoming "an eccentric with a taste for prophecy" or reverting to an infantile attitude, cutting himself off from human society. Second, the warrior might *reject* the shadow, resorting to "regressive restoration of the persona," eschewing all further risk. The person tries to patch up his old persona within the boundaries of a much more limited personality, "doing inferior work with the mentality of a scared child." Third, the person may *identify* totally with his unconscious, becoming overpowered by it. The identification pattern is in a sense an inversion—the shadow becomes the face the person presents to the world, and his previous persona becomes the repressed shadow. Jung also calls this pattern "schizophrenia" and notes that it is generally accompanied by a dramatic sense of "psychic inflation" or powerful "godlikeness," the result of attaining the knowledge of the universal collective psyche, particularly the knowledge of good and evil.

We contend that *individuation*—the gradual "coming to selfhood" achieved when the person aims at a living cooperation of previously unconscious and conscious factors would be most probable for the postwar warrior who entered the battle with a strong persona, because his shadow would be less likely to overcome it. The individuated person learns to accept both his uniqueness and his "indissoluble communion with the world at large"—that is, the aspects of himself that he shares with the collective psyche. The individuated person feels power, but of a fundamentally different kind from the person who identifies with his shadow. Jung explains the difference:

> It is precisely the strongest and best among men, the heroes, who give way to their regressive longing and purposely expose themselves to the danger of being devoured by the monster of the maternal abyss. But if a man is a hero, he is a hero because, in the final reckoning, he did not let the monster devour him, but subdued it, not once but many times. Victory over the collective psyche alone yields the true value—the capture of the hoard, the invincible weapon, the magic talisman, or whatever it be that the myth deems most desirable. Anyone who

identifies with the collective psyche—or, in mythological terms, lets himself be devoured by the monster—and vanishes in it, attains the treasure that the dragon guards, but he does so in spite of himself and to his own greatest harm.[28]

In the following analysis of "The Deer Hunter," we shall focus only on three of these patterns—(1) regressive restoration of the persona, (2) identification, and (3) individuation—for these are the three patterns of postwar change exhibited by the three main characters.

The Analysis

We can now examine "The Deer Hunter" in terms of our critical model. We explore, first, the psyches of the major characters; second, the initiation rituals in terms of their mythic potential, as well as how the characters experienced them; and, third, the changes in the characters' psyches as a result of war.

Psyches of the Characters

The three main characters in "The Deer Hunter" are the good friends, Michael, Nick, and Steven. Michael and Nick share the most intimate relationship. Reflecting to Nick about the others going on the deer hunt, Michael muses, "They're all assholes." The bond between Michael and Nick does not extend to Steve. In the prison camp in Vietnam, Michael initially tells Nick to forget about Steven— "He won't make it," he warns. Subtle reminders of the intimacy between Michael and Nick occur throughout the film. For example, in the initial bar scene where the two buddies shoot pool, the jukebox croons,"You're just too good to be true, can't take my eyes off of you." And, in a tender moment after Steve's wedding reception, Michael runs drunken and naked through a city street, collapsing under a street light:

> Michael: Hey, Nick, think we'll ever come back?
> Nick: I love this fuckin' place. Don't leave me over there—you gotta promise.

And, of course, Michael does promise.

The ties between Nick and Michael run deeper than friendship. At the outset of the film, they share an interesting complementary relationship: In the terms of our model, Michael's shadow is projected into Nick's persona, while Nick's shadow is projected into Michael's persona. Such an attraction is not unusual. Mahoney explains: "You can fairly surmise which spouses, sweethearts, inseparable friends and intimates are living testaments to the irresistible attraction-of-opposite functions, *as though responding to a hidden command to find completion however vicariously through experiencing their opposite, inferior function,* expressed in another person."[29] The special closeness of Michael and Nick is expressed symbolically in their mutual (and mutually reciprocal) attraction to Linda.

Michael's persona is characterized by the qualities of self-control or discipline ("You're a control freak," Nick chides him just before the deer hunt), rationality (he stalks the deer strategically), leadership (he attempts—successfully—to control the activities of the Clairton gang), and detachment (he is primarily an onlooker in the raucous wedding festivities). That these persona features are highly valued by the culture is demonstrated by the fact that Michael's leadership of his community is never questioned, though it changes in form. Michael's shadow qualities are spontaneity, empathy, vulnerability, and involvement. Michael remarks to Nick concerning the deer hunt that he doesn't like "surprises." Initially, he is painfully awkward and inept with women and seems disdainful of any form of weakness. In the first part of the film, Michael does resemble the stereotype of the small steel town macho man.

Dominant aspects of Nick's persona are spontaneity ("Wanna get married?" he asks a startled Linda at Steve and Angela's wedding reception), empathy (he is compassionate when Linda seeks comfort after being beaten by her father), vulnerability (he isn't ashamed to express his fears about going to Vietnam), and involvement (he actively participates in the wedding reception). Nick's qualities are vital to Michael, who is tacitly aware he is unwhole without him. "You're the only one I'll hunt with," Michael professes, although it is obvious to both men that Nick derives little pleasure from the hunt itself. In sum, the predominant features in Nick's persona are the repressed features of Michael's shadow.

Similarly, Nick's unconscious shadow qualities are the elements in Michael's persona. Nick abhors self-discipline, rationality, leadership, and detachment. When Michael angrily refuses to lend Stan his boots for the hunt, scolding him for not being prepared, it is Nick who finally ends the argument by tossing the boots to Stan and asking Michael, "What the fuck's the matter with you?" In his abandoned singing and his relationship with his friends, Nick is empathic and involved; he seems uncomfortable with too much reflection.

Although Nick's persona is the opposite of Michael's, it would be a mistake to say that Nick is not masculine. He is a lover *par excellence.* Not only does he win the group's most attractive woman, but there is a hint that Nick is the father of Steve's bride's baby. The fatal flaw in Nick's character is that, though his persona is probably a more diversified and androgynous one than Michael's, it is not composed of qualities *relevant to war.* Nick is pacifistic at home; he never fires a shot during the deer hunt, although, being with Michael, he has ample opportunity. Thus, even though he has some qualities that are valued by the culture, his is not a *warrior* persona.

Steve does not share the interdependence of a complementary relationship with either Michael or Nick. Lacking that interdependence, he is less crucial to the film, and his personality is delineated less completely. He is important, however, because he exemplifies the possible fate of someone totally unprepared for war. The available glimpses of Steve's persona suggest that he is best described as childlike. The Clairton guys treat "Stevie" like a small mascot they are fond of, and he in turn seems to look to them as a surrogate family. He drinks beer with the gang, but his mother collars him out of the bar and into his wedding. None of the guys expects him to go on the deer hunt; the only initiation Steve relishes is his wedding, and much of that revolves around women's activities. He probably did not even father his own child, who is blonde like Nick. Michael plays the protective father to Steve, piggybacking him out of the prison camp and, later, wheeling him out of the Veterans Hospital. If Steve is consciously childlike, then, his adulthood is buried in his shadow—Steve does not seem to want to grow up, and maybe the group needs a kid, too.

Rituals

"The Deer Hunter" is structured around seven major initiation rituals: a wedding, two deer hunts, a war, and three games of Russian roulette.

The Wedding. The first third of the film seems curiously to dwell upon a ritual that is apparently unrelated to war. The relevancy of the wedding to the film's theme is complex; the wedding itself is a holistic initiation rite different from war. Rather than requiring its actors to experience the depths of the unconscious in order to enter the spirituality of adulthood in the culture, marriage is mythically a restoration of integral wholeness—an imitative celebration of the union of heaven (the husband) and earth (the wife). Marriage is associated with the fertility of the earth as well as of women, and thus symbolically regenerates the seasonal year and confers fecundity, wealth, and happiness upon the entire community,[30] The animated celebration of the wedding festivities contrasts ironically with the stark lifelessness of war.

The wedding lends more to the film than dramatic irony, however. Although "The Deer Hunter" is above all a man's film, *this* wedding, typical in modern American culture, is mainly a woman's ritual. Women carry the cake ceremoniously to the church. The camera playfully pauses on the bridesmaids chattering excitedly as they float down a dirty urban street in their pastel organdy gowns, and on the bride as she checks her bulging white profile in the mirror before catching her veil in the screen door. Steven's matriarchal mother oversees the entire ritual.

The significance of the wedding, then, is in the *male* characters' participation in it. Michael, characteristically, stands back from the festivities, detached. Both Nick and Steve celebrate with gusto. His wedding is the only ritual Steve participates in before the war. His passage to adulthood is not only an initiation rite irrelevant to preparing his persona for battle, but it is mainly a ritual for women in this culture. It is not surprising that Steve is the least able of the trio to cope with the horrors of war.

The Deer Hunt. From the film's title to the anthems accompanying the ritual, it is clear that deer hunting is much more than an annually recurring pastime for the young men of Clairton. What makes deer hunting so special is that to complete the rite successfully by killing a deer demands manly qualities and skills highly valued by the culture. These qualities include discipline (planning in advance and self-control, as in Michael's "one shot" motto), rationality (strategically stalking the prey), leadership (as shown by Michael's independence from the other guys), and detachment (a singlemindedness of purpose). Deer hunting is a partial intitiation-into-manhood rite that strengthens the personae of those who take it seriously as a sacred activity defining the mythic qualities demanded of the warrior.

The sacredness of the rite is lost on all except Michael. Michael's buddies, except for Nick, get drunk, shoot wildly, and make a lot of noise. Stan symbolizes the unpreparedness of all of them by forgetting his boots. Even Nick experiences the hunt profanely. The crucial distinction between Michael and Nick is captured on the evening of the wedding and the day before the hunt. Michael enters the shack he and Nick share, and after sharply admonishing Nick for not having prepared adequately for the hunt, he reminds Nick of the "one shot" credo. Nick's response is prophetic:

> Nick: I don't think about one shot much anymore.
> Michael: You have to. I try to tell the guys, but they don't listen.
> Nick: I like the way the trees are, y' know?

Again Michael attempts to make the connection for Nick between deer hunting and the impending war:

> Michael: Y' know—I wouldn't mind gettin' it in the mountains.
> Nick: Why the fuck are we talking about hunting with Steve getting married and us goin' to war?

The consequences of Michael's and Nick's differing attitudes toward deer hunting are profound. Michael approaches the mountaintop as a pinnacle of spirituality; there he is reenergized for his tasks in the valleys of human existence.[31] His insistence on "one shot" represents the mythic significance of the entire hunt—the optimal way to complete the ritual. Michael fortifies those aspects of his persona needed to complete the deer hunt and to compete in the war successfully. Campbell puts it well: "By and large, hunting people are warrior people."[32] For Nick, deer hunting is an aesthetic experience, but one devoid of sacred import. He follows Michael across the mountains preoccupied with their beauty, without ever firing a shot. Campbell pinpoints the problem Nick faces:

> One of the great problems . . . of our own variously troubled society is just this, that youths brought up to function in the protected fields of peacefully domestic life, when suddenly tapped to play the warrior role, are provided with little or no psychological induction. They are therefore spiritually unprepared to play their required parts in this immemorial game of life and cannot bring their inappropriate moral feelings to support it.[33]

Nick's impending tragedy is amply foreshadowed in his attitude toward deer hunting.

The War. One of the most recurrent patterns in criticisms of "The Deer Hunter" has been devaluation of the film for its historical inaccuracy and political naivete on the Vietnam War.[34] But "The Deer Hunter" is *not* primarily about the Vietnam War, the Vietnamese people, or even about the Russian subculture in Pennsylvania. The film *is* about War—especially about the consequences of this ultimate holistic rite of initiation for those differentially prepared to enact it. Experienced sacredly, war is a universal ritual that, through the act of killing a worthy opponent, revitalizes and regenerates the identity and uniqueness of both the warrior and his culture.[35]

Russian Roulette. But war, as "The Deer Hunter" agonizingly demonstrates, is not a sacred ritual for most people in modern times. By far the most mesmerizing and horrifying ritual in the film is Russian roulette; it is a microcosm of war as a profane ritualistic experience. If war as a sacred rite reaffirms personal uniqueness and cultural identification, then war as a profane game dramatizes with an equal fervor the total dehumanization of the participants and decay of the cultures at battle. The ancient Greek athletic games versus American professional football—recently portrayed in the film "North Dallas Forty"—comes to mind as an analogy. As Kroll puts it, "The VC soldiers are shown as savages, but the image of the Americans holding a gun to their temples is a gut-wrenching symbol of a society committing moral suicide."[36]

Russian roulette is a game of chance with its own mythic significance. In a life versus death game of chance, no human qualities or skills can affect the outcome. If men are equally impotent to control it, then the players lose all semblance of uniqueness or individuality. It is no accident that those connected with the game were presented in stereotypical sameness. Dehumanized sameness is a consequence of experiencing war profanely—as an exercise in Russian roulette.

Changes in Characters' Psyches

Given a sense of the characters of Michael, Nick, and Steven—particularly the complementary relationship between Michael and Nick—as well as a conception of the major rituals they experienced, we track the changes in the three men's psyches both as they confront war and afterwards.

Survival—The Prison Hut. P.O.W.'s at the prison camp get their choice: Either play Russian roulette against an equally luckless opponent at the brutal orders of the Vietcong in a steamy bamboo hut of death or slowly rot in a cage in the filthy rat-infested river below. Along with darkness, the womb, cosmic night, and the belly of a monster, a hut often symbolizes initiatory death, expressing regression to a previous state of being[37] (for example, the witch's, or shadow's, hut in "Hansel and Gretel"). But the game inside could be found only in the profanest of initiations. Kroll captures the scene well: "The suspense and horror are agonizing as the prisoners, quaking with fear, press the pistols to their heads, pulling the trigger to the click of an empty chamber or the roar of an explosion that blasts a fountain of blood from their heads."[38]

Michael, Nick, and Steven do regress to a latent mode of being; from deep within the bowels of this ultimate profanity, the shadows of all three spring forth. All must deal with their darkest personalities immediately, without the comfort and guidance of a therapist, priest, lover, or parent. Michael finds himself almost out of control—both of the ritual and of his emotions. He feels fear, rage, and hatred. His shadow, however, does not totally take over Michael's psyche. His persona has been "prepared" for this task as well as anyone's can be.

In a moment fused with hysterical, but "creative," insight, Michael invents a plan to take control of the ritual—in effect, to change it from a game of chance to a game of skill. He mumbles, as much to himself as to Nick, "Three bullets. We've gotta get them to play with three bullets." This apparently suicidal plan is nothing of the sort. Now cognizant of his unconscious (in the mythic sense, having gained the knowledge of Good and Evil), Michael *believes* that his will can, in fact, determine where the macabrely spinning cylinder will stop.[39] The audience can almost see the inner conflict of personalities as Michael's facial expressions shift from wild hate, to calm rationality, to fear, to self-control. When he takes control of the game, he turns the ritual into a sacred event for himself, and he survives with his persona and shadow intact.

When Michael explains his three-bullet ploy to Nick, Nick shakes his head and replies, "I'm not ready for this." But play he must—ready or not. In the desecrated carnage of the prison hut, Nick's shadow also emerges. As Michael almost coerces him to play the game, Nick's shadow—his discipline, rationality, and cold detachment—takes over, and, under Michael's leadership, both survive a ritual that meant almost certain death.

Steve does not fare so well. Totally unprepared for such an ordeal, his shadow (adulthood) tries to emerge, but in battle with his childlike persona, he rejects it and turns into a terrified and whining infant. Even with Michael screaming "Do it, Stevie, *do it!*" the petrified Steve cannot play the game; at the last instant, he tilts the pistol up and the loaded chamber only grazes him. For his "effort," Steve is relegated to the river coffin. Michael saves the half-dead Steve, but the harrowing escape effort costs Steve his legs, his manhood, and his power.

Postwar Changes. It is one thing to survive physically an ordeal such as the prison camp; it is quite another to survive psychologically. In a hospital in Vietnam, Nick's persona fights a gallant but losing battle against his shadow.

For Nick's shadow was released upon a weak and ill-defined persona in a holistically profane ritual, and his psyche, to borrow Jung's metaphor, is "succumbing to the dragon." Nick tries to keep in touch with his consciousness— to remain sane—as he keeps looking at Linda's picture and makes one last abortive attempt to call her in America. But the telephone connection is not made, and he is then swallowed up mystically into the Saigon nightlife as more and more he *identifies* with his shadow and with the collective unconscious.

Nick searches for Michael, or, just as accurately, for his other half, and for an explanation for his own gradual transformation into Michael's former persona. Nick is drawn to the same ritual that gave him his "godlikeness." With the aid of an opportunistic Frenchman, a Mephistophelean character intent on buying his soul,[40] Nick finds another Russian roulette game, controlled by professionals, in the Saigon underground. The players appear to be destitute young Vietnamese men for whom the monetary rewards outweigh the unspeakable risks.

After watching a player click an empty chamber at himself, Nick stumbles forward, grabs the pistol, clicks a second empty chamber at an astonished Vietnamese player, and then clicks still a third empty chamber at his own temple. Nick seems compelled to test that rush of awesome power he felt when he and Michael took control of the first roulette game. If there was any doubt in his mind over his power to control his own destiny, that doubt vanishes with this scene.

Michael, too, is at this game—unbeknownst to Nick. But there is a difference. Having prepared himself for war, Michael's persona is strong enough to "subdue the monster" and remain a part of his psyche. Unlike Nick, Michael tests the legitimacy of his control over the first game as a spectator. This is because the compassionate and vulnerable aspects of his emerging shadow allow Michael to keep distance on the deadly rite; he can identify with the players as humans rather than automatons. Ironically, it was Michael-the-player and Nick-the-spectator in deer hunting. And because of that pattern, it is Nick-the-player and Michael-the-spectator in this second round of Russian roulette.

The "setting" of the patterns of change in both Michael and Nick is captured symbolically in a poignant scene. After his impromptu act, Nick runs out of the game and is picked up by the Frenchman. Michael fights his way through the excited onlookers and begins chasing Nick through the Saigon streets. After cavalierly throwing his money out of the speeding auto to the street urchins (a sign that he is no longer rooted in material reality), Nick tosses his wallet out as well. Michael tenderly retrieves the last remnant of Nick's former identity. Symbolically, at that moment, Nick's psyche becomes totally dominated by his shadow, while Michael's psyche begins the gradual process of *individuation*.

After this incident, Michael returns home and finds a paraplegic Steve in the veterans hospital. Steve apparently prefers the safety of playing bingo to the uncertainty of facing his catatonic wife at home. Having rejected his shadow, he now has restored his childlike persona in a *regressive* way; he is more infantile than before, he eschews all risk, and dares nothing. He cries in protest when Michael wheels him home—out of the womb of the hospital.

Meanwhile, Michael begins an awkward courtship with Linda. He seems sensitive that she was Nick's girl, and is empathic over her loss. When she says tearfully, "Did you ever think life would turn out like this?", Michael shows compassion born of experience. The guys are awed at Michael's uniform and at the war stories they sense he could, but does not, tell. They seem still to accept Michael as their leader, but he does not resume the same disciplined, powerful role. They go on another deer hunt—this time without Nick. But the Nick in Michael is firmly intact. In a moment of enlightened realization, he chooses not to shoot a stag he has strategically and successfully stalked. He no longer needs to.

Still the haunting reminders of Nick persist—most notably in the money Steve mysteriously receives monthly from Saigon. Michael, who has made a promise not to leave Nick "over there," goes back to Saigon to look for Nick and encounters the Frenchman. After bribing the Frenchman to set up a game between Michael and "The American," Michael embarks on a desperate barge trip through the sewers of a burning Saigon.[41]

Finally, the two old friends meet. Nick has completely lost contact with any reality apart from the roulette game.[42] A tragic symbol of mechanical inhumanity, he seems to personify the consequences of profaning the most powerful rituals. He does not recognize Michael and is annoyed at Michael's attempt to "contact" him. Nick seems intent only on playing until his opponent kills himself.

Michael knows that only the roulette game is a wrenching enough ritual to rekindle Nick's slumbering sanity. But he has forgotten the very lesson he tried to teach Nick before the war; namely, that Nick's unprepared psyche cannot endure the type of change Michael must ask for. Nick's shadow has become the totality of his psyche and its life-preserving feature has given him control over his own mortality—at least within the roulette ritual. To disturb that fragile psyche would be to lose its saving dimension. It is a risk that Michael must take.

As the game begins, the pistol points to Nick. "Don't do it," Michael implores. But Nick does. Indifferently, he clicks off an empty chamber as his vacant eyes stare at Michael. Michael's turn. Michael picks up the pistol and looks at Nick: "This what you want?" With that, Michael presses the barrel against his temple, and, saying "I love you, Nick," clicks off an empty chamber.

As the two face each other, Michael tries one final time: "We don't have much time, Nick. Come on home. Remember the trees?" A glimmer of recognition crosses Nick's face, the old gentle smile returns for one fleeting instant: "Yeah, one shot." One final time Nick presses the gun to his head. He begins the journey back to consciousness, but the control is gone and the odds have too long been against him.

The Epilogue

The funeral is over, Michael, Steve, Linda, and the remainder of the clan sadly gather in the bar for final goodbyes. Hesitantly, first one and then another begins singing "God Bless America." The image is of the warrior returning to his tribe. They are shattered and broken, but it is a far richer and stronger Michael who leads them now than led them at the film's onset. By being psychologically prepared, Michael experienced war sacredly, and, in so doing, reaffirmed the mythic qualities in himself and in his community. But rebirth comes slowly and painfully. Only Michael knows the extent to which they all owe their rebirth to Nick. In his final toast, "To Nick," Michael seems to be saying, "To him who gave what he was so that I might become what I am."

Implications

We now consider some implications of our analysis for future studies in criticism.

Rhetoric of War

Of all aspects in "The Deer Hunter," critics are most divided over the film's posture toward the Vietnam War. Some critics are appalled at the stereotyped Vietnamese characters and the glorification of the American soldier. Others see the film as a brutal denunciation of the horrors of any war. Kroll, for instance, writes that " 'The Deer Hunter' is the first film to look at Vietnam not politically, but as the manifestation of an endemic murderousness."[43] Both views have merit. Although we have argued that the film is not about the Vietnam War in particular, certain political implications concerning War in general follow from our model and analysis.

When people experience war as a profane ritual, analogous to a game of Russian roulette, it is hideous. If roulette is taken as the central metaphor, then the film indeed condemns war as "an endemic murderousness." War as an ultimate profanity does destroy good people like Nick and Steve; it does disrupt and threaten even the most close-knit communities; and war as roulette does force a community to the very edge of despair and disillusionment.

We have argued that a complete understanding of the film demands a model that stresses the *aesthetic form* of war as a universal initiation rite. To view war aesthetically raises several serious problems. As a sacred ritual, war *can* perform positive functions: The mythic values of the culture are reaffirmed, societal unity is reinforced, and heroes are provided with a chance to confront their own personal dragons. It does not follow from this, however, that all values reaffirmed through war are good. There is little question that under the tutelage of Adolph Hitler many of the German people experienced World War II as a sacred event brimming with mythic significance.[44] Clearly, however, the values reaffirmed by Hitler are not those that morally responsible persons would endorse. There is also little doubt that Michael, the sole figure in "The Deer Hunter" who experiences the sacred link between deer hunting and war, fares better than the other characters. The film seems to say: "If you want to survive in war, be like Michael." We might question, however, the emphasis placed on developing a warrior-type persona in young men of our society.

It also does not follow that war is the sole or best ritualistic *means* for serving these "positive functions." Other rituals, if experienced sacredly by the culture—for example, political elections, national holiday celebrations, etc.—reaffirm values and unite the society in a much less costly, though possibly less profound, manner. Still other rituals, when experienced sacredly by the individual—for example, therapy or religious rites—can effect a rebirth of the total Self without the risk of being killed or the immorality of killing another. The historical truth and rhetorical efficacy of purification and personal rebirth through killing is well-documented, most notably by Burke.[45] When the enemy (or shadow) within must be externalized and killed in order for a person to be "born again," and particularly when such externalization is sanctioned by a culture in the form of war, then culture is faced with the ultimate immorality.

In sum, "The Deer Hunter" offers a complex rhetorical stance on war. It is not undeniably clear whether the film is rabidly antiwar, whether it merely portrays what war does to people under both sacred and profane experiences and proclaims nothing, or whether it implicitly advocates personal and societal transcendence through killing. On whatever level one chooses to interpret the film, however, the aestheticizing of war as a universal ritual remains bothersome. As Benjamin writes, "The logical result of Fascism is the introduction of aesthetics into political life."[46] We are not claiming that "The Deer Hunter" is a Fascist film. Ironically, however, in bypassing the politics of Vietnam, the film may have unwittingly allied itself with a heinous political ideology.

Psychological/Ritual Model

In model criticism, the critera for interpretation arise from the model and not from the intrinsic structure of the critical object.[47] "Our end is accomplished," Crane notes with regard to poetry, "when we have established the presence in poems of patterns of action, character, and imagery concerning which we can say that they are patterns originating not in the artistic purposes and inventions of the poets but in antecedent history or prehistory or in human nature itself, our assumption being that the profounder meanings of poems are a function always of the original meanings of the archetypes which they embody."[48] One recurring inference made from this feature of model criticism is that the method inhibits the critic's capacity to *evaluate* the critical object. If the meaning of a critical object is derived from perspectives outside of the structure of the object, there are no intrinsic grounds for evaluation.

The question is whether critical evaluation is an inherent incapacity of the model methodology. Although we acknowledge that the primary function of the explanatory model is interpretation, evaluation can follow logically from the model perspective, as the foregoing critique demonstrates. If the model required to explain a critical object fully reveals methods in that object that imply a questionable moral posture, then that model itself invites a negative assessment of that object and its methods. Insofar as the model required to explain "The Deer Hunter" uncovers methods that depict war aesthetically as a holistic initiation ritual, the model alerts the critic that some aspects of the film need to be devalued. Thus, our analysis demonstrates one way in which model criticism facilitates evaluation as well as explanation.

The model also implies a heuristically stimulating linkage between film and dreams. Dreams, art, and religion are well-known means of expressing archetypal images and symbols. Film is an art form particularly well-suited to expressing archetypes: It is primarily visual; it is experienced in darkened, dreamlike conditions; and, through special techniques, it can simulate the surrealistic plasticity of dreams. As such, both films and dreams can deal with what Jung calls the "collective unconscious":

> In addition to our immediate consciousness, which is of a thoroughly personal nature and which we believe to be the only empirical psyche . . . there exists a second psychic system of a collective, universal, and impersonal nature which is identical in all individuals. This collective unconscious does not develop individually but is inherited. It consists of pre-existent forms, the archetypes, which can only become conscious secondarily and which give definite form to certain psychic contents.[49]

If dream imagery expresses individual awareness or "personal knowledge" of the collective unconscious, then film imagery expresses one form of public awareness or "social knowledge" of the collective unconscious.[50] The Psychological/Ritual Model implies that effective social change agents must "see" the relationships between the archetypal images in their personal knowledge of the collective unconscious, as expressed in dreams, and the social knowledge, as expressed in rituals. The understanding of these relationships, though not essential to an individual's personal growth, is important if that person is to function as an instigator of social change.

In fact, the relationship between the personal and social knowledge of the collective unconscious may be more active than we realize. Kauffmann concludes his remarks on "The Deer Hunter" by lamenting the gap between what the film is as opposed to what it could have been. For us, Kauffmann's stance is far less interesting than the image he chose to express his concern. Paraphrasing T. S. Eliot, Kauffmann concludes, "Between the idea and the reality fell the shadow."[51]

Notes

1. Silvia Feldman, "Eloquent Visions of War," *Human Behavior,* Feb. 1979, p. 77; and David Denby, *New York,* cited in Tom Buckley, "Hollywood's War," *Harper's,* Apr. 1979, p. 85.
2. Denby, p. 85.
3. Jack Kroll, "Life-or-Death Gambles," *Newsweek,* 11 Dec., 1978, p. 113.
4. Ibid., p. 115.
5. Marsha McCreadie, "The Deer Hunter," *Films in Review,* 30 (1979), 242.
6. Pauline Kael, "The God-Bless-America Symphony," *New Yorker,* 18 Dec. 1978, p. 66.
7. Buckley, p. 88.
8. Studs Terkel, "On Seeing *The Deer Hunter,*" *Chicago,* May 1979, p. 210.
9. Wayne Brockriede, "Rhetorical Criticism as Argument," *Quarterly Journal of Speech,* 60 (1974), 170–71.
10. Ibid., p. 171.
11. Although we are not attempting a complete Jungian analysis of the characters, we do believe that the film presents enough evidence to cast the characters as broad types. Thus, we use only that part of the vastly complex Jungian system that facilitates our critical analysis. Our principal sources on Jung are: David Cox, *Modern Psychology: The Teachings of Carl Gustav Jung* (New York: Barnes & Noble, 1968); C. G. Jung, *Memories, Dreams, Reflections,* trans. Richard and Clara Winston (New York: Random House, 1962); C. G. Jung, *The Undiscovered Self,* trans. R. F. C. Hull (Boston: Little, Brown, 1958); Maria F. Mahoney, *The Meaning in Dreams and Dreaming* (New York: Citadel, 1966); and *The Portable Jung,* ed. Joseph Campbell, trans. R. F. C. Hull (New York: Viking, 1971).
12. Buckley, p. 85.
13. Mahoney, p. 36.
14. *The Portable Jung,* pp. 105–06.
15. Cox, p. 142.
16. Mahoney, p. 110.
17. C. G. Jung, *Shadow, Animus and Anima,* cited in Mahoney, p. 108.
18. Cox, pp. 153–54.
19. *The Portable Jung,* pp. 121–38. In the more complete model, Jung identifies two levels of the unconscious: the *personal unconscious* and the *collective unconscious.* The shadow, anima, animus, and persona are archetypes that have both personal and collective manifestations. Furthermore, the persona is dominated by one of the four functions (Thinking, Feeling, Intuition, or Sensation), whereas the shadow is dominated by the antithesis of the persona function. Thinking and Feeling are opposites, as are Intuition and Sensation. Ibid., pp. 59–162; 178–269.
20. Mircea Eliade, *The Sacred and the Profane,* trans. Willard R. Trask (New York: Harper & Row, 1961), pp. 101–02. Eliade explains that his usage of the term "archetype" differs from Jung's. Whereas Jung uses archetypes as the universal symbols of the collective unconscious, Eliade's archetypes refer to "exemplary models" or "paradigms." See Mircea Eliade, *The Myth of the Eternal Return,* trans. Willard R. Trask (Princeton: Princeton Univ. Press, 1954), pp. xiv-xv.
21. Mircea Eliade, *Myths, Rites, Symbols: A Mircea Eliade Reader,* Vol. 1, ed. Wendell C. Beane and William G. Doty (New York: Harper & Row, 1975), p. 174; Mircea Eliade, *Rites and Symbols of Initiation: The Mysteries of Birth and Rebirth,* trans. Willard R. Trask (New York: Harper & Row, 1965), pp. 1–4; C. G. Jung, *Four Archetypes,* trans. R. F. C. Hull (London: Routledge & Kegan Paul, 1972), esp. pp. 45–81.
22. Eliade, *Rites and Symbols of Initiation.*

23. Joseph Campbell, *Myths to Live By* (New York: Bantam, 1972), p. 177.

24. Eliade, *The Sacred and The Profane,* P. 208.

25. By contrast, in the protracted ritual of psychotherapy, C. A. Meier claims, "The stronger the *Persona* is, the more rigid it becomes and the more the bearer is jeopardized from influences from within." See "The Cutter Lectures," Andover Newton Theological School, Newton Center, Massachusetts, cited in Mahoney, p. 106.

26. *The Portable Jung,* p. 116.

27. All four of these patterns are discussed in ibid., pp. 83–138.

28. Ibid., p. 119.

29. Mahoney, p. 95. It is also common for a person to hate, rather than be attracted to, another onto whom one has projected one's shadow.

30. Eliade, *The Myth of the Eternal Return,* pp. 23–27.

31. The association of the mountaintop motif with spiritual heights is common in mythology, literature, and rhetoric; e.g., the gods of Mount Olympus, Moses receiving the Ten Commandments from Mount Sinai, Martin Luther King, Jr's., "I Have Been to the Mountaintop" speech of 3 April 1968, etc. For a discussion of this motif, see Maud Bodkin, *Archetypal Patterns in Poetry: Psychological Studies of Imagination* (London: Oxford Univ. Press, 1934), pp. 99–104.

32. Campbell, p. 176.

33. Ibid., p. 177.

34. For example, see Peter Arnett, " 'Deer Hunter' is good drama, but bad history," *Chicago Sun-Times,* 29 Apr. 1979, p. 7; Terkel (p. 210) is the most graphic: "In fact, the movie may actually justify to some audiences, especially the young, our adventure in Indochina. They may wonder, If these gooks and slopes are such bastards why didn't we bomb the bastards back to the Stone Age? Was Curtis Le May a consultant on this film?"

35. Kenneth Burke, "The Rhetoric of Hitler's Battle," in *The Philosophy of Literary Form: Studies in Symbolic Action,* 3rd ed. (Berkeley: Univ. of California Press, 1973), pp. 191–220.

36. Kroll, p. 113.

37. Eliade, *Rites and Symbols of Initiation,* pp. xii–xv.

38. Kroll, p. 113.

39. The belief that one has mystical control over chance events is not unusual. Jung cites numerous examples of "ego-inflated" persons who believed they possessed unusual powers in the initial phases of coming to grips with their shadows. See *The Portable Jung,* pp. 83–103.

40. Jung calls the confrontation of the conscious with the unconscious the "Faustian problem"; see ibid., p. 117. "Mephistopheles is the diabolical aspect of every psychic function that has broken loose from the hierarchy of the total psyche and now enjoys independence and absolute power," ibid., p. 343.

41. The "night sea journey" is a common motif in fairy tales and literature, usually symbolizing a trip toward unity—e.g., the hero journeys to meet his bride (anima). It is prophetic, of course, that this night sea journey is polluted.

42. In providing a glimpse of Nick's needle-tracked arm, writer/director Cimino, we believe, committed one of the few serious artistic errors in the film. If Nick's ultimate dehumanization is due to drugs, then neither Nick nor society can be held responsible for his acts.

43. Kroll, p. 113.

44. The classic rhetorical example of the sacredness of the war is Leni Riefenstahl's "Triumph of the Will." Of that film, Marsha Kinder and Beverle Houston comment, "The final night rally takes on the appearance of a religious ceremony as the hall, darkened by shadows, becomes like a cathedral and the camera cuts to

the twisted cross of the swastika as Hitler says of the party, 'Its total image will be like a holy order.' " *Close-up: A Critical Perspective on Film* (New York: Harcourt Brace Jovanovich, 1972), p. 118.

45. Kenneth Burke, *A Rhetoric of Motives* (Berkeley: Univ. of California Press, 1969); Kenneth Burke, *The Rhetoric of Religion: Studies in Logology* (Berkeley: Univ. of California Press, 1970).
46. Walter Benjamin, *Illuminations,* trans. Harry Zohn (New York: Harcourt, Brace & World, 1968), p. 243.
47. For some consequences of this perspective for literary criticism, see R. S. Crane, *The Language of Criticism and the Structure of Poetry* (Toronto: Univ. of Toronto Press, 1953), esp. pp. 120–39.
48. Ibid., p. 135.
49. *The Portable Jung,* p. 60.
50. Thomas B. Farrell, "Knowledge, Consensus, and Rhetorical Theory," *Quarterly Journal of Speech,* 62 (1976), 1–14.
51. Stanley Kauffmann, "Stanley Kauffmann on Films," *The New Republic,* 23 and 30 Dec. 1978, p. 22.

The Rhetorical Structure of
Frederick Wiseman's *High School*

Thomas W. Benson

The room darkens, the title flashes briefly upon the screen, and then we are traveling along a suburban street listening to Otis Redding sing "Dock of the Bay" ("sitting on the dock of the bay, wasting time. . ."). Then there is a chain link fence, a parking lot, and a factory-like building. A brief glimpse of a crowded hallway; we are in the school. Then a teacher's face, and the first speech of the film.

> First thing we want to do is to give you the daily bulletin. You might be surprised. A little notice that you think doesn't concern you might change your whole life. It might decide what college you'll go to, or it might decide on what activity. And then Joyce has a few things to say, right, Joyce? All right. The thought for the day: "Life is cause and effect. One creates his tomorrows at every moment by his motives, thoughts, and deeds of today." And this question of cause and effect, you know what they say, you might read something that might change, uh, your life.

Cut to a woman's face. She pronounces a sentence with exaggerated clarity, in Spanish, emphasizing the word *"Existentialista."*

"Wasting time." "Cause and effect." *"Existentialista."* We are less than two minutes into Frederick Wiseman's *High School*. There has been no explanatory narration, nor will there be any, but already we have heard a statement that may serve not so much as the theme of the film as its epigraph.

Frederick Wiseman is one of the most productive and consistently successful documentary filmmakers in the history of the medium. His films about American institutions now form a considerable body of work: *Titticut Follies* (1967), about a prison for the criminally insane; *High School* (1969); *Law and Order* (1969); *Hospital* (1971); *Basic Training* (1971); *Essene* (1972); *Juvenile Court* (1973); *Primate* (1973); *Welfare* (1975); *Meat* (1976); *Canal Zone* (1977); *Sinai Field Mission* (1978).

This essay explores the rhetorical structure of *High School*. I will argue that, for the American adults who form the film's primary audience, the film offers a powerful rhetorical appeal that is realized through the structure of the film.

In a 1974 interview with Ira Halberstadt, Wiseman commented that his films, though based on real events, are constructed fictions presenting a theory about the material being considered.

Reprinted from *Communication Monographs,* Volume 47, 1980, by permission.

WISEMAN: . . . So you are creating, hopefully, a form which has a life of its own, and that form is a fiction because it does not exist apart from the film.

HALBERSTADT: How would you describe the way in which you work?

WISEMAN: Well, it's the structural aspect that interests me most, and the issue there is developing a theory that will relate these isolated, nonrelated sequences to each other. That is partially, I think, related to figuring out how it either contradicts or adds to or explains in some way some other sequence in the film. Then you try to determine the effect of a particular sequence on that point of view of the film.

Presumably, if a film works, it does so because the structure works. . . .

That overall statement is what the point of view of the film is. And what the point of view of the film is, is also an expression of a theory or an attitude toward the experience that constitutes the film. In relating the sequences in a particular way, you are developing a theory which in turn provides a form for this kind of experience. The abstractions you are dealing with are abstractions that are related to the structure of the film and that emerge from the structure of the film.[1]

High School calls upon viewers to exercise a variety of skills to derive meaning from the experience. They must draw upon their skills as viewers of film, acquainted with the elements of film language, and they must be able to look through the film language to the social behavior recorded there—the use by human beings of speech and gesture in a context familiar to most viewers. Our question then becomes: How does Wiseman draw upon the skills and contexts of his viewers to invite them to experience a particular complex of meanings as they view *High School?*

If we are to make any sense of the way *High School* means for its audience, we must take two risks. One is the risk of assumed linearity, the other of overinterpretation. *High School* is a film, not verbal discourse. The film argues, but does so in the context of a concrete audiovisual experience. As a film, and especially as a film often placed with others in the tradition called cinema verite, *High School* is coherent, but as a film it borrows from actuality an awkward concreteness that resists the forms of linear, propositional argument. I will try to show that *High School* is about power without reducing the film to an oversimplified pseudolinearity, but also without broadening the concept of power until it is without any coherence whatever. In film, the formal is always at war with the material, and it is in the filmmaker's resolution of the relation of form and matter that particular meanings emerge.

The risk of overinterpretation arises from the critic's temptation to impose meanings for his own convenience. Selecting a detail here or there and calling it a symbol is a particularly antiaesthetic form of criticism, a kind of shell game in which the critic substitutes his or her own obsessions or ambitions for the common language of art or literature, and for the common evidence of the senses. As a general rule, an element should be admitted to critical interpretation as a symbol only when the context requires it, either through repetition of the same or parallel or contrasting symbols, or when failure to account for the symbol makes the element in question incoherent, implausible, or distracting.

In order to answer the question of how *High School* means, I will present a detailed analysis of two levels of symbolic activity: the film as a structure, and the social behavior recorded in the film as another structure. The film is a rhetorical structure about a rhetorical structure. In order to avoid confusion, however, it is well to be clear about the perspective of this analysis. The only evidence we have about the actors in the film comes from the film itself. Hence, although I will comment in detail upon the behavior of the actors in the context of the film, I can make no claims for the referential accuracy of the actions depicted. We know, of course, that the actors behaved as we see them. The film is evidence of that. But the behaviors we see are contextualized by Wiseman, and are out of the context in which they occurred for the participants. The film was shot in Northeast High School, Philadelphia, in 1968. But in the comments that follow about the meanings of the social behaviors recorded in *High School* I make no claims about Northeast High Schol, about the intentions of its teachers and students, or about their relations to one another.

High School may be more or less accurate about Northeast High School. It may also be more or less accurate about "high school" as a generalized institutional experience shared by virtually every American who sees the film. The film is a powerful experience for most viewers, and its power probably derives from the film's evocation of at least part of the experience of high school. Still, this essay is about *High School,* and not about Northeast High School or "high school."

Because this essay is about the meaning of *High School,* it is important to be clear *whose* meaning we are talking about and *what* meaning we are attributing to the film. Whose meaning? This essay is an inquiry into the states of thought and feeling an audience is invited to experience. We are not particularly interested in the psychological predispositions of the filmmaker, though the film provides considerable inferential evidence about the filmmaker's rhetorical intentions. Nor can we speak with authority about the way the behaviors of the characters in the film may reveal the psychologies of those characters. *High School* is a created reality. But for the audience of *High School* the characters may seem quite real, their behaviors quite significant. It is into this seeming reality that we are inquiring. Our perspective is, then, an audience perspective. But the evidence for the audience's responses, as well as the evidence for the filmmaker's designs, will be sought in the film itself. All of the themes that I will discuss in the following essay as forming the fabric of ideas in *High School* have been mentioned by other writers: power, authority, identity, alienation, sexuality, boredom. What I hope to do is to develop the presence and the function of these thematic elements in more detail than have previous writers, to show how the details of the film relate to one another to form a structure, and to offer an account of how the structure may invite a rhetorical response.[2]

High School is a film about power as it is exercised in an institution whose ostensible mission is to educate.[3] An audience is invited to perceive the institution's exercise of its power as absurd and hurtful. Wiseman reveals his theme and invites us to share in a bitter laughter about the packaging of American adolescence through a remarkable filmic structure built upon accumulation, comparison, and contradiction. This seemingly simple, episodic film can be seen, upon close examination, to exhibit a startling coherence, based upon a series of dialectical relations that gain force with each additional sequence.

As Wiseman has said, *High School* "is both a theory and a report on what I have learned."[4]

The beginning and ending of the film show the school as a factory turning out a product. In the first sequence, a series of traveling shots, Wiseman opens the second shot with a closeup of the back of a milk truck advertising "Penn Maid Products," a pun for the Pennsylvania-made products turned out by the school. And when the school first appears (Figures 2, 3), it looks like a factory.[5] The end of the film shows us the product: students adapted to military service, which seems to stand as a symbol for alienated conformity. The middle of the film explores how the factory processes its students into willing members of the social order. Wiseman revealed in his interview with Rosenthal that this pattern was consciously imposed on the film: "You begin the film showing a factory process, and you end up with a view of the perfect product."[6]

The Theme of Power

The theme of power is introduced unmistakably in sequence 6 of the film (see Figure 100 for a list of the sequences in the film). Sequence 6 is the first of the film in which we see an extended face-to-face interaction. A student attempting to get excused from compulsory gym class is being confronted with the power of the school in the form of an administrator. The administrator sits behind a desk, the stereotype of a retired sergeant. His heavy face is topped by a crew cut and he speaks in commands. He is framed in the shot so that we see his face and next to it, on the wall, a picture of the American flag (Figures 21, 22, 23, 24, 25). The student protests, and the administrator rises from his chair, pointing finger and fist at the student's face as he approaches. "Don't you talk and you just listen." Again he orders the student to report for gym. Then he repeats it. Barely audible, the student says, "I said I would." This continued bit of protest, which the teacher rightly translates as "I said I would; stop scolding me," draws an immediate response. "You're suspended." The oppressiveness of the school is symbolized in unmistakable terms in this sequence. And there are other sequences in which oppressive power is revealed, or in which school officials are engaged not in instruction but in admonition. In sequences 10 and 24 the administrator of sequence 6 is again acting the role of the school disciplinarian. In sequence 11 we follow a teacher

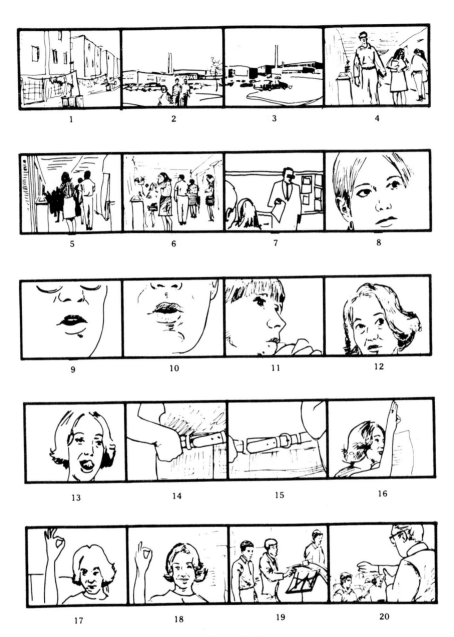

1   2   3   4

5   6   7   8

9   10   11   12

13   14   15   16

17   18   19   20

Figures 1–20.

on hall patrol duty as he examines passes and regulates hall traffic. In sequence 25 a mother and daughter attend a disciplinary conference with a school official. But if these sequences—6, 10, 11, 20, 25—are about power, discipline, and control of students they are only five sequences out of a total of forty-three in the film. What of the other thirty-eight?

The power exercised so absurdly and hurtfully by the institution is not simply the power to discipline as it is represented plainly in sequences 6, 10, 11, 20, and 25, although these sequences serve the function of placing power unmistakably before the viewer. Power in the high school extends to the power of the school and its representatives to control the setting and define the situation. Their power is the power they try to achieve over the lives—the minds and spirits—of their charges. Such power is exerted in virtually every scene of *High School,* through all the means of face-to-face communication: language, gesture, costume, setting. And it is a power that is exercised in ways much more pervasive than simply requiring students to accept a simple and single code of thought and behavior. The school presented by Fred Wiseman is one in which students are required to obey a code that is by its very nature contradictory, from their point of view. Whatever they do is likely to be a mistake. The students are thus not merely required to obey a rule: they are required to be mixed up, stupid, confused, in the wrong—and subject at any time to the authority of the school. The school does not simply tell the students what to do; it tells them who they are. The school, of course, does not achieve total control. It does not have the students fulltime, nor is it entirely competent to extend its confusion, nor, truly, do its agents seem to understand the situation they seem to control. And the students have their own resources of subversion and alienation. Hence, the school does not produce robots, but rather very confused, oddly loyal, and self-sacrificial human victims, ready to take their places as the next generation of housewives, beauticians, astronauts, soldiers, secretaries, and high school teachers.

The Double Bind: Distorted Communication

At its most damaging, the school exercises its power through a method that is similar to what Bateson and others have called the double bind.[7] The double bind was first posited as part of an interpersonal dynamic that contributed to the development of schizophrenia. In the double bind, the victim is sent inconsistent messages by those in authority in a situation where the victim must make some response to the messages but is prohibited from drawing attention to the contradictory nature of the messages and from withdrawing from the situation. The result is that the victim becomes schizophrenic. Wiseman does not, of course, claim that Northeast High School is breeding schizophrenics, but the structures of power that he discovers in the school fit the double-bind hypothesis remarkably well.

One of the ways in which the schoolmasters exercise double-binding control is through the use of language, making nonsense of ordinary discourse. Teachers and administrators invoke contradictory commonplaces to gain momentary advantage in discourse, remove words from their proper signification, reduce poetry to technique, and just plain miss the point of their own sanctimonious homilies.

In sequence 10, an administrator is talking with a boy, Michael, who has been sentenced to a detention for talking back to a teacher.

MICHAEL: I don't feel I have to take anybody screaming at me for nothing.
ADMINISTRATOR: No, well, there's a point to that, but in the meantime it's time you showed a little character of your own. Right?
MICHAEL: Yes.
ADMINISTRATOR: I would take the detention and then you can come back and say now I took the detention may I speak with you.
MICHAEL: I can't . . .
ADMINISTRATOR: Well, you can try.

Michael returns to a description of the situation in which he got into trouble, and tries to show that he was not in the wrong. The administrator returns to his own agenda:

ADMINISTRATOR: See, we're out to establish something, aren't we?
MICHAEL: Yes.
ADMINISTRATOR: We're out to establish that you can be a man and you can take orders. We want to prove to them that you can take the orders.
MICHAEL: The way I see it you have to stand for something.
ADMINISTRATOR: Yeah, well, the principles that are involved here, I think it's a question now of proving yourself to be a man. It's a question here of how do we follow the rules and regulations. I think you don't fight this teacher, I think you ask permission to talk, and you ask him to listen to you. Now this is what you didn't do. Now if you had taken your detention, and, after all, they didn't require much from you. The teacher felt you were out of order, and in her judgment you deserved a detention. I don't see anything wrong with assigning you a detention. And I think you should prove yourself. You should show you can take a detention when given.
MICHAEL: . . . I'm doing in my opinion what I feel is right.
ADMINISTRATOR: Are you going to take the detention? I feel that you should.
MICHAEL: I'll take it but only under protest.
ADMINISTRATOR: All right then, fine. You'll take it under protest. That's good.

Michael does not seem to realize what has happened to him. The administrator has twisted an act of protest by reversing Michael's meanings, asking to "establish that you can be a man and you can take orders," when Michael obviously wants to prove to himself that he can pursue his rights, and, equally important, pursue what is right. The administrator's tactic of seeming to agree with the student, seeming to take his side, is particularly insidious. It is in bad faith and makes nonsense of the language by which the student is attempting to understand his reality.

Linguistic nonsense also occurs in sequence 9, where a father and mother are discussing their daughter's grade with another administrator. The father shows that the daughter earned high marks on her papers, even being told that one was "fabulous," only to find out that she had failed the course. He seeks an explanation and is met, not with a clear inquiry into all the elements that went to make up the grade, but obfuscation:

ADMINISTRATOR: I can only say this. That the teacher, upon reading these papers, thought they were fabulous, but that the total mark involves more than just those papers. That's all I can tell you.
FATHER: Well I think this is a rather unique situation, wouldn't you say so? Rather unique?
ADMINISTRATOR: Will you be happy if I say it's unique?
FATHER: I'd be happy.
ADMINISTRATOR: I would say somewhat unique.

The administrator speaks good sense when telling the father that grades are based on many types of student performance. As with the administrator in sequence 10, he seems to announce a principle, a commonplace, that in itself is unobjectionable. But in this case he uses it as a cloak to prevent further inquiry. The commonplace is "all I can tell you," rather than the introduction to an examination of the other work done by the daughter. And then the dialogue loses focus and turns into complete nonsense, as father and administrator spar over whether the situation is "rather unique" or "somewhat unique"— both, of course, meaningless qualifications of a word whose usefulness depends upon its absoluteness.

Sequences 20 and 25 present an unresolved contradiction of commonplaces that we are invited to see as confusing and inconsistent. In sequence 20, a girl is told not to be individualistic, and then in sequence 25 another girl is told not to go along with the crowd. In sequence 34 a teacher reading the "thought for the day" seems to miss the point of it completely.

The function of these linguistic absurdities in the film is not simply to show up the teachers and administrators as inept. In each sequence, the misuse of language occurs in a setting where it works to confuse the issue. Students subjected to such language are at a disadvantage in the power game that the school is playing with them. In the world of the film, as in the world Alice finds in Wonderland, words and their meanings are under the arbitrary control of those at the top of the hierarchy, with the result that the person in charge stays in charge. And in this world where they cannot do anything right, it is no wonder that the responses of students are pinched and apathetic—small acts of misbehavior or cautious conformity.

So far I have argued that *High School* is a film about power, a power exercised through direct control of behavior, as well as more subtly through the definiton of setting and situation, and the confusion of issues by obfuscating language. These elements alone may be enough to account for the apathy of the students and the rage on their behalf that we are likely to feel as viewers. But there is more to the film than this.

The Rhetoric of Power and Sexuality: An Explication

In *High School* the theme of power is related to a pervasive secondary theme of sexuality. Thematically, the film might be taken as a set of binary structures relating power and sexuality in a proposition: in *High School,* those who have social power maintain it by engaging those with an emerging sexual potency in a double bind. Students are ostensibly told to grow up and accept the responsibilities of adulthood, but they are subjected to constant warnings about the dangers of adult sexuality. The contradiction that seems so silly when heard at the level of power alone ("be a man and take orders") becomes devastating when the power of the school invades the confused adolescent sexual identities of its students. The confusion created by the double-binding of the school's contradictory directions results in the apathy, alienation, juvenility, and inversion that are evident in the behavior of the students. Almost every scene in the film deals explicitly with some element of the curious relations between sex and power in the school, and the few that do not deal with related issues.

I am claiming that most of the audience is moved by a rhetorical structure that has not previously been adequately described. The meaning of the film is about institutional power—that much has been evident to every viewer and critic. But the vehicle by which that meaning is made into a powerful experience is the relation of power to sexuality through a series of mostly invisible, but powerfully affecting, rhetorical structures.

High School invites viewers to experience the structural relations of the themes of power and sexuality, and the subordinate manifestations of these themes in distorted interpersonal communication, twisted language, confused identities, militarism, and boredom. But the film is not simply the themes. The critic can abstract themes from the film, but to present each theme separately, together with examples that support its presence, though it would simplify this analysis, would also seriously distort Wiseman's structure. Instead, I will proceed sequence-by-sequence through the film, presenting a detailed explication that will suggest the ways in which Wiseman invites his viewers to experience the meanings of *High School* as structures.

The presence of sexuality in *High School* is exceedingly complex, ranging from possibly accidental dirty jokes to bodily awareness, the formation of gender identities, and an undercurrent of courtship rituals. Though some of the sexually relevant scenes are unmistakable, as when a gynecologist lectures on the dangers of sex, most of the instances I will cite are marginal in their intimations. It is impossible to divine Wiseman's intentions or predispositions with any certainty, and equally impossible to be certain that an ordinary viewer would ascribe a sexual relevance to much of the material. And it has been all too easy, since Freud, for a critic to find sexual symbolism in every random tree, telephone pole, and railway tunnel. It is well to remember Freud's reminder that sometimes a cigar is just a cigar. I will argue that the repetition of sexual elements, and the way they are placed in context, is likely to predispose the viewer to decode them in something like the way I am describing. But I must strain the reader's credulity further by arguing that the sexual material works on the viewer of the film much as it works on the student in the school: for the student, it exists as part of the double-bind that reinforces the school's power while remaining just at the edge of consciousness. And for the film viewer the sexual material is also usually just out of conscious awareness, inviting us to feel angry about the power of the school without quite realizing why we feel so angry.

High School speaks in a rhetorical vernacular in which concepts of alienation and repression become the commonplaces of audiences who have probably never read Marx or Freud. Alienation and repression are part of the conceptual apparatus of *High School,* but Wiseman does not require of the audience a first- or even second-hand knowledge of philosophy or psychology; the concepts have seeped into ordinary discourse as part of the apparatus of contemporary conventional knowledge.

As soon as Wiseman enters the school, he presents the issue of bodily awareness. In sequence 2, a hallway, we see students walking. A girl stops and looks into her handbag (Figure 4). Then she turns to look into a glass, perhaps a glass doorway, and combs her hair (Figures 5 and 6). She is performing a grooming activity which is not particularly significant in itself but which will accumulate with other images in the film into a repeated pattern of gender-specific self-stroking and grooming. A *meaning,* once established, begins to absorb neutral or ambiguous signs. So with the theme of sexuality in *High School*—many gestures that are, in themselves, neutral, seem to take on relevance to the general awareness of sex, gender, and bodily awareness that pervades the film.

In sequence 3, a teacher reads the daily bulletin. Underneath the speech in this sequence there runs a visual undercurrent of bodily attention. The first shot of the sequence presents the teacher in a mid-shot (Figure 7). Wiseman cuts from the mid-shot of the teacher to a closeup of a female student, looking at something off camera (Figure 8). By the logic of film, the next shot should reveal what she is looking at. Cut to Figures 9 and 10, a big closeup of the teacher's mouth, then cut to Figure 11, another student gazing with concentration at the teacher's mouth. It would be forcing the issue to argue that these images unambiguously represent sexuality. But they do guide our awareness. Attention is focused, by the intercutting of gaze and its object, the teacher's mouth, on the existence of some sort of relation between eyes and lips. In a fictional film, such images would certainly be understood as foreshadowing sexual desire.

89

The hints of sequences 2 and 3 are made more explicit in sequence 4. We cut to a woman talking Spanish. She tilts her head, her eyes widen (Figure 12), and then her tongue, pointed, caresses her upper lip (Figure 13). Then, without cutting, the camera tilts down to reveal, in Figure 14, the teacher's hand on her belt, thumb hooked into the belt and hip thrust to the side. The camera then pans right, across the belt line, to discover the teacher's elbow (Figure 15). Later in the same sequence, the teacher leads the class in choral repetition of Spanish words, keeping time with her hand making the "ring gesture": thumb and index finger forming a circle, tips touching, with the other fingers erect (Figures 16, 17,and 18). The ring gesture is repeated four times in one shot.

The widened eyes and protruding tongue are unmistakable courtship routines, and it is significant that the cameraman instantly recognizes this by tilting the camera down to discover the teacher's hand hooked in her belt. At the very least, such courtship routines seem to call attention to the gender of the actor, and to imply that gender is somehow relevant to the interaction that is taking place. Do they imply more than gender identification in this sequence?

Albert Scheflen has pointed out that the gestures whose origin and frame of reference have to do with courtship are not always used as the instruments of seduction. Instead, they are converted into "quasi-courtship behavior," in which courtship behaviors are qualified to make clear that they are not seductive but rather meant to encourage a positive interaction. According to Scheflen, social occasions often require the maintenance of a sense of mutual attractiveness and attentiveness. "This state is necessary to group cohesion and the completion of tasks that are not immediately gratifying. Some of the different terms used to describe this state are attractiveness, attentiveness, sociability, readiness to relate, and quasi-courtship."[8] According to Scheflen, quasi-courtship behavior is always available as a way of increasing the sense of attentiveness in groups, and a corresponding complex of decourting behaviors is available to lessen the degree of involvement.

It is not clear, by the time one has reached the fourth sequence in *High School,* how a viewer is likely to understand the courtship behaviors of the Spanish teacher. Would they be seen as simple quasi-courtship intended to maintain a high level of attention among the students to the group task? Or would they be seen, consciously or not, as having a seductive quality? It must be remembered that we are not searching for what the behaviors meant in the actual classroom situation, but for how they are likely to appear to a viewer of the film. Surely the film viewer would not be likely to think that the teacher was actually trying to seduce her students. But possibly the teacher's behavior does at least cross into an ambiguous area of sexual awareness. As film viewers, we have been trained by all of our film watching to look for the signs of sexual involvement on the screen. Bing Crosby, priest though he seemed, allowed us romantic fantasies in his partnership with Ingrid Bergman in *The Bells of St. Mary's*—the involvement may not have been sexual, but there was about it an element of romantic longing that was rendered perfectly safe by the use of dog collar, nun's habit, and Hollywood convention. But Dustin Hoffman and Anne Bancroft demonstrated another, and more consequential, pattern of courtship in an early scene from *The Graduate*. Bancroft, as Mrs. Robinson, engages in a highly ambiguous display of sexually aggressive non-involvement that contrasts with Hoffman's desperately juvenile decourting behaviors. Finally, when the audience has been given a chance to explore the special pleasures, the dangerous excitement, of wondering whether Bancroft is really courting, can be trusted, or is worth desiring, Hoffman asks, "Mrs. Robinson you're trying to seduce me. Aren't you?" She maintains control of the situation, prolonging the terror of the young man, by replying, "Well no, I hadn't thought of it." Other examples from other films could be cited, but the point is clear: as film viewers we have been trained to be aware of the signs of courtship. Whether the behaviors of a particular actor are likely to be seen as seductive, quasi-courting, or ambiguous depends upon one's experience in watching films, one's social experience, and upon the way the filmmaker provides a context for his own images.

The Spanish teacher's behaviors are at least quasi-courting. And as Wiseman develops his context, they seem to go beyond quasi-courting to contribute to an atmosphere in which social power is exerted through the exchange of signals having to do with sexuality and its confusion, repression, or inversion.

The Spanish teacher's ring gesture also has a variety of possible meanings. In *Gestures: Their Origin and Distribution,* Desmond Morris and his associates traced the meaning of the gesture in several European cities. They found that the gesture meant "Ok—good" to 700 informants; "orifice," anal or vaginal, to 128 informants; "zero—worthless" to 115 informants; and "threat" to 16 informants. Morris and his associates also found that the gesture was used as a "baton signal," where speakers were making a fine point or requesting greater precision in some way.[9]

In the context of the Spanish class, the baton signal appears to be the most appropriate content for the ring gesture: the teacher is keeping time with the raising and lowering of her hand, and signaling the need for precision with the ring. But in the context of the courtship behaviors that have just preceded, it, the ring gesture may be seen by Wiseman and the viewer as ambiguously referring also, in some measure, to the "ok," "orifice," and "threat" aspects of the gesture. And even if the ring gesture is understood only as the baton signal, the earlier presence of the courtship behaviors—widened eyes, tongue thrust, hand in belt, hip swing—creates a complex of meanings that goes beyond simple group attentiveness. The behaviors that we have observed in this scene are not performed mutually by teacher and students, but rather are the behaviors of a person in authority signaling a relation to a classroom of students. Aggressive courtship behaviors, together with the baton signal, assert the relation of power and sexuality. Further, Wiseman has chosen a situation in which the response of the students is mechanical: they are a chorus, repeating by rote the words that the teacher is pronouncing.

Wiseman uses the baton signal as a bridge to sequence 5. He cuts from the hand of the Spanish teacher beating time with the ring gesture to an orchestra (Figure 19) being led by another teacher (Figure 20). This cut not only reinforces by parallelism the interpretation of the Spanish teacher's ring gesture as a baton signal, but also indicates to the audience that the filmmaker is likely to seek meaningful associations when he cuts from one sequence to another.

In sequence 8, a French teacher is discussing, in French, the domestic life of France and America. As he talks, Wiseman's camera and editing build another courtship relationship. In Figure 26, the young woman in the foreground with glasses raises her left hand to stroke the back of her head, a preening gesture. The camera pans left to Figure 27, in which the teacher is presenting his palm, another courtship gesture. Wiseman cuts from Figure 27 to Figure 28, an even more definite courtship gesture by a young woman who preens her hair while presenting her palm. This palm-forward hair preening is, in American culture, a strong courtship gesture, and is reserved exclusively for females.[10] Wiseman cuts from Figure 28 to Figure 29, a closeup of the teacher's face. The framing and cutting relate these two shots not only to indicate that the two faces are regarding one another, but that one dominates the other. The girl in Figure 28 is looking slightly upward and occupies a diagonal lower right segment of the screen. The teacher in Figure 29 occupies an upper left diagonal section and looks down.

In sequence 9, the sexual comedy is complicated by an element of pathos. A mother and father are trying to understand why their daughter failed a course. This is the same sequence we examined earlier, in which the administrator conceded to a "somewhat unique" situation. In our earlier examination of the sequence, we concentrated on the way language was manipulated to maintain control of the situation. An examination of the speech in relation to the images of the sequence reveals the presence of an even more humiliating struggle. In Figure 30, the father is pleading his case, palms held forward in a defensive gesture. The administrator replies (Figure 31), with his elbow on the desk, arm blocking his body, fingers pointed toward the father, palms up— he is shrugging off an inquiry. The father (Figures 32 and 33) leans forward slightly to press his point. Mother is looking on with an encouraging grin. This time the administrator responds with greater gestural emphasis (Figure 34), extending his right arm and forming a fist. Then the administrator attacks:

ADMINISTRATOR: Because she failed on all these tests. We can only judge on the basis of performance. You may have hidden talent in you, sir, but if you don't perform, we don't know.
FATHER: That's true.
ADMINISTRATOR: The world will recognize you only by your performance.
FATHER: That true, that's true.

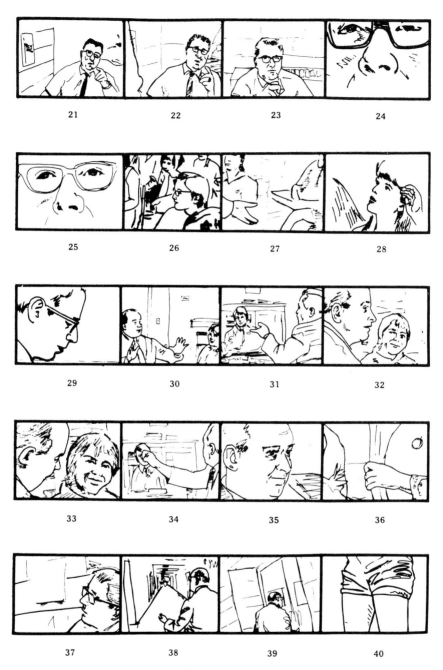

Figures 21–40.

As the administrator presses his argument directly at the question of the father's hypothetical performance, the father begins to concede "That's true," and Wiseman moves in for a closeup. The father's eyes widen, and he appears to be on the verge of tears (Figure 35). The father then bows his head in apparent submission. Wiseman cuts to a closeup of the mother's hand, which is grasping the vertical wooden member on the back of her chair, on the side of the chair which is between her and her husband. Her hand gently strokes the post up and down (Figure 36). The sequence then continues to a closeup of the mother's face, then to the father's face, still almost in tears, and a pan right across the desk to a big closeup of the administrator's fist.

Wiseman captures here the personal defeat of the father when the administrator turns from his "what can I do?" approach to a direct challenge of the father's performance. But the ambiguity in American talk about the word "performance," when applied to an adult male, allows Wiseman another chance to stress the relationship between power and sexuality. The administrator has challenged the father's manhood, with startling results: the father is reduced almost to tears, and Wiseman shows the mother stroking her chair in a gesture that, in the filmic context, invites an interpretation of it as a sexual caress.

The next sequence, sequence 10, has already been discussed in the context of the way the schoolmasters twist the language. It is in this sequence that Michael is encouraged to be a man and take orders. Earlier, the sequence was discussed as representing linguistic distortion, but we can now see that in the developing context of the film, the appeal to Michael's manhood is consistent with the sexual theme of the film, in which students are encouraged to be confused about their developing gender identities, in order that they can be more easily controlled by the teachers and administrators.

The next six sequences are linked to amplify Wiseman's meditation on sex and power. In sequence 11, a male teacher is patrolling the corridors, asking to see passes, and stopping to tell one student to finish a telephone conversation (Figure 38). Wiseman cuts to a girl walking down the hallway, then back to the teacher. The sequence is cut to make it appear that the teacher is girl-watching. The teacher continues down the corridor, and music is heard on the sound track. The teacher stops at a double door and looks through the windows in the door (Figure 39). By the logic of the film, the next shot should reveal what he is looking at. Wiseman cuts to sequence 12, where the camera is recording closeups of girls exercising in a gymnasium to a recording of "Simple Simon Says," the song that faded into the sound track at the end of sequence 11. Wiseman's cutting makes it appear that the teacher of sequence 11 is looking through the window at girls' bottoms (Figures 40 and 41).

From the regimented but sexually charged athleticism of sequence 12, Wiseman cuts to sequence 13, in which an English teacher is reading "Casey at the Bat" in a mechanical, singsong voice (Figures 42 and 43). As the teacher continues to read, Wiseman explores the attitudes of the students in the classroom. He discovers the girl in Figure 44, her heavy eye makeup imitating a

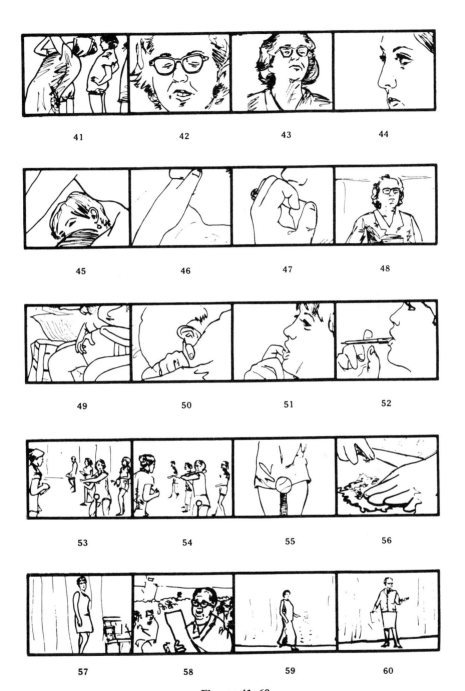

41   42   43   44

45   46   47   48

49   50   51   52

53   54   55   56

57   58   59   60

Figures 41–60.

95

maturity at odds with the innocence implied by the poem. From Figure 44, Wiseman cuts to the sleepy inattention of the girl in Figure 45, then pans up to the face of a boy with his hand over his mouth (Figure 46). The boy moves his hand, stroking his lips with his knuckles (Figure 47). Wiseman cuts back to the teacher (Figure 48), then cuts to two girls and pans down to focus on one whose hand rests on her half-exposed thigh (Figure 49). A moment later Wiseman presents a closeup of a boy asleep, his head resting on his arms (Figure 50). The logic of film might tell us that the next image will show us what he is dreaming about. Wiseman cuts to the face of a girl who is caressing her opened lips with her finger (Figure 51). As the shot continues, the girl takes her finger out of her mouth and begins to suck on the end of her pen (Figure 52). All of these images in sequence 13, when seen in the context of the sexual imagery preceding this sequence, seem to add up to a description of a world in which the teachers drone on and on against a background filled with the unacknowledged sexual daydreams of the students. The daydreams are turned inward, finding their expression in a visible but tacitly ignored pattern of self-stroking. The inverted sexuality implied by the self-stroking of sequence 13 creates the link to sequence 14.

In sequence 14, Wiseman returns to the gymnasium. In the foreground a girl is taking batting practice with a softball perched on a flexible post. In the opening shot of the sequence (Figure 53), she whacks at the ball. Then the girl at the left of the frame puts another ball on the post (Figure 54). Whack again. Wiseman then cuts to a closeup of the ball on the post (Figure 55). Whack.

Sequence 13 is linked to the sequence before it by the theme of baseball. But there is another link. By placing his camera so that the softball is framed at the batter's crotch, Wiseman escalates the sexual joke. The implication is that the sexual confusion engendered by the school's use of power (oppression) and sex (repression) turns these women into what street talk calls "ballbreakers," mutilating for themselves whatever chance they might have for a fully mature sexual intimacy. In my view an audience would be unlikely to get this implication, since it depends for its force not upon the social sensitivity that makes us aware of courtship behaviors but upon a visual pun. But it is hard to doubt that Wiseman understood the implications of the batting practice sequence.

The ballbreaking joke of sequence 14 is taken one step further when Wiseman cuts from Figure 55 to Figure 56, the first shot of sequence 15. In large closeup, a pair of hands, a knife, and chopped nuts. We realize that this is a cooking class and think that we have gone from girls batting balls to girls chopping nuts. The joke gets another twist as Wiseman cuts back to reveal that it is indeed a cooking class, but that the choppers are two boys. The sexual destruction of sequence 14 carries forward to an implied self-mutilation in sequence 15. Once again it seems unlikely that an audience would catch this joke, but it is also clear that Wiseman has allowed very few accidents into this film: his framing and cutting are highly structured, and the interpretations I have placed on sequences 14 and 15 are supported by everything that comes before and after them in the film.

The home economics teacher of sequence 15 appears as the central character of sequence 16, and provides a link between the two sequences. But there is also a thematic bridge. In sequence 16, the teacher instructs a group of girls who have designed and constructed dresses and who are rehearsing for a fashion show. Everything the teacher says encourages the girls to see their own bodies as imperfect objects which must be costumed and manipulated so as to project an illusion of grace and beauty. The teacher advises girls not to wear culottes when they have heavy legs, asks another girl to find someone with slimmer legs to wear her outfit, and advises another girl to wear pink stockings to make her legs seem slimmer (Figures 57 and 58). Another girl crosses the stage (Figure 59) and we hear that she has "a weight problem," and then she is congratulated on designing her costume to disguise the problem. Then the teacher takes to the stage and gives a short lesson in how to walk, stand, and turn gracefully (Figure 60). The teacher is obviously a woman of good humor, affection, and modesty, but the message she is sending to the girls is consistent with the rest of what Wiseman shows us: success is the result of treating one's self as an object.

Sequence 16 ends as the teacher asks, "Any questions?" Wiseman cuts to sequence 17 as another teacher asks, "Any questions?" (Figure 61). We are in a typing class, looking over the shoulder of an adenoidal and pasty young teacher who presides over several rows of machines. Wiseman indulges himself in a standard rack-focus shot down a long row of typewriters that draws our attention once again to the regimented quality of the high school. But he also discovers, in the midst of these machines, a Veronica Lake closeup (Figure 62) that reminds us of the presence of sexuality.

In sequence 18, a male teacher is describing to a group of boys the sociology of American families, emphasizing the division of responsibility between mothers and fathers. The scene is a straightforward lesson in gender roles.

In sequence 19, Wiseman reveals, in closeup, a woman speaking about sex to an auditorium of girls (Figure 63). Her speech is slightly disorganized, but constitutes a clear warning about the dangers of sexuality and promiscuity. She tells the girls to practice self denial. As the speaker rambles on through her warnings, Wiseman slowly zooms out on the speaker, to reveal her in a long shot behind the lectern (Figure 64). A motto engraved on the lectern serves as Wiseman's ironic caption for the scene: "Whatsoever thy hand findeth to do, do it with thy might."

Sequence 20 has already been mentioned in the discussion of distorted language. But it must also be mentioned here in the context of sex and gender, since the girl who is being reprimanded is accused of wearing too short a skirt to a formal dance. In Figure 65, she demonstrates where she thought the hem should be. Two teachers tell her, and then tell her again and again, how wrong

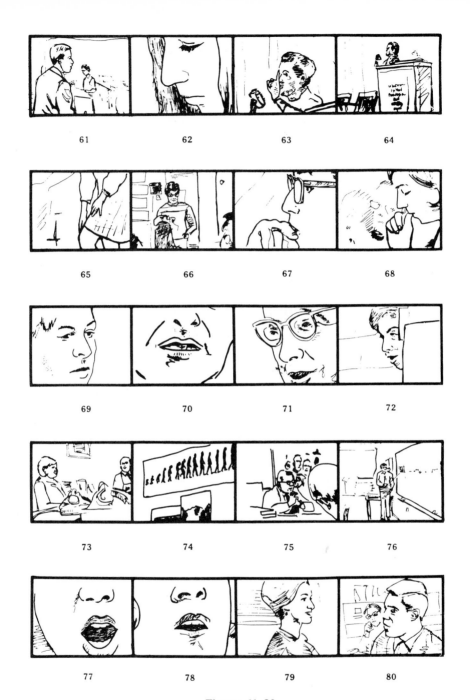

61   62   63   64

65   66   67   68

69   70   71   72

73   74   75   76

77   78   79   80

Figures 61–80.

she was. One of the teachers, a woman, describes the sacrifices she makes to convention in wearing a formal dress: "I can't walk in it, I can't get in a car comfortably." It is not clear whether she is bragging or complaining, but it is clear that her sacrifice gives her the right to criticize the student, and that the student has been presented with a rule that confuses her not only about "style" and "individuality" but also about what it means to be a woman.

The critical woman teacher of sequence 20 provides the bridge to sequence 21, in which she is the gym teacher encouraging a group of girls to see how long they can hang with bent arms from sets of rings. To the girls who let go first she says, "Oh boy, you're feminine." As she counts off the seconds, she shouts encouragement to those who hang on longer: "Tarzan!" "Super Tarzan!" Whatever these girls do is wrong. If they opt for femininity, they fail at the classroom task by falling off the rings too early. If they opt for success, they forfeit their femininity and become "Tarzans."

Critics have disagreed about what Wiseman intends with sequence 22, in which a teacher describes the poetry of Simon and Garfunkel (Figure 66).[11] Is she to be contrasted with the teacher who read "Casey at the Bat" in sequence 13? Critics who believe so point out that she has chosen material that is relevant to her students. But perhaps her "relevancy" is only an unsuccessful attempt to co-opt her students. As we hear her describe the song, the camera records a poster on the wall: "Rock with Shakespeare." And on the blackboard the song is reduced to mechanics: theme, metaphor, images, figurative language. The teacher's sincerity is evident, but she is not the only well-meaning teacher in the film who may be contributing to the boredom and alienation of her students. The attitudes of the students who listen to the song are also unclear. Taken out of context, they might seem to be merely attentive (Figures 67 and 68). But in the context of the other images in the film, the self-stroking of the students seems to hint at an infantile tactility in contrast to the teacher's attempt to rationalize song into technique.

In sequences 24 through 27, Wiseman develops the theme of communication between generations as it occurs in the context of confusion about sex and power. This group of sequences is set apart from the rest of the film by two transitional sequences: sequence 23 shows a woman dragging a trash bin down a school corridor as the music from sequence 22 fades out. Sequence 28 shows a janitor working in a hallway. The hallway sequences provide a structural reinforcement for the setting apart of sequences 24 through 27, and their thematic similarities help to reinforce the coherence of this group of sequences.

In sequence 24, the dean of discipline is reprimanding a student who started a fight (Figure 69). The student replies with formality, speaking in what sounds like military courtesy, as he begins and ends most of his replies with "sir."

ADMINISTRATOR: Hey, you, turn around, pal.
STUDENT: Sir.
ADMINISTRATOR: Don't sir me. Don't feed me that sir business. . . .

ADMINISTRATOR: That's why you're going to be suspended, for throwing the first punch.

STUDENT: Yes, sir.

ADMINISTRATOR: Don't give me that yes sir business. I don't like the sir business, you know why? Because there's no sincerity behind it.

The administrator's demand to be treated with respect is perhaps reasonable, and he is perhaps even within his rights in asking the student to refrain from using "sir." But in the context of the film, his demand that the student be sincere is absurd. One of the classic illustrations of the double bind is the command, "Be spontaneous." The command cannot be obeyed. Similarly, if the student were sincere in this situation, he might tell the administrator just what he thought of him, which would get him in even worse trouble. The command "Be sincere," though not structurally impossible to obey, as the "Be spontaneous" command is, would nevertheless be dangerous to obey, and is clearly not what the administrator wants. Whatever the student does in response to the demand to be sincere is going to be disobedient.

In sequence 25, a mother and daughter are in a disciplinary conference with a female administrator. When the girl says she was just "messing around," the mother wants to know what that means. The term, of course, is impossible for the girl to define. Then the girl is told by what standards she should govern her conduct. The mother says that respect for adults is most important. The administrator tells the girl to be an individual, to lead the crowd away from trouble. Once again the advice is perfectly sensible when taken in its own context, but when placed in the context of the film it is clear how difficult it is for the students to discover a general standard of conduct. The girl in sequence 20 whose skirt was too short was told that she ought to conform: "Around here we are going to do what the majority decides." But here another girl is told that she should not go along with the crowd. What rule applies? Wiseman seems to invite us to take the point of view of the students, from which the demands of adults are double binding. The adults speak a different language, and they make impossible demands. It is not surprising that students respond with apathy. As if to emphasize the adults' garbled speech and distorted vision, Wiseman focuses on the mouth of the mother (Figure 70) and the coke-bottle glasses of the administrator (Figure 71).

In sequence 26, a girl and her parents are discussing college plans with a counselor. As if to emphasize the barriers to communication, Wiseman frames the counselor peeping out from behind a row of books (Figure 72).

In sequence 27, the mother and father of sequence 9 are shown with their daughter and the administrator. Wiseman jokes about the difficulties of communication by framing father and daughter so that two telephones loom up between them in the foreground of the shot (Figure 73).

Sequences 29 through 34 are grouped between the hallway transitions of sequence 28 and sequence 35. In this group of sequences, the dominant element appears to be the discussion of social issues and attitudes, though the

100

contexts of power, sexuality, and communication are also interwoven into the form and substance of the sequences. Once again, the teachers are made to look absurd.

In sequence 29, a group of teachers in the lunchroom discuss foreign aid. They agree that foreigners ought to be more grateful for American help. Wiseman makes one teacher look foolish by recording him as he drips food on the heel of his hand and licks it off.

In sequence 30, the dean of discipline is teaching a class about labor-management relations. Why, he asks, were unions necessary? The correct answer, it turns out, was "lack of communication" and "lack of security," which of course is precisely the condition of the high school. After the scenes in which we have already seen this teacher, his comments on communication and insecurity have an ironic edge. And Wiseman plays another visual joke in sequence 30. The sequence opens with a shot of a chart on the wall at the back of the classroom. The chart represents the rise of man from ape to *homo sapiens* (Figure 74). *Homo sapiens* is on the right side of the frame. The camera then begins to pan to the left, from *homo sapiens* to ape, and comes to rest (Figure 75) on the dean of discipline dispensing homilies about social studies. The effect has been to descend from *Homo sapiens* to ape to teacher. From a bulletin board behind him, Leonid Brezhnev, Jackie Onassis, and Ho Chi Minh look over his shoulder.

In sequence 31, the teacher who read the daily bulletin in sequence 3, and who dribbled his food in sequence 29, discusses poverty and race relations with his class. How many, he asks, would join a club in which a minority of members were black? The students glance around at each other and most raise their hands. How many would join if an equal number of blacks and whites were in the club? The students glance at each other again. Fewer hands go up. If blacks were the majority? More glances. Fewer hands still. Then the teacher tells the students not to worry, that there is no right or wrong answer, and that he is just trying to determine attitudes. His statement seems disingenuous in the atmosphere of conformity revealed by the visual images. As if to reinforce our sense that the teacher's questions about attitudes are not an open search for values but rather an exercise in peer pressure, Wiseman cuts to sequence 32, in which a music teacher (Figure 76) leads a class through the scales. As the teacher stands at the blackboard pointing to one note after another, Wiseman cuts to big closeups of disembodied mouths singing out in chorus the names of the notes (Figures 77 and 78). The dominant tone of sequence 32 has to do with regimentation, though it appears that in the context of the film as a whole, in which Wiseman has established mouths as having sexual relevance, the closeups shown in Figures 77 and 78 help to maintain the film's overtone of misdirected eroticism.

In sequence 33 a teacher (Figure 79) is discussing Northeast High School with a group of students. The students speak out against the moral and intellectual atmosphere of the school, and it appears that here at last is a sign

101

of rebellion that runs counter to the rest of the film in which students have been badgered into passivity. But Wiseman dashes our hopes. Though the students make brave speeches, they are unable to get through to the teacher or each other. A young black man is recognized by the teacher and begins to talk about the school. But before he has a chance to finish, the teacher interrupts him and makes a speech of her own. Wiseman keeps the camera on the black student's face as the teacher's loudmouth interruption continues (Figures 80, 81, and 82). He stops speaking, then looks on with surprise, and finally displays a cowed grin. A young woman looking on over his shoulder contemplates his reactions, and as she does so her hand moves from her chin to her mouth.

At another point in the sequence, Wiseman shows what seems at first to be an exception to the atmosphere of stifled sexuality that he has constructed throughout the rest of the film. A student in dark glasses makes some disparaging remarks about the school. He has been sitting with his arm around a girl. The girl cuddles toward him (Figure 83), and he kisses her on the forehead (Figure 84). Is this to be taken as a healthy display of affection? In context, I think not. The student's wise-cracking attitude about the school, his beads and dark glasses, are, it is true, signs of rebellion from the confines of the school, but dark glasses, beads, and kiss appear in the context of a classroom discussion as a demonstration rather than as an authentic act of politics or human intimacy. The girl is part of his audience, and part of the costume that he displays to the rest of his audience. He is not, in this context, capable of authentic affection, but instead comes off as a smug pseudorebel playing it cool. If Wiseman's rhetoric has been successful up until this point, the audience will not simply condemn the student for his inauthenticity, however. If it has been persuaded that the school has abused its power, then the school must seem to blame for the poverty of his response. If the school is to blame, he is simply another one of its products, groping unsuccessfully for a way to become fully human in a political situation that robs him of that opportunity. Sequence 35 returns once more to the corridor as students crowd through it between classes. In the foreground a policeman looks at his watch in apparent boredom (Figure 85).

The film's undercurrent of concern about sexual repressiveness continues with sequence 36, which opens with a shot from the rear of an auditorium looking toward the stage. Amid cheers and music, a group of cheerleaders runs down the aisles and begins to dance on the stage (Figure 86). When Wiseman moves in for a closer look (Figure 87), we see that this is a group of boys dressed in girls' cheerleading outfits.

In sequence 37, a man who seems perfectly cast as a feminist's stereotype of the male chauvinist gynecologist is warning an auditorium filled with boys about the dangers of sexual intercourse (Figures 88 and 89). He stands in the classic postures of male dominance: arm akimbo, hand on hip, fingers pointing to his genitals. Wiseman cuts to a member of the audience, who is apparently worried by the warnings of the doctor (Figure 90). But the tone taken by the

81   82   83   84

85   86   87   88

89   90   91   92

93   94   95   96

97   98   99

Figures 81–99.

gynecologist is at odds with his message. At the same time that he warns the boys about the dangers of pregnancy, he brags about his access to female genitals. He talks about inserting his fingers into vaginas, and says, "I happen to be a gynecologist and I get paid to do it," with a smirk on his face. He holds up the fingers that have explored so many women (Figure 91) and tells the boys to use birth control or abstain.

In sequence 38, Wiseman shows excerpts from an animated film that is explaining the dangers of venereal disease (Figures 92 and 93).

The last five sequences of the film are tied together by their common emphasis on the theme of militarism, though even here there are hints about the way sexuality and bodily imagery mingle with the theme of violence. These five sequences seem to build toward Wiseman's vision of the product of the school: good soldiers. This is not to say that Wiseman reduces *High School* to an antimilitaristic tract. Rather the scenes of militarism help to symbolize and summarize the alienation that grows out of the experience of the school as he depicts it.

The concluding sequences begin with a pair of sequences that are related to each other by a typical Wiseman irony. In sequence 39 a Vietnam veteran is standing at the edge of a playing field talking with a coach (Figure 94). They are discussing the wounding of a former student, and for a moment it appears that the coach, who obviously feels sympathy for the wounded man, is hinting at a tone of regret about the war. Then Wiseman cuts to sequence 40, where the same coach is refereeing a violent game between two massive teams who fight to move a huge ball back and forth in a gymnasium (Figure 95), and it is evident that the coach is encouraging the students to learn the skills of battle.

In sequence 41, three boy astronauts emerge from a simulated flight in a space capsule (Figure 96). The military ambience of the scene is clear, but the military theme is synthesized with the issue of gender identity when the boys remove their space helmets. One of the boys who has been assisting from outside the capsule cries, "The beard. Look at the beard." The astronauts have raised a stubble in their days of simulated flight. They are men.

There is another bit of byplay in the astronaut sequence that demonstrates how to be a man. As the boys emerge from the capsule, one of the students on the sidelines, apparently asking for a pose so that he can take a picture, asks the teacher in charge of the group to put his arm around one of the astronauts. The teacher obviously hears the request, but chooses to ignore it, saying instead that he will help the astronaut remove his helmet. The request for a physical display of affection between the teacher and his student is emphasized by the way it is brushed off. Later in the scene a woman gives one of the boys a motherly kiss.

In sequence 42, a drum major (Figure 97) prances onto a stage, then stands before the camera, and pumps his baton, held vertically before his body, up and down in rhythm to the music. The militarism of the scene is parodied by the jerking motions of the boy's symbol of authority. Wiseman then cuts to an ambiguous closeup (Figure 98), as a hand grasping a rifle butt moves back and forth in the frame, revealing on each swing a patch of uniform on the torso of the person with the rifle. Then Wiseman completes his joke by panning up to reveal that the rifle is in the hand of a pretty girl (Figure 99), and our expectations about gender are once more reversed as they have been in some earlier scenes.

In the final sequence, Wiseman reveals what all of the preceding sequences add up to. The school principal is standing behind a lectern reading a letter to a group of teachers in the school auditorium. The author of the letter is a young man about to be dropped behind enemy lines in Vietnam. In his letter he tells how much the school has meant to him, and says that he has bequeathed his military life insurance to a scholarship fund for the school. Of his attitude toward himself as a man and a soldier, he says, "I am only a body doing a job." The principal comments: "Now, when you get a letter like this, to me it means that we are very successful at Northeast High School. I think you will agree with me."

The Rhetorical Structure

The final sequence of *High School* completes Wiseman's design. It is important to observe that Wiseman chose to reserve the principal's reading of Bob Walters' letter until the final scene. Had the letter scene come at the beginning of the film, as the first sequence, say, or the second, it would have served as a heavy-handed announcement that this film was going to show how the school made "good soldiers," that is, tractable adults. Had Wiseman tipped his hand in this way, the audience experience would have been very different. It would have been clear that Wiseman disapproved of the school and that the audience was expected to do the same. The body of the film would have served as proof for a more or less clearly stated proposition. By structuring the film as he has, Wiseman allows the audience to work its own way through the ambiguous discomforts of the school's oppressiveness and repressiveness. In this way the film becomes an experience before it becomes evidence. And when the letter scene is finally presented, the audience can gasp at the revelation that the school meant, all along, to produce "good soldiers." And the audience can clinch the job of persuasion it has been allowed to perform upon itself by congratulating itself that its theory about the school is confirmed by the principal's reading of the letter. The placement of the letter scene is the climactic stroke in Wiseman's rhetorical design.

Wiseman's rhetorical design is more complicated than it appears, because it has to achieve a delicate balance between obscurity and overstatement to convey its impressions. Wiseman's rhetorical structure can best be appreciated if we review Wiseman's "theory" about Northeast High School and then describe in abstract terms how an audience can be expected to experience the presentation of that theory in *High School*.

Wiseman's "theory," of course, resists simple verbal expression. That is why it is expressed in a film rather than an essay. But at the risk of reductionism, the theory seems to run as follows: In Northeast High School, the teachers and administrators work to control the students. They control the students in the school, and they try to build in a system of control that will last the students for a lifetime. Control is exercised by constantly placing students in the double bind, where the students receive inconsistent directions in a situation in which they are dependent, in which they must try to obey the directions, and in which they cannot call attention to or even conspicuously notice what is happening. Power is exercised in the high school through direct orders, humiliating reprimands, absurdly manipulated language, mechanical teaching that reduces learning to a stultifying process of repetition, and, most hurtfully, through a constant confusion of thought and feeling about sex and gender. The students are unable to bring any of the school's tyrannies into clear enough focus to combat them directly. The student response, for the most part, is to disconnect, to resort to daydreams, narcissism, and apathy.

That this statement of Wiseman's theory is approximately correct has been borne out, I hope, by the detailed examination of the film. But the viewer of the film does not have the same experience as a student in the high school, nor does he or she have the same experience of the film as a critic who takes it apart bit by bit on an editing table. A rhetorical examination of Wiseman's film would be seriously incomplete if it were to stop with a statement of what a critic was able to discover in the text. To stop here, to allege that a detailed examination, having revealed Wiseman's "theory," has thereby revealed the structure of his rhetoric, is to ignore the audience, and to be guilty of over-reading. Even if a critic can find a signficant detail, and can relate it to other details to argue that it is part of a pattern, one's understanding of a work of rhetoric is inadequate without some attention to what an audience would be likely to make of the detail and the pattern.

The success of *High School* as a rhetorical structure seems to depend upon the audience's apprehending the film at different levels of consciousness. At the conscious level, the audience understands that *High School* is about power, and it sees the students being oppressed, reprimanded, manipulated, humiliated, and bored. But audiences typically are not consciously aware of the prevalence of sex and gender as elements of the film. Rather, the recurring images of courtship and the repressive warnings about the dangers of sexuality are mostly just beyond conscious awareness. Although they are out of conscious awareness, the sexual images in the film magnify the audience's felt discomfort with the film they are experiencing, because for the audience, as for the students, the presence of sexuality in interpersonal and intrapersonal conduct is at the core of the sense of self but carefully blocked from conscious attention.

The presence of sexuality as an issue in *High School* seems to function as a way of deepening the audience's feelings about those parts of *High School* that they do allow themselves to notice: the parts that have to do with the exercise of power. It is the genius of the film that it enables viewers to re-experience the tensions of adolescence, and to adopt sufficient distance from that experience to condemn the high school for its role in enforcing an institutional tyranny. But *High School* does not create so much distance from the experience that it makes the whole "theory" of repression immediately clear to viewers. It is the great strength and the great weakness of filmic persuasion that it can create an experience, and an attitude toward that experience, but that it would be likely to diminish the felt response to the experience and the attitude if it were to provide a clearly stated, linear explanation of its point of view. Wiseman helps us to feel the institutional claustrophobia and the sexual panic of these teenagers, giving us just enough distance from them to feel outraged on their behalf, and perhaps somewhat liberated from the remembered defeats of our own adolescent years. The power of the double bind is broken when the victim can call attention to what is happening.

If Wiseman had been explicit about the suggested meanings of his treatment of sexuality, the power of his film as an appeal to shared experience would be dissipated. Suppose that in sequence 4 (Figures 12–18), a voice-over commentator told us that this teacher was employing courtship behaviors that were likely to be confusing to her students. Our immediate response would be, quite properly, suspicion of the claim, arguing that this particular teacher is shown out of context, that it is reasonable to explain her behavior simply as a way of making faces and gestures to retain the amused attention of her students, and that, in any case, she may have been mugging for the camera. However, Wiseman never tells us that these are courtship behaviors, and we are unlikely to notice them at a conscious level. Rather, they exist for us just out of awareness, as they tend to do in face-to-face interaction, making us vaguely attentive to our sexuality and hers but never conscious of what is happening.

Similarly, if Wiseman had pointed out the courtship gestures of sequence 8 between the French teacher and the two girls in his class (Figures 26–29), we would object that there is a cut between these images, and that we have no way to be sure that teacher and students were actually directing these gestures at each other, or that they were particularly significant. And so on with the other sequences in which attention to sexuality and gender identity hovers just at the edge of conscious awareness.

Some of the scenes having to do with sex, as I have argued, are likely to be almost totally disregarded by the audience, as in sequence 15 when boys in cooking class are chopping nuts, or when in the first shot of the film Wiseman shows a street scene with garbage cans and a line of laundry on which there hangs a football jersey with the numeral 69. But if all the scenes about sexuality were as obscure as this, constituting a sort of private joke, our argument would be reduced to critical over-reading, wherein a text or image is treated as a challenge to the ingenuity of the critic, a sort of secret code planted in the work by an artist. Although Wiseman does crack some private jokes in *High School,* most of his sexual imagery has a rhetorical function, inviting the viewer to experience a tension that can occur only when the images are apprehended but when part of the experience is kept out of conscious awareness.

The most explicit statements of sexual warning in the film are, of course, available to viewers at a conscious level. The lecturer of sequence 19 and the gynecologist of sequence 37 are stating directly what so many other sequences in the film display implicitly: sex is dangerous, and is better left to adults, who seem to hold the secret to its powers.

If my description of *High School,* of Wiseman's "theory," and of the audience's experience are convincing, then we can claim to have discovered the rhetorical structure of *High School.* What final assessment can be made of the film?

An evaluation of Wiseman's *High School* must acknowledge the immense power of the film to evoke the experience of adolescence and to call into question the power exercised by high school. But Wiseman's rhetorical success is achieved at the expense of certain contradictions.

Wiseman takes advantage of the conventions of cinema verite to create a sense that we are observing social reality. The photographic surfaces of the film bespeak an atmosphere of naturally occurring behavior. There are no actors, no special lights, no enormous film crews. The feel of actuality is present as a condition of the recording of the images. And yet the documentary texture of the film is contradicted by its dialectical structure. It is not simply that the filmmaker has selected these images from among the many hours he recorded. The film is not simply selected, it is carefully structured within and between scenes to take advantage of the conventions of narrative and documentary film that enable a filmmaker to imply sequence, causation, and point of view. Wiseman employs the conventions of cinema verite to establish the evidentiary value of his images, to assure us that what we see is true to the material reality of Northeast High School. Then Wiseman draws upon the structural conventions of narrative and documentary film to relate the images so that they take on meanings they would not have if seen in isolation or at random. Are such combinations of generic conventions for the filmmaker's purposes objectionable?

Insofar as Wiseman leaves his viewers believing that they know the truth about a particular group of human beings who taught and studied at Northeast High School in 1968 he may be misleading. But insofar as he uses Northeast High School as a source of images out of which to fashion a film, *High*

1. Exterior traveling shots along streets to exterior of Northeast High School. Sound: Otis Redding singing "Dock of the Bay."
2. Interior: Hallway with students.
3. Male teacher reading daily bulletin.
4. Female Spanish teacher discussing existentialism.
5. Orchestra.
6. A school administrator directing a student to report for gym class, then suspending student.
7. Hallway with students.
8. Male French teacher discussing French and American domestic life.
9. Father and mother in administrator's office, arguing about their daughter's failing grade.
10. School Administrator (same man as in sequence 6) convincing student who talked back to a teacher to accept a punishment.
11. Male teacher patrolling hallway.
12. Girls exercising in gym to "Simple Simon Says."
13. Female teacher reading "Casey at the Bat."
14. Girls in gym taking batting practice.
15. Boys in cooking class.
16. Rehearsal for school fashion show.
17. Test in typing class.
18. Male teacher telling a classroom of boys about family life.
19. Woman lecturer discussing promiscuity to auditorium of women students.
20. Two teachers scolding a girl about the length of a dress she chose for a formal dance.
21. Girls hanging from rings in gymnasium.
22. Female teacher lecturing on poetic devices in Simon and Garfunkel.
23. Hallway: girl walks by, then woman pulls trash bin down the hall.
24. The administrator of sequences 6 and 10 reprimands a student who hit another student.
25. A mother, her daughter, and a teacher discussing the girl's "messing around."
26. A female counselor with parents and their daughter discussing plans for college.
27. The parents of sequence 9, with their daughter, meeting with the administrator who also appeared in sequence 9.
28. Hallway, with janitor.
29. Teachers in lunchroom discussing foreign aid.
30. Administrator of scenes 6, 10, and 24 teaching a class on labor-management relations.
31. Teacher of sequence 3 discussing social issues and attitudes with a class.
32. Girl singers being led through scales by male teacher.
33. Students and teacher in discussion about Northeast High School.
34. The teacher of sequence 13 reading the thought for the day.
35. Hallway: a policeman looks at his watch.
36. School auditorium: boys in costumes of girl cheerleaders.
37. A gynecologist lecturing to auditorium of male students.
38. Animated scenes from instructional film about venereal disease.
39. Exterior: Vietnam veteran and coach discussing the wounding of a former student.
40. Boys in gym with enormous ball.
41. Boy astronauts at the end of simulated flight.
42. Drum major with band and color guard.
43. Woman reading letter from school alumnus about to be dropped into Vietnam.

Figure 100 Sequences in *High School.*

School, which evokes for his viewers the conflicts of their own adolescent years, and thereby helps them to understand and transcend those conflicts, perhaps Wiseman is speaking a larger truth.[12]

Another anomaly about *High School* is that it speaks out for the importance of the individual through a filmic method that ridicules some individuals and fragments others. The teacher who reads "Casey at the Bat," the one who licks a bit of food from the heel of his hand, and the one who gives a lesson in how to walk gracefully down a hallway—all of these people are caught at moments when they look foolish. And at other times Wiseman uses big closeups of eyes or mouths to make a point in his description of a scene, at the expense of fragmenting his subject. Wiseman has fabricated a humanistic vision out of fragmentary bits and pieces of behavior and physiognomy. His humanism is compromised by his occasional willingness to sacrifice the full humanity of his subjects to make a point.

The paradoxes and anomalies of Wiseman's rhetorical method are flaws in *High School,* but they are flaws that share their existence with a comic vision that goes beyond the lampooning of Northeast High School to make an important statement about American social experience. Perhaps the best response to *High School* is to be charitable to Northeast High School and at the same time bitterly alert to the uses of power and repression revealed by the film. If we can do this, perhaps we can at the same time be alert to the potential deceptiveness of Wiseman's rhetoric and still celebrate his brilliant achievement. It is too much to ask that Wiseman resolve all the social and aesthetic paradoxes he has uncovered. We can, without forfeiting the right to continue the debate about Northeast High School, *High School,* and "high school," declare our gratitude to Wiseman for creating a rhetorical masterpiece. Fred Wiseman's rhetorical acuity is evident in his presentation of the rhetoric that operates among the characters in *High School* and in the way he has structured the experience of his audience.

Notes

1. Ira Halberstadt, "An Interview with Fred Wiseman," in *Nonfiction Film: Theory and Criticism,* ed. Richard Meran Barsam (New York: E. P. Dutton, 1976), p. 303.
2. Among the critics of *High School,* see: Richard Meran Barsam, *Nonfiction Film: A Critical History* (New York: E. P. Dutton, 1973), pp. 275–277. But Barsam garbles some of the details of the film and misses the point of others. Stephen Mamber, *Cinema Verite in America: Studies in Uncontrolled Documentary* (Cambridge: MIT Press, 1974), pp. 224–229, has a fuller commentary on *High School* but fails to integrate the elements of the film, partly because of an a priori claim that "The events in cinema verite are uncontrolled and editing generally attempts to avoid the imposition of value judgments" (p. 228). To those who have read his essay, it will be evident that my view of *High School* differs from the quantitative, generic analysis offered by Bruce Gronbeck in "Celluloid Rhetoric: On Genres of Documentary," in *Form and Genre: Shaping Rhetorical Action,* ed. Karlyn Kohrs Campbell and Kathleen Hall Jamieson (Falls Church, Virginia:

Speech Communication Association, 1978), pp. 139–161. See also: T. R. Atkins, "The Films of Frederick Wiseman," *Sight and Sound,* 43 (1974), 232–235; Donald E. McWilliams, "Fred Wiseman," *Film Quarterly,* 24 (1970), 17–26; Stephen Mamber, "High School," *Film Quarterly,* 24 (1970), 48–51; Bill Nichols, "Fred Wiseman's Documentaries: Theory and Structure," *Film Quarterly,* 31 (1978), 15–28; Susan Swartz, "The Real Northeast," *Film Library Quarterly,* 6 (1972–73), 12–15.

3. In his interview with Rosenthal, Wiseman spoke at length about the theme of power: "A high school, like any institution, is a self-contained society and you have to hunt out the places where power is exercised. That's where you're going to find the real values of the institution expressed. In one way the film is organized around the contrast between the formal values of openness, trust, sensitivity, democracy, and understanding, and the actual practice of the school which is quite authoritarian." Alan Rosenthal, *The New Documentary in Action: A Casebook in Film Making* (Berkeley: The University of California Press, 1971), p. 71.

4. Rosenthal, *The New Documentary in Action,* p. 70.

5. Figures 1–99 are line drawings representing frames from *High School.*

6. Rosenthal, *The New Documentary in Action,* p. 73.

7. For descriptions of the double bind, see Gregory Bateson, Don Jackson, Jay Haley and John Weakland. "Toward a Theory of Schizophrenia," *Behavioral Science,* 1 (1956), 251–264; John H. Weakland, "The 'Double-Bind' Hypothesis of Schizophrenia and Three-Party Interaction," in *The Etiology of Schizophrenia,* ed. Don D. Jackson (New York: Basic Books, 1960), pp. 373–388; Albert E. Scheflen, with Alice Scheflen, *Body Language and Social Order: Communication as Behavioral Control* (Englewood Cliffs, New Jersey: Prentice Hall, 1972), pp. 184–198. I am not arguing that Wiseman imposes the double-bind theory on his material. In fact, in describing his working methods, Wiseman has often said that he makes little use of social science. But Wiseman has discovered a structure in his material that is remarkably similar to the double-bind. Wiseman's structure and the double-bind hypothesis are thus not only confirming one another but are also likely to exercise a forceful appeal to audiences whose own experience of social institutions has been double-binding.

8. Albert Scheflen, "Quasi-Courtship Behavior in Psychotherapy," *Psychiatry,* 28 (1965); reprinted in Shirley Weitz, ed., *Nonverbal Communication: Readings with Commentary* (New York: Oxford University Press, 1974), pp. 192–193.

9. Desmond Morris, Peter Collett, Peter Marsh and Marie O'Shaughnessy, *Gestures: Their Origin and Distribution* (New York: Stein and Day, 1979), pp. 100–105.

10. Scheflen, "Quasi-Courtship Behavior in Psychotherapy," p. 186.

11. Barsam, *Nonfiction Film: A Critical History,* p. 276; Gronbeck, p. 147; Mamber, *Cinema Verite in America,* pp. 227–228.

12. This is not the place to debate with Wiseman the merits of American secondary education, or the accuracy of his depiction of the school. But some brief comments on the matter are relevant to understanding *High School.* Wiseman's condemnation of the oppressiveness and repressiveness of Northeast High School is not simply a call for permissiveness or sexual freedom. All societies educate their offspring to cope with systems of contradictions, and Northeast High School is not to be blamed insofar as it presents to adolescents the necessity to face the tensions of social and sexual maturity. Insofar as Wiseman indicts high school, he seems to charge that the school perniciously invades the territory of the family, simultaneously abandoning its own calling to uphold intellectual standards, and that, rather than simply exercising the discipline needed to get on with the job of educating, the school places the students in a double bind from which there is no escape except into the claustrophobic, dizzying, haven of their own narcissistic passivity.

Hiroshima, Mon Amour: From Iconography to Rhetoric

Martin J. Medhurst

Hiroshima, Mon Amour was first shown at the 1959 Cannes Film Festival, where it won critical acclaim and captured the International Critics' Prize. The following year it opened in New York City, won the New York Film Critics' Award, and was proclaimed by one reviewer to be a work that "may well turn out to be a landmark in the history of the film form."[1] The reviewer was also a prophet for "in retrospect 1959 can be seen as constituting as great a watershed in the cinema as 1929."[2] One of the primary reasons for this watershed moment was Alain Resnais' now classic film, *Hiroshima, Mon Amour.*[3]

Narrative structure, more than anything else, propelled *Hiroshima, Mon Amour* to the forefront of the emerging New Wave movement, a movement which Resnais found interesting but which he predated by more than a decade. While Truffaut, Goddard, and Rivette were finishing their secondary education, Resnais was accepting an Academy Award for his first 35 mm. film, *Van Gogh.*[4] Consequently, the cinematic theories which motivated the young critic/directors associated with *Cahiers du Cinéma* differed from the cinematic agenda that produced *Hiroshima, Mon Amour.* Film, for Resnais, was a medium with which "to visualize the complexity of the mechanism of thought."[5] Thus, while the young New Wave directors sought to extend film outward to encompass political and cultural concerns, Resnais turned his lens inward to explore questions of epistemology and metaphysics, to investigate how art in general and film in particular help humans achieve true knowledge and distinguish the real from the illusory.

Hiroshima, Mon Amour is not a film about the city of Hiroshima or atomic war. Nor is it a film about the nature of love or the specific love affair which forms the core of the narrative. To approach the film from either of these perspectives is to lay oneself open to the initial rebuke spoken by the male lover to his female consort: "You saw nothing in Hiroshima."[6]

To understand *Hiroshima, Mon Amour* or, for that matter, any Resnais film, one must learn *how* to see. Resnais, first and foremost, is a teacher, a persuader who has a goal clearly in mind. "If I made the films I dream of making," says Resnais, "it would be less to destroy or demolish than to provoke the spectator to question his own assumptions. My aim is to put the spectator in such a state that a week, six months or a year afterwards, placed before a problem, he would be prevented from cheating and obliged to react freely."[7]

From *The Quarterly Journal of Speech,* Volume 68, 1982. Reprinted with permission of the Speech Communication Association and the author.

In *Hiroshima, Mon Amour,* Resnais seeks to prevent the spectator from cheating when presented with the problem of comprehension, of coming to know reality. That he sets his story in Hiroshima, birthplace and symbol of the problem that threatens to destroy humanity and populates it with lovers who practice the one act that sustains humanity, is only of secondary importance insofar as the central message of the film is concerned. It is the attempt to understand this central message which has led to multiple and sometimes contradictory interpretations of the film's meaning. For the majority of critics the film is a portrait of "the difficulties of living in time."[8]

Unlike most of Resnais' interpreters, however, I do not believe that the primary message of *Hiroshima, Mon Amour* is the interrelated problems of "memory and the corrosive effects of time."[9] Neither do I join chorus with Resnais' detractors who charge him with "deliberate ambiguity,"[10] "unnecessary romantic vagueness,"[11] and "a rather sensational treatment of some only partly digested psychological commonplaces."[12] Instead, I contend that *Hiroshima, Mon Amour* is a film about the problem of knowing reality.

For Resnais, humans know reality imperfectly, incompletely, but continually strive to capture it, label it, and use it as a basis for future action. This effort to capture and label reality is "art" in the broadest sense of the term. Art, for Resnais, is the human being's attempt to capture and express existence and experience. It is an effort at expressing and codifying human reality. But, says Resnais, there is a problem. Art codifies mankind's existence and thereby helps it to remember and feel. Soon, however, because of the limitations of the human mind, it comes to function as a propositional statement, a metaphysical statement of the way things are, divorced from the sentiment of creation and unresponsive to the flow of time. Art proclaims reality, but in the very proclamation falsifies it.

Herein lies the paradox and the heart of man's epistemological and metaphysical problem. Humans cannot give meaning or expression to their existence without "saving the appearances"[13] of the moment, be it in a cave painting, book, song, or film. But no sooner has the appearance been saved and recorded than humans forget that it is an appearance and start to act as though it is reality, as though the thing symbolized is the thing itself.[14]

By substituting marks for reality, we enthrone empirical method, allowing facts, figures, and documents to explain existence and condition memory, the basis for future action. We become what our art—our marks—proclaim us to be. Resnais teaches that we are caught in the paradox of being the animal who marks existence—*animal symbolicum*—while at the same moment being the animal who apprehends reality only through those marks.

That we are caught in this paradoxical situation of being the "art-created art creator"[15] is the central message of *Hiroshima, Mon Amour.* What makes the film "a 'classic,' a text which demands multiple readings,"[16] is not the message per se, but the techniques by which the message is conveyed. From the outset, Resnais set himself a most difficult task: the use of an artistic medium to call into question the propositional nature of art. How the director invites the audience to understand his message without contradicting his own thesis—that art lies—is the central concern of this essay.

It is my contention that Resnais constructs the entire film around the metaphor of "marking time." *Hiroshima, Mon Amour* is a poetic recitation on the various ways humans mark time and thereby make it meaningful. It is also a rhetorical argument that all such marks present a necessarily distorted view of reality and should therefore be suspect. We must be taught to "see" correctly, but sight is an act of mind, of imagination based in feeling. To see only the artifact without experiencing the feeling and imagination behind it is to mistake illusion for reality.

First, I shall reconstruct the narrative structure of the film. Second, I shall identify the various icons, images, sounds, and acts that constitute "marks" in time, a process which corresponds with the first two steps of iconographic criticism as outlined by Erwin Panofsky.[17] Finally, I shall examine these marks in context to show how they function rhetorically to invite the critical spectator to understand the central message or, as Panofsky calls it, the "intrinsic meaning"[18] of the film.

Narrative Structure and Meaning

It was the unorthodox narrative structure of *Hiroshima, Mon Amour* that first distinguished it as a landmark in cinematographic technique when, for "perhaps for the first time, a film explored the full possibilities of cinematic time."[19] Even today, *Hiroshima mon amour* [sic] . . . remains by far Resnais' most complicated, difficult, confusing, and treacherous essay in the social, political, and linguistic semiological ramifications of film."[20]

As the opening credits fade to black and the piercing score segues into a slow pastoral theme, the viewer witnesses a gradual fade in. The image is ambiguous: limbs in a contorted position, entangled, enmeshed, fused in such a fashion that one cannot tell a shoulder from a thigh or an arm from a leg. Suddenly the limbs begin to glow and thoughts of radioactivity race through the spectator's mind. Still no word, no sound, only the pastoral theme interpreting what now seem clearly to be the movements of love.

"You saw nothing in Hiroshima . . . nothing," repeats the male voice. "I saw everything . . . everything," answers the female. No faces are visible, only a pair of hands resting on bare shoulders. One hand is flat and calm, the other tense and clawed, digging into the flesh. Thus the dialectical opening sets the stage for the rest of the film—nothing or everything, the open hand of reason or the clawed fist of emotion.[21]

From this oblique opening, the viewer is whisked into the mind of the heroine as she recalls for her lover the sights of Hiroshima: the hospital, where victims of the bomb calmly await their death; the museum, with its tortured iron, burnt flesh, and photographic reconstructions; the people of Hiroshima, who bear deformed children, eat contaminated food, and fear the rain which falls from above; the tourists, who buy mementoes, shoot film, and take tours past shadows etched in stone, tourists who try so hard to remember the meaning of Hiroshima. But the vision of a tourist is suspect, as seven times the man interrupts the woman's internal monologue to deny her assertions.

Suddenly, fifteen minutes into the film, the viewer sees for the first time the faces of these two lovers, a French woman and a Japanese man. They begin to talk, and little by little their stories emerge. She is an actress who has come to Hiroshima to perform in a film about peace. He is an architect who served with the Japanese Army and whose family was in Hiroshima on that fateful day.

The screen fades to black then quickly fades in again to the woman now dressed in a kimono and standing on a sun deck. She turns and walks back to the doorway, gazing at her lover, who lays face down on a bed with hand upturned. Suddenly an image flashes on the screen: the upturned hand of a dead German soldier lying in the arms of a young woman. The image is on the screen less than 3½ seconds. But it is the first of what will be numerous images to come, images from out of the woman's past.

The man awakens. They shower together and begin to talk, once more, of the past. We learn that they met the night before in a cafe; that the woman was in Paris at the time of the bombing, having just left her hometown of Nevers; that the woman is planning to leave Hiroshima the next day and that the man wants her to stay. As they prepare to leave the hotel room, the man asks if she is returning to Nevers, to which she responds, "I don't go to Nevers anymore." We learn that once she was mad in Nevers and that her madness ended shortly after the war. The man implores her to stay, but she hails a taxi and disappears.

The director cuts to a closeup of a man with cupped hands, apparently calling out instructions. The man is a film director. We see the actress sleeping under a tree and witness the approach of her Japanese lover. Together they watch the final crowd scenes being shot. We see placards opposing nuclear weapons: a burned hand, a hairless head, a woman and child. The paraders pass. Some carry drawings, some doves, some dance while others march. The man and woman are caught up in the crowd, lose sight of one another momentarily, and are then reunited. The placards pass once again and the screen fades to black only to fade in again inside the man's apartment.

We learn that both the man and the woman are married—happily, they claim. Soon the conversation turns to the woman's past, to her experience in wartime Nevers. Once back in bed, the woman again recalls the images of fourteen years earlier. We learn of her German lover, his death, her punishment for giving comfort to the enemy, and her subsequent madness and incarceration in a cellar. As the lovers prepare to leave, he places his hand on her shoulders and says, "All we have to do now is kill time." The director dissolves into a long shot of the River Ota where people stand on the banks fishing and gazing across to the bright lights of Hiroshima.

115

We see the outside of a tea room and then find ourselves inside with the man and woman sitting at a table, gazing into one another's eyes. "Is there any other meaning to Nevers in French?" asks the man. "No . . . none," replies the woman.[22] Thus begins another excursion into images long repressed, thoughts long suppressed, as the man quizzes his companion on her experiences in Nevers. As the conversation continues, the woman begins to respond as though she is talking to her dead German lover. She recalls the small cellar, the clawing of her hands against the walls, the people as they pass above her, unknowing, unsuspecting. She recalls her screams, how she called out her dead lover's name, and how the townspeople, out of a sense of duty, cut off her hair to reveal her shame. She recalls how they were to meet by the river, and how she discovered the wounded German near death. She recalls being forced to leave for Paris by bicycle and arriving when "the name of Hiroshima is in all the papers." Having relived her past, the woman rises from the table and departs.

The screen fades to black and fades in again as the woman, now alone, enters the Hotel New Hiroshima, site of their earlier rendezvous. She walks up the steps to her room, starts to enter, hesitates, and returns to the stairwell. Again she hesitates, turns around, and walks back up to her room where she enters the bathroom and buries her face in running water. "You think you know," she says, "but you don't . . . fourteen years, I searched for an impossible love. . . ." The camera cuts and we see the woman emerging from the hotel and walking into the darkness. A spotlight sweeps the landscape and we find the woman sitting outside the tea room, now closed, talking to herself. Her Japanese lover approaches, asks her to stay with him, then walks away. The woman rises and walks down the dark alleyway as the man follows, silently stalking her every step. She continues to walk down the streets, now neon lit, her paramour nowhere in sight. Again, the images of Nevers reappear now interspersed with the neon lights of Hiroshima. Mental images of the past are made present and contrasted with the images of physical sight.

The director cuts to black then tilts up to reveal the woman standing outside the tea room. Her Japanese lover approaches and asks, once again, if it is possible for her to stay. "You know quite well," she replies, "it's even less possible than to go." Again, she walks away from him as the director cuts to the inside of a train station where the French woman sits next to an elderly Japanese lady. The man enters and sits next to the elderly lady. He reaches across the lady and offers a cigarette to his French lover. Immediately, images of Nevers begin to emerge from her subconscious and the internal monologue returns. "Little shorn head from Nevers," she thinks, "I forget you here and now."

The director cuts again and we see the French woman entering a cab which, at the next cut, arrives at the club Casablanca. She exits the cab and enters the club with her Japanese lover arriving seconds later in another cab and following her into the dimly lit nightclub. The man takes a table opposite the

Table I

film/movies	writing
newsreels	public address
photographs	banners
phonograph records	placards
cards	billboards
paintings	drawings
architecture	statuary
books	

woman and watches her. They look at each other, but remain silent, motionless. Dawn arrives and the director cuts to reveal the woman back in her hotel room pursued, as before, by the Japanese. They enter the room and sit on the bed. "I'll forget you! . . . I already havė," she exclaims. He grabs her hands as she looks into his eyes and says, "Hiroshima is your name." He returns the gaze and replies, "Yes, that's my name . . . and your name is Nevers . . . Nevers . . . in . . . France." On that note, the film comes to an end.

This scene by scene description is an accurate account of the narrative structure, plot, and characterizations in *Hiroshima, Mon Amour*. Its main function, however, is to demonstrate the complete inadequacy of traditional literary categories to account for the rhetoric of film. Film is not literature and literary categories cannot explicate a serious film; that is, a film that makes extensive use of the resources of cinematographic language.

Though it may be true that Resnais "represents the most literary cinema that ever existed,"[23] it is equally true that "a technical exegesis of the film is necessary because Resnais is a director who expresses emotions" and ideas "*through* the montage and composition of the individual shots."[24] And even though "he has collaborated with the best literary minds of his generation . . . his films," as Alan Stanbrook points out, "do not emerge as illustrations, more or less bolstered by an apt musical score. They are transformed into original creations in which the perfect symmetry of each aspect of production attests the controlling hand of a single, dedicated personality."[25]

The task for the rhetorical critic, therefore, is to show how the film director uses iconography, editing, framing and other resources of cinematic language to advance ideas and arguments to that portion of the audience who understands, or who can be helped to understand, the language and logic of cinematic form. The task is to explicate the artistic movement from iconography to rhetoric. Thus, the next step is to describe and explicate the cinematic means employed by Resnais to advance his thesis that all art is a form of marking time that is paradoxical in nature being, at one and the same moment, propositionally false and poetically true.

Table II

Sight	Sound	Touch	Taste	Smell
hands	jukebox	clawing shoulders	blood	burning refuse
			-German	
hair	bells		-Girl	burnt flesh
		embracing	-Japanese	
clocks	scream			dead fish
		slapping		
water				

Marks In Time. In *Hiroshima, Mon Amour,* Resnais uses a complex calculus of icons, images, and sounds to invite the audience to question its perception of reality and to recognize the paradoxical nature of artistic expression. Because humans tend to interpret and judge on the basis of sense perceptions, Resnais intentionally manipulates audience perception of the five senses—sight, sound, touch, taste, and smell—to deny the absolute validity of empirically-based knowledge. He challenges all forms of perception and communication while at the same time demonstrating that communication of one's perception of reality is central to the human condition.

In *Hiroshima, Mon Amour,* Resnais introduces fourteen different means of communication by which humans mark the span of their existence. Table I illustrates the different ways in which humans attempt to share their perceptions and register their existence. Mankind marks time, but time also marks mankind. Who we are at any one moment is dependent on who we have been and what we have done in the past. The past marks us just as surely as we have marked it. Resnais attempts to demonstrate this principle through image composition, intellectual montage,[26] and aural/visual counterpoint, using the narrative of a love affair as a vehicle for his ideas about human perceptual and communicative abilities.

Table II illustrates the major elements of image composition and sound arranged according to the physical sense the spectator uses to apprehend each element. The senses of touch, taste, and smell cannot, of course, be communicated directly, but are strongly suggested by the power of the imagery through which they are connoted. As we will see, no one particular sense nor any combination of senses can yield adequate knowledge, knowledge which can be used as the basis for further action. Through the repetition of these images which invites the participation of the entire sensorium, Resnais constructs an intellectual montage the central message of which is "the impossibility of documenting,"[27] in any adequate way one's own experience, one's own quest to know, one's own interpretation of reality. In Resnais' world, facts divorced from feeling yield only deformity.

Marks as Structure and Meaning

The Sense of Sight. Let us examine the four images which the viewer *sees* repeatedly throughout the film: hands, hair, clocks, and water. We first see the hand motif in the initial sequence where the man and woman are enmeshed in the motions of love. The woman's hands grip the man's shoulders and with each surge of emotion her left hand claws into his flesh. Her right hand, however, remains calm throughout the sequence. The opening is a visual analogy proclaiming the inadequacy of knowledge divorced from emotion. Such knowledge is defective, productive only of intellectual deformity. The hand functions in a symbolic capacity throughout the film to remind the audience of the necessity of integrating emotion into one's view of reality.

The woman is intellectually deformed because she has sought to suppress the emotional reality of her love affair with the German soldier. Not being able to feel properly has diminished her ability to "see," to comprehend reality. Thus, when she recalls the sights of Hiroshima all she can recite are facts gathered from museums and tours, but these facts fail to reveal the great human tragedy of Hiroshima.

While the woman babbles on about tortured iron and burnt flesh, Resnais creates an ironic comment concerning her perceptions. As the camera tracks down the row of exhibits inside the museum the viewer sees the flesh that fell from the bomb victims. But as the internal monologue draws attention to the foreground, Resnais makes his comment in the background with the letters ABC. For the woman it's all so cut and dried, as simple as ABC. She can claim to see "everything" because it is all so clear, so neat and ordered.

But the woman's sight is flawed. As she recalls her visit to the museum she claims to have seen "people walk around deep in thought." As she says these words, a person walks briskly past the displays. Visual evidence contradicts the verbalized memory. She speaks of seeing the photographs and reconstructions. "What else was there," she asks, as two children—human reconstructions—enter the frame.

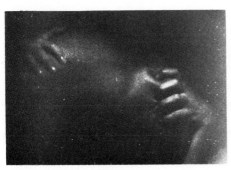

Figure 1

Figure 2

"Four times at the museum in Hiroshima . . . I looked at those people . . . I, too, looked thoughtfully," she says, as the director cuts to visual evidence which contradicts her assertion. She saw documents, but she missed their message as demonstrated in shots 24 and 25.

#24—Camera tracks left while trained on a model airplane suspended from the ceiling. The effect of the moving camera is to give the illusion that the plane is moving.

CUT

#25—Closeup of a reconstruction of the bomb site. First one child, then a second, then a third enter the frame.

As the woman claims to have looked thoughtfully, Resnais shows the viewer the real message: an airplane banking to bomb innocent children. To see through the woman's eyes is not to see at all.

Resnais uses the image of the hand (figure 4) as a constant reminder of the woman's deformed perceptions. Just as the victims of Hiroshima were physically deformed, so the woman is emotionally deformed. Resnais first shows an example of a physically deformed hand, then recreates imitations of that deformity throughout the film. Figures 5, 6, and 7 are illustrative.

Though the physical resemblance is to the victims of Hiroshima, the image functions as a metaphorical reminder of the woman's emotional deformity resulting from the death of the German and her subsequent punishment. It is the memory of the German's *hand* which triggers all her recollections of Nevers. Thus, Resnais attaches a double signification to hands, though both participate in the idea of deformity and both are echoed in the image of the hand clawing the lover's back, an image which demonstrates in itself the paradoxical nature of emotion. Only emotion allows one to truly love, or truly know, but an emotion based totally in the past deforms the act of love just as it distorts perception, resulting in adultery and pseudocommunication. Thus, hands function symbolically to remind us of both the necessity and dangerous role of emotion in our perception of reality.

Hair functions in a manner similar to hands. It carries a double signification as an emotional mark in time. Clumps of hair mark the Hiroshima tragedy. As the hair fell from the heads of those exposed to the bomb, so too did it fall from the woman's head during her hour of debasement. In both cases the perpetrators considered it their duty to take retributive action. In both cases the consequences were unforseen, coloring each future moment for those involved.

Newsreels can show hair falling out. Photographs can capture the results of radiation exposure. But mere marks in time can never adequately express the reality of those who suffered such a fate. Mankind's art helps to recall part of the reality, but it is not the reality itself. Only those who have personally felt and experienced can really know the reality, and then only to the degree that they can remember those feelings and experiences.

Figure 3 **Figure 4**

Figure 5 **Figure 6**

Figure 7 **Figure 8**

Table III

Shot #	Description	Shot #	Description
#30	anonymous hair in museum	#164	Japanese runs hand through his hair
#31	closeup of anonymous hair	#186	French woman touches hair after seeing placard
#53	newsreel of victim with hair falling out	#186	Japanese touches woman's hair and pulls off scarf
#56	hairless victim of bomb	#205	hairless victim on placard
#68	man losing hair	#211	woman flips hair in circle
#69	man pulling out woman's hair	#303	Japanese touches woman's hair at cafe
#70	woman pulling out her own hair	#303	woman touches own hair
#138	woman flips hair in circle	#304	young girl touches her short hair
#147	Japanese man runs hand through hair	#306	girl having hair cut
#151	man and woman in shower run hands through her hair	#351	hair in hotel sink

The hair image marks the woman's perception of reality just as surely as the image of the hand. She carries within her the marks of a past which is never totally eclipsed but lurks always in each present moment. She can repress the past, but she cannot forget it. Memory is a part of the current configuration and interpretation of reality whether one wishes it to be or not. Resnais demonstrates this principle, as illustrated in Table III, through repetition of the hair image.

The hair image, like that of the hand, is symbolic of both physical and mental deformity, a deformity one carries, consciously or unconsciously, through time. The past intrudes on the present despite efforts to kill time. It is with the third image, the clock, that Resnais most forcefully articulates this principle.

Though art, for Resnais, can effect a poetic realization of the past it, too, is dependent on memory. To remember what gave rise to the artistic expression, the mark in time, is to participate to some degree in the feeling that produced it. To forget the creative impulse, however, is to allow art to function propositionally as a statement of fact, to allow it to function as that which it is not. As more and more time passes between the mark and its interpretation the greater becomes the possibility of the symbol being mistaken for the thing symbolized. Resnais indicates that when one is unable to recall the feeling that gave rise to the mark, art passes from poetry to proposition, from index of truth to proclaimer of lies.

In *Hiroshima, Mon Amour* clocks and wristwatches are used to indicate this ever-present threat to truth. Humans cannot escape time or its effects. To live in a spatio-temporal world is to live in a world where "marks" are demanded as indexes of existence, but where those same marks are subject to misinterpretation and atrophy. Hence, the symbolic representations of time are, like the hand and hair images, paradoxical, being both the impetus to poetic truth and the barrier to propositional fact.

Table IV demonstrates the frequency with which the clock image is employed. There are so many visual and verbal references to time that some critics have inferred, incorrectly I believe, that the theme of *Hiroshima, Mon Amour* is "the interaction between past and present."[28] Although the effect of time is certainly part of Resnais' message, it is not the complete message nor even the primary thrust. The symbolic use of clocks is, like the images of hands and hair, a subtext which forms but a part of the whole. By exploring both the positive and negative effects of time, Resnais is able to get at the heart of the "epistemological problem . . . of how man knows reality and how he assesses the accuracy of his perceptions."[29] Two examples will suffice.

In figures 10–14 the man and woman are sitting in the tea room discussing her experiences in Nevers. Figure 10 is a closeup of two pairs of clenched fists. The shot shows a wristwatch on each person's arm. As the woman says "hands become useless in a cellar," she reaches across the table and obliterates the view of the man's watch. The director then cuts to the next shot which is the woman's memory of having clawed at the cellar wall until her hands are red with blood. Resnais then cuts again, a form cut from the clenched, bleeding fist of the cellar to the clenched fists of the lovers at the cafe table. The woman removes her hand, but the man's watch has disappeared from sight. The woman's "eternity" in the cellar obliterates time, both psychologically and literally. Her memory of the cellar functions as a mark in time which helps her recall the feelings of the past while, at the same time, deforming her life in the present. Thus, the interlocked hands of the lovers resemble the earlier shot of the Hiroshima victim. Time shapes our perceptions, both forming and de-forming, revealing some aspects of reality while hiding others.

Table IV

Shot #	Description	Shot #	Description
#100	clock—atomic bus tour	#303	man's watch revealed at cafe
#117	wristwatch on student with skin cancer	#303	man's watch again revealed at cafe
#159	2 wristwatches lay on nightstand	#306	watch on young girl's father
#160	man picks up watch and listens to it	#314	woman's watch revealed at cafe
#162	watch on man's wrist	#318	man's watch revealed at cafe
#163	woman adjusts her wristwatch	#318	man's watch revealed at cafe
#164	watch on man's wrist	#325	man's watch revealed at cafe
#167	man's watch against stone street backdrop	#348	woman's watch revealed at hotel
#186	woman's watch revealed	#387	old man in train station checks watch
#187	woman's watch revealed	#389	man's watch revealed at train station
#199	film director enters frame with watch on	#390	man's watch revealed at train station
#207	watch on parade participant	#399	man's watch revealed at train station
#221	man's watch revealed after embrace	#410	man's watch revealed at Casablanca Club
#270	man's watch revealed at cafe table	#411	woman's watch revealed at Casablanca Club
#278	both watches revealed at cafe	#422	woman's watch revealed in hotel room
#291	man's watch revealed again at cafe	#422	man's watch revealed in hotel room
#292	man's watch revealed again at cafe	#422	both watches side by side in hotel room
#301	woman's watch revealed at cafe		

Figure 9

Figure 10

Figure 11

Figure 12

Figure 13

Figure 14

Figures 15–17 function similarly. In this, the next to last shot of the film, Resnais again uses the clock image to comment on the effect time has on perception and communication. The shot, which lasts one minute and thirty-five seconds, shows the woman trying to strike the man. He catches her arm as she strikes out, revealing the watch on her wrist. The man then reaches up to touch her cheek and in so doing covers her watch with his hand, the same hand on which he wears a watch. He then lowers his arm and we see both watches side by side. The interlocked hands again look deformed as the woman says, "Hiroshima is your name," and the man affirms, "Yes, that's my name . . . and your name is Nevers . . . Nevers . . . in France."

The intellectual montage which arises from the action within this single shot suggests, once again, the dual nature of time. Time past is overshadowed for a moment by time present. But the final resolution is past and present resting side by side, each present, each real, each informing and modifying the other. Time cannot be destroyed. The name for the Japanese—his "mark"—is Hiroshima. He is defined by his past just as surely as the woman is defined by her experiences in Nevers. His mark or name is Hiroshima, hers is Nevers. One's reality, one's defining mark, determines the label used; one's perception of reality shapes language which, in turn, doubles back and shapes reality. Like it or not, Resnais says, the past is the present, and the present the past. Epistemology is intimately linked with metaphysics and communication. The act of coming to know cannot be divorced from the mind of the knower or the means used to register—to mark—the existence of that knower. That time both destroys and creates humanity is further illuminated in the fourth central image—water.

Resnais does not employ water imagery as frequently as that of hands, hair, or clocks. Nevertheless, the symbolic function of water is central to the message of the film. The four individuations of this symbol are the rainfall, the River Ota, the Loire River, and the water that flows from the shower and faucet in the woman's hotel room.

Rainfall is linked with destruction through time. The immediate effects of the bomb, displayed in the woman's recollection of her visit to Hiroshima, are shown to be ever-present in the falling rain. Fourteen years after the event, the rain still carries the seeds of destruction. Time has not erased the effects of the bomb. "Rain produces panic," says the woman, "ashes rain over the Pacific . . . the ocean turns deadly." A time once marked by the dropping of the bomb intrudes into the present. The past is present having become, quite literally, part of nature.

Even as the rain feeds the rivers that produce the food, it carries the germs of destruction. Life and death coexist with past and present, war and peace.[30] The ashes of war fall on a pacifistic people in a time marked by the absence of war. Time is one, indivisible, absorbing man's marks and turning them, eventually, into a song.

Figure 15   **Figure 16**

Figure 17

The rivers Ota and Loire function in much the same manner. Physically deformed by the bomb and its aftermath, the Ota was dried up, bereft of fish, dead. The Loire, too, represents deformation through time, an internal deformity of the mind. It was by the banks of the River Loire that the young girl met her German lover, and it is the personal identification with the river that prompts the woman to describe it as a body "with no navigation at all." The river, like her mind, cannot be traversed "because of its irregular course and the sand bars." It was by the river that she was to meet her lover and elope to Bavaria. And it was by the same river that she found him with a mortal wound, a wound which she has internalized and carried with her since. As the war in the Pacific physically deformed the River Ota, so the war in Europe mentally deformed the young woman who rendezvoused with her lover by the Loire. The effects of both deformities continue to the present.

The fourth representation of water occurs inside the woman's hotel room. There are two separate instances. In the first instance the man and woman shower together after making love. The sequence is shot in closeup to allow the filmmaker to register his point. The man and woman speak of their meeting the night before. "I didn't notice whether you spoke Japanese or not," says the man. "You see that people always notice things to suit themselves," observes the woman. "No," retorts the man, "all I saw . . . was you!"

Figure 18   **Figure 19**

Figure 20

There are two points to note about this exchange. First, the man proves the woman's point through his response. He noticed precisely what suited himself—the woman. But more important is what the film viewer notices or fails to notice. As the dialogue demonstrates the difficulty of recognizing and accepting truth when it is heard, the visual imagery announces the difficulty of perceiving truth even when one is looking at it.

By shooting the sequence in closeup, Resnais eliminates all background save the tiled walls of the shower stall. As the lovers run their hands through the woman's hair and speak of noticing what suits the observer, the filmmaker constructs a prison-like backdrop. The man and woman are imprisoned in their perceptions. They cannot escape the "reality" in which they live. The visuals give the lie to the man's response just as surely as do the words he utters. Resnais invites the audience to understand the problems of human perception by bringing together the hand, hair, and water imagery in a visual prison.

The second instance of water imagery within the hotel room functions in a similar manner. The woman has returned to the hotel from the tea room. With great hesitation, she enters the room and immediately goes to the bathroom where she turns on the water and buries her face in the sink. The screen is filled with hair as the viewer watches the back of her head. When she raises her head, dripping with water, and looks into the mirror, we once again experience the prison imagery. This time the bars of the prison are reflected in the mirror as the woman speaks of going to Bavaria—a trip she never made. She reflects on the past, a past which has imprisoned her memories, just as surely as one witnesses her reflection in the mirror. Physical reflection and mental reflection, physical bars and mental bars are associated in one powerful image.

Through these four images—hands, hair, clocks, and water—Resnais teaches the viewer that the sense of sight is not perfect. What appears to be truth at first glance may not be true at all or may be only part of the truth, a distortion of reality. Just as Resnais denies our ability to know through sight, so he denies the validity of knowing through sound. In addition to the musical themes on the soundtrack,[31] three sounds are central to the film—the ringing of bells, jukebox music, and one lone scream.

The Sense of Hearing. Bells are first heard as the man and woman sit on the bed discussing morality. "You see," says the woman, "my morals are rather dubious." "What do you mean?" the man inquires. "I am dubious of the morality of others," she replies. During this short exchange church bells ring in the background. The woman, according to the logic of the dialogue, is guilty of dubious morality simply because she questions the morality of others. To question, to inquire, is to be guilty. One should accept moral standards as given be they those of church or culture.

The woman, in this instance, speaks truthfully for according to both church and culture her morals are suspect. She is an adultress and a collaborator with the enemy. According to traditional, abstract standards she is an immoral preson. But the bells, like the condensation symbols associated with sight, invite the viewer to think further, to reflect more deeply.

It was the bells of St. Stephens that rang to announce the liberation. As her German lover lay dead in the bed of a truck the bells rang and rang celebrating, as it were, his death as a prelude to victory. After her incarceration in the cellar, her imprisonment for loving an enemy, the bells continued to ring every night at six. Traditional morality, Resnais seems to indicate, is often self-contradictory. While proclaiming "thou shalt not kill," it celebrates death. While admonishing to "love thy enemy," it condones the punishment of those who take the command too literally.

The reality which the bells purport to represent is not as clear cut or obvious as one is led to suspect. Moralities, like other aspects of social reality, are dubious and should be doubted, questioned, and probed. The viewer is invited to "see" and understand the real by questioning the reality portrayed. The sound of the bells proclaims a truth, a mode of knowing, which upon closer examination is dubious indeed.

The music of the jukebox inside the tea room is a second instance of the unreliability of aural peception. As the man and woman discuss her ordeal at Nevers, the man selects a gay French tune on the jukebox. As the director cuts to a closeup of the record dropping onto the turntable, we see the number 20 affixed to the record-changer. The music is light, happy, and carefree. It invites a feeling of joy.

To the woman, however, the music has an entirely different meaning, a different feeling tone. "Oh, how young I was once," she says. Immediately the images of the cellar prison return. The music represents a different reality for her; not happy, not carefree, not joyous. At age 20 she was humiliated, locked away, ostracized. The view of reality offered to the spectator by the music is abstract, divorced from any concrete experience. But for the woman it is a voice from the past, real, vital, and tragic. Time has passed. Youth is gone. Memory fades, but the feeling and imagination remain. To truly know, the viewer must learn to feel, imagine, and strive to remember. Appearances, whether of sight or sound should be saved, but they must not be mistaken for reality.

The third sound that functions rhetorically to invite the audience to know reality is the scream uttered by the young woman in the square at Nevers. The scream differs from all other sounds in *Hiroshima, Mon Amour* because it is the only piece of the Nevers experience, the only evidence from the past, that comes directly to the viewer in first person narrative. All other evidences are in the present tense as recalled by the woman. The scream, however, is in the past tense. We hear it as it happened then, not as it is remembered now.

The scream is pure emotion. It is poetic, not propositional. It invites us to understand feelings, not facts. Any other sound, dialogue, or recollection would be but one more mark in time subject to the same limitations as all art. But the scream is the director's statement about the truth of the woman's experience. It is the director's art that allows the scream to be heard as the film demolishes space and time to reveal truth. The emotion is pure knowledge. Any description of it would be something less than truth, less than real. Hence, Resnais demonstrates once again the necessity of bringing feeling and imagination into the interpretation of reality. One knows reality, he says, by understanding its poetic dimension, the realm of feeling and form.[32]

Neither what is seen nor what is heard can be taken as propositional fact. Only poetry reveals truth. To know reality, says Resnais, requires an act of the imagination, a participation in the feeling and form of creation. Just as sight and sound are unreliable indexes, so too are touch, taste, and smell. Resnais stretches the cinematic medium to its fullest by using image and sound to invite the spectator to feel, taste, and smell reality, then transcends the invitation by denying the validity of these perceptions.

The Sense of Touch. As Linda Williams has pointed out, there is "a broad metaphoric system of touch that runs throughout the film."[33] This system is best exemplified in three images, two of which recur throughout. The images of hands clawing flesh, people embracing, and the man slapping the woman all connote strong tactile impressions. Not only do these images *show* touch, but they invite *feelings of touch;* feelings often associated with pain.

Figure 21   Figure 22

...they put me in the cellar...

Figure 23

The first distinct image in the film is that of the woman's hand gripping her paramour's shoulder during the act of love. This image of the clawing hand recurs eight times in different contexts. In each context, however, it is associated not with love, but with pain and death. Figures 1, 22, and 23 are illustrative.

In figure 1 the woman's hand digs into the man's shoulder with each surge of emotion. The image connotes a reaction to love and affection. It carries a positive valence throughout the first segment of the film where images of lov-emaking are intercut with the woman's recollections of her visit to Hiroshima. But as the film continues, the meanings associated with the claw hand begin to shift.

In figure 22 the image of a claw hand appears on a placard during the shooting of the crowd scene. It is the hand of one who has experienced the atomic bomb: burned, deformed, and clawing for life. But what has this to do with the man and woman? The next two appearances of the image provide the answer.

131

In figure 12 the viewer sees the young French girl literally clawing the wall of the cellar. Her hands bleed; the blood becomes an index which points to the death of her lover. She tastes her own blood to establish a mark in time; a mark that will help her remember the past. But it is not until figure 23 appears that one fully understands the import of the claw hand.

In figure 23 the girl's mother grabs her by the shoulders in much the same manner that she, fourteen years later, grips the shoulder of her Japanese lover. The mother claws the shoulder not in love, but in anger and shame. She grabs the girl for one purpose only—to propel her into the cellar; to punish her for loving the enemy. Thus, it is not until the film has run its course that the full meaning of the clawing hand becomes evident.

Any one image by itself is inadequate. Images in isolation lie. It is only when past images are brought to bear on present reality that the truth emerges. To know that the clawing of the shoulder was the action that preceded the young girl's incarceration and led to her mental deformity is to understand the link with the physical deformities of Hiroshima and the emotional deformity of her later life. The woman digs into the shoulder with one hand and massages with the other because she is two people: the young girl who loved a German and the woman who died of love at Nevers. After the cellar experience, she could never again be the same.

The second set of images that Resnais uses to invite strong tactile associations are the bodily embraces that run from the opening sequence to the end of the film. Like the image of the claw hand, the sense of touch associated with any one embrace is a distortion of reality. One cannot know the full implications of any one embrace apart from an examination of each individual act of embracing. In *Hiroshima, Mon Amour* there are eighteen such acts. Figures 1, 24, 25, 26, and 27 are illustrative.

In Figure 1 the man and woman embrace as they engage in sexual relations. The opening image is, deceptive, however. What one sees at first glance is not necessarily what one should see, but rather one element of an overall gestalt whose meaning emerges only through the interaction of subsequent images of embrace.

As the film progresses, Resnais invites the viewer visually to associate the embrace of the lovers in Hiroshima with the lovers in Nevers. But that is not all. We are also invited to associate the Hiroshima lovers with the relationship between the girl and her mother. What is the link? It is the idea of dissociation or apartness. It is the opposite of the embrace. It is the lack of human contact, the lack of being connected to something outside the self.

As a young girl the woman was connected to the German. But the war brought his death and their separation. Likewise, the young girl was connected to her mother. Then the discovery of her love affair led to the dissolution of familial bonds and her banishment first to the cellar and then to Paris. The embrace is not a symbol of togetherness, but of the search for a lasting re-

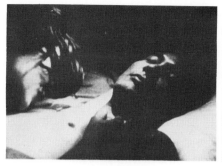

Figure 24   Figure 25

Figure 26   Figure 27

Figure 28

lationship. What appears to be an image of physical intimacy is actually a representation of emotional and psychological separation. Nowhere is this better demonstrated than in figure 28.

As the man and woman attempt to depart from the location where the crowd scenes are being shot, they become separated by the surging masses. They look one way and then the other, unable to find one another. Finally, they fight through the crowd and grab one another by the arm. The embrace is the direct outcome of the separation. It is a clinging informed by past separations. So too are the embraces which open the film. Though appearing at first to be images of intimacy, in context, they are merely images of longing, longing for connections long since broken, for embraces only half remembered. To correctly interpret the present, one must first understand the past and the marks of it humans have left behind.

The third image that invites strong tactile associations is the slap which the man administers to the woman at the tea room. Like the previous examples, this powerful image of touching behavior is not what it first appears to be. Just as the embrace is not a symbol of intimacy or closeness, so the slap is not a symbol of anger or violence. On the contrary, it is an antidote to pseudoreality and false communication. As the images of clawing and embracing announce the truth claims of the past, so the slap proclaims its limitations. One cannot truly know without recourse to the past. But neither can one truly know by living in the past alone. One must remember, but one must also learn how to forget.[34]

As the man and woman sit in the tea room talking about Nevers, the woman lapses into a description of the German's death. She tells how she became one with his dead body, not being able to feel, as she says, "the slightest difference . . . between his dead body and my own." She so totally identifies with this moment from the past that she is unable to distinguish the present. This is illustrated throughout by her habit of responding to the questions of the Japanese as though he were, in fact, the German.

When she cries out, "He was my first love," the Japanese slaps her twice across the face. The slaps function as reminders of the difference between past and present. Though one cannot know reality without recourse to the past neither can one know reality without recourse to the present. This tactile stimulation is not what it appears to be in isolation. Touch, interpreted out of context, is misleading to the spectator just as surely as are sight and sound. For sense perceptions to be useful, one must take the feelings and imagination of the past and apply them to the present. One must strive to remember by making marks that echo and evoke the feeling of their creation. This, for Resnais, is art at its highest, a poetic realization of feeling and form. To know is to be forced to go beyond surface appearances and to grapple with the dynamics of the creative impulse. It is the slap that forces the woman to abandon her self-contained world of past memories and return to the struggle of the present.

The Sense of Taste. The tactile sense is suspect, but so too is the sense of taste. Resnais creates a strong invitation to experience and question the gustatory capacity by applying human blood to the palate. There are four images of tasting blood throughout the film. Two of the images are explicit, the other two are implicit. One must understand the interrelationships of these images, however, to comprehend the reality they depict.

Figure 29

Figure 30

Figure 31

Figure 32

The two explicit images of tasting blood seem rather straightforward. As the woman recalls her cellar experience she says, "I already know the taste of your blood. . . ." In figures 9 and 30 the viewer sees dried blood on the woman's face; the blood of her German lover. Closely related to these images is the shot of the girl tasting her own blood. "Hands are useless in a cellar," she says, "they claw . . . they get skinned on the wall . . . until they bleed." The girl tastes her own blood because, as she says, "it's all I can do for myself . . . and it helps me remember." Her blood functions as a mark in time, a mark which helps to recall the feeling of the past.

If these were the only images of taste, there would be no need to seek a deeper meaning. But there are two other shots which implicitly invite the audience to taste blood and which must be considered before adopting an interpretation. Each of these shots involve the woman and the Japanese man. They are suggestive rather than demonstrative, but read in the context of the visual narrative the two shots function to formally complete the blood image.

In shots 160 and 161 the lovers are in the man's apartment talking about the film in which the woman is performing. "What is this film of yours?" he asks. "It's about peace. . . . What else would they make in Hiroshima?" the

135

woman replies. As she utters these words she moves to the bed, rubs the man's hand, and places her lips on the inside of the man's arm at the elbow. A strange place to kiss, it seems, but a very common place to draw blood. The woman is dressed as a nurse. The conversation is about a film on peace. What is the connection with the taste of blood? Shot 303 provides the missing link.

As the man and woman sit at the cafe, the woman recalls her madness at Nevers. She exclaims that she is "mad,—with longing for you," and places her lips on the man's hand—the second most common place to draw blood, next to the inside of the elbow. Now the pattern starts to emerge—film, peace, madness, blood, and hand. In figures 30 and 31 the images of tasting blood functioned as reminders of the German's death. The taste of her own blood helped the woman remember the taste, the feeling associated with her love affair. Now, fourteen years later, she is replaying the tasting of blood with the Japanese lover. An image, a film, has been continually running through her mind since the day of the German's death. Since that time she has had no peace. The film which runs through her mind will not allow peace. The taste of the blood has ceased to function as a poetic mark to ease the pain and has become, with the passing of time, a proposition which defines for the woman the nature of reality. Her reality is the taste of fourteen years before. Blood, the mark of that taste, has haunted her and haunts her still. The constant replaying of the mental film has become, for her, a deformity. Just as the imagery of hands and hair show that the deformities of the past are still present, so the imagery of tasting blood shows the need for exorcising the root of those deformities: the mental film of the German bleeding to death.

This exorcism is accomplished by providing new blood, a new taste, a new feeling for life. Thus, Resnais builds into the film images of vampirism to demonstrate the blood transfusion that is taking place as the woman pours out her story. The Japanese man helps to save the woman's life by providing a substitute for the bad blood, the horror film, she has been carrying since Nevers.

Understanding the taste of blood is, therefore, more complex than simply linking it to a point in the past. Resnais invites the spectator to understand that the taste of blood has turned bitter, that reality has been distorted through the constant repetition of a horror film, and that a new taste of blood, a new view of reality, is needed if the woman is to escape from her nightmare. People must remember the past if they are to act wisely in the present, but they must not let the past haunt them.

The Sense of Smell. The final sense that Resnais invites the spectator to experience and transcend is smell. Again, the filmmaker uses sight and sound to connote olfactory impressions. Three images are particularly evocative: burning refuse, dead fish, and burnt flesh. In each case the image one sees is reality as processed through the deformed mind of the woman. The spectator sees only what the woman recalls having seen.

Figure 33   Figure 34

Figure 35   Figure 36

Figures 34, 35, and 36 illustrate the power of film to evoke sensations of smell. The burning city, the dead fish, and the scorched flesh are the smells of death. The odor is a mark that lingers after the icons of destruction have been rebuilt, buried, or replaced. But the odor is not Hiroshima anymore than the twisted iron, photographs, or reconstructions. Precisely because the smell is so arousing, so memorable, it easily asserts itself as a proposition, as a testimony to the nature of the real. The images of burning refuse, dead fish, and burnt flesh are diabolical because they encourage spectators to remember that which they have not experienced and could not possibly feel.

It is not the spectator whose home was destroyed. It is not the spectator whose food supply was poisoned. It is not the spectator who bears the scars of a skin graft or lives in daily fear of developing cancer. The mark—be it of sight, sound, touch, taste, or smell—is not the reality. It is a mark in time only; a mark which indicates a presence, an existence, a mind. It is a mark which grew out of an impulse, a feeling, a belief. To see, hear, touch, taste, or smell the mark is to take only the first step toward knowing the feeling and imagination behind it. To claim knowledge based on the mark alone is to mistake illusion for reality. To look at the newsreels and museums and claim to have seen Hiroshima is to be engaged in a process of self deception. To think that one can smell the refuse, gag on the aroma of dead fish, or experience the odor of burnt flesh simply by viewing a film is to be deceived. To make any mark in time and offer it as a metaphysical statement of the way things are is to practice deception. This is the artist's dilemma; the same dilemma that confronts all symbol-using creatures.

Conclusion

As the woman could not possibly have known or comprehended Hiroshima nor the man known or comprehended Nevers, so, Resnais seems to indicate, are we all condemned to marking time and mistaking those marks for reality. Not even great art can escape the effects of time which transforms the emotion of creation into a proposition of existence. The best that art, mankind's marks in time, can hope to accomplish is to provoke the spectator to realize the paradox of existence and the inherent distortion of all such marks. This is precisely what Resnais has done.

As James Monaco has noted, *Hiroshima, Mon Amour* is a film about "the impossibility of making the film."[35] Through image composition, intellectual montage, and aural/visual counterpoint, Resnais has built into the film the very paradox which forms its thesis. How can a filmmaker who believes that art lies dare to make a statement about mankind's perceptual and communicative abilities through a work of art? Is not Resnais caught in the very dilemma he proclaims?

No. Resnais escapes between the horns of the dilemma. By taking seriously the notion that art lies, Resnais has been able to take his thesis and transform it into a cinematic resource. Lies abound throughout the film.[36] The soundtrack says one thing which the images promptly contradict. The woman admits that she lies. The viewers are led, time and again, to believe they know the truth about Hiroshima, Nevers, the man and the woman, only to have each of their perceptual apparati called into question. Things are never quite what they seem to be. The film raises many questions but provides few answers.

To know reality, Resnais seems to be saying, is no easy task. One must learn how to see; a process that requires the stripping away of surface appearances and the will to seek out the feelings and forms that lay behind those appearances. Mankind's marks in time—paintings, books, photos, architecture, film—are all necessary. None, however, is sufficient as a basis for action. Before humans can act they must discover the truth that lies beneath the image. In their quest to arrive at such truths humans must continue to create, to remember, to forget, and to go on living.

One thing only is certain. Time remains, implacable. Caught in such a dilemma, what can the artist do? Resnais gives his answer in figure 37. Two young boys appear as part of the parade for peace. The film director jumps in front of them to stop their progress. Immediately, they begin to mark time. This is the task of the artist. To slow down the world. To create marks in time. And to invite the audience to imagine and thus create a truth not yet in existence.

Figure 37

Notes

1. Paul V. Beckley, "'Hiroshima, Mon Amour,'" *New York Herald Tribune,* 17 May 1960, p. 23.
2. Roy Armes, *The Ambiguous Image: Narrative Style in Modern European Cinema* (Bloomington: Indiana Univ. Press, 1976), p. 230.
3. *Hiroshima, Mon Amour* was produced by Samy Halfon for Argos Films, Como Films, Daiei Motion Picture Company, and Pathe Overseas Productions; Starring Emmanuele Riva and Eiji Okada with Stella Dassas, Pierre Barbaud, and Bernard Fresson; Directed by Alain Resnais; Screenplay and dialogue by Marguerite Duras; Photography by Sacha Vierny and Takahashi Michio; Music by Georges Delerue and Giovanni Fusco; Edited by Henri Colpi and Jasmine Chasney; Set Design by Esaka/Mayo/Petri; Sound Engineering by P. Calvet and R. Renault.
4. Resnais made several 16mm films prior to *Van Gogh.* A complete listing of his 35mm films follow: *Van Gogh* (1948); *Guernica* (with Robert Hessens, 1950); *Gauguin* (1951); *Les Statues meurent aussi* (with Chris Marker, 1953); *Nuit et Brouillard* (1955); *Toute la Memoire du Monde* (1956); *Le Mystere de l'Atelier 15* (with Andre Heinrich, 1957); *Le Chant du Syrene* (1958); *Hiroshima, Mon Amour* (1959); *L'Annee derniere a Marienbad* (1961); *Muriel ou le Temps d'un Retour* (1963); *La Guerre est Finie* (1966); *Loin du Vietnam* (one episode, 1967); *Je t'aime je t'aime* (1968); *Stavisky* (1974); *Providence* (1977); *Mon Oncle d'Amerique* (1980).
5. Eugene Archer, "Director of Enigmas: Alain Resnais," in Lewis Jacobs, ed., *The Emergence of Film Art* (New York: Hopkinson and Blake, 1969), p. 340.
6. Dialogue quoted in this essay is transcribed directly from the subtitles of the English version of *Hiroshima, Mon Amour.* Any discrepancies between the English subtitles and the French/Japanese/English dialogue have been noted. References to individual shots are from the author's own framic analysis of the film and have been checked against the shot list in Raymond Ravar, ed., *"Tu n'as rien vu a Hiroshima!"* (Brussels: Free University of Brussels, 1962), pp. 249–306.
7. Resnais quoted in Roy Armes, *The Cinema of Alain Resnais* (New York: A. S. Barnes, 1968), p. 82.
8. John Ward, *Alain Resnais, or the Theme of Time* (New York: Doubleday and Co., 1968), p. 14. See also John Howard Lawson, "Time and Space," in *The Movies as Medium,* ed. Lewis Jacobs (New York: Farrar, Straus and Giroux, 1970), pp. 163–177; Robert Gessner, "The Faces of Time," *The Movies as Medium,* pp. 135–143; Bruce F. Kawin, *Telling It Again and Again: Repetition in Literature and Film* (Ithaca: Cornell University Press, 1972), p. 157; Stanley Cavell, *The World Viewed: Reflections on the Ontology of Film* (Cambridge: Harvard University Press, 1979), p. 137.

9. Alan Stanbrook, "The Time and Space of Alain Resnais," *Films and Filming,* 10 (1964), 35.

10. John J. Michalczyk, "Alain Resnais: Literary Origins from *Hiroshima* to *Providence,*" *Literature/Film Quarterly,* 7 (1979), 17.

11. A. H. Weiler, " 'Hiroshima, Mon Amour,' " *New York Times,* 17 May 1960, p. 43.

12. Robert Hatch, "Films," *The Nation,* 28 May 1960, p. 480.

13. I have borrowed this phrase from Owen Barfield's excellent book by the same title. The book, itself, directly relates to the thesis of 'Hiroshima, Mon Amour.' See Barfield, *Saving the Appearances: A Study in Idolatry* (New York: Harcourt, Brace and World, 1965).

14. The human propensity for mistaking the symbol for the thing symbolized is stressed by Kenneth Burke when he writes: "But can we bring ourselves to realize . . . just how overwhelmingly much of what we mean by 'reality' has been built up for us through nothing but our symbol systems? Take away our books, and what little do we know about history, biography, even something so 'down to earth' as the relative position of seas and continents? What is our 'reality' for today (beyond the paper-thin line of our own particular lives) but all this clutter of symbols about the past combined with whatever things we know mainly through maps, magazines, newspapers, and the like about the present? . . . Though man is typically the symbol-using animal, he clings to a kind of naïve verbal realism that refuses to realize the full extent of the role played by symbolicity in his notions of reality." See *Language As Symbolic Action: Essays on Life, Literature, and Method* (Berkeley: University of California Press, 1966), p. 5.

15. I have borrowed this phrase from Robert Joyce, author of *The Esthetic Animal: Man The Art-Created Art Creator* (Hicksville, N.Y.: Exposition Press, 1975).

16. Godelieve Mercken-Spaas, "Destruction and Reconstruction in *Hiroshima, mon amour,*" *Literature/Film Quarterly,* 8 (1980), 244.

17. See Erwin Panofsky, *Meaning in the Visual Arts* (Garden City: Doubleday, 1955), pp. 26–54. Panofsky, *Studies in Iconology* (1939; rpt. New York: Harper and Row, 1962), pp. 3–31. Panofsky developed iconographic criticism as a technique for unravelling the multiple layers of meaning in Renaissance art works. The method is equally revealing, however, when applied to other visual forms, particularly film. Panofsky details a three step process for the criticism of visual phenomena: pre-iconographical description, iconographical analysis, and iconological interpretation. It is this method of analysis, with minor modifications, which I employ in this essay.

Pre-iconographical description involves the recognition and identification of "pure *forms,* that is: certain configurations of line and colour, or certain peculiarly shaped lumps of bronze or stone, as representatives of natural *objects.* . . . The world of pure *forms* thus recognized as carriers of *primary* or *natural meanings* may be called the world of artistic *motifs.* An enumeration of these motifs would be pre-iconographical description of the work of art." (*Studies in Iconology,* p. 5).

Iconographical analysis, the second step in the process, involves the connection of the "artistic *motifs* and combinations of artistic motifs . . . with *themes* or *concepts*" (*Studies in Iconology,* p. 6). In *Hiroshima, Mon Amour,* for example, hands function as a motif. But it is not until the viewer connects the hand motif with the idea of the German's death that the movement from description to analysis takes place. Iconography is, therefore, nothing more nor less than "a description and classification of images . . . which informs us as to when and where specific themes were visualized by which specific motifs." (*Meaning in the Visual Arts,* p. 31). Pre-iconographic description and iconographic analysis are preparatory for the third step: iconological interpretation.

Iconological interpretation reveals the "intrinsic meaning" of the artifact under study. One is in the realm of iconology, says Panofsky, "whenever iconography is taken out of its isolation and integrated with whatever other method, historical, psychological or critical, we may attempt to use in solving the riddle of the sphinx." Iconology is iconography "turned interpretive," arising from "synthesis rather than analysis." (*Meaning in the Visual Arts,* p. 32). I shall show, in the pages to follow, how this third level of Panofsky's method—the iconological—is actually part of the *rhetoric* of visual forms. The critical movement, therefore, is not from iconography to iconology, but from iconography to rhetoric.

18. Panofsky, *Studies in Iconology,* p. 7. The "intrinsic meaning" or iconology of an art form arises from the correct description and analysis of the visual forms and motifs by which it is comprised. Panofsky, himself, recognized that the combination of motifs with generalized themes or concepts corresponded to what "the ancient theorists of art called *'invenzioni.'* " (*Studies in Iconology,* p. 6). The connection which Panofsky failed to make, however, was that between the theories of visual forms and those of oral persuasion, between iconology and rhetoric.

It is the iconographic forms and the iconological content that visual rhetors—filmmakers, painters, cartoonists—use to construct appeals to the viewing audience. Working within a particular medium, the artist first discovers the available means of persuasion or communication then shapes those means by the conscious application of tools and principles peculiar to that medium. For Panofsky's iconology to function as the overarching interpretive scheme he wishes it to be, it must necessarily transcend invented content to encompass the related arts of disposition and stylization; that is, it must make the move from iconography to rhetoric.

For recent attempts to explicate the rhetorical dimensions of visual forms see Martin J. Medhurst and Michael A. DeSousa, "Political Cartoons as Rhetorical Form: A Taxonomy of Graphic Discourse," *Communication Monographs,* 48 (1981), 197–236; Michael A. DeSousa and Martin J. Medhurst, "Political Cartoons and American Culture: Significant Symbols of Campaign 1980," *Studies in Visual Communication,* 8 (Winter 1982), 84–97; Martin J. Medhurst and Thomas W. Benson, *The City:* The Rhetoric of Rhythm," *Communication Monographs,* 48 (1981), 54–72; Thomas W. Benson, "The Rhetorical Structure of Frederick Wiseman's *High School,"* *Communication Monographs,* 47 (1980), 233–261.

19. Armes, *The Cinema of Alain Resnais,* p. 87.

20. James Monaco, *Alain Resnais* (New York: Oxford University Press, 1979), p. 34.

21. Following the example of Edward P. J. Corbett, "The Rhetoric of the Open Hand and the Rhetoric of the Closed Fist," in Douglas Ehninger, ed., *Contemporary Rhetoric: A Reader's Coursebook* (Glenview: Scott, Foresman & Co., 1972), pp. 202–210, I have reversed the descriptions of logic and rhetoric provided by Zeno for the purpose of making a "rhetorical" point.

22. This is just one of many lies uttered by the French woman. In addition to the name of a town, "Nevers" is a variety of tulip. It is perhaps significant that following the bombing Hiroshima was "carpeted with flowers."

23. Wolfgang A. Luchting, " 'Hiroshima, Mon Amour,' Time, and Proust," *Journal of Aesthetics and Art Criticism,* 21 (1962–63), 308. See also Michalczyk, "Alain Resnais: Literary Origins from *Hiroshima* to *Providence,"* pp. 16–25.

24. Peter Cowie, *Antonioni, Bergman, Resnais* (New York: Barnes and Co., 1963), p. 142.

25. Alan Stanbrook, "The Time and Space of Alain Resnais," p. 35. The critical opinion concerning Resnais' position vis-a-vis *auteur* theory is mixed. Roy Armes, one of Resnais' best interpreters, correctly points out that "in the sense in which the term author *(auteur)* has come to be used in French film criticism—to denote a

complete creator as opposed to a 'mere' director—it is clear that it cannot mean-ingfully be applied to Resnais. He is, in terms of this distinction, a director *(met-teur en scène)* and recognises himself as such." *The Cinema of Alain Resnais,* p. 9. Such a distinction becomes quite pernicious, however, when a film historian such as Parker Tyler uses it to conclude that "Resnais has no personality of his own" or when Geoffrey Nowell-Smith asserts that Resnais is "a scrupulous interpreter rather than an original creator." See Tyler, *Classics of the Foreign Film: A Pic-torial Treasury* (New York: The Citadel Press, 1962), p. 222; Nowell-Smith, "Alain Resnais," *New Left Review,* No. 27 (Sept.–Oct. 1964), 86. All depends, of course, on precisely what one means by a creator. If it is true, as John Francis Kreidl claims, that "none of Resnais' films retains even half the intent of the original screenplay," but exists solely "to provide a basis for Resnais' work," then perhaps *auteur* theorists would do well to rethink their definitions. See Kreidl, *Alain Res-nais* (Boston: Twayne Publishers, 1977), preface. My own position concerning Resnais' authorial "status" is succinctly expressed by Richard Roud when he says that "in spite of the contributions of Duras, Robbe-Grillet, etc., Resnais is still very much the *author* of his films." See Roud, "Alain Resnais," in Richard Roud, ed., *Cinema: A Critical Dictionary,* 2 (New York: The Viking Press, 1980), p. 860.

26. I use the term "intellectual montage" in the same sense I understand Sergei Ei-senstein to have used it. Eisenstein wrote that intellectual montage "is montage not of generally physiological overtonal sounds, but of sounds and overtones of an in-tellectual sort: i.e., conflict-juxtaposition of accompanying intellectual affects." Ei-senstein developed this category of montage, it seems, from Lenin's synopsis of the elements of Hegelian dialectics. Eisenstein cites five points from Lenin's synopsis, the first three of which are: "1) an endless process of revealing *new* aspects, re-lationships, etc.; 2) an endless process of deepening human perception of things, appearances, processes and so on, from appearance to essence and from the less profound to the more profound essence; 3) from co-existence to causality and from one form of connection and interdependence to another, deeper, more general." See Sergei Eisenstein, *Film Form: Essays in Film Theory,* ed., trans. Jay Leyda (New York: Harcourt, Brace and Company, 1949). pp. 82, 81. This description of intel-lectual montage seems to conform in all essentials with Resnais' cinematic tech-nique in *Hiroshima, Mon Amour.* The film is literally an endless process of revealing relationships both within and among the protagonists and of deepening both their and the audiences' perceptual abilities. Resnais invites the audience to juxtapose conflicting interpretations of the motifs, motives, and memories of the characters to reveal causative factors and thus clarify interrelationships. The idea which emerges from the clash of the varying perspectives is a general sentiment about human modes of knowing and the artist's role in helping to foster (or retard) that knowing. Perhaps it was this ability to exemplify, so completely, Hegelian prin-ciples which led Jean Collet to conclude that *Hiroshima, Mon Amour* was the first Marxist film, the first materialist film and the first film devoid of any spiritual implications. See Jean Collet, "Hiroshima san amour," *Téléciné,* Fiche 362, pp. 12–13.

27. Kreidl, preface.

28. Luchting, " 'Hiroshima, Mon Amour,' Time, and Proust," p. 301. See also Rene Prédal, "Alain Resnais," *études cinématographiques,* 64–68 (1968), 120–144; Catherine Duncan, [Review of *Hiroshima, Mon Amour*], *Film Journal* (Aus-tralia), 15 (1960), 54–55; Alan Stanbrook, "The Time and Space of Alain Res-nais," 35–38.

29. Frederick Joseph Sweet, "Narrative In The Films of Alain Resnais and Contem-porary Fiction," Diss., University of Michigan, 1973, p. 7.

30. These are just the tip of one iceberg in a sea full of dialectical icebergs that lurk just beneath the surface of the film. As Michel Delahaye observes: "One can say not only that each moment in a Resnais film is the consequence or indication of another moment, but also that each moment, each film 'is' another moment, another Resnais film, just as inevitably as Nevers 'is' Hiroshima and as the Japanese is the German, as sweetness is cruelty; memory, amnesia; silence, screaming; the individual, society; preservation, destruction; movement, stillness; document, fake; the cinema, literature. . . ." Delahaye quoted in Cowie, pp. 154–55.

31. For insights into the use of the soundtrack as a counterpoint to the visual imagery see Henri Colpi, "Musique D'Hiroshima," *Cahiers du Cinema,* 18 (1960), 1–14; René Predal, "Alain Resnais," 64–68 (1968), 29–42; Henri Colpi, "Editing *Hiroshima, Mon Amour*," *Sight and Sound,* 29 (1959–60), 14–16.

32. For a theoretical discussion of how art creates knowledge see Susanne K. Langer, *Feeling and Form* (New York: Charles Scribner's Sons, 1953).

33. Linda Williams, "*Hiroshima and Marienbad:* Metaphor and Metonomy," *Screen,* 17 (1976), 35.

34. The tension between memory and forgetfulness runs throughout Resnais' *oeuvre.* As John Ward points out: "Resnais contemplates the difficulties of living in time, with the past hovering over us when we want to forget and receding into the shadows when we need to remember." See *Alain Resnais, or the Theme of Time,* p. 14. Or, expressed in a slightly different way, "one of Resnais' *universalia*" is "that forgetting is as necessary as living—which, among other things, consists precisely of experiences that seem unforgettable." See Luchting, " 'Hiroshima, Mon Amour,' Time and Proust," p. 304.

35. Monaco, p. 37.

36. For a theoretical explanation of the interrelationships between film and lying see Kari Hanet, "Does the Camera Lie?: Notes on *Hiroshima Mon Amour*," *Screen,* 14 (1973), 59–66.

3
Rhetoric of Radio

When Guglielmo Marconi arrived in England with his little black box in 1896 neither he nor his British hosts suspected that "wireless" would soon become the basis for a multi-million dollar business, a means of communication with a mass audience, or a powerful means of political persuasion. But it became all of these things and more. Radio was used for propaganda purposes in World War I, became an instrument for communication with a mass audience in 1920, and was being used by educational, religious, and political persuaders by 1925. The primary means of persuasion was, of course, the human voice—disembodied, authoritative, personal.

Unlike the radio of today which is composed primarily of music, news, and an occasional talk show, broadcasting in the golden age of radio, roughly 1928 to 1946, consisted of comedy, variety, drama, religious and political harangues, educational debates, news, discussions, and, during certain periods, outright propaganda. Radio was for the second quarter of the twentieth century what television has been for the third: the primary means of entertainment, enlightenment, and instruction for the mass audience. As such, its role as inculcator of values, inspirer of ideas, and influencer of attitudes, beliefs, and opinions was substantial. The essays by J. Fred MacDonald and Gary Saul Morson explore the persuasive potential of the radio medium by examining two of the most influential programs of all time: *Treasury Star Parade* and the *Mercury Theatre on the Air* production of "The War of the Worlds."

MacDonald focuses on rhetoric as propaganda; as the intentional use of persuasive tactics to arouse and move a mass audience. He takes as his case study one of the most widely-aired programs of World War II, *Treasury Star Parade*. Using recordings of the actual broadcasts, MacDonald identifies six propaganda techniques employed by the writers and producers of the program. In so doing, he raises some substantial questions about rhetorical theory, practice, and criticism. What, for example, is the proper role of government persuaders during times of national crisis? MacDonald seems to argue that blatant persuasive attempts by government officials, even during times of war, are dangerous and perhaps unethical. He seems to assume that standards for rhetorical persuasion are more or less independent of situations and that certain techniques may be inherently destructive of human capacity for rational decisionmaking; that is, that certain persuasive techniques may be anti-rhetorical if by rhetoric we mean a cultural ideal reflecting a commitment to shared decisionmaking, rational discussion of available options, and freedom to refuse assent. Upon what grounds does MacDonald warrant his stance? Does the author imply different standards of rhetorical behavior for public agencies than for private ones? If so, what reasons does the author give for maintaining this distinction?

MacDonald identifies six elements in the persuasive strategy of *Treasury Star Parade:* appeal to basic American values, appeal for domestic unity, intimidation by direct threat, the enemy as demonic, the nobility of the Allies, and uplift through entertainment. Are these elements inherently propagandistic regardless of medium or situation? Are there any situations in which some or all of these tactics could be used in conformity with the notion of rhetoric as a cultural ideal? Take, for example, intimidation by direct threat. Often we think of intimidation more in terms of coercion than of persuasion; we believe it to be anti-rhetorical. But is this necessarily so? And what is the role and responsibility of the listener in all of this? One differing perspective is provided by Morson.

In his critique of the H. G. Wells novel and the Orson Welles radio production of "The War of the Worlds," Morson shows how direct intimidation both within the work of art (Martians attacking the Earth) and between the artist and his audience (Orson Welles intentionally provoking fear and panic) functions to promote an ideal vision of social relations. Here an anti-rhetorical means or technique seems to be used to secure an end that is compatible with the notion of a rhetorical culture: one which realizes its limited vision, seeks for human unity, and guards against nationalistic hubris and racial superiority. If a technique such as direct intimidation is not an inherently anti-rhetorical or unethical tactic, then the question can be seen as one of ends versus means. Rhetoric, as both MacDonald and Morson realize, involves both.

Persuaders, whether governments or playwrights, have purposes and intentions—goals they wish to accomplish. They also have means, rhetorical and non-rhetorical, artistic and inartistic, for achieving these goals. Rhetorical theorists and critics seek to describe, interpret, and evaluate how the means do, in fact, relate to the ends in any given persuasive effort and in the world of rhetoric at large.

The role of the audience in both criticism and theory building is central to the rhetorician's task. Morson asserts that the "lesson" of "The War of the Worlds" broadcast is that we must become more responsible listeners. MacDonald, on the other hand, appears to be saying that the way to secure responsible listeners is to insist on responsible speakers. But can one judge either speakers or listeners apart from the historical and communicative context within which persuasion occurs? Both Morson and MacDonald note that the historical context affected the way listeners heard and responded to the broadcasts under study. And Morson points specifically to the communicative context of radio and the use of "defamiliarized frame markers" as a factor in audience interpretation and influence. If the medium, itself, has characteristics that affect listener response, then these, too, must become part of the rhetorical situation which the critic seeks to explain and interpret.

Morson shows quite clearly that the novel by Wells and the radio production by Orson Welles, though quite similar in content, were much different in effect because of the limitations of the particular medium of expression. It is Morson's belief that the use of radio and the specific effect achieved by "The War of the Worlds" broadcast was an intentional ploy specifically designed by Orson Welles to deliver a political warning. But what if it was not? What if Welles was truly as surprised by the event as everyone else? Is Morson's critique any less valid? Does the playwright's or radio producer's intention necessarily structure audience response? What is the critic's main interest: uncovering authorial intent or accounting for persuasive effect?

Government Propaganda In
Commercial Radio—
The Case of *Treasury Star Parade, 1942–1943*

J. Fred MacDonald

The boundary between federal regulation and federal manipulation of broadcasting has been strongly delineated in the United States. Recognizing its function to represent public interest without stifling private initiative, government has generally refrained from manipulating the persuasive potential of broadcasting systems. Such a condition has resulted in part because of the laws of the nation. It has also resulted from the fact that broadcasters, themselves, have traditionally supported the general values, directions, and institutions of American society.

In a certain sense all broadcasting is filled with material supportive of the governmental system. Because of the commercial nature of American mass culture, it is necessary for the competitive media to appeal to customers by reflecting, espousing, and defining attitudes and sensitivities that are popularly shared. In this way the content of American broadcasting propagates interpretations helpful to a bourgeois society with a liberal-democratic political, social, and economic system. Whether it is formulaic sitcom or innovative science fiction, the protection of private property, the rightness of the cause, the individuality of the hero, and the justness of the resolution are anticipated and usually predictable.

Yet, when the federal government oversteps this boundary and becomes actively involved in the production of patently propagandistic media fare, the significance of broadcasting and its persuasive qualities needs deeper consideration. Nowhere was this truer than in the case of the wartime radio series, *Treasury Star Parade,* a flagrantly-propagandistic program that was sponsored by the Department of the Treasury during 1942 and 1943. Ostensibly designed to persuade listeners to puchase government War Bonds, the series also sold World War II to a citizenry which had been isolationist at least until Pearl Harbor.

From its beginnings, *Treasury Star Parade* was a carefully-manufactured, quality series. The Radio Section of the Treasury Department Defense Savings Staff was the government agency which coordinated the series. The first and longest-lasting producer of the program, however, was William A. Bacher, an experienced radio writer-producer whose credits included two successful variety series, Maxwell House *Show Boat* and Campbell's *Hollywood Hotel.*

Reprinted from the *Journal of Popular Culture,* Volume 12.2, 1979, with permission of The Popular Press, Bowling Green, OH.

William A. Bacher was the first producer of *Treasury Star Parade.*

The entertainment industry co-operated, providing the biggest names in show business. From motion pictures (e.g., Bette Davis, Edward G. Robinson, Walter Pidgeon), the legitimate stage (Alfred Lunt, Lynn Fontaine, Judith Anderson, Maurice Evans), Broadway musicals (Alfred Drake, Todd Duncan), radio (Fibber McGee and Molly, Gertrude Berg, Eddie "Rochester" Anderson, Amos and Andy), popular music (Paul Whiteman, Dinah Shore, Perry Como, Tommy Dorsey), and classical music and opera (Igor Gorin, Kenneth Spenser) came the outstanding talents who appeared in over 300 fifteen-minute shows during the life of the series.

Treasury Star Parade featured stirring original plays by writers such as Norman Rosten, Violet Atkins, and Joseph Ruscoll, as well as adaptations from the works of Stephen Vincent Benet, John Steinbeck, Alice Duer Miller, and Thomas Mann. It drew from newspaper and magazine articles, as well as poetry, classical music, motion pictures, and the popular and patriotic music of the day. According to Henry Morgenthau, Jr., the Secretary of the Treasury, such artistic quality was intentional. His goal was to make the entertainment and the entire program so good, people would become "as fond of War Bonds as they are of Coca-Cola or Lucky Strikes."[1]

Although no direct relationship between the broadcasts and the successful sale of War Bonds can be substantiated, *Treasury Star Parade* was well received. In May, 1942, it was cited by the Women's Press Club of New York

City as one of the "outstanding radio programs" on wartime radio. That same year Farrar & Rinehart published an anthology of twenty-seven plays from the series. Perhaps the most fitting appraisal came from John D. Hutchens, radio critic for *The New York Times,* who lauded "the intelligence, skill and fervor that have gone into" the series. Terming the program "one of the brighter chapters in American radio history," Hutchens commended *Treasury Star Parade* for being "just about the best of all those domestic wartime programs whose task it is to awaken, convince, entertain, and not incidentally, to sell war bonds and stamps."[2]

This was not the only radio program produced for the Treasury Department in order to sell War Bonds.[3] Since May 1, 1941, when the first United States Defense Bonds and Stamps were placed on sale, the federal government utilized commercial radio to spur sales. In the months before Pearl Harbor, programs like *Millions for Defense* (an NBC network series), *America Preferred,* and *For America We Sing,* as well as innumerable spot announcements, raised public consciousness about bonds. During the war, War Bonds (née Defense Bonds) were peddled on features such as *Treasury Song for Today, Over Here, Music for Millions, Treasury Salute, Treasury Bondwagon,* and the limited dramatic series produced in conjunction with the fifth war loan drive, *Four for the Fifth.* In all cases, the performers donated their energies and talents; electrical transcriptions of the programs were distributed without charge to any American radio station requesting them; playtime was donated by those stations airing the shows; and the undated shows were broadcast whenever, and as often as, the participating outlets desired. And these programs reached a wide audience. At its height, for example, over 830 stations carried *Treasury Star Parade,* making it one of the most widely-heard programs in wartime radio.

Above all, the program was a propagandistic triumph which blended patriotism, dire warning, entertainment, and technical artistry in an emotional melange reflective of the urgency of the time. The principal goal of the series was clear: to compel or persuade Americans to sacrifice spare cash by loaning it to the war effort through the purchase of bonds. To accomplish this, the series utilized several methods of approach. In analyzing these methods, it becomes clear that in *Treasury Star Parade* the federal government more blatantly than ever in its history manipulated a supposedly-free and responsible mass medium, commercial radio, in order to disseminate the message it wanted. Specifically, in six distinct approaches *Treasury Star Parade* demonstrated itself as a powerful instrument of domestic mass propaganda.

I. Appeal to Basic American Values

The overriding theme of the programs was that this was a democratic nation waging a just war through its unified army of free and equal commoners. It was a battle being fought at home and abroad by legions of average people, little people, of the plain folk who constituted the United States. Edward G.

Edward G. Robinson appeared as "Joe Doakes" in two *Treasury Star Parade* broadcasts in 1942.

Robinson, portraying cab driver Joe Doakes in "Joe Doakes and the White Star" (#60), suggested this mentality when he audaciously picked up the telephone and demanded to talk to the Japanese leader.

> Hello, Tokyo, ah, let me talk to Hirohito. Yeah, the Emperor. What do you mean he don't talk to nobody? How does he order a short beer? OK, OK, comb the rice outta your hair, will ya, and let me talk to premier Tojo. Well, then, oh nuts! Just let me talk to Japan. Hmmm? This is Joe Doakes over in the USA talkin'. . . . You know, Joe the butcher, the baker, the barkeep, the bricklayer. Joe the busboy, Joe on the subway, Joe on the prairies, on the merry-go-round, Joe on a half-a-pound of sugar a week. Joe in Kansas, ah, Joe in the bleachers, Joe in Macy's basement, Joe in a jeep. Can ya hear me?

This sense of nobility-among-the-commoners was painted most romantically in "The Second Battle of Brooklyn" (#94) when one character declared,

> And, like I said, all the little people of the world was in that battle. The Collinses and the Kellys, and the Smiths and the Joneses—Joe Doakes and George Feldon—all the gentle, beautiful, little people—This is a "little guys" war, Eddie. Hitler ain't fightin' kings and queens no more. . . . We're the only ones that can win it, Eddie. Only us—the little people, all dressed up in our haloes and gas masks.

This army of "little guys," in the interpretation of the series, reflected a nation that was homogenous despite its multi-ethnic background. Some shows dealt with specific racial or religious groups—such as the Broadway cast of *Porgy and Bess* (#33) and the skit enacted by the radio cast of *The Goldbergs* (#86). Usually, however, the appeal was made to as wide an audience as possible. In the musical production, "Hands" (#26), baritone Blair McKlusky and a chorus touched several groups.

MCKLUSKEY: Native born, alien, Negro and White. . .
Shoulder to shoulder in an all-out fight.
CHORUS: Protestants, Catholics, Quakers, and Jews. . .
With everything to gain and everything to lose. . .
It's all for one, and one for all. . .
United we stand, and divided we fall. . .
Men working together. . . .

Even more dramatically, inter-ethnic unity was the message delivered by Fredric March in his fictional conversation with the Nazi propagandist, Dr. Joseph Goebbels, and a chorus of average Americans, in "A Report on the State of the Nation" (#16).

CHORUS: We're the Swedes from Minnesota, the Irish from Manhattan, the French from Louisiana, the Germans from Wisconsin. We are the Spaniards from California, the Armenians down in Fresno, the Indians in Nevada, the Poles in old Chicago! Czechs and Syrians, Greeks and Russians. . . .
MARCH: This is a nation of many nations, a race of many races, singing the full, the goodly song.
GOEBBELS: (in Germanic accent) Wait!
CHORUS: What was that?
MARCH: That was the voice of Joseph Goebbels, Hitler's Minister of Propaganda!
CHORUS: What's he saying?
MARCH: He says nothing will be easier than to produce bloody revolution in North America. No other country has so many social and racial tensions. We shall be able to play on many strings there.
CHORUS: (whispering) Can they do it?
MARCH: I don't know—you are the people. What's the answer?
CHORUS: (shouting) No!
MARCH: They think that because we're the conglomerate nation, enriched with the bloods of all the races, that we are easy to trap and snare. But they forgot that out of this fusion of many races has come this one united nation of men, not slaves—American!

This unity even infected American street gangs, according to the rousing broadcast, "Education for Life" (#36). Here a street punk patriotically announced,

I'm no Boy Scout, but I've got a job, too! I rounded up all the gangs in my neighborhood—Italians, Negroes, Jews, Swedes—everybody! And they're plenty tough. But I told 'em we got no time for private fights now! No use kiddin' ourselves—we gotta win this war!

Another social value openly exploited by *Treasury Star Parade* was the Judeo-Christian religious foundation of the American nation. As Fredric March termed it when speaking Thomas Mann's words in "A Christmas Letter to the German People" (#19), the war was "a struggle of the great Christian peoples of the world." In "Education for Death" (#29), narrator Henry Hull concisely contrasted American children with those educated in the enemy Nazi state.

HULL: Our children believe in prayer—in the *Bible,* in God!
GERMAN: God is an outworn myth. Our Bible is *Mein Kampf.* Our God is Hitler!

The quest for religious freedom present in the earliest settlers of the New World was worked into the script of "A Report on the State of the Nation" (#16): "They came to the waiting land, bringing with them faith, and industry, and belief." This was also the essence of the prayer of the first Pilgrim kneeling on American soil in "American Design" (#289).

We thank Thee, O Lord God of Hosts. We thank Thee for that Thou art brought us safely across the watery kingdom of Leviathan. And beached us on this New World, with a new life and a new freedom to be ours to make (CHORUS: Amen, Amen).

Given the state of the world in 1942, the appeal to the religious faith was poignant when a Russian slave laborer in Nazi Germany begged God to smash the dams and flood the Ruhr valley in "The Earth Shall Be Sweet Again" (#290).

Dear God, punish these transgressors. I don't ask you to save Andrusia or myself. Perhaps it is too late for us. But for the sake of all our mothers and sons, for the sake of all those whom the Nazis would enslave, place Your Almighty Hand heavily upon them. Open up the flood gates of Your Wrath. Give us the earth clean again, Dear God, Dear God.

It was also effective in the Dutch mother's prayerful grace uttered over her last family dinner before Nazi invaders took power (#94).

Our Dear Father in Heaven, bless this food that is before us. We thank Thee for it. And bless this our house. Give us wisdom and hope through this long night. Bless our soldiers at the front. Bless our flag. Bless our freedom. Amen.

The most compelling merger of religious values and the war was "The Price of Free World Victory" (#79), a dramatization of a speech by Vice-President Henry A. Wallace. As narrated by Vincent Price, the program boldly asserted such messages as 1) "the idea of freedom is based upon the *Bible,* with its extraordinary emphasis upon the dignity of the individual," 2) "Democracy is the only true political expression of Christianity, but that which was sensed by the prophets many centuries before Christ was not given complete and powerful political expression until our nation was formed as a federal union a century and a half ago," and 3) "The people's revolution is on the march! And the Devil and all his angels cannot prevail against it. They cannot prevail for on the side of the people is the Lord." The playlet ended with a chorus and full orchestra playing "Onward, Christian Soldiers," while Price declared,

> He giveth power to the faint. To them that have no might, He increaseth strength. They that wait upon the Lord shall mount up with wings as eagles. They shall run and not be weary. They shall walk and not be faint.
> Strong in the strength of the Lord. We who fight in the people's cause will not stop until that cause is won.

The successful propagandist knows that rather than create new concepts, the most potent avenue of communication lies in the manipulation of pre-existing principles and beliefs. Thus, the writers, actors, and musicians of *Treasury Star Parade* exploited the values and dispositions that were accepted by most Americans. The death of the member of a loving family—be it by enemy bombardment or by an emotionless Nazi's pistol—was a powerful disruption of idealized family feelings. Portraying the Japanese invaders of China as rapists as well as murderers of innocent school girls in "A Lesson in Japanese" (#53) was antithetical to the concept of the sanctity of human life and dignity, as well as being repugnant to the sense of chivalrous concern for the protection of women and children. Political concepts like freedom, liberty, democracy, and equality were consistently used to paint the enemy in black and the American in white terms. This was most obvious when actress Florence Eldridge read "Freedom" (#8), a poem by a twelve-year old girl from Kentucky. With the orchestra playing "America" softly in the background, Eldridge confidently concluded, "Freedom—it's you!"

The writers of *Treasury Star Parade* often utilized social activities as metaphors in making their emotional points. Sports was handled occasionally in this manner. In "The Second Battle of Brooklyn" (#94) the heroine scolded her boyfriend by likening the world war to the World Series:

> Eddie, it's goin' to be the biggest World Series we ever seen. And we gotta win this second battle of Brooklyn, even if we gotta drag old Daffy Vance outta the bullpen. . . . This ain't for peanuts and a hot frank out in the bleachers, Eddie. This is for all or nothin'. This is for our life, liberty, and the pursuit of happiness. This is for democracy. This is so the meek, the little people, can inherit the earth.

In a group of programs dedicated to college football fight songs (#284–286), narrator Jimmy Wallington spoke about the war exploits of former college football stars in terms of the gridiron. In this manner, he admonished the Japanese that getting Lt. Woody Adams of Texas Christian University "shoved into the lineup against them is just one of the penalties on the Japs for clipping at Pearl Harbor—not only an all-conference tackle, but a Marine: double trouble!" And of Capt. Clint Frank, an all-American halfback at Yale in 1938, he noted that in "the African arena" Frank "played a good game in taking the ball away from the enemy on downs, and now the home team is out to do some fancy rushing and razzle-dazzle." The tragedy of wartime death was also part of the sports metaphors used in the *Treasury Star Parade.* Wallington morosely saluted a former University of Washington halfback who had been killed in action in the Pacific: "Well done, Fritz Waskowitz, well done. We'll all talk it over in the Great Locker Room one of these days." More believable, however, was his lament for the loss of Nile Kinnick who had crashed at sea in mid-1943: With "Auld Lang Syne" in the background, he said of the former All-American at the University of Iowa:

> Student, athlete, leader, Phi Beta Kappa—the perfect American, the ideal of Americans. . . . They won't be seeing Nile around old Iowa anymore. Sing, sons of Iowa, for a college comrade, and for an ideal that did not die in the deep waters with him. Bury your heads and bury your hearts. And stand while old number 24 trots off the field, because you won't be seeing him anymore.

In appealing to basic national values, this governmental series often directed its pitch at specific social and economic groups with their own particular attitudes. Women were the target of those shows which lauded historical and contemproary contributions by women to America. Heroines from the past such as Molly Pitcher (#97), and Mary Dwyer (#15) appeared with present-day women called upon to make heroic sacrifices, whether it be a mother saying "Good-bye" to her son entering the military (#61), a woman donating her time to help raise money for bonds (#270), or a generalized salute to the women of America "who march shoulder-to-shoulder with their men" (#23). Other shows spoke to children who, despite their lack of financial independence, were still urged to play a role in the war by buying less-expensive savings stamps or by collecting scrap metal, rubber, and fats. Youthful radio characters such as Henry Aldrich and Maudie Mason, the heroine of *Maudie's Diary,* also appeared in dramas illustrating the ways in which youngsters could aid the war effort.

Among the various economic groups that were targets of the series, farmers were strategic. They were shown their importance, as "America's first duty is to produce food" was the theme of Fredric March's dramatization of "The Average American" (#11). Laborers and factory workers were also urged to greater output—a "guerrilla production program"—in a broadcast where the announcer concluded, "Let's get to peak production; we've got to keep our factories running twenty-four hours a day if we're going to win this war!" (#10). *Treasury Star Parade* also offered special salutes to taxi drivers (#67), RFD mailmen (#63), and the merchant marines (#257).

II. Appeal for Domestic Unity

While the overwhelming majority of Americans sympathized with the anti-Fascist side of the war, until December 7, 1941, most citizens were strongly opposed to intervention. Despite momentary emotionalism, after the American entry there was no guarantee that internal dissension would not reappear and threaten the co-ordination of military efforts overseas and supportive activities at home. It was therefore important to the war that domestic unity be forged and maintained. *Treasury Star Parade* helped to meet that need.

Apathetics, slackers, and grumblers were regularly assailed. To the man, woman or child who felt there was little to contribute, there were many shows offering constructive information. It might be a 12-year-old son nagging his indifferent parents about their wartime responsibilities in "Tommy Tucker, Patriot" (#39); in another skit it might be Robert Montgomery portraying a truck driver whose inconsiderate speeding wasted that one gallon of gasoline which might have saved the two American flyers whose plane ran out of fuel and crashed seven miles short of their base. Singers as disparate as Carmen Miranda, the Almanac Singers, and Gladys Swarthout performed songs treating all aspects of the war. And in case a listener became too engrossed with artistry and forgot the intention of the broadcast, statements made throughout the shows—"It's your country, keep it yours"; "Find your job! Do it! And then do a little bit more"; "Buy United States Savings Bonds and Stamps, that is one of the true patriot's jobs today"—were brusque reminders of the serious purpose of the series.

Of particular interest to the program was the problem of dealing with dissenters. National leaders were lionized. As well as portraying Franklin D. Roosevelt as "that strong, gentle, humane man in the White House who watches over us" (#36), *Treasury Star Parade* suggested that governmental and military leaders were carrying "the greatest load on their shoulders since Christ started up the slope of Calvary" (#10). But people who scoffed at the war were not tolerated. In "It Isn't Peanuts," Edward G. Robinson returned as Joe Doakes to chide two pretentious women critical of federal policies and leaders.

> I don't say you shouldn't criticize. You should—we all should, we're Americans. Only, ladies, be sure you're not repeatin' things and sayin' things that the enemy wants you to say and is spreadin' around—things to make us distrust each other and the men who're workin' for us. Gee, because if that thing starts happenin', why—look, did you ever hear that expression they use, "divide and conquer?"

Closer to the expressed purpose of the *Treasury Star Parade,* cynicism about the sale of War Bonds was directly confronted by Lionel Barrymore playing a stingy, self-interested character, in "A Modern Scrooge" (#52). After a night of apparitions, including one in which his soldier-nephew urgently pleaded for more bullets—"Hurry, for God's sake, hurry!"—he had a change of heart, bought $500 worth of Bonds, sent his nephew a package of gloves and socks, and then became an air raid warden.

156

The goal of such rhetoric was at once persuasive and confirmative. Those who doubted or were uninformed found in these programs enough information, emotional and rational, with which to decide. Those already committed to the war effort on the homefront found in the broadcasts enough justification to rededicate their time, energy, and money.

More than a sales vehicle for War Bonds, however, *Treasury Star Parade* was selling the American military commitment. This was strikingly clear in "The Awakening of Johnny Castle" (#57), the story of a conscientious objector. As narrated by Charles Coburn, listeners heard Johnny's naive sincerity in maintaining "I haven't got anything against anybody—even Hitler." He was fired from his job, ridiculed by his soldier-brother—called by the latter a "crackpot," "slacker," "wise guy," and "screwball"—and rebuked by his wife—now called "jellyfish," and "worm." Johnny's father rejected him with the statement, "son, I'm ashamed of you." And a colonel at the draft board blasted him, saying "Thank goodness there's not many like you, or Lord help the U.S.A.!" Amazingly, Johnny was converted only after a bad dream showed him the perfidity of the enemy. After a quick morning trip to the draft board, Johnny insisted that he be assigned to the front lines where he could "shoot those black-hearted cutthroats."

III. Intimidation by Direct Threat

While *Treasury Star Parade* relied principally upon implorations to sacrifice and projections of positive role models, the series often resorted to threatening statements and overtly intimidating images. Horrendous views of the United States after a Nazi victory, statements about the global consequences of defeat, descriptions of the "Nazi Revolution" in action—all proferred overwhelming examples of the enemies' hideous direct threat to American freedom.

Radio dramatist Arch Oboler, whose *Lights Out!* series had raised the level of radio drama since the mid-1930s, heightened the intensity of *Treasury Star Parade* when his "Chicago, Germany" (#59) was produced in the Spring of 1942. Oboler was an advocate of a more strident style of radio propaganda for, as he told a radio conference that same season, American broadcasting needed "an injection of hatred and passionate feeling."[4] His play for the Treasury Department envisioned Chicago after its occupation by German conquerors in 1944. Starring Joan Blondell, the program watched the disintegration of a family—one sister turned to prostitution to support the family, a boyfriend never heard from again, a second sister relegated to slave-labor at a local office—and it predicted mass murder, starvation, the forced Germanization of the city, the institution of racial laws, and the creation of slave-labor camps. The threat was enunciated in poignant fashion when Blondell, with a German officer's voice off-mike categorized the annihilation of the American way of life.

Joan Blondell gave a remarkable performance in Arch Oboler's
emotional piece, "Chicago, Germany."

BLONDELL: What is there in life for somebody "just plain ordinary" like me?
To marry someone you love.
OFFICER: Verboten!
BLONDELL: To have children.
OFFICER: Verboten!
BLONDELL: To have a home.
OFFICER: Verboten!
BLONDELL: To walk in the park with your kids.
OFFICER: Verboten!
BLONDELL: To go shoppin' on pay day.
OFFICER: Verboten!
BLONDELL: If you haven't got the money, window shop.
OFFICER: Verboten!
BLONDELL: And see the children growin' up and goin' to school.
OFFICER: Verboten!
BLONDELL: And gettin' smarter than you, and they grow older, and you grow
older with the man you love—and just livin' like human beings. But now I'm not
a human being anymore. They said so. "Verboten"—everything "Verboten" for
me, for people like me who are just plain Americans! . . . This was their world—
they'd won—they'd won . . . there wasn't any place left in the world for us.

The threat in Oboler's story was underscored by the announcer's final statement: "This has been a play about an America that must never happen—that
will never happen—NEVER!!"

At the conclusion of each program, the various announcers usually made pointed appeals to urge listeners to purchase bonds. In these statements are found some of the most threatening language of the series. In one broadcast (#22), the narrator spoke bluntly: "Today, now, we are meeting the supreme test of whether democracy and the American way of life can survive, or deserve to survive. It's up to us." Listeners were warned in one show (#58) that wastage of vital materials was a threat to the entire war effort. "Blood in your tank!," remarked the announcer. "Remember that whenever you think about going out joyriding. Don't use any more gas than you have to." And another announcer (#62) summarized the issues at stake in the war.

> What we're fighting for is our right to live. Our right to have children and homes— our right to work and to laugh and play. What we're really fighting for is our inalienable right to be normal, happy human beings. . . . We must work, fight, and save—this is your country, keep it yours!

Conjuring up images of jackbooted conquerors and inhumane deprivation, one speaker concluded (#29),

> How would you feel if you had to step into the gutter to let the Nazis pass? How would you feel working sixty hours a week for thirty-hours pay? How would you feel watching your wife go hungry and your children faced with the prospect of a lifetime of slavery? NEVER—I can almost hear you say that—we must never let that happen in America!

In its portrayal of the Nazi system, *Treasury Star Parade* was relentlessly hostile. Many shows depicted life in occupied countries where brutality had replaced reason, where slavery had been substituted for human dignity. In "Education for Death" (#29), however, the program projected the threat that the German educational system was to the civilized world. Based on a book by an American educator who had taught in Berlin, the broadcast was a shattering indictment of a system educating its children in hatred, death, intolerance, and militarism. Here listeners encountered forceful sterilization of women, eugenics used to create a master race, state-raised children, the eradication of love, forced pregnancy for the betterment of State and Fuhrer, and chanting robot-like young Germans. As Henry Hull emotionally concluded, the threat to America was obvious. Hitler "is making fanatical monsters," said Hull, "we must make reasonable human beings." That this particular broadcast struck a responsive chord in the American audience was evidenced several weeks later when the series presented "Education for Life" (#36) as an American children's answer to the Hitlerian challenge.

The intimidating warnings in the propagandistic rhetoric of *Treasury Star Parade* were not always negative suggestions of the brutal reality of the Axis systems. Positive threats, challenges hurled at the enemy, could also be emotional persuaders. Thus, Paul Henreid, as a German-American patriot, warned the would-be conquerors in "Two Way Passage" (#56) that he was carrying back to the exploding Old World the tolerant, democratic principles of the New World. With "God Bless America" in the background, he rallied: "And we are coming back. Do you hear that over there, you liars, you gangsters, you traitors and murderers? WE ARE COMING BACK!!" In concluding remarks, the announcer augmented this threat.

> That is America's message to the world. The two-way passage—to take liberty and freedom again to all the oppressed, the downtrodden peoples of the earth. We have pledged ourselves to that task and we shall *not* fail.

In a more poetic fashion, the challenge to the world conquerors was levelled in "The Earth Shall Be Sweet Again" (#290).

> Beware, beware, oh enemy of mankind, for the time is coming when the whelming wrath of mankind shall break upon you in all its awful rage. We will have the earth sweet, the earth shall be sweet again.

And in religious tones, the positive threat was implicit when Conrad Veidt in "Return to Berchtesgaden" (#64)—with a choir and orchestra slowly rising in crescendo behind him—supplicated the Heavens,

> Suffer not, oh my Lord, that injustice triumph on earth. Permit not the unleashed hordes of the anti-Christ to corrupt nations, lay waste countries, dishonor women, destroy children. Suffer not violence to conquer so that men will be forced to put their faith in violence instead of love. Suffer not, oh Lord, that the Lie be stronger than the Truth! Though earth is not Heaven, it cannot be Thy Will that it be Hell. It cannot be Thy Will that all those who bear Thy Name shall be destroyed. For Thou art not only the Kingdom and the Glory, but the Power! Amen.

IV. The Enemy as Demonic

The image of the enemy contained in the *Treasury Star Parade* was bellicose. Although it seldom treated Mussolini or the Italian enemy, the series uncompromisingly attacked the Nazis and the Japanese for, as one character remarked (#276), "it ain't men we're fightin' with in this war, it's monsters." It is interesting, however, that in approaching these two enemies, the program differed significantly in its approach.

In viewing Germany, the *Treasury Star Parade* singled out the Nazi Party and its leaders for the brunt of its criticism. It showed the citizens of captured nations unmercifully handled by the victors, and it suggested that the average German citizen, himself, was a Nazi captive. Although the series directly attacked Nazi officials like Joseph Goebbels and Gestapo leader Heinrich Himmler, the preferred target for rebuke was Adolf Hitler. In one program (#64) he was seen as the repulsive blasphemer, screaming out that "There is no God! I am God. I will hound this God-lie to the ends of the earth and

160

destroy it!" Later, Hitler was heard screaming maniacally of religion, "I will erase it from the earth! I will burn every *Bible* and put away all preachers . . . until I wipe out religion and all its evils." In another broadcast (#51), his fiendish voice was heard describing his favorite type of "music."

The sweet hum of Heinkels. A roar of Messerschmitts. The Blasting of Stukas. The bombs screaming to earth. The pounding of great guns across the Channel. The bursting of shells. A moan of the stricken. The unbearable agony of the bereaved. And the silence of great cities when the flames have died and life is gone.

In those propagandistic broadcasts dramatizing life under the Nazi victors, life was always shown as torment. The din of marching guns offered projections of the mass slaughter of innocent citizens. Wives, daughters, and sweethearts were often lustfully regarded by German soldiers. Slave-labor conditions were brutally envisioned, and a generalized bestiality marked the German invaders. In a conscientious objector's nightmare in "The Wakening of Johnny Castle," (#57), the hero encountered slavery for himself and sexual abuse for his wife in occupied Poland. In Nazi France he was among one hundred innocent people taken off the street to be shot in revenge for the killing of a German officer. And in China, he endured bombardment from the skies and the death of his wife.

The ultimate enemy was Nazism and the so-called "revolution" it proclaimed. Most movingly the Hitlerian movement was painted in terms of evilness and the diabolical in "The Price of Free World Victory" (#79). Stressing the theme that "Satan has turned loose upon us the insane," this program sketched Nazism as the anti-Christ.

Through the leaders of the Nazi Revolution, Satan is now trying to lead the common men of the whole world back into slavery and darkness. For the stark truth is that the violence preached by the Nazis is the Devil's own religion of darkness.

Concurrent with this attack on Fascism, the German people were often depicted as being duped, coerced, even captured by the Nazis. In "The Bishop of Munster" (#34), a condemned cleric declared that "we are the people—we are Germany and Austria . . . and they, our rulers, are the enemy. . . . Pray not for my liberation, but for the liberation of a great people." In "The Silent Women" (#47) it was alleged that "Hitler has silenced the women of Germany, too—has even ordered them not to weep for their own dead." In "I Can't Sleep" (#49) listeners encountered a pitiful, misguided middle-aged German who reported to the Gestapo two of his friends who listened illegally to British radio transmissions. He exposed his friends not from any zealous commitment to a cause, but out of his robot-like "duty to the State."

With great eloquence this attitude was summarized in Fredric March's powerful reading of Thomas Mann's "Christmas Letter to the German People" (#19). Written originally in 1940, this epistle urged the citizens of Germany to reject their Nazi masters. Mann attacked "this war which your present leaders have foisted upon you and the world," and condemned "your masters, who in your name, have plundered the continent they have overrun." The broadcast reached a climax when Mann wrote of Justice, Freedom, and Truth—those values "that make not only a Christian a Christian, but quite simply, a human being a human being."—for, in his words, the misled Germans "believed in a miserable forger of history, a counterfeit conqueror . . . who tells you that through him and through you a world shall dawn. . . ."

The devastating effect of the Nazis in Germany was often illustrated in the attitude of German immigrants living abroad. In a scene from the movie *The Invaders* (#22), one character spoke for all Germans living in Canada when he told a band of Nazi agents: "You and your Hitlerism are like the microbes of some filthy disease, filled with some longing to multiply yourselves until you destroy everything healthy in the world. No! We are not your brothers." A similar hostility to Nazism by German expatriates was notable in an excerpt from Lillian Hellman's successful play and motion picture, *Watch on the Rhine* (#12). In this drama a German-American who had been active in the underground inside Germany, gave up his new American home and security to return to Germany to help friends escape the Nazis, "the sick of the world." Certainly, the *Treasury Star Parade* showed Germans usually sympathetic and cooperative with Nazism. Yet, the persistence of this image of 'good Germans' but 'bad leaders' suggests that American propaganda held out the hope that historic German sensibilities would inevitably overcome Fascism.

While propagandists in *Treasury Star Parade* differentiated the German people from their governmental leaders and philosophy, no similar distinction was made with the Japanese. Rather than stress the twisted leadership in Tokyo, and applaud the civilized people who produced great poetry, drama, literature, and art, the Japanese were seen as inveterate barbarians. The programs frequently made use of racial epithets ("Nips" and "Japs"), physiological disparagement ("yellow bellies," "little brown men," "yellow midgets," and "flat eyes"), as well as analogies with the animal kingdom ("monkeys," "rats," and "reptiles"). One program (#53) even declared that all Japanese spoke with a natural hiss as it explained that "the hiss . . . is a basic characteristic of Japanese speech."

The racist overtones in such remarks are obvious. Undoubtedly, wartime feelings were intense. The propaganda levelled at the Germans was certainly not tepid. But with the white European enemy there was no criticism of racial characteristics. Anti-Japanese racism was also unchecked by organized criticism within the United States. With most Japanese-Americans confined to so-called "relocation camps," there existed no self-interested constituency to protest the broadcasting of racial slurs. Thus, the civility demonstrated in depicting the Germans was absent when dealing with the Oriental threat.

If the Nazis were pictured as madmen, the Japanese were depicted as both butcherous and subhuman. One of the strongest examples of wartime radio propaganda was the episode entitled "And No Birds Shall Sing" (#288). It was first aired in November, 1943, and was a lurid description of the Japanese bombardment and invasion of Hong Kong two years earlier. The program flamboyantly spoke of "the screams and the blood, and the stench and the crushed skulls of the little children on the streets of Hong Kong." It described the invaders, "massacring as they came," as the "beast that burned and bled Hong Kong . . . beast that ripped and tore." Listeners heard the enemy machine-gun a nurse, bayonet doctors, and slaughter 52 helpless, injured men as they invaded a hospital. All the nurses were then carried off by the Japanese. After satisfying their captors' physical lusts, the nurses were executed.

This type of animalism was also ascribed to the "Japs" in another broadcast, "A Lesson in Japanese" (#53). Ostensibly a dramatization of the "evil" Japanese code of living, "Bushido," the episode appealed to listeners' emotions by depicting the barbarism of the enemy and his leader, "Hirohito, sometimes Hiro-Hitler." The Japanese were heard murdering an American POW in Java. One vignette portrayed them as rapist-murderers of five hundred women from a Chinese college. The "little Japanese men" were ridiculed and reviled. Narrator Fredric March even questioned the civilized quality of the Japanese.

> Have you ever watched a well-trained monkey at a zoo? Have you seen how carefully he imitates his trainer? The monkey goes through so many human movements so well that he actually seems to be human. But under his fur, he's still a savage little beast. Now, consider the imitative, little Japanese, who for seventy-five years has built himself up into something so closely resembling a civilized human being that he actually believes he is just that.

V. The Nobility of the Allies.

Treasury Star Parade was unflaggingly positive in its portrayal of the soldiers and people of the Allied nations. Whether they were fighting or enduring Axis aggression, these descriptions told listeners that the cause for which they fought was a moral one, and that the struggle against Fascism was a noble international endeavor. A French woman shot for her activities in the resistance was compared to Joan of Arc (#55); Chinese peasants helping a wounded American flyer spoke admiringly of Abraham Lincoln (#282); and a Czech mother felt the same pain and pride known to American mothers as she watched her son go off to fight Nazism (#73). Be it the projection of saintly historical images, or the analysis of an emotion common to mothers of soldiers, the Treasury Department series showed the United Nations in crusade.

In portrayals of the miserable conditions faced by those in the captured nations, American listeners found self-sacrificing heroes who stood as role models. Certainly the notion of "it can happen here" was important to spurring the purchase of War Bonds, but such characters also preached sacrifice, struggle, and honor. In "Bonus for Berlin" (#274) it was Englishwoman Betty

Matthews never losing her spirit or will-to-work despite her two legs being crushed during a bombardment. For Zoya, the Russian high school girl who had become a guerrilla fighter (#47), it was the power to make a ringing speech from the scaffold—after her Nazi captors had flogged, burned, and otherwise tortured her—as she was about to be hanged.

> Comrades, comrades, hear me. Do not grieve, I am happy to die. Do as I have done. Kill Them! Destroy them! Burn them! . . . . You German soldiers, surrender. Surrender before it is too late. Victory will be ours! VICTORY!! VIC . . (agh) . . . (agh).

The world war was depicted as an effort of united peoples fighting barbarism. Broadcasts spoke praisefully of the Free French forces of General Charles de Gaulle, the bravery of the Australian military, the valor and dedication of the Chinese troops of Chaing Kai-Shek. Radio stars Amos and Andy lauded all resistance movements as they thumbed through a postage stamp album (#71). In "The Silent Women" (#47) a continent on the march was described as a pattern of confident voices proclaimed: "We are the guerrilla fighters, the anti-Quislings, the invisible army marching from the English Channel to the Russian front. From Narvik to Athens, Yugoslavia, Greece." Racial prejudice was totally absent when "Ballad for Bataan" (#43) praised the fighting spirit of the Philippine fighters who stood with American defenders to battle the Japanese. "Brown and white they stood together," spoke the narrator, "under the blazing sun and the hot wind—and the sun burns them all the same color— and their blood is of the same color."

Even the fires of anti-Communism, which had kept the United States and the Soviet Union apart for over two decades, were abated in the reconciliation compelled by Fascism. Russians were depicted as fighting for a return to pre-war freedom. The Red Army was warmly lauded in one broadcast (#66), and the anthem of international communism, the "Internationale," was even blended into the musical arrangement of another (#79). The "bogey men" of slave-labor camps, unloving automatons, and international warmongers—the cliches of anti-Communism—were shelved by American propagandists for the duration of the war.

This spirit of Allied nobility and purpose was most dramatically expressed in "The Songs of the United Nations" (#72). Here, Igor Gorin sang for the first time on the air "The Song of the United Nations," written by Dmitri Shostakovitch "on the Russian battlefields." With lyrics such as "a new day for mankind is dawning, our children shall live proud and free," the composition was a utopian masterpiece. In this program, too, happy songs of an earlier day became defiant songs of a day to come. From Czechoslovakia, Poland, the Netherlands, and the Soviet Union popular music revealed the common purpose of waging war. With "America" hummed in the background, narrator Vincent Price melded the energies generated by the show into a final note of dedication.

There will be no sacrifice too great, no effort too mighty that we will not make it to achieve that end. In our hands is the future peace and happiness of the earth. And we have sworn to preserve it with our own effort, and with the help of God. Amen.

VI. Uplift Through Entertainment

The propagandists of *Treasury Star Parade* understood that moral indignity and solemn affirmation could be carried to a point of diminishing returns. Frequently, therefore, they constructed their broadcasts around lighter forms of entertainment. These programs usually featured music from the top bands and pop singers of the day, or situation comedy from well-known radio personalities. While these shows certainly contained an appeal to patriotic feelings, they avoided serious dramatic skits, and added variety and a sense of balance to the entire series.

From Harry James and Bob Crosby, to Vaughn Monroe and Kay Kayser the infectious sound of "swing" music was performed in the name of Treasury Bonds. In a milder vein, the traditional rhythms of Ted Lewis and Vincent Lopez, the Latin beat of Xavier Cugat, and the sedate quality of Fred Waring and His Pennsylvanians judiciously blended pop and patriotism. Big-name singers like Jane Froman, Frank Parker, and Rudy Vallee also recorded programs. On these occasions *Treasury Star Parade* became a pulsating jukebox offering listeners recognizable hit tunes and freshly written war songs.

This record label appeared in transcriptions of at least 300 different 15–minute programs from the Treasury Department during the first years of World War II.

Radio comedy was a significant change-of-pace for the series. Fibber McGee and Molly (Jim and Marian Jordan) jested, and George Burns and Gracie Allen punned when they made their respective appearances on the series. When the cast of *Blondie*—the popular CBS series starring Arthur Lake as Dagwood Bumstead, and Penny Singleton as his wife, Blondie—performed in late 1943, the skit sounded more like a topical sitcom than a stark drama, the traditional fare of the Treasury series. But such levity was needed. Ultimately, emotional bombardment from *Treasury Star Parade* could become unnerving. Listeners with loved ones in the war could become increasingly apprehensive had the series relied solely upon heavy-handed propagandistic approaches. The musical programs were energetic and uplifting without overlooking the purpose behind the broadcasts. The guest bandleaders and singers made speeches throughout the quarter-hour, reminding listeners of the need to buy bonds. And the radio comedians, in their comic routines and direct appeals, also underscored the true goal of the program.

As aired during World War II, *Treasury Star Parade* was the longest-running and most overtly-propagandistic program in broadcast history. During the months before the attack on Pearl Harbor, the Nazis and the Japanese were as brutal as they were after that date. But in the pre-war period, commercial broadcasting steered as neutral a course as possible. Even newscasters were warned against showing bias when reporting the details of Axis aggression. Within ten weeks of the American entry into the war, however, *Treasury Star Parade* was broadcasting statements and plays charged with hate, indignation, and patriotism. Nothing like it had even been heard on American radio.

During this fearful period of American history, many voices were raised in support of using commercial radio to communicate propaganda to American listeners. Perhaps the fullest expression of this attitude was found in Sherman H. Dyer's book, *Radio in Wartime*. Writing in 1942, Dyer warned that "public support cannot be mobilized on an exclusive diet of truth, news and information." He called for "a judicious admixture of propaganda, for propaganda endeavors to convert initial decision into mass concurrence and united action." Dyer argued for what he called, "democratic propaganda," the emotional manipulation of democratic ideals by a cadre of trained technicians which understood that it could "respect no single fact, no truth, so much that it will refuse to alter it, if it does not fit into the total emotional pattern it is designing."[5]

One might dismiss the government and its sponsorship of *Treasury Star Parade* as a product of the time, an aberration produced in an atmosphere of tension and apprehension. This argument becomes even more creditable when it is recalled that many responsible citizens felt that commercial radio should be totally controlled by the government in time of war. Nevertheless, the fact remains that *Treasury Star Parade* was a dangerous precedent. Even though the various programs were written, produced, and enacted by non-governmental talents, the series was coordinated from Washington and bore the seal of the federal administration. And given the fact that later administrations would also utilize broadcasting to further their own crusades—be it anti-Communism, the Korean or Vietnamese wars, or naked political self-preservation—the implications of this radio series are evident. A free system of broadcasting should not tolerate such dire governmental propagandizing as was found in *Treasury Star Parade*. When it does, it becomes an adjunct of the state rather than a conduit for truthful information and genuine entertainment. This was a lesson that was lost on wartime America, and unfortunately, on much of the post-war era, too.

Notes

1. Geoffrey T. Hellman, "Profiles: Any Bonds Today?" *The New Yorker,* January 22, 1944, p. 29.
2. It should be remembered that the Department of the Treasury was not the only government agency producing programs for commercial radio. The Office of War Information produced informational shows, and the Department of War produced *This Is the Army* and the long-running variety series, *The Army Hour.* Other direct government incursions into commercial broadcasting came from the Office of Civilian Defense, Department of Labor, Department of Justice, Office of Emergency Management, and the Co-ordinator of Inter-American Affairs. According to the National Association of Broadcasters, American radio stations during the period May through July 1942, carried 1,541,640 spot announcements and 186,075 live and transcribed programs in support of federal war projects. This represented a total of 35,995 hours of free air time. See *Variety,* September 9, 1942, p. 47.
3. Those numbers cited after references to specific broadcasts are the program numbers assigned by the Department of Treasury. The recordings used for this analysis are from a personal collection of more than 140 of the first 300 programs in the *Treasury Star Parade* series.
4. *Variety,* May 6, 1942, p. 29.
5. Sherman H. Dyer, *Radio in Wartime.* (New York, Greenberg, 1942), pp. 84–87.

The War of the Well(e)s

Gary Saul Morson

The facts are well-known: when Orson Welles broadcast his dramatization of H. G. Wells' novel *The War of the Worlds,* millions of listeners believed that an actual invasion from Mars was taking place. A fictive newscast was mistaken for a real newscast, a represented apocalypse for the Apocalypse. The key to this mass delusion lies in the fact that Welles did not simply dramatize the novel, he parodied it. And he did so in such a way as to question the nature of both mass communication and twentieth-century historical ideology. Welles' *War* ironically recontextualizes Wells' *War* and, in the process, also raises questions about the significance of contexts—both historical and communicative—for a narrative's meaning.

Apocalyptic narratives may be regarded as a way of considering the nature of the historical process by imagining its cessation. In much the same way that nonsense systems may inform about logic—that is, by violating and thereby calling attention to the deductive rules usually taken for granted—apocalyptic models of history may inform about the ways we assume events to follow from, rather than simply follow, each other. To use the language of the Russian Formalists, apocalypse "defamiliarizes" and "disautomatizes" our beliefs about the historical process, and so renders them "perceptible" and the object of attention.

When we imagine the end of history, we imagine a moment that is unlike all other moments in that its meaning neither depends on what may follow nor is subject to continual re-interpretation and re-evaluation in the future. The time "when there shall be time no longer" (*Revelation,* 10:6) is the moment when, sure that there is nothing unexpected to consider, we may pass certain judgments about history, society, and morality. The certainty that the apocalypse promises is perhaps most clearly embodied in the image of the Last Judgment, in that final weighing of evidence when—at last—our verdict will coincide with the verdict of the One who sees from beyond history.

It should be stressed that it is possible to use the *concept* of an apocalypse for thinking about history and society without believing that a literal apocalypse will ever take place. On the contrary, the concept of an apocalypse has often been used in "thought experiments," models, or fictions that readers have been enjoined *not* to take literally. For to believe in an imminent apocalypse is to risk madness—and, when the belief is widespread enough, to risk either

mass destruction or totalitarianism. Whereas fictive apocalyptic works characteristically use the idea of a vantage point outside history to imply the possibility of radically different views of social and moral problems, literal ones emphatically reject relativism and skepticism for a doctrine regarded as infallible.

> *H. G.* Wells' War of the Worlds *is an*
> *example of a modern apocalypse that is*
> *framed unambiguously as a fiction.*

The principal goal of Wells' novel is to defamiliarize its readers' assumptions about society and history. His method for doing so is to present his text as a "mere" fiction and so to induce his readers to entertain beliefs they would probably not entertain if those beliefs were presented in a non-fictive text. (The "safe" entertainment of beliefs that are radically different from conventional beliefs is, in fact, one of the principal social functions of literature's "entertainment.")

For a brief period, Wells' real readers assume the position and attitudes of his implied readers, who live after the Martian invasion; the real readers consequently are permitted and encouraged to adopt a point of view from which present beliefs appear naive. After the readers have put the novel aside, they may, of course, return to their original set of beliefs, but now with the consciousness that it is but one among many possible sets. In short, like all didactic fictions, Wells' novel relies on "leakage" from the fictive frame.[1] Because of such leakage, a fictive apocalypse may lead to real doubt about the foundations of accepted historical models.

In Wells' novel, European civilization, which has formulated scientific and historical models that describe nineteenth-century European man as the summit of nature and culture, is subject to a "surprise attack" from the unknown universe that European models have excluded from consideration. In combatting an enemy the possibility of whose existence it had not entertained, Europe must take cognizance of what it did not wish to know. *The War of the Worlds,* then, like most figurative apocalypses, is an epistemological parable—in this case, a parable about how much we do *not* know about a universe in which we ourselves may be insignificant citizens. That universe, Wells' parable implies, has probably not been made for our benefit or constructed according to models that would appear logical, symmetrical, or comforting to the human mind. When Europe does manage to survive the Martian invasion, it must adjust its self-image to reflect an epistemological modesty tinged with doubt and sadness. As the novel's epigraph, a citation from Kepler in *The Anatomy of Melancholy,* tells us: "But who shall dwell in these worlds if they be inhabited? . . . Are we or they Lords of the World? . . . And how are all things made for man? (7, p. 4).

It is on such a note of modesty and doubt that the novel's narrator, writing after the Martians have been destroyed by an epidemic disease, begins his account. To him, it is not the Martian invasion that appears strange; on the contrary, that invasion is now the center of his picture of history. What is strange to him is, rather, the way Europeans, himself included, thought about themselves and their history before the invasion. For instance, when the Martians invade, the narrator is writing an article about "the probable development of Moral Ideas with the development of the civilising process. . . . 'In about two hundred years,' I had written, 'we may expect—' The sentence ended abruptly" (p. 169). The sentence ends just as abruptly, we might stress, as the historical process whose necessity it assumed.

The narrator's article would have been, of course, utterly unexceptional for its time. Like all the influential historical models of the nineteenth century, from Buckle to Marx, it took for granted the concept of "society's" (read "Europe's") inevitable progress. As man has evolved from lower animals, over whom he now properly rules, so, the narrator and his nineteenth-century audience reasoned, Europe has progressed from earlier stages of civilizaton, over whom it now properly rules. The narrator comes to learn, however, that the same arguments that justify our imperialism and our exploitation of lower animals would also justify the Martians' doing the same to us. Martian conquest of Earth, he comes to realize, is simply another form of colonialism, and who are Europeans to object to colonialism? (p. 9).

This anti-imperialist argument suggests the logic of the analogy on which the novel is based and which the narrator so often explicitly invokes: as men are to "lower" animals (his comparisons range from monkeys to microbes) and Europeans are to "inferior" races and more "primitive" civilizations, so Martians are to men. There is, therefore, a profound irony in man's rescue by "the humblest things that God, in his wisdom, has put upon this earth" (p. 162), that is, by disease-producing infusoria. The apparently purely rhetorical comparison of men to microscopic creatures in the novel's first paragraph turns out to be the key to the plot: we, whom the Martians scrutinize "perhaps as narrowly as a man with a microscope might scrutinise the transient creatures that swarm and multiply in a drop of water" (p. 7), are preserved by those transient creatures we so resemble—preserved, to extend the irony, by agents of putrefaction. Or, to take the metaphorical significance of our unexpected rescue one step further, we are saved, "after all man's devices had failed" (p. 162), by something the human eye cannot see.

> *How men learn, or fail to learn, of the reality*
> *of what they have not seen constitutes*
> *the essential story of Wells' novel.*

At first, men will not credit the fact of the invasion; even those who, like the narrator, have seen the Martians, rapidly return to the state of mind of "a decent ordinary citizen" and regard the evidence of their own eyes as "a dream": "I asked myself had these latter things indeed happened? I could not credit it" (p. 30). Even when the reality of the invasion cannot be doubted, its seriousness is discounted, since men cannot, or will not, accept the possibility of so radical an interruption of the social and historical processes they regard as natural and inevitable. Although the news of the invasion was sensational, the narrator recalls, it was much less so than the news of an ultimatum to Germany would have been; and an aristocratic lady who flees England wonders whether she may, after all, be safer with the Martians than with the French.

The newspapers, the organs of mass information and, metaphorically, of collective awareness, describe the Martian invasion as nothing more than an extraordinary event (not *the* extra-ordinary Event). That is, they try to make it fit the system of knowledge and history they take for granted—systems always have ways of comprehending occasional exceptions—instead of realizing that the Apocalypse renders all such systems inapplicable altogether. "A MESSAGE RECEIVED FROM MARS: Remarkable Story from Woking" (p. 18) reads the absurdly understated headline of a London newspaper; and we wonder if the newspaper contains other, "ongoing" stories as well.

The narrator must pay the usual price for the newspaper announcing the end of the world—as if money, the value of which is entirely based on social convention and the promise to honor it, could possibly be worth anything when the social order itself is destroyed. Wells' novel, in fact, plays subtly and frequently on the two meanings of the word *credit:* (a) to believe and (b) to promise to pay. What is common to both meanings is the concept of expectation, that is, the reliance on the future's being more or less like the past. One is less likely to credit, or to give credit, in uncertain or unpredictable situations. Both kinds of credit, in other words, depend on our being reasonably sure of the course of history—an assurance that Wells' novel attacks and which the Apocalypse renders absurd. Credit becomes worthless when nothing can be credited, when all is incredible—just as insurance becomes meaningless when there is nothing of which we can reasonably sure. In Wells' novel, however, complacent Europe goes right on with its usual commerce as if there will be a future in which money, even promises to pay money, will have value. The milkman making his usual delivery speaks for his short-sighted culture when he tells the narrator that the damage caused by the Martians will "cost the insurance people a pretty penny before everything's settled" (p. 37).

Because Wells' novel is about the naiveté of our social and scientific models, the most telling changes in "mental habits" are those of the narrator, who is a social philosopher, and Oglivy, who is an astronomer, or natural philosopher. Their reluctant conversion to a belief in the radical strangeness of the universe and in the possibility of its non-conformity to human models and needs both represents and anticipates the conversion of society as a whole. Predictably, Ogilvy and the narrator "scoff" (p. 11) at the possibility of life on Mars, and when the Martians do invade, the narrator underestimates the danger. He is, however, among the first to understand that this apparent end of history is a real end to our historicisms, and that the narrowly avoided apocalypse must become the occasion for epistemological and moral self-reflection. He writes in the epilogue:

> It may be that in the larger design of the universe this invasion from Mars is not without its ultimate benefit for men; it has robbed us of that serene confidence in the future which is the most fruitful source of decadence . . . and it has done much to promote the conception of the commonweal of mankind. . . . The broadening of men's views that has resulted can scarcely be exaggerated (p. 172).

In other words, the experience of an apocalypse has given the Europeans the possibility of viewing their history as if it were over—that is, as if from outside of it, from a metahistorical position. Moreover, the readers of Wells' novel occupy an analogous vantage point, inasmuch as the fictive frame allows them, too, to read about history as if from outside of it. Occupying a similar position to those who have lived through an apocalypse, those who have lived through the reading of an apocalypse are implicitly invited to learn a similar lesson.

The audience of Welles' **War of the Worlds** *broadcast was invited to learn a different lesson.*

In 1938, it must have seemed that the greater danger lay not in the refusal to entertain beliefs different from accepted ones, as H. G. Wells had asserted, but, on the contrary, in the readiness to believe anything, however preposterous. The criticism of reason's adequacy to comprehend the universe had been,

Orson Welles implies, all too successful. More skeptical than H. G. Wells, he saw the potential dangers in apocalyptic fantasies of any sort. When clearly understood as a fictive tool, apocalypse can be, as I suggested earlier, useful in defamiliarizing historical assumptions—but only insofar as it does not itself become an *alternative* to historical models. When it does become an alternative, metahistory becomes confused with history, and the confusion can have catastrophic consequences.

The central point of Orson Welles' broadcast, it seems to me, is that the frame that defines apocalypse as a useful fiction can never be made secure *enough*. H. G. Wells' novel may seem to be sufficiently unambiguous as a fiction, but, as with all apocalypses, the frame of fictionality is unstable. There simply is no safe way, Orson Welles implies, to play with apocalyptic fire. When the message "this is play" is all that stands between social order and social chaos, then those who wish to create chaos may attempt to exploit the weakness of the fictive frame. And what the educated take as a fiction may turn out to be more like a magical incantation, whose description of a non-existent state of affairs brings that state of affairs into being. This was, indeed, what actually happened with Orson Welles' broadcast.[2]

The remarkably wide-spread panic that resulted from Welles' broadcast (a study made at Princeton University shortly after the broadcast estimated that 28 percent of the approximately six million listeners believed an actual invasion from Mars was taking place; see 2, p. 58) is, it seems to me, persuasive evidence that Welles' fears about the intellectual limitations of mass audiences were justified. Welles and CBS, in the face of threatened law suits for damages caused by the panic, piously denied that Welles had anticipated his audience's error. I think it is likely, however, that he did anticipate it, and that his denials were (a) made because of the law suits, and (b) so overstated and ironic as to take on the character of another performance.[3] My contention about Welles' broadcast is that, inasmuch as two of his central themes were the credulity of audiences and the weakness of the fictive frame, he staged a drama in which the chief actors were his own deluded audience, deluded because they could not tell the representation of a newscast from a real newscast. The "worlds" that are at war in Welles' broadcast are, in fact, the worlds of fiction and reality; and the central action of Welles' drama was its reception, its planned misapprehension by much of its audience. Its "plot" was a "plot" against its own audience, designed to demonstrate the danger and possible success of more sinister contemporary conspiracies whose "fictions" would never be acknowledged as such.

There were, as CBS later pointed out, four announcements during the broadcast stating that the broadcast was fictitious, one of a series of fictions presented by "The Mercury Theatre on the Air." Moreover, newspaper listings of scheduled radio programs described the broadcast in advance as a dramatization of H. G. Wells' novel, and, of course, anyone who took the trouble to check other stations would have discovered that the apocalypse was taking place only on CBS. The insufficiency of such explicit statements of fictionality and the inability or refusal of a large portion of the audience to make obvious checks were, I think, Welles' central point. Welles' last statement of the broadcast "bares the device" of this hoax and, somewhat archly, asks his audience to learn an important and "terrible" lesson:

> This is Orson Welles, ladies and gentlemen, out of character to assure you that the *War of the Worlds* has no further significance than as the holiday offering it was intended to be. The Mercury Theatre's own radio version of dressing up in a sheet and jumping out of a bush and saying Boo! Starting now, we couldn't soap all your windows and steal all your garden gates, by tomorrow night . . . so we did the next best thing. We annihilated the world before your very ears, and utterly destroyed the Columbia Broadcasting System. You will be relieved, I hope, to learn that we didn't mean it, and that both institutions are still open for business. So good-bye everybody, and remember, please, for the next day or so, the terrible lesson you learned tonight. That grinning, glowing, globular invader of your livingroom is an inhabitant of the pumpkin patch, and if your doorbell rings and nobody's there, that was no Martian . . . it's Hallowe'en (pp. 42–43).

> *Welles' principal strategy for teaching*
> *his "terrible lesson" was to*
> *exploit metafictional devices*

Characteristically for metafictions, Welles played upon a confusion of frames in order to defamiliarize frame markers and the process of their correct identification. He created the possibility of error in order to show how important is the correct identification of frames; those who made the errors were themselves "framed," and, by becoming actors as well as listeners, were "taken in." Welles' broadcast, in fact, made it likely that frames would be missed by creating a dizzying sequence of them, and by rendering frame markers ambiguous and thus easy to mistake. For this reason, the same kind of markers that were used to indicate boundaries *within* the fictive broadcast were also used to indicate the boundaries of the real broadcast, and it therefore became easy to confuse the two. The announcer who introduced "this week's episode of the Mercury Theatre on the Air" and interrupted the episode at its midpoint, for instance, sounded a lot like announcers who introduced and interrupted the fictive interviews about the Martian invasion. Moreover, because the information about the Martian invasion came in the form of news flashes interrupting "the music of Ramon Raquello and his orchestra" (the orchestra plays "Stardust") the frame-marking significance of music, which indicated breaks in the Mercury Theatre on the Air, also became problematic. Interviewed later, many of the deluded listeners reported that they had thought the Mercury Theatre on the Air was being interrupted by news flashes about a Martian invasion. That is, even many of those listeners who heard the initial announcement that this was to be a Mercury Theatre dramatization *still* mistook the fictive broadcast for a real one![4]

That mistake, as we might expect, was even more common among those who missed the opening announcements, and so tuned in late to a radio program that represented a radio program interrupted by news flashes. Denials by Welles and CBS notwithstanding, Welles probably knew that at a time when news flashes about the unstable political situation in Europe were so frequent, and when radio, moreover, was still a relatively young medium, the possibility of confusion was not to be discounted. I believe, in other words, that Welles knew how people do usually listen to radio, and took advantage of that knowledge. He understood, for instance, that people frequently tune in late, often listen to radio programs inattentively—especially programs like "the music of Ramon Raquello and his orchestra"—and commonly miss the frames that might distinguish fiction from factual reporting. Radio demands redundancy, and four widely spaced announcements of the frame are *not* much redundancy. Welles probably understood, furthermore, that one often listens to a radio program while doing other things—particularly great confusion existed among drivers who believed the fictive but highly specific "traffic reports"—and that one cannot re-hear what one has missed as one can re-read parts of a novel.

To pursue the contrast between novel and broadcast, the frame of a novel is always physically present on the title page of the book that one has, in any case, oneself selected and chosen to read at that time—just as the curtain and stage of the theatre and the fact that one has bought a ticket and gone to see a play make it almost impossible to mistake the play's representation of action for real action. But a radio dramatization, a "theatre *on the air,*" is quite a different thing from a novel or a play. On radio, there are no physical markers, since a broadcast extends only temporally, but not spatially; its listeners sometimes tune in to whatever might be on the air and so may not always be aware of the genre or fictive status of what they have begun to hear.

No doubt, the content of Welles' broadcast should have been enough of a clue to its fictionality; but it was Welles' genius to know that for many listeners it would not be. As for the possibility of tuning in to other stations as a check, many deceived listeners reported that they had not done so because an announcer in Welles' broadcast had explicitly told them that CBS was the only network left on the air, and that they should stay tuned for information that this last network might not get a chance to repeat (2, p. 100). Welles may also have anticipated that those who panic often do not think of taking rational action or making obvious checks. It is a tribute to the effectiveness of Welles' metaliterary devices that CBS announced, in response to the furor that arose about Welles' broadcast, that it would no longer employ the "play within a play" technique (4, pp. 94–95).

That ban on Welles' technique, however, suggests that CBS may have missed, or pretended to miss, Welles' central point. The principal danger against which Welles' broadcast implicitly warned was not metaliterary hoaxes but political deceptions,[5] and political deceptions do not usually rely on the "play within a play" technique. They do, however, use radio, and those who practice political deception may understand the nature and psychology of listening well enough to abuse the considerable power of radio over a credulous audience. The man who was soon to make *Citizen Kane* well understood the power of mass media. That film, like Welles' broadcast of the *War*, is rich in self-referential ironies, and is deeply aware of its own medium: *Citizen Kane* begins with a film within the film, and its plot deals with a journalist who discovers the deceptions of journalism. The theme and self-referential devices of *Citizen Kane*, like those of *The War of the Worlds*, calls attention to the conditions in which fact and fiction can be confused, and to the power of mass media to exploit those conditions.

> *It could, indeed, be said that the central subject of Welles'* **War of the Worlds** *is its own medium—radio itself.*

The Martians, at least, seem to understand radio's importance: although they avoid destroying cities, they take special care to "paralyze communication, and [thus] disorganize human society" (p. 24). For this reason, a central drama of the broadcast is the network's attempt to keep broadcasting. Communication is repeatedly lost and regained; the reporter Carl Phillips is killed by a Martian heat ray in the midst of his transmission; and at last, the destruction of CBS headquarters in New York marks the end of human resistance. By the end of the first half of the program, the simple ability to indicate that the lines of communication are still open itself becomes the most important information that can be communicated. When transmission becomes intermittent, "phatic" language becomes emphatic. So the network's "last words" on the air contain considerable dramatic power in their simple repetition of identification signals in a doomed attempt to continue to speak and be heard (p. 31):

> OPERATOR 4: 2X2L calling CQ. . . .
> 2X2L calling CQ. . . .
> 2X2L calling CQ . . . New York.
> Isn't there anyone on the air?
> Isn't there anyone. . . .
> 2X2L----------

The ensuing silence, of course, carries the most important information of all. There is, therefore, considerable irony in the next sound that is broadcast—the real identification of the program and the network (p. 32):

> ANNOUNCER: You are listening to a CBS presentation of Orson Welles and the Mercury Theatre on the Air in an original dramatization of *War of the Worlds* by H. G. Wells. The performance will continue after a brief intermission. This is the Columbia . . . Broadcasting System.

As it takes in its own audience, Welles' metabroadcast assimilates its own frames.

Welles knew that listening, like interpretation, is an action that, like every other action, can be performed skillfully or ineptly. The "terrible lesson" of his broadcast is that we must become responsible, not just responsive, listeners.

Notes

1. On metacommunicative messages and fictive frames, see(1, 3, and 6); on "leakage" in didactic fictions see (5).
2. I use the text of Welles' broadcast as it appears in Cantril (2). Cantril's text differs slightly from the text published by Welles' scriptwriter Howard Koch in 1970 (4). Cantril's is the text of Welles' broadcast, Koch's of his script for that broadcast.
3. The *New York Times* of October 31, 1938 (also in 4, pp. 18–21) quotes Welles saying that he "hesitated about presenting it . . . because it was our thought that perhaps people might be bored or annoyed at hearing a tale so improbable." Made on Hallowe'en, does this denial echo Welles' closing statement in the broadcast that he was engaged in a Hallowe'en prank? Koch's book also includes a photograph of Welles, making what I take to be a theatrical gesture of innocence and surprise; the photograph is captioned, "I had no idea. . . ." (4, p. 84).

   In contrast to Welles, however, Koch evidently did not anticipate the possible mass reaction. On the contrary, his 1970 account makes clear that (a) he imagined he was writing a dramatization, not a parody of Wells' novel, and (b) that, like Wells but unlike Welles, he regards events *like* those in Wells' novel, as being not at all impossible. (His book begins with an interview with Arthur C. Clarke, in which both men agree that there is "considerable likelihood" of life on Mars.)

   The idea for the broadcast was Welles', and so was the technique of using news flashes, as Koch explicitly states (p. 13). The way in which Koch's script became Welles' quite different (even if verbally identical) broadcast is itself a good example of how meaning depends on context, on how conditions of performance can become enabling conditions for parody. Koch also makes clear that Welles often edited and partially re-wrote his scripts.
4. According to Cantril's study (2), twelve percent of listeners who tuned in from the beginning still believed that Mercury Theatre was being interrupted by real newscasts. He attributes the error to the fact that the technique of interrupting programs for news reports became common during "the radio reporting of the war crisis in October, 1938 [i.e., the month of the broadcast]" (pp. 77–79).
5. Judging from the news coverage of the broadcast, it was indeed effective as political commentary. Moreover, even if Welles did not intend to deceive his audience—he made, to my knowledge, no explicit statement that he did—the work nevertheless *functioned* as a politically pointed attack on the utopian tradition. In her widely read column, for instance, Dorothy Thompson, who apparently believed the broadcast's effect was not intended by Welles, still drew a "terrible lesson" from it: "All unwittingly Mr. Orson Welles and the Mercury Theatre of the Air have made one of the most fascinating and important demonstrations of all time. They have proved that a few effective voices, accompanied by sound effects, can so convince masses of people of a totally unreasonable, completely fantastic proposition as to create nation-wide panic. . . . The newspapers are correct in playing up this story over every other news event in the world. It is the story of the century. And far from blaming Mr. Orson Welles, he ought to be given a Congressional Medal

and a national prize for having made the most amazing and important of contributions to the social sciences. For Mr. Orson Welles and his theater have made a greater contribution to an understanding of Hitlerism, Mussolinism, Stalinism, anti-Semitism, and all the other terrorisms of our times than all the words about them that have been written by reasonable men" (The *New York Tribune,* November 2, 1938; reprinted in 4, pp. 92–93).

References

1. Bateson, Gregory. "A Theory of Play and Fantasy." In *Steps to an Ecology of Mind.* New York: Ballantine, 1972.
2. Cantril, Hadley, Hazel Gaudet, and Herta Herzog. *The Invasion from Mars: A Study in Psychology of Panic, with the Complete Script of the Famous Orson Welles Broadcast.* Princeton, N.J.: Princeton University Press, 1952 [1940].
3. Goffman, Erving. *Frame Analysis: An Essay on the Organization of Experience.* New York: Harper, 1972.
4. Koch, Howard. *The Panic Broadcast: Portrait of an Event.* Boston, Mass.: Little, Brown, 1970.
5. Morson, Gary Saul. "The Reader as Voyeur: Tolstoy and the Poetics of Didactic Fiction." *Canadian-American Slavic Studies,* 12 (1978), 465–480. See also Gary Saul Morson, *The Boundaries of Genre* (Austin: University of Texas Press, 1981).
6. Shklovskij, Victor B. *O Teorii Prozy* [On the theory of prose]. Moscow/Leningrad: Krug, 1925.
7. Wells, H. G. *The War of the Worlds.* New York: Berkeley, 1964.

4
Rhetoric of Graphic Arts

It has been said that "a picture is worth a thousand words," and for graphic artists and their audiences the cliche often has proven accurate. Though the study of persuasion has been limited largely to the spoken or written word, scholars from several disciplines—semiotics, rhetoric, anthropology, literature, and film to name only a few—have begun to map the contours of what is often referred to as "visual language." Rhetoricians and semioticians, in particular, have been interested in the persuasive dimensions of visual culture; how people create various sorts of "signs," organize those signs according to an agreed upon "code," and use such signs and codes to invite particular responses from viewers.

The study of visual language has ranged over many fields and its principles have been applied to various artifacts: film, television, painting, architecture, sculpture, comics, and cartoons being the genres most widely explored. In the field of rhetoric and communication studies, however, the principles of visual language have been applied primarily to the nonverbal dimensions of interpersonal interactions. Study of "body language"—facial expressions, eye movements, gestures, spatial relations, and so forth—have become quite popular. Rhetorical scholars are now trying to extend their understanding of visual language to other communicative forms.

In this section two scholars, one a semiotician and the other a rhetorician, explore the persuasive dimensions of a prominent cultural artifact: the political or editorial cartoon. Alette Hill examines the cartoon treatment given to Jimmy Carter during the 1976 presidential primaries. Michael DeSousa looks at the Iranian crisis of 1979–1981 and the understanding of it and its leader, the Ayatollah Khomeini, offered by American cartoonists.

Both Hill and DeSousa are interested in how cartoonists use signs (icons, indexes, and symbols to use the typology of C. S. Peirce) or rhetorical devices (metaphor, metonymy, synecdoche, irony) to invite readers to render judgments about the person or event depicted. Hill's purpose is to test a theoretical position; DeSousa's to argue a proposition. Both turn to cartoon texts for support of their ideas.

Hill wishes to test a theory of interpretation which holds that the study of lies can reveal much about our ability or inability to communicate the truth. Inasmuch as caricature is based, in large part, on the distortion of physical

179

features, on a particular sort of lie, Hill has decided to use cartoons and caricatures to explore the viability of the theory. She has chosen cartoons about Jimmy Carter produced during the 1976 presidential primaries as her data base.

Carter, according to Hill, became a "cultural unit" during his run for the presidency inasmuch as he could be reduced to a "series of iconic signs." Such signs included Carter's smile, thick lips, and alleged southern drawl all of which, Hill claims, were used to indicate specific attributes about Carter's personality or motives. Cartoonists, using both mimetic and analogic coding systems, were able to impute status (or lack of it) by manipulating the signs and their internal relationships. Recognizing signs and systems of codes helps the reader to understand the cartoons, Hill seems to imply, though it is "the configuration of facial features that passes final judgment."

DeSousa is also interested in signs, though he does not use that term, as a means of analyzing how American cartoonists tried to communicate information about Ayatollah Khomeini to their readers. Instead of starting with specific signs (turban, long beard, and flowing robes), DeSousa begins by searching for the general grounds or starting points which inspired cartoonists to construct specific caricatures. He starts with the general themes or commonplaces to which cartoonists returned time and again to give form to their ideas about Ayatollah Khomeini.

According to DeSousa, three commonplaces recurred on a regular basis from the beginning of the Iranian hostage crisis to its conclusion. Khomeini was imaged as a madman, a religious fraud, and a political manipulator. DeSousa argues that all three commonplaces were fertile ground for the cartoonists' imaginations, but that the information conveyed did not really provide insight into the nature and meaning of the crisis. Instead, the author argues that the cartoons provided only "an illusion of meaning" which functioned to perpetuate beliefs already held and thereby retard real understanding of what was happening in Iran.

Both Hill and DeSousa point to the use of rhetorical devices as means by which the cartoonists attempted to structure their messages to the reader. After reading their essays, can you tell precisely how such rhetorical figures as metaphor, metonymy, synecdoche, and irony work to convey the artist's message? Do Hill and DeSousa agree about the nature and function of these devices? After examining the cartoons in each essay which of these rhetorical figures seem to be used most often? Can more than one be used in the same cartoon?

Another issue which both authors raise, either implicitly or explicitly, is the problem of meaning construction and communication in the graphic arts. Hill and DeSousa both offer interpretations of several cartoons. Do you agree with their interpretations? If not, what evidence do you have that they are wrong? From where did your evidence originate: the cartoon itself, the artist's testimony about his cartoon, the author's interpretation, comparison with some other cartoon by the same artist, your personal knowledge of the topic being portrayed, or from some other source?

Do DeSousa and Hill agree about how cartoons "mean" or the ways in which an audience might gain access to that meaning? Is it possible that the artist could mean one thing, but the reader interpret the drawing to mean something different? If so, who is right—the cartoonist or the reader? If a reader misunderstands what a cartoonist is trying to say, then are we to conclude that the cartoonist is a poor communicator or that the reader is ignorant? How can the theory and practice of rhetoric guide us through some of these questions?

The Carter Campaign in Retrospect: Decoding the Cartoons*

Alette Hill

With the hindsight of Carter's phenomenal victory not only at the Democratic Convention, but also in the Presidential election, it is now easy to view his success as inevitable. During the spring of 1976, however, it was by no means obvious that Carter would be the winner, and cartoons produced during this period reflect the ambivalence of artists in interpreting the candidate to the public.

Though political cartoons are frequently negative, inasmuch as they belong to the realm of visual satire, there are many degrees of negativity ranging from gentle irony to angry condemnation. (To be sure, some cartoonists drew approving or at least neutral pictures of Carter at this time, and the victories in July and November brought out more positive views of the new President, as would be expected after any race in which the underdog reaches the goal first despite tremendous handicaps.) The cartoons that appeared during the spring campaign of 1976 are peculiarly negative, revealing Carter as a 'foreigner' and therefore an anomaly among the other candidates. The South has been *terra incognita* to much of the nation for more than a century, and the suspicions and fears of some of our most prolific cartoonists are revealed in the depictions of the Georgia peanut farmer who couldn't possibly become President.

What follows is an analysis of certain key cartoons, with the purpose of testing a theory of interpretation. Cartoons belong to a genre that lends itself to analysis by an approach through semiotics, for the following reasons:

(1) Umberto Eco says that sign-codes must be able to lie, and cartoons are traditionally distorted and therefore to a degree mendacious.[1]

(2) Cartoons often seem to project unconscious desires and fears, and semioticians like Eugen Bär have studied the language of the unconscious as revealed by psychotherapy. Bär (1971:265) says that works of art can be used to decipher 'discourse U'.[2] Cartoons, as a branch of art, can be scanned for symptoms of primal expression even though esthetically they may seldom rate a showing in our more prestigious museums.

(3) Julia Kristeva (1975) has said that linguistics in its emphasis on code should *not* be a model for semiotics because it stresses the social function of language to the exclusion of "play, pleasure, or desire".[3] Cartoons contain within

Reprinted from *Semiotica,* Volume 23:3/4, 1978, by permission of the author.

themselves elements of play, pleasure, and desire, even though on the level of propaganda and satire they would seem to perform a purely social function. E. H. Gombrich, in his study of the origins of cartoons (1961), shows how the play principle, incorporating the accidental and whimsical, contributed to the development of this genre.[4]

(4) Cartoons rely upon the principles of physiognomy, which purport to analyze character and fortune through facial features. Semiotics, whose etymology can be traced to Galen and the diagnosis of pathological symptoms, has a fundamental connection with physiognomy in the history of science.[5]

(5) Umberto Eco (1975) makes the ambitious claim that semiotics should ultimately provide a logic of culture. Cartoons, as an enduring, though lately developed, part of popular culture, should provide clues to an overall apprehension of the structure of our society.

Michael Wood in an article (1976) about westerns that appeared almost simultaneously with the Democratic Convention makes the following statement: ". . . westerns (and by implication other films and other forms of popular entertainment) offer versions of social *thought,* that is, are not merely reflections of prejudice or fantasy but are narrative vehicles for the display and displacement of what worries us." The same may be said of cartoons, but whereas the traditional western glorifies the cowboy as a lonely hero, the cartoonist depicts political candidates more often as non-heroes or even as villains.

The cartoons of Jimmy Carter during the closing months of the Democratic campaign show that he worried artists more than he heartened them. Cartoonists displayed their condescension through pictures that trivialize the candidate, or they displaced their fear that he might win by lampooning him, as if with their potent magic, he would thereby fail and then disappear.[6] Whatever the real Carter was in the spring of '76, he rapidly became a 'cultural unit' (to borrow a phrase of Eco's), which was presented to us in a series of iconic signs that reveal, I suspect, not only the fears of cartoonists but of large portions of the electorate as well. It is illuminating to compare cartoon illustrations of Carter around convention time with photographic representations of him in the same magazines. The photographs are almost entirely flattering, and so are the articles that accompany them. We find photographs in living color of Amy, Rosalynn, Miss Lillian, the Carter peanut acreage, and the Plains Baptist Church. The articles tell us about the candidate's natural unspoiled childhood in rural America, his determination to go to the Naval Academy, his interview with Hyman Rickover, and his unflagging zeal not only to become governor of Georgia but to run a tight ship once in office. In the very same magazines, sometimes on the same page with the panegyric prose of the biographical articles, we find cartoons of Carter as Id monster and crook. Cartoonists seem to be natural Freudians, who suspect everyone's real motives while expressing themselves in graphic Jungian symbols.

Europeans and others outside the U.S. who interest themselves in our presidential politics may well have wondered whether Carter was a devil or a savior. Semioticians need only reply that Carter the 'cultural unit' was both. The 'real' Carter, being a mere mortal, is obviously not to be judged from cartoons; but projected fears and wishes about his character and personality are clearly discernible in pre-Convention caricatures.

Two types of encoding systems are evident in the cartoons: (1) mimetic, based upon the features of Carter's face as seen in photographs, and drawn from beliefs about what faces betray about character and intelligence; and (2) analogic, which often make Carter's body into something very different from the articles about the candidate. The face must be recognizable as Carter's, whereas the body can depart from mere distortion into the realm of fantasy and myth-making. To be sure, the subject may appear as a farmer or as a politician, both of which represent real aspects of his career, but more often he is transformed into a guise that is analogical rather than representational, for example, Carter as a faith healer or as a peanut. He shares some property that allows the cartoonist to encode a simile that will be read as an imputation of status. If the facial expression does not fit the message of the rest of the cartoon, we have what amounts to pictorial catachresis, a kind of mixed metaphor in which the elements of the two codes are at war and the overall impression on the viewer is ambiguous.

A few cartoons do not show Carter present, such as the one by Freden in *The New Yorker,* in which two men at a bar have been discussing his qualifications. The one wearing a Carter button says, "I like him *because* he's an unknown" (June 7, 1976, p. 35). I leave these cartoons out of the discussion, because it is my belief that the physiognomy or facial features of the subject supplies the essential message, and these cartoons lend no evidence either to support or refute this claim, unless one might construe the absence of the subject as a 'zero' morpheme.

In the March 8 issue of *Time* magazine Witte caricatured Carter as a peanut (Fig. 1), to illustrate an article entitled "Jimmy Carter: Not Just Peanuts" (p. 15). His features are superimposed on the familiar 'Planter's Peanut' man, an ad that had already paved the way for Carter to be accepted as sophisticated although a farmer. Three rhetorical modes are implicit in this cartoon: (1) metaphorical: Carter could be represented as a peanut because they're small, insignificant, and cheap, and Carter, at least early in the campaign, was considered trivial;[7] (2) metonymical: Carter as a peanut farmer could be associated with the crop he cultivates. There is contiguity between the candidate and the peanut;[8] and (3) ironical, which is explicit in the article title. There is a contradiction or negation of the peanut as trivial or hickish. Planter's Peanuts by dressing up its man in top hat, monocle, gloves, cane, and spats had already elevated the lowly peanut to dandy or urban sophisticate. It remained only for the cartoonist to supply Carter's features to produce a politically relevant restatement of this irony.

Figure 1. Planter's Peanut Man. (Illustration of Jimmy Carter, 1976; illustration for *Time* by Michael Witte.)

A similar irony can be seen in a mini comic strip by Wright, which originally appeared in the Miami *News* and was reprinted in *Time* on May 10 (p. 19). The peanut becomes an animated cocoon or Mexican jumping bean from which Carter launched as a rocket: the peanut shell gives birth to an upwardly mobile candidate. A photograph in *Newsweek* (July 26, p. 24) shows three placards for Carter at the Democratic Convention, two of which are shaped in the form of peanuts. The one to the left is held by a smiling member of the Georgia Delegation and says, "Georgia Peaches Love Jimmy Carter," in which 'peaches' means 'ladies'. The one on the right looks like a blow-up of a real peanut wearing a representational Carter grin. The middle sign, "Grits and Fritz in 76," encodes a second agricultural product associated with the South and coins a catchy slogan by rhyming what Carter eats for breakfast with Walter Mondale's nickname. If irony is present, it is of the tale-turning variety: Carter as the winner can now be presented by his supporters as the homely legume that earlier in the year was used by his opponents to make him look foolish.

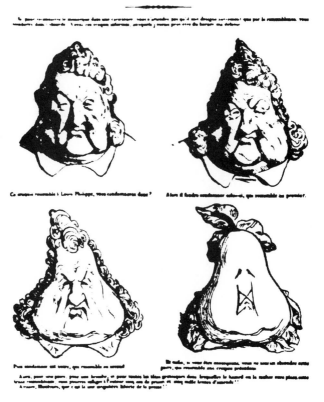

Figure 2. *Les Poires.*

Carter as peanut might be compared with a famous cartoon series of King Louis Philippe as a pear, executed by Charles Philipon in 1834 (Fig. 2).[9] Philipon ran afoul of the law and was harassed by the King through both fines and imprisonment because of his rendition of the monarch's features. However, the insult depended not so much on the graphic comparison of the King with a piece of fruit, but upon a verbal pun, inasmuch as *poire* in French argot means 'fathead' (Gombrich 1961:344). *Le roi bourgeois* only drew more attention to his pear-shaped visage by making war on Philipon, with the result that fellow journalists took up their cudgels and formed a society to protect freedom of the press as it affected cartoonists. One of the masterpieces that ensued from this skirmish between the King and fourth estate is an elaborate lithography by J.-J. Grandville and Albert Desperret published in 1833 showing the 'pear king' like the 'sun king', enthroned in splendor and surrounded by his minions, but substituting a pear for the radiant sun that would have been appropriately streaming upon Louis XIV.[10]

Figure 3. Hayseed marching ahead of donkeys. (Cover of *Newsweek,* July 19, 1976. Courtesy of Newsweek, Inc.)

Again peanuts are introduced into a Carter cartoon, but here the artist, Lou Grant of the Los Angeles *Times,* makes the candidate into a con man playing the old shell game with the issues, manipulating peanuts instead of the usual walnut shells. Dishonesty is imputed to Carter by the very nature of the scene, but the face also tells us something else: the thick lips indicate lack of culture, a feature that is also found in cartoons of George Wallace.

Fig. 3 appeared on the cover of *Newsweek* on July 19, after he had won the Democratic nomination for President. The victorious hayseed is smiling as he leads a troop of Democratic donkeys through New York, indicated by a background of skyscrapers. Robert Grossman, the artist, apparently wanted to stress the incongruity of Carter's rural origins with his success in the big city. This caricature reduces Carter to one aspect of his career, and the worst that might be said of the Pinocchio face is that it appears rather foolish.

Oliphant, on the other hand, drew a devastating picture of Carter as a farmer whose face wears quite another expression (Fig. 4 from *Newsweek,* June 21, p. 16). Carter sits on a wooden porch in Plains greeting visitors: George Wallace has already passed by in his wheel chair (note that both Southerners are given thick lips); Mayor Daley approaches with violin case, Mafia style; and

187

Figure 4. Carter as farmer greeting Wallace, Daley, and Jackson.
(Copyright, 1976, Universal Press Syndicate. Reprinted with
permission. All rights reserved.)

a third character bears a tuba. The caption reads: ". . . And, Ah declare,
here's Georgey Wallace . . . and Good ol' Ricky Daley . . . and who do Ah
see comin'? . . . Why it's ol' Scoopey Jackson!" One little creature on the
porch comments to the other, "Us'uns are headed fo' th' Whitey House." (Oliphant seems to think that Southerners speak baby talk.) Carter's clothing is
that of a farmer, but his face is that of a grotesque opportunist.

Oliphant's attitude toward the South is confirmed by Fig. 5, in which the
Republican Delegation of Mississippi is placed in the same setting as the preceding cartoon: a rural porch with one man seated, barefoot and disheveled,
and a visitor approaching, President Ford. Mississippi differs from Georgia in
that it's trashed out (Georgia is poor but neat), less friendly (at least to out-
landers: two scruffy dogs bark and jump viciously at Ford); and the owner of
the cabin is barefoot and apparently dressed in his underwear as he sprawls
on a dilapidated arm chair. At least he doesn't speak baby talk: "Hang on a
second, Ron—I think I got me a visitor." The balloon caption of the two little
creatures is "He better have come to say pretty please!" (*The Denver Post,*
July 26, p. 18).

One aspect of Carter's value system that apparently worried the press was
his religion—not that a President shouldn't be a churchgoer, quite the reverse—but he isn't supposed to take it seriously. The Presidents until Kennedy

188

'HANG ON A SECOND, RON — I THINK I GOT ME A VISITOR.'

Figure 5. Mississippi delegation depicted as farmer greeting Ford.
(Copyright, 1976, Universal Press Syndicate. Reprinted with
permission. All rights reserved.)

were Protestants, for the most part nominal or conventional Christians. Carter's evangelical strain brought out fears and snickers from many cartoonists. One of the more innocuous examples is Mauldin's imaginary scene of Carter as a youthful fisherman, in which fish magically jump into his hat. Two men farther up the bank remark, "That Carter kid's gonna be President some day." (*The New Republic,* June 6, p. 15).

In Fig. 6 he is a Southern preacher attempting to heal a sick Democratic donkey, with allusions to *imitatio Christi* in the caption: "Heal! In the name of J.C. (Jimmy Carter, that is) Ah say, Heal!" Carter is revealed as a Southerner by the spelling of the first person pronoun 'Ah'. Regional dialect aside, the caption is unidiomatic, since the preacher is telling the donkey to heal instead of *be* healed. Carter's facial expression is sanctimonious and suspect (Keefe, *The Denver Post,* July 18, p. 19). Another one by the same cartoonist (Fig. 7) shows Carter at the Convention preparing to be hoisted up as a theatrical agent, with the caption, "Glory, Glory, Hallelujah' . . . That's your cue!" (*The Denver Post,* July 14, p. 24). Here the expression is enthusiastic, but in the context of a rigged dramatic event the smile can be construed as that of a trickster.

Figure 6. Carter as faith healer of sick Democratic donkey.
(Reprinted by permission of Michael Keefe.)

Greg Scott on the cover of *Rolling Stone* projected Carter as the Convention winner on June 3, dressing the candidate in white baptismal garb with a Confederate flag draped over his shoulders like a Roman toga. (Fig.8). For once, the smile is not encoded with negative connotations.

Oliphant shows Carter at the convention receiving the name of his Vice Presidential running mate from the hand of God (Fig. 9). The caption, "The envelope please. . . ," the phrase used at Academy Award ceremonies, supplies a theatrical touch that ironically belies the motto on Carter's podium— "Trust Me". The lips are thick, the eyes seemingly closed in mock solemnity, and the two little creatures at the lower right say, "Oh, the suspense" (*The Denver Post,* July 12, p. 16).

J. E. Anderson depicted Carter in medieval iconic tradition as a preaching Christ holding an open book that reads, "Have ye all faith in me and give thy vote to me. We'll talk about the issues later. Not for nothing are my initials J. C.! Amen." (Fig. 10). This cartoon, which appeared in a student newspaper, reflects the extreme skepticism about the candidate's sincerity, also loudly expressed in editorials before the Convention (*Colorado Daily,* April 27, p. 6). For once Carter is serious and 'concerned' (note the lines in the furrowed brow and the dignified crow's feet), as befits the Son of God. A caption was necessary to place in contrast the 'sincere' physiognomy and the intentions behind the mask.

" 'GLORY, GLORY, HALLELUJAH' . . . THAT'S YOUR CUE!"

Figure 7. Carter as theatrical angel. (Reprinted by permission of Michael Keefe.)

Figure 8. Carter on cover of *Rolling Stone* as newly baptized. (Reprinted by permission of the Rolling Stone.)

THE ENVELOPE PLEASE.

Figure 9. Carter receiving V.P. envelope from hand of God. (Copyright, 1976, Universal Press Syndicate. Reprinted with permission. All rights reserved.)

Carter's smile, so frequent in his photographs, was a logical feature for caricaturists to develop, since they ordinarily establish a public figure with as few strokes of the pen as possible. Once established as a sign for Carter, the smile could be reduced to teeth alone, irridescently shining in the dark in Simpson's ingenious cartoon for the Tulsa *Tribune,* and given a domestic application by the caption: "Dammit Jimmy, Cut it out and go to sleep!" (reprinted in *Time,* May 10, p. 19). Edmondson in *The New Republic* gave Carter a smiling mouth and a nose but no eyes, implying a lack of vision or even of intelligence (May 8, p. 8). Curtis showed Carter with a talk balloon containing a picture of Carter talking, the message being that he is substituting personality for the issues (*National Review,* April 16, p. 377).

Carter's smile could also be compared with other famous smiles: Guaerke makes a comparison with Eleanor Roosevelt, in which an unshaven man looking at a Democratic campaign poster imagines the smiling face of Mrs. Roosevelt. The caption reads, "Happy Days Are Here Again" (*National Review,* May 14, p. 493). Alfred Gescheidt concocted a trick photograph in which Carter's face is superimposed upon the body of John F. Kennedy. This collage, with Kennedy hair and characteristic arm gesture, looks at first glance exactly like JFK until one looks more closely at the eyes, nose, and mouth (*The Star,* June 22, p. 31).

Carter's grin could be transplanted to animals: Wright put it on the Democratic donkey (*Time,* July 26, p. 10); Herblock used it in a game scene in which the Democratic donkey is gloating over his selection of a running mate

Figure 10. Carter as medieval Christ. (Reprinted by permission of the Colorado Daily.)

(indicated by a completed jigsaw puzzle—'Carter and Mondale'), while a distraught Republican elephant in the foreground has gotten no further with his puzzle than 'and'. (*Newsweek,* July 26, p. 25). The Carter grin was attributed to the Cheshire Cat, an enigmatic animal that showed the cartoonist's wish to label Carter's personality as mystifying. Willy used this motif to illustrate a suprisingly pro-Carter essay in the *National Review* (May 14, p. 504), but a superior rendering of the same scene was produced by Conrad for the Los Angeles *Times,* in which Alice stands before the familiar tree looking at the cat who has disappeared all but for the teeth, which are Carter's. This cartoon is captioned with the original lines from Lewis Carroll: " 'Well! I've often seen a cat without a grin,' thought Alice; 'But a grin without a cat! It's the most curious thing I ever saw!' " (reprinted in the *Boulder Town and Country Review,* July 21, p. 4).

Carter's smile with emphasis on the teeth would seem to have of necessity a negative or threatening connotation, yet Bassett featured teeth in a positive way by depicting Carter as a champion boxer: his teeth are intact, whereas his Republican sparring partners have suffered a few losses. Ford is lacking one tooth: Reagan, two (*U.S. News and World Report,* July 19, p. 15). Carter's smile eventually became the symbol for Democratic victory. Joseph R. Smith drew a smiling Carter literally steamrolling to Convention victory to illustrate an article entitled "Startling Surge for Carter." It is interesting that Smith dresses Carter as a businessman rather than as farmer or blue collar worker, as if the candidate's credentials as a member of the middle class, the governing class, and even the Establishment are now being acknowledged. Likewise, the face is refined and well groomed (*Time,* May 10, p. 12).

Conversely the big smile could become a symbol of possible Republican defeat, as Herblock shows in his cartoon of President Ford trying to grin broadly by pulling his lips apart with his fingers. Two advisers judge the performance with the caption, "Well, what do you think?" (*Newsweek,* May 10, p. 28). Bob Engelhart of the Dayton *Journal Herald* made up a four-frame comic strip of Carter teaching Mondale to smile: (1) "You've got to try harder, Walt" (both men are serious); (2) "You've got to put your heart and soul into it" (Carter is patting Mondale's shoulder, and Mondale is covering his eyes with his hands in a gesture of defeat); (3) "O.K. Let's try it again (both men are frowning in discouragement); (4) "Perfect" (both men are smiling from ear to ear). The caption reads: "The Democratic team: 'We're a lot more compatible than is generally realized.' " (*Newsweek,* July 26, p. 27).

The famous smile, however, could be made sinister. MacNelly paints a macabre picture of Carter who sneakily takes over the Presidential rostrum, while a solemn Ford in the audience says to the lady on his right, "Yea . . . I think Hubert is gonna jump in the race at the last minute.—Say . . . what brings you to Washington, Mrs. Carter?" (Richmond *News-Leader,* reprinted in *Newsweek,* May 20, p. 28). Carter wears a truly wicked smile in Fig. 11 (by Taylor Jones) while scrubbing the Washington Monument. The teeth have been elongated and made more jagged, which injects a feral note while the eyes, though crinkly, are not jolly. They are cunning, even sadistic, and resemble those of the cartoons lampooning Bobby Kennedy during his days as hounder of Hoffa. This is a smile which connotes lust for power and the joy of revenge (Boulder *Sunday Camera,* June 13, p. 1).

Keefe paints a ghoulish smile on Carter and makes his body massive and muscular, as befits a grave digger of Democratic liberalism (Fig. 12). Carter's face appears vicious and cruel, a figure of evil and destruction. There is a contradiction in this cartoon, since Carter is both burying Democratic liberalism and "digging up" a running mate, according to the caption. The message of the verbal part of this cartoon is complicated, if not unintelligible, but the message of the physiognomy leaves no doubt as to Keefe's opinion of Carter's character (*The Denver Post,* July 15, p. 22).

Keefe's attitude toward the South as well as toward its famous representative is shown in this scene of Carter buying lemonade from his daughter (Fig. 13). Amy's sign reads, "lemnade Demcrats 5c Evbody else $1.15," which is supposed to be illiteracy Georgia-style. Georgia dialect is attempted in the caption as well: "Wahtuhgate? I don't intend to make Wahtuhgate an issue . . . Let us fo'get Wahtuhgate . . . Wahtuhgate . . . Wahtuhgate . . . !"

Figure 11. Carter scrubs Washington Monument.

Jimmy's lust for power is reflected in the greedy daughter, whose pop eyes stare at the coin in her father's hand while her fingers nervously twitch in anticipation of receiving it (*The Sunday Denver Post,* July 25, p. 15).[11]

A pro-South cartoon appeared after the Democratic Convention by Conrad, who depicts Carter as Robert E. Lee at Appomattox, except that he is the victorious general rather than the one who surrenders. Carter, handsome, confident, and smiling, addresses his 'party regulars', who are attired as Union soldiers, with, "Your men may keep their mules. . . . They'll need them for fall campaigning." (Los Angeles *Times,* reprinted in the Boulder *Town and Country Review,* July 21, p. 4). Similarly, MacNelly depicts Carter as a Confederate general clasping hands in victory with Mondale, who is clad as a Yankee. Carter's face is grinning from ear to ear and looks like a jackass, whereas Mondale's handsome features have been made into a hardly recognizable character with sleepy eyes and enormous nose (*The Richmond News Leader,* reprinted in the Boulder *Camera,* July 30, p. 5). Conrad's Carter as a debonair General Lee implies that the Democrats have chosen a worthy candidate; MacNelly's gives the impression that the winning team have the mentalities of Disney comic strip characters: Carter is the grinning Goofey, and Mondale as Dopey afflicted by his fellow dwarf Sleepy with perpetual lethargy.

'IT'S SURPRISING HOW FAR YOU HAVE TO GO TO DIG UP A RUNNING MATE!'

Figure 12. Carter as grave-digger of Democratic Liberalism. (Reprinted by permission of Michael Keefe.)

These two views of the Democratic candidate in July of 1976 augur two very different futures of the Executive branch of the Federal Government: one of confidence and savoir-faire; the other, of incompetence and bungling. The idea that face and fortune are related is implicit in the artistic encoding of both Conrad and MacNelly, as well as of the other cartoons discussed above. This belief has been around for so many centuries that we hardly question its validity, even though the 'signs' that can be read in faces may have been reinterpreted as to what constitutes an honest or intelligent face as opposed to what can be read as a deceitful or stupid one. It is instructive to consult the monumental work of the Swiss divine, Johann Caspar Lavater, *Essays in Physiognomy* (1789–98), the subtitle of which reads: "Designed to Promote the Knowledge and the Love of Mankind . . . God created Man after His Own Image."[12] Yet we have only to see the engraving of Judas Iscariot (I, p. 186) to find out that Lavater apparently exempts Jews from mankind, since his description of the caricature of Judas, with its exaggerated hooked nose and crafty expression, is interpreted as a very un-Godlike creature:

> Had we never been told that this is the portrait of Judas Iscariot after Holbein, had we never seen a face that bore the least resemblance to it, a primitive feeling would warn us at once to expect from it neither generosity, nor tenderness, nor elevation of mind. The sordid Jew would excite our aversion, though we were able neither to compare him with any other, nor to give him a name. These are so many oracles of feeling.

196

**WAHTUHGATE? I DON'T INTEND TO MAKE WAHTUHGATE AN ISSUE...
LET US FO'GET WAHTUHGATE... WAHTUHGATE... WAHTUHGATE...!**

Figure 13. Carter talks to reporters while Amy sells lemonade.
(Reprinted by permission of Michael Keefe.)

Although we have veered away from crude stereotyping of minorities, such as
is exhibited in the lithograph of Judas, we still show prejudice toward Southerners as 'rednecks' and women as 'birdbrains'. More important, though these
prejudices are frowned upon in 'liberal' circles, they emerge in popular culture
in blatant forms and in more 'refined' forms of art by innuendo and allusion.
The key to the interpretation of cartoons seems to lie in a sophisticated appraisal of the nuances included by the artist, not by resorting to historical
cliches, since manners and mores have moved in the direction of skepticism
of stereotypes, especially as they concern classes, occupations, and native
origins. Cartoons reveal the changing nature of our esthetic and moral conventions and are a rich source of information for those interested in gauging
the national psyche in the last quarter of the twentieth century.[13]

The early cartoons of Jimmy Carter form a unique configuration of signs,
which are for the most part pessimistic and wary. They present a loaded view
of the candidate that suggests a dim future for the nation. Cartoonists are
constrained by the conventions of their code: they must convince the viewer
that there is some element of truth in their pictures or else their message will
be rejected. They may depict the signified in the metonymical mode and generate the signifiers as literal figures. For example, Carter cultivates peanuts,
and therefore he can be shown as a farmer. Or, from this same context, the
signifier can be treated as a metaphor, as in the cartoons of Carter as a peanut.

In the context of religion, Carter is ironically imagined as a precocious and spell-binding fisherman, a revivalist faithhealer, God's messenger, a theatrical angel, and Jesus Christ, which call into question Carter's self-confessed belief in God and the power of prayer. Only the cartoon of Carter on the cover of *Rolling Stone,* dressed as newly baptized with a Confederate flag as stole, and climbing above the other candidates, reflects true-to-life facts, namely, that he has been baptized, he represents the Confederacy, and he wins the Democratic nomination. A grinning angel draped in a foreign flag is an incongruous character in Presidential politics; yet the expression on Carter's face, the ubiquitous grin, do not belie the body, garments, and background to which they are the key. Even though the likeness is not particularly accurate, the physiognomy is in harmony with the 'message' of this captionless cartoon.

The most widely encoded sign for Carter to emerge from the cartoon is his face reduced to a smile, which is a form of synecdoche: "He's all mouth." The big smile became a shorthand symbol that could be transplanted to the Democratic donkey or the Cheshire Cat. Or, by selection and substitution of features, Carter's face could be likened to that of JFK or Eleanor Roosevelt or even George Wallace, with whom he shares a resemblance, however tenuous. E. H. Gombrich says that the art of caricature requires the ability to differentiate equivalence from likeness.[14] From mimesis of the real Carter based upon photographs to a reductionist equivalence of Carter as smile, cartoonists were able to signify Carter's presence within any animal or type of person, and even within vegetables and inanimate objects.

A variety of statements about Carter can be deduced from the cartoons, but they do not arrange themselves neatly according to the images employed. That is, the connotations of the entities with which Carter is compared do not necessarily express the artist's opinion of the candidate. It is the configuration of facial features that passes final judgment, good or bad. Carter as the peanut man of Planter's Peanut advertisement conveys an affable intelligent impression, whereas Oliphant's farmer welcoming Mayor Daley looks untrustworthy and sinister. In fact, the peanut looks more like the real Carter than does the farmer, showing the power of the caricaturist to project likeness with a few strokes of the pen and to find equivalence in the most fanciful similes.

Since the ultimate deduction about the candidate's values can be derived from his facial expression, the ancient theory that a man's character can be read in his face must still be in force. If the cartoonist and his viewers did not share a code of signifying faces, the genre of caricature would be possible, but it would not be useful for political cartoons. Candidates could be shown with distorted features but could not be endowed with character. It is the character of the candidate that is of interest to the voters, and therefore of central concern to the cartoonist.

Whatever metaphorical guises the subject may assume, no matter how ingenious the use of symbols and settings to make timely comments on newsworthy figures, it is the face of the person cartooned that affects us most powerfully. Symbols, emblems, regalia, and allusions may be misinterpreted, but seldom the physiognomy.[15] This can be seen in the picture of Carter cleaning up the Washington Monument (Fig. 11). One has to scrutinize it to decipher the brush, the canteen, and the monument, but the interpretation of Carter as ruthless and even sadistic leaps out from the face even before one can tell exactly what he's doing. The artist has used the trick of hieratic scaling by making the face disportionately large—even gigantic—in comparison with the body and background, as if to emphasize the physiognomic message. Though the idea of cleaning up the Capital is generally approved of as standing for reform of corruption, the features and expression on Carter's face reduce this laudable activity to a pretext for the candidate's revenge.

The semantics of these cartoons is not to be derived from the metaphorical figures of Carter as peanut, rocket, con man, or Jesus Christ so much as from the eyes and mouth of each. The negative smiles of Carter exhibit connotations of stupidity, cunning, sadism, ghoulishness, greed, and hypocrisy. The positive smiles convey genuine affability and good will. There were many more negative Carters than positive ones in the spring and summer of 1976, which is to be expected of the cartoons of any candidate since the genre is largely satirical, but these caricatures show more detestable personality attributes than the facts of Carter's career could possibly warrant.

This discriminatory treatment can be explained by the national paranoia about the region he represents. Oliphant is one of the few who openly enshrined his contempt for the South, and Keefe is another. For most critical cartoonists it was sufficient to show Carter as a rural hick or a religious hypocrite and supply him with a face that reveals a character flaw or intellectual defect without setting the scene in Georgia. Perhaps in the next Presidential election it will be unfashionable even remotely to ridicule or slander a candidate for his place of birth. The South has already been partly decoded with the message 'slow-witted' and 'treasonable' and encoded with signs of 'shrewd' and even 'honorable'. If Carter should fulfill his early promise as chronicled by Hunter Thompson in *Rolling Stone,* we may even find Uncle Sam's features changing from those of Lincoln to the now familiar smile of the man from Plains.[16]

Notes

*On the subject of cartoons and their origins see E. H. Gombrich and Ernst Kris 1940. This brief book traces the development of comic art from ancient times to the twentieth century. The authors point out that though the poor and deformed have routinely been held up to ridicule, the rich and powerful were not derided by artists until fairly modern times. To be sure, there are distorted faces and bodies carved on medieval cathedrals in the form of gargoyles; there are also humorous creatures in the margins of illuminated manuscripts. But not until the seventeenth century were individuals rather than types or classes subjected to pictorial satire. G. L. Bernini drew a sketch of Cardinal Scipio Borghese in which the smiling mouth is rendered by a single line (Gombrich and Kris 1940:13), yet the sketch was not intended to be insulting. On the other hand, Gombrich and Kris reproduce an etching of King Louis XIV from an anti-royalist pamphlet in which the Sun King is riding through the Zodiac but is clearly being mocked by the fact that he is leaning on crutches in a broken chariot (*ibid.*:16); nevertheless, the king's facial features are not in the least disfigured. It was William Hogarth (1697–1764) who combined the techniques of physiognomic distortion with the poking of fun at the socially elite and powerful: "Before Hogarth all barriers fell. For him not only the outcast, the low and the servile were funny, but every fool whatever his social position might be. . . . When caricature came to England it was a more or less sophisticated joke. . . . When it left England to conquer the world, it had developed not only into a branch of art, but also into a weapon." (*ibid.*:17, 18). For a detailed discussion of political cartoons as they evolved in England see George 1959. An account of one of America's most influential cartoonists can be found in Keller 1968.

1. "*. . . semiotics is in principle the discipline studying everything which can be used in order to lie.* If something cannot be used to tell a lie, conversely it cannot be used to tell the truth: it cannot in fact be used 'to tell' at all. I think that the definition of a 'theory of the lie' should be taken as a pretty comprehensive program for a general semiotics." (Eco 1976:7).

2. In the so-called 'Signorelli incident' Freud is unable to recall the name of the artist who painted the Judgment frescoes in the cathedral at Orvieto and displaces it with the names 'Botticelli' and 'Boltraffio' instead. Bär says that "the scenes painted by Signorelli are fairly universally expressive of the representatives of the life and death instincts formed in a particular cultural environment". (Bär 1971:265).

3. Semiotics "cannot simply go on following the linguistic model alone, or even the principle of systematicity if it aims also at tackling signifying practices which, although they do subserve social communications, are at the same time the privileged areas where this is put to non-utilitarian use, the areas of transgression and pleasure: one thinks of the specificity of 'art', of ritual, of certain aspects of myths. . . ." (Kristeva 1975:48).

4. Gombrich 1961, Chap. 10, "The Experiment of Caricature", pp. 330–58, and especially pp. 336–42—his account of the inventor of the comic strip, Rodolphe Töpffer of Geneva, whose treatise on physiognomics was published in 1845. Töpffer used doodling as a method of expanding his repertoire of facial expressions (p. 340).

5. Semiotics still considers symptoms as signs, and the diagnosis of symptoms as a branch of semiotics as well as of medicine. See the interesting paper by Ostwald (1964) and the subsequent "Discussion Session on Psychiatry" at the Indiana University Conference on Paralinguistics and Kinesics in 1962. See also Evans 1969, especially pp. 24–26 on Galen. Evans believes that satirists used the principles of physiognomics in their characterizations of personality, though they may not have done so consciously (p. 71).

6. It was the theory of E. H. Gombrich and Ernst Kris that cartoons appeared relatively late in the history of art because of "the fear of image magic, the reluctance to do as a joke what the unconscious means very much in earnest. . . ." (Gombrich 1961:343).

7. Walt McDougall depicted (and labelled) a high state official of Pennsylvania, Freddie Pusey, as a 'small potato' in *The* [Philadelphia] *North American* of January 30, 1903. Reprinted in Hess and Kaplan 1968:48, plate I–47.

8. I am taking the liberty of defining 'metonymy' rather loosely, according to the discussion of this and other tropes by Hayden White (1973:35): "In Metonymy, phenomena are implicitly apprehended as bearing relationships to one another in the modality of part-part relationships, on the basis of which one can effect a *reduction* of one of the parts to the status of an aspect or function of the other. To apprehend any given set of phenomena as existing in the modality of part-part

relationships (not, as in Metaphor, object-object relationships) is to set thought the task of distinguishing between those parts which are representative of the whole and those which are simply aspects of it."

White's example of a metonymical trope is "the roar of thunder," in which the sound is reduced to the effect of a cause—thunder. If Carter's career is seen to include the activity of peanut-farming, then the relationship of farmer to peanut is clearly metonymical, whereas Carter depicted *as* a peanut is metaphorical (cf. "my love, a rose," White's example of metaphor, p. 34). I prefer White's four tropes to the dyadic approach of Roman Jakobson and Morris Halle, in which synecdoche and irony are subsumed under metonymy. (See "The Metaphoric and Metonymic Poles" in Jakobson and Halle 1971:90–96.) On the one hand, the application of the concept of 'contiguity', stressed by Jakobson and Halle, is invaluable for my purposes here, although I believe their definition of metonymy is too broad; on the other hand, while I acknowledge my debt to Hayden White, I cannot subscribe to his emphasis on cause-and-effect reductionism as the dominant characteristic of the metonymical mode.

9. *"Les Poires"* from *"Le Charivari"* (1834), reprinted in Gombrich 1961:344, Plate 282.

10. See Bechtel 1952, Plate XI. The caption begins, *"Adoremus in aeternum sanctissimum philipoirum. . . .",* thus making a pun out of Philip's name as well as a 'fathead' of his physiognomy.

11. This cartoon was placed over a crude article called "Love and Justice in the White House," purportedly a humorous look at the Carters as First Family. Georgia dialect is sprinkled with "that thar's" that belong to Dog Patch or to the Rockies, but hardly to Sumter County. Rosalynn speaks a gushing feminine idiolect, with the exclamation "Lordy to goodness." Jimmy wants corn pone, black-eye peas, grits, and "souther' fried chicken" served to Mrs. Gandhi. His sister Gloria needs a place for "frog giggin," but the Rose Garden won't do because it's full of peanuts and "worm diggins." A cotton gin has been installed on the south lawn, and thirty relatives are camped on the White House grounds. The Carters are presumably a southern version of the Beverly Hillbillies.

12. See Chap. VII "Of the Mouth and Lips" and the conclusions about character drawn from the illustrations (none of which particularly resembles Jimmy Carter), Vol. III, Pt. 2, pp. 394–405. The author attaches great significance to this part of the physiognomy: "The mouth is the interpreter and the representative of the mind, and of the heart. It combines, both in a state of rest, and in the infinite variety of its motions, a world of characters. It is eloquent even in its silence." (p. 394).

13. It goes without saying that the nuances of caricature, that is, of facial features, is one of the prime targets for the 'message'. Gombrich's opinion is that physiognomy is one of the most challenging of all artistic accomplishments: ". . . if there is one effect more difficult to analyze than the impression of texture it is that of physiognomic impression. . . . In the earliest treatise on painting, Alberti's *Della Pittura,* we read that it is hard for the painter to distinguish a laughing from a weeping face. Even today the rendering of the exact nuance of facial expression is notoriously difficult. Portrait painters know those tiresome relatives of their sitters who 'can't see him like that' and complain that there is something around the mouth which is not quite right. Nor does this difficulty apply only to a copy from life. Max Friedländer tells the revealing story of the bank official who insisted that German bank notes should retain a portrait head of their design. Nothing, he said, was harder for the forger to imitate than precisely the right expression of these artistically quite insignificant heads, nor was there a quicker way of discovering a suspect note than simply observing the way these faces look at you. I believe the same is true of forged paintings. They look at you with a 'modern' look which, for

those who like to converse with the figures of the past, is easy to spot but extremely hard to analyze. The reason is plain. We respond to a face as a whole: we see a friendly, dignified, or eager face, sad or sardonic, long before we can tell what exact features or relationships account for this intuitive impression. I doubt if we could ever become aware of the exact changes that make a face light up in a smile or cloud over in a pensive mood simply by observing the people around us. For . . . what is given us is the global impression and our reaction to it; we 'really' see distance, not changes in size; we 'really' see light, not modifications of tone; and most of all we really see a brighter face and not a change in muscular contractions. The very immediacy of the impression stands in the way of analysis, and so the discovery and simplification of facial expression provide the best example of the course taken by an artistic invention. It is also an example of an invention the history of which has not been attempted. I dare say to write it seriously would present great difficulties, precisely for the reasons alluded to. Expression is hard to analyze and harder to describe unequivocally. It is a curious fact, moreover, that our immediate reaction results in firm convictions, but convictions which are rarely shared by all—witness the pages of interpretation that have been devoted to Mona Lisa's smile." (Gombrich 1961:333–34).

14. "The invention of portrait caricature presupposes the theoretical discovery of the difference between likeness and equivalence. This is how the great seventeenth-century critic Filippo Baldinucci defines the art of mock portraiture: 'Among painters and sculptors,' he explains in his dictionary of artistic terms, which came out in 1681, 'the word signifies a method of making portraits, in which they aim at the greatest resemblance of the whole of the person portrayed, while yet, for the purpose of fun, and sometimes of mockery, they disproportionately increase and emphasize the defects of the features they copy, so that the portrait as a whole appears to be the sitter himself, while its components are changed.' " (Gombrich 1961:343–44).

15. See the cartoon of Hitler as Achilles with the map of Italy at his left boot in E. H. Gombrich 1972: "Political cartoons are a special branch of symbolic imagery. They often lose their impact as the circumstances that engendered them are forgotten. The wit of Vicky's 1942 cartoon 'Achilles' Heel' is lost on those who do not know the situation to which it refers" (p. 92). Yet the expression on the warrior's face— one of angry perplexity—conveys the ultimate message. It reveals the cartoonist's intention even more potently than the much larger shield embossed with the swastika or the military uniform and geographical clues, all of which take up the largest proportion of the total picture as compared with the relatively small face of the Führer.

16. Thompson's article, "Fear and Loathing on the Campaign Trail '76: Third-Rate Romance, Low-Rent Rendezvous," is probably the single most perceptive and prophetic piece written about the candidate before the Democratic Convention. See *Rolling Stone,* June 3, pp. 54–88. A cartoon of Jimmy as Cheshire Cat illuminates the first capital letter on p. 54, but the section devoted to Carter begins on p. 58, where Thompson recounts his meeting with Carter in May of 1974 at the governor's mansion in Atlanta.

References

Eugen Bär, "The Language of the Unconscious According to Jacques Lacan," *Semiotica* 3, 241–68, 1971. [Reprinted in Eugen Bär, *Semiotic Approaches to Psychotherapy,* 31–58. Bloomington: Indiana University, 1975.]

Edwin de T. Bechtel, *Freedom of the Press and L'Association Mensuelle.* New York: The Grolier Club, 1952.

Umberto Eco, "Looking for a Logic of Culture," in *The Tell-Tale Sign*, ed. by Thomas A. Sebeok, 9–17. Lisse: Peter de Ridder Press, 1975.

. . . *A Theory of Semiotics*. Bloomington: Indiana University Press, 1976.

Elizabeth C. Evans, *Physiognomics in the Ancient World* (= *Transactions of the American Philosophical Society*, N.S. 59, Pt. 5), 1969.

M. Dorothy George, *English Political Caricature 1793–1832: A Study of Opinion and Propaganda*. 2 vols. Oxford: Clarendon Press, 1959.

E. H. Gombrich, *Art and Illusion: A Study in the Psychology of Pictorial Representation*. 2nd rev. ed. New York: Pantheon Books, 1961.

. . . "The Visual Image," *Scientific American* 227, 82–96, 1972.

E. H. Gombrich and Ernst Kris, *Caricature*. Hammondsworth: Penguin, 1940.

Stephen Hess and Milton Kaplan, *The Ungentlemanly Art: A History of American Political Cartoons*. New York: Macmillan, 1968.

Roman Jakobson and Morris Halle, *Fundamentals of Language*. 2nd rev. ed. The Hague and Paris: Mouton, 1971.

Morton Keller, *The Art and Politics of Thomas Nast*. New York: Oxford University Press, 1968.

Julia Kristeva, "The System and the Speaking Subject," in *The Tell-Tale Sign*, ed. by Thomas A. Sebeok, 47–55. Lisse: Peter de Ridder Press, 1975.

John Caspar Lavater, *Essays on Physiognomy*, transl. by Henry Hunter. 3 vols. London: n.p., 1789–98.

Peter F. Ostwald, "How the Patient Communicates about Disease with the Doctor," in *Approaches to Semiotics*, ed. by Thomas A. Sebeok, 11–49. The Hague: Mouton, 1964.

Hayden White, *Metahistory: The Historical Imagination in Nineteenth-Century Europe*. Baltimore: The Johns Hopkins Press, 1973.

Michael Wood, "Hi ho, Silver!" *The New York Review of Books*, July 15, 29, 1976.

Symbolic Action and Pretended Insight: The Ayatollah Khomeini in U.S. Editorial Cartoons

Michael A. DeSousa

The Iranian crisis of 1979–1981 remains for many Americans a collage of vivid and painful images: the first photographs of blindfolded American diplomats being herded by Iranian "students"; revolutionary guards carrying trash hammock-like in a captured American flag; the nightly TV news from Tehran featuring a sea of angry faces denouncing Carter, the Shah and the United States; the charred remains of men and machines, horrible wreckage of the abortive rescue attempt.

The "picture" of what was going on in Iran was conveyed to the American people by a wide variety of mass media: newspapers, magazines, TV, radio and film. How these media covered this event and the rhetorical implications of that coverage have been the subject of several recent studies.[1] It is clear that the media, through their power to select, structure, and present the news, have great influence on audience perception of reality and predisposition to act either to change or maintain that reality. But what happens when the media representatives are relatively ignorant of their subject, restricted in their ability to gather information, yet still charged with the task of structuring and presenting a story to an audience that is even less knowledgeable than they?

The answer is as old as rhetoric itself. When faced with an unfamiliar situation and the need to present new information to an audience unprepared to receive it, orators have traditionally turned to the commonplace. A commonplace is just what its name implies: a common, traditional topic or saying about the subject under discussion.

Throughout history the commonplace has provided direction to the orator who is at a loss for what to say. Recent studies have shown that commonplaces are also used by graphic artists, visual rhetors who draw upon a storehouse of common words and images to communicate with their readership.[2] In this essay I want to explore how U.S. editorial cartoonists used commonplaces to generate and structure their graphic caricatures, caricatures which, as we shall see, embodied a rhetoric of their own concerning the ways in which Americans should "understand" the Ayatollah Khomeini and his revolution.[3]

My argument has two parts. First, I will demonstrate the existence of three commonplaces to which American political cartoonists regularly turned in their attempts to explain the Ayatollah to their readers. These commonplaces, I will argue, were effective means of communication if by communication one means imparting information in such a manner that an audience can understand the intended meaning. The second part of my argument, however, is that the meanings or interpretations invited by these caricatures were not conducive to a balanced portrayal of reality, and functioned more as a means of supporting American foreign policy and reinforcing American values than as vehicles for understanding the true implications of the events in Iran. However, while these caricatures may not have provided genuine *understanding* of the Ayatollah and the Iranian crisis, it will be argued that the cartoons may have functioned as a powerful and perhaps necessary form of symbolic aggression.

Rhetorical Functions of Cartoons

The persuasive dimensions of cartoons and caricatures have been recognized for many years, but not until the mid–1960s did scholars begin to explore such dimensions systematically. In the last twenty years the editorial cartoon has become the focus of research into the nature of political campaigns and the evolution of social issues within a culture.[4] A wide variety of functions have been attributed to the cartoon, ranging from outright persuasion,[5] to agenda-setting,[6] to serving as a barometer of the changing political climate.[7]

The major function of cartoons for readers, however, is as a frame for encompassing complex issues and events. These frames are a condensation of a number of interrelated themes, ideas, and motives into one easily apprehended image. Such images often function as root metaphors for the larger, more complicated drama. All of the dramatic elements cannot be imaged, but those which seem to distill the essence of the event can be captured and made to stand, metonymically, for the entire cast. Metonymy is a rhetorical figure in which an idea is evoked through reference to some associated idea. For example, as will be demonstrated in this essay, the Ayatollah Khomeini can be made to stand metonymically for Iran, Islam, religious fanaticism, and a host of other concepts for which he serves as a compressed argument. The concepts which a graphic artist chooses to distill out of all those possible is determined, in part, by the audience he wishes to reach.

"Editorial cartoonists," as DeSousa and Medhurst noted in an earlier essay, "must achieve a concrete understanding, a *Verstehen,* with the reader almost immediately. To achieve this the cartoonist must concoct imagery that is at once compelling and powerful, drawing frequently from potent symbols within the political and cultural mythology."[8] This is precisely what editorial cartoonists did with respect to the crisis in Iran: they turned to commonplace images from within American culture to explain what was happening in a foreign land. The way U.S. cartoonists chose to portray the Ayatollah Khomeini is especially revealing of both the power and danger of communication by commonplace.

Many images of the Ayatollah emerged during the nearly fifteen months that elapsed between the takeover of the American embassy on November 4, 1979, and the return of the hostages on inauguration day, January 20, 1981. For editorial cartoonists, however, three commonplaces were repeatedly employed to invite audience "understanding" of Iran's new leader. In the language of graphics, the Ayatollah was a madman, a religious fraud, and a manipulator.[9] The selection and development of these themes by American cartoonists constitute a persuasive mosaic whose individual frames are both entertaining and effective, but whose collective vision tells us as much about ourselves as it reveals of the Iranian leader.[10]

Khomeini as Madman

One of the most consistently powerful ways in which major syndicated cartoonists portrayed the Ayatollah Khomeini was as a lunatic, a madman whose irrationality might possibly be related to the creeping senility associated with advanced age.[11] The theme of madness or lunacy is, of course, a commonplace way of accounting for behaviors that seem removed from the norm. If a person is insane, there is no need to seek rational or more substantive explanations for his behavior. To appropriate the label of madness is to simultaneously describe and explain. It is a way of shortcircuiting further attempts to understand. Once we realize that a person is "not all there," as the saying goes, further attempts to account for his or her behavior and motives seem superfluous.

Once madness has been accepted as a frame of reference for encompassing the Ayatollah's actions, both artistic creativity and audience interpretation become restricted. If the subject is mad, then the artistic task is clear: to account for the madness and take stock of its potential consequences. There is no longer any need to ponder other motives for actions or the socio-political context of those actions. To be mad is to be controlled by forces beyond reason and to act from psychological or physical *causes* rather than consciously chosen acts inspired by rational motives. The artistic task reduces itself to accounting for the causes of the psychopathology and its potential effects.

In framing Khomeini as a madman, cartoonists may have been reflecting other American media or attempts by the U.S. government to characterize the Iranian leader. That the highest levels of U.S. government shared a perception of Khomeini as a lunatic is at least intimated in the recollections of key American officials, most notably those of Jimmy Carter. In his published memoirs Carter speaks of the Iranian leadership as "those suspicious and irrational men who refused to communicate directly with me." Commenting on Khomeini's leadership during the early days of the embassy takeover Carter adds, "Although Khomeini was acting insanely, we always behaved as if we were dealing with a rational person."[12]

Figure 1. Mike Peters, *Dayton Daily News*. (Copyright © 1980. Reprinted with permission.)

Whether the cartoonists were simply reflecting a viewpoint held by officials in the highest levels of government or were projecting an image which later became adopted by those officials, we cannot know.[13] What is clear is that such an image was repeatedly presented to the reading public by the corps of nationally syndicated American cartoonists. Artists took the commonplace of madness and presented variations upon it by drawing from the cultural resources and social knowledge available to their readers.

Cartoonists, acting as publicists for an emerging rhetorical pose regarding Khomeini, constructed both humorous and unnerving portrayals of the Iranian leader as a madman. One major cluster of cartoons illustrating this commonplace feature the Ayatollah in the stock postures of the mentally imbalanced. In Figure 1 Mike Peters appropriates a familiar icon of institutional madness, the psychiatrist's couch, to present Khomeini confronted with that staple of modern psychiatry, the double bind. In a cartoon borrowing yet another stock symbol of lunacy, the *Philadelphia Inquirer's* Tony Auth caricatures Khomeini's flowing religious robes to fashion a straight jacket securely embracing the Islamic leader. Not only is Khomeini the resident of a madhouse, but he is bound (both literally and figuratively) by a religion which ends in insanity.

"You're right, doc. . . . There's definitely something wrong with his head!"

Figure 2. Jim Borgman, *Cincinnati Enquirer.* (Reprinted by permission of Jim Borgman.)

Just as Peters and Auth drew from American culture familiar *visual* images of madness, so Jim Borgman of the *Cincinnati Enquirer* uses a *verbal* expression as the basis for his cartoon. Figure 2 shows hostage Richard Queen, who would be released early because of his medical condition, surrounded by the Iranians who, themselves, have a physical problem. In the foreground Khomeini says to a physician: "You're right doc. . . . There's definitely something wrong with his head!" The visual pun here (upside down heads) is based on the popular verbal expression about "having your head screwed on right" or "having your head together." In the case of the Iranian captors the outward deformity is meant to imply a mental deficiency. Queen may be physically ill, but his captors are psychologically sick.

Patrick Oliphant uses a more obscure expression of madness to lead readers to the same conclusion when he images the Ayatollah "chewing the carpet." Following Reagan's electoral victory, an apoplectic Khomeini gnaws a persian rug while ranting, "Tell them I refuse to deal with some irresponsible, old, over-the-hill extremist, conservative crazy! Tell them I demand a recount!" His comment, of course, is meant to be self-applicable. It is implied that the cause of Khomeini's insanity may lie in his age and his commitment to extremist politics. In either case the end result is the same: the Ayatollah has gone mad.

Many other cartoons continue to explore the theme of Khomeini's irrationality by associating him with illogical or erratic behaviors. Mike Peters offers us a grumpy Khomeini instructing an aide: "My coffee's cold, seize the

Brazilian embassy." Paul Conrad of the *Los Angeles Times* invokes a memorable literary allusion in a cartoon captioned "Iranian Tea Party." The cartoonist recalls the rampant illogic and confusion of the tea party in Lewis Carroll's classic tale of Alice in Wonderland. In Conrad's version of the scene, a confused Jimmy Carter in the Alice role awaits the antics of the Ayatollah and his minister Bani-Sadr, who is costumed as the Mad Hatter.

Just as some cartoonists searched for the causes of Khomeini's alleged insanity, so others speculated on its potential consequences. For example, cartoonists Auth and Herblock both offer cartoons in which the lunatic policies of Khomeini are seen as replacing the Shah's brutality with a new form of brutality. Other cartoonists see Khomeini's obsession with the Shah as ultimately counterproductive. Paul Conrad draws the Ayatollah literally "painting himself into a corner" with a paint bucket labelled "Return the Shah." One consequence of Khomeini's obsession (itself an attribute of an irrational mind), Conrad implies, is a return to the state of affairs that produced the takeover in the first place: the Ayatollah will lose everything he has gained.

While irrational acts and ridiculous poses are naturally the province of popular *visual* representations of madness, some cartoonists extended the madness frame to include even darker implications. Such cartoons implied that self-destruction (and by extension national destruction) is the logical outcome of this state of irrationality; allusions to suicide, therefore, predominate in these cartoons. Suicide can be a political as well as psychopathological act. But nowhere in the cartoonist's arsenal is suicide so presented. The destruction of the self is not a consciously chosen act referenced to outside social or political events, but a spontaneous result of the failure to think clearly. Self-destruction, the cartoonists imply, is the predictable outcome of Khomeini's insanity.

In Figure 3, for example, Auth images suicide by self-immolation. Khomeini is presented as "playing with fire" by allowing the volatile mobs to run free while striking the match (his oratory perhaps?) which will inflame the masses. At first glance this cartoon may seem to be referenced to political reality. But look at Khomeini's face. He is oblivious to what he is doing, not recognizing that he is about to destroy himself and his people. His potential suicide arises from his inability to see the situation for what it is, to recognize the danger that lurks about him. His behavior is not a conscious political act, but the consequence of a mind that is either too mad or too far removed from reality to realize what it is doing. In a strikingly similar cartoon that continues the self-immolation theme, Pat Oliphant pictures Khomeini and an Iranian follower in the midst of flames which Khomeini has just ignited. While the Iranian leader broods the follower rationalizes the act: "Whatever you say, Imam. I guess you know what you're doing."

Lee Judge of the *San Diego Union* settles for a more contemporary mode of metaphorical suicide in his suggestion that Khomeini will provoke a deadly U.S. response. In Figure 4 the Ayatollah does not seem to be aware of what

Figure 3. Tony Auth, *Philadelphia Inquirer.* (Reprinted by permission of Tony Auth.)

Figure 4. Lee Judge, *San Diego Union.* (Reprinted by permission of the *San Diego Union.* Copyright, 1979.)

"And this one says, 'Congratulations on being voted political leader for life. Very best wishes.' Signed, President-for-life Idi Amin."

Figure 5. Wayne Stayskal, *Chicago Tribune.* (Reprinted by permission of Chicago Tribune. Copyright, 1979.)

he is doing. His eyes are nearly closed. Two chambers of the pistol have already been tried yet he persists in his self-destructive course. Audience members familiar with the Russian roulette scene from the movie *The Deer Hunter,* released only a year before the Iranian crisis, will be cued to both the insanity of the actor and to the likely outcome of his behavior.

Though other cartoonists during this period liken Khomeini to notorious contemporary dictators associated with irrationality and megalomania—dictators like Uganda's Idi Amin (see Figure 5) or Central Africa's Emperor Bokassa—it is the *Chicago Tribune's* Dick Locher who, in Figure 6, most neatly synthesizes the madness and suicide themes within a single frame. Locher's cartoon recalls Philipon's famous caricature of King Louis-Philippe in which, in four stages, the French king's paunchy features are exaggerated until he becomes a pear, "pear" being a French colloquial term for a fathead or dolt.[14] With a transformation as sinister as Philipon's was humorous, Locher presents Khomeini as a moral if not ideological equivalent to an infamous American religious fanatic. Locher visually traces the evolution from Jim Jones to the Ayatollah, from Jonestown to Tehran. If the religious fervor of Jonestown led to mass destruction, Locher implies, the Ayatollah's religious rantings could lead to the same end.

There are three primary reasons for the amplification of the madness commonplace by U.S. editorial cartoonists. First, the iconography of the Ayatollah Khomeini closely parallels the visual imagery of madmen in western cultures. Visually speaking, nothing is more striking about Khomeini than his

211

Jonestown.   **Tehran**

Figure 6. Dick Locher, *Chicago Tribune.* (Reprinted by permission of Chicago Tribune. Copyright, 1979.)

very inappropriateness in the modern, technological world. His turbaned head, religious robes, and patriarch's beard make him, to modern sensibilities, a walking anachronism. His medieval visual ethos easily is made analogous to similar visual types like the eccentric, the crank, the hermit and the zealot. One is reminded how doomsayers (a type of harmless lunatic) are typically portrayed in the robes and beards of ancient prophets. Khomeini's appearance, then, is ripe for rhetorical manipulation. Khomeini's non-western, archaic appearance is offered as evidence of abnormality if not madness, and helps cue reader interpretation.

The second reason the madness commonplace was appropriated during the Iranian crisis is because it allowed cartoonists to do what they do best: deprecate. Madness is a stock device among graphic artists who wish to evoke derisive laughter from their audience. To be mad is to be subjected to abuse. A madman does crazy things in crazy ways which an audience may find humorous. In Figure 7, for example, Peters draws on our social knowledge of the late night pitchman both to deprecate and to entertain. To liken Khomeini to the typically frantic used car dealer of our airwaves is to momentarily suspend the gravity of the Iranian situation while having a laugh at Khomeini's expense. Though the Ayatollah's actions were, in reality, anything but humorous, his physiognomy could be caricatured in humorous ways and his reasoning abilities deprecated in a manner both funny and revealing. We expect madmen to look and act in peculiar ways and we enjoy poking fun at them since to do so is to assert our own "normalcy," thus superiority.

The third reason why madness was appropriated as a commonplace for Khomeini is more complex, but no less rhetorical in nature. The charge of madness channeled audience perceptions along certain predetermined lines,

Figure 7. Mike Peters, Dayton Daily News. (Copyright © 1980. Reprinted with permission.)

and away from other lines of thought. As Kenneth Burke says, "A way of seeing is also a way of not seeing."[15] To be invited to understand Khomeini as a madman is to be encouraged to limit our vision to what is going on in his head, to become amateur psychologists. The question becomes not *if* Khomeini is mad, but what accounts for his madness (e.g., senility) and what is likely to result from it (e.g., mass destruction). By choosing to emphasize this theme, cartoonists implicitly direct reader attention away from other topics which might well have provoked a more accurate understanding of both Khomeini's actions and the nature of the Iranian revolution.

If it is true that ideas have consequences, then it is no less true that images have consequences since they invite readers to form ideas about how the world is. Images of madmen, for example, invite interpretations that locate the source of the problem in the realm of psychology; the problem is in the Ayatollah's head. In so doing, these images direct audience attention away from political and social realities that may have greater explanatory value for understanding the Iranian revolution, but which are more difficult to communicate graphically. Moreover, to label Khomeini as crazy is to vitiate, to some degree, his charges of U.S. support of the oppressive Pahlavi regime and his accusations that some of the hostages were in fact C.I.A. agents rather than diplomats. If Khomeini is crazy, then such troubling charges can be dismissed as the products of a mind unhinged.

Khomeini as Religious Fraud

The second commonplace used by American cartoonists to encompass the Ayatollah Khomeini was that of a religious fraud. If something is fraudulent its value is degraded and its credibility shattered. American consumers are continually warned to beware of the fake or imposter and hold out for the original. Our popular culture teaches us that "Coke is the *real* thing," that "Mama's *original* recipe" is better, and that "it's ingenious, it's *genuine* Bell." The Ayatollah presents himself as a holy man, a religious leader, but according to American cartoon rhetoric he is neither: he is a fraud. Cartoonists attempted to convey the message that, though Khomeini undoubtedly held the titular role as supreme Islamic leader in Iran, that role itself was both a parody and perversion of what religious leadership should be. The term "Ayatollah," denoting a specific class of mullahs or Islamic religious leaders, would become an almost generic term for villainy in the U.S. national vocabulary.[16]

It is fitting, perhaps, that cartoonists should focus on the task of invalidating Khomeini's religious ethos since it is that facet of his character that is most dominant pictorially. Khomeini's dark religious robes, sage-like beard and stern visage recall western visualizations of old testament prophets. In a cartoon appearing just after the Shah's death, Paul Conrad renders the deposed Shah in the heavens awaiting judgment from an Ayatollah-like deity. Since Khomeini genuinely *looks* the part of the ascetic religious figure, the rhetorical device of contradiction is most often used to contrast Khomeini's appearance with his fraudulent nature.[17]

The commonplace of fraud is interesting because it carries with it an implicit acknowledgement that the real thing exists as well as an implied set of standards for determining the object's genuineness or lack thereof. If the Ayatollah is not a real holy man, then who is? If Khomeini's actions do not measure up to the standards of "holiness," then whose actions do and what are those standards? These questions are never raised explicitly by the cartoonists, but they are implicit in the theme of religious fraud.

In Figure 8, for example, Auth emphasizes the blackness of the robes, the hollowed eyes, and the long, claw-like fingers which support the hypocrite's halo. Not only does the cartoonist violate our notions about the way holy men should look, but he has the Ayatollah doing something that a true holy man should not do: proclaiming his own self-righteousness. The paraphrase and inversion of Jesus' Sermon on the Mount almost amounts to rhetorical overkill since the visuals alone invite negative evaluations.

The *Washington Post*'s Herblock employs a similar contradiction between label and deeds in his cartoon depicting the firing squad execution of prisoners under the gaze of a Khomeini poster. The cartoon caption simply states: "Spiritual Leader." Khomeini's religious stature is called into question given his role in such secular matters as executions. The *Chicago Sun-Times'* Bill Mauldin offers readers a wanted poster on which the Iranian leader is accused

Figure 8. Tony Auth, *Philadelphia Inquirer.* (Reprinted by permission of Tony Auth.)

of numerous crimes including "kidnapping, murder, extortion, conspiracy, piracy," and concluding with the charge of "impersonating a holy man." Since the wanted poster announces a $3 reward, the cartoonist also evokes audience recall of the colloquial expression, "phoney as a three dollar bill." Here the dollar amount carries a double signification, implying both counterfeit status and worthlessness. Whereas Auth pictures the Ayatollah violating a religious tenet, Mauldin clearly charges the Iranian leader with secular crimes which contradict religious principles; Khomeini is only a criminal masquerading as a holy man.

To communicate the ways in which the Ayatollah failed the tests for religious legitimation, American cartoonists often turned to Christian standards for criteria. This, in itself, is interesting since it invites audience members to form judgments about Islam and its practice by comparing it with the values and practices of Christianity and Judaism. In Figure 9, for example, Auth presents the Old Testament imagery of the Ten Commandments written on stone tablets. The Commandments are, of course, inverted and several new ones added for good measure. That the last commandment is more political in nature seems to be Auth's way of saying that politics is hiding under the cloak of religion, or perhaps that politics and religion are indivisible in Iran.

Even when cartoonists explicitly recognize the different religious values that motivate the Ayatollah, values based on the Koran and the teachings of Islam, they do so in ways that evoke Christian iconology. Figure 10 is a prime example. Here Bob Englehart specifically pictures the Koran and inverts one of

Figure 9. Tony Auth, *Philadelphia Inquirer.* (Reprinted by permission of Tony Auth.)

Figure 10. Bob Englehart, *Dayton Journal Herald.* (Copyright © 1979. Reprinted with permission.)

its teachings regarding proper treatment of guests within an Islamic state. The interesting point here is not so much that the cartoonist accuses Khomeini of not practicing his own religion, but the way in which he does so. The Koran is pictured as a thick, black book with enlarged Gothic letters and commandments written in the hortatory negative. The inverted *content* is Islamic, but the *form* is still Christian.

Still other means for the pictorial attack on Khomeini's spiritual credentials feature expressions of U.S. ethnocentrism concerning eastern religions. In these cartoons Khomeini is paired with stereotypical visual devices associated with primitive or exotic religious practices. In some cases Khomeini is linked with practices we associate with "black magic" or the dark side of the spiritual world. For example, one Herblock cartoon presents the Ayatollah as an evil wizard tending a boiling cauldron that is producing a hateful potion for an ailing Iran. The coincidence of the early period of the embassy takeover with the American holiday of Halloween prompts cartoonist Bill Mauldin to seat Khomeini on a broomstick. In both of these examples Khomeini is represented as playing a devalued spiritual role as a conjurer or a witch.

Continuing the association with lowly regarded quasi-religions, Pat Oliphant pictures a vengeful Khomeini sticking pins, voodoo fashion, into an Uncle Sam doll; this association of Khomeini with evil religious practices is made despite the cultural inaccuracy of linking Khomeini with primitive *Caribbean* rites. Nowhere is the message of Khomeini's supposed distortion of the religious and spritual *anima* more subtly stated, however, than in Paul Conrad's elitist cultural allusion in Figure 11. Conrad "paraphrases" the work of a pretty fair renaissance cartoonist in his update of Michaelangelo's "Creation" which adorns the Sistine Chapel. In place of God the father extending his index finger to the reclining Adam, Conrad fashions a darkly menacing Khomeini cloaked in a host of terrorists while extending a digit with a very different signification. The Christian deity offers life; Khomeini and his armed revolutionary guards threaten violence and death.

The commonplace of religious illegitimacy serves to deprecate Khomeini's spiritual qualifications through the skillful evocation of western, specifically American attitudes and expectations about religious figures. First, our culture demands that clergy, above all other citizens, be free of the taint of secular sins. A priest or rabbi who is caught, say, cheating on his income tax, is destined for more public outcry than a tax cheater with a more secular occupation. Since Khomeini is consistently linked with such wrongs as lying, blackmail, kidnapping, and the like, his clerical credentials are clearly suspect.

Second, our national policy dictates a clear separation of church and state. Since Khomeini flaunts this sacred bifurcation by occupying the dual roles of head of state and supreme religious leader, he is once again revealed as a counterfeit clergyman, a bogus spiritual leader. How can he claim religious credentials, Americans wonder, when he is so involved in the running of not just the government, but a revolution?

Figure 11. Paul Conrad, *Los Angeles Times.* (Copyright, 1979. Reprinted with permission.)

Third, the frequent use by cartoonists of Judeo-Christian religious symbols (stone tablets, the Bible, scriptural verse) allows readers to evaluate the Ayatollah in terms of Judeo-Christian standards. The inversion of Christian religious symbols is used to communicate that Khomeini is indeed the antithesis of humanistic religious principles. Thus, not only the Ayatollah but his religion is devalued in light of its poor comparison with the tenets which supposedly guide Christian America. The discrediting of Islam through its Iranian leader provides an opportunity to assert the moral superiority of the dominant religious force within this nation.

Khomeini as Manipulator

The third commonplace employed by American cartoonists is that of the manipulator. As an explanation for what was happening in Iran the theme of manipulation has to compete with those of madness and fraud. The manipulation commonplace may have been easily accepted by an American audience because they themselves felt victimized and manipulated by various principals in the hostage crisis, most notably the Ayatollah. Madness could account for some of Khomeini's actions and religious fraud might explain his method of

Figure 12. Patrick Oliphant, *Washington Star.* (Copyright, 1979 Universal Press Syndicate. Reprinted with permission. All rights reserved.)

controlling the populace, but America's failure to deal effectively with Khomeini could only be explained by his desire and ability to manipulate the hostage drama. A madman can be dismissed and a fraud exposed, but a successful manipulator is one who has a goal and intends to achieve it using any means at his disposal.

The commonplace of manipulation is typically communicated by cartoonists through the use of stock metaphors: puppetry, animal training, snake charming, and rigged games of chance. A typical example would be a Locher cartoon that features a wary Uncle Sam at the "Foreign Policy Circus" approaching a shifty-looking Ayatollah who is running the "shell game" booth. Skillful manipulation of the shells will allow the clever Khomeini to consistently dupe the gullible Uncle Sam. These cartoons, which focus on Khomeini as a manipulator, are especially significant since the majority of them pair the Ayatollah with another principal in the hostage drama: Jimmy Carter. As will be demonstrated, it is this pairing of political foes which illustrates the potential power of the editorial cartoon as a reflector of national consciousness.

Given the preeminence of the hostage situation as a U.S. media event, it is perhaps predictable that Khomeini would be criticized as a manipulator of the mass media. One recalls the "spontaneous" demonstrations which filled both the streets of Tehran and American television screens. There were the raucous protests outside the U.S. embassy which fell strangely silent when western TV cameras stopped taping; the staged hostage press conferences and propagandized Christmas visitations were also condemned by U.S. officials as

Figure 13. Jeff MacNelly, *Richmond News Leader.* (Reprinted by permission: Tribune Company Syndicate, Inc. reserved.)

cynical manipulations. For example, in Figure 12 Oliphant employs the puppeteer metaphor to imply that Khomeini has been controlling the U.S. media for his own ends. Note both the NBC network logo on the camera pack and the discussion in the foreground of the need for "extras."

Employing a stock metaphor for control associated with eastern, exotic cultures, Jeff MacNelly concocts a Khomeini whose tool of control is the television camera, not the fakir's flute. The significance of the snake in Figure 13 is oddly ambiguous. Does it symbolize a dangerous Iranian populace which must be carefully controlled? Or does the cobra signify a distracted America, swaying to Khomeini's media tune? In either case, the television medium is asserted as a powerful device for manipulation, a device that Khomeini wields with some degree of skill.

That Khomeini's control of the foreign media was seen as essential to his exploitation of the hostage situation is nicely depicted in an ironic Oliphant cartoon. The Ayatollah is pictured addressing his apparently nervous minister: "Ghotbzadeh, I had the craziest dream last night. I held a press conference and nobody came because some stupid turkey had expelled all the American newsmen. So, naturally, I had the klutz executed, whoever he was. . . ." This same minister would be executed in 1982 for the graver error of plotting against

Figure 14. Michael Keefe, Denver Post. (Reprinted by permission of Michael Keefe.)

Khomeini. Wayne Stayskal of the *Chicago Tribune* parodies Khomeini's control of American television in a cartoon which poses a typical American husband complaining about the hostage interviews which NBC aired. "I wonder what NBC will do next?" he queries while his TV set blares "And now, heeeeeeeere's Khomeini!"

Besides the charge of media manipulation, a second, more significant scenario of manipulation features the beleaguered American president, Jimmy Carter. In a startlingly familiar succession of cartoons, American popular culture and idiom are raided to convey the persistent message that Khomeini has become the shrewd manipulator in this crisis; Carter, on the other hand, has become the too easily manipulated victim. While a few cartoons do feature an Uncle Sam figure or an "Average American" in the role of dupe or victim, it is Jimmy Carter who is frequently on the receiving end of Khomeini's manipulations.

Many cartoonists use almost identical visual metaphors in communicating Carter's role as inept respondent to Khomeini's demands. For example, in Figure 14 the *Denver Post*'s Michael Keefe sees Carter as the hapless performer in a perverse game of diplomatic "Simon Says." Carter is relegated to the status of respondent, one who simply reacts to another's commands. In a similar vein MacNelly features Khomeini holding a large hoop which an obliging Carter has attempted to leap through unsuccessfully. While Carter crashes in the sawdust Khomeini observes: "Be patient . . . He's doing the best he can."

Khomeini has Carter jumping to his commands in the manner of a trained seal. Continuing the master/mastered format, Oliphant represents Khomeini as the commanding master, Carter as the obedient performer. In Figure 15 Khomeini puts the docile Carter through his paces. In Figure 16 Locher borrows a recurring scene from the popular "Peanuts" cartoon strip with the trickster Lucy/Ayatollah once again playing Charlie Brown/Carter for the fool.

Locher images Khomeini using the hostages as a "political football." He holds out their possible release as an inducement to the president, then withdraws the offer when an attempt is made to redeem it. The comment placed in Carter's mouth makes it clear that this has happened before. The Ayatollah is manipulating the possibility of a hostage release to make the American president do his bidding. In the process he is making the president look like a fool for who else but a fool would be taken in twice by the same gambit?

Still other cartoons in this cluster picture Carter in the role of inept respondent to Khomeini's actions. In a Locher cartoon Carter makes a fumbling grab for a yoyo labelled "Hostages" which a stern Khomeini maneuvers expertly. A Herblock cartoon images Carter being shoved off a precipice by Khomeini while complaining to the Iranian: "one of these days you're gonna push me too far!" This last cartoon neatly summarizes the message of these caricatures: Carter is too easily conned, tricked, or "pushed around" by Khomeini. Carter's victimage and humiliation, we realize, extend to the American people.

Besides the use of stock formulae for representing manipulation (shell game, puppetry, jumping through a hoop), there is also one other important rhetorical device being employed by the cartoonists. In addition to the obvious conclusion that Khomeini is the *controller* in these scenes and Carter the *controlled,* there is also the issue of pictorial stature as a symbol for political stature. While Khomeini is consistently represented as an adult, full-sized figure in the cartoon frames, Carter is frequently presented in the diminutive mode as a child, a pet, or a pint-sized leader. This tendency to use size as part of the rhetorical arsenal parallels earlier research into the graphic resources available to editorial cartoonists.[18] Carter is, in the language of the cartoons, too easily manipulated because he lacks the stature of a strong, active leader.

While cartoons utilizing the commonplace of manipulation do indeed cast some aspersions on Khomeini's honesty and intentions, such cartoons are even more revealing of cartoonists' (and their audiences') estimations of Carter's leadership in the hostage crisis. A corollary to this position, of course, would be that candidate Ronald Reagan would be perceived by cartoonists as capable of providing more leadership in the crisis. This appears to be the case. Though Reagan was certainly not immune to cartoonists' barbs during the 1980 campaign, artists seem united in the perception that Reagan would take

Figure 15. Patrick Oliphant, *Washington Star.* (Copyright, 1979, Universal Press Syndicate. Reprinted with permission. All rights reserved.)

Figure 16. Dick Locher, *Chicago Tribune.* (Reprinted by permission of the *Chicago Tribune.* Copyright, 1980.)

a tougher stand with Khomeini. For example, a Tony Auth cartoon just after Reagan's election offered a new twist on the compliant performer metaphor noted in Figures 14 and 15. In Auth's version an obedient Carter leaps through a hoop for Khomeini only to be yanked offstage by a vaudeville hook. Carter's replacement is a pistol-toting Cowboy Reagan with a lasso who startles the Ayatollah with the line, "Role change, towel-head!" The *Los Angeles Times'* Conrad also suggests Khomeini's fear of Reagan in a cartoon displaying a grim Ayatollah counting off with hashmarks the "Days Until I Have To Deal With Reagan." The cartoon is captioned "Hostage." The tables have apparently been turned, implies Conrad, the Ayatollah will soon discover what it's like to be a political victim.

Finally, an Oliphant cartoon from the post-election period reinforces the perceived contrast between the apparently submissive Carter and the supposedly militaristic Reagan. An Iranian adviser queries Khomeini: "Hey Immam, I got one for you . . . What is flat and glows?" Khomeini: "OK, I'll bite, What is flat and glows?" "Iran on Inauguration Day," the aide retorts. "I don't get it," Khomeini mutters. "There are those of us who wish you would ponder it, Immam," concludes the aide.

One could argue that the commonplace of manipulation, originally adopted to describe and explain the Ayatollah's actions, also became a functional argument for the election of Ronald Reagan. The cartoons "instructed" readers as to who was the manipulator (Khomeini), who the manipulated (Carter). They further suggested who was likely to terminate Khomeini's manipulations (Reagan). To the degree that the hostage crisis was a pivotal issue in the 1980 election, the "votes" cast by editorial cartoonists forecast the eventual outcome.

The American people will tolerate a broad range of character flaws in their leaders, but weakness or indecision are among the most despised presidential traits. By continually emphasizing Khomeini's *success* as a manipulator of events, the editorial cartoonists were also drawing attention to Carter's *failure*. The commonplace of manipulation thus functioned to support a change of national leadership by framing Carter as a compliant victim who was too foolish or weak to respond in an appropriate manner. If to be "presidential" means to act, to be in control, then Carter's presidential stature was surely deflated by his consistent portrayal as a hapless victim of the Ayatollah's machinations.

Conclusion

Throughout the fifteen months of the Iranian crisis, American editorial cartoonists employed three commonplaces to describe and explain the Ayatollah Khomeini to their readers. He was a madman, a religious fraud, and a manipulator. All of these commonplaces were effective means of communicating to the American audience some of the apparent characteristics of the Ayatollah and his revolution. American readers were familiar with the madman.

They had seen him on television, read about him in the newspapers, and seen him used as a foil in numerous cartoons and comedy routines. Readers were likewise familiar with the religious fake. The iconography of the prophet and the suspect nature of the guru were, by 1979, hardly cause for surprise. Political manipulators had long been a part of American society and that image, too, found ready acceptance.

Cartoonists fell back on these commonplaces because they were a means of connecting the unknown and strange with the known and familiar. They were analogs, points of comparison, which could be used to explain Iran and its leader to the American people. But the commonplace can be a dangerous device. In the act of rhetorical invention the substitution of commonplace sayings or images for genuine reflection can lead to the adoption of ideas that are *too* simple, *too* glib, and thus misleading. In many ways the use of the madman, religious fraud, and political manipulator images were over-simplifications.

To communicate in cartoon form is, by definition, to distill one clear idea from a multitude of competing ideas, to condense and reduce complex issues into a simple visual design. By reducing complex issues to simple analogic or metaphoric forms, the cartoonist provides the reader with an attractive illusion of understanding. Such understanding often serves as a touchstone for subsequent thought and action, and it is this rhetorical function that is most in need of further exploration.

By being repeatedly told that Khomeini was a madman, a religious fraud, and a political manipulator, American readers were invited to respond in several ways, most of them counterproductive to genuine understanding of Khomeini or his revolution. If Khomeini was a madman, then anything he said or did could be dismissed as the mere rantings of an unbalanced mind. There was no need to consider his charges, reflect upon American involvement with the Shah, or acknowledge U.S. espionage in Iran. A madman is crazy and so, by implication, is anything he says. By adopting this commonplace, cartoonists invited their readers to "understand" Khomeini in such a way as to rob him of the legitimacy of his case.

Use of the religious fraud commonplace produced much the same result. Cartoonists were able to deprive Khomeini of his religious authority by playing on American presumptions about how clergy behave and what the relationship should be between church and state. Artists used Christian symbols and their attendant values to suggest judgments of an Islamic cleric; they also relied on American legal tradition to imply that the Ayatollah was playing an inappropriate political role in Iranian affairs. Such cartoons encouraged the audience to understand that Islam is not Christianity and Iran is not America, but did little to further real understanding of the role of clergy or the relationship between church and state in other cultures.

The commonplace of political manipulation was, in some ways, both the most effective and the most accurate. It was most effective in that it reflected the American sense of frustration and also projected an instrumental way to relieve that frustration. The message communicated by the commonplace was functional because the audience could actually, if only indirectly, do something about their frustration: change national leaders. Use of the commonplace also invited a more balanced understanding of who Khomeini was and what he was doing. To acknowledge someone as a manipulator, though unflattering, is still to recognize him as a conscious agent who makes choices and who might be persuaded to make different choices given the proper inducement. For many cartoonists the proper inducement appears to have been the election of Ronald Reagan and to that end, too, the commonplace of manipulation may have proved effective. By picturing Khomeini as a successful manipulator, cartoonists implied that Jimmy Carter was inept, and in doing so they presaged the electoral judgment of November, 1980.

Though two of the three commonplaces used to characterize the Ayatollah did little to help American readers actually *understand* the leader or the roots of the hostage crisis, the cartoons may well have served a more emotional need: symbolic aggression. Exhibiting a unity of purpose that typifies that nationalism found during times of crisis, editorial cartoonists gave the American people avenues for venting hostilities that might otherwise have turned into more violent expressions.

The importance of other avenues for symbolic punishment is heightened by the diplomatic constraints which prevented the U.S. administration from engaging in vitriolic political rhetoric aimed at the Khomeini regime. The Carter administration could not vilify Khomeini without risking harm to the hostages. President Carter's political ideology also may have constrained responses to Khomeini. As historian Theodore White has observed, "it is impossible in the rhetoric of liberal American politics, of which Carter was a true expression, to disdain or denounce people of other traditions as inherently evil, genetically inferior, or culturally vicious."[19] As a result, it was up to *unofficial* echoes of the national consciousness—columnists, artists, comedians, media personalities, cartoonists—to articulate the hostilities resulting from what White has called our "National Humiliation."

It is difficult to gauge the impact of the popular arts as vehicles for the expression of both hostility toward Iran and American national unity during the period of crisis. Certainly one may object to the ways patriotism itself was commercialized as parodied in Figure 17. Yet the obscene bumper stickers, the Ayatollah dart boards, the ubiquitous yellow ribbons, the hostile pop songs (e.g., *Bomb, Bomb Iran* to the tune of the Beach Boys' *Barbara Ann*), T-shirts, and cartoons served important functions for a frustrated American public. The importance of the cartoons and other means for catharsis became vital when we realized, after the disastrous rescue attempt, that "there was no way Americans could punish their Iranian tormentors."[20]

Figure 17. Lee Judge, *San Diego Union.* (Reprinted by permission of the *San Diego Union.* Copyright, 1979.)

In lieu of punishment, then, was the opportunity to vilify the Iranian Revolution's most revered political symbol: the Ayatollah Ruhollah Khomeini. With the aid of the traditions of visual caricature and rhetorical commonplaces, Khomeini could be ridiculed as a madman, a religious fraud, and a cynical manipulator of people and events. Or the dark, gaunt physiognomy of the Iranian leader could metamorphose to become the inhuman, lone benefactor of the tragic rescue attempt as represented by Conrad in Figure 18.

While a valid argument could be made for the position that Americans did not receive a balanced perspective of the crisis in the cartoons surveyed here, that finding should not be surprising. As the anthropologist Edward Hall noted almost thirty years ago in his book *Silent Language,* the major benefit of studying a foreign culture is learning more about one's own society. Similarly, the study of U.S. cartoonists' portrayals of the Iranian hostage crisis tells us far more about the American people, their values and traditions, than it illuminates the crisis or explains its leader.

Americans are often accused of ethnocentrism, of viewing the world through red, white, and blue lenses.[21] If the rhetoric of the editorial cartoons during the Iranian hostage crisis is any indication, then such charges seem justified.

Figure 18. Paul Conrad, *Los Angeles Times.* (Copyright © 1980. Reprinted with permission.)

By relying on commonplaces from American culture and supporting them with values drawn from the Judeo-Christian tradition, cartoonists were able to communicate their negative evaluations of the Ayatollah in an effective and often entertaining manner. But communication is more than effect. Images, like words, are invitations to knowledge.

During the Iranian crisis of 1979–1981, American editorial cartoonists invited their readers to know the Ayatollah, but provided only the illusion of understanding. By labelling Khomeini mad, we implicitly vindicated our own foreign policy. By picturing him as a religious fraud, we asserted the moral superiority of our own religious tradition. By emphasizing his skill as a manipulator of our president, we may have nudged ourselves toward a change in national leadership. The majority of cartoons examined in this study, a small portion of which are offered as illustrations, demonstrate the communicative potential of this visual form. Cartoons offer an audience what has been called "the satisfaction of pretended insight," not necessarily the truth, but a palatable version of reality demanded by a mass readership. In this case that readership was a nation enduring a crisis of purpose and in deep need of unity and reassurance.

Notes

1. Robert C. Johnson, " 'Blacks and Women': Naming American Hostages Released in Iran," *Journal of Communication,* 30 (1980), 58–63; Ernest G. Bormann, "A Fantasy Theme Analysis of the Television Coverage of the Hostage Release and the Reagan Inaugural," *Quarterly Journal of Speech,* 69 (1982), 133–145; D. Ray Heisey and J. David Trebing, "A Comparison of the Rhetorical Visions and Strategies of the Shah's White Revolution and the Ayatollah's Islamic Revolution," *Communication Monographs,* 50 (1983), 158–174; Edward W. Said, *Covering Islam: How the Media and Experts Determine How We See the Rest of the World* (New York: Pantheon, 1981).

2. For an examination of the visual commonplaces from the 1980 presidential campaign, see Michael A. DeSousa and Martin J. Medhurst, "Political Cartoons and American Culture: Significant Symbols of Campaign 1980," *Studies in Visual Communication,* 8 (1982), 84–97; Martin J. Medhurst and Michael A. DeSousa, "Political Cartoons as Rhetorical Form: A Taxonomy of Graphic Discourse," *Communication Monographs,* 48 (1981), 197–236.

3. See Robley D. Rhine, "Ethnocentrism Expressed in American Editorial Cartoons During the Iranian Hostage Crisis," Speech Communication Association Convention, Louisville, Kentucky, 1982; Michael A. DeSousa, "The Satisfaction of Pretended Insight: The Iranian Crisis in Selected U.S. Editorial Cartoons," Speech Communication Association Convention, Louisville, Kentucky, 1982; available through Eric Reports. Conclusions reported here are based on a study of 244 editorial cartoons treating the Iranian Crisis from the period Nov. 1, 1979 through Nov. 30, 1980. To ensure geographical and ideological diversity, cartoons were obtained from the *Washington Post,* the *Chicago Tribune,* the *Los Angeles Times* and the Davis, California *Enterprise.* This cartoon sample included the work of 23 syndicated cartoonists.

4. Alette Hill, "The Carter Campaign in Retrospect: Decoding the Cartoons," *Semiotica,* 23 (1978) 307–332; Katherine Meyer, John Seidler, Timothy Curry, Adrian Aveni, "Women in July Fourth Cartoons: A 100 Year Look," *Journal of Communication,* 30 (1980), 21–29; Janet L. Jacobsen, "What Are They Saying About Us: How Cartoons Over The Years Have Depicted Male/Female Relationships," W.H.I.M. Conference, Tempe, Arizona, 1982.

5. See Matthew C. Morrison, "The Role of the Political Cartoonist in Image Making," *Central States Speech Journal,* 20 (1969), 252–260; Kathleen J. Turner, "Comic Strips: A Rhetorical Perspective," *Central States Speech Journal,* 28 (1977), 24–35. For a study which attempts to correlate artistic intention and reader interpretation see LeRoy M. Carl, "Meaning Evoked in Population Groups by Editorial Cartoons," Unpublished Dissertation, Syracuse University, 1967; Carl, "Political Cartoons: 'Ink Blots' of the Editorial Page," *Journal of Popular Culture,* 4 (Summer 1970), pp. 39–45. A more recent study of the editorial cartoon's persuasive effect is Michael A. DeSousa and Martin J. Medhurst, "The Editorial Cartoon as Visual Rhetoric: Rethinking Boss Tweed," *Journal of Visual Verbal Languaging,* 2 (1982), 43–52.

6. DeSousa and Medhurst, "Political Cartoons and American Culture," p. 92.

7. See, for example, two studies which examined the impact of the Watergate Crisis on caricatures of Richard Nixon: Mary E. Wheeler and Stephen K. Reed, "Responses to Before and After Watergate Caricatures," *Journalism Quarterly,* 52 (1975), 134–136; Mitchel Goldman and Margaret Hagen, "The Forms of Caricature: Physiognomy and Political Bias," *Studies in the Anthropology of Visual Communication,* 5 (1978), 30–36. For cartoon treatment of an international scandal, see James D. Steakley, "Iconography of a Scandal: Political Cartoons and the Eulenburg Affair," *Studies in Visual Communication,* 9 (1983), 20–51.

8. DeSousa and Medhurst, "The Political Cartoon as Cultural Form," p. 93.

9. Of the 244 cartoons examined, 186 feature the Ayatollah pictorially or verbally. Of these cartoons 43 evidence the madness commonplace, 38 represent the religious fraud commonplace, and 40 utilize the manipulation commonplace. Commonplaces do, of course, overlap in selected cartoons.

10. A statement indicative of the lack of a national "definition" of Khomeini at the time of the embassy takeover—thus the opportunity for such a definition to be supplied by cartoons and other media—comes from Captain Gary Sick, National Security Council expert on Iran: "Khomeini was beyond the experience, if not the imagination, of anyone in the United States government." As quoted in Theodore H. White, *America in Search of Itself: The Making of the President 1956–1980* (New York: Harper and Row, 1982), p. 16.

11. The tendency of American cartoonists to engage in stereotypical portrayals of the aged is noted in Jerry Adler et al., "The Finer Art of Politics," *Newsweek,* 13 Oct., 1980, p. 78.

12. Jimmy Carter, *Keeping Faith: Memoirs of a President* (New York: Bantam, 1982), p. 459.

13. An interesting question here concerns the role editorial cartoons play as conduits for an official or governmental point of view. For further development of this idea, see Richard A. Cherwitz, "The Contributory Effect of Rhetorical Discourse," *Quarterly Journal of Speech,* 66 (1980), 35–50.

14. For a discussion of Philipon and other pioneering caricaturists, see Judith Wechsler, "Caricature, Newspapers and Politics: Paris in the 1830s," *Studies in Visual Communication,* 7 (1981), esp. pp. 5–7.

15. Kenneth Burke, *Permanence and Change* (1935; rpt. Indianapolis: Bobbs-Merrill, 1965), p. 49.

16. A discussion of the evolution of the term "Ayatollah" into a full fledged visual and verbal devil term is found in DeSousa, "The Satisfaction of Pretended Insight: The Iranian Crisis in Selected U.S. Editorial Cartoons," pp. 12–14.

17. Contradiction as rhetorical device is elaborated in Medhurst and DeSousa, "Political Cartoons as Rhetorical Form," pp. 207–210.

18. Medhurst and DeSousa, pp. 213–214.

19. White, p. 16.

20. White, p. 23.

21. For an example of foreign cartoon depiction of American issues and characters, see Yeshayahu Nir, "U.S. Involvement in the Middle East Conflict in Soviet Caricatures," *Journalism Quarterly,* 54 (1977), 697–702+726.

5
Rhetoric of Music

The relationship between the arts of rhetoric and music is both ancient and complex. Pythagorean musical theory, formulated in the sixth century B.C., gave birth to the terms "figure" and "trope" which were later applied by Gorgias of Leontini to the art of rhetoric. In ancient musical theory a "figure" was a specific arrangement of notes. When generalized to rhetoric, "figure" came to mean primarily the arrangement of words in certain patterns. Throughout the history of rhetoric certain "rhetorical figures"—metaphor, simile, analogy, metonymy, and so forth—have been widely discussed. Hence, from the outset, rhetorical thought was indebted to musical theory.

Aristotle, the first great systematizer of the art of rhetoric, adopted many of the terms originally derived from music theory in his effort to explain the arts of rhetoric and poetic. In addition to figures and tropes, Aristotle wrote about movement, rhythm, and harmony: all concepts that originated with musical studies. From a theoretical standpoint, then, rhetoric and poetic were greatly indebted to the art of music.

If ancient thinkers borrowed from the principles of one art (music) to help explain other arts (rhetoric and poetry), then it is equally true that contemporary critics have sought to repay the debt by bringing the insights of rhetoric and poetic to bear on musical texts. Songs and chants long have been recognized as persuasive media. More recently, the lyrics of ballads, folk hymns, campaign songs, and rock music have been examined from rhetorical perspectives.

In this section Michael McGuire focuses critical attention on the field of rock music and one of its more controversial practitioners: Bruce Springsteen. McGuire conducts a structuralist/thematic critique in which he claims to find three recurring ideas that interact to fashion a unique rhetorical message. The author "reconstructs" these ideas in such a manner as to form three coherent themes: despair, optimism, and responsibility.

McGuire's method of reconstructing and identifying these themes is, he claims, a sort of structuralist approach similar to Kenneth Burke's method of cluster analysis. Having first isolated three primary clusters, McGuire then describes their interactions and discusses how interpretation of one theme impinges on the intepretation of the other two.

In the process of conducting his analysis McGuire raises some interesting questions for both the theory and practice of rhetorical criticism. The first issue he raises concerns the relationship between words and music. Traditionally, rhetorically oriented studies of music have focused almost exclusively on musical *lyrics*. McGuire, too, focuses reader attention on lyrics, but notes that the sound of the music is also part of the message. In McGuire's view can music function argumentatively in and of itself or is its role simply to extend and reinforce arguments made in the lyrical mode? If music does argue apart from the lyrics that accompany it, does the author give us any hints as to how such music might be analyzed?

Another issue raised in this essay concerns the interrelationships between words, thoughts, and feelings. McGuire explicitly argues that Springsteen's music expresses feelings and thereby opens up "a universality by focusing, not on what makes us feel, but how we may feel, even if each for our own reasons." McGuire seems to be arguing that the reasons for feeling are secondary to the feelings themselves. But if this is the case, then how does the rhetorical critic manage to describe or interpret feelings through the medium of the written word? If Springsteen chooses to express his message in music because it is through that medium that he can best express feelings, is it possible for the critic ever to analyze accurately the elements of that message apart from the musical code within which it is encompassed? Put differently, can analysis of lyrics alone ever reveal feelings, whether those of the artist or of his listeners, if such feelings are conveyed or invited primarily through the music? Such a question immediately raises another: Is it possible to do *rhetorical* criticism of music and song without reference to lyrics?

Finally, McGuire argues that Springsteen's audience closely identifies with the feelings and themes expressed in his music, and cites as evidence an instance of audience participation at a Springsteen concert. Earlier in the essay, however, McGuire argues that much of Springsteen's lyrics call for a metaphorical or symbolic interpretation. If that is true, how can the critic know with which message the audience is likely to identify—the literal message (as in the example of the concert audience supplying the precise words) or the metaphorical message (as in several of the interpretations offered by the author)?

If invitations to self-knowledge are offered by the singer on various interpretive levels, then how is the critic to know to which of the possible levels any particular audience is responding? How many levels is the critic responsible for explicating? Is the best criticism that which reveals what a particular audience actually understands or that which reveals the greatest number of possible interpretations? Is any one interpretation "better" than any other and if so, what are the criteria by which we may discriminate the "better" from the "worse" interpretation?

'Darkness on the Edge of Town': Bruce Springsteen's Rhetoric of Optimism and Despair

Michael McGuire

Investigation of the rhetorical dimensions of music and song is still in its infancy. The few studies that have been conducted to date focus primarily on social protest music; songs that are blatantly didactic in purpose, method, and content.[1] Consequently, artists perceived primarily as musicians rather than musical orators have received less attention than might otherwise be warranted. One such artist is Bruce Springsteen.

During the week of October 27, 1975, Springsteen appeared on the covers of both *Time* and *Newsweek* where, among other accolades, he was proclaimed the new Bob Dylan.[2] That same year John Landau, music editor of *Rolling Stone,* wrote: "I have seen the future of rock 'n roll, and its name is Bruce Springsteen."[3] Nearly a decade later, Springsteen remains a rock phenomenon. His concerts are sellouts and his album sales run into the hundreds of thousands. He is on the verge of becoming a cultural myth as well as a rock legend. References to "the Boss" punctuate prime-time television, and an educational album featuring "Bruce Stringbean" has recently been produced by Jim Henson and the Muppets.

In this essay I offer a rhetorical analysis of the three themes that bind together most of Springsteen's music: despair, optimism, and responsibility. To understand Springsteen's message is not only to recognize these central themes, but to appreciate the complex, dialectical relationships between and among them. We will focus on three of Springsteen's most popular albums: *Born to Run* (1975), *Darkness on the Edge of Town* (1978), and *The River* (1980).[4] Realizing that lyrics cannot be criticized *in vacuo* as if they were poetry independent of important musical accompaniment, we will observe relationships between the words and music. However, our purpose is to uncover the *synthesis* Springsteen structures among his three major themes of despair, optimism, and responsibility by observing first the nature of each theme and then their interrelationships.

A few words about our method of inquiry are in order at the outset. We will not focus on the chronological growth of Springsteen as an artist or the sequential development of his music, as if we saw it reaching toward some goal or endpoint. Such discussions could prove interesting and valuable, and popular authors have been providing them to demonstrate Springsteen's development, especially as a composer and producer.[5] But with contemporary rock music we confront an art form especially suited to nonsequential analysis. The average rock album contains from eight to twelve songs, and even when we consider what has come to be called a "concept album," there is not usually a necessary sequence of songs.[6] The "concept" generally is one of instrumental or lyrical unity which does not require serial or diachronic presentation to be grasped. To grasp the thematic unity of a single rock album often requires a restructuring of its units; the same observation applies to an attempt to isolate themes that recur in a number of albums.

This sort of structuralist approach to rhetorical criticism has been both advocated and illustrated. In *The Philosophy of Literary Form* Kenneth Burke discusses finding "associational clusters" in artistic works and a process for examining such clusters to disclose "what goes with what."[7] The disclosure of clusters usually involves some deconstruction and reconstruction of an author's works to put together the parts of the clusters which fit thematically but not narratively. A similar process of reconstruction is the heart of structuralist criticism, which seeks out thematic units and the relationships among them.[8]

I

To Springsteen fans it will come as no surprise that the musician offers pictures of despair as a form of social criticism. Such images are rendered subtle by their essentially individual, existential nature. Without becoming blatantly didactic and advocating changes or assigning blame, Springsteen sings of people in despair and the situations which have produced such an outcome. The label *despair* was chosen for the theme being reconstructed here because it best encompasses the breadth of images ranging from hopelessness to ennui— from a deeply and personally felt despondency to a sort of bored surrender to the monotony of modern life. Springsteen's critical attitude toward these images will emerge in the analysis which follows and be discussed in summary; what remains by way of introduction is to comment about the narrative structures in this theme.

Within the despair theme, we find both first and third person narration. Generally, first person narration conveys the extreme of hopelessness and third person shows people the singer regards as being in hopeless circumstances, whether they are aware of them or not. The songs which provide the images for this theme are not addressed to a specific person, but once or twice a comment is made to a specific woman within the narrative, and one first person plural is addressed to a friend named Eddie. We will consider first the more personal and extreme images of the despair theme.

Broken loves and broken dreams and promises are the sources of some of the most intense expressions of despair in Springsteen's music. This deeply felt hopelessness is not always clearly attributed to a specific cause, unless we could say that high hopes dashed is the supreme cause from which all others follow. A convenient touchstone for the theme of despair is expressed in the intensity of feeling in "Streets of Fire."[9]

"Streets of Fire" resembles some of Springsteen's earliest work in the sense that it does not offer narrative development, but only images of feelings. There is no story of "she done me wrong" or "the whole world is falling apart," but only one voice located in no particular time, place, or plot crying out about what happens when "you realize how they tricked you this time/And it's all lies." Neither "they" nor "it" is defined by any other part of the song; however, no mood of flaming paranoia is developed, either. The singer finds the world empty, but it may be the world of his own making, he says. That is, he tells us that when "the weak lies and cold walls you embrace/Eat at your insides and leave you face to face with/Streets of fire," that's when "you don't care anymore." In sum, there is a hopelessness to existence built on fabrication penned in by the coldness which only genuine emotions can thaw. But this singer finds nothing genuine: "I live now, only with strangers/I talk to only strangers/I walk with angels that have no place." Strangers are those we know only through lies, not "really." "Streets of Fire" is a metaphor for the isolation and desperation of anyone who ever felt totally betrayed. Its mood, considered lyrically, vocally, or instrumentally, ranges from soft and somber to intensely wailing.

Just as "Streets of Fire" affirms no particular time or place, it expresses no particular cause of despair. The song offers a glimpse into the mind of a person betrayed and bitter. The song expresses a feeling; it does not tell any story. The effect of this unspecified situation may be to open up a universality by focusing, not on what makes us feel, but how we may feel, even if each for our own reasons. Life is often symbolized by travel, paths, or roads; the sojourner singing this song to us finds the trip sufficiently punishing to conceptualize it as "Streets of Fire," as he wanders "a loser down these tracks." The music sets the mood for us to receive this unhappy, anguished message. "Streets of Fire" is a reminder that things and people are not always what they seem, and that betrayal may lead one to a false consciousness or bad faith ("the weak lies and cold walls you embrace") resulting ultimately in despair.

Not all despair is inflicted on us by others, however. Most people can relate to the experience of feeling betrayed, but an even more common experience may be the disappointment of unfulfilled hopes. Springsteen tells his audience about dreams, in connection with despair, dreams that do not come true. Two examples of this rhetoric are especially clear. The song, "Racing in the Street" is the story of a man who competes for money by racing his car in the streets.[10] The racer seems to assert that he has triumphed over problems that others experience, primarily boring lives. He will "only run for the money, got no strings attached." But this very quality, built carefully in details for the first two thirds of the song, gives way to an ironic and tragic picture. Suddenly there is mention of a woman he met "on the strip three years ago/In a Camaro with this dude from L.A." When he won the race, of which he boasts, she rode away with him. It was, we gather, her dream to ride to the top with the winner, and it was a mistake: "But now there's wrinkles around my baby's eyes/And she cries herself to sleep at night." Here is a rhetoric, not of betrayal, but of misperception and wrong expectations; he still has "got no strings attached" because he never promised them to her. Her despair is described as total:

> She sits on the porch of her daddy's house
> But all her pretty dreams are torn,
> She stares off alone into the night
> With the eyes of one who hates for just being born.

Her life's streets aren't for racing; they are dead ends. Her life is so awful to her with her dreams ended that she "hates for just being born."

He is aware of her plight and understands it. In the next section of the song he holds out some hope of fulfilling her dreams: "Tonight my baby and me are gonna ride to the sea/And wash these sins off our hands." But that expression is spoken, not to the woman, but to the song's audience. That it is a hollow promise is made clear by the final chorus telling us, "summer's here and the time is right/For racin' in the street." We can only expect the situation shown to us to continue unchanged; the very thing which makes him feel alive has destroyed her. This slow-paced, somewhat mournful song matches lyrical tragedy with instrumental and vocal sadness. The tone is more thoughtful or meditative than sympathetic; that is, our narrator understands the woman's plight and even its origins. Yet his analysis of the situation is self-centered:

> Some guys they just give up living
> And start dying little by little, piece by piece,
> Some guys come home from work and wash up,
> And go racin' in the street.

Our narrator is unwilling to die in a mundane life; the result is that his woman suffers while he goes "racin' in the street." The situation is not a betrayal; it is a case of delusion which has run its course, leaving nothing.

The two examples of despair we have examined thus far show us the personal, experienced, or felt side of despair. These descriptions have two rhetorical qualities. First, the sound and meaning of each song are *expressive* of how hopelessness feels—both can serve a cathartic function for some audiences. Second, both songs can serve rhetorically as warnings. Neither picture is a happy one: the singer of "Streets of Fire" and the woman in "Racing in the Street" have given up on life. The audience, while invited to look at despair, is simultaneously cautioned against it. Nevertheless, the examples we have considered thus far are intensely personal statements of feelings. Somewhat different from these personalized accounts are Springsteen's descriptions of how social systems and expectations can wear people down.

One of Springsteen's most vivid descriptions of the endless ennui which can overtake and numb people in mass society is "Factory."[11] A poignant, third person narrative, "Factory" is the story of "man," whose life is started every day by the factory whistle he hears telling him it's time to get up: "Man rises from bed and puts on his clothes,/Man takes his lunch, walks out in the morning light/It's the working, the working, just the working life." The man is summoned into his repetitive routine as another faceless, lunch-box-carrying blue collar worker.[12] The motivation for "man" to walk through the "mansions of fear" and "mansions of pain" is the same as most of his kind: "Factory takes his hearing, factory gives him life." The kind of life it provides is suggested again by the last verse of the song; the factory whistle "cries" out the end of another day, and: "Men walk through these gates with death in their eyes,/And you just better believe, boy, somebody's gonna get hurt tonight/ It's the working, the working, just the working life." The song is sung to the beat of a dirge, which reinforces the lyrical message of depression and monotony.

This picture of despair is complex as it reveals how a social system can simultaneously support and crush someone. The singer feels despair for the worker who trudges dutifully, unthinkingly off to the job which deafens him, but puts groceries on his table; a job which provides his family with shelter from the weather and hunger, but not from his own rage or fists. "Factory" is a picture of how some people live in a contemporary, lower class, not-too-quiet desperation. "Factory" is a protest against that lifestyle, but it is individual or existential, not social. We hear Springsteen sing mournfully and decide, "that life's not for me," but he never says "don't be like this," nor does he call upon Congressmen, Senators, workers, Americans, or anybody else. He just describes the desperate situation at the individual level. Neither music nor lyrics hint at any hope that this life will change. The repetitions in the chorus ("It's the working, the working, just the working life") reinforce the impressions of monotony and endlessness. The life of the factory worker is one of ennui—listlessness and dissatisfaction resulting from a total lack of interest.

There are many more images and stories of despair in Springsteen's works, but we have seen examples of the two dominant types of despair with the limited examples we have considered. "Factory" is a criticism and rejection of "the working life" in assembly line plants; but this social criticism focuses on the effects of the social system on the individual and family. Springsteen's examples are not used to generalize about the whole society, but to illustrate one slice of life; and nowhere evident are the typical bombast and assignment of blame which characterize so much protest and propaganda music. The song remains within a single, existential universe which can be felt personally. In the last analysis, if blame is or can be assigned for the despair of "Factory" or "Streets of Fire" or other of Springsteen's songs, it appears to lie within the individual. Social systems ranging from factory labor to interpersonal commitment exert pressure on individuals to conform or surrender: "Some guys just give up living." But as Springsteen says to a victim in another song, "You took what you were handed and left behind what was asked/but what they asked, baby, wasn't right, you didn't have to live that life," and "did you forget how to love, girl, did you forget how to fight?"[13] Springsteen's socially critical images of despair acknowledge the pressures that can grind people down, but he does not absolve either the system or the individual of some responsibility for what happens. Whether the individual can triumph over social systems is a question not answered by the songs in which the despair themes appear. But individual triumph is the very core of the optimism which other Springsteen songs depict, and it is to those we turn now.

II

A buoyant optimism pervades some of Springsteen's music and lyrics, telling us "that it ain't no sin to be glad you're alive."[14] Springsteen advocates saying "yes" to a life infused with value. Optimism is a theme built on images of hopefulness, success, and independence. Here feelings of power and pictures of overcoming dominate. That a rhetoric of approval is operating is signaled by the exclusive reliance on first person narrative; the singer is himself involved in these messages. The dominant sources and expressions of optimism in Springsteen's music contrast sharply and directly with the causes of despair. These songs explore the promise of love, in contrast to the broken promises and shattered dreams we saw leading to despair. Here are songs which declare an escape from and break with the monotony of daily working life—not surrender to modern life, but triumph over it. These two different optimistic tendencies very frequently occur within a single song, and sometimes in direct comparison with despair.

One of the songs that reveals the promise of love and the strength to conquer a reality that drags others down is "Thunder Road."[15] The hero-singer of "Thunder Road" addresses his message to Mary, whom he is trying to persuade to run away with him. As the narration opens, the singer has come to Mary's house where, appropriately, she is dancing to Roy Orbison's "Only the Lonely," which is playing on the radio:

Roy Orbison singing for the lonely
Hey that's me and I want you only
Don't turn me home again
I just can't face myself alone again.

Loneliness, especially like that felt by the singer of "Streets of Fire," is a source of despair for which the solution is companionship. The singer claims that only Mary's companionship will help him and his comments illustrate that an ongoing relationship of some kind exists which he wants to escalate. He urges her:

Don't run back inside
Darling you know just what I'm here for
So you're scared and you're thinking
That maybe we ain't that young anymore
Show a little faith, there's magic in the night
You ain't a beauty, but hey you're alright
Oh and that's alright with me.

Again we see that some continuity of relationship between the two exists, so she knows exactly what he wants—to run off with total commitments. People might tend to associate such an impulse or desire with youthfulness; Springsteen attributes such a skepticism to Mary, but offers the rebuttal, "Show a little faith, there's magic in the night." Even if broken dreams and promises lead to despair, we are told that dreams and promises are our hope.

Dreams and promises hold out hope for the future only if one can overcome both dwelling on the past and dreaming of perfection. He tells her:

You can hide 'neath your covers
And study your pain
Make crosses from your lovers
Throw roses in the rain
Waste your summer praying in vain
For a saviour to rise from these streets.

But he does not advocate that she crucify herself on a cross of lost love or dwell on her pain, hoping for the perfect saviour. Instead, he says, "I'm no hero," and "All the redemption I can offer girl/Is beneath this dirty hood." He urges her, however, to take the chance and go with him:

With a chance to make it good somehow
Hey what else can we do now
Except roll down the window
And let the wind blow
Back your hair.

The answer is to leave, and he urges her on. "These two lanes will take us anywhere," and what he has in mind is "heaven's waiting on down the tracks." He says he is "riding out tonight to case the promised land." This theme of escaping is stated clearly and powerfully in the last two lines of "Thunder Road": "It's a town full of losers/And I'm pulling out of here to win." Those lines are sung in a confident and loud voice, and followed by a triumphant saxophone solo to reinforce the mood of power and success. The individual plans to escape the sort of mundane existence of "Factory" and the pain of "Streets of Fire." Finally, the song offers other lyrical evidence that these are not young people or people lacking a long history together. The singer, urging Mary to take the chance with him, tells her "we got one last chance to make it real," and he acknowledges, "I know it's late we can make it if we run."

In sum, "Thunder Road" is a picture of someone believing that escape is the route to happiness. He is optimistic that heaven awaits if he can run away with Mary and escape the "town full of losers" like the man in "Factory." "Thunder Road" is representative of Springsteen's approach to optimism. On the same album, the title song, "Born to Run," contains the same themes. The man singing is tired of a life in which "In the day we sweat it out on the streets of a runaway American dream" and a town which "rips the bones from your back/It's a death trap, it's a suicide rap." Like the singer of "Thunder Road" he is sure that "Someday, girl, I don't know when, we're gonna get to that place/Where we really want to go/And we'll walk in the sun." He adds the refrain, "But till then tramps like us/Baby, we were born to run," suggesting that he sees the need to flee a desperate situation and look for something better. Both songs offer the audience optimism about the chances of the singer's success, and both bind the optimism to a love relationship.

As the despair found in Springsteen's music is not necessarily love-related, so neither is the optimism imagery necessarily contingent upon such relationships. The singer of "The Promised Land" has in mind no relationship, but a break with a dead end life that has no more specific goal than "the promised land."[16] The singer seems to view his life as one that has been aimless and over which he needs to exert control. He says he has been "just killing time/Working all day in my daddy's garage/Driving all night, chasing some mirage/Pretty soon little girl I'm gonna take charge." If this singer can take charge he will be doing more than the man in "Factory." A dream of control lures him away from his misery, as described by the song's chorus:

> The dogs on main street howl, 'cause they understand,
> If I could take one moment into my hands
> Mister, I ain't a boy, no, I'm a man,
> And I believe in a promised land.

What the dogs on main street must understand is that our singer has been living their kind of life. That life is like the lives of those in despair.

The singer has been trying to "live the right way" by getting up and going to work like the man in "Factory." He cannot give in, however:

> But your eyes go blind and your blood runs cold
> Sometimes I feel so weak I just want to explode
> Explode and tear this town apart
> Take a knife and cut this pain from my heart
> Find somebody itching for something to start

His weaknesses are caused by conforming to the work and the town instead of following his own instincts to escape. Surrender to these social systems is weakness; strength can be felt only in opposing them. His opposition is expressed by his resolve to leave: "I packed my bags and I'm heading straight into the storm." The storm he sees ahead is, perhaps, reflective of himself—a "twister to blow everything down":

Blow away the dreams that tear you apart
Blow away the dreams that break your heart
Blow away the lies that leave you nothing but lost and brokenhearted.

Those lines are followed by the chorus and refrain, "I believe in a promised land." The promised land is different from other dreams and lies. The twister, the storm envisioned by our singer, will blow away everything "that ain't got the faith to stand its ground." In "The Promised Land" we see, as we did in the despair imagery, that some dreams are hollow, some promises broken, some faith misplaced. What has "the faith to stand its ground" endures, and that is the promised land. Faith in the self has strength, while faith in the "runaway American dream" or the factory is bad faith which leads to despair.

In stark contrast to the images of despair, the optimism we have found in Springsteen's music suggests that the chance for happiness is not out of reach. Perhaps it is more to the point to observe that Springsteen describes feelings of intense despair and feelings of enthusiastic optimism. Both are part of the human situation, and if despair is optimism's failure, optimism is also the drive to escape despair. Springsteen shows us a powerful, optimistic faith in the self and the ability to escape the loneliness of life without love, as well as the boring depression of life servicing machines or false dreams. "Thunder Road" and "Born to Run" show the hopefulness of strength to love and be loved—at least, gladly to take the risk, if blindly, too. "The Promised Land" shows the optimism with which we all may start journeys, real or metaphorical, to escape from slavery and misery into freedom and joy.[17] Optimism in Springsteen's music is a theme with recurrent images of strength of self and triumph of the individual. There are many optimistic songs on Springsteen's albums, and they all emphasize either success at love or the achievement of independence. Yet success at love and the achievement of independence do not come free of charge in this life. The third major theme of Springsteen's musical rhetoric is a theme of responsibility and realism to which we now turn our attention.

III

Between oppressive despair and enthusiastic optimism must lie some middle ground. At the very least we need to understand why particular people occupy either end of the continuum from despair to optimism. The answer lies in the third major theme of Springsteen's music, responsibility. Responsibility may seem an unlikely theme for music, but the theme as conceptualized here is hinted at by the songs we already have examined. Responsibility here refers to individual choice making and the need to acknowledge its two-sided nature. On one hand, choice is a prerogative and privilege which allows us to seek rewards, and on the other hand, every choice precludes other possibilities, and so entails two prices: first, one loses the possibilities not selected; second, one must accept responsibility for one's own outcomes, good or bad. Responsibility is first and foremost responsibility to one's self; the "responsibility" of the factory worker to others and his job is false, and produces despair. We will see that Springsteen challenges the individual to accept responsibility to the self as the necessary first step in escaping despair, and as a moderating check on naive optimism.

In "Thunder Road," which we considered above, the singer is urging Mary to run away with him. We observed that the people in that song are not adolescents, but adults, in contrast to the couple in "Born to Run." One other sign of their maturity is what he says while urging her to get into his car:

> And my car's out back
> If you're ready to take that long walk
> From your front porch to my front seat
> The door's open but the ride it ain't free

Those lines, while they are sufficient when understood literally, beg for a metaphoric or symbolic interpretation. How much Mary's front porch life is like that of the woman in "Racin' in the Street" is unclear, but it certainly represents her stable or stagnant past and present. And it's a long walk from one's own front porch to another's front seat; from the certainty of one lifestyle to the uncertainty of taking the chance on someone else. Even when the other opens wide the door, entry is never free; something must be lost, given up. The singer wants to persuade Mary that she is giving up something hopeless if she comes with him to chase a better life. Even in his optimistic message, assuring her they can make it to a promised land, he acknowledges that the ride *ain't free*. His plea to her is that she owes herself enough that she should go; what she will owe him when she does is unstated.

A similar entreaty occurs in "Prove It All Night," when the singer tries to persuade a woman to run off with him for "a gold ring and pretty dress of blue."[18] He wants "a kiss to seal our fate," and he acknowledges the price she must pay. After he tells her he knows she wants and deserves more than she has, he says:

> But if dreams came true, oh, wouldn't that be nice,
> But this ain't no dream we're living through tonight,
> Girl, you want it, you take it, you pay the price
> And prove it all night, prove it all night. . . .

That is not an altruistic offer, but a proposal to trade; he wants her commitment to him, and not for a one night stand, but for life. And he tells her she will have to have strength to resist when she hears "the voices tell you not to go/They made their choices and they'll never know/. . . What it's like to live and die/To prove it all night. . . ." Individuals' choices introduce the theme of responsibility in Springsteen's music as people are challenged to take risks and make strong decisions, even when those go against the grain of social mores.

242

The clearest single illustration of the responsibility theme is Springsteen's "I Wanna Marry You."[19] The song is a first person narrative addressed to a specific but unnamed woman in a situation not uncommon today. He tells her he sees her walking down the street with her baby carriage and knows that she is alone, and perhaps wants a man. As he sees her, she is unhappy:

You never smile girl, you never speak
You just walk on by, darlin', week after week
Raising two kids alone in this mixed up world
Must be a lonely life for a working girl

In spite of the implication that he does not know her well—if at all—the chorus asserts repeatedly, "Little girl, I wanna marry you." Furthermore, his proposal explains at length his very realistic attitudes toward the situation:

Now, honey, I don't wanna clip your wings
But a time comes when two people should think of these things
Having a home and a family
Facing up to their responsibilities
They say in the end true love prevails
But in the end true love can't be no fairytale
To say I'll make your dreams come true would be wrong
But maybe, darlin', I could help them along

His modest proposal merits our consideration.

In contrast to a "promised land," the singer offers facing up to the responsibilities of family, which the woman already has. Facing reality is the entire point of his proposal: "true love can't be no fairytale," and he knows he can't make dreams come true. Here is a rhetoric of moderation and realism; we can, after all, help each other toward many of the goals we set in life, even though we cannot make life perfect.

Not all responsibility is responsibility to others; as the introduction to this section of our exploration observed, the self is a central concern of the images which make up the theme of responsibility. "Independence Day" expresses most clearly an individual's decision to act against a social system and in behalf of himself.[20] Both personal and social pressures are involved in the singer's decision to leave home and hometown:

Cause the darkness of this house has got the best of us
There's a darkness in this town that's got us too
But they can't touch me now
And you can't touch me now
They ain't gonna do to me
What I watched them do to you

243

Our best referent for what *they* did to the father being addressed is the picture of the man in "Factory." We are told in the same song that our singer is not alone, that "There's a lot of people leaving town now." The singer does not dwell on his inability to get along with his father, but observes:

Now I don't know what it always was with us
We chose the words, and yeah, we drew the lines
There was just no way this house could hold the two of us
I guess that we were just too much of the same kind

That observation acknowledges responsibility, shared responsibility, for what has happened to the two: "yeah, *we* drew the lines."

The singer is leaving for reasons both personal and external. Responsible to and for himself, he acknowledges that "It's Independence Day all boys must run away," and "All men must make their way come Independence Day." To grow up strong enough to set out on life's roads alone is natural. Leaving the nest may be accelerated by extra-familial factors: "Because there's just different people coming down here now and they see things in different ways/ And soon everything we've known will just be swept away." As the world changes, responsible people must somehow make significant changes for their own well being. The man declaring that it's independence day is not running blindly out of fear, nor is he leaving with a declared expectation of finding heaven. He's just got to go.

The responsibility theme, then, shows pictures of responsibility both to others and to self. That is not said to imply that responsibility toward others excludes or precludes responsibility toward self. Rather, within the theme of responsibility in Springsteen's music we have found acknowledgement that there are always prices one must pay to be free *or* to be committed. Above all, the choice must be conscious and deliberate. The man leaving home in "Independence Day" is exhibiting responsibility no less than the man singing "I Wanna Marry You," but the two are in very different circumstances. In fact, one way for us usefully to view the responsibility theme is to see it as a mediator of the contradiction between optimism and despair. That view will establish the relationships among the themes we have been examining in Springsteen's music.

IV

What has gone before has established three themes that emerge with clarity from Springsteen's music: despair, optimism, and responsibility. But in at least two ways, that view is incomplete. First, the overall rhetoric of Springsteen's music is more complex than these themes alone; the interactions among them are necessary to understand the total picture. Second, analysis at the thematic level necessarily neglects other things which may be of value. The second of these issues we will address below; here it remains to conclude thematic analysis by putting together the three themes we have isolated.

By any yardstick, despair and optimism are contradictory. Two of the songs we chose to illustrate despair, "Streets of Fire" and "Factory," seem to offer no connection with optimism except contradiction. "Racing in the Street," on the other hand, afforded us a view of a situation in which one man's optimism and life caused one woman's despair. One connection between despair and optimism is their dialectical necessity to one another; that is, without high hope there can be no contrasting despair, and vice versa. But that is a simple, perhaps obvious connection, and one based upon abstract form, not concrete content. Springsteen's pictures of optimism and despair suggest an unusual set of causal relationships.

First, both despair and optimism may be brought about by the same things. The deeply felt despair of "Streets of Fire" and "Racing in the Street" has the same root cause as the optimism of "Thunder Road" and "Born to Run": the quest for love as salvation. To be sure, we are shown different stages of the quest. Second, the form of despair we saw in "Factory" and called *ennui* plays a role in the songs about optimism. The singer of both "Thunder Road" and "Born to Run" wants to grab love and leave the "town full of losers," the "death trap," before he gets stuck in a "Factory" lifestyle. Like the singer of "The Promised Land," he believes that just getting up and going to work every day is not all there should be to life. The voice speaking to us out of the songs of optimism encourages us to dream and promise, and to flee, to run, in pursuit of those dreams and promises. But if we do, as we just observed above, we may end up *feeling* that "it's all lies." Nonetheless, the ennui and unhappiness lying about on the edges of the optimism theme play a motivating role for characters developed there.

How can we say that the contradictory nature and mutual causation of optimism and despair are mediated by the theme of responsibility? First, both despair and optimism as presented in Springsteen's songs are *extreme*. On that very quality hinges at least a substantial part of their mutually causal relationship. To illustrate, we would have to say that only the dashing of very high hopes would cause one to "stare off alone into the night with the eyes of one who *hates for just being born*"; and likewise, the powerful hope of "Born to Run" is strengthened or made more extreme because the place—the life— that *has to be* escaped is "a death trap, a suicide rap," and not merely a minor irritant. The themes of optimism and despair are extreme, and so is the music to which they are set: "Factory" is a dirge, while "Born to Run" sounds like an accelerating motor.

Between these extremes is set the possibility of something more calm, which we have argued is a theme of responsibility. Between "Streets of Fire" and "The Promised Land" is reality. That is not to deny the reality or the legitimacy of feelings of despair or optimism, but to underscore that the very unreality of the most extreme dreams is what prevents their realization and fulfillment: such extremes are certainly real inside the head, but the impossibility of a promised land is exactly what leads to despair. Springsteen expresses a more responsible view: "To say I'll make your dreams come true would be wrong/But maybe, darlin', I could help them along."

The other principal component of the responsibility theme is acknowledgment of choice. The relationship of choice to despair and optimism is complicated. The images of despair involve people who have refused or denied choice. That is, the man in "Streets of Fire" blames others ("they tricked you") for his condition; the man in "Factory" lives in bad faith, allowing the employment machine to dictate his life instead of choosing it. These people are like those Springsteen mentions in "Racing in the Street": "Some guys they just give up living/And start dying little by little, piece by piece." Viewed from this perspective, the perspective of choosing, the people in despair have given up their prerogative to choose, and are denying life. Within the songs making up the despair theme we are invited to adopt a sympathetic view to the man ground down by the factory or the man whose life is nothing but streets of fire. From the perspective of responsibility and choice, however, we are given a less sympathetic perspective.

The songs which make up the optimism theme share a more complex relationship with the issue of choice. In these songs we seem to hear someone choosing and asserting strength of life. The men in "Born to Run" and "Thunder Road" are telling women of two choices: first, the choice to leave the place where they are, and second, the choice of a woman companion. The man in "Promised Land" is so angry with his place that he wants "to explode," and so is leaving. We seem invited to approve these instincts of strength and the choice to say, "It's a town full of losers/And I'm pulling out of here to win." But when we consider these messages within the vision of responsibility and choice, we may see a different picture. These people are running away in pursuit of unrealities—of "heaven waiting on down the tracks" and "the promised land." In contrast, the young man in "Independence Day" is simply leaving, and keeps imploring his father, "Just say goodbye, it's Independence Day." He doesn't describe the place he is leaving with hatred at all. And the man in "I Wanna Marry You" isn't running away at all; he believes life can be improved, but dreams can't come true. In sum, the characters expressing optimism have had their choices dictated to them by running *away* and not *toward*. And they are chasing dreams in their flight, not working to improve real situations. The optimistic characters appear irresponsible when we consider them in this light.

What, then, shall we say about the thematic quality of Springsteen's musical rhetoric? Above all, we must not emphasize the posture of advocate in Springsteen's music. Springsteen *describes* the three themes we have examined, but he does not *prescribe* any of them explicitly or condemn any of them. Springsteen's approach is to show the audience possibilities, not to tell his hearers what to think or do. This is a narrative rhetoric, not a didactic one.

Its thematic unity and focus are derived from the very different subjectivities of despair, optimism, and responsibility being displayed vividly for our examination. Whether these are our only alternatives is moot; that they are possible attitudes toward life is what is important. These feelings may be unavoidable for adults to experience at some time. That fact may account for a certain ambivalence on the part of audience and artist toward the themes. It also points us toward considering, by way of conclusion, what sort of audience is invited by these themes, and what aspects of music, especially Springsteen's, are not disclosed fully by thematic analysis.

V

Both the complexity of Springsteen's message and the themes themselves define and limit his audience. Springsteen's message does not have meaning for adolescents or children; an adult audience may relate to lines like, "I lost my money and I lost my wife/Them things don't seem to matter much to me now," but high school students are not likely to.[21] Stylistic detail and thematic force solicit the identification of an adult audience. Yet in stylistic details or background, Springsteen also excludes many adults.

The stylistic details of Springsteen's musical rhetoric center around urban American lower class people and values. Gangs meet "'neath that giant Exxon sign"; one man's sixty-nine Chevy waits outside the 7–11 store; downtown "the black and whites . . . cruise by"; Roy Orbison is on the radio; and "In the day we sweat it out on the streets of a runaway American dream." Album and song titles also suggest America: on *Greetings from Asbury Park, N.J.* is "Mary Queen of Arkansas"; on *Born to Run* is "Thunder Road"; on *Darkness on the Edge of Town* is "Racing in the Street"; on *The River* is "Cadillac Ranch"; on *Nebraska,* in addition to the title song, is "Atlantic City." The background images of Springsteen's lyrics are not universal. Millions of Americans can relate to racing in the street in a '69 Chevy with a 396, but the imagery would be lost on many foreigners; there are not many 7–11 stores outside the United States; and Cadillac Ranch is a freakish exhibit of cars nose down in the dirt near Amarillo, Texas. While these images of American scenes may trigger sweeping meanings for listeners familiar with the movie *Thunder Road* or Roy Orbison's "Only the Lonely," they are not Springsteen's focus. Springsteen's rhetoric is not centered around fast cars and street life; those are elements of the background in which people find themselves. They do lend a sense of concrete reality to the lyrics, and are interesting for us as detail; but they are setting, not action. Springsteen is not writing idylls.

In addition to the many specifically American references, Springsteen has a focus on lower class people. These are people who drive to the unemployment office, live on welfare checks, load crates on the dock, work in a factory. Readers will have noticed the frequency of ungrammatical language in the passages explicated in this essay. The language of the lower class American is full of the casual contraction "ain't" and double negatives; it is in that language that Springsteen writes, which makes his work all the more amazing or impressive. There may be much ungrammatical in his lyrics, but he is not inarticulate or unimaginative.

Springsteen writes about what he knows first hand. The themes, background, and emotions reflect his background and life. The audience that identifies most with his rhetoric is made up of people close to his own age (34 in 1983) who are familiar with urban, lower class, American street life. Springsteen's audience consists of people who like rock 'n roll music and concerts. Concert audiences demonstrate high familiarity with his music. During his 1978 tour when playing "Thunder Road," he would stop after the line "So you're scared and you're thinking that maybe we ain't that young any more" and point his microphone at the audience, which would chant the next lines: "Show a little faith, there's magic in the night/You ain't a beauty but, hey you're alright."[22] Springsteen's audience evidences knowledge of his lyrical message.

We have been able here to catch only a glimpse of the rhetorical aspects of music *not* written expressly to advocate social changes. Springsteen serves as an example of a broader phenomenon. Music expresses meanings, especially lyrically, in which act it becomes rhetorical. Music functions both as an expression of the artist and as an invitation to the audience to identify with the themes, ideas, and emotions expressed. If rhetoric is conceptualized either as constructing or interpreting reality, music is a powerful part of that process, even when it is not part of a propaganda or agitative campaign. Springsteen's music is one example of the rhetorical potentialities of non-didactic lyrics, and as such merits continued investigation.

Notes

1. See James R. Irvine and Walter Kirkpatrick, "The Musical Form in Rhetorical Exchange," *Quarterly Journal of Speech,* 58 (1971), 272–289; Cheryl Irwin Thomas, " 'Look What They've Done to My Song, Ma': The Persuasiveness of Song," *Southern Speech Communication Journal,* 27 (1974), 260–268; G. P. Mohrmann and F. Eugene Scott, "Popular Music and World War II: The Rhetoric of Continuation," *Quarterly Journal of Speech,* 62 (1976), 145–156; Mark W. Booth, "The Art of Words in Songs," *Quarterly Journal of Speech,* 62 (1976), 242–249; Stephen A. Smith, "Sounds of the South: The Rhetorical Saga of Country Music Lyrics," *Southern Speech Communication Journal,* 45 (1980), 169–182; David A. Carter, "The Industrial Workers of the World and the Rhetoric of Song," *Quarterly Journal of Speech,* 66 (1980), 367–374; Ralph E. Knupp, "A Time for Every Purpose Under Heaven: Rhetorical Dimensions of Protest Music," *Southern Speech Communication Journal,* 46 (1981), 377–389; Roth Lane, "Folk Songs as Communication in John Ford's Films," *Southern Speech Communication Journal,* 46 (1981), 390–396; Alberto Gonzalez and John J. Makay, "Rhetorical Ascription and the Gospel According to Dylan," *Quarterly Journal of Speech,* 69 (1983), 1–14. Most of these studies deal minimally, if at all, with music. Irvine and Kirkpatrick suggest that the interaction of lyrical and musical elements should be studied, but they don't do so; Booth observes that lyrics have to live with music

and should not be evaluated independent of that fact; Gonzalez and Makay provide a few guitar chords Dylan plays, but their descriptions of instrumentals (p. 13) are too brief and undescriptive to capture the sound one would hear. In defense of the studies mentioned, most focus on protest or propaganda music in which, to paraphrase Booth, the music *as music* is the lesser half at best. Springsteen has a message, but he is first and last a musician; he is nowhere the social protester in the classic sense, as our analysis will reveal.

2. In the week of October 27, 1975, *Time* ran its story, "Backstreet Phantom of Rock," and *Newsweek,* adopting a slightly different angle, printed "Making of a Rock Star." Over the weeks following, both magazines were deluged in mail about their matching cover stories, and the editors were prompted to reply. There had been only four previous instances of *Time* and *Newsweek* having the same cover story (other than political stories). On November 17, 1975, letters to *Newsweek* included these comments: "Why not put a picture of the real Bob Dylan on your cover instead of an imitation named Springsteen?" "We cannot understand why a prestigious magazine of your calibre will waste its cover on a 'freak' like Bruce Springsteen." "It was a pleasure to see *Newsweek* take the initiative and do a cover story on the most deserving Bruce Springsteen. Maybe now he'll receive the recognition he's earned." One week later, a reader consoled the editors, "Take it easy— don't worry about your recent cover match-up with *Time.* It simply proves the point that Bruce Springsteen is a new rock 'n roll sensation." Letters to *Time* were similar in the November 17 issue: "I am beginning to wonder about the intellect of *Time*'s editors when they are so quick to put a mush-mouthed, off-key nothing like Bruce Springsteen on their cover and yet take five years to bestow that honor on the one who deserves it most—Elton John." "Please do not imply that American youth is eating up the products of 'rock's new sensation.' I am not." "Bruce Springsteen is a living example of Longfellow's, 'All things come round to him who will but wait!' "

The letters are revealing to those who know about Springsteen's career and music. Both studio hype and early critical attention compared Springsteen with Dylan. Peter Gambaccini, *Bruce Springsteen* (New York: Quick Fox, 1979), p. 31 observes, "The 'new Dylan' tag on Springsteen began early; indeed, it was so prevalent that Dylan . . . was at times referred to as 'the old Springsteen.' " Some people resented the comparison. Springsteen's physical apearance resembled Dylan in 1973, although by 1975 he had a somewhat harder, urban look which some people may have found freakish. The young man who complained to *Time* that American youth was not enthralled with Springsteen reflected the fact that Springsteen's music appeals to an older crowd than most pop or rock music. We will consider that fact later in this essay.

3. Landau quoted in Gambaccini, *Springsteen,* p. 50.

4. Springsteen has released six albums to date: *Greetings from Asbury Park, N.J.,* Columbia Records, KC 31903, 1973; *The Wild, The Innocent, and The E Street Shuffle,* Columbia Records, KC 32432, 1973; *Born to Run,* Columbia Records, PC 33795, 1975; *Darkness on the Edge of Town,* Columbia Records, JC 35318, 1978; *The River,* Columbia Records, PC2 36854, 1980; *Nebraska,* Columbia Records, TC 38358, 1982. Lyrics quoted are taken from printed lyric sheets accompanying the albums, even when those differ slightly from what is sung on the album; *E Street Shuffle* does not have a printed lyric page. Also in my possession are illegally reproduced tapes and records which cannot be identified practically. Such widely available "bootleg" recordings are of concerts and interviews, e.g., in San Francisco and Cleveland during 1978.

5. See, for example, Gambaccini.

6. An exception would be *Tommy,* MCA Records, MCA2–10005, 1972 (previously Decca, DXSW7–205), a rock opera by The Who.

7. *The Philosophy of Literary Form* (Baton Rouge: Louisiana State University Press, 1941), p. 20.
8. Michael McGuire, "Mythic Rhetoric in *Mein Kampf:* A Structuralist Critique," *Quarterly Journal of Speech,* 63 (1977), 1–13.
9. *Darkness on the Edge of Town.*
10. *Darkness on the Edge of Town.*
11. *Darkness on the Edge of Town.*
12. The faceless "man" is Springsteen's own father, as the line "See my daddy walking through them factory gates in the rain" suggests. In concert, Springsteen introduces this song by talking about his childhood and his father.
13. "Point Blank," *The River.*
14. "Badlands," *Darkness on the Edge of Town.*
15. *Born to Run.*
16. *Darkness on the Edge of Town.*
17. Springsteen's music contains abundant Biblical imagery which an Aristotelian analysis undoubtedly would connect with his childhood in Catholic schools. There are many references to "promised land" and "angels," one song on *Darkness on the Edge of Town* is called "Adam Raised a Cain." These details may be important, but they lie in the background of the music, and this method of reconstruction cannot deal with them adequately.
18. *Darkness on the Edge of Town.*
19. *The River.*
20. *The River.*
21. "Darkness on the Edge of Town," *Darkness on the Edge of Town.*
22. This is an observation based on personal experience. There is a study of the effects of audience members' participation with rock music which rhetorical critics have failed to cite or consider to date: John E. Hocking, Duane G. Margreiter, and Cal Hylton, "Intra-Audience Effects: A Field Test," *Human Communication Research,* 3 (1977), 243–249.

6
Rhetoric of Magazines

From the advent of the penny press in the 1830s until the present, newspapers and magazines have played a leading role in reflecting and shaping popular attitudes. Though scholarly attention to the various forms of popular literature was rather restricted throughout the middle ages and the renaissance, the eighteenth and nineteenth centuries brought about a renewed awareness of the persuasive potency of such written forms as the broadside, the political tract, and the newspaper. This renewed interest was due in large measure to the spread of literacy, the enfranchising of the common man (and later woman), and the growing power of the press. Both teachers and practitioners of persuasion began to pay heed to the distinctly rhetorical dimensions of popular writing.

In this section an essay by Roderick Hart, Kathleen Turner, and Ralph Knupp, and another by Virginia Kidd examine some of the rhetorical dimensions of popular magazines. Hart and his associates employ content analytic techniques to understand the rhetoric of religion as presented by *Time* magazine. They extend their study over a thirty year period and examine such issues as the denominational, topical, and presentational focus of the articles as well as the orientations expressed toward conflict, role, gender, theology, and geography. Kidd, on the other hand, uses a fantasy theme approach to isolate two rhetorical visions of interpersonal relations found in twenty-five popular magazines. Her study covers a twenty year period.

On the surface there are several similarities between the study by Kidd and that by Hart, Turner, and Knupp. Both deal with popular magazines with circulation figures in the millions. Both span a long time period. Both deal with the treatment of a single subject: religion in one case and advice about interpersonal relations in the other. Finally, both use some form of content analysis and random selection to reduce the mass of information to a more manageable size and help to insure the generalizability of the results.

There are three aspects, however, in which these essays differ to a greater or lesser degree: the specific methodology employed, the conclusions offered about the rhetorical functioning of mass circulation magazines, and the role accorded to non-linguistic or extra-linguistic rhetorical dimensions such as placement on the page, amount of space utilized, and the various aspects of graphic design.

Methodologically, the authors of these two essays appear to proceed in much the same manner. But do they? Hart, et. al. take two full paragraphs to discuss the content analytic techniques employed. The authors specify the total number of articles within the universe surveyed, the total number of articles randomly selected, and the safeguards employed to guard against systematic bias and cyclical trends. Throughout the article charts are provided that delineate frequency counts and the percentages of each sub-category with respect to the total configuration.

Hart and his co-authors specify that 648 articles were subjected to content analytic techniques. Given the information provided by Kidd, is there any way to know exactly how many articles she examined before discovering the existence of visions I and II? Would it make any difference if the actual number of articles examined was 100, 200, or 400 out of the total surveyed? What other facts would one need to know before answering such a question?

The point is this: content analysis, whether used as a method in and of itself (à la Hart, et. al.) or as a pre-critical technique to generate data that can then be interpreted through the use of some other critical paradigm (à la Kidd), must be subject to certain procedural rules. If the rules are not followed the data generated is, at best, flawed and the conclusions based upon that data are, at best, misleading. To guard against such a possibility, the critical reader should demand full disclosure of all relevant procedures.

But methodological considerations aside, there are other interesting contrasts between these two studies, including the view taken toward the rhetorical functioning of magazines. Both articles emphasize the importance of repetition and formula, but in somewhat different ways. Kidd focuses on the repetition and evolution of an ideology or philosophy. She traces the dogma or tenets of the philosophy as it manifests itself in the rhetoric of articles. By doing so, Kidd is able to reconstruct the overall vision that animated popular thought on the subject of interpersonal relations and to identify the general point in time when vision I began to give way to vision II. Though both visions were distinctly formulaic, the rhetorical role of repetition was significantly different. In vision I repetition functioned to instantiate and perpetuate an ideal. In vision II repetition was used to destroy the very notion that such things as ideals or norms even exist. The role of repetition in the first instance was constructive of meaning whereas in the second it was destructive.

Hart, Turner, and Knupp also see repetition and formulae at work, but place more emphasis on institutional constraints and definition of audience. The rhetoric of religion in *Time* has as much to do, they seem to argue, with the type of publication *Time* considers itself to be, the type of "news" believed to be most appealing to its readers, and the principles of rhetorical appeal which have stood the test of time regardless of subject matter. Whereas the "reality links" identified by Kidd led to an eventual change in the rhetoric of inter-personal advice, the social facts uncovered by Hart and his associates seem to have had little, if any, effect on the reporting of religious topics. Why might the audience be an active force for rhetorical change in the first instance, but not in the second?

Finally, there are differences with regard to the non-linguistic dimensions of magazine rhetoric. Though neither essay emphasizes such dimensions, both allude to the fact that persuasion involves more than the words and the order in which they are presented. Hart, Turner, and Knupp implicitly recognized the importance of placement by controlling for feature versus non-feature articles. The very fact that an article appears in the first column on the left hand side of the page, or is set off from the surrounding materials by one or more graphic devices, affects the reader's perception of its importance. Such factors may, indeed, go far in helping to determine whether the article is read, skimmed, or simply passed over. As Kidd notes, a short article carries with it a connotation of ease and simplicity which may affect the interpretation of the subject matter being presented.

The rhetorical dimensions of popular magazines involve a multitude of factors: constraints imposed by the medium, perceptions of audience, the rhetorical history of the particular organ, standard formulae, interaction with "reality links" in the social order, and the non-linguistic aspects of layout and design. To study adequately the persuasive dimensions of newspapers or magazines necessitates a methodology that allows the critic to range over long spans of time and large masses of data. Content analytic techniques provide one possible avenue. The identification of fantasy themes is another. What other approaches to the analysis and interpretation of popular writing might prove beneficial to the rhetorical critic?

A Rhetorical Profile of Religious News:
Time, 1947–1976
Roderick P. Hart, Kathleen J. Turner, and Ralph E. Knupp

Religion is generally agreed to both affect and be affected by the mass media, but systematic examinations of these relationships have been few. A number of books and articles have severely criticized the media's treatment of religious matters (e.g., 4, 7, 14, 16, 25). The few scholarly studies in the area have focused upon either the denominational press (e.g., 19, 20, 27) or upon journalistic training in seminaries (23). Studies by Whaten (26) and Buchstein (6) have attempted to understand how the secular press has treated religious matters, but they too were rather unsystematic.

We investigated how one media outlet, *Time* magazine, has "constructed" American religion over roughly the past thirty years. In doing so we posed a number of questions about *Time*'s treatment of religion. As presented by *Time* magazine, what is the essential nature of religion, of religious personnel? Of the many characteristics of religion, which does *Time* select for presentation and which does it consistently ignore? Is *Time*'s reporting of religious activities clearly affected by temporal or denominational realities? What combination of social, political, economic, and rhetorical factors explains *Time*'s portrayal of religion? *Time* was chosen because it has the largest circulation of any news magazine in the United States, because it has covered religious activities since its inception, and because its philosophy of "group journalism" (whereby no single individual is responsible for gathering, writing, or editing the news) has given it a rare form of stylistic consistency over time.[1]

A detailed inspection of every issue of *Time* from January 1947 through December 1976 indicates that religion has been a consistently popular commodity. *Time* carried a religion section almost weekly in the first decade, did so slightly less frequently in the second, and in the seventies included a religion section about sixty percent of the time. Since each religion section carried an average of two or three substantive articles, the population from which we drew our sample consisted of approximately 3000 articles. From this grouping we selected 648 articles for content analysis. Our sample was stratified across time so that each of the thirty years was represented equally; to guard against

Reprinted from "A Rhetorical Profile of Religious News: *Time, 1947–1976*," by Roderick P. Hart, Kathleen J. Turner, and Ralph E. Knupp in the *Journal of Communication,* Volume 31, Issue 3, 1981.

systematic bias, feature (the first article in each section) and non-feature articles were included in our sample on an equal basis. Care was also taken to prohibit seasonal reporting preferences from biasing the sample. Thus, our sample consisted of roughly one out of every five articles appearing in *Time*'s religion section between 1947 and 1976.

In addition to coding each article by date and by its feature or non-feature status, each article was measured in column centimeters and in number of paragraphs so that both absolute and relative coverage could be determined. Every article was also coded in each of the following areas: *denominational focus*—Roman Catholic, Jewish, mainstream Protestant, ecumenical, etc.; *topical focus*—pastoral or ministerial activities (church as social agent: draft counseling, soup kitchens, etc.), liturgical activities (religious ceremonies, modes of worship, scriptural translations), doctrinal matters (matters of faith and morals, theological disputes, canon law), institutional affairs (religious personalities, meetings, elections, bureaucratic struggles); *conflict orientation*—intra-denominational or inter-denominational strife, church/society conflict, etc.; *presentational focus*—focus on a particular denomination, on a religious person, some other focus; *role orientation*—role played by persons profiled (church leader, local cleric, layperson, etc.); and *gender orientation*—male vs. female focus of attention. In addition, frequency counts were made of *theological orientation*—references to God versus references to human beings; and *geographical orientation*—references to the United States, Europe, southern states, and so on.

> *As portrayed in* Time, *religion in America is an overwhelmingly institutional affair.*

Table 1 lists the overall characteristics of the 648 *Time* articles. These data show that religion is portrayed as more concerned with institutional matters (34.7 percent) than with pastoral matters (13.8 percent). Overall, the *Time* religion section is only slightly more involved with doctrine (24.1 percent) than with liturgical matters (16.6 percent). Religion is presented as a here-and-now phenomenon which is twice as likely to focus on its human adherents (65.7 percent) as on its gods (34.3 percent). Theologians (16.9 percent) and church leaders (38.6 percent) outnumber local clerics (24.1 percent) by about two to one. With laypersons featured less than eight percent of the time, and religious men appearing seven times as often as religious women, religion is depicted as an ecclesiastical enterprise enjoyed by only a select few.

In terms of location, religious activity occurs four times as frequently in the eastern United States as it does in the South and twice as often in the East as in the Midwest or West. Moreover, religion is depicted as an essentially Euro-American matter in the vast majority of the cases; about 80 percent of

Table 1. Rhetorical features of *Time* articles on religion, 1947–1976.

Item	N	% of Category
Topical focus (n = 648)		
Pastoral	90	13.8
Liturgical	108	16.6
Institutional	225	34.7
Doctrinal	156	24.1
Other	69	10.6
Denominational focus (n = 648)		
Non-denominational	101	15.5
Ecumenical	154	23.8
Other Protestant	49	7.6
Mainstream Protestant	101	15.5
Catholic	187	28.8
Jewish	23	3.5
Other denomination	33	5.0
Temporal focus (n = 648)		
Present	614	94.7
Past	34	5.3
Conflict orientation (n = 648)		
No conflict	132	20.3
Intra-church	173	26.7
Inter-church	58	8.9
Church/society	184	28.4
Other conflict	101	15.6
Presentational focus (n = 648)		
Denominational	220	33.9
Personal	153	23.6
Other	275	42.5
Role orientation (n = 153)		
Theologian	25	16.9
Church leader	59	38.6
Local cleric	37	24.1
Mystic	5	3.3
Layperson	11	7.2
Other	16	10.5
Gender orientation (n = 153)		
Female	19	12.4
Male	138	87.6

Table 1.—*Continued*

Item	N	% of Category
Geographical orientation (n = 3659)		
General U.S.	317	8.7
Eastern U.S.	636	17.4
Southern U.S.	163	4.5
Midwestern U.S.	341	9.3
Western U.S.	311	8.5
Europe	1185	32.4
Other	706	19.3
Theological orientation (n = 4016)		
Individualistic references	2640	65.7
Deistic references	1376	34.3

the religion articles involve only about 25 percent of the world's inhabitants. Moreover, 84 percent of *Time*'s articles focus upon issues within particular denominations and only five percent venture outside of the Judeo-Christian tradition. Given that most of the ecumenical articles (i.e., those in which two or more denominations received equal focus) involved one of the mainstream Protestant groups, mainline Protestants outnumber their "fringe" brethren by five to one in the pages of *Time*. No matter which denomination is featured, however, conflict—a stock-in-trade of all mediated messages—is pervasive. Four out of every five articles on religion in the past thirty years were primarily concerned with conflict. Most of the conflict has been intra-denominational, although conflict between church and society has also received attention.

Perhaps because of *Time*'s well-established journalistic style, the religion sections appearing in 1947 tend to resemble those appearing thirty years later (for more information see 13). *Time* has long been written in a sprightly style and its essays on religion continue to have an upbeat tempo. Throughout the period, religious males who are institutionally "connected" have been featured and *Time*'s news sources and their presentation have basically remained the same. Still, several noteworthy changes in focus have taken place in the last three decades.

There has been some amount of waxing and waning in the coverage of denominations over the years (see Figure 1). General denominationalism has increased steadily, ecumenism peaked in the 1960s, and the Protestants outside the mainstream shared more of the national limelight in the late sixties and seventies. The attention devoted to mainstream Protestantism has fallen

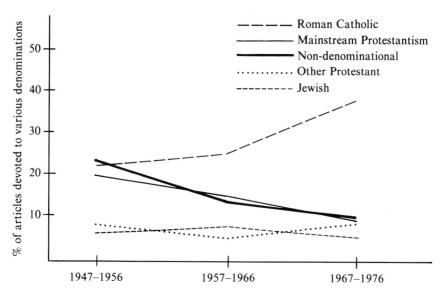

Figure 1. Denominational focus in *Time* articles on religion, 1947–1976.

over the years, the slack presumably being picked up by Roman Catholics, who were more recently featured in almost two out of every five articles. No dramatic change in proportional membership patterns accounts for the increase in the space devoted to Catholics, although theologically revolutionary events such as Vatican II undoubtedly have had their influence on *Time*'s reportage.

One of the most interesting chronological trends is the steady increase in intra-church skirmishing reported by *Time* (see Figure 2). Whereas the earlier articles focused on the disagreements between organized religion and secular society, contemporary reporting has emphasized conflict within the churches themselves, especially within the Catholic church.

On the surface, *Time* has treated the denominations even-handedly. No significant differences were observed in the amount of space-per-article devoted to the denominations and no religion received feature status significantly more often than any other. In other areas, however, differences are apparent.

Table 2 charts the denominational affiliations of the individuals who have been profiled in *Time* articles on religion. The Catholic church appears to have within it more media-prone personalities than do the other religious persuasions. Similarly, the ecumenical movement is depicted by *Time* primarily as a parade of celebrities. In terms of topics, Jews and Protestants outside the

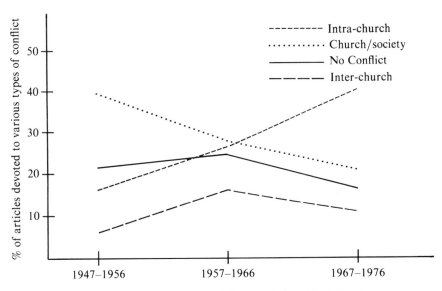

Figure 2. Conflict in *Time* articles on religion, 1947–1976.

Table 2. Role orientation of persons profiled in *Time* articles on religion by denomination (n = 153).

	Non-denom-inational %	Ecu-men-ical %	Other Pro-test-ant %	Main-stream Protes-tant %	Roman Catholic %	Jewish %	Other %
Theologian	49.7	14.8	0	15.7	11.1	0	12.4
Church leader	20.1	45.3	50.5	37.4	40.8	19.9	50.2
Local cleric	20.1	10.1	35.7	31.1	24.2	60.2	0
Mystic	0	4.7	0	0	7.3	0	0
Layperson	5.1	15.0	0	6.4	1.7	19.9	37.4
Other	5.0	10.1	14.3	9.4	14.9	0	0

mainstream denominations more often are depicted as having pastoral concerns than are either Catholics or mainstream Protestants (see Table 3). Such Protestants also are portrayed as less concerned with matters of doctrine than are the establishment groups, although as we have already seen, doctrinal exegesis has never been *Time*'s real reportorial emphasis. In terms of liturgical issues, only those groups falling outside of the Judeo-Christian tradition have been featured heavily in the pages of *Time*. Also, Judaism as portrayed in *Time* is much less conflictive than the other groups; when Jews are described

Table 3. Topical focus of *Time* articles on religion by denomination (n = 648).

	Non-denominational %	Ecumenical %	Other Protestant %	Mainstream Protestant %	Roman Catholic %	Jewish %	Other %
Pastoral	16.4	18.1	22.5	16.3	16.9	23.9	13.6
Liturgical	23.8	14.0	11.2	12.9	11.8	13.0	18.2
Doctrinal	36.2	30.5	13.3	25.7	27.9	23.8	19.8
Institutional	10.9	33.4	47.0	43.6	36.8	39.1	39.4
Other	12.9	3.9	6.1	4.0	3.7	0	9.1

as engaging in conflict, secular society rather than other Jews or Christians is usually involved. Only the fringe Protestants, besides Jews, are portrayed as being in conflict more with the world at large than among themselves because of their sectarian status.

Ecumenical events in *Time* are set twice as often in the East as anywhere else in the United States. The most likely explanation for this is that the most active ecumenical spokespersons live in and around Manhattan. As Epstein (9) has suggested convincingly, the "geography of news" is largely dictated by economic considerations, and it is much less expensive to interview a New York-based prelate than one who lives in the hinterlands.

Differences among the denominations are especially sharp when we consider the personal profiles *Time* has produced during the last thirty years (Table 2). Judaism, for example, is depicted as a "grass roots" religion in that significantly more members of its laity have been profiled than have members of Christian churches, and local Jewish clerics outnumber national Jewish leaders three to one. Among Catholics, however, twice as many national leaders as local communicants are profiled. However, more Protestant than Catholic laity are profiled and Protestant pastors and church leaders are featured in nearly equal numbers. Whereas mainstream Protestants had a large number of newsworthy theologians, their less well-established Protestant counterparts had none. Finally, religious women were featured only among Jews and Catholics, and mystics only among the former.

> ***How closely do the portrayals of
> denominations in** Time **correspond to
> their actual numbers in the U.S. population?***

As shown in Table 4, during the past thirty years *Time* magazine has represented Catholics and Jews in its religion section at twice their national strength and Episcopalians at seven times their relative numbers. Presbyterians have also been slightly over-represented, and Methodists and Lutherans

Table 4. Actual versus rhetorical density of American religious denominations.

	Reported National Membership[a]	% of U.S. Population[b]	% of Eastern U.S. Population[c]	No. of *Time* Articles	% of *Time*'s Denominational Articles[d]
Roman Catholic	40,871,000	22.6	37.7	187	48.7
Jewish	5,500,000	3.0	8.8	2.3	6.0
Methodist	12,352,000	6.8	4.8	25	3.6
Presbyterian	4,203,000	2.3	2.5	16	4.2
Episcopalian	3,127,000	1.7	2.5	52	13.5
Baptist	20,879,000	11.6	4.9	7	1.8
Lutheran	8,021,000	4.4	3.3	12	3.1
Other Protestant	16,499,000	9.1	5.2	40	10.4
Total	111,452,000	61.5	69.7	351	91.3

[a]Figures given are 1960 figures from (17, pp. 250–272).
[b]Total population in the United States in 1960 (roughly the mid-point of this study) was approximately 180,000,000.
[c]Total population in the eastern United States in 1960 was approximately 51,000,000. Percentages given are extrapolations of figures provided in (10, pp. 57–58 and 17, pp. 250–272).
[d]Excludes non-denominational and ecumenical articles.

have been slightly under-represented. Baptists, a fourth of whom are black and over half of whom are Southern, have received one-sixth of the media exposure that might be considered justified by their national membership.[2]

Although some media apologists claim that "magazines place events in a national perspective" and they "have fostered a sense of national community and furnished Americans across the nation with a common fund of subjects for discussion" (21, p. 192), our data reveal no such cosmopolitanism. In contrast, our findings indicate that religious coverage in *Time* is best predicted by discovering which churches are attended with greatest frequency on the east coast of the United States. The eastern-oriented Episcopalians and Jews have been shown to be better educated, wealthier, and more highly placed in business than any other religious grouping (22, pp. 448–451). Catholics, too, are now beginning to enjoy material advantages and greater educational possibilities; in addition, half of them live on the East coast and one-third are urban dwellers. When such facts are coupled with *Time*'s reportorial preferences, there can be little doubt that *Time* typically responds to its immediate environment when writing religious "news." In doing so, of course, *Time* may be presenting an understanding of the religious impulse which seems foreign to many of its readers.

Some might argue that our interpretations here are misguided and that *Time* refers to the East five times more often than the South (see Table 1) because the most important religious activity occurs in New York City. It is true that the national headquarters of most major denominations are located in New York City and Washington, D.C. Because of that fact, some might suggest, *Time* should be charged with elitism, not favoritism. The data presented in Table 4, however, reveal graphic *denominational* differences, so that if *Time* is elitist, it is selectively so.

Time's differential coverage of the various denominations is better explained when we consider data made available in *Ulrich's International Periodical Dictionary*. In its 1977 version, the directory lists 224 popular English-language magazines sponsored by mainstream Judeo-Christian groups in the United States. Of these, 44 percent are Catholic periodicals. Episcopalians produced eight percent of the magazines (even though Episcopalians account for only three percent of the mainstream community) and eleven percent of the periodicals were published by Jewish groups (compared with their six percent representation in the mainstream grouping). Methodists, Presbyterians, Baptists, and Lutherans published at, or under, their membership strength.

These data suggest that some amount of "journalistic contagion" may exist among publishers of religious news. When 63 percent of the mainstream publications are produced by only three religious bodies, it stands to reason that *Time* magazine's adjacency to the centers of publishing in the United States might have narrowed its sources of information and thus biased its coverage. It may well be the case that all news, including that of religion, travels in a relatively tight journalistic circle, the nucleus of which is the Time-Life Building in New York City. *Time* writers may thus be transmitting what is local news for them into national news for the American people.

A number of explanations for the trends noted here can be rather easily dismissed. A gatekeeping explanation would hold that coverage of religion in *Time* is a direct function of the individual editing the religion section. Because of *Time*'s philosophy of group journalism, however, the selective power of an individual "gatekeeper" is minimized. Neither would a straight-news explanation be plausible as there is not a one-to-one correspondence between what goes on in the theological world and what appears in print. *Time* largely dismissed America's Baptists from its pages, even though they are the largest Protestant denomination in the United States. Also, *Time* disregarded religious activity in the American South despite the fact that every major opinion poll documents anew the religious fervor found there, especially in contrast to the East. *Time* consistently ignored the American laity, apparently on the assumption that an interview with Billy Graham or a papal pronouncement has greatest significance to the everyday reader. Thus, a straight-news explanation fails to explain all of *Time*'s coverage patterns.

A third explanation is political in nature. Championed by such persons as Spiro Agnew (1) and Edith Efron (8), the political hypothesis holds that a small cadre of leftist ideologues controls what is seen and read in the mass media and that news has a resultantly liberal cast to it. Our data, however, render the political hypothesis less compelling. Most of *Time*'s tempests, for example, have occurred in the denominational teapot. Despite what may have happened in Berkeley or San Francisco in the 1970s, religion in *Time* magazine has become increasingly denominational over the years.

A more sophisticated interpretation is that certain bureaucratic forces within the news organization inexorably dictate its journalistic operations. Accordingly, as an old-line East coast organization, *Time* slants its news in an Episcopalian direction. But since there is a great deal of Judeo-Catholic news, and since *Time* is a popular newsweekly written by *teams* of authors and reporters, its rather homogenized news is normally not easily suited to points-of-view. Thus, though corporate nuances of *Time* may affect its coverage, the "massified" nature of its news just as surely prevents it from becoming, say, an Episcopalian house organ.

For a sociological explanation, *Time*'s reportage would be treated as an oblique measure of America's religious unconscious, or an unobtrusive social index of religiosity. However, *Time* has been clearly shown to be a highly selective reporter of religious news.

A more convincing and inclusive explanation for *Time*'s religious coverage would be of a rhetorical nature (for studies of the rhetorical strategies available to the mass media, see 2, 3, 5, 12, 15, 24). A rhetorical explanation would hold that any communicative transaction—including the reporting in a popular news magazine—involves selecting and shaping messages for particular others. We are thus encouraged to treat *Time*'s articles as messages which grow out of, and are aligned to, certain generic (or class-bound) rules. These generic rules not only place constraints upon how ideas are expressed but they also constrain what kinds of ideas are likely to be expressed. Over the years, these generic structures become entrenched (if they are socially rewarded) and messages emanating from them become self-reflective and, necessarily, formulaic.

Because of such constraints, *Time*'s treatment of religion differs little from its treatment of other subject matters. Whether discussing sports, show business, or religion, *Time* specializes in contemporary excitement. Because its guiding rhetorical protocol demands action, conflict, and personality, each *Time* essay succeeds in responding to its own rhetorical history and, therefore, in preserving it. *Time*'s articles become mini-dramas in which great athletes, great politicians, and great preachers compete on a scale which dwarfs the lives that mortals lead.

Time emphasizes Catholicism, for example, because the Roman Catholic Church has within it all of the ethnic diversity, theological determinism, monolithic bureaucracy, and socio-political intertwining necessary to fashion entertaining news reports. *Time* neglects oriental scriptures, prosaic pastoral activities, and abstruse theological arguments because they lack the color and excitement upon which it thrives.

Time follows its rhetorical formula because that formula consistently attracts five million subscribers. Although the formula occasionally embraces—by some standards—irrelevant and distorted social facts, it does produce the kind of information many readers find engaging. In knowing how *Time* describes religious activity, then, we see that religious news receives no special dispensation from the processes of selection and adaptation which shape all varieties of news.

Notes

1. In fact, *Time* does not designate a religion editor *per se*. Rather, the magazine employs a senior "staff writer" for religion; above him or her are associate and senior editors who interchangeably edit *Time*'s various sections. In such a system, therefore, it becomes almost impossible for one person to impress his or her will upon the pages of *Time* (18).
2. Gaustad (11) found that Presbyterians and Episcopalians enjoy three and four times their "deserved" strength in the U.S. House of Representatives, while Baptists and Lutherans have but a fraction of the representation they would have were the House apportioned on the basis of religious predilection.

References

1. Agnew, S. "Television's Coverage of the News." In K. Campbell (Ed.) *Critiques of Contemporary Rhetoric*. Belmont, Cal.: Wadsworth, 1972.
2. Anderson, R. L. "Rhetoric and Science Journalism." *Quarterly Journal of Speech* 56, 1970, pp. 358–368.
3. Berg, D. M. "Rhetoric, Reality, and Mass Media." *Quarterly Journal of Speech* 58, 1972.
4. Bockle, F. (Ed.) *The Manipulated Man*. New York: Herder & Herder, 1971.
5. Brown, W. R. and R. E. Crable. "Industry, Mass Magazines, and the Ecology Issue." *Quarterly Journal of Speech* 59, 1973, pp. 259–272.
6. Buchstein, F. D. "The Role of the News Media in the 'Death of God' Controversy." *Journalism Quarterly* 49, 1972, pp. 79–85.
7. Drinan, R. F. "Renewing the Moral Resources of Our Nation." *Journal of Church and State* 14, 1972, pp. 430–439.
8. Efron, E. *The News Twisters*. Los Angeles: Nash, 1971.
9. Epstein, E. J. *News from Nowhere*. New York: Random House, 1973.
10. Gallup Opinion Index. *Religion in America*. April 1971.
11. Gaustad, E. "America's Institutions of Faith: A Statistical Postscript." In William McLoughlin and Robert Bellah (Eds.) *Religion in America*. Boston: Houghton Mifflin, 1968.
12. Gregg, R. B. "The Rhetoric of Political Newscasting." *Central States Speech Journal* 28, 1977, pp. 221–237.
13. Hart, R. P., K. J. Turner, and R. E. Knupp. "Religion and the Rhetoric of the Mass Media." *Review of Religious Research* 21, 1980, pp. 256–275.
14. Haseldon, K. *Morality & The Mass Media*. Nashville, Tenn.: Broadman Press, 1968.
15. Kidd, V. "Happily Ever After and Other Relationship Styles: Advice on Interpersonal Relations in Popular Magazines, 1951–1973." *Quarterly Journal of Speech* 61, 1975, pp. 31–39.

16. Kuhns, W. *The Electronic Gospel: Religion and the Media.* New York: Herder & Herder, 1969.
17. Landis, Benson Y. (Ed.) *Yearbook of American Churches for 1961.* New York: National Council 1960.
18. Medina, Sara, *Time* magazine. Telephone interview, April 1978.
19. Mohan, V. "The Lutheran Standard: 125 Years of Denominational Journalism." *Journalism Quarterly* 45, 1968, pp. 71–76.
20. Real, M. R. "Trends in the Structure and Policy in the American Catholic Press." Journalism Quarterly 52, 1975, pp. 265–271.
21. Rivers, W., T. Peterson, and J. Jenson. *The Mass Media and Modern Society* (second edition) San Francisco: Rinehart, 1971.
22. Rosten, L. (Ed.) *Religions of America.* New York: Simon and Schuster, 1975.
23. Sellers, J. E. "Religious Journalism in Theological Seminaries." *Journalism Quarterly* 35, 1955, pp. 464–468.
24. Tuchman, G. "Introduction." In Gaye Tuchman (Ed.) *The T.V. Establishment: Programming for Power and Profit.* Englewood Cliffs, N.J.: Prentice-Hall, 1974.
25. Wall, A. "How Can the Religious Press Be a More Effective Conscience for America?" *Catholic Mind* 72, 1974, pp. 19–23.
26. Whalen, J. W. "The Catholic Digest: Experiment in Courage." *Journalism Quarterly* 41, 1964, pp. 343–352.
27. Whalen, J. W. "The Press Opens Up Vatican II." *Journalism Quarterly* 44, 1967, pp. 53–61.

Happily Ever After and Other Relationship Styles: Advice on Interpersonal Relations in Popular Magazines, 1951–1973

Virginia Kidd

The *Reader's Digest* in November of 1972 blazed across its front cover the legend "Three Ways to Save a Marriage."[1] The *Saturday Evening Post,* November, 1953, featured the article, "So You're Not Speaking to Each Other."[2] *Seventeen* in June of 1963 pondered the question "Why Can't I Talk to My Mother?"[3] The articles fulfilling these titles lack the detailed development of scholarly treatises, but they touch upon subject matter common to comunication scholarship. Quite obviously, advice on interpersonal relations is being offered in massive doses through the media of public rhetoric, and this advice reaches and potentially influences readers numbering in the multi-millions.

Such articles contribute to the development of what Ernest Bormann has termed "rhetorical visions,"[4] concise interlocking dramas which fuse into a symbolic reality of the world. The rhetorical visions thus derived provide for those who accept them an understanding of the world, motivation for behavior, and most importantly, cues for meaning to be given to various verbal and nonverbal interaction. Bormann urged critics to examine "the social relationships, the motives, the qualitative impact of that symbolic world as though it were the substance of social reality for those people who participated in the vision."[5]

Popular magazines indicate social realities readers may come to accept. Kenneth Boulding, in *The Image,* explained the process by which such rhetorical visions in the mass media assume importance:

> The burnt child receives a vigorous message from nature regarding the relationship between heat and pain. The unburnt child, however, likewise dreads the fire because it has been taught to do so by its elders who speak with the voice of authority. Probably by far the larger portion of our relational image comes with the authority of the transcript not with the authority of the experience.[6]

Mass media become the "authority of the transcript"; they provide what Walter Lippmann termed "pictures in our heads—pictures which are representations of the real world."[7] Through these representations a composite image of "reality" is constructed, a rhetorical vision which has its base not so much in "reality" as in rhetoric.

From *The Quarterly Journal of Speech,* Volume 61, 1975. Reprinted with permission of the author.

Popular magazines, reaching vast numbers of readers, are an important element in the furthering of rhetorical visions. They can be presumed both to reflect and to inspire attitudes in their readers, and while an examination of the rhetorical visions of popular journals is not a verification of the beliefs of the readers, it is an indication of popular mood.

This study examined rhetorical visions of interpersonal relations in popular magazines over the last twenty years. The twenty year time period allowed for the tracing of derivations and development of particular lines of thought while at the same time focusing on contemporary attitudes.

Journals were selected for inclusion in this study on the basis of two criteria: (1) Inclusion in the *Reader's Guide to Periodical Literature*. The *Reader's Guide* has traditionally offered access to the popular journals, indexing the major large circulation magazines and excluding specialized periodicals. As such, it provided a useful cross-section of the popular visions as presented in contemporary journals. Magazines not included in the *Guide* for the entire twenty years were examined only during the years of inclusion in the *Guide*. (2) Having a circulation of over 1,000,000. This dividing point allowed a broad enough circulation for each magazine to have a significant influence on the "mass culture" and at the same time included a large enough number of magazines to supply the information needed.[8] A random selection of ten percent of all articles dealing with human relations in these journals for two year periods between 1951 and 1973 was analyzed.

Two rhetorical visions describing interpersonal relations were evidenced in the popular journals from 1951 to 1973. Vision I dominated the journals in the 1950s and early 1960s and continues to be operative today. Vision II is newer, appearing sporadically in the early Sixties, gaining impetus in the late Sixties and assuming a major position in the last few years. Each vision included explanations for appropriate behavior in caring relationships, specific suggestions for face to face interaction, and provided readers models of meaning in exchanges between persons. Despite the similarities of function, the specific advice each vision proffered was unique to it.

Dramas presented in Vision I were set in a world which was relatively unchanging. Behavioral patterns were described as continually repeating, and the repetition established a pattern of normality. This standard of normality was indicated through the continually reappearing assumption that any given dramatized situation had only one correct line of action for the characters. Behavior was dramatized on a bipolar continuum. Issues were right or wrong, left or right, and behavior was acclaimed or condemned. Regular columns, such as *Better Homes and Gardens'* "What's Wrong with This Family?" and *Ladies Home Journal's* "Can This Marriage Be Saved?" presented relationship situations in which experts revealed the right behavior to the confused participants. Journals regularly gave readers the opportunity to test their mastery of appropriate behavior through quizzes which offered as a matter of course only one correct answer to each question.

Even more revealing of the single standard was the Vision I presentation of sex roles. Females and males were expected to behave according to traditional patterns, and when one did not do so, it was not the pattern but the individual's sexuality that was at fault. Dr. Margaret Mead's report on the Arapesh culture, for instance, where males are "gentle, always cooperative rather than competitive and never aggressive," was so out of line with the Vision I image of woman as the passive homemaker and man as the aggressive breadwinner that it was entitled "Where Men Must Have Feminine Traits."[9] So pervasive was this standard as a basis for relationships that Robert Coughlan could write in *Life,* 1956, of the violation of the norm, "In New York City the 'career woman' can be seen in fullest bloom and it is not irrelevant that New York City also has the greatest concentration of psychiatrists."[10] Such an argumentative leap was permissible in Vision I because deviation from the norm literally communicated emotional problems. The dramas offered dire predictions for those who dared to violate Vision I standards. In terms of the working wife, for example, Coughlan wrote, "She may find many satisfactions in her job, but the chances are that she, her husband and her children will suffer psychological damage, and that she will be basically an unhappy woman."[11] Through such ominous rhetoric, Vision I indicated the power of the standard it set up, and Vision I authors reinforced the rhetoric by giving the sex role standard empirical bases. Reported Dr. Clifford R. Adams in *Ladies Home Journal,* 1957, "Generally a fourth of a wife's married happiness and a third of her husband's, depend on the sexual adjustment they make. The greater importance to the male is probably due to his greater sex drive. . . ."[12] Researching such a hypothesis might prove a challenge to scholars throughout the discipline of speech communication, but it was no problem for Vision I authors: the standard was so well accepted that no one would question it.

Though examples of the dominance of the single standard are most readily evident in sex role relations, the standard existed in relationship situations throughout Vision I, providing the foundation on which the vision rested. The single standard gave clear meaning to behavior. Characters in Vision I dramas had only to conform to the standard of normal to communicate the specific meaning such normal behavior aroused. Violations of the standard were immediately deviant and suspect.

Given a knowable and known standard against which behavior could be monitored, authors in Vision I were able to prescribe appropriate behavior easily. Basically, Vision I drama indicated how to create an image which most closely resembled the ideal in order to have high value on the interpersonal marketplace.[13] To help readers create such an image, authors developed an elaborate catalogue of prescriptions for interpersonal communication which, if followed, would develop readers into the heroes and heroines of Vision I dramas. The "ten easy steps" genre of article grew in prominence as authors explained how simple changing Cinderella into a princess really could be.

Fundamental to Vision I's ideal interaction was that an individual should make "others" happy. Paramount among the suggestions for accomplishing this goal was the admonition, "Above all, think of the other's problems before you think of your own."[14] This putting aside of self was defined as loving behavior, and conversely thinking of self first was unloving and displayed lack of genuine concern for others.

Intertwined with what was dramatized as a genuine desire to create happiness for others was the implied promise that those who brought such kindliness would be rewarded. When *Coronet,* 1953, proclaimed the virtue of compliments, for example, the author suggested, "We may even make some of them so memorable that they will still bring pleasure to the recipients long after we've spoken them," then added pragmatically, "A compliment has greater purchasing power than money."[15] Even listening could be pursued for profit as well as friendship. *Reader's Digest,* September, 1965, showed how a listener could benefit from an otherwise dull conversation:

> There is no such thing as a worthless conversation provided you know what to listen for. The attentive listener . . . listens for what people unconsciously reveal about themselves while they're talking. Thus he can derive meaning from a conversation even though the other person may be talking nonsense.[16]

The goal was not to break through the nonsense to the speaker, but rather to give the speaker the courtesy of appearing to listen while searching for personal advancement from the interchange.

An extension of "putting the other first" was an attempt to avoid any incident which might cause the other discomfort. Disagreement or conflict was seen as indicating serious relationship problems, and journals described at length alternatives to confrontive behavior. *Seventeen* explained to its readers:

> If you really want to get rid of a fellow, there are some effective ways that will avoid deeply hurt feelings or the embarrassment of constantly running into someone you've had an argument with. One way is never to make a date with him. You never make dates far in advance, you tell him, and just this week you happen to be awfully busy with lots of things. Not dates. Just "things." So he waits a week, and somehow or other, you're so busy again. In a while he'll take the hint. And meanwhile, you haven't really rejected him outright.[17]

Motivation for this behavior was generally in the best interests of the "other." Marion Hilliard, in the *Reader's Digest,* 1957, urged women to deceive their husbands deliberately during sexual intercourse. She explained, "A man can feel kinship with the gods if his wife can make him believe he can cause a flowering within her. If she doesn't feel it she must bend every effort to pretend."[18] Dr. Hilliard sanctified such manipulation of facts. It was, she wrote, "the worthiest duplicity on earth."[19]

A final Vision I criteria of ideal interaction in a relationship was simply being with others in the relationship. Vision I writers were the agents who spawned "togetherness." Acting together in mutual concerns was held up as the symbol of family solidarity; it was dramatized as uniting a family to the point that its members found in each other's company pleasure "so great you don't even *want* a night out."[20] Those who did want a night out were manifesting relationship problems.

Vision I presented a consistent, coherent picture of the world of relationships which dominated much thought between 1951 and 1970. Characters in the dramas of the time interacted through social norms which praised selflessness, absence of open confrontation, and strategic interaction as positive relationship behavior. Since individuals compared the behavior of those with whom they related to a preconceived standard in order to give meaning to behavior, meaning-giving was fairly consistent for all persons. Vision I's weakness as a communication system came when individuals did not wish to convey by their behavior what the preconceived notion demanded. Vision I offered little outlet for creativity in communication, for formulating new ways of expressing relationship messages, or for forming new ways of relating which were not prescribed by the vision. In addition, the Vision I emphasis on creating a good impression, putting genuine personal feelings aside, and living up to a predetermined standard could easily destroy honest responses between people as well as any beneficial change which might result from honest feedback. (One can well imagine, for instance, that moment when the wife who did not feel a flowering within as a result of her husband's lovemaking finally stabbed him through the heart with the butcher knife in a fit of frustration. Suggesting changes in his behavior seems a lot simpler.)

Beginning slowly in the early Sixties and increasing steadily thereafter, a new notion of appropriate interpersonal relations evolved to challenge the dominant position previously held by Vision I. Henry Miller articulated the basic position of Vision II in a 1966 *Esquire* article: "The idea of permanence is an absurd illusion. Change is the most permanent thing you can say about the whole universe."[21] Vision II authors always assumed, and often directly asserted, that life was ever changing and so were relationships. Consequently, so was meaning. Standard preconceived meaning could no longer adequately be applied to human interaction. Meaning was therefore negotiable, and the task of Vision II dramatists was not to prescribe to readers how to match a specific standard but rather how to function in negotiation of meaning.

Articles indicated this change in philosophy in their descriptions of relationships. A discussion of marriage in *Redbook,* 1968, for example, was a far cry from the prescriptive lists of the Fifties:

> Specialists who study family life now agree that it is pointless to compare real marriages with some imagined ideal. The model marriage is a myth. . . . We must begin with a basic fact. Not all marriages are alike and they cannot be measured by the same standards.[22]

Erich Fromm not only rejected the preconceived standard, but cast it as a villain in his metaphor of plant care in *McCall's,* 1967: "If I have preconceived ideas of 'what is good for the plant'—for instance, the idea that lots of water is good for everything—I will cripple or kill the plant. . . ."[23] Thus the ordered dramatic scene of Vision I, with its prescribed meanings for human relationships, was replaced in Vision II by a world in which universal conventions ought not be applied to all relationships and indeed carried possible harmful effects when applied.

In such a setting the "we can talk it out" theme became paramount. What was once "conversation" was now the "miracle" or "magic" of communication, and authors echoed such ideas as those of John Lagemann, who wrote in the *Reader's Digest,* 1966, that ". . . when people talk together honestly and intensely the human spirit is lifted and refreshed."[24] Characters were dramatized as coming together in unity when they established "an atmosphere of openness so that everyone feels free to discuss and express his feelings."[25] *Redbook's* monthly "Young Mother's Story" typified the attitude in a drama of marital problems resolved through communication entitled "Please Talk to Me."[26]

Conflict was included in this talking out behavior. Vision II authors dramatized burying conflict and denying disagreement as causing dissension to fester and grow. Representative of this approach was a 1972 *Redbook* article: "Unpleasant feelings, petty resentments and frustrations do not go away simply because one refuses to let them show. Rather, they can build up a deadly store of bitterness."[27]

In a world without prescribed meaning for interpersonal behavior, where individuals had to confer meaning, the individual was vital. "Being your real self," "self-fulfillment," "being more yourself" were cue words for wise, alive behavior. Often the "self" was equated with an individual's feeling. Consequently, expression of feeling was cherished in Vision II dramas and constraining such feeling was negative behavior. Obviously the self-sacrifice practiced in Vision I was antithetical to this philosophical position; it was pictured as resulting in resentment and possessiveness.

As the self increased in importance, social institutions were subordinated and lost their power to define relationships. For example, *The New York Times Magazine* in 1972 described the "new breed of marriage counselors" whose motto was "Save the spouses, rather than the marriage."[28]

Indicative of Vision II ideals was its depiction of negative behavior. The truly villanous act of Vision II dramas was the failure to become involved with others. Lee Salk, for example, advised his *McCall's* readers in 1972 that hate was not the opposite of love, "Indifference is."[29] Fromm asserted, "Suffering is not the worst thing in life—indifference is."[30] Symptoms of indifference were displayed in dramas where living, growing beings were unrecognized by the villains of the piece who treated them as "objects" rather than people. Clearly, a rhetorical vision which functions on the basis of human exchange, which demands negotiation of meaning for interpersonal relationships to progress, cannot tolerate the absence of such interaction. Building such refusal to interact into a highly negative behavior was necessary for the vision's success.

Vision II's strength as a communication system was the emphasis it placed on the communication process. In a world of change, constant movement and reassessment of values, the traditional roles and norms of community were no longer pervasive. Meaning could not be accurately conferred on words or actions by comparing them to preconceived definitions. Rather, individuals had to arrive at a consensual meaning. The resultant exchanges between individuals could at times, unfortunately, be highly confusing. Meanings had to be deciphered from a complex morass of possibilities and were subject to constant redefinition. Despite the potential confusion of the system, meaning was more flexible than in Vision I and offered participants a greater freedom of expression. As well, Vision II allowed for more direct expression. Individuals were expected to describe their reactions in relationship situations in order to negotiate meaning; such description functioned as clarifying behavior. Vision II's weakness as a communication system was its almost simplistic approach to some communication situations, ironic in a vision based so firmly in the recognition of the world as complex. Vision II equated talking about problems with resolution of problems and suggested that the only element involved in "talking it out" was a decision to talk. The authors did not dramatize problems which discussion could not resolve, did not envision human interaction made less satisfying by open revelation of feelings, and did not portray characters incapable of expressing themselves.

In order for a rhetorical vision to gain credence as a belief system, it must perform two functions: (1) it must offer the potential believer some benefit for accepting the vision, some reason for believing, and (2) it must do so while adequately taking into account "reality links," the tangible events in an individual's life which exist outside the world of rhetoric. An examination of how Vision I and Vision II fulfilled these two functions indicates how Vision II gained acceptance against the once unquestioned authority of Vision I.

Vision I offered its adherents a world hierarchy which gave them significance and security. Significance was available through identification with characters in the dramas. Anyone could be the heroine or hero if she or he was willing to abide by the definitions the vision offered. Everyone was rhetorically allowed a role that could be center stage, if not immediately, then at the apex of a life of effort and careful advancement. As well, Vision I offered security. The world was taken from a state of random chaos and given pattern and thus meaning. The future was predictable and controllable. To believe in such a vision gave followers a way to understand human interaction.

Not all readers, however, were willing to identify with the characters Vision I dramas depicted. Increasingly through the Sixties, groups of individuals outside the magazine world were not identifying with the traditional lifestyles. Women's liberation groups rejected the dramatization of women, individualists ridiculed "togetherness," "the establishment" was assaulted on multiple fronts. And in the press of these reality links, Vision I continued to offer the same rhetoric. No changes in the vision indicated the changes historically occurring outside the dramas because Vision I had no provision for change. If meanings could fluctuate, then the whole foundation of Vision I crumbled.

Vision II offered an explanation of the world for those who could no longer find identity in Vision I. Like Vision I, it offered its believers significance. Each character bore internally the promise of a wondrous identity, and the confusion of a chaotic world which so plagued Vision I was readily assimilated into the newer vision as a potential source of growth for the individual.

Vision II has not completely replaced Vision I, however, though it continues to challenge. Perhaps this lack of complete acceptance stems from its weaknesses as a rhetorical explanation with which readers could identify. The significance Vision II offered in its dramas was offered only to the strong. Unlike Vision I, Vision II did not provide identity for all. The average American was not the hero of Vision II; rather, the special person was. The vision offered no heroes or heroines who were indecisive, unable to handle difficulty, insecure, afraid or unable to speak their minds. Characters who were unable to function at an optimum level interpersonally were presented in a negative light. Individuals who believed themselves to be inadequate in some aspect would find little comfort in the vision dramas which provided no identity for weakness, no rationale for failure. In addition, Vision II did not offer the security that Vision I offered so well as a belief system. The vision authors dramatized characters who put their faith in growth, change, and the individual's ability to deal with the future, yet in so doing they lost the vast persuasive rhetoric that security offers.

Assessing the exact influence of dramas presented in popular magazines on their readers is clearly impossible. To make such an assessment, a critic would have to know to what extent readers accepted what they read in their own lives. In addition, the critic would have to separate the influence of popular magazines from all other sources of influence on other magazine readers. To do either is clearly impossible.

Anyone can speculate, however, about probable reactions to the magazine influence. Two general observations seem particularly relevant. First the impact of any popular journal is limited and somewhat defined by the journal's readership. With the exception of the *Reader's Digest* and *Coronet,* the magazines carrying the bulk of the articles on interpersonal relations had predominantly female readerships.[31] The result of this readership weighting was that articles were generally slanted toward the woman reader, accenting the woman's role in the dramas presented. The extension of this journalistic slanting is that the articles taken as a whole seem to be suggesting that the woman bears a greater responsibility in human relations than does her male counterpart. Dramas in both visions featured examples of how women could resolve problems and how women could interpret behavior. The modeling process provided by these dramas left little doubt as to who bore the responsibility for solving relationship difficulties or enhancing relationships in general, and implied by the absence of modeling examples that the male's responsibility was negligible. Whether women readers believed what they read or not, they were at least sensitized to communication situations in ways that non-readers were not.

Second, the short length of magazine articles, fundamental to the journal's form, lends itself to the deception that communication in close human relationships can be attained so easily that the process can be explained in two thousand words or less with space left over for the toothpaste ad.

Both Vision I and Vision II testify to the kind of interaction to be expected in the society that creates the visions. As well, they speak to the aspirations of that society. The rhetorical visions of interpersonal relations expressed in popular magazines have at their core the belief that somehow people can be close, that some techniques tried at the right time and in the right manner, will allow individuals to reach through the barriers of human separation to feel the emotional pulse of a loved one. Popular magazine authors are attempting to help people make that contact, and the enormous readership of these journals makes them far too significant to be put aside as skeletons-in-the-closet of communication scholarship.

The massive amount of published material this survey represents attempts to deal rhetorically with the fundamental issue of human isolation. The need for such articles emphasizes one repeated comment, the despairing observation that life is somehow, at the innermost core of our most significant relationships, unsatisfying. The urgency of that issue is reflected in the prominence of such articles, in the continual popularity of potential relationship elixirs which describe how individuals might reach other individuals and might go on reaching them year after year. The problem is that the elixirs offered are often so inadequate. In the final analysis, the popular magazine articles, the rhetorical visions they foster, and ultimately the expectations about relationships given into the minds of believing readers through the visions, do no more than skim the surface in their approaches to human encounters. Neither vision ever confronts the awesome possibility that human separation may be unavoidable, may in fact be necessary, in some self-preserving way. All the advice of Margaret Blair Johnstone, Ann Landers, Benjamin Spock, Lee Salk, and Erich Fromm together is meaningless if isolation is the ultimate refuge of sanity.

Notes

1. Ruth Stafford Peale, "Three Ways to Mothproof a Marriage," *Reader's Digest,* Nov. 1972, pp. 105–107.
2. H. A. Smith, "So You're Not Speaking to Each Other," *Saturday Evening Post,* 7 Nov. 1953, pp. 22–23ff.
3. "Why Can't I Talk to My Mother?" *Seventeen,* June 1963, pp. 100–101ff.

4. Bormann's description of the rhetorical vision critical techniques is explained in detail in Ernest G. Borman, "Fantasy and Rhetorical Vision: The Rhetorical Criticism of Social Reality," *Quarterly Journal of Speech*, 58 (1972), pp. 396–407. Bormann uses the methodology to examine an issue in the 1972 Presidential campaign in "The Eagleton Affair: A Fantasy Theme Analysis," *Quarterly Journal of Speech*, 59 (1973), pp. 143–159. This article not only illuminates the issues surrounding the removal of Senator Tom Eagleton from the Democratic Presidential ticket; as well it exemplifies the rhetorical vision methodology.

5. Bormann, "Fantasy and Rhetorical Vision," p. 401.

6. Kenneth Boulding, *The Image*, Ann Arbor Paperbacks (Ann Arbor: University of Michigan Press, 1956), p. 70.

7. Cited by Rod Holmgren and William Norton, eds., *The Mass Media Book* (Englewood Cliffs, New Jersey: Prentice-Hall, Inc., 1972), p. 4.

8. Journals included in the analysis were *American Home, American Magazine, Better Homes and Gardens, Colliers, Coronet, Cosmopolitan, Ebony, Esquire, Farm Journal, Field and Stream, Good Housekeeping, Ladies Home Journal, Life, Look, McCall's, Newsweek, New York Times Magazine, Parents Magazine, Reader's Digest, Redbook, Saturday Evening Post, Scholastic, Seventeen, Time,* and *Woman's Home Companion.*

9. Judson T. Landis and Mary G. Landis, "The U.S. Male—Is He First Class?" *Colliers*, 19 July 1952, pp. 22–23ff.

10. Robert Coughlan, "The Changing Roles in Modern Marriage," *Life*, 24 Dec. 1956, p. 110.

11. *Ibid.*, p. 116.

12. Clifford R. Adams, "We Agree On Almost Everything Except Sex," *Ladies Home Journal*, June 1957, p. 54.

13. The metaphor of the marketplace was common to Vision I. Ernest Havermann in *Reader's Digest* and *Life*, 1961, cited sociologist Clifford Kirkpatrick, who "feels that courtship can best be regarded as essentially a bargaining process; you go looking in the open market for the best possible mate to whom your own qualities entitle you." "Modern Courtship: The Great Illusion?" *Reader's Digest*, Dec. 1961, p. 82. Even Rosalind Russell got into the act, explaining in *Reader's Digest*, 1959 that "the girl who shops carefully, for a husband or a dress, generally gets better value. . . ." "I'm Glad I Didn't Marry Young," *Reader's Digest*, Feb. 1959, p. 75.

14. Lynn Mighell and Marjorie Holmes, "What's Your Paycheck Doing to Your Marriage?" *Better Homes and Gardens*, March 1954, p. 65.

15. Helen Colton, "Making Friends with Compliments," *Coronet*, July 1953, p. 108.

16. J. N. Miller, "Art of Intelligent Listening" *Reader's Digest*, Sept. 1965, p. 85.

17. Jimmy Wescott, "Good-by, My Love," *Seventeen*, May 1963, p. 22.

18. Marion Hilliard, "The Act of Love—Woman's Greatest Challenge," *Reader's Digest*, June 1957, p. 45.

19. *Ibid.*

20. Marjorie Holmes, "Can Husband and Wife Be Friends?" *Better Homes and Gardens*, Oct. 1953, p. 194.

21. David Dury, "Sex Goes Public, A Talk with Henry Miller," *Esquire*, May 1966, p. 121.

22. Wells Goodrich with Robert J. Levin, "What Makes a Marriage Succeed," *Redbook*, Dec. 1968, p. 44.

23. Erich Fromm, "Do We Still Love Life?" *McCall's*, Aug. 1967, p. 108.

24. John Kord Lagemann, "Conversation Can Nourish Your Life," *Reader's Digest*, June 1966, pp. 131–132.

25. Lee Salk, "You and Your Family," *McCall's,* Nov. 1972, p. 68.
26. "Please Talk to Me," *Redbook,* April 1972, pp. 28ff.
27. *Ibid.,* p. 34.
28. M. W. Lear, "Save the Spouses Rather than the Marriage," *New York Times Magazine,* 13 Aug. 1972, pp. 12–13ff.
29. Lee Salk, "You and Your Family," *McCall's,* Sept. 1972, p. 64.
30. Fromm, "Do We Still Love Life?" p. 110.
31. The journals carrying the heaviest proportion of articles about interpersonal relationships were *Cosmopolitan, Ladies Home Journal, McCall's, Parents Magazine, Reader's Digest, Redbook, Seventeen* and, while they were in publication, *Coronet* and *Woman's Home Companion.*

7

Rhetoric of Public Letters

For over two millenia the principles of rhetoric have been applied to various forms of writing. Though rhetorical theorists did not produce treatises exclusively dealing with the persuasive dimensions of the written word until the fourth century A.D., the principles of oral rhetoric had long been assumed to apply to writing as well as speaking. As James J. Murphy notes in his seminal work *Rhetoric in the Middle Ages:* "It is not surprising . . . that the ancient world produced no separate rhetorical doctrine about writing. Ancient education—and Roman schools especially—aimed at preparing a student to be adept in both writing and speaking. Eloquent letters, like eloquent speeches, were expected to be the product of broad rhetorical education."[1]

In this section Richard Fulkerson and F. Forrester Church demonstrate how rhetorical theories of the classical period, theories developed primarily for the education of orators, have been used from classical to contemporary times to invent, arrange, and stylize public letters. Fulkerson looks to the recent past as he examines the structure, logic, and style of Martin Luther King Jr.'s "Letter from Birmingham Jail." Church, on the other hand, takes the reader back to the first century A.D. to consider the rhetorical structure of St. Paul's epistle to Philemon. Both authors look to classical rhetorical theories to help explain the persuasive dimensions of written discourse. Both are concerned with matters of structure, logic, and style.

Fulkerson turns to the classical pattern of *narratio, propositio, confirmatio, refutatio,* and *peroratio* to explain the structure and function of King's "Letter from Birmingham Jail." In so doing, he raises the important question of audience or, more accurately, the question of audiences. Who were the audiences, both real and apparent, for the letter? How does the structural pattern developed take these multiple audiences into account? And how does the structure, in and of itself, function as a means of persuasion? Fulkerson suggests answers to all of these questions as he probes the techniques King used to refute one group while simultaneously appealing to a much larger constituency.

Church, like Fulkerson, is interested in questions of rhetorical structure and how such structures can help to explain the compositional principles followed by St. Paul. But Church has a larger purpose in mind as well. He proposes to demonstrate through his critique that rhetorical theory is a better

1. James J. Murphy, *Rhetoric in the Middle Ages* (Berkeley: University of California Press, 1974), p. 195.

explanatory system—a better way of accounting for why Paul's letter to Philemon was written the way it was written—than competing explanations. Church uses rhetorical analysis as both an alternative to and supplement for the more traditional literary, formal, and higher critical methods of biblical interpretation. Rhetoric, for Church, is more than a technique for explaining persuasive structure; it is a body of theory with both explanatory and predictive force. If one knows the situation to which Paul was responding, one can both explain why he wrote as he did and predict the probable effects of such writing based upon historical precedent, classical testimony, and audience analysis.

Church identifies the pattern of exordium, proof, and peroration and shows how Paul actually argues a case under the guise of deliberating what should be done with the runaway slave, Onesimus. Church believes that the letter clearly falls within the deliberative genre.

Both Fulkerson and Church deal with matters of logic and argument. Fulkerson describes the refutative logic practiced by King. He reconstructs the syllogistic forms of the arguments to which King is ostensibly responding and shows how the letter writer attacked both minor and major premises in order to destroy the claims put forward by the opposition. Both Fulkerson and Church emphasize the interaction among the modes of proof. Logic, by itself, cannot account for the overall effect of the discourses. Though refutation explains why King was able to maintain the logical consistency of his position, and admonition and implication account for Paul's internal logic, one must turn to matters of style to understand how audience evaluation transcended substance alone.

In both letters style functioned argumentatively. Fulkerson shows, through introduction of possible alternatives, why King's word choices were the most appropriate given the rhetorical situation he faced. King used stylistic factors to bolster his ethos with both the clergymen to whom he was ostensibly responding and to the mass of moderate and liberal whites who would ultimately determine the success or failure of his movement. Elements of King's style functioned as arguments about his character, intellect, motivations, and intentions.

St. Paul also used stylistic factors argumentatively, as Church shows, but in a more implicit and implicative fashion than King. By playing on the sounds and meanings of particular Greek words, Paul was able to imply to Philemon what his actions should be with regard to his escaped slave. On the surface it may appear that Paul's stylistic strategies were extremely subtle, so much so that his meaning might have been missed. But is there a reason why a style that placed heavy reliance on rhyme, similarities of vowel sounds, and "interidentification" of terminology might be effective for Paul's audience but not for King's? Might stylistic choices and effectiveness be determined, at least in part, by whether the letter is to be read aloud or printed for silent consumption?

The art of letter writing poses several interesting questions for rhetorical theory and criticism. Both Church and Fulkerson refer to the phenomenon of multiple audiences that is often associated with the public letter. The letter writer must "fictionalize" his audience, must make certain assumptions about who they are, what capacities they have, and how best to appeal to them. But in the very act of fictionalizing an audience the letter writer also projects an image of himself. The audience, in a sense, creates the writer just as much as the writer creates the audience. Nor can the writer ever be sure that the audience he has projected as his target is, in fact, the same as the audience he will succeed in reaching.

Paul believed himself to be writing to Philemon, though he clearly recognized that his epistle would be read to others. King constructed his letter as a refutation to the Birmingham clergymen, but clearly understood that the letter would be printed for all to read. Yet neither Paul nor King could have foreseen the distant audience. Paul did not know that his letters would be collected, canonized, and read by the faithful for the next two thousand years. King did not know that his letter would become a classic of the civil rights movement and be reprinted in college anthologies for the next quarter century or more. Neither man could have foreseen the true scope of his audience, or fictionalized even a small portion of it, or adjusted his ideas to men and women of all times and places. Yet the letters endure. They are read, studied, and imitated. Why? There is something about the language, the style, structure, and logic that transcends time and place. Is it possible that effective rhetoric can also be beautiful poetry? Are situational effectiveness and universal permanence mutually exclusive concepts?

Rhetorical Structure and Design in Paul's Letter to Philemon

F. Forrester Church

What has Paul to do with Quintilian? For a host of scholars this question would answer itself, rhetorically.[1] A stock device, the rhetorical question has long been favored in argument. Even Paul is no exception. "Where is the wise man?" he asks. "Where is the scribe? Where is the debater of this age? Has not God made foolish the wisdom of the world?" (1 Cor. 1:20). Paul would appear to be dismissing everything his contemporary, Quintilian, stood for. Yet one point remains. As Cicero once wrote of Plato, "it was when making fun of orators that he himself seemed to be the consummate orator."[2] The following, a rhetorical study of the letter to Philemon, will suggest that Paul too employed basic tactics of persuasion taught and widely practiced in his day.

Why Philemon? There are three reasons. First, acting upon Robert Funk's suggestion that "the investigation of Philemon would be a promising point of departure in uncovering the structure of the Pauline letter," John White has recently subjected it to a rigorous structural analysis, tracing its components to patterns reflected in the Hellenistic papyri.[3] Philemon does offer a promising point of departure; and White's contribution to Philemon studies provides a ready contrast to my own appraoch. Second, Philemon shows no trace of dialogical style, the one aspect of Paul's letters where, with credit to the work of Johannes Weiss and Rudolf Bultmann, the influence of rhetorical conventions, particularly those of the Cynic-Stoic *diatribe,* has generally been admitted by the new critics.[4] There is an advantage in this. If, without reference to dialogical style, the impact of rhetoric on the structure and design of the *whole* of Philemon can be demonstrated, then, where it does appear, its presence may less conveniently be explained away by consignment to those "sections of the Pauline letter which draw on a nonepistolary tradition."[5] Third, while Philemon has been recognized, even by those who place least credence in Paul's art, as a well-crafted and carefully woven piece, the consensus remains that it "owes nothing to the graces of rhetoric."[6]

By definition, there are three kinds of rhetoric. The object of deliberative rhetoric is to exhort or dissuade; of forsenic, to accuse or defend; of epideictic, to praise or blame.[7] They are appropriate, respectively, to the forum, where one's hearers must judge the future; to the courts, where they must judge the past; and to the marketplace or amphitheater, where they, as spectators, must

Used by permission of the author, F. Forrester Church. Originally appeared in *Harvard Theological Review,* 71 (1978).

judge the art of the orator present before them.[8] Of course, deliberative oratory is equally appropriate to anyone who might need or seek advice. Quintilian, who speaks interchangeably of deliberative *(pars deliberativa)* and advisory *(pars suasoria)* rhetoric, claims that this type of oratory offers "a more varied field for eloquence, since both those who ask for advice and the answers given to them may easily present the greatest diversity."[9] It is equally important to those who would "take part in the counsels of their friends," as to those who would "speak their opinions in the senate, or advise the emperor."[10] Thus, it is to deliberative rhetoric, as the genre that is least elaborate and most conducive to Paul's hortatory purpose, that one should look for patterns that may underlie his argumentation.[11]

In deliberative rhetoric, success rests on establishing two primary motives for action, honor *(honestas)* and advantage *(utilitas)*.[12] These are supported by the skillful use of proofs, or appeals to the reason and emotions of one's hearer. The three proofs ($\pi \acute{\iota} \sigma \tau \epsilon \iota s$), or "means of carrying one's point," are *ethos, pathos,* and *logos.*[13] In deliberative oratory, the two appeals to the emotions are especially necessary, in that "anger has frequently to be excited or assuaged and the minds of the audience have to be swayed to fear, ambition, hatred, reconciliation."[14] *Pathos,* expressed in Latin by *adfectus,* is a stirring appeal to the heart.[15] *Ethos,* or *mores,* does not admit of a simple definition. It is essentially a reflection of one's own good character.[16] The key is to demonstrate love or friendship and to induce sympathy or goodwill, in order to dispose the hearer favorably to the merits of one's case.[17]

In structure, the deliberative speech divides into three parts: the exordium ($\pi \rho o o \acute{\iota} \mu \iota o \upsilon$); main body or proof ($\pi \acute{\iota} \sigma \tau \iota s$); and peroration ($\epsilon$'$\pi \acute{\iota} \lambda o \gamma o s$).[18] The exordium is often reduced to a mere prelude, intended primarily to establish the appropriate mood and to secure the goodwill of the hearer, both by praise itself and by linking that praise to the subject in question. "If the case affords us the means of winning the favor of the judge," Quintilian adds, "it is important that the points which seem most likely to serve to our purpose would be selected for introduction into the exordium."[19] In the main body or proof, the argument is formally advanced, with primary reference to the motives of honor and utility, and by appeal to *ethos, pathos* and *logos.* The peroration consists of four elements: restating one's appeal; securing the hearer's favor; amplifying one's argument; and, setting the hearer in an emotional frame of mind.[20] Here, factors alluded to in the exordium and adduced in the proof are restated a third time with all possible force. If, in the exordium, "any preliminary appeal to the compassion of the judge must be made sparingly and with restraint, . . . in the peroration we may give full rein to our emotions."[21] Such are the outlines of ancient deliberative rhetoric as described by Aristotle, Cicero, and Quintilian.

Philemon, the briefest of Paul's collected letters, concerns the case of a runaway slave, Onesimus. Upon having fled from the household of his master Philemon, a prominent Christian of Colossae (Phlm 1), Onesimus was converted to Christianity by Paul (v 10), who was then in prison (v 9), perhaps in Ephesus.[22] During this period, Paul was well served by Onesimus and grew close to him (vv 10–13). Paul's letter is an appeal to Philemon, that he welcome back Onesimus as he would welcome Paul himself, a beloved brother (vv 16–17), regardless of any wrongs incurred in the past (vv 18–19).

Paul's appeal to Philemon is framed in the deliberative manner, as adapted to the requirements of his own particular epistolary structure and style. The thanksgiving (vv 4–7) serves the purpose of an exordium; the main body (vv8–16), of a proof; and the body-closing (vv 17–22), of a peroration.[23] Of course, Philemon is not a school exercise or a set piece written for applause. Its artifice is not contrived from handbooks. Yet, that its design should reflect the commonplaces of a living rhetorical tradition is not surprising. Whether he was trained in school or acquired his talent through a natural course of observation and imitation, Paul was a master of persuasion.[24] It is hardly surprising that this mastery should be grounded in the widely practiced rhetorical tradition of his time.[25]

The Exordium (vv 4–7). In Philemon, Paul faces what the ancients would call, interchangeably, a "difficult," "discreditable," or "scandalous" case, "one which has alienated the sympathy of those who are about to listen to the speech."[26] Even, as seems unlikely from the context (v 18), had Onesimus fled with nothing more of his master's property than himself and his services, this alone would constitute a serious infraction of law and a betrayal of Philemon's trust. In such a case, "some kind of palliation is required."[27] Accordingly, Paul seeks from the outset not only to mollify Philemon, but also to insinuate the principles upon which he will base his argument.

> I give thanks to my God always when I remember you in my prayers, for I hear of your love and faith which you have in the Lord Jesus and for all the saints. May your imparting of the faith become effective in the knowledge of all the good that is ours in Christ. For I have derived much joy and comfort from your love, because the very hearts of the saints have been refreshed on account of you, my brother.

Three things appropriate to the exordium in deliberative rhetoric are accomplished here by Paul. First, by praising Philemon, he establishes good will between them. Second, he fashions that praise for the furtherance of his case by stressing those of Philemon's qualities upon which its outcome depends. Third, to set up his argument, he alludes to particulars which later will be adduced in the proof and underscored in the peroration. If, as Quintilian writes, "the sole purpose of the exordium is to prepare our audience in such a way that they will be disposed to lend a ready ear to the rest of our speech,"[28] Paul accomplishes this with economy and tact.

Paul begins with mention of reports that he has received, crediting Philemon for his faith in Christ and the love he has shown to all the saints. By dropping "hope" from the triad of graces and by structuring his sentence in a chiastic manner, he places special emphasis on Philemon's love (ἀγάπη), a quality that will take on particular importance as Paul develops his appeal.[29] "This adroit acknowledgement of the practical Christian love of Philemon," in the words of Gordon P. Wiles, is rendered even more effective for being enveloped in Paul's intercessory prayer report.[30] It is Philemon's partnership with the faithful that Paul makes the object of his prayers.[31] Then he returns to Philemon's love and the joy and comfort he derives from it, "because the very hearts of the saints have been refreshed on account of you, my brother." John Chrysostom, who captures the rhetorical nuance in Paul better than most modern commentators, writes of this passage, "nothing so shames us into giving as to bring forward the kindnesses we have bestowed on others."[32] In his thanksgiving, Paul has put Philemon to the blush.

While fulfilling its function of directed praise, Paul's opening also serves the purpose of an exordium by introducing the elements of his argument. John Knox describes it as an "overture in which each of the themes, to be later heard in a different, perhaps more specific, context, is given an anticipatory hearing."[33] This can be shown graphically as follows:

Exordium	Proof	Peroration
in my prayers (4)		to your prayers (22)
τῶν προσευχῶν μου (4)		τῶν προσευχῶν ὑμῶν (22)
of your love (5)	for love's sake (9)	
σου τὴν ἀγάπην (5)		
τῇ ἀγάπῃ σου (7)	διὰ τὴν ἀγάπην (9)	
from your love (7)		
παντὸς ἀγαθοῦ (6)	the good deed (14)	
of all the good (6)	τὸ ἀγαθόν (14)	
ἡ κοινωνία τῆς πίστεώ σου (6) your imparting of the faith (6)		if you consider me a partner (17) εἰ οὖν με ἔχεις κοινωνόν (17)
τὰ σπλάγχνα τῶν ἁγίων ἀναπέπαυται διὰ σοῦ, ἀδελφέ (7) the very hearts of the saints have been refreshed on account of you, my brother	Ὀνήσιμον . . . τὰ ἐμὰ σπλάγχνα . . . ἀδελφὸν ἀγαπητόν (11, 12, 16) Onesimus . . . my very heart . . . a beloved brother (11, 12, 16)	ναί, ἀδελφέ, ἐγώ σου ὀναίμην ἐν κυρίῳ ἀνάπαυσόν μου τὰ σπλάγχνα (20) yes, brother, let me have this benefit of you in the Lord. Refresh my very heart (20)

283

If this studied repetition of key concepts gives coherence to Paul's argument, it also provides a control for rhetorical analysis. First, Paul strives to secure Philemon's favor, by introducing the motifs of "love," "good," "partnership," etc., in such a way that they redound to Philemon's credit. "We shall derive our greatest supply of openings designed either to conciliate or to stimulate the judge from topics contained in the case that are calculated to produce emotions," Cicero writes, "though it will not be proper to develop these fully at the start, but only to give a slight preliminary impulsion to the judge, so that the remainder of our speech may find him already biased in our direction."[34] A perfect example of this is the way in which Paul employs the word σπλάγχνα, which I have translated as "very heart."[35] This striking and evocative term is introduced three times during the course of Paul's appeal, once each in the exordium, proof, and peroration. Taken together they constitute a syllogism that is itself the touchstone of Paul's argument: if Philemon refreshes the very hearts of the saints (v 7); and, if Onesimus is Saint Paul's very heart (v 12); then, to refresh Paul's very heart, Philemon must refresh Onesimus (v 20). By this interpretation the rhetorical effectiveness of Paul's exordium becomes evident. Nothing in it is extraneous to his appeal. As Cicero writes that it should be, the thrust of Paul's opening is not "drawn from some outside source but from the very heart *(ex ipis visceribus)* of the case."[36]

The Proof (vv 8–16). In Philemon, the main body or proof corresponds with Paul's request period. As White has shown, certain formal items within his request roughly reflect the structural elements of those requests found in the papyri.[37] But there are differences as well. "I do not recall, ever, running across such an inordinately long request in the papyri, either in private letters of request or in actual petitions," White admits. "The request is so oblique, so faltering, that one has difficulty in determining what it is, precisely, Paul requests."[38] To account for this descrepancy, White's explanation is simply that "Paul's own creativity working in conjunction with conditions prevailing in his ministry at the time and in relation to the established epistolary conventions, determine the difference in form and function."[39] He claims that this does "not imply, necessarily, that Paul was dependent on a literary convention other than the private Greek letter."[40] It is here that rhetorical form criticism can substantially supplement an outline-critical analysis. Paul is not only making a request, he is also advancing an argument. This argument conforms, both in structure and in function, to the conventional and commonplace canons of deliberative rhetoric. By such standards his request, if no less oblique, proves far from faltering.

Paul opens with a perfectly balanced appeal to *ethos* and *pathos*, expressed, as has been recognized by Ulrich Wickert, through the device of tautological parallelism (8, 9a; 9bc, 10a).[41]

284

Therefore, though I have full	although I am none other than
authority in Christ to command	Paul, an ambassador, and moreover
you to do what is required,	now a prisoner for Christ Jesus,
I prefer to beseech you	I beseech you for my child, whom I
for love's sake.	have begotten in prison, Onesimus.

In addition to the tautological parallelism, two further rhetorical figures are brought into service here by Paul. The first is a type of what is called by some ἀντίφρασις, namely the open abandonment of an apparently strong line of argument.[42] Compare Cicero's "I will not plead against you according to the rigor of the law, I will not press the point which I should perhaps be able to make good."[43] Here, Paul waives his authority, as both Christ's ambassador and now, in addition, a prisoner for Christ, preferring to rely upon Philemon's free compliance with his request. This has the effect of establishing an *a fortiori* argument, reinforcing everything that follows. Paul could command Philemon to receive Onesimus as a brother, but pointedly declines to do so. Instead, he offers an appeal filled with *ethos* and *pathos* that cannot help but affect his hearer. "For who would not receive with open arms a combatant who had been crowned?" as John Chrysostom asks. "Who seeing him bound for Christ's sake, would not have granted him ten thousand favors?"[44] In this the second figure alluded to above comes into play, a form of reduplication, or *conduplicatio,* which is defined as "the repetition of one or more words for the purpose of amplification or appeal to pity."[45] By doubling the verb παρακαλῶ, Paul pulls Philemon's heart-strings not once, but twice. In the exordium, Paul commended Philemon for the love he had shown toward all the saints. Now it is for love's sake, and his child, whom he had begotten in prison, that Paul appeals, offering Philemon the opportunity to demonstrate that love.

It is not until the very end of Paul's twice-stated appeal that he finally chooses to introduce Onesimus' name. By suspending mention of it until this point, he has allowed himself full opportunity to prepare Philemon for his request. Then, when he does bring up the name, Paul at once works a play on its meaning, "profitable." Onesimus,

who formerly was useless to you
but now is useful indeed, both to you and to me,

henceforth will be true to his name (v 11).[46] Reluctance by some to consider this a pun must be attributed to the scruples of those for whom it is somehow inconceivable that the elegant simplicity of Paul's heartfelt utterance might allow for any artifice.[47] Far more crucial to his proof is that Paul establishes the motive of *utilitas* and a secondary motive as well, *affectio,* defined as "change in the aspect of things due to time, so it seems that things should not be regarded in the same light as they have been."[48] Onesimus' case has been affected by his conversion to Christianity and his service to Paul. "Formerly" he was useless to Philemon; "now" he is useful indeed, both to Philemon and to Paul.

Next, Paul offers up the motive of honor, or *honestas*. Not only has time changed things and Onesimus become profitable to Philemon, but also Philemon is given the opportunity to do a good deed (vv 12–14).

> I am sending him back to you, that is my very heart. I would have been happy to keep him with me, so that he might serve me in your place during my imprisonment for the gospel, but I preferred to do nothing without your consent, in order that your good deed might stem not from compulsion but be of your own free will.

Paul is literally forcing a point of honor. While ostensibly avoiding even the appearance of constraint, his argument is designed to do just that, yet without robbing Philemon of the opportunity to act on his own in a truly honorable fashion. To accomplish this, Paul equates himself even more intimately with Onesimus than before. Not only is Onesimus Paul's son, begotten in his bonds (v 11), but his very heart, that is, his very self. Cicero suggests that "if the scandalous nature of the case occasions offence, it is necessary to substitute for the person at whom offence is taken another who is favored, . . . in order that the attention of the auditor may be shifted from what he hates to what he favors.[49] Paul does more than this. He doesn't substitute himself for Onesimus; he embodies himself in him. Then Philemon too is bound by this relationship. Onesimus' service to Paul has been rendered in Philemon's stead (ὑπὲρ σοῦ). Moreover, by sending Onesimus back to Philemon, Paul will lose that service. Thus, it is at some cost to himself that Paul commends by his own actions the quality of selfless love he wishes to instil in Philemon.[50] With considerable persuasive force, he now has established grounds for mutual reciprocity between Philemon, Onesimus, and himself, a reciprocity based upon service in the Lord.

To close his proof, Paul submits an additional motive not alluded to by the ancient authorities: the hand of Providence (vv 15–16).

> For, perhaps the reason that he has been separated from you for awhile, is that you may have him back forever, no longer as a slave, but as more than a slave, as a beloved brother, most of all to me, but how much more to you, both in the flesh and in the Lord.

White, who breaks the request at the end of verse 14, considers the above two verses as the "body-middle" of the letter, admitting both that "this brief middle section is without parallel in Paul's letters," and that "the ambiguity of Paul's request continues unrelieved in this section."[51] One danger of rigid outline criticisms is that there exists a tendency to identify "sections" that do not exist in order that the specific text may be made to accord with the generic form. There is no so-called "body-middle" in Philemon.[52] As Lightfoot noted a century ago, these verses are intimately connected with those immediately preceding them, with the γάρ introducing an "additional motive which guided the Apostle's decision."[53] Actually, this is nothing less than the capstone of Paul's proof. It is designed to motivate Philemon, not to account for Paul's actions. Not only does Philemon stand to gain by the loss that for awhile he had incurred, but by receiving Onesimus back as a beloved brother, he is completing God's designs. Moreover, by turning it all to Providence with his employment of the passive ἐχωρίσθη, Paul frees Onesimus from the onus of his crime. Philemon may indeed have lost the services of an unfaithful slave, but in recompense he stands to receive the faithful services of one whose worth can now be measured only by hyperbole (μάλιστα ἐμοί, πόσῳ δὲ μᾶλλον σοὶ).[54] [most of all to me, but how much more to you.]

The Peroration (vv17–22). "It is in the peroration, if anywhere," Quintilian writes, "that we must let loose the whole torrent of our eloquence. For, if we have spoken well in the rest of our speech, we shall now have the judges on our side, and shall be in a position, now that we have emerged from the reefs and shoals, to spread all our canvas."[55] Paul's closing statement fulfils each of the four requirements of a rhetorical peroration. He restates his request (v 17); he amplifies his argument (vv 18–19); he sets the hearer in an emotional frame of mind (v 20); and, he secures the hearer's favor (vv 21–22). This is done with a maximum of *pathos,* as is appropriate to the close of a deliberative appeal:

> Therefore, if you consider me your partner, receive him as you would me. If he has wronged you in any way or owes you anything, reckon it to my account. I, Paul, write this with my own hand; I will repay you—not to mention that you owe to me your very life besides. Yes, brother, let me have this benefit of you in the Lord. Refresh my very heart in Christ. Confident of your obedience I write to you, knowing that you will do even more than I say. At the same time, prepare a guest room for me, for I am hoping that, thanks to your prayers, I will be restored to you.

These verses correspond to the "body-closing" section as identified by White. Paul restates his request, introduced by the conjunction οὖν, at the beginning of v 17. As White points out, "since the message of Philemon is a request, we anticipate some reiteration of that request in the closing to the body."[56] This holds equally well for the peroration of a deliberative appeal. In the exordium, Paul had prayed that Philemon's "imparting (κοινωνία) of the faith" might become effective. Now he makes it clear that, if Philemon considers Paul his partner (κοινωνός), he must receive Onesimus as if he were receiving Paul himself. Thus, in reiterating his request, Paul conveys the essence of its purport. He, Philemon, and Onesimus are coequal partners in the Lord.

Paul amplifies his argument by employing two devices of powerful rhetorical effect: anticipation and *praeteritio.* The former is defined by Aristotle as "the method by which you anticipate the objections that can be advanced against your arguments and sweep them aside. You must minimize the other party's arguments and amplify your own, . . . making those of your opponents weak and trifling."[57] *Praeteritio* "occurs when we say that we are passing by, or do not know, or refuse to say that which precisely now we are saying."[58] To anticipate any possible objections, Paul writes that he will recompense Philemon for whatever Onesimus had cost him. However pivotal such a pledge may appear when taken out of its rhetorical context, it remains totally irrelevant to the main body of Paul's argument.[59] There he demonstrates how Philemon had gained, not lost, as a result of Onesimus' flight and subsequent conversion. Here he is doing nothing more than painting the blush on a rose he has already plucked. It is to remind Philemon that the ledger has already been more than balanced by Onesimus' service to Paul (not to mention the fact that Philemon, presumably through conversion, owes Paul his very life as well), that Paul, rhetorically, offers to requite Philemon for his pains.

Paul follows the above *tour de force* with a direct appeal that Philemon be of benefit to Paul by refreshing his very heart in Christ. Again playing on the name of Onesimus (ὀναίμην), whom he earlier had described as "my very heart," Paul here, while appearing to plead for himself, is actually sustaining his case on Onesimus' behalf. This continuing inter-identification between the three parties carries a purpose in addition to the theological statement of unity in the body of Christ that it implies. Aristotle states the obvious when he writes that we shall make the judges "well disposed towards us, . . . by summarily showing on what occasions we or our friends have done or are doing or are going to do good to the judges themselves or persons whom the judges care for, and by explaining to them that now there is an opportunity for them to repay us a return for the services we have rendered."[60] By his earlier arguments, Paul has certainly convinced Philemon to receive Onesimus back as a beloved brother; but, if for any reason he had not, here in the peroration he obliges him to do so. Having established Philemon's indebtedness and then begged for satisfaction, Paul goes on to place full confidence in Philemon's obedience. Surely he will do even more than Paul has asked. By this, Philemon's good will, together with his good offices, is assured. "When we are pleading before a judge, who has special reasons for being hostile to us or is for some personal motive ill-disposed to the cause which we have undertaken, although it may be difficult to persuade him, the method which we should adopt in speaking is simple enough," writes Quintilian. "We shall pretend that our confidence in his integrity and in the justice of our cause is such that we have no fears."[61] This has nothing to do with the return of Onesimus to Paul, or his manumission.[62] It simply serves to trump Paul's argument in a flattering and very persuasive way. And that is the fourth requirement of a deliberative peroration.

In closing, Paul expresses the hope that he may soon visit Colossae and stay with Philemon and his household. By asking for the aid of their prayers to this end, Paul concludes his peroration, and with it, the entire request, in a poignant manner. For the time being he remains in prison. In his stead he commends to them a once errant brother, Onesimus, his very heart. Paul will follow if he can.[63]

Fortunately, for the sake of comparison, we have an example of a similar letter, Pliny's appeal to Sabinianus, like Philemon written on behalf of an errant servant.[64] The two contrast sharply in their rhetorical approach to the "difficult" case. No less carefully wrought, Pliny's letter takes a different tack, that of the *deprecatio,* or plea for pardon. To give an indication of how other ancient letters may display rhetorical structure, and to set Philemon in relief, I quote it here in full.

> The freedman of yours with whom you said you were angry has been with me, flung himself at my feet, and clung to me as if I were you. He begged my help with many tears, though he left a good deal unsaid; in short, he convinced me of his genuine penitence. I believe he has reformed, because he realizes he did wrong. You are angry, I know, and I know too that your anger was deserved, but mercy wins most praise when there was just cause for anger. You loved the man once, and I hope you will love him again, but it is sufficient for the moment if you allow yourself to be appeased. You can always be angry again if he deserves it, and will have more excuse if you were once placated. Make some concession to his youth, his tears, and your own kind heart, and do not torment him or yourself any longer—anger can only be a torment to your gentle self.
>
> I'm afraid you will think I am using pressure, not persuasion, if I add my prayers to his—but this is what I shall do, and all the more freely and fully because I have given the man a very severe scolding and warned him firmly that I will never make such a request again. This was because he deserved a fright, and is not intended for your ears; for maybe I *shall* make another request and obtain it, as long as it is nothing unsuitable for me to ask and you to grant.[65]

Structurally, Pliny's argument contains a direct opening, in which he briefly notes the circumstances leading to his appeal; a proof, in which the major points of his argument are advanced; and a peroration, replete with prayer and *praeteritio,* which displays each of the four characteristics present in Phlm 17–22. In every respect, Pliny's letter to Sabinianus accords with the requirements of the rhetorical *deprecatio.* As Quintilian writes, in the plea for mercy "there are three points based on the circumstances of the accused which are most effective. The first is drawn from his previous life, . . . or if there is good hope that his conduct will be blameless for the future and likely to be of some use to his fellow men."[66] To this end, Pliny avers that Sabinianus' freedman "has reformed." The man once was worthy of his love; in the future he will be so again. "The second is operative if it appears that he has . . . repented of his sin." Sabinianus' servant "realizes he did wrong," and Pliny is convinced of his "genuine penitence." Third, "we may base his appeal on his external circumstances, his birth, his rank, his connections, his friendships." Here, the principal "connection" is Pliny himself, whose very interest in the case cannot help but have an effect upon his friend's decision. "It is, however, on the judge that we shall pin our highest hopes, if the cirumstances be such that acquittal will result in giving him a reputation for clemency rather than for regrettable weakness." And so it is with Pliny's appeal. Sabinianus is justifiably angry, "but mercy wins most praise when there was just cause for anger." We know that Pliny won a favorable hearing from Sabinianus from a brief acknowledgement written shortly thereafter.[67]

How is it that Paul, the Christian, makes no mention of forgiveness in Philemon, whereas Pliny, the pagan, rests his very case upon it?[68] Here, a sensitivity to rhetorical patterns can prove useful. First, Philemon is not a plea for mercy. Such would have no place in Paul's argument. Pliny writes to Sabinianus, "You loved the man once, and I hope you will love him again, but it is sufficient for the moment if you allow yourself to be appeased." The Christian case for love and real equality between persons, be they slave or free, would hardly be served by such an appeal, no matter how artful its advocate. Second, Philemon is a public letter.[69] It represents far more than one man's intervention on another's behalf. Onesimus may be the subject of Paul's plea, but its objects are love and brotherhood. Paul has seized the opportunity to instruct an entire community in the principle of practical Christian love. One need not invent a hidden agenda to follow his argument.[70] It accords with the common-sense logic of contemporary rhetorical practice. Nor should this be particularly surprising. As Robin Scroggs has written recently of Paul, "he is first of all a preacher, a rhetorician. Both his style and structure betray the typical marks of the preacher as we know him today and of the rhetorician as he was known to the Mediterranean world in the first Christian century."[71] It is not a question of going by the book. Paul was not a student of dead rhetoric, but a practitioner of the living word. The question is, whether attention to rhetorical patterns and forms as described by the ancient authorities can give any insight into the shape and design of Paul's letters. I believe it can.

Notes

1. Among others, see Franz Overbeck, "Über die Anfänge der patristischen Literatur," *Historische Zeuschrift* 48 (1882) 443; and Amos Wilder, *Early Christian Rhetoric* (New York: Harper & Row, 1964) 15.
2. *De oratore* 1.11.47, trans. H. Rackham (LCL; Cambridge: Harvard University, 1942).
3. "The Structural Analysis of Philemon: a Point of Departure in the Formal Analysis of the Pauline Letter" (SBLASP; Missoula: Scholars Press, 1971) 1–47, citing Funk on pp. 1 and 26. For other illustrations of this same approach, see Robert W. Funk, *Language, Hermeneutic, and Word of God* (New York: Harper & Row, 1966). Beda Rigaux, *Letters of St. Paul: Modern Studies* (Chicago: Franciscan Herald, 1968); Chan-Hie Kim, *Form and Structure of the Familiar Greek Letter of Recommendation* (SBLDS 4; Missoula: Scholars Press, 1972), John White, *The Form and Function of the Body of the Greek Letter* (SBLDS 1; Missoula: Scholars Press, 1972); and, for a recent survey, William G. Doty, *Letters in Primitive Christianity* (Philadelphia: Fortress, 1973).
4. Weiss, "Beiträge zur paulinischen Rhetorik," *Theologische Studien: Bernhard Weiss Festschrift* (Göttingen: Vandenhoeck & Ruprecht, 1897) 165–247; Bultmann, *Der Stilder paulinischen Predigt und die kynisch-stoische Diatribe* (Göttingen: Vandenhoeck & Ruprecht, 1910). See also Friedrich Blass, *Die Rhythmen*

der asianischen und römischen Kunstprosa (Leipzig: A. Deichert, 1905); H. J. Rose, "The *Clausulae* of the Pauline *Corpus*," *JTS* 25 (1923) 17–43; and, following Blass, P.-L. Couchoud, "Le style rhythmé dans l'éptre de Saint Paul à Philémon," RHR 96 (1927) 129–46.

5. White, *Body of the Greek Letter, 75.*

6. J. B. Lightfoot, *St. Paul's Epistles to the Colossians and to Philemon* (8th ed.; London: Macmillan, 1886) 317. See also John Knox, *Philemon Among the Letters of Paul* (New York/ Nashville: Abingdon, 1959) 7; Gordon P. Wiles, *Paul's Intercessory Prayers* (Cambridge: Cambridge University, 1974) 216; and, for a minority view, P. C. Sands, *Literary Genius of the New Testament* (Oxford: Clarendon, 1932) 128. Among those who acknowledge Paul's artistry in Philemon are Ernest Renan *(L'Antéchrist* [Paris: Michel Lévy Fréres, 1873] 96, cited by Lightfoot, *Colossians and Philemon,* 316), who finds it "a true little chef d'oeuvre of the art of letter-writing." He is echoed by Maurice Goguel (*Introduction au N.T.* [4 vols.; Paris: Leroux, 1923–26] 4.423, cited by Théo Preiss, *Life in Christ* [STB; London: SCM, 1954] 32), who terms Philemon, "with respect to style, perhaps the best of Paul's epistles, a true chef d'oeuvre of tact and heart."

7. See Aristotle, *Art of Rhetoric* 1.3.3–4.

8. To expand upon a stock example, the question "Should a person marry?" might provide a topic suitable to epideictic oratory; "Should Cato marry?" is a deliberative question; "Did Cato Marry?" could prove crucial to a forsenic defense of Cato wherever bigamy is considered a crime punishable by law.

9. Quint. 3.8.15, trans., H. E. Butler (LCL; Cambridge: Harvard University, 1922). For deliberative rhetoric in general, see Cicero, *De inventione* 2.157–78; *De oratore* 2.342–49; and also Cicero, *Rhetorica ad Herennium* 3.2–15. Friedrich Solmsen ("Aristotelian Tradition in Ancient Rhetoric," *Rhetorika,* ed. Rudolf Stark [Hildesheim: Georg Olms, 1968] 335) observes that deliberative rhetoric, like epideictic, is, on the whole, "less affected by the innovations of Post-Aristotelian theorists," than is forensic rhetoric.

10. Quint. 3.8.15. See also Aristotle *Rhet.* 1.3.4–6.

11. For a different view, see Hans Dieter Betz's ground-breaking article, "The Literary Composition and Function of Paul's Letter to the Galatians," *NTS* 21 (1975) 353–79, where Galatians is interpreted as an "apologetic letter," composed along the structural lines of ancient forsenic rhetoric.

12. The emphasis placed on each as a primary motive varies. See Aristotle *Rhet.* 1.3.4–6; Cicero *De inv.* 2.52–4; *De or.* 2.82.334; *Rhet. ad Her.* 3.2.3; and Quint. 3.8.1

13. Solmsen, "Aristotelian Tradition," 337. See also his "Aristotle and Cicero on the Orator's Playing upon the Feelings," *Classical Philology* 33 (1938) 390–404. Of these three motives Aristotle writes: "The first depends upon the moral character of the speaker, the second upon putting the hearer into a certain frame of mind, the third upon the speech itself, in so far as it proves or seems to prove." *(Rhet.* 1.2.3, trans. John Freese [LCL: Cambridge: Harvard University, 1926]).

14. Quint. 3.8.12.

15. Quint. 6.2.9–12.

16. Quint. 6.2.11–14, where he writes: "The *ethos* which I have in my mind and which I desiderate in an orator is commended to our approval by goodness more than anything else and is not merely calm and mild, but in most cases ingratiating and courteous and such as to excite pleasure and affection in our hearers, while the chief merit in its expression lies in making it seem that all we say derives directly from the nature of the facts and persons concerned and in the revelation of the character of the orator in such a way that all may recognise it. This kind of *ethos*

should be especially displayed in cases where the persons concerned are intimately connected, whenever we tolerate or pardon any act or offer satisfaction of admonition, in all of which cases there should be no trace of anger or hatred."

17. Aristotle *Rhet.* 2.4–7.
18. Similar to forensic oratory, with the exception of the narration, which, in most cases, is dropped, "because no one can narrate things to come; but if there is a narrative, it will be of things past, in order that, being reminded of them, the hearers may take better counsel about the future" (Aristotle *Rhet.* 3.16.11). See also George Kennedy, *The Art of Persuasion in Greece* (Princeton: Princeton University, 1963) 11–13.
19. Quint 4.1.23. Cicero writes that "an exordium is a passage which brings the mind of the auditor into a proper condition to receive the rest of the speech. This will be accomplished if he becomes well-disposed, attentive, and receptive" *(De inv.* 1.15.20). See also Quint. 3.8.6–10; and *De inv.* 1.16.22. Both draw from Aristotle, *Rhet.* 3.14–19.
20. Aristotle *Rhet.* 3.19.
21. Quint, 4.1.28; cf. Aristotle *Rhetoric to Alexander 36.*
22. Among recent commentaries on Philemon see esp. Eduard Lohse, *Colossians and Philemon* (ed. Helmut Koester; Hermeneia; Philadelphia: Fortress, 1971); and G. Bouwman, *De Brieven van Paulus aan de Kolossenzen en aan Filemon* (Amsterdam: Roermond, 1972); C. F. D. Moule, *The Epistles of Paul the Apostle to the Colossians and to Philemon* (Cambridge Greek New Testament Commentary; Cambridge: Cambridge University, 1958).
23. The traditional division is thanksgiving (vv 4–7); body (vv 8–20); closing (vv 21–25): see, e.g., Lohse, *Colossians and Philemon,* 187; and Bouwman, *Kolossenzen en Filemon,* 158 (ignore typographical error in his initial statement of divisions 8–21, 22–25 [p. 158]). Alternatively, Kim (*Letter of Recommendation,* 124) treats of Philemon as a Greek letter of recommendation, with the body of the request contained in vv 8–17. However, he admits that compared to the papyrus letters of recommendation "Philemon generally does not show the same form and structure." Kim concludes that "It may be possible to identify vv 8–16 as the background and v 17 as the request period, in accordance with the general structure of the body of the papyrus letter; but such a division is secondary and arbitrary, for the body of Philemon exhibits the Pauline commendation formula as found also in all six of the other Pauline passages of recommendation" (125–26). My division follows most closely that of White, with the only exception v 7 which he assigns to the introductory body ("Philemon," 34); elsewhere, however, he considers it, as I do, a part of the thanksgiving, or a transitional verse leading into the body-opening (*Body of the Greekk Letter,* 76).
24. As Robin Scroggs ("Paul as Rhetorician: Two Homilies in Romans 1–11," in *Jews, Greeks and Christians: Essays in Honor of William David Davies,* ed. by Robert Hamerton-Kelly and Scroggs [Leiden: Brill, 1976] 272) notes, "Paul can speak out of Hellenistic rhetorical practice as easily as he can support a point with the most subtle rabbinic hermeneutic."
25. As my space is limited, the following exegesis will be limited in scope as well, focusing upon the practicability of rhetorical form criticism as a supplementary aid to the interpretation of Paul's letters. So sharp a focus, if restrictive, is required by the relative novelty of this approach. I hope shortly to bring out a second piece on Philemon that will cover these bones with a bit of theological muscle and sociological flesh.
26. Cicero *De inv.* 1.15.20; cf. *Rhet. ad Her.* 1.3–6.
27. Quint. 4.1.41; cf. Cicero *De inv.* 1.16.21.

28. Quint, 4.1.5; as Quintilian notes elsewhere (3.8.59), "Do not begin to shriek, but endeavor as far as possible to win the assent of the man who is considering the question by a courteous and natural opening."

29. The absence of the word "hope" corresponds to a lack of explicit eschatological reference anywhere in Philemon. On this, and the thanksgiving prayer-report in general, see Wiles, *Paul's Intercessory Prayers,* 215–25. For the chiastic structure, see Lohse, *Colossians and Philemon,* 193; Moule, *Colossians and Philemon,* 141. As Wiles remarks, "This sentence, written in a highly condensed style, literally directs both Philemon's love and his faith, both to Jesus and to all the saints. So uncharacteristic of Paul would this be, that it is best interpreted in a chiastic manner: your faith towards the Lord Jesus, and your love toward all the saints." For a chiastic structural interpretation of the entire letter, see Nils Wilhelm Lund, *Chiasmus in the New Testament* (Chapel Hill: University of North Carolina, 1942) 219–20, with a critique by Joachim Jeremias, "Chiasmus in den Paulusbriefe," *Abba* (Göttingen: Vandenhoeck & Ruprecht, 1966) 154–55.

30. *Paul's Intercessory Prayers,* 218. According to Quintilian (4.1.17), "in pleading for a man of good birth we shall appeal to his own high rank, in speaking for the lowly we shall lay stress on his sense of justice." In commending the person of a beloved brother, himself one of the saints, to the attention of a man whom he has wronged, Paul could do much worse than to praise that man for the love he has shown to all the saints.

31. For this difficult verse, see Moule (*Colossians and Philemon.* 142–43), who presents various options and their respective advocates. For κοινωνια (participation, impartation, fellowship), see Friedrich Hauck, *TDNT* 3 (1965) 797–809; J. Y. Campbell, "KOINONIA and its cognates in the N.T." in *Three New Testament Studies* (Leiden: Brill, 1965) 1–28; Heinrich Seesemann, "Der Begriff KOINONIA im Neuen Testament." *BZNW* 14 (1933) 79–83. I have chosen "impartation" to draw attention to the stem's recurrence in v 17, where Paul writes, "if you consider me your partner, receive him as you would me."

32. *Hom. in Phlm.* 2.1.7. Bouwman (*Kolossenzen en Filemon,* 163) aptly describes this as *captatio benevolentiae.*

33. *Philemon,* 22. This image, adapted to the requirements of ancient music, is inverted by Cicero, but the point remains: "the opening passage should be so closely connected wth the speech that follows as to appear to be not an appendage, like the prelude to a piece of music, but an integral part of the whole structure" (*De or.* 2.80.325).

34. *De or.* 2.79.324.

35. Martin Dibelius *(An die Kolosser, Epheser, an Philemon* [HNT 12; 3rd ed. by Heinrich Greeven; Tübingen: Mohr-Siebeck, 1953] 104) perceives in this usage "orientalisierend-pathetischen Stil." For a complete discussion, see Helmut Köster, "σπλαυχνον," *TDNT* 7 (1971) 548–59. A "very strong and forceful term which occurs only when Paul is speaking directly and personally, . . . the word is again used [in Philemon] for the whole person which in the depths of its emotional life has experienced refreshment through consolation and love," Koster writes. "It is as if Paul, in the runaway slave, came to Philemon in person with his claim to experience love" (555).

36. *De or.* 2.,78.318.

37. "Philemon," 36; idem, *Body of the Greek Letter,* 78. Kim (*Letter of Recommendation,* 125) identifies vv 8–16 as the "background," and v 17 as the request period proper, but White ("Philemon," 36) has shown that all the elements of a request period are present in vv 8–14. I extend that period two verses, but agree that v 17 constitutes a reiteration of Paul's request, and not its original statement.

38. "Philemon," 35–36.
39. "Philemon," 36; idem. *Body of the Greek Letter,* 79 n. 17. As Betz has observed ("Literary Composition of Galatians," 354), "Scholars of the later twentieth century seem in basic agreement that Paul's letters are 'confused', disagreeing only about whether the confusion is caused by emotional disturbances, 'Diktierpausen' or 'rabbinic' methodology."
40. *Body of the Greek Letter,* 79 n. 17.
41. "Der Philemonbrief-Privatbrief oder apostolisches Schreiben?" *ZNW* 52 (1961) 235. Following Wickert's reading, it would seem clear that "ambassador" and "prisoner" are titles, replacing that of apostle (cf. v 1). On this see Moule, *Colossians and Philemon,* 140; and White, "Philemon," 29. For the reading "old man" for πρεσβυτης see Lohse, *Colossians and Philemon,* 199.
42. Quint. 9.2.47.
43. *Verrine Orations* 5.2.4, cited by Quint. 9.2.47.
44. *Hom. in Phlm.* 2.2.9.
45. Cicero *Rhet. ad Her.* 4.28.38; cf. Quint., 9.3.28–9.
46. See Lohse, *Colossians and Philemon,* 200; on the name Onesimus as common to slaves, see Lightfoot, *Colossians and Philemon,* 308–9.
47. Such reluctance is epitomized in BDF 488.1.b: "Paul is not playing upon the name of the slave Onesimus, although he uses ὀναίμην only here (Phm 20); at most the recipient could make the obvious word-play himself from ἄχρηστον . . . εὔχρηστον." But see Bouwman, *Kolossenzen en Filemon,* 166–67; and Lohse, *Colossians and Philemon,* 200 n. 35. In addition Paul employs here a type of paronomasi (when the same word stem recurs in close proximity) in the juxtaposition of ἄχρηστον and εὑρησγογ, and *homeoptoton* (when, in the same period, two or more words appear in the same case and with like terminations) in the sequence 'Ονήσιμον . . . ἄχρηστον . . . εὔχτηστον (See BDF 488.1: and Cicero *Rhet. ad Her.* 4.20.28).
48. Cicero *De inv.* 2.58.176.
49. *De inv.* 1.17.24; cf. Quint. 6.1.24–5: "Sometimes the advocate himself may even assume the role of close intimacy with his client, as Cicero does in the *pro Milone,* . . . [where he] himself assumed the role of suppliant."
50. See Quint. 2.6.18.
51. "Philemon," 37.
52. Philemon also fails to fit the formula since it lacks both an eschatological climax to the thanksgiving and any hint of paraenesis. Attempts to pinpoint the former in v 6 and the latter in v 21 (Doty, *Letters,* 43, etc.) are closely related to the illusive search for the "body-middle." As Scroggs ("Paul as Rhetorician," 273) writes, "the *structure* of the *body* of Paul's letters is not as a whole much clarified by the letter model."
53. *Colossians and Philemon,* 340.
54. Strictly speaking, this is not hyperbole, but simply a form of amplification that consists in passing beyond the highest degree *(supra summun adiectio).* For other examples use Quint. 8.4.5–6.
55. Quint. 6.1.52.
56. "Philemon," 38.
57. *Rhet. ad Alex.* 36 (trans. H. Rackham [LCL: Cambridge; Harvard University, 1937]).
58. Cicero *Rhet. ad Her,* 4.27.37. See S. Bartina, " 'Me debes más' (Flm 19). La deuda de Filemón a Pablo," *Studiorum Paul. Congressus Inter. Cath.* 2 (1963) 143–44; Bouwman, *Kolossenzen en Filemon,* 170. Of course, as Adolf Deissmann has demonstrated, there is another formal convention reflected here as well; in *Light from the Ancient East* ([New York: George Doran, 1927] 84; 331–32), he identifies vv 18–19 as a "memorandum of debt," or χειρόγραφον: "A stereotyped formula in

these documents is the promise to pay back the borrowed money, 'I will repay', and they are in the debtor's own hand. . . . It now becomes clear that S. Paul, . . . is in the letter to Philemon (18f.) humorously writing him a sort of acknowledgment of debt (332–33)." The juxtaposition of this handwritten I O U, with its obvious legal ramifications, and the stated "passing over" of any mention of Philemon's much greater debt to Paul, is rife with rhetorical finesse. To punctuate the sentence differently (ἐμοὶ ἐλλόγα . . . ἵνα μὴ λέγω σοι ὅτι), as advocated in BDF 495.1 and elsewhere (see Lohse, *Colossians and Philemon,* 204 n. 75, for a discussion), not only glosses over the otherwise obvious *praeteritio,* but misses the legal formula behind Paul's construction as well.

59. Typical is the interpretation of Preiss (*Life in Christ,* 35): "Whoever keeps with him a runaway slave makes himself an accomplice of a serious infringement of private law. He owes the owner the value of each day's work lost. This is what Paul solemnly undertakes to make good." Cf. William J. Richardson, "Principle and Context in the Ethics of the Epistle to Philemon," *Interpretation* 22 (1968) 308.

60. *Rhet. ad Alex.* 36.

61. Quint. 11.1.75.

62. As suggested by John Knox (*Philemon,* 1–33). For a discussion see White. "Philemon," 36–37; P. N. Harrison, "Onesimus and Philemon," *ATR* 32 (1950) 268–94; Heinrich Greeven, "Prüfung der Thesenvon J. Knox zum Philemonbrief," *ThLZ* 79 (1954) 373–78.

63. Funk refers to this recurring component in the closing of Paul's letters as the "apostolic *parousia*" ("The Apostolic Parousia: Form and Significance," in *Christian History and Interpretation: Studies Presented to John Knox,* ed. W. R. Farmer, C. F. D. Moule, R. R. Niebuhr [Cambridge: Cambridge University, 1967] 249–68). In its full form (see White, "Philemon," 38–45), the "apostolic *parousia*" comprises the close of Paul's peroration, effectively reinforcing Paul's argument.

64. *Epist.* 9.21.

65. Trans. Betty Radice (LCL; Cambridge: Harvard University, 1969).

66. Quint. 7.4.18–19; cf. Cicero *Rhet. ad Her.* 2.17.25–6.

67. *Epist.* 9.24.

68. One overwrought explanation (Richardson, "Ethics of Philemon," 310) is that "we can hardly make too much of the fact that accompanying this letter was one which said: 'As the Lord has forgiven you, so you also must forgive' (Col 3:13)."

69. See Wickert, "Der Philemonbrief," for a demonstration of this point.

70. As Knox (*Philemon,* 20) does, in part drawing upon a comparison of these same two epistles: "Pliny says exactly what we should expect such a note to say. Paul, on the other hand, does not say some things we should certainly expect and says others which seem scarcely relevant. . . . Paul says not one word about any repentance on the part of the slave and there is no explicit appeal for forgiveness or pity on the part of the master. In other words, the terms we should expect such a letter to contain in abundance are simply not there at all. This fact alone should lead us to suspect a rather deeper purpose in the letter than the obvious one generally assigned."

71. "Paul as Rhetorician," 273. As Robert Funk has noted (*Language,* 242), citing Amos Wilder (*Early Christian Rhetoric,* 29), "the letter form as such . . . 'is almost as flexible as oral speech itself,' and the style of Paul betrays on every page the marks of oral expression." Cf. Sands (*Literary Genius of the New Testament,* 133): "Oratory is only pleading, and in his letters Paul sees his correspondents present before him, and pleads with them."

The Public Letter as a Rhetorical Form: Structure, Logic, and Style in King's "Letter from Birmingham Jail"

Richard P. Fulkerson

In Birmingham, Alabama, on 12 April 1963, the Reverend Martin Luther King, Jr., in order to have himself arrested on a symbolic day (Good Friday), disobeyed an Alabama Supreme Court injunction against demonstrations.[1] That same day in the *Birmingham News,* King saw a public letter signed by eight leading (white) Birmingham clergymen calling on the protesters to cease their activities and to work through the courts for the redress of their grievances.

On the morning following his arrest, while being held in solitary confinement, King began to write in response to the clergymen the now famous "Letter from Birmingham Jail." As he wrote later, "Begun on the margins of the newspaper in which the statement appeared while I was in jail, the letter was continued on scraps of writing paper supplied by a friendly Negro trusty, and concluded on a pad my attorneys were eventually permitted to leave me."[2] The "Letter" was completed on Tuesday, and the American Friends Service Committee had 50,000 copies printed for distribution.[3] Later, after polishing, it became a central chapter in King's *Why We Can't Wait* (1964).[4]

Judged by the frequency with which it has been reprinted, the "Letter" has already become an American classic.[5] It has been characterized as a "compelling argument,"[6] "a virtuoso performance,"[7] "a model of effective persuasive writing,"[8] and "one of the strongest pieces of persuasive writing to come out of twentieth-century America."[9] Despite these comments, the "Letter" has been the subject of only one rather cursory study.[10] Most of the published commentary on it constitutes praise rather than criticism.

The "Letter" deserves more extensive study, for it is an instance of superb rhetoric in action. Designed apparently as a refutative response to the clergymen, King's essay actually addresses two audiences simultaneously: the limited and precisely defined group of eight clergymen and a broader and less exactly defined group of intelligent and religious moderates. The purposes of this study are, first, to consider the nature and relationship of King's two audiences and the rhetorical benefits King gained from using one audience to provide a focus through which the other could be addressed, and second, to demonstrate how carefully and effectively King adapted his presentation to suit both audiences on three levels: structural, logical, and stylistic.

From *The Quarterly Journal of Speech,* Volume 65, 1979. Reprinted with permission of the Speech Communication Association and the author.

The Clergymen's Letter

In their letter, the eight clergymen, representing both Christian and Jewish faiths, address not the issue of racism, but the propriety of civil disobedience and the timing of the protest. A restrained document of seven paragraphs and slightly more than 400 words, the clergymen's letter supports the theses that "these demonstrations are unwise and untimely," and that, "When rights are consistently denied, a cause should be pressed in the courts."[11] It is a clear statement of the moderate position: Injustice may exist, but the methods of remediation must lie in compromise and in the appropriate legal channels. Typically moderate also is the tone of optimism; the clergymen refer to a "new constructive and realistic approach" and "increased forbearance" which make these "days of new hope." Such positive signs, along with the patience and restraint now being shown by the police, make this an especially inappropriate time for protest.

Specifically the clergymen accuse King and his followers of (1) being led "in part by outsiders," (2) failing to negotiate, (3) inciting hatred and violence, (4) choosing an inappropriate time to act, (5) using extreme measures, (6) ignoring the courts as the correct avenue of redress, and (7) not observing the principles of "law and order."

Two "Fictionalized" Audiences

Since King's response to these charges is a "Letter" to "My dear Fellow Clergymen," one might assume the eight clergymen to be the audience. On the other hand, it is a public letter in the tradition of Emile Zola's Dreyfus letter. Thus, because the letter has an apparent audience (the clergymen) and a larger, more diverse one (King's public reader), the question of audience is complex.

Ong has recently argued that "the writer's audience is always a fiction," since no writer addresses the audience at the moment of writing but must imaginatively project both the audience and its potential response.[12] This becomes more true and thus presents a more difficult rhetorical problem as the distance between writer and reader widens. While seeming to address the clergymen and to respond to their charges, King had also to address his broader readership; thus as he wrote he had to fictionalize two audiences, one sharing his clerical perspective, the other more diverse. Such a perspective obviously creates some difficulties. The writer, for example, must not assume (i.e., fictionalize) anything about the ostensible audience that would not also apply to the broader real audience. Structure, logic, and style, all have to be appropriate not just for a single defined audience but for the larger one as well.

Yet King turned the rhetorically complex situation into an advantage. Had he chosen to defend his actions directly to a public audience, he would have had to fictionalize his audience with virtually no guidelines. Instead, he wrote as if he were addressing the clergymen, about whom he could reasonably make certain assumptions; he took them—or rather his fictionalized image of them—as a metaphor for his broader readership.

By using the clergymen as his ostensible audience, King found the guidelines for fictionalizing the broader audience, much the more important one to address under the circumstances. The clergymen, of course, were religious, white, moderate, educated leaders of public opinion. Thus they were representative of only a segment of the broader public, but it was a segment which King had both a need to and a possibility of persuading. Little, if anything, was to be gained in addressing white segregationists, black revolutionists, or people indifferent to civil rights. The situation called instead for an address to as wide a range of moderate-to-liberal, involved readers as possible; so much the better if a substantial number of them were also leaders of public opinion.

All social movements face the potential problem of splintering; and the civil rights movement, then in its infancy, was in danger of falling apart because of disagreement over the propriety of King's tactics. In addition to persuading a broad public, King thus needed also to unify civil rights proponents by persuading the more moderate among them that his course of action was the right one. By answering the clergymen, he in effect answered the mental reservations held by those whose dedication to equality fell short of support of public demonstrations.

The rhetorical advantages of addressing the broader audience in terms of the clerical audience are clearer if King and the clergymen are perceived as opponents in a written debate. Debaters seem to address each other, and they do respond to each other, but the response is determined by its intended effect on a third party, the judge or audience.

Despite the complexity resulting from the dual audience, this debater's stance gave King five argumentative advantages. First, the already existing document defined the key issues. Instead of having to fictionalize all potential arguments that an audience might hold against protest, King had only to respond to assertions in the clergymen's letter. Fortunately for his purposes, their letter was a synthesis of almost every likely criticism. This allowed King the fullest range of issues to discuss and thus allowed the greatest opportunity for persuasion; had the clergy disagreed with King on only one matter, such as timing, he could have answered that charge, but his reponse could not have become a refutative manifesto for a broader audience, a defense of his movement and the theory of peaceful civil disobedience on which it was based.

Second, refutation of an existent paper allowed a clear, easy to follow, point by point organization. Purely by enumeration, if King wished, he could handle each argument as it had been brought up by the opponents. The only necessary scaffolding was the transition, "You also argued. . . ."

Third, refutation worked particularly well since the clergymen were in a weak position to begin with. They could not deny the charge that Birmingham was a thoroughly segregated city; at best they could argue that the means being used to remedy segregation were improper and/or that they were pursued at the wrong time.

Fourth, it is simpler to disprove someone else's moral argument than to build a case for one's own. Demonstrating that an opponent's position is unsoundly argued does not logically validate one's own argument, but rhetorically it often seems to a reader to do so. A reader-judge does not engage in argument but, rather, compares the two cases presented. Instead of listening to King to decide whether he is right, a public reader is more likely to judge which of two presentations is the more persuasive. And, although a reader might be unconvinced by the "Letter" as an independent entity, when it is compared with the clergymen's argument, King's case is clearly superior on all counts.[13]

Finally, adapting his presentation to his ostensible audience, instead of having to launch it into the dark, allowed King to create a warm, personal tone. His essay is stylistically and tonally a real letter with a real personality behind it.

The "Letter's" Structure

King's essay is primarily a series of refutations of the arguments made by the clergymen, a point made by several commentators.[14] But saying this tends to obscure its more subtle features. In constructing his essay King, by design or accident, adapted the pattern of the classical oration to suit the situation in Birmingham, the clergymen's letter, and the wider audience as well. He reduced the classical *confirmatio* to utmost brevity and expanded the *refutatio* to carry the burden of argument.

The letter opens without an impassioned *exordium,* and this seems entirely appropriate to the already heated circumstances. Instead, the salutation, "My dear Fellow Clergymen," establishes immediately the warm, tactful tone prevalent in the essay. How different would have been the more formal "Dear Sirs," or "Dear Clergymen," or even "My Fellow Clergymen." The body of the letter begins with the classical *narratio,* "the exposition of the state of affairs at the moment,"[15] the facts that have motivated the writing. Subtly emphasizing the irony of a minister's being in prison, King notes, "While confined here in the Birmingham City Jail, I came across your recent statement calling our present activities 'unwise and untimely.' . . . I would like to answer your statement in what I hope will be patient and reasonable terms." Both the "patient and reasonable" tone and the intimacy of direct address continue throughout the essay.

King quickly deviates (pars. 2 and 3) from the pattern of the classical oration, however, by addressing one point in the clergy's letter: "I think I should give the reason for my being in Birmingham, since you have been influenced by the argument of 'outsiders coming in.' " The reason for refuting this argument before presenting the constructive case seems clear; if the argument about "outsiders" has any validity in the minds of either audience, then King has no right to discuss circumstances in Birmingham. He must earn the right to talk.

After his response to the "outsiders" argument, King states (par. 4) his *propositio,* that the Negro in Birmingham has had no choice but protest. Then, using the classical *partitio,* King notes (par. 5) that four steps are necessary in a protest campaign: "(1) collection of the facts to determine whether injustices are alive; (2) negotiation; (3) self-purification; and (4) direct action." King now takes up successively (pars. 5–7) the first three steps to show that in fact the Birmingham protesters had gone through them before determining to use direct action (par. 8).

These few paragraphs constitute King's unusually brief *confirmatio,* his constructive case for civil disobedience in Birmingham at this time, an argument built on what Bosmajian has called the "Method of Residues."[16] Altogether, proposition, partition, and confirmation comprise only five of the essay's forty-eight paragraphs.

King now turns (par. 9) to the first of six major issues: "You may well ask, 'Why direct action? Why sit-ins, marches, etc.? Isn't negotiation a better path?' " This was not the first point raised by the clergymen, but King wisely adapts the order of his main arguments to move from the obvious to the more complex, presumably for the benefit of the wider audience. By agreeing, King logically and gracefully turns the argument back on the clergymen: Certainly negotiation is desirable; the *goal* of the protest is precisely to make the other side willing to negotiate. In the succeeding paragraphs (10–20), King handles the second and third major issues, the charges that the protests were ill-timed and violations of "law and order."

At this point King interrupts his refutative pattern with one of the personal sections that Larson calls digressions.[17] If the section is digressive, it is progressive at the same time; and such asides, merged into the rigid refutative structure, enhance the feeling that this is a personal letter in which personal feeling and digression (of sorts) are acceptable. In this "digression," King moves by association from the clergy's "law and order" argument to the first of "two honest confessions." He feels compelled to "confess" (par.21) that he has been profoundly disappointed in the Southern white liberal for making arguments such as the "law and order" one instead of joining the Negro cause. Suddenly the clergy are on the defensive; not just their argument but their inaction is criticized. King does not attack angrily; he is merely forced (against his own good will) to admit that he has been saddened by such behavior and "almost" made to conclude that the people who make up his audiences are more dangerous to the Negro than outright segregationists. This tone of sadness and compulsion is effective precisely because it allows King to attack without seeming aggressive.

After two paragraphs (21–22) on his first disappointment, King returns (par. 23) to his refutative strategy and disposes of the argument that his nonviolent actions are evil because they precipitate violence from others. Then he refutes (pars. 24–25) what he calls "the myth of time," an argument that Negroes should wait for the natural course of social evolution to solve their problems. The clergymen had not made this argument, although it might have been suggested in their assertion that the protest in Birmingham was untimely. So to provide this view explicitly, and consequently maintain his refutative pattern, King quotes another letter, one from "a white brother in Texas" who had argued, "All Christians know that the colored people will receive equal rights eventually, but is it possible that you are in too great of a religious hurry? It has taken Christianity almost 2000 years to accomplish what it has." The "white brother," and perhaps the clergymen, is answered quickly. Then King devotes three paragraphs (26–28) in response to the argument that his actions are "extreme."

His second "disappointment," this one sadder and more pointed, follows; it is not only disappointment with the white liberal Southerner, but also disappointment with the Southern white church, which King sees as having sacrificed the "extremism" of moral commitment historically typical of the Christian faith. In the characteristic sad tone, King devotes twelve paragraphs (30–41) to the irony of the Southern churches' professing equality in the eyes of God, and the spirit of Christian fellowship, while allowing the ungodly and immoral practice of segregation to continue unopposed. By implication this is a direct attack on precisely the behavior of the eight clergymen to whom he is responding, for they profess a religiously rooted equality and fellowship but are arguing to allow the continuation of an ungodly segregation. King cannot understand such an "other-wordly religion which made a strange distinction between body and soul, the sacred and the secular."[18] Whereas the major *confirmatio* received only five paragraphs, the *refutatio* with its two attendant confessions extends for thirty-three paragraphs.[19]

King then begins (par. 42) his moving *peroratio,* stopping once (pars. 43–44) to refute the clergymen's praise of the restraint shown by the Birmingham police. The peroration, in its apology for having written at such length, recalls both the calm tone and the prison reference of the opening: "what else is there to do when you are alone for days in the dull monotony of a narrow jail cell other than write long letters, think strange thoughts, and pray long prayers?" The closing paragraph reasserts the identity of his viewpoint with that of his ostensible audience and speaks confidently of the future, when they may all meet and the "deep fog of misunderstanding will be lifted from our fear-drenched communities."

Schematically, then, the essay's structure looks like this:

A. *Narratio* (pars. 1–4)
    1. Clergy's letter
    2. King's reasons for being in Birmingham
B. *Propositio*—"the white power structure of this city left the Negro community with no other alternative" (par. 4)
C. *Confirmatio*—the four steps to protest (pars. 5–8)
D. *Refutatio* (Pars. 9–41)
    1. Negotiation
    2. Timing
    3. Breaking laws
        (First "Confession":Disappointment in white liberals for not breaking laws)
    4. Precipitating violence
    5. The myth of time
    6. Extremism
        (Second "Confession": Disappointment in white Southern church for not being extreme)
E. *Peroratio* (pars. 42–48)
    1. Confidence in the future
    2. Clergy's praise for police (refuted)
    3. Hope to meet in a better future

The interjection of the two "disappointments" into the six main refutations, as well as the length of some of the refutations, may create the impression of looseness.[20] So may the informal, epistolary style. But the essay is actually tightly and elaborately structured. It combines the clarity, efficiency, and persuasive force of the classical oration with the personal warmth and associative structure of a letter to a friend.

The "Letter's" Refutative Logic

Even more impressive than the overall arrangement of the "Letter" is its internal logic in each refutative segment. King characteristically refutes the charges brought against him with a dual pattern. Never satisfied with one response, he answers each argument on at least two levels, usually a practical, immediate level, perhaps most appealing to a public audience, and an abstract, philosophical level involving unstated moral premises, an argument appealing more to the ostensible audience and others with some concern for philosophical abstractions. Multiple refutation is especially effective for the onlooking audience because it creates the impression that the other side's reasoning is not just weak but so unsound as to be unacceptable.

For example, in response to the charge that he is an outsider who has no business in Birmingham, King has four answers. First, he explains that the black leaders of Birmingham had invited him to come assist in the protest (rather than being a cause of it); second, that as president of the Southern Christian Leadership Conference of which the Alabama Christian Movement for Human Rights is an affiliate, "I am here because I have basic organizational ties here." These are the practical answers. They establish (if accepted) that he is not in fact an outsider, or at least not a complete outsider. But, beyond these, King moves to attack the concept of the "outsider." Thus his third response is that, in the tradition of Paul and other Christian prophets and missionaries, he has gone wherever there was need. Such a view is the direct consequence of a historical, religious precedent that neither of his audiences could reject. Fourth, since all communities and states in the modern world are interrelated, King argues, no man can be an outsider in his own nation. With that he has turned to the attack: "Whatever affects one directly affects all indirectly. Never again can we afford to live with the narrow, provincial 'outside agitator' idea."

For refutative purposes King, here and throughout, expands the clergymen's enthymemes into syllogisms, without using the dry and formidable phrasing of formal logic. In formal terms their reasoning had to be as follows:

Outsiders have no right to protest
King is an outsider.
Therefore, King has no right to protest.

In response, King first attacks the minor premise by showing the ties that make him other than an outsider in Birmingham. But if this is not convincing, he also attacks the major premise by citing the tradition of Christian missionary work and by arguing that in our interdependent nation, no citizen is an outsider anywhere.

Perhaps the clearest example of King's strategy of dual refutation is his answer to the label "extreme measures." The phrase masks a full syllogism:

Extremism is wrong.
King and his followers' actions are extreme.
Therefore, their actions are wrong.

At first King attacks the minor premise by pointing out that in fact among the Negro community his is precisely the moderate position, midway between the passive complacency of some older Negroes and the violent militance of the young. Then, upon rethinking the matter, King attacks the unstated major premise by citing historical precedents of great extremists whom his opponents and the observing audience cannot help but revere: Christ, Paul, Martin Luther, John Bunyan, Lincoln, Thomas Jefferson. To deny first that one is an extremist, and then to argue that in fact extremism in moral matters is desirable, not wrong, seems self-contradictory. Actually King works on two definitions of extremism: The first is holding a position far from the norm (which King says he does not); the second is holding a view, no matter what, without compromise. Since the clergymen's brief letter did not define the term, King takes the two possible definitions and shows his own position superior in either case. His position is not an *extreme* one, but he holds to it with extreme commitment.

Throughout the essay similarly, precise meanings of key terms are used as the bases for arguments. In answering the most important charge, that it is improper to break a law, in this instance a court-ordered injunction, King graciously acknowledges the apparent inconsistency: "Since we so diligently urge people to obey the Supreme Court's decision of 1954 outlawing segregation in the public schools, it is rather strange and paradoxical to find us consciously breaking laws." Because this is in fact the central issue and the one probably most likely to evoke disagreement, King devotes the longest refutation to it, eight paragraphs, and gives the greatest number of different answers. This time King cannot attack the minor premise; he had in fact broken a law. Instead he answers the implied major premise (that it is always wrong to break the law) on several levels, each carefully calculated to persuade both his ostensible and his observing audiences, both of whom were likely to be hostile to such a claim.

King's fundamental answer is drawn from the premise that laws are not *ends* in themselves but *means* of achieving justice. If so, justice, and not the law per se, must be served. In fact, he asserts, initiating another key distinction, there are just laws and unjust laws, and it is one's moral duty to disobey unjust laws because they subvert the purpose of law-justice. By subtle implication then, if he is right, his audiences have not lived up to their moral duties.

King offers three definitions of the difference between just and unjust laws, presumably in the event that one of the distinctions proves less than persuasive. First, "A just law is a man-made code that squares with the moral law or the law of God. An unjust law is a code that is out of harmony with the moral law." Second, an unjust law is any law forced on a minority not followed also by the majority. And third, an unjust law is any law that a minority had no voice in making.

On all three counts, King argues, segregation laws (and presumably laws against or used against public protests) are unjust. His audience might not agree with his definitions, but few could deny that some laws are unjust. However one defines injustice, the opponents of protest are in the untenable position of defending at least temporary obedience to unjust law.

King then turns again to historical tradition for key instances of disobedience to patently unjust laws. Several examples from the Judeo-Christian tradition can scarcely be rejected by the ostensible audience, and probably not by most members of the wider one. As a more current instance King alludes to Hitler, who in persecuting the Jews was following the law. Anyone who does not accept, at this point, the notion that it is sometimes moral to break the law must also accept the implication of defending on similar grounds obedience to the antisemitic decrees of the Nazi regime.[21]

In this instance King's argument rests on premises similar to those underlying the "Higher Law" argument of the nineteenth century abolitionists and the "Natural Law" argument of the eighteenth century revolutionists. Thus, in outline, the argument is one with which his audience was likely to be familiar and sympathetic. King's position, consequently, is well adapted to both of his audiences and increases his chances of being persuasive. Moreover, King's use of the historical tradition here (as throughout) has the rhetorical virtue of presenting him as a traditionalist, an image likely to be valued by his moderate audience, who tend to regard him as a radical bent on "extreme measures."

Reading the "Letter" a first or second time, one is not yet fully aware of the shape of King's refutation, but, as in many affective situations, awareness is not requisite. King's combination of definition, precedent, and multipremise refutation is rhetorically effective, both directly and indirectly. Because the refutation seems at once precise, clear, and elegant without ostentation, the reader-judge is encouraged to assume not only "this is a sound position," but also "this is a master at work. He knows his subject, he knows his audience, he knows his art." And, I believe, a reader comes unconsciously to feel that "a man who can perform these tasks is able and honest and worthy of belief." In short, as he argues, King not only adapts to a fictionalized audience, but creates for that audience an image of himself through his adaptation. In classical terms, he creates his *ethos*. To extend Ong's argument, in any instance of *written* communication, the rhetor—whether the image be true or false—is always a fiction created for the audience and based on the writer's fictionalizing of them.

Any rhetorical choice thus has two dimensions. A choice effective in its own right becomes doubly effective because it fictionalizes a writer as the sort of person who makes such choices—a wise, shrewd rhetor worth listening to. Likewise, a choice that fails presents an image of a rhetor who had no better judgment than to make that choice. Persuasion results not only from the *logos* of content but also from the *ethos* created through the performance, and King's "Letter" is outstanding on both grounds.

Style as Persuasion in the "Letter"

The positive ethical image does not result only from the chosen audience conceptualization and refutative strategies discussed above, however. It also results from the essay's style. Although this is not the place for a complete descriptive analysis of King's stylistic versatility in "Letter from Birmingham Jail," I would like to highlight some of its more striking stylistic features and to speculate on the ways they reinforce the total persuasive effort. The essay's style is supple and sophisticated yet readable. An audience is likely to be favorably impressed, without being overwhelmed. The stylistic manipulations both create an image of competence and sincerity and operate on the reader's emotions.

Like all rhetorical choices, stylistic decisions have multiple effects. But to clarify the relation between stylistic choice and persuasion, it may be useful to assert that an effective stylistic choice will work in one or more of the following three ways. It may adapt the style in order to carry meaning more effectively to the audience as fictionalized by the rhetor, such as a decision to use a simpler synonym in place of a more elaborate equivalent. This is the *adaptive* dimension of style. Or the choice may operate on the reader's emotions in a less than obvious way, such as in a decision to use words that alliterate. This is the *affective* dimension of style, as I hope to clarify below. Finally the stylistic choice may be effective primarily because it helps enhance the rhetor's image and thus the rhetor's credibility. This is the *ethical* dimension of style. These three varieties of stylistic impact correspond closely to the three classical modes of persuasion; the adaptive choice is a rational technique (logos), the affective choice works on the emotions (pathos), and the ethical choice is a technique for enhancing ethos.

To illustrate these three persuasive dimensions of King's style, it may be well to start with an obvious and relatively simple feature of the essay. A reader can scarcely help noticing how often King refers to other famous men whom he expects his reader to recognize. These allusions are directly effective in their adaptive and affective appeals to both the limited and broader audiences and indirectly effective in the image of him they help create.

King unabashedly puts himself into a great tradition of protest beginning with Socrates, referred to three times, and extending down through primarily Christian history, from the early prophets to Christ himself, to Paul, to Aquinas, Augustine, Martin Luther, and Bunyan. In addition to such historical allusions, King also buttresses his argument by quoting or paraphrasing Reinhold Niebuhr, Martin Buber, and Paul Tillich, leading modern spokesmen from both Christian and Jewish faiths and thus presumably adaptive references for all of the eight clergymen at one time or another as well as to virtually all of King's broader audience. He even manages to quote an unidentified justice of the United States Supreme Court and T. S. Eliot. This man, who is potentially suspect as an outsider, a rabble-rouser, even a criminal, reveals himself to be educated, wise, and widely read. At least that is the impression such allusions make in discourse. They have multiplicative ethical impact, since an auditor assumes they are a carefully chosen sample drawn from a much larger store of information.

King's style in the essay is also marked by the extensive use of metaphors, generally of two types: either enduring archetypal metaphors or metaphors drawn from contemporary technology. Two archetypal patterns are dominant, that of depth versus height and dark versus light. The present system and segregation are repeatedly characterized as being *down* and *dark,* while the hope for the future involves rising and coming into the *light.* The Negroes live in a "dark shadow" and must "rise from the dark depths." They are "plunged into an abyss of injustice where they experience the bleakness of corroding despair." Policy must be lifted from "quicksand" to "rock," and "we have fallen below our environment"; Negroes are in a "dark dungeon"; in the emphatic and optimistic final paragraph (quoted below) America now suffers under the "dark clouds of racial prejudice" in a "deep fog of misunderstanding," but "tomorrow the radiant stars of love and brotherhood will shine."

As Osborn has argued, "Because of their strong positive and negative associations with survival and developmental motives, such metaphors express intense value judgments and may thus be expected to elicit significant value responses." Such "argument by archetype" also appeals to an audience's desire for simplification through its built-in, two-valued orientation.[22]

Other metaphors come from modern technology. The nations of Africa are moving forward with "jet-like speed" while we go at "a horse and buggy pace"; and the church stands "as a tail light behind other community agencies rather than a headlight leading men to higher levels of justice." The church is now merely a "thermometer" recording popular opinion instead of what it once was, "a thermostat that transformed the mores of society."

Specifically medical metaphors unite the technological imagery with the archetypal metaphor of disease and health. Segregation is a disease and later a boil that must be exposed to the healing sun. The liberal argument to wait has "been a tranquilizing thalidomide, relieving the emotional stress for a moment, only to give birth to an ill-formed infant of frustration."[23] Some whites have sensed the need for "antidotes" to segregation, but others have remained silent "behind the anesthetizing security of stained glass windows." All told, I count seventy-two metaphors, including both explicit and suppressed forms. Almost none are presented through cliches (common verbal formulas). They share several stylistic functions. On the adaptive level they are memorable for their ingenuity, and they help make an abstract philosophical argument vividly concrete. On the affective level, the archetypal metaphors speak to fundamental urges in us all and thus enhance the message indirectly. Finally, like all rhetorical choices, the stylistic decision to use metaphors also affects King's image. The archetypal references create the image of a sincere man of deep feeling who is fundamentally like the reader and who has confidence both in his own moral judgment and in the inevitability of a better tomorrow. The technological images help build an identification between King and his readers; both speaker and listener inhabit the same world of jet planes, thermometers, and wonder drugs, a world of rapid change in which only one element—the status of blacks—has not kept up.

This same identity of rhetor and reader is also enhanced by a series of stylistic choices which, taken together, constitute the conciliatory tone that characterizes the essay and serves to unite a variety of other tones. From the salutation onward, King is not out to criticize or belittle, but merely to explain patiently and sadly to those who do not (yet) see the light of the truth. Throughout the essay King may be righteous, hurt, disappointed, ironic, sorry that he must say some unavoidably critical things, but neither angry nor despairing. He has "almost reached the regrettable conclusion that the Negroes' great stumbling block in the stride toward freedom is not the White Citizens' 'Counciler' or the Ku Klux Klanner, but the white moderate"; almost but not quite. And he has paid his clerical audience the compliment of having listened carefully to their views. His essay thus fulfills Carl Rogers' demand that one must first hear a position and be able to repeat it with understanding and clarity before real communication can occur.[24] Throughout the essay King shows his respect for his reader. He knows that his clerical audience is composed of sincere and devout men, men who share his basic religious values and whom he can call "My dear Fellow Clergymen" and "My Christian brothers." King even praises some by name for their own (limited) efforts to move toward integration. He can criticize such men only with regret. Echoing through the essay are phrases such as "I must say" and "I feel impelled to mention." Such a stylistic stance flatters him as well as his addressees. It serves the positive image he wants; this writer is not a shouting, belligerent, trouble-maker, but a sincere and understanding human being whose views are forced out of him by his concern for their misguided positions.

The identification with the audience and the conciliatory tone are further created by one of the most subtle stylistic elements in the "Letter," the use of personal pronouns. Since the "Letter" is a deeply personal apologia, it is not surprising that *I* occurs regularly—139 times to be exact, 100 times as the subject of a main clause. Similarly King often addresses his ostensible audience directly: in rephrasing their arguments ("you stated"), in asking for understanding ("I hope that you can see"), in direct address ("Each of you has taken some significant stands"), and in personal appeal ("I beg you to forgive me." "I hope this letter finds you strong in the faith."). There are forty uses of *you* to refer to the clergymen, not to mention other generic uses of the word, which also carry personal overtones. The net effect is an impression of informality as well as personal commitment on the part of the *I*.

More subtle still is King's manipulation of ambiguous first-person-plural pronouns. Often *we* and *our* and *us* in the essay refer clearly to some or all of the Birmingham protesters: "Several months ago our local affiliate here . . . invited us to be on call . . . We readily consented." In other places, the *we* is more general, as in "Never again can we afford to live with the narrow, provincial 'outside agitator' idea." Yet frequently a *we, our,* or *us* seems to refer to the protesters but may also include the audience, in effect reinforcing the frequent direct addresses by gathering King and his opponents into a unit sharing a single outlook. Consider this sentence: "I have tried to stand between these two forces saying that we need not follow the 'do-nothingism' of the complacent or the hatred and despair of the black nationalist." *We* here at first seems to mean "we the moderate protesters," but it may equally well mean "we who recognize the problem and want to see it solved." We, all of us, you clergymen as well as my followers, may take this middle road. The union is subtle, but is at least subconsciously forced on the reader by King's choice of pronouns.

A similar movement from "I-you" to *we* operates in the closing paragraph of the essay in conjunction with extended archetypal imagery:

> *I* hope this letter finds *you* strong in the faith. *I* also hope that circumstances will soon make it possible for *me* to meet each of *you,* not as an integrationist or a civil rights leader, but as a fellow clergymen and a Christian brother. Let *us* all hope that the dark clouds of racial prejudice will soon pass away and the deep fog of misunderstanding will be lifted from *our* fear-drenched communities and in some not too distant tomorrow the radiant stars of love and brotherhood will shine over *our* great nation with all their scintillating beauty (italics added).

In the first two sentences, the current separation between *I* and *you* is both stated and reinforced by the pronouns, but after the conciliatory "fellow clergymen," in the third sentence, both groups merge in a vision of future unity in "our communities" and "our great nation" under the scintillating beauty of the high, bright stars.

King's style in the "Letter," as Larson has pointed out,[25] is primarily characterized by variety. It shows in the allusions and metaphors already discussed and in the range of tones united by the dominant conciliatory stance, but it is nowhere more obvious than in the essay's syntactic structures.

The original published text of King's "Letter" consisted of 48 paragraphs, 325 sentences, and 7,110 words, with a moderate average sentence of 22 words and an average paragraph of almost 7 sentences or 149 words. The average sentence, not so long as that of normal American intellectual prose, is consequently appropriate for King's extensive audience. But such statistics mask the variety of King's syntax. Of the 325 sentences, many are short; 62 have 10 or fewer words. Some are aphoristic, such as "We are caught in an inescapable network of mutuality tied in a single garment of destiny. Whatever affects one directly affects all indirectly." Thus parts of the essay are quite easy to read and eminently quotable. On the other hand, 18 sentences are more than 50 words long and 2 exceed 100 words. I know of no other modern public prose including sentences of such length. Although some readers are likely to stumble over such sentences, my impression is that, overall, the style is clear and vivid and relatively easy to read but with no hint of condescension. The extreme variations in sentence length as well as similar variety in clausal construction and levels of formality seem primarily to work on the ethical level. That is, they dramatize for the readers a rhetor who is a master manipulator of language.

The one syntactic feature that emerges as common within the variation is elaborate parallelism. In it, as in the metaphors, it is easy to hear the cadences of the evangelist, another dimension of King's self-dramatization through style. Sometimes King's parallelism is tight and aphoristic as in "Shallow understanding from people of good will is more frustrating than absolute misunderstanding from people of ill will," or "Whatever affects one directly affects all indirectly." More often, however, it is spread out and rhythmic: "I say it as a minister of the gospel, who loves the Church; who was nurtured in its bosom; who has been sustained by its spiritual blessings and who will remain true to it as long as the cord of life shall lengthen." Or,

> I have almost reached the regrettable conclusion that the Negroes' great stumbling block in the stride toward freedom is not the White Citizens' "Counciler" or the Ku Klux Klanner, but the white moderate who is more devoted to "order" than to justice; who prefers a negative peace which is the absence of tension to a positive peace which is the presence of justice; who constantly says "I agree with you in the goal you seek, but I can't agree with your methods of direct action"; who paternalistically feels that he can set the time-table for another man's freedom; who lives by the myth of time and who constantly advises the Negro to wait until a "more convenient season."

Frequently this extended parallelism continues through several sentences:

> They have left their secure congregations and walked the streets of Albany, Georgia, with us. They have gone through the highways of the South on torturous rides for freedom. Yes, they have gone to jail with us. Some have been kicked out of their churches and lost the support of their bishops and fellow ministers. But they have gone with the faith that right defeated is stronger than evil triumphant.

In all, I count 15 instances of sustained parallelism, some involving as many as 6 sentences and one (discussed below) a single sentence of more than 300 words.

The effects of such parallelism must be largely conjectural, but it is difficult to imagine that they can lie in the adaptive domain. That is, there seems to be no reason to think that parallel syntax is any more clear or easy to follow than are other syntactic structures. On the other hand, the rhythms and balance created by parallelism, especially when a series of parallel constructions is used to build to a climax, probably have an affective impact, much as they would in oral discourse but to a lesser degree. The major effect is ethical, portraying the rhetor as a man who can balance various views and who has his ideas under complete control.

The "Letter's" most impressive stylistic feat is its longest sentence. Unique form serves to emphasize unique content since it is the one place in the essay where the evil of segregation, rather than the necessity of protest, is delineated. Because it contains in miniature so much that is syntactically and metaphorically characteristic of the essay, I quote it in full. It occurs (par. 12) within the refutation of the argument that now is not the proper time for protest. It opens, as do many of the sentences, with a conjunctive turn:

> But when you have seen vicious mobs lynch your mothers and fathers at will and drown your sisters and brothers at whim; when you have seen hate filled policemen curse, kick, brutalize, and even kill your black brothers and sisters with impunity; when you see the vast majority of your twenty million Negro brothers smothering in an air-tight cage of poverty in the midst of an affluent society; when you suddenly find your tongue twisted and your speech stammering as you seek to explain to your six-year-old daughter why she can't go to the public

amusement park that has just been advertised on television, and see tears welling up in her little eyes when she is told that Funtown is closed to colored children, and see the depressing clouds of inferiority begin to form in her little mental sky, and see her begin to distort her little personality by unconsciously developing a bitterness toward white people; when you have to concoct an answer for a five-year-old son asking in agonizing pathos: "Daddy, why do white people treat colored people so mean?"; when you take a cross country drive and find it necessary to sleep night after night in the uncomfortable corners of your automobile because no motel will accept you; when you are humiliated day in and day out by nagging signs reading "white" men and "colored"; when your first name becomes "nigger" and; your middle name becomes "boy" (however old you are) and your last name becomes "John," and when your wife and mother are never given the respected title "Mrs."; when you are harried by day and haunted by night by the fact that you are a Negro, living constantly at tip-toe stance never quite knowing what to expect next, and plagued with inner fears and outer resentments; when you are forever fighting a degenerating sense of "nobodiness";—then you will understand why we find it difficult to wait.

This most impressive periodic sentence of 331 words is highlighted through contrast with the preceding sentence of 19 words and succeeding sentences of 33, 11, 13, and 6 words. Its nine major subordinate clauses are each addressed directly to the audience with "when you," and they comprise an elaborate catalogue, frequently with metaphor, of the injustices suffered daily by the Negro in America. The sentence builds to a climax after detail is piled on detail, only to end with the one main clause of magnificently understated direct address: "then you will understand why we find it difficult to wait." Here the pronouns create no union: *you* are distinctly not *we*. It is appropriate that this single indictment of American racism, the only point in the essay at which pathos is used as a major suasive mode, should be the longest sentence. But it is also appropriate that it not be dominant. For the subject of the essay is not racial injustice. That is, except here, a given.

Conclusion

Presumably a public letter, to be credible, must suit the ostensible audience; one of the virtues of the form is that it provides a relatively well-defined (ostensible) audience on which rhetorical and stylistic choices may be based. But this fact in turn both defines and controls the onlooking audience. We can never know who King's readers were (or will be), but we can deduce who his fictionalized audience must have been. The refutative logic, discussed above, is careful and complex. Precise definitions are used involving careful distinctions. Uncommon (primarily Christian) allusions, some impressive vocabulary, complex syntax, and elaborate metaphor mark this, not as a piece of popular propaganda, but as a moral argument carefully designed for an audience of some sophistication.

The "Letter" lacks the elaborate pathos that might be persuasive to a purely popular audience, the emotional fireworks it could easily have employed about the evils of segregation. It uses instead a combination of logical and ethical persuasion, effective for a broad but generally well-educated audience, "sincere" readers "of genuine good will." Further, it is written for a concerned religious audience, an essentially conservative and traditional audience who would generally oppose civil disobedience but who would take the time to listen and not be alienated by extensive citing of other thinkers.

To lose the moral and social content of King's argument in critical analysis of nuances would, of course, be a mistake. Central to this examination is the attempt to bring about a more refined appreciation of King's text as an instance of rhetoric in the classical sense, a conspicuously compelling effort to persuade. It cannot be fully understood in isolation. As a public letter it stands in the context of its time and place, and it has a precise dialectical relationship to the document which provoked it. It is thus a very real effort to use language as a medium of social-problem solving, as a medium of change. Nevertheless, it also exists, especially for readers today, as a permanent articulation of human perception of an issue, which justifies examining it in all of its eloquent, rhetorical complexities. As an exercise in clarity and logic, King's essay well deserves the fame it has gained. Its structure makes it both readable and thorough. Its refutative stance makes it alive with the fire of heated but courteous controversy, and the dual nature of the refutation makes it simultaneously persuasive and logically compelling. Its stylistic variety and nuance portray a personality in print, manipulate a reader's emotions, and create a union of reader and rhetor.

Notes

1. David L. Lewis, *King: A Critical Biography* (New York: Praeger, 1970). p. 182.
2. Martin Luther King, Jr., *Why We Can't Wait* (New York: Harper & Row, 1963), p. 78.
3. Alan F. Westin and Barry Mahoney, *The Trial of Martin Luther King* (New York: Crowell, 1974), p. 140.
4. My analysis is based on the first published version. In all major respects the two versions are almost identical. King's editing was restricted to minor alterations of diction and syntax in more than 200 sentences. Six other sentences were deleted, and one was added. In fourteen instances two sentences were combined in revision; and four original sentences were divided. The changes seem to have been made in the interests of economy and a move toward slightly more formality. Anyone reading the two versions, however, must search carefully to find the changes. The overall difference in impact is negligible.
5. The "Letter" is included in a number of college anthologies: Charles Muscatine and Marlene Griffith, eds., *The Borzoi College Reader,* 3rd ed. (New York: Knopf, 1976); Arthur M. Eastman et al., eds., *The Norton Reader,* 4th ed. (New York: Norton, 1977); Caroline Shrodes, Harry Finestone, and Michael Shugrue, eds., *The Conscious Reader,* 2nd ed. (New York: Macmillan, 1978); Richard E. Young, Alton L. Becker, and Kenneth L. Pike, *Rhetoric: Discovery and Change* (New York: Harcourt, Brace & World, 1970); Halsey P. Taylor and Victor N. Okada, eds., *The Craft of the Essay* (New York: Harcourt Brace Jovanovich, 1977); and Forrest D. Burt and E. Cleve Want, eds., *Invention & Design: A Rhetorical Reader* (New York: Random House, 1978). It also appears in Edward P. J. Corbett, *Classical Rhetoric for the Modern Student,* 2nd ed. (New York: Oxford, 1971);

Staughton Lynd, ed., *Nonviolence in America: A Documentary History* (Indianapolis: Bobbs-Merrill, 1966); George Ducas and Charles Van Doren, eds., *Great Documents in Black American History* (New York: Praeger, 1970); and Herbert J. Storing, ed., *What Country Have I? Political Writings by Black Americans* (New York: St. Martin's, 1970).

6. Craig Bradford Snow, *A Guide to The Norton Reader, Fourth Edition* (New York: Norton, 1977), p. 173.

7. Richard L. Larson, *Rhetorical Guide to The Borzoi College Reader* (New York: Knopf, 1967). p. 87.

8. Burt and Want, p. 354.

9. Taylor and Okada, p. 310.

10. Haig A. Bosmajian, "Rhetoric of Martin Luther King's Letter From Birmingham Jail," *Midwest Quarterly,* 8 (Jan. 1967), 127–43.

11. The clergymen's letter along with the earlier version of King's response is reprinted in Muscatine and Griffith, pp. 233–34.

12. Walter J. Ong, "The Writer's Audience Is Always a Fiction." *PMLA,* 90 (1975), 9–21.

13. I do not mean to imply that a reader of King's essay must be familiar with the clergy's letter. It is quite enough to "know" their letter through King's restatements of its main points. He "responds" to the clergy's arguments but does not allow them to structure his essay; they only seem to do so. If one knows the clergy's letter well, it is even clear that King slightly restates some arguments to make them more refutable.

14. The refutative structure has been pointed out by Larson and Bosmajian.

15. Corbett, p. 27.

16. Bosmajian, p. 130.

17. Larson, p. 84.

18. It may not be too farfetched to argue that these two digressions actually constitute the real constructive case of the essay. They do not directly support the proposition as I have described it, but they do make a case for concerted action against, rather than endurance of, segregation. And motivating such action may be the real implicit purpose.

19. Actually one of the clergy's corollary claims, that King and his followers had ignored the courts, is never answered. Since King, in fact, had chosen protest in the streets rather than action in the courts, he can scarcely answer such a charge directly. The whole letter is, however, a justification of ignoring the courts.

20. Larson, in his valuable set of notes on the essay, has characterized it as "randomly interconnected" (p. 84); obviously, I disagree.

21. In his revision, King added a further historical example, the Boston Tea Party.

22. Michael Osborn, "Archetypal Metaphor in Rhetoric: The Light-Dark Family," *Quarterly Journal of Speech, 53* (1967), 117.

23. In the revised version, King cut out three of his metaphors, apparently because they were too harsh. Both the "thalidomide" and the "tail light" images were omitted, as was a reference to the few whites who had joined the black protest as "the leaven in the lump of race."

24. Carl R. Rogers, "Communication: Its Blocking and Its Facilitation," in Young, Becker, and Pike, pp. 284–89.

25. Larson says, "It is, indeed, unfair to speak of the 'tone' of the 'Letter,' for in its varied tones the 'Letter' is more like a musical performance than a piece of argument" (p. 86). True, but, as in a piece of music, the varied tones are all brought into harmony by the tonic note, in this instance the generous, conciliatory stance with which King states his uncompromising case.

8
Rhetoric of Literature

Rhetorical dimensions in literature have been recognized for centuries. Even before Aristotle cross-referenced his *Poetics* with his *Rhetoric,* theorists of the language arts had recognized that poetics was not a purely mimetic enterprise nor rhetoric a purely pragmatic one. Elements of each art could be found within the other. Though the majority of theorists from Aristotle to Horace identified the ends of literary works as the imitation of life through the evocation of feeling and emotion, some, including Plato, clearly recognized the didactic or persuasive functions of literature. Literature could lead to action as well as thought; could foster change as well as celebrate permanence and beauty. In later years critics came to recognize that the rhetorical dimensions of literature were more pervasive than matters of effect alone, extending even to the choices made by the author in the process of composition.

In this section Bayer, Benson, and Taft-Kaufman consider the rhetorical potentials of three literary genres: the novel, autobiography, and drama. These are but three of the many forms—poetry, short stories, biography, critical essays, and so forth—that constitute literature proper. Each has rhetorical potentials that are shared with other members of the poetic family as well as dimensions that are unique to the particular form. The essays presented in this section represent attempts to understand the rhetorical functioning of poetic forms while, at the same time, respecting the unity and integrity of the literary object. None of the authors seek to reduce literature to technique or claim to account for all important aspects of the work by considering its potential to move an audience to belief or action. The authors do find, however, that different aspects of the rhetorical tradition help to open the literary artifact, help to explain its functioning as communication, in ways that a purely internal, literary analysis cannot.

One question that is addressed by all three authors concerns the interrelationships among the poet, the literary artifact or creation, and the source materials used to construct that artifact. Bayer considers the role of source materials on two levels: those used as theoretical guides in the construction of the text, and those used as raw materials for inventing or locating the actual content. Both levels function rhetorically. By relying on the rhetorical theory of Hugh Blair and the grammatical principles of Lindley Murray, Bayer shows how Hawthorne structured his work around the principles of oral rhetoric. Hawthorne opened with an exordium in which he emulated Blair's advice for dealing with a hostile audience: flattery, deprecation of self, and establishment of common bonds. In so doing, Hawthorne constructed a reading audience whose values, assumptions, and predispositions prepared it to function in the manner needed to transform a historical narrative into a moral lesson. Likewise, Bayer points to Hawthorne's use of the commonplace book and personal diaries or notebooks as inventional sources for *The Scarlet Letter.* Though Bayer does not pursue the precise influences of the notebooks on the novel, it is clear that certain themes and their treatment originated in Hawthorne's personal notebooks and his collection of commonplace sayings.

Benson, like Bayer, is interested in the influence of outside sources on the construction of the literary object, but goes considerably beyond questions of literary origin. While Bayer is primarily interested in using the rhetorical tradition to explain Hawthorne's compositional choices and the effects achieved by those choices, Benson starts with the nature of rhetorical discourse and compares *The Autobiography of Malcolm X* with the notion of rhetoric as a synthetic art that allows one to know the world, constitute the self, and exercise influence over others. The question for Benson is whether Malcolm's *Autobiography* achieves a synthesis of these three rhetorical roles in such a manner as to allow the *Autobiography* to serve as a persuasive model for its readers.

To be successful as rhetoric, Benson argues, Malcolm must structure his *Autobiography* in such a way as to overcome the audience's predisposition to dismiss Malcolm as a religious fanatic, a charlatan, or a misguided ideologue. Since Malcolm displayed all three of these elements in his public rhetoric, the reading audience might well be inclined to interpret his *Autobiography* in light of his earlier behaviors. If that is allowed to happen, Benson argues, the *Autobiography* fails as a rhetorical document. The task then becomes, from Benson's perspective, to find a reading of the *Autobiography* that avoids allowing the reader to dismiss Malcolm and compels the audience to recognize a principle of action which transcends the *Autobiography* itself, modeling forth a plan of action for the reader to adopt as his or her own.

Implicit in Benson's analysis is the view that for autobiography to function successfully *as rhetoric,* it must transcend the formal requirements of the genre. It is not enough that autobiography simply constitute the self or encompass one's view of the world. To be successful rhetoric, Benson seems to argue, autobiography must transcend both the particular idiosyncrasies of the self as well as the universal appeal of generic form to invite the reader to recognize and accept a belief, attitude, or plan of action that has implications *beyond* the world constructed by the author.

While Bayer looks to the author's background and training to account for rhetorical form, and Benson isolates the dialectical movement between conflicting visions of the self to explain Malcolm's model of action, Taft-Kaufman conducts an intensive analysis of Shakespeare's method of shaping his source materials. Starting from the critical consensus that identifies Arthur Brooke's poem, "The Tragicall Historye of Romeus and Juliet," as the immediate source for Shakespeare's play, Taft-Kaufman explores the rhetorical implications of the changes Shakespeare made when transforming the poem into a play. She is interested in the choices Shakespeare made, and why he made them as he did.

Taft-Kaufman argues that by understanding the effect of these changes we gain insights into how the audience is apt to interpret the ongoing action. The playwright, she seems to argue, is able to guide audience reaction by the way he selects, structures, and stylizes his production. Consequently, what Shakespeare deletes from Brooke's poem, and what effect that deletion has on the perceived meaning of the play becomes just as important as what he adds. Likewise, the ways Shakespeare invites audience interpretation through the structuring of scenes and acts and the stylistic devices he assigns to particular characters constitute purposeful changes in the original source material. Why these changes were made and how they control the rhetorical invitation to the audience, the invitation as to how the viewer is to understand and value the action, constitutes the focus of Taft-Kaufman's essay.

Inasmuch as each of these articles deals with the interrelationships among artists, their creations, and their audiences, certain common questions arise. Is rhetorical functioning necessarily dependent on knowledge of source materials? If we did not know, for example, that Hawthorne had been exposed to Blair's *Rhetoric* as part of his college curriculum, would that lack of knowledge significantly impair our ability to interpret the rhetorical structure and design of *The Scarlet Letter?* What is the relationship between the reader or viewer's prior knowledge of the author and his or her predisposition to recognize and respond to rhetorical structure? Benson, for example, argues that there is a reading of Malcolm's *Autobiography* that allows it to fulfill the functions of effective expression. But what evidence is there that a reader familiar with Malcolm only through his various public personae would likely make such a reading of the *Autobiography?* Is it possible for the author's ethos to be so pronounced as to vitiate any attempts to transcend it? Finally, how can we be sure that audience members, even if they do recognize the persuasive structure implicit in the work of art, are able (or willing) to abstract the principles or lessons from the world of literature and apply them to their daily lives? What would constitute external evidence that literature not only has persuasive dimensions, but that such dimensions are transferred from the world of art to the arena of action and affect human choice and decision-making?

Narrative Techniques and the Oral Tradition in *The Scarlet Letter*

John G. Bayer

Hawthorne's preface to the second edition of *The Scarlet Letter,* dated March 30, 1850, is a brief defense of "The Custom-House" in which he refuses to recant for allegedly indiscreet portrayals of his political enemies. Yet his rebuttal is by no means vociferous; with the first line of the preface, he sets the same disarmingly humble tone that permeates the Custom-House sketch itself:

> Much to the author's surprise, and (if he may say so without additional offence) considerably to his amusement, he finds that his sketch of official life, introductory to THE SCARLET LETTER, has created an unprecedented excitement in the respectable community immediately around him.[1]

Tonal ambiguity is but one enigma in "The Custom-House." Except for the now classic definition of the romance, the intent of *The Scarlet Letter* "Introductory" has troubled critics, and the tendency has been to ignore the remainder—primarily, it would seem, because Hawthorne himself encourages such a dismissal.[2] In the second edition preface he remarks: "The sketch might, perhaps, have been wholly omitted, without loss to the public, or detriment to the book . . ." (I). But if the personal essay format surrounding the theory of the romance adds little to our understanding of *The Scarlet Letter* itself, it promises much concerning Hawthorne's sensitivity to an assumed audience. In the Custom-House sketch he "speaks" directly to his reader in a familiar, at times jocular, manner as if he were conversing with a friend and confidant.[3] That such familiarity is mere pose has been observed, for one, by Jesse Bier, who concludes that Hawthorne's "soft-spoken and unassuming tone" is "deceptive."[4] This view is borne out by Hawthorne's own comments during the preparations for publishing *The Scarlet Letter.* In a letter to his publisher, James T. Fields, he betrays his lack of confidence in the book by proposing that its title be printed in red ink. This, he hoped, would be "attractive to the great gull we are endeavoring to circumvent" (xxii). While writing "The Custom-House" Hawthorne found himself in the awkward position of having to court an audience that he assumed to be hostile and for whom he felt contempt. The combative tenor of his comment to Fields seems to be reflected in the decidedly oral-aural cast of the beginning of "The Custom-House," in that

John G. Bayer, "Narrative Techniques and the Oral Tradition in *The Scarlet Letter*," in AMERICAN LITERATURE 52:2, pages 250–263. Copyright © 1980 by Duke University Press.

oral-rhetorical prescriptions derived from the ancients are polemically oriented, directed toward persuasion. Hawthorne refers to himself as a "speaker" and to his reader as a "listener," with whom he must "stand in some true relation" lest "thoughts are frozen and utterance benumbed" (4). He conceives of his audience as an adversary that must be won over and commits himself to finding the proper rhetorical tools of persuasion to render his audience sympathetic. The confusion over the purpose of the Custom-House sketch *in toto* can be allayed once it is understood as an exordium for the romance proper, an atavistic reminder of oral modes of composition.

In the corpus of critical work on Hawthorne, his ties with the oral tradition have received little attention, perhaps because literary romanticism in America has often been defined as a movement pitted against the eighteenth century's preoccupation with classifying the oral-rhetorical prescriptions of antiquity. Hawthorne is ranked among our first great writers precisely because the vision and shape of his works abandoned the static conventionality of the neo-classical period in favor of an original treatment of the short story and the novel-romance. During the first few decades of the nineteenth century, as advances in print technology enabled publishers to widen distribution, the public came to depend less on the spoken word and more on the printed one. Still, the process was gradual, and the oral milieu that spawned the lyceum movement continued to manifest itself, however covertly, in the compositional and thematic concerns of romantic writers.

Hawthorne's anxiety about the audience he projected for *The Scarlet Letter* is one such manifestation. In order to cope with his hostile reader, he apparently relied on Blair's *Rhetoric,* published in 1783, which contained persuasive tactics inherited from a time when oratory dominated writing. Blair's lectures are a typical product of the eighteenth century's drive to regularize the conventions of rhetoric as writing principles and yet are also, paradoxically, a primary source of Hawthorne's familiarity with the oral tradition. From his college years when he read Blair, Hawthorne acquired the habit of keeping commonplace books, a practice also prefigured long before in oral, preliterate societies. He recorded in his notebooks ideas for projected scenes in order to maintain, like his predecessor in the art of narration the oral performer, a storehouse of pre-readied themes that could be shaped into dramatic plot during the act of composition. Moreover, in *The Scarlet Letter* the plot is itself imbued with the resonance of the spoken word, as Hawthorne uses Arthur Dimmesdale's oratorical virtuosity to suggest the evocative power of the sermon in the Puritan community. *The Scarlet Letter* is not only a lasting monument of the romantic movement in American letters, but residual elements from the oral tradition make it a paradigm of America's last great age of oratory.

Although the concepts of audience, reader, and narratee have come to be used interchangeably, it is valuable for purposes of this inquiry to make distinctions among them similar to the accepted distinctions between author and

319

narrator. Thus, *reader* is probably best understood as the counterpart of *author*—that is, the flesh-and-blood being who actually reads the novel, short story, or epic. Similarly, just as the *narrator* is, to use Wayne Booth's phrase the author's "implied version of 'himself,' " so too is the *narratee* an idealized reader.[5] The term *audience* can best be reserved as a generic concept that denotes listeners or viewers (in whatever special way these terms might pertain to a particular narrative).[6]

In "The Custom-House" Hawthorne manipulates the reader-narratee relationship; and only later, in the romance proper, does he expand his focus to include the more general concept of audience. So excessive is his initial attention to the reader that one is persuaded he was more than a little anxious about "converting" his reader to narratee. From the beginning his tone is apologetic, as he, "the intrusive author," seeks an audience with "the indulgent reader" (3). He seems to presuppose a reader as uncooperative and downright hostile as the pair of spectators in his "Main-Street" (a sketch mentioned later in "The Custom-House"). In that piece an unlucky showman suffers the boorish barbs of two patrons unwilling, or unable, to contribute any of their own imagination to his performances. When the showman suggests to one that he lacks "the proper point of view," he receives the scornful reply: "I have already told you that, it is my business to see things just as they are."[7] The second spectator is no less critical of historical inaccuracies in the skits. A tandem more ill-suited to entertain a Hawthorne romance is probably not to be found, and it is apparently just such a readership Hawthorne addresses in the Custom-House sketch. He conceives of a reader akin to his own ancestors, whom he portrays as specter-critics contemptuous of his craft:

No aim, that I have ever cherished, would they recognize as laudable; no success of mine—if my life, beyond its domestic scope, had ever been brightened by success—would they deem otherwise than worthless, if not positively disgraceful. "What is he?" murmurs one gray shadow of my forefathers to the other. "A writer of story-books! What kind of business in life,—what mode of glorifying God, or being serviceable to mankind in his day and generation,—may that be? Why, the degenerate fellow might as well have been a fiddler!" (10)

It is clear that Hawthorne assumes a reader in "The Custom-House" whose skepticism and insistence on "reality" are meant to reflect the hard-bitten practicality of many nineteenth-century Americans. How is such a reader won over? Surely Hawthorne's self-imposed burden in this regard is greater than most, and his persuasive strategy will, accordingly, have to be more painstaking. And so it proves to be, as he employs both overt and covert modes of manipulation. His most obvious ploy is outright flattery. Professing great concern lest he violate his "reader's rights" (4), he is patronizing in his use of the conventional appellations "indulgent reader" (3) and "honored reader" (8). As mentioned above, Hawthorne likens his reader to his own forebears in that both parties disdain his profession. Yet at the end of the imagined attack by his Puritan ancestry he includes a qualifier: "And yet, let them scorn me as they will, strong traits of their nature have intertwined themselves with mine" (10). The suggestion is that Hawthorne and his progenitors—and by identification, his reader—are not so estranged after all. There may indeed be some similarity of sentiment in spite of differences in values. What follows this comment are various autobiographical asides, all intended to establish common ground between Hawthorne and his reader. A prime example is Hawthorne's insistence that his children must set down roots somewhere other than Salem because "human nature will not flourish, any more than a potato, if it be planted and replanted for too long a series of generations, in the same worn-out soil" (11–12). This urgent call for change and new growth echoes throughout "The Custom-House." During his tenure as surveyor of the Salem Custom House, Hawthorne had learned this lesson, an especially valuable one for "a man who has dreamed of literary fame" because he will discover "how utterly devoid of significance, beyond his circle, is all that he achieves, and all he aims at" (26–27). Such self-depreciation is hardly incidental. Hawthorne intends his reader to apply this same lesson to his own circumstance, to question whether his own reality-bound preoccupations might not also benefit from exposure to an altogether different perspective.[8] If the reader can be made to sympathize with Hawthorne's personal experience and to see the value of challenging one's stubborn ways—if these effects are managed—the reader will be more receptive to his role as narratee in *The Scarlet Letter*.

Hawthorne seeks his reader's sympathy in yet a third way: by adopting the pose of editor of Surveyor Pue's manuscript. That he includes the romance convention of the found manuscript is once again indicative of his sensitivity to his readership. What has been called quite simply the public's "distrust of fiction" in the nineteenth century is, as already noted, a prejudice shared by Hawthorne's reader.[9] Given this attitude of resistance, Hawthorne places the starting point of his narrative in the public domain; that is, he invites his reader to share in the discovery of the Pue manuscript. He attempts to engender some commonality of experience between the reader and himself in order to prepare for their respective roles in the romance (i.e., narratee and narrator).

All of Hawthorne's devices aimed at enlisting reader sympathy are, furthermore, conscious efforts to build toward closure in the narrative. Hawthorne seems to be aware intuitively that written narrative lacks the immediacy of existential involvement that obtains in an oral performance (as in the case of epic narrative). Early in "The Custom-House" he observes: "as thoughts are frozen and *utterance* benumbed, unless the *speaker* stand in some true relation with his *audience*—it may be pardonable to imagine that a friend, a kind and apprehensive, though not the closest friend, *is listening* to our *talk* . . . ." [emphasis added] (4). Hawthorne seems to find the dynamics of oral performance desirable, though only up to a point. Because, as a writer, he must maintain esthetic distance, he is prompted to place himself in what he calls a "true position as editor" (4). The editorial pose functions so as to persuade the reader that Hawthorne himself cannot be held accountable for any discrepancies of historical fact (such as those criticized by the "Main-Street" spectator); the story of Hester Prynne is Surveyor Pue's story, and Hawthorne is simply its editor—a mediator whose sole purpose for "assuming a personal relation with the public" is to reveal the significance of the historical record (4). A reader willing to accept Hawthorne's role as editor is more likely to blame any historical deficiencies on Pue and to respond more willingly to the suggestions of Hawthorne's retelling. By placing the source of his narrative in the public domain, Hawthorne reminds his reader that "real life" events are often ambiguous and unintelligible. The upshot of these tactics will be, if Hawthorne has calculated rightly, to soften his reader's skepticism.[10] Beneath this skeptical veneer Hawthorne ultimately assumes his reader to be "kind and apprehensive," and it is to this latent sympathy that he directs his attention (4). In sum, an essential function of "The Custom-House" is to characterize a composite reader and in turn to prepare that reader for his narratee role in *The Scarlet Letter*. Without such preparation, Hawthorne's artful structuring of his romance would be less evocative. Until the reader steps into the carefully delimited role of narratee, the closure that distinguishes tightly plotted narrative will remain merest potential.

A profile of Hawthorne's reader would include these characteristics: skepticism, discrimination, Yankee practicality. Yet, to be a suitable counterpart to the narrator of *The Scarlet Letter,* he must also display compassion, understanding, imagination. He must cooperate with the writer in spite of the typically American tendency to discredit that which cannot be apprehended through the senses. In order to act as a narratee in a romance, he is required to acknowledge his more sympathetic other half, to consciously sustain an internal counterpoise between tough-mindedness and sensitivity that attunes him to the mixing of reality and ideality in the romance itself. Hawthorne's reader is incapable of entering "a neutral territory, somewhere between the real world and fairy-land" until he can bring with him a mind set that is correspondingly neutral, or balanced (36). It is in this sense that the reader fictionalizes himself. The narratee of *The Scarlet Letter* is a figure of precisely defined proportions who, because of his close identification with the narrator, is privy to knowledge about events in the narrative that eludes both the central characters and the Puritan community at large.

Unlike the oral performer of the epic, who was a perpetual recounter and preserver of historical events, the narrator of *The Scarlet Letter* orchestrates an investigation into the moral implications of events. He is "consistently more interested in meaning and significance than in realism or factual accuracy," and is thus wholly a by-product of the romantic tradition.[11] Robert Scholes and Robert Kellogg trace the origin of this narrator type to the Greeks, whose *histor* "examine[d] the past with an eye toward separating out actuality from myth."[12] Whereas the traditional oral bard had to confine himself to a version of his story formulated through mnemonic device (indeed, he could conceive his role in no other way), the *histor* could present conflicting reports in his search for truth. Similar to this method is what Yvor Winters calls Hawthorne's "formula of alternative possibilities."[13] Hawthorne's editorial function in pivotal scenes in *The Scarlet Letter* frequently consists of summarizing various accounts ostensibly gleaned from witnesses. The most striking instance of this technique is the climactic public confession of the Reverend Arthur Dimmesdale, after which the members of the community speculate widely as to the causes for the "letter" that appears on his breast. Here, as elsewhere in the romance, Hawthorne recommends implicitly that the reader exercise his own acumen in choosing from among the suppositions of the crowd. The faceless Puritan community functions as a source of information from which the narrator, the editor, picks and chooses—only to defer final judgment to the reader.

The citizens of Boston function further as a chorus, whose attitudes alternately coincide and stand apart from those shared by the narrator and narratee. The value matrix that establishes the bond between narrator and narratee is centered on sympathy and tolerance. From the beginning of *The Scarlet Letter,* the narrator empathizes with Hester's plight; and the narratee, lest his identification with the narrator after having read "The Custom-House" be incomplete, is encouraged by the callousness of the Puritan community also to side with Hester. The community is in fact an audience in the sense defined earlier: they are viewers and listeners, subject to the innate limitations of sight and hearing. Hawthorne's narrator offers this editorial comment on these limitations:

> When an uninstructed multitude attempts to see with its eyes, it is exceedingly
> apt to be deceived. When, however, it forms its judgment, as it usually does, on
> the intuitions of its great and warm heart, the conclusions thus attained are often
> so profound and so unerring, as to possess the character of truths supernaturally
> revealed. (127)

The multitude is "uninstructed" in that it lacks the "supernatural" knowledge shared by the narrator and narratee. As a result, its sight (i.e., insight) is distorted. When the crowd relies exclusively on this impaired faculty, as in the scene when Hester's shame is made a "spectacle" on the scaffold, its obsession with guilt precludes compassionate response. Although the members of the community are sometimes equally deceived by what they *hear,* their compassion is nonetheless consistently awakened by the spoken word. When Hester is publicly shamed, she stands quietly, and the heart of the community is hardened. In contrast, when Dimmesdale subsequently entreats Hester to name her partner in sin, his impassioned words "vibrate within all hearts, and [bring] the listeners into one accord of sympathy" (67). At this point the public's view of Dimmesdale is of course still false; they see him as a paragon of moral rectitude. It is only later, in the crucial revelation scene, that sight and sound combine to enhance the people's knowledge and understanding. As Dimmesdale bares his breast, and his soul, the crowd-audience's "great heart [is] thoroughly appalled, yet overflowing with tearful sympathy . . ." (254). They are appalled by what they see and deeply touched by what they hear. As Dimmesdale completes his confession with his dying breath, the Puritan gathering responds with a paroxysm of collective catharsis: "The multitude, silent till then, broke out in a strange, deep voice of awe and wonder, which could not as yet find utterance, save in this murmur that rolled so heavily after the departed spirit" (257). Just as the great heart of the people responds directly to the spoken word, so too are its deepest feelings uttered in spontaneous harmony.

The profound effect of Dimmesdale's dying confession is certainly generated in part by the very fact that he dies. He is revered by his congregation, in spite of his admitted sin, and his untimely death in and of itself leaves them grief-stricken. Yet at the moment of death they no longer stand in mute despair; their voices join in a communal utterance of pity and fear. This spontaneous response can be accounted for only by recognizing the dynamics of the spoken word. Had Dimmesdale died quietly, the crowd would more than likely have remained silent as well. There is a kind of law of inertia that operates in the relationship between speech and silence which states: an absence of speech from a person is usually met with silence from another, but once one speaks the other is obliged to reply. That is, verbal utterance is marked by reciprocity. A discerning examination of "auditory synthesis: word as event" is offered by Walter Ong in *The Presence of the Word*.[14] Father Ong notes that speech evokes reciprocal responses as very few other human activities can. In the absence of oral confession, Dimmesdale's death would have been quite literally a dead event. This is not mere word play, for, as Ong also observes, "sound unites groups of living beings as nothing else does."[15] The Puritans at the scaffold are captivated by the startling admixture of sermon and sin in Dimmesdale's speech. Spellbound by the spectacle, they are totally immersed in a flood of emotion only because Dimmesdale speaks. The rightness of this dramatic scene is confirmed by the fact that "sound situates man in the middle of actuality and in simultaneity, whereas vision situates man in front of things and in sequentiality."[16] The experience of the congregation during Dimmesdale's confession is inclusive, and stands in bold relief when compared with their simply *watching* Hester on the scaffold, an experience of half measure.

Except for the intensifying influence of Dimmesdale's death, the effect of his earlier Election Day sermon is almost identical to that produced by his confession of guilt. It is Dimmesdale's vocal eloquence that causes the similarity of response:

> The eloquent voice, on which the souls of the listening audience had been borne aloft, as on the swelling waves of the sea, at length came to a pause. There was a momentary silence, profound as what should follow the utterance of oracles.

324

Then ensued a murmur and half-hushed tumult; as if the auditors, released from the high spell that had transported them into the region of another's mind, were returning into themselves, with all their awe and wonder still heavy on them. (248)

The congregation sit in respectful silence in the church, but once outside "their rapture broke into speech" (248). Although all speakers anticipate and expect audience recognition, the inspirational influence wielded by Dimmesdale is obviously utterance of a higher order: it is oratory. He is blessed with greater powers than most clerics, for he has received "the gift"—the Pentecostal Tongue of Flame— "symbolizing, it would seem [says Hawthorne], not the power of speech in foreign and unknown languages, but that of addressing the whole human brotherhood in the heart's native language" (141–42). He is all the more unique because his burden of sin has paradoxically enhanced his ability to empathize with his parishioners, such that "his heart vibrate[s] in unison with theirs . . . and sen[ds] its throb of pain through a thousand other hearts, in gushes of sad, persuasive eloquence" (142). A positive sympathy is generated by the bond of sin, and Dimmesdale's affinity with his flock is compounded by a strange blend of saintly breath and wretched flesh.

Not only are the dynamics of plot in *The Scarlet Letter* energized by the power of oratorical display, the structure of the tale has been informed by the oral tradition as well. Hawthorne's composition of his finest romance was guided by entries in his notebooks and journals—commonplace books whose collation very likely grew out of habits engendered while he was a student at Bowdoin College. The curriculum at Bowdoin in 1822, Hawthorne's sophomore year, included classes in Murray's *Grammar* and Blair's *Rhetoric*.[17] The custom of keeping commonplace books for such courses of study can be traced to the proliferation of commonplace collections during the Renaissance, when the print revolution stimulated the urge to catalogue the knowledge of previous, orally dominated generations. The educated among the New England Puritans compiled commonplace books on matters of theological and moral concern, and the efficacy of the practice survived as a pedagogical device in Hawthorne's time, nourished by an oratorical, revivalist spirit. Early nineteenth century heroes, both secular and orthodox, were often great speakers: Henry Clay, Daniel Webster, John C. Calhoun and Lyman Beecher, William Ellery Channing, Theodore Parker. The age's passion for the spoken word required that declamation remain a part of the college curriculum; and though Hawthorne shied from classroom performance at Bowdoin, he was for a time secretary of the Salem Lyceum, where he maintained good standing by occasionally presenting talks. Temperamentally unsuited for the speaker's platform he nonetheless benefitted as a writer from his lessons in Blair's *Rhetoric*.

Of particular interest as a probable source for the composition of "The Custom-House" is Lecture XXXI: "Conduct of a Discourse in All Its Parts." It has been demonstrated earlier in this discussion how Hawthorne uses "The Custom-House" in order to prepare his reader for the role of narratee. That he relied on Blair's rhetorical methods to accomplish that task can also be illustrated. From the ancients Blair derived two kinds of exordia for a discourse: *Principium* and *Insinuatio*. The former is a straightforward presentation of the speaker's objective. The latter is used in the special case of a hostile audience. Blair advises: "presuming the disposition of the Audience to be much against the Orator, he must gradually reconcile them to hearing him."[18] Hawthorne appears to have learned this lesson well, for "The Custom-House" shows his masterful ability to, as Blair puts it, "render [the audience] benevolent."[19] Derivative oral-polemical features in "The Custom-House" associate Hawthorne with the Puritan sermon in a manner that sheds new light on his debt to his forbears. Puritan ministers did not think of their congregations as openly hostile, but they were aware that their flock had to be wooed away from the vicissitudes of the workaday world before they would be receptive to the Word. The ancient rhetoric of persuasion served equally well the purposes of Puritan divine and latter-day romancer.

Because Hawthorne found compensatory value in sinfulness, he would seem to stand, on a moral plane, at a far remove from his Puritan ancestors. Yet the matter of sympathy is most certainly a concern shared by Hawthorne and the Puritans. Evidence of this is to be found in their common regard for the efficacy of the spoken word. The preeminent position of the sermon in the life of a Calvinist is well documented, as is the fact that the clergy carefully constructed their sermons to appeal not just to the intellect but also to the heart. Perry Miller contends that in discussing a sermon the Puritans most often dwelt on the manner in which it aroused the affections, or the passions.[20] Appeals to the affections placed the heart in proper sympathy with the doctrinal premise of the sermon. It is about the purpose of exciting the affections that some Puritans and Hawthorne disagree. The extent of this disagreement is made clear when the theme of *The Scarlet Letter* is seen as "the conflict in a soul between the pride which would contract it to harsh and narrow limits and the affections which would reach out and bind it to the natural society of its kind."[21] Hawthorne has romanticized and secularized the notion of affection in such a way that its proper purpose is not to serve as a possible aid toward individual salvation but instead to assert one's fellowship in the whole human community. Perhaps the best illustration of Hawthorne's redefining is his description of Hester's alienation from humanity:

> . . . there seemed to be no longer any thing in Hester's face for Love to dwell upon; nothing in Hester's form, though majestic and statue-like, that Passion would ever dream of clasping in its embraces; nothing in Hester's bosom, to make it ever again the pillow of Affection. (163)

Whereas the stirring of the affections was a sermonic strategy for the Puritan clergy, it became in Hawthorne's romance a central theme—needful human sympathy born of the recognition of common sinfulness.

The theme of sympathy is but one among many dramatized in *The Scarlet Letter*. Recent attention to Hawthorne's notebooks has provided a clearer understanding of how these themes were conceived. In the Centenary Edition of Hawthorne's *American Notebooks,* Claude Simpson has briefly outlined Hawthorne's method of working from notes to manuscript:

> During more than a decade before he wrote *The Scarlet Letter* Hawthorne repeatedly recorded notes bearing on the central relationships developed in that romance and elsewhere in his work: the insidious control of one person by another; the ironic contrast, often hypocritical, between man's social self and his inner anxieties. Other themes similarly treated—the failure of romantic expectations, the zeal for vengeance, the destructiveness of good intentions—suggest the power of ideas, not their translation into dramatic terms.[22]

Hawthorne's method of composition emulates that of Francis Bacon and other Renaissance writers, who augmented the work of encyclopedists by compiling their own commonplace books on various topics of universal concern, called commonplaces. The codification of these *topoi,* or *loci communes* began with the Sophists, Aristotle, Cicero, Quintilian and others, and found its way to Bacon via the Middle Ages, when scribes worked doggedly to amass the wisdom of the oral past under generic headings. Like Bacon, Hawthorne in turn collected personal bits of insight and stored them to be later filtered through the half-lights of the romance landscape. In the notebook entries related to *The Scarlet Letter,* begun in 1838 and accumulated over the next eleven years, he stressed ideas, not dramatic situations.[23] The notebooks contain the germ for many a scene that blossomed forth in the romance atmosphere, just as the ancient poet's mnemonic storehouse served as a foundation for each new performance. Very early in the history of narrative, oral performers such as Homer used commonplaces as thematic units to be strung together in a loose, rhapsodic approximation of the more tightly plotted written narrative of the novel. Although *The Scarlet Letter* is a strongly unified work, its episodic, highly scenic structure is a reminder of the cumulative drift of oral composition.

The dramatic features of *The Scarlet Letter* have often been noticed, but the relation of Hawthorne's narrative stagecraft to the oral roots of America's native literary tradition has not been accounted for. A close reading of "The Custom-House" and the romance itself reveals that Hawthorne was a writer drawn between America's literary future and her oral past. As shown earlier, the scaffold scenes depicting first Hester's and later Dimmesdale's guilt are charged with the existential dynamics of speech. Disagreement among critics concerning the purpose of "The Custom-House" has stemmed from the seeming incongruity between it and the romance proper. Once seen as an exordium designed to enlist reader cooperation, its complete function emerges clearly. These oral dimensions are altogether consistent with Hawthorne's rhetorical apprenticeship in college and confirm the judgment that *The Scarlet Letter* is a fictional exemplar of a residually oral age.

Notes

1. Nathaniel Hawthorne, *The Scarlet Letter,* Vol. I of *The Centenary Edition of the Works of Nathaniel Hawthorne,* ed. William Charvat et al. (Columbus: Ohio State Univ. Press, 1962), p. 1. All subsequent references are to this edition and are included parenthetically in the text.

2. Critics who have questioned the importance of "The Custom-House" to *The Scarlet Letter* are identified in Sam S. Baskett, "The (Complete) Scarlet Letter," *College English* 22 (1961), 321. Baskett argues for the relevance of "The Custom-House," as does John E. Becker in *Hawthorne's Historical Allegory* (Port Washington, N.Y.: Kennikat Press, 1971), pp. 61–87.

3. Malcolm Cowley, in his introduction to *The Portable Hawthorne* (New York: Penguin Books, 1977), pp. 6–7, suggests that Hawthorne carried on an "inner monologue" when he conceived his romances, and projected a second part of himself as a participating audience.

4. "Hawthorne on the Romance: His Prefaces Related and Examined," *Modern Philology,* 53 (1955), 17.

5. *The Rhetoric of Fiction* (Chicago: The Univ. of Chicago Press, 1961), p. 70.

6. Three useful analyses of the nature of narrative audience are: Walter J. Ong, "The Writer's Audience Is Always a Fiction" in *Interfaces of the Word* (Ithaca: Cornell Univ. Press, 1977); Gerald Prince, "Notes Toward a Categorization of Fictional 'Narratees,' " *Genre,* 4 (1971), 100–106; Walker Gibson, *Tough, Sweet and Stuffy* (Bloomington: Indiana Univ. Press, 1966), pp. 28–42.

7. "Main-Street," Vol. XI of *Works,* p. 57.

8. A related study is Joseph C. Pattison, "Point of View in Hawthorne," *PMLA,* 82 (1967), 363–69, which argues that dream is the proper "angle of vision" for Hawthorne's reader to adopt.

9. Harry C. West, "Hawthorne's Editorial Pose," *American Literature,* 44 (1972), 211.

10. West, 209.

11. Ibid.

12. *The Nature of Narrative* (London: Oxford Univ. Press, 1966), p. 242.

13. Cited in West, 217.

14. (New Haven: Yale Univ. Press, 1967), p. 111.

15. Ong, *Presence,* p. 122.

16. Ong, *Presence,* p. 128.

17. Randall Stewart, *Nathaniel Hawthorne* (New Haven: Yale Univ. Press, 1948), p. 11.

18. Hugh Blair, *Lectures on Rhetoric and Belles Lettres* (Carbondale, Ill.: Southern Illinois Univ. Press, 1965), II, 159.

19. Blair, p. 158. The art of letter writing, taught in medieval schools and derived from older oratorical structures, included an element called *benevolentiae captatio,* or "the winning of good will." See Walter J. Ong, "Tudor Writings on Rhetoric, Poetic, and Literary Theory" in *Rhetoric, Romance, and Technology* (Ithaca: Cornell Univ. Press, 1971), p. 54.

20. *The New England Mind: The Seventeenth Century* (Boston: Beacon Press, 1961), p. 300.

21. Carl Van Doren, *The American Novel, 1789–1939* (New York: The Macmillan Company, 1940), p. 63.

22. Vol. VIII of *Works,* p. 679.

23. A notebook entry that prefigures the Chillingworth-Dimmesdale relationship reads: "The influence of a peculiar mind, in close communion with another, to drive the latter to insanity" (Vol. VIII of *Works,* p. 170).

Rhetoric and Autobiography:
The Case of Malcolm X

Thomas W. Benson

Rhetoric is a way of knowing, a way of being, and a way of doing. Rhetoric is a way of knowing the world, of gaining access to the uniquely rhetorical probabilities that govern public policy and personal choice for oneself and others; it is a way of constituting the self in a symbolic act generated in a scene composed of exigencies, constraints, others, and the self; it is a way of exercising control over self, others, and by extension the scene.[1] Taken by itself, any one of the rhetorical modes of action is incomplete. Knowledge alone becomes decadent and effete, existence alone becomes narcissistic and self-destructive, and power alone becomes dehumanized technological manipulation. Perhaps only when rhetorical knowing, being, and doing are present together can a rhetorical act truly be said to take place. In a given rhetorical event the balance among being, knowing, and doing is a function of the structure of the act and its relation to audience, scene, agent, agency, and purpose.[2]

The constituents of rhetorical action are illustrated with special force in *The Autobiography of Malcolm X,*[3] which, I shall argue, achieves a unique synthesis of selfhood and rhetorical instrumentality.

The general outline of Malcolm's life is familiar to many Americans. He was born Malcolm Little in 1922, the son of a Baptist minister who was later killed by the Ku Klux Klan. After a boyhood in Michigan, Malcolm moved to Boston, where he worked as a shoeshine boy, soda fountain clerk, busboy, and railroad kitchen crewman, and drifted into a life of hustling, numbers running, pimping, and burglary. Finally arrested, he was sent to prison. There he became a convert to Islam, and after his release from prison became the leading spokesman for Elijah Muhammad's Lost-Found Nation of Islam in North America (the Black Muslims), and the country's most widely heard black advocate of racial separation. Then in November of 1963, Malcolm referred to the assassination of John F. Kennedy as "chickens coming home to roost," and was publicly silenced by Elijah Muhammad. Shortly afterwards, Malcolm broke with the Muslims and undertook a pilgrimage to Mecca. He returned to America to announce that he would henceforth work for the brotherhood of all men, and set about organizing a movement to achieve his ends, hinting that violent means might be necessary.

When Malcolm X was assassinated in February of 1965, he was a much-publicized but little-understood leader who seemed temporarily to have lost his following. Cut off from the Black Muslims, spurned as a black racist by

From *The Quarterly Journal of Speech,* Volume 60, 1974. Reprinted with permission of the author.

moderate Negro leaders and most of the press, Malcolm nevertheless appeared at the threshold of either national leadership or increasingly bitter notoriety. His death seemed to end all that, temporarily promoting him to a compromised martyrdom that might well, because of the seeming ambiguity of his final position, have led to a quick eradication of his influence.

But a few months later Grove Press published *The Autobiography of Malcolm X,* written "with the assistance of Alex Haley." This book quickly restored Malcolm to a position in the ranks of such black leaders as Douglass, Washington, DuBois, and King. Why? Here is an autobiography, moreover an autobiography whose authorship is clouded by collaboration, exhibiting the signs of a rhetorical work, and managing to solve a rhetorical problem of great complexity. How could Malcolm meet the most serious challenges posed to his life and work? The challenges that he changed his position so abruptly, near the end of his career, that he was without audience or program? And the challenge not only to create a place for himself in the pantheon of black leaders, but to further the development of revolutionary masses?

Let us first examine the foundation of the rhetorical problem and then try to find a reading of the *Autobiography* which illuminates his strategy.

1

For most of his audience, whether white or black, Malcolm's greatest needs were to establish his credibility and to explain his program. What stands in the way of satisfying these needs is the suspicion that he had no program and was not worth believing. Herbert W. Simons, for instance, sees Malcolm as impaled on the dilemma of needing to be both consistent and fresh. "When, in one year, Malcolm X broke with Elijah Muhammad, shifted positions on integration and participation in civil rights demonstrations, and confessed his uncertainties on other issues, he inevitably alienated some followers and invited charges of weakness and inconsistency from his enemies."[4] One option for the readers of Malcolm's *Autobiography* is to explain Malcolm's apparent inconsistency by arguing that he was either a blind fanatic or an irresponsible charlatan.

One of the greatest rhetorical potentialities of the autobiographical genre lies in its ability to take a reader inside the writer's experience, and to show how early mistakes led to later enlightenment. But this very advantage also presents a danger, since later actions may be judged as variations on those earlier mistakes. In Malcolm's case, some readers may be tempted to see his conversion to Islam and his later advocacy of brotherhood as self-serving extensions of his former career as a street hustler. And there are elements of the hustler in Malcolm as he reveals himself even after his conversion to Islam.

Malcolm has an irritating propensity for opportunism in debate, cleverly setting up a situation to score a point when that point may be inconsistent with another position. For instance, late in the *Autobiography* when he is describing his visit to Africa in 1964, Malcolm tells of a press conference: "I stressed to the assembled press the need for mutual communication and support between the Africans and Afro-Americans whose struggles were interlocked. I remember that in the press conference, I used the word 'Negro,' and I was firmly corrected. 'The word is not favored here, Mr. Malcolm X. The term Afro-American has greater meaning and dignity.' I sincerely apologized. I don't think that I said 'Negro' again as long as I was in Africa."[5] As it stands, this episode is unobjectionable. And yet during his ministry with the Black Muslims, Malcolm had, in his speech at Cornell University in March of 1962, for instance, repeatedly referred to America's "so-called Negroes," on the grounds that Negro was a white man's word which he refused to be ensnared by.[6] His sincere apology of 1964, not an outright reversal, nevertheless misleads his readers for the convenience of making his point. And earlier in the *Autobiography* Malcolm makes much the same point in reporting a speech by Elijah Muhammad. The white man, says Muhammad to a group of Muslims, "has taught you, for *his* benefit, that you are a neutral, shiftless, helpless so-called 'Negro.' I say *'so-called'* because you are *not* a *'Negro.'* There is no such thing as a race of *'Negroes.'* You are members of the Asiatic nation, from the tribe of *Shabazz! 'Negro'* is a false label forced on you by your slavemaster!"[7]

With considerable relish, Malcolm boasts of some of his debater's tactics when responding to white reporters; "I might copy a trick I had seen lawyers use, both in life and on television. It was a way that lawyers would slip in before a jury something otherwise inadmissable."[8]

To prove that blacks did not really want integration, Malcolm said in his *Autobiography* that "the black masses prefer the company of their own kind," and as for the charge of "vain, self-exalted white people . . . that black people want to sleep in bed with them—. . . that's a lie!"[9] And yet at Cornell in 1962, when he wanted to prove that white society had corrupted black culture, Malcolm charged that the black man in America had been made into a monster. "He is black on the outside, but you have made him white on the inside. Now he has a white heart and a white brain, and he's breathing down your throat and down your neck because he thinks he's a white man the same as you are. He thinks that he should have your house, that he should have your factory, he thinks that he should even have your school, and most of them even think that they should have your woman, and most of them are after your woman."[10]

For some readers of the *Autobiography,* Malcolm's enormous interest in his speaking appearances at American universities may seem to betray the crude ambitions of the autodidact to establish his intellectual status.[11]

After he left Elijah Muhammad, Malcolm undertook the traditional Hajj pilgrimage to Mecca, where among other thoughts he records the following reflection:

> Behind my nods and smiles, though, I was doing some American-type thinking and reflection. I saw that Islam's conversions around the world could double and triple if the colorfulness and true spiritualness of the Hajj pilgrimage were properly advertised and communicated to the outside world. I saw that the Arabs

are poor at understanding the psychology of non-Arabs and the importance of public relations. The Arabs said *"insha Allah"* ("God willing")—then they waited for converts. Even by this means, Islam was on the march, but I knew that with improved public relations methods the number of new converts turning to Allah could be turned into millions.[12]

Coupled with his opportunism in debate, his inconsistencies, his earlier career as hustler, pusher, and pimp, and his ministry of millennial anti-white black nationalism, Malcolm's confession of the urge to market Islam with the tools of American public relations may seem the final proof in branding him as a charlatan. We are reminded early in the *Autobiography* that Malcolm first sees the Muslims as a hustle. His brother, Reginald, wrote to him, "Malcolm, don't eat any more pork, and don't smoke any more cigarettes. I'll show you how to get out of prison." Malcolm's first response was that his brother "had come upon some way I could work a hype on the penal authorities."[13] Even in the last pages of his book, Malcolm speaks of how much he "cherished" his " 'demagogue' role," and hints that he sees himself as another Elijah Muhammad.[14]

Was Malcolm merely reducing Islam to a hustle, or was he a blind fanatic who was so absorbed in black racism that he would not allow logic to stand in his way?

After Malcolm's death, USIA director Carl T. Rowan called Malcolm a fanatic,[15] and there are passages in the *Autobiography* that a judicious reader might take as evidence for fanaticism. There is, for instance, Malcolm's sense that his life is worked out according to divine guidance. While he was in prison, Malcolm had a vision:

> I prayed for some kind of relief from my confusion.
> It was the next night, as I lay on my bed, I suddenly, with a start, became aware of a man sitting beside me in my chair. He had on a dark suit. I remember. I could see him as plainly as I see anyone I look at. He wasn't black, and he wasn't white. He was light-brown skinned, an Asiatic cast of countenance, and he had oily black hair.
> I looked right into his face.
> I didn't get frightened. I know I wasn't dreaming. I couldn't move, I didn't speak, and he didn't. I couldn't place him racially—other than that I knew he was a non-European. I had no idea whatsoever who he was. He just sat there. Then suddenly as he had come, he was gone.[16]

Malcolm's own sense that he is a chosen leader is sometimes striking. He speaks of his brother Reginald, who recruited him into Islam and then was cast out by Elijah Muhammad, and was finally placed in an institution. Malcolm says of his brother: "I believe, today, that it was written, it was meant for Reginald to be used for one purpose only: as a bait, as a minnow to reach into the ocean of blackness where I was, to save me."[17] And Malcolm says that Elijah Muhammad "virtually raised me from the dead."[18]

Malcolm often speaks of his life as "written." After describing his arrest for robbery, Malcolm says, "I have thought a thousand times, I guess, about how I so narrowly escaped death twice that day. That's why I believe that everything is written."[19] The incident took place before his conversion, he says, but "Allah was with me even then."[20] Malcolm talks of having "previsions" while in prison of addressing large crowds.[21]

Malcolm's pilgrimage to Mecca, after the break with Elijah Muhammad, is full of talk of the signs of divine guidance. On the plane from America, Malcolm's seatmates were Muslims. "Another sign!"[22] And later, in Egypt, "I considered it another of Allah's signs, that wherever I turned, someone was there to help me, to guide me."[23]

One curious mark of Malcolm's faith in divine guidance was his belief in the significance of numbers. He speaks of attending the Cassius Clay-Sonny Liston fight: "Among the eight thousand other seat holders in Miami's big Convention Hall, I received Seat Number Seven. Seven has always been my favorite number. It has followed me throughout my life. I took this to be Allah's message confirming to me that Cassius Clay was going to win."[24] Variations on the theme of seven appear here and there in the *Autobiography*. For instance, on his pilgrimage he was a guest at the Jedda Palace Hotel. He is careful to report that he was in suite number 214 (the sum of whose digits is seven).[25]

In the face of evidence that Malcolm was a hustler or a religious fanatic, how were those of Malcolm's followers who believed his descriptions of the white man as a devil to interpret the final year of his life? Malcolm quotes from speeches he made during this period: " 'Since I learned the *truth* in Mecca, my dearest friends have come to include *all* kinds—some Christians, Jews, Buddhists, Hindus, agnostics, and even atheists! I have friends who are called capitalists, Socialists, and Communists! Some of my friends are moderates, conservatives, extremists—some are even Uncle Toms! My friends today are black, brown, red, yellow, and *white!*' "[26]

How could Malcolm's diverse audiences, the audiences of his last year and beyond, of all colors and politics, be expected to understand and assent to his final appeals to them? For somehow, although he did make enemies, although his organizational following at the time of his death was smaller than during his ministry for Elijah Muhammad, Malcom's influence has continued to grow.

2

For all the difficulties that Malcolm poses to credibility, the charge that he is a fanatic or a charlatan will not stick. He was too good humored for a fanatic, and in fact he spoke in his last days of the danger of assuming that anyone is divinely guided.[27] He made more painful sacrifices than could have been borne by a charlatan. Some larger reading of his *Autobiography* is needed, one that will accept his traces of fanaticism and charlatanism without supposing that they account for the full impact of the *Autobiography* and the elevation of Malcolm to a leading role in America's tragic struggle over racial injustice.

One way out of our difficulty at this point is to find the solution in a direct refutation of charges against Malcolm's credibility. There are patterns in the *Autobiography* which support a version of Malcolm as a magnificent anti-hero, an existentialist saint, a mythic witness to America's oppressive racism.

Malcolm's existentialist credentials are strong. He often speaks as if action constitutes the man, and he was a man of action. He says, "I've never been one for inaction. Everything I've ever felt strongly about I've done something about."[28] And again, "Our Nation of Islam could be an even greater force in the American black man's overall struggle—if we engaged in more action. . . . I felt that, wherever black people committed themselves, in the Little Rocks and Birminghams and other places, militarily disciplined Muslims should also be there—for all the world to see, respect, and discuss."[29]

Not only did Malcolm demonstrate the virtues of courage, wit, and dedication, but he was willing to change his position when he thought it necessary. The autobiographical mode is uniquely suited to explaining and justifying how Malcolm was led from one stage of life to another, just as it is suited to keeping the focus upon Malcolm as its central figure. We are made to understand how Malcolm evolved from a troubled but promising black youth through the underworld of crime and drugs to an urgent and original agent of social redemption. Far from denying his changes, Malcolm makes "change" a major theme of his *Autobiography,* developing a pattern which tempts one to think in messianic terms. There is in the *Autobiography* a tension between the particularity of Malcolm's experience, depicted with passion and eloquence, and the sense of universal, almost mythical, patterns into which Malcolm's life is rendered, forming an archetypal cycle of innocence-initiation-corruption-salvation-disillusionment-redemption-death and, ultimately, vindication.[30]

But to describe Malcolm as a hero or martyr, reading the *Autobiography,* in effect, as a novel or a sacred text of existential revelation, for all that the *Autobiography* suggests such patterns, especially in the context of contemporary literary and popular culture, is to derail the book as rhetoric. For if we find the principle of Malcolm's life in his existential heroism or in a repetition of universal cycles, we shall have built a monument and destroyed a leader. Malcolm would be elevated above the problem posed by his inconsistencies, but his elevation would be either too personal or too universal to exercise a truly rhetorical function, that is, to contribute to the wisdom of a contemporary social movement much in need of direction. And so if Malcolm can rescue himself from the charges of fanaticism and charlatanism only by reconstituting himself in the role of hero or saint, he has allowed the autobiographical genre to triumph over its rhetorical purpose and has left the movement without any clue as to how to apply his experience to today's problems.

If Malcolm contained the principle of change within himself, how can his audience know that he would not have changed again, had he lived? Might the humanism of Malcolm's last year not be simply one more stopping place along an obscure trail whose markings only Malcolm could read? Does *The Autobiography of Malcolm X* become literature at the expense of fulfilling its rhetorical possibilities?

At this point we must pause to consider more fully the relation of rhetoric and literary forms, particularly in autobiography. Certainly it would be misleading to argue that literature and rhetoric are separated by impenetrable barriers. In the literature of experience, whether poetry, drama, journalism, fiction, or autobiography, rhetoric can provide the purpose, content, or principle of organization. In practice, literature may always be in part rhetorical. Wayne Booth has demonstrated the necessity of separating the implied from the actual author, and he has shown that where literature does not directly address an audience, at the very least it requires the audience to participate in the moral world of the literary work.[31] And yet the language of criticism would be impoverished if we overcompensated for old dichotomies by substituting the slogan that all literature is rhetorical. Slogans are still slogans, and even if it is true that all literature is rhetorical, literature and rhetoric are not identical. In a given case such imprecise terms as literature and rhetoric must be distinguished before they can be related.

In the case of any symbolic form, a set of conventions helps to create the context for a response. What conventions operate in autobiography, and what sorts of responses do they invite? Theorists of the genre, and there are few, seem to agree that autobiography is a literary genre more important for the form it gives to felt experience than for the accuracy with which it records actual events or the extent to which it influences public or private behavior.[32] And most theorists sharply distinguish between autobiography proper and such associated forms as reminiscence, memoir, confession, and apologia.

Roy Pascal is willing to grant that autobiography must "give us events that are symbolic of the personality as an entity unfolding not solely according to its own laws, but also in response to the world it lives in,"[33] but he is quite clear in his insistence that autobiography "is in fact not at all a suitable vehicle for the exposition of a doctrine, for by its very form we are led to appreciate the ideas and insights expounded in it (e.g., with Augustine, Wordsworth, Croce, Schweitzer) not in their objective truth but as true for this particular man, as true of him."[34] It is this sense of the single self generated symbolically in terms of a literary genre that prompts Richard Ellmann to argue that "autobiography is essentially solitary," whereas "biography is essentially social."[35]

The conventions of autobiography are constantly working to focus the reader's attention upon an individual, and even at that, an individual who is created in the work and not necessarily as he appeared in "real life." Where the external world is an element, it is most readily seen as a part of the author's experience, rather than as a real place shared with the reader. Indeed, the more fully realized the work as autobiography, as distinguished from such related genres as memoir, reminiscense, confession, or apologia, the more the reader may be impelled to a literary, as opposed to a rhetorical response. The literary response holds the pleasures of formal apprehension and psychological insight, whereas a fully rhetorical response ends in a responsibility which goes beyond the work. Or so, at least, the theorists of autobiography seem to tell us.

Perhaps Maurianne Adams suggests a false dichotomy when she states her preference for autobiographers when "as imaginative writers they are more concerned with the controlled articulation of subjective impressions and responses than with outer, public events and achievements."[36] Her allegiance is given to a convention which "enables autobiography to be a form of literature that we enjoy for its own sake, not as an adjunct to our knowledge of politics, military history, or public affairs."[37]

What may appear to Adams as the vexing intrusion of actuality into the rarified atmosphere of "authenticity, fidelity, coherence, and thematic design," is likely to appear to a rhetorical critic as a quite inevitable tension whose resolution it is up to the autobiographer to produce. In a rhetorician's view, the aim is not to purify the work of any taint of the real world. It is not how close to pure form the autobiography becomes, but how the work *relates* form to audience and external world that holds the interest of the rhetorical critic.

In Malcolm's case we can observe a reinvention and extension of the genre, recapitulating as he does the development of a literary form through religious confession and political apology to a final discovery of the self. But Malcolm does not stop with the revelation of his selfhood, and it is his ability to transcend the confines of pure literature even while meeting its formal requirements that constitutes his rhetorical genius.

For Malcolm's rhetorical purposes, either of the readings of the *Autobiography* so far proposed would amount to failure. For those who would reject Malcolm as a hustler or fanatic, the rhetorical problem is to establish credibility. For those who would promote Malcolm into a virtually fictional hero, Malcolm must avoid the more subtle failure of succeeding too well at remaining within the traditions of autobiography as literary form, and thereby isolating himself from the experiential world of the reader.

Both of the readings we have so far proposed are supportable by reference to the *Autobiography,* but both are too narrow to account fully for the work. Is it possible to develop a view of the book that acknowledges the attraction of contrasting, even inconsistent, alternate readings? Such a reading would have to accept Malcolm's opportunism and his deep commitment, his ordeal of corruption and his sacrifice in blood, his evident ambition and its accompanying self denial. The reading we seek does not lie "somewhere between" the two so far proposed, but is generated out of them. Because it must be approached in a dialectical fashion, the view now proposed takes its support not only from the direct evidence of the text, but also from the evident clash of two persuasive but conflicting readings.

3

At the first level, our proposed final or synthetic reading is simple: Malcolm's life is a drama of enlargement. In this view, Malcolm is a gifted but flawed man whose natural powers and sympathies undergo a gradual but powerful opening up to embrace wider scenes of action and larger groups of people. What makes Malcolm's life a drama—an enactment of conflict—rather than a mere growth, is the presence of racism, the agency of constriction, domination, and injustice. We reject the figure of growth because it is essentially passive, suggesting the involuntary fulfillment of a destiny. What is important about Malcolm is his achievement through willed action and reflection, in the face of hostile forces. Malcolm, in this view, is not a creature of circumstantial corruption, nor is he a Sisyphean figure whose life takes on a mythical distance from the immediate scene. He is a man in conflict with a condition whose nature he comes to understand and transcend as motive passes from his environment to him. Such a view, if we can accept it, gives Malcolm's life a continuity that may be extended beyond his death, and it reconciles our two previous readings.

Given this reading, the elements of fanaticism and hustlerism in his early career do not detract from Malcolm's credibility, but rather lend authenticity to a humanism which, alone, might seem anemic.

If Malcolm's life as a pimp and hustler, as a black nationalist rabble-rouser, and as a spokesman for human brotherhood can be seen as the general unfolding of a consistent pattern, then the *Autobiography* has succeeded as rhetoric, signaling the response to a human institution of which racism is the most pressing extension. Malcolm would thus not have to be dismissed as a frantic true believer or elevated—another form of dismissal—as a sainted scapegoat of racist America. Rather, he could be read as a gifted leader of men who develops a rhetoric transcending racism, a rhetoric of human purpose and brotherhood. Most importantly, perhaps, the reading gives us the principle behind Malcolm's "changes," which are now seen as consistent steps forward rather than as random and untrustworthy conversions by faith. Malcolm's readers are not reduced to admiring him; they can pick up where he left off.

As Malcolm came to understand that racism had caused him to act as he had, its power to control his actions passed over to him. Motive, previously located in his condition, was now in the hands of a conscious agent. With the *Autobiography,* Malcolm shares that motive with his readers, giving them a principle of action they can carry into the confrontation with racism as it conditions their own lives.

Thus far we have shown that to explain Malcolm's *Autobiography* as a drama of enlargement will plausibly synthesize variant readings and suggest the source of the book's power over readers. But every critical reading must pass a further test. If the notion of enlargement is to be useful, it must help us to open up the text. This it can do in a variety of ways.

First, enlargement is the pattern of Malcolm's career itself. Starting as a small-time hustler, whose power was active but restricted, Malcolm sought wider and wider stages for his actions. Moving from Michigan to Boston to Harlem to black nationalism, pan-Islamism, and the United Nations, Malcolm also enlarged his loyalties from self and family to gang, race, religion, and all mankind. Seen in this light, Malcolm's sense of brotherhood with all men is not the weakening of militancy or a softening of commitment, but an extension of potency.

The force against which Malcolm's power grew and exercised itself was racism, which Malcolm came to understand in broader terms as but the central manifestation of injustice and domination. Where racism appeared simply as the condition denying Malcolm money and prestige, he could combat it by conking his hair and resorting to a life of crime. Where racism was conceived as an institution created by white oppressors, he could turn to black nationalism. And where racism grew to appear as the symptom of a disease afflicting a social system, Malcolm could look for the healing power of revolution and social redemption.

Supporting the movement of Malcolm's life to ever larger stages is a counter-theme of thwarted growth. Before his two most important changes, Malcolm was placed temporarily in positions of impotency or confinement. It was while he was in prison that he converted to the Islamism of the Black Muslims, and later it was during an enforced silence imposed by Elijah Muhammad that Malcolm incubated his transformation into the larger world of a pilgrimage to Mecca, a political tour of Africa, and a return to America as the potential leader of an extended search for racial justice. And of course racism itself appears throughout the work in all of its forms as a constricting element that invites conflict and growth. Counter theme reinforces theme, thwarted power grows into larger power.

The pattern of enlargement is imitated in the structure of the chapters of the *Autobiography* as well as in its major movements. Typically, a chapter opens with a narrative section, which then gives way to a series of amplifications or generalizations on a theme growing out of the narrative. Chapter Three, "Homeboy," narrates Malcolm's first days in Boston and Roxbury, leading to a description of his first conk, applied by his friend Shorty. The chapter ends with an extended peroration depicting the hair-straightening process as a self-defacement, a natural product of racism. And along the way, even during the narration, there extends out from concrete particulars the larger world of values suggested by the vocabulary of a racist society: black, white, Crispus Attucks, Uncle Tom.

An early paragraph illustrates the book's movement, a movement repeated at the levels of sentence, paragraph, chapter, and section. Malcolm is describing his father, as remembered from his earliest years:

It was in his role as a preacher that my father had most contact with the Negroes of Lansing. Believe me when I tell you that those Negroes were in bad shape then. They are still in bad shape—though in a different way. By that I mean that I don't know a town with a higher percentage of complacent and misguided so-called "middle-class" Negroes—the typical status-symbol-oriented, integration-seeking type of Negroes. Just recently, I was standing in a lobby at the United Nations talking with an African ambassador and his wife, when a Negro came up to me and said, "You know me?" I was a little embarrassed because I thought he was someone I should remember. It turned out that he was one of those bragging, self-satisfied, "middle-class" Lansing Negroes. I wasn't ingratiated. He was the type who would never have been associated with Africa, until the fad of having African friends became a status-symbol for "middle-class" Negroes.[38]

This paragraph is worth our close attention. Here a recollection from his early childhood leads Malcolm to a larger theme which then incorporates an enlarged temporal scheme as he speaks directly from a later point in time (the incident at the United Nations did not happen, say, "many years later," in the usual formula for such things, but "just recently"). We note also that we are again in the presence of what at first appears as Malcolm's own snobbery, but by the end of the paragraph his worries about his own status, no doubt stirred by bitter memories of early snubs, have been transcended by turning the tables and by referring to the wider themes of Africa, the United Nations, and the fight against racism. The paragraph displays enlargement both as a dispositional strategy and as a struggle to confess and work from his own confining concern for status and retribution towards a principle of active change.

Malcolm's choice of figures is also governed by themes of growth and their contraries. Chapter Fifteen is climaxed by the image of Icarus, who reminds Malcolm that however high he flies his wings were supplied by Islam.[39] Earlier in the chapter, describing a period when he was at the peak of his success as a minister of Elijah Muhammad, and therefore just about to leave the brotherhood, Malcolm devotes a section to his relations with the press: "I developed a mental image of reporters as human ferrets—steadily sniffing, darting, probing for some way to trick me, somehow to corner me in our interview exchanges."[40] The image goes no further, and Malcolm instead continues by illustrating how he outwitted the press. Yet if the reporters were ferrets, Malcolm implies that he saw himself as a burrowing prey, retreating into a dark tunnel from which he was soon to emerge in a new form.[41]

What bothered Malcolm most about prison were the bars, the visible sign of his confinement. "Any person who claims to have a deep feeling for other human beings should think a long, long time before he votes to have other men kept behind bars—caged. I am not saying there shouldn't be prisons, but there shouldn't be bars. Behind bars, a man never reforms. He will never forget. He never will get completely over the memory of the bars."[42]

Later, when he had converted to Islam while in prison, Malcolm began to study, educating himself from the prison library. "Anyone who has read a great deal can imagine the new world that opened. . . . Months passed without my even thinking of being imprisoned. In fact, up to then, I had never been so truly free in my life."[43] And still later, when Malcolm undertook his Hajj pilgrimage, he arrived in Cairo, and "the effect was as though I had just stepped out of a prison."[44]

But there is more to the theme of enlargement and confinement than images, for Malcolm's *Autobiography* goes beyond the closed world of literary form towards the open forum of rhetorical address. The relation of the theme of confinement to the predicament of American blacks is stated clearly in the following passage: "Human rights! Respect as human beings! That's what America's black masses want. That's the true problem. The black masses want not to be shrunk from as though they are plague-ridden. They want not to be walled up in slums, in the ghettos, like animals. They want to live in an open, free society where they can walk with their heads up, like men, and women!"[45]

When speaking to black audiences in the last year of his life, Malcolm went beyond the Islamic faith "to embrace all who sat before me."[46] He was, he said, "for whoever and whatever benefits humanity *as a whole*."[47] In the face of opposition and harassment, he declared that he was against "strait-jacketed thinking, and strait-jacketed societies."[48]

Malcolm's *Autobiography* is constructed in terms of the contradictions between open and closed, constriction and enlargement, confinement and action. The dialectical structure of the book is a major rhetorical accomplishment, since it allows Malcolm to transcend the challenges which his own life in the context of a secular and a racist society posed to his credibility and relevance.[49]

After he left Elijah Muhammad, in the last three chapters of the *Autobiography,* Malcolm's images change, to become variations on the concept of healing, with Malcolm seeking a symbol to reconcile an intensified religiosity and a growing sense of the need for secular action. He speaks of racism as a disease, a metaphor that for him makes possible a symbolic transcendence in which violence is weighed as a radical surgery for the "cancer" which grips America—an America which he no longer hates but now seeks to mend. The image of cancer itself becomes especially meaningful when we see it in the light of Malcolm's theme of enlargement, where it takes on resonances of the perverted growth of an evil and uncontrolled malignancy. The dialectical symmetry of the cancer metaphor is, in context, unmistakable.[50]

These final themes are not resolved, nor had Malcolm, at the end of his life, yet found a perfectly unified and straightforward synthesis for the contradictions of his life. But he had found the principle of synthesis in his actions, and had set it forth in a pattern of symbols that, like his own life, possesses the capacity to evolve.

I have not attempted a full critical exploration of the immensely rich rhetorical works of Malcolm X. Rather, I have addressed the preliminary question of how to account for Malcolm's enduring influence by suggesting the presence in *The Autobiography of Malcolm X* of a dialectical rhetoric, in which a drama of enlargement saves Malcolm from being dismissed as a fanatic, a charlatan, or an existential anti-hero, and instead renders his life as the embodiment of a principle of rhetorical action. And the form of action Malcolm achieves in the *Autobiography* transcends the rhetorical fractions of which we spoke at the beginning of this essay. If we see hustling as a parody of rhetorical Doing, fanaticism as a corruption of rhetorical Knowing, and existential sainthood as a variation of rhetorical Being, we are able to see the *Autobiography* as a synthesizing act which resolves and transcends the fractions, producing a fully rhetorical action to which Being (and becoming), Knowing, and Doing contribute equally.

Malcolm has created a work which is formally consistent, authentically autobiographical, and yet rhetorically effective. Symbolically, Malcolm continually enlarges his powers and sympathies; dialectically, Malcolm's recurrent changes are shown to be transcendent movements which reconcile his own contradictory masks as hustler, religious mystic, and existential rebel, and the polarities of America's ordeal of racism; rhetorically, Malcolm seizes motive from the scene and makes it available to his readers, who are invited to assume their roles as actors in the drama of enlargement and reconciliation.

Confinement and enlargement. In *The Autobiography of Malcolm X* these are the symbolic vehicles for an essentially rhetorical mode of knowing, being, and doing in the world. They stand as the symbols for Malcolm's discovery of himself through the act of addressing his fellow men. As Malcolm's sphere of action, a rhetorical sphere, enlarges, as he seeks in return to rob, hustle, convert, and join in brotherhood with ever larger constituencies, there is a parallel enlargement of his world view. At the end of his life, the Malcolm of the *Autobiography* stands at the threshold of both power and vision. Some men grow by appropriating the power and space of other men and women. Malcolm X, born Malcolm Little and assassinated as Brother Malcolm, El-Hajj Malik Shabazz, was one of those rare men the growth of whose power was consistently accompanied by a growing vision of freedom and brotherhood for all people.

Notes

1. Thomas W. Benson and Gerard A. Hauser, "Ideals, Superlatives, and the Decline of Hypocrisy," *QJS*, 59 (Feb. 1973), 99–105; Lloyd F. Bitzer, "The Rhetorical Situation," *Philosophy and Rhetoric*, 1 (Win. 1968), 1–14; Kenneth Burke, *A Rhetoric of Motives (1950; rpt. Berkeley: Univ. of California Press, 1969);* Richard B. Gregg, "The Ego-Function of the Rhetoric of Protest," *Philosophy and Rhetoric*, 4 (Spr. 1971), 71–91; Gerard A. Hauser, "Rhetoric as a Way of Knowing," *Today's Speech*, 19 (Win. 1971), 43–48; Robert L. Scott, "A Rhetoric of Facts: Arthur Larson's Stance as a Persuader," *Speech Monographs*, 35 (June 1968), 109–121; Alexander Sesonske, "Saying, Being, and Freedom of Speech," *Philosophy and Rhetoric*, 1 (Win. 1968), 25–37; Herbert Wichelns, "The Literary Criticism of Oratory," *The Rhetorical Idiom*, ed. Donald C. Bryant (Ithaca, New York: Cornell Univ. Press, 1958), pp. 5–42.

2. Similarly, a rhetorical critic may place major emphasis upon any one or more of the relationships present in the rhetorical event, at one time assessing the causal force exerted by the act, at another following the form of the act itself, the actor, or for example, the relation between act and agency. See Lawrence W. Rosenfield, "The Anatomy of Critical Discourse," *Speech Monographs,* 35 (March 1968), 50–69.

3. Malcolm X [Malcolm Little] with the assistance of Alex Haley, *The Autobiography of Malcolm X* (1965; rpt. New York: Grove Press, 1966). Hereinafter referred to as *Autobiography.*

4. Herbert W. Simons, "Requirements, Problems, and Strategies: A Theory of Persuasion for Social Movements," *QJS,* 56 (Feb. 1970), 6–7.

5. *Autobiography,* p. 354.

6. *The Rhetoric of the Civil-Rights Movements,* ed. Haig A. Bosmajian and Hamida Bosmajian (New York: Random House, 1969), pp. 70, 77, 84, 86. Cf. Robert D. Brooks and Thomas M. Scheidel, "Speech as Process: A Case Study," *Speech Monographs,* 35 (Mar. 1968), 1–7.

7. *Autobiography,* pp. 253–254.

8. *Ibid.,* pp. 269–270.

9. *Ibid.,* p. 273.

10. Bosmajian and Bosmajian, pp. 76–77.

11. *Autobiography,* pp. 3, 281–287.

12. *Ibid.,* p. 345; see also pp. 195–196.

13. *Ibid.,* p. 155.

14. *Ibid.,* p. 381.

15. *Ibid.,* pp. 446–447.

16. *Ibid.,* pp. 186–187.

17. *Ibid.,* p. 188; see also p. 295.

18. *Ibid.,* p. 296. But near the end Malcolm says he sees the danger of ascribing divinity to Elijah Muhammad or any human, including, by implication, himself. *Ibid.,* p. 365.

19. *Ibid.,* p. 149.

20. *Ibid.,* p. 148.

21. *Ibid.,* p. 365.

22. *Ibid.,* p. 320.

23. *Ibid.,* p. 322.

24. *Ibid.,* p. 307.

25. Ibid., p. 333. And later he speaks of the trip home. "The Pan American jet which took me home—it was Flight 115 $[1 + 1 + 5 = 7]$—landed at New York's Kennedy Air Terminal on May 21, at 4:25 in the afternoon" [May, the fifth month, plus $2 = 7; 2 + 1 + 4 = 7; 2 + 5 = 7$]. *Ibid.,* p. 360. The Muslim mysticism in these passages is compounded with Malcolm's former experience as a numbers runner. *Ibid.,* pp. 84–85.

26. *Ibid.,* p. 375.

27. *Ibid.,* p. 365.

28. *Ibid.,* p. 170.

29. *Ibid.,* p. 289. On the theme of action, existentialism, and oppressed peoples, see also Lionel Abel, "Sartre vs. Lévi-Strauss:" *Claude Lévi-Strauss: The Anthropologist as Hero,* ed. E. Nelson Hayes and Tanya Hayes (Cambridge, Mass: The M.I.T. Press, 1970), pp. 235–246.

30. Thomas W. Benson, "Violence: Communication Breakdown?" *Today's Speech,* 18 (Win. 1970), 46. Alfred Kazin writes of Malcolm's *Autobiography* that "the book is an astonishing example in our time of autobiography as a religious pilgrimage, of a man seeking his way up from his personal darkness to some personal light." "The World as a Novel: From Capote to Mailer," *The New York Review of Books,* 8 Apr. 1971, p. 28.

31. Wayne Booth, *The Rhetoric of Fiction* (Chicago: Univ. of Chicago Press, 1961); see also Hugh D. Duncan, *Communication and Social Order* (London: Oxford Univ. Press, 1962); Edward P. J. Corbett, ed., *Rhetorical Analyses of Literary Works* (London: Oxford Univ. Press, 1969); and the works of Kenneth Burke.

32. See Maurianne Adams, *Autobiography* (Indianapolis: Bobbs-Merrill, 1968), p. 5. See also James M. Osborn, *The Beginnings of Autobiography in England* (Los Angeles: William Andrews Clark Memorial Library, n. d.), pp. 3–4.

33. Roy Pascal, *Design and Truth in Autobiography* (London: Routledge & Kegan Paul, 1960), p. 185.

34. *Ibid.,* p. 182.

35. "That's Life," *The New York Review of Books.* 17 June 1971, p. 3.

36. *Adams,* p. 5.

37. *Ibid.,* p. 5. But compare Leo Lowenthal, *Literature and the Image of Man* (Boston: Beacon Press, 1957), pp. ix-x: "Memoirs, autobiographies, diaries, and letters might be offered as sources of data at least as personal and specific as the contents of imaginative literature. In such personal documents, however, rationalization and particularly, self justification often blur or distort the image of social reality. It is the artist who portrays what is more real than reality itself."

38. *Autobiography,* p. 5.

39. *Ibid.,* pp. 287, 291–292.

40. *Ibid.* p. 269.

41. The ferret imagery also appears in *Ibid.,* p. 109.

42. *Ibid.,* p. 152.

43. *Ibid.,* pp. 172–173.

44. *Ibid,* p. 321. See also pp. 205–206, where Malcolm quotes Elijah to the effect that "the Bible's words were a locked door, that could be unlocked, if only we knew how."

45. *Ibid.,* p. 272.

46. *Ibid.,* p. 364.

47. *Ibid.,* p. 366.

48. *Ibid.,* p. 372.

49. He had not, even at the end of his life, entirely resolved his difficulties. He said to Alex Haley in 1965, of other black leaders: "They won't let me turn the corner! . . . I'm caught in a trap!" *Autobiography,* p. 424. Cf. Simons, pp. 6–7.

50. *Autobiography* pp. 341, 379, 382. Cf. Edwin Black, "The Second Persona," *QJS,* 56 (Apr. 1970), 109–119.

Rhetorical Implications of Shakespeare's Changes in His Source Material for *Romeo and Juliet*

Jill Taft-Kaufman

The story of doomed love upon which Shakespeare based *Romeo and Juliet* can be traced to the third century A.D. One Xenophon of Ephesus, a writer of Greek romance, produced a work titled *Ephesiaca* which contains plot elements similar to those in Shakespeare's play. Later, Renaissance writers revived the theme of star-crossed lovers, reworked it, and presented it to reading audiences several years before Shakespeare wrote his famous play.[1] Past critics have disagreed about which of these previous versions Shakespeare read before writing his play,[2] but in recent years there has been consensus that he relied upon Arthur Brooke's long narrative poem, "The Tragicall Historye of Romeus and Juliet."[3]

Critics agree that the changes Shakespeare made while transforming a narrative poem into a play turn the work into a more engrossing tale. Notable among these changes are the compression of time in the story from several months to four days, and the change of Juliet's age from sixteen to thirteen.[4] These two major changes draw the audience into the play in a way the poem never did, and critics have thus studied them as early indications of Shakespeare's skill at creating an absorbing dramatic experience for his audience. Largely ignored, however, are those more subtle transformations that were not made out of dramatic necessity. These changes create effects that are equally crucial to the play's impact and to potential audience response. Awareness of these other changes and their patterning in the play can illuminate *Romeo and Juliet* as a compelling illustration of Shakespeare's emerging skill at controlling his material to gain maximum rhetorical effect.[5]

Shakespeare usually departed from his source material in such major ways that comparing source to play often provides little more than an illustration of different uses of the same story. *King Lear*, for example, resembles the earlier *Leir* (1594), only vaguely, despite certain common plot elements. Likewise, Shakespeare's deviations from *The Taming of a Shrew* (between 1592 and 1594), in *The Taming of the Shrew* are so numerous that, again, examining the two side by side merely provides an example of comparative use of the same theme. When Shakespeare composed *Romeo and Juliet,* however, he preserved much more of his source, adopting nearly every plot element from Brooke's narrative. Consequently, the changes that he did make stand out in bold relief. Clearly some changes were made to facilitate the move from one genre to another: to transpose a poem into a work for the stage. Yet the difference between Shakespeare's play and Brooke's poem is not just one of genre. The changes create a radically different work which invite audience response in substantially different ways.

In this essay, I shall describe and interpret the rhetorical significance of the five primary changes that Shakespeare made from Brooke's material, changes which transcend those of mere theatrical necessity. These include: 1) changes in the development of major characters through the use of distinct styles of diction to suggest individual character thought; 2) changes in the development of major characters through speeches which emphasize character attitude; 3) changes in the development of foil characters and the addition of new foils; 4) imposition of explicit inter-character assessment of Romeo through the dialogue of various characters; and 5) four small but significant plot modifications that are closely linked with changes in character. The effect of these changes, as we shall see, is to do more than arouse anxiety and elicit pity for the lovers—the end of Brooke's narrative. Instead, the audience is invited to recognize the stylized information and behavior provided by the playwright, and to respond critically and emotionally to the artistic and rhetorical pattern developed.

"Romeus and Juliet" as Shakespeare Found It

The story line of Brooke's poem re-emerges with few changes in Shakespeare's play. The poem's young hero is persuaded to forget an unrequited love affair by going to a dance held at the home of a family whose members are enemies of his own household. At the dance he meets the daughter of his enemy. Their romance gradually flourishes, and after a few weeks they are secretly married, with the aid of a garrulous nurse who delights in trickery and a wise friar who is a friend to both their houses.

After several more weeks, during which the lovers continue to meet secretly, Romeus is forced to kill his wife's maniacal cousin in self-defense. For this act, he is banished to Mantua, where his life is tolerable in spite of his separation from Juliet.

Juliet, who is betrothed to another by her parents, finds her requests for immediate help from Romeus unanswered and takes a sleeping potion given to her by the Friar. News of her "death" brings Romeus back to Verona, where he consumes poison purchased from an apothecary. Upon awakening in her family tomb, Juliet learns from the Friar that Romeus is dead, and while the Friar runs from the tomb in fright, Juliet kills herself. The Friar, who must defend himself against charges of murder, tells the story of the lovers, is pardoned, and spends the rest of his life in seclusion. The Nurse is banished and the apothecary hanged. The deaths of the lovers bring an end to the enmity between the Capulets and Montagues.

At first there seems to be no question about the ostensible aim of Brooke's tale. He promises the reader a story of culpability and its consequences, one that suggests that his characters are responsible for their actions. In a brief introduction, Brooke tells the reader to expect a story about:

> a coople of unfortunate lovers, thralling themselves to unhonest desire, neglecting the authoritie and advise of parents and frendes, conferring their principall counsels with dronken gossyppes, and superstitious friers (the naturally fitte instruments of unchastitie) attemptyng all adventures of peryll, for thattaynyng of their wished lust, usyng auriculer confession (the kay of whoredome, and treason) for furtheraunce of theyre purpose, abusyng the honorable name of lawefull marriage, the [sic] cloke the shame of stolne contracts, finallye, by all meanes of unhonest lyfe, hastyng to most unhappy deathe.[6]

What the reader discovers in the next eighty pages of the poem itself, however, is that the expectations aroused by this introduction are entirely reversed. Brooke is not only sympathetic to his characters, but he tells a tale in which they are not responsible for their lives. The reader comes to know them as passive creatures, manipulated and controlled by events, situations, and stresses against which they have no choice but to submit and react. Brooke's proposed saga illustrating "evil actes of the wicked" becomes instead a story in which the actions of the characters are only reactions to fate. Thus, it is not surprising that Brooke's work evidences little character development. What need has the reader for understanding well-developed motivation and thoughts of characters who will not be acting as a result of interior motivation or thought? Portraits of Brooke's characters take shape as much from descriptions of external qualities and actions as from narration of the slender substance inside of them. Romeus is respected for his beardless beauty; Tybalt is recognized by his "body tall and strong" (366), his intentions forecast by his "strayned voice and mouth outstretched" (368); and Mercutio is distinguished only by his cold hands.

While the narrative is liberally sprinkled with characters' speeches and dialogues, the style of these utterances does not differentiate the personalities who speak them. In the following exchange, for example, the substance of what the two speakers say differs, but the styles of their diction and their tones suggest that Romeus, the speaker who poses the rhetorical question, is essentially of the same temperament as the friend who responds to him with another rhetorical question:

Romeus: What booteth me to love and serve a fell unthankfull one,
               With that my humble sute and labour sowede in vayne,
               Can reape none other fruite at all but scorne and proude disdayne? (77–80)

Friend:	What meanst thou Romeus (quote he) what doting rage
	Dooth make thee thus consume away, the best part of thine age,
	In seking her that scornes, and hydes her from thy sight,
	For forsing all thy great expence, ne yet thy honor bright. . .
	(105–108).

Not only do the characters speak similarly to one another in diction and tone, but they also speak much like the narrator.[7] When the narrator shifts from presenting Romeus's confessed misery about his unrequited love to the story teller's own description of the young man's state, for example, there is little tone change or stylistic alteration other than that from first person to third person:

Romeus:	Perhaps mine eye once banished by absence from her sight,
	This frye of myne, [sic] that her pleasant eyne is fed
	Shall little and little weare away, and quite at last be ded.
	But whilest he did decree this purpose still to kepe,
	A contrary repugnant thought sanke in his brest so depe
	That doutefull is he now which of the twayne is best (86–91).

This uniformity of style among as well as between characters and narrator allows dialogue to serve the same purpose as narration and description: it primarily reports events rather than revealing the nature of distinctive personalities. Even when characters speak about themselves, the substance of what they have to say minimizes personal thought, feeling, and motivation. In Brooke's poem, character description and ostensible self-disclosure are used simply to facilitate the unfolding of a sequence of dire incidents which strike the lovers through no fault of their own.

Shakespeare's play, on the other hand, presents to the audience a cause and effect relationship between character, action, and consequence. Although in the Prologue he promises "star-crossed"[8] lovers, in the play itself, Shakespeare rhetorically presents the characters in such a way that the audience is invited to perceive them as having a good measure of control over what happens to their lives.[9]

Distinct Styles of Diction and the Development of Character Thought

Shakespeare develops audience understanding of cause and effect in *Romeo and Juliet* as he develops character. Towards that end, one of the major changes he makes in Brooke's material is to give each of the seven primary figures in the story a distinctive style of diction.[10] Distinct styles of diction, and the thought reflected by these styles, emerge as soon as the first two major characters, Tybalt and Benvolio, appear. Tybalt's diction is composed of terse *epithets*. The *epithet* (a characterizing word or phrase which may accompany or replace the name of an object, event, or person) may be used to elevate or disparage a person. In this instance, Tybalt's abusive epithets demean those around him and indicate hasty passion as a motive for action. Seeing Benvolio using his sword, he yells:

What, art thou drawn among these heartless hinds?
Turn thee,
Benvolio, and look upon thy death. . . (1.1.73–74)
Have at thee coward! (1.1.77–79)[11]

The style of Benvolio's response, in which Shakespeare emphasizes the *distributio,* suggests a syntax of rationality. He tells Tybalt, "I do but keep the peace; put up thy sword/ Or manage it to part these men with me" (1.1.75–76).

Distributios, or the divisions of concepts or actions and apportioning of their parts, come to distinguish Benvolio in nearly all his appearances. Forever considering an alternative to a thought or an action, he is seen urging Romeo to seek a woman against whom to compare Rosaline, and when Romeo protests, the thoughtful Benvolio vows, "I'll pay that doctrine, or else die in debt" (1.1.244). In the lull before the death-charged fight of Act Three, it is Benvolio who distributes reasons for leaving the streets: ". . . good Mercutio, let's retire:/ The day is hot, the Capulets abroad,/ And, if we meet, we shall not 'scape a brawl' " (3.1.1–3). When the Capulets do indeed appear and the entire group verges on conflict, it is again Benvolio who is made to appear rational, not only by what he says, but by how he says it. Clearly he distributes the choices for the bellicose Mercutio and Tybalt. "We talk here in the public haunt of men./ Either withdraw unto some private place,/ Or reason coldly of your grievances,/ Or else depart" (3.1.53–56).

The *epithets* which predominate in Tybalt's opening speech characterize that persona in his brief stay in the action. Although we see him only twice more, both of those occasions are ones in which he reduces Romeo, the object of his hatred, to a series of names that suggest Romeo is worthy of that hatred and contempt. On hearing Romeo's voice at the Capulet ball, Tybalt's dialogue with his uncle reflects his desire to categorize Romeo as objectionable:

Tybalt:	Uncle, this is a Montague, our foe;
	A villain. . .
Capulet:	Young Romeo is it?
Tybalt:	'Tis he, that villain Romeo.
Capulet:	Content thee, gentle coz, let him alone, . . .
	Show a fair presence and put off these frowns,
	An ill-beseeming semblance for a feast.
Tybalt:	It fits, when such a villain is a guest:
	I'll not endure him (1.5.63–77).

When we see Tybalt again for the next and last time in Act Three, it is once again the *epithet* that marks him as a character who desires to reduce his enemy from a person to a name, the better that he might attack him:

"Romeo, . . . thou art a villain" (3.1.63–64). When Romeo responds, ultimately by a swearing of revenge for Mercutio's death, Tybalt reduces his opponent to a new insulting tag: "Boy" (3.1.69), . . . and later: "Thou, wretched boy" (3.1.134).

Having established Benvolio's rationality and Tybalt's hot-headed passion as extremes of attitude in the play, Shakespeare creates an array of character stances in-between in which the diction implicitly suggests to the audience how the character will behave. This connection between diction, thought, and behavior is particularly significant as it applies to Romeo. For that lover, Shakespeare fashions a style of expression that revolves around three primary figures of speech: *hyperbole* (exaggeration), *oxymoron* (a paradox in which contradictions are linked as adjective-noun phrases), and *personification*. Romeo's first lengthy exclamation in the play, for example, describes the hazards of love through heavy reliance upon *personification* and *oxymoron*:

Alas, that love, whose view is muffled still,
Should without eyes see pathways to his will! . . .
Why, then O brawling love! O loving hate! . . .
Feather of lead, bright smoke, cold fire, sick health!
Still-waking sleep, that is not what it is!
This love feel I, that feel no love in this (1.1.177–187).[12]

In fact, while Romeo is smitten with Rosaline, nearly every speech out of his mouth functions to reveal to us that it is the idea of love and not Rosaline herself that appeals to him. Whether he is describing love as "A choking gall and a preserving sweet" (1.1.200), claiming that in his Rosaline's vow to forswear loving that he lives "dead," or maintaining to Benvolio that his love is so fair that the "all-seeing sun/ Ne'er saw her match since first the world begun" (1.2.97–98), Romeo is revealed to us as a young man who is using language to convince himself and others that he is indeed a lover.

Shakespeare sustains Romeo's use of *hyperbole, oxymoron,* and *personification* and the Petrarchan sentiments they convey as the object of Romeo's love switches from Rosaline to Juliet. In response to Juliet's simple questioning of Romeo at her balcony, for example, the reply Romeo gives is filled with *personification* and *hyperbole*:

Juliet: By whose direction found'st thou out this place?
Romeo: By love, that first did prompt me to inquire;
          He lent me counsel, and I lent him eyes,
          I am no pilot; yet, wert thou as far
          As that vast shore wash'd with the farthest sea,
          I would adventure for such merchandise" (2.2.79–84).

Shakespeare invites the audience to tune its ear to the familiar strains of the conventional lover, similar to the ones Romeo emitted when in love with Rosaline.

We get a stronger sense of the characteristic thought that Shakespeare was creating for Romeo, however, if we turn to the last act of the play. Romeo's warning to his servant reflects the extremes to which his emotion has carried him. In a rush of hasty fury, he vows to Balthasar:

. . . . if thou, jealous, dost return to pry
In what I farther shall intend to do.
By heaven, I will tear thee joint by joint
And strew this hungry churchyard with thy limbs;
The time and my intents are savage-wild,
More fierce and more inexorable far
Than empty tigers or the roaring sea (5.3.33–39).

The speech, like so many of Romeo's, revolves around *hyperbole*. Yet here, the hyperbolic has become an extreme that defines the dramatic situation. Shakespeare presents us with a Romeo who does indeed seem wild enough to kill someone, and in fact, does take the life of Paris. Shakespeare moves our perception of Romeo from that of a character whose language alone conveys the identity he seeks, to one whose language is matched by extreme action— murder and suicide.

Shakespeare also continues his heavy use of *personification* in Romeo's final speeches. Through the extended use of *personification*, Shakespeare has fashioned both the excited elation and frantic despair of the lover whose passions make the world and every quality and state in it seem intensely alive to him. Indeed, Romeo's entire final utterance is an *apostrophe* or address to Death, who is personified as both an advancing conqueror and an amorous contender for Juliet against whom Romeo will prevail: "For here lies Juliet, and her beauty makes / This vault a feasting presence full of light./ Death, lie thou there, by a dead man interr'd" (5.385–87). This final speech, as well as Romeo's extolling of the tomb that holds Juliet as a "triumphant grave" (5.3.83), reveals that the conventional *oxymorons* which characterized Romeo's early speeches have matured into statements that capture the paradoxical nature of a love that can be preserved perfectly only by death. Shakespeare's abandonment of the shallow *oxymoron* for the use of *paradox* in Romeo's final lines suggests a character who has grown to recognize one of the apparent contradictions of experience. In this instance, a tomb still holds life for him. For the audience, the significance of this *paradox* is underscored by the irony it captures since they are well aware that Juliet looks alive because she *is* alive.

For Juliet, Shakespeare creates, at first, a style of speech that is, for the most part, direct and simple. Once Juliet falls in love with Romeo, however, that direct diction changes to a style that echoes Romeo's. The balcony scene serves as a useful illustration of this change. It begins with Juliet's concern for Romeo, voiced in questions and practical statements with little rhetorical adornment:

How cam'st thou hither, tell me, and wherefore?
The orchard walls are high and hard to climb,
And the place, death, considering who thou art,
If any of my kinsmen find thee here. (2.2.62–64). . .
If they do see thee, they will murder thee. (2.2.70). . .
I would not for the world they saw thee here. (2.2.74). . .
O, swear not by the moon, th' inconstant moon. (2.2.109). . .
Do not swear at all; (2.2.113)

The plainness of Juliet's diction reflects her practical concern for Romeo's safety and her worry over the evanescence of a love that lies in words alone. By the end of the scene, however, at Romeo's insistence on professing love in an extreme manner, Juliet indulges in the *hyperbole* and *personification* that show her new abandonment to emotion:

Bondage is hoarse, and may not speak aloud;
Else would I tear the cave where Echo lies,
And make her airy tongue more hoarse than mine,
With repetition of 'my Romeo!' (2.2.161–64)

As the play continues, Juliet's style of diction becomes an extension of her lover's. Shakespeare draws the audience into the cohesion and the urgency of the union by diminishing the initial differences he had carefully created.

The three remaining major characters—Mercutio, the Nurse, and the Friar—are also imbued with their own ways of speaking that serve to crystalize the quality of their thought and distinguish it from Romeo's. For Mercutio, Shakespeare's major device is the *pun* which presumes, as one scholar points out, "a realization of the ambiguous relationship between language and experience that is generally a Renaissance phenomenon. . . . When it is not merely a conversational tic, it functions to control discourse indirectly."[13] While Mercutio is too bold a creation to seem indirect, his discourses with Romeo concerning love do reduce the high blown sentiments of his friend to the more easily circumscribable notion of sex:

Romeo:	Under love's heavy burthen do I sink.
Mercutio:	And, to sink in it, should you burthen love;
	Too great oppression for a tender thing.
Romeo:	Is love a tender thing? it is too rough
	Too rude, too boisterous, and it pricks like thorn.
Mercutio:	If love be rough with you, be rough with love;
	Prick love for pricking, and you beat love down (1.3.22–28).

In short, Mercutio is not impressed with the conventional ploys of eloquent passion behind which he perceives that "drivelling love . . . runs lolling up and down to hide his bauble in a hole" (2.4.97–98). It is only when Romeo engages in some highly structured punning with him (2.4.56–91), that Mercutio acknowledges in his friend the control over speech and behavior that he admires— "Why, is not this better, now than groaning for love? now art thou sociable, now art thou Romeo" (2.4.92–93).

Shakespeare balances Mercutio's cynicism by infusing him with a passion that is as extreme as Romeo's passion for love. Mercutio's flamboyant bellicosity knows no control. To parade that portion of Mercutio's nature, Shakespeare once again makes use of the *epithet*. The *epithet* for Mercutio functions as it did for Tybalt and as it usually does in conflict; calling people names dehumanizes them until they become mere name, a target deserving of destruction. As Tybalt reduces Romeo, likewise Mercutio reduces Tybalt. "Why, what is Tybalt?" Benvolio queries (2.4.18), and Mercutio replies, "More than prince of cats, I can tell you . . . the very butcher of a silk button . . . the pox of such antic, lisping, affecting fantasticoes; . . ." (2.4.19–29). And to Tybalt's face, he spews out enough names to provoke the fight he wants:

Mercutio: Tybalt, you rat-catcher, will you walk?
Tybalt: What wouldst thou have of me?
Mercutio: Good king of cats, nothing but one of your nine lives (3.1–78–80).

In his last moments alive on the stage, it is not surprising that Mercutio exercises his control over the situation and his contempt for Tybalt through the *pun* and the *epithet:*

Ask for me to-morrow, and you shall find me a grave man.
I am peppered, I warrant, for this world— . . . Zounds, a dog,
a rat, a mouse, a cat, to scratch a man to death! a braggart,
a rogue, a villain . . . (3.1.101–106).

The Nurse, who imprints upon the play a loquacious color to rival Mercutio's, is drawn linguistically primarily by Shakespeare's use of *repetition,* particularly of sexual innuendos. Our introduction to her, as she recalls Juliet's childhood, amply indicates her effusive bawdiness:

And then my husband-God be with his soul!
A was a merry man-took up the child:
'Yea,' quoth he, 'dost thou fall upon thy face?
Thou wilt fall backward when thou hast more wit;
Wilt thou not, Jule?' and, by my holy-dam,
The pretty wretch left crying, and said 'Ay.' . . .
I never should forget it: 'Wilt thou not Jule?' quoth he;
And, pretty fool, it stinted, and said 'Ay.' . . .
To think it should leave crying, and say 'Ay:' . . .
'Yea,' quoth my husband, ;'fall'st upon thy face?
Thou wilt fall backward when thou comes to age;
Wilt thou not, Jule?' it stinted, and said 'Ay' (1.3.39–57).

Finally, Shakespeare develops Friar Lawrence, that figure some critics see as the voice of reason in the play,[14] by endowing him with repeated aphoristic statements. These statements are expressed primarily in a form in which reason is condensed to an easily grasped general truth about behavior. As a kind of folk wisdom, the *sententiae* (concise and weighty sayings) which predominate in the Friar's speeches, offer sensible dictums to those in the play, to Romeo in particular, and to the audience of the play as well. They consist of pithy wisdom, such as, "virtue itself turns vice, being misapplied" (2.3.21); "Wisely and slow; they stumble that run fast" (2.3.94); ". . . violent delights have violent ends" (2.6.9); and ". . . madmen have no ears" (3.3.61). But while these condensations of decorum and sense do provide a counterpoint to the extremes of passion that Romeo vents, they are, after all, condensations. The audience might well feel that there is a disparity between the importance of what is being said and the time it takes to say it. Shakespeare's Friar is a voice of wisdom, yet that wisdom is reduced too quickly for the audience to embrace it as the full truth on how to act. It comes from a character who, by the status of his vows to the church, is removed from the necessity for acting in the social world. Significantly, however, once the Friar makes vows to help Juliet out of her predicament, we no longer hear those *sententiae*. Rhetorical form is linked directly to social position. It is not so easy to sum up the truth about the way to live when one is caught in the flow of necessity and despair.

For Shakespeare, then, the sameness of the diction of Brooke's characters was a phenomenon to be recast into differences and variety. On the simplest level the creation of distinctive styles of diction provides a way for the audience to distinguish the characters from one another. On another level, it underscores the quality of thought and emotion which the characters convey in their speeches. Thus, a Romeo speaking in extremes about extremes, helps the audience to experience more vividly the information which the character conveys and to anticipate implicitly the action based upon that style.[15]

Emphasis on Character Attitudes

In *Romeo and Juliet,* Shakespeare's emphasis on a character's thought, revealed implicitly through style of diction, is indicated explicitly by speeches about that thought—still another deviation from his source. Brooke's material provided characters who speak only minimally about what they think or feel. Even at Romeus's most ardent moment, for example, he stands at Juliet's window and tells her simply, "I love, you honor, serve and please" (514) [sic]. The discussions and individual musings of Brooke's characters reflect, primarily, a concern for what they have done in the past and what they will attempt in the future.[16] Even when Brooke, as narrator, steps in to explain these characters to the reader, his accounts are not, for the most part, filled with their thoughts, but with summaries of the incidents that have befallen them.

Shakespeare, in contrast, keeps his central characters' discussions of events to a minimum and maximizes their attitudes towards the events. Each major character may thus be perceived as the sum of his or her distinctive thoughts, feelings, and judgments about experience, rather than as a passive figure to whom experiences merely happen. When actions in the storyline finally do occur, their occurrence has been foreshadowed by the characters' attitudes. Attitude, as a basis for action, or, as Burke would call it, attitude as "incipient action,"[17] is particularly emphasized in the depiction of Romeo, whose passionate idealism about love is a focus for audience perception before any calamitous action occurs. For example, it is not surprising that Romeo kills himself to be with Juliet, for the audience has heard him announce his extreme feelings many times throughout the play—from his reckless vow at Juliet's balcony that "My life were better ended by their hate,/ Than death prorogued, wanting of thy love" (2.2.77–78), to his pre-wedding vow "Do thou but close our hands with holy words/ Then love-devouring death do what he dare/ It is enough I may but call her mine" (2.6.6–8), to his post-wedding pronouncement of "Let me be ta'en, let me be put to death;/ I am content, so thou wilt have it so" (3.5.18–19).

Shakespeare establishes the importance of Romeo's attitudes by making them the primary subject of the first two acts of the play. This is not to say that Romeo is depicted as a complex character simply because Shakespeare gives him so much to say about what he thinks and feels. On the contrary, this central character is presented as a personality with profuse, yet restricted, thoughts and feelings; responses to his world emerge primarily as attitudes towards love, whether it be the self-consciously posed love over Rosaline or the idealistic, extreme love of Juliet.

Presentation of Romeo as a character obsessed with the idea of feeling represents an alteration of the priorities which Brooke initially establishes for his Romeus. As soon as we learn of Brooke's Romeus, we discover he is preoccupied with a particular lady "Whose beauty, shape, and comely grace, did his heart entrappe" (58). Shakespeare, however, alters this focused obsession to reveal a Romeo who is initially more concerned with feeling the part of the lover than he is with a particular woman. His first speeches are not about the *object* of his affection, but about the *nature* of it. The audience, on meeting Romeo, is treated to a lengthy listing of oxymoronic statements on the nature of love (1.1.171–175), followed by a description of the classic symptoms of the disease (1.1.183–187). And it is not until Benvolio urges the revelation of Romeo's lady that Romeo bothers to add, "In sadness, cousin, I do love a woman" (1.1.197). The audience's attention is thus directed towards the character's ideas about emotion rather than towards his emotional attachment to a particular woman. While we first glimpse Romeus pursuing a woman, we initially view Romeo pursuing an emotional ideal.

Creation of Foils: Expansion of Existing Characters, and Development of New Ones

Romeo's attitudes about emotion take on significance for the audience as they are contrasted with other characters' stances on the subject. In a major modification of his source material, Shakespeare creates an array of foils whose diction and attitudes stand in opposition to Romeo's. In so doing, he changes Brooke's format of character introduction. Brooke introduced each of his characters scene by scene as he needed them to play out their parts in the course of events. In Shakespeare's hands, however, the majority of the characters are introduced in the first scene. The audience is thus allowed more opportunity to become familiar with their distinctive stances and with the polarization of the stances among them. With the early and simultaneous introduction of contrasting sets of attitude, diction, and action, Shakespeare provides multiple perspectives from which to react. Benvolio, Mercutio, and the Friar convey to the audience the idea that there are alternative views and courses of action towards love besides the extreme passionate ones voiced by Romeo. In short, Shakespeare seems to recognize "what is needed to set off the intended shape against the nonintended ground" by developing a relationship of contrast.[18]

Benvolio is constructed by Shakespeare from a character who is so unimportant in Brooke's poem as to remain nameless. A friend of Romeus's, he is used to facilitate Romeus's appearance at the Capulet party; that is all. As Shakespeare fleshes him out and expands his role, however, Benvolio comes to represent a practical, rational approach to love and life, in contrast to the more idealistic stance espoused by Romeo. Shakespeare's Benvolio implicitly functions in the play to invite the audience to make comparative judgments of Romeo. Explicitly, Benvolio urges upon Romeo the action that Shakespeare, at another level, urges upon the audience. Benvolio recommends to the love-sick Romeo that he sample the beauty of other women in order to put Rosaline into perspective, much as Shakespeare invites the audience to sample the attitudes of all the major characters in order to understand Romeo's attitudes on love. Benvolio's advice is to:

Compare her face with some that I shall show
And I will make thee think thy swan a crow (1.2.91–92).

. . . you saw her fair, none else being by,
. . . But in that crystal scales let there be weigh'd
Your lady's love against some other maid
That I will show you shining at this feast,
And she shall scant show well that now shows best (1.2.99–104).

The audience's context for interpreting Romeo's thoughts and behavior is broadened by perceiving him in relationship to Mercutio. For the creation of Mercutio, Shakespeare expanded a nondescript character at the Capulet ball into a strong and significant foil to Romeo. The playfulness, wit, and cynicism by which Mercutio is characterized function to point up still another kind of contrast to Romeo's intensity, single-mindedness, and idealism. To Mercutio, Romeo's intensity is predicatably conventional: "Romeo! humours! madman! passion! lover!" he mocks. "Appear thou in the likeness of a sigh!" (2.1.7–8)

In creating the Friar, Shakespeare found more source material with which to work than in his depictions of Benvolio and Mercutio. Brooke's Friar is described as a learned scholar and philanthropic member of the community, with strongly botanical and somewhat pedagogical interests. Shakespeare reverses these priorities for his Friar, creating a character who, while somewhat interested in botany, appears primarily pedagogical. In his creation of the Friar, Shakespeare has taken the moralistic offerings which Brooke initially advances in his address to the reader and has placed them in the mouth of one character. By centralizing these warnings about cause and effect, Shakespeare keeps the notions of responsibility and culpability within the mainstream of the play and allows them to exist as another perspective on the passion of Romeo.

Finally, Shakespeare alters drastically the personality of Brooke's Juliet. The change creates another significant foil to Romeo. Unlike Shakespeare's heroine, the Juliet of Brooke's poem weeps at the slightest upset, falls into trances, and frequently threatens death, appearing to be more of a model for Shakespeare's Romeo than for his Juliet.[19] While Brooke's Juliet behaves far more emotionally from the start, she implicitly has a good reason for her extremes. Brooke tells us she loves Romeus more than he loves her. Shakespeare, however, changes this uneven distribution of passion by equalizing the feelings between the two lovers. Since attitude is connected with action in his characters, Shakespeare's depiction of an unequal passion might well serve as an understandable justification for a lover's extreme behavior. Yet in redressing the imbalance of passion, Shakespeare allows the audience, in the balcony scene, to compare and contrast different styles of behavior towards a love that is held to be equally strong. In making his Juliet's practical attitudes and straightforward expression of those attitudes different from those of her predecessor's, Shakespeare creates one more striking foil to Romeo, even though she remains as such for only a short time.[20]

These juxtapositions of differing attitudes towards passion become more significant if we note that this configuration of foils remains in the play only for the first two acts. In the third act, Mercutio is killed, taking from the play his cynical mockery about Romeo's passion. Benvolio walks off, never to return, eliminating the rational, thoughtful approach to behavior. Juliet's practicality and simplicity about passion last only as long as the end of the balcony scene. Even the cautious Friar throws off his sententious philosophizing in the fourth act, when he implicates himself in the action. As thoroughly as Shakespeare initially provides alternative views on extreme emotion to provoke a kind of critical audience awareness on the subject, he then just as thoroughly eliminates those alternative perspectives. He thereby smoothes over possible conflicting interpretations of Romeo so the audience, like the characters, has no choice but to see narrowly the course ahead of them. Romeo, who could previously be viewed as immoderate next to Benvolio, foolish beside Mercutio, extreme when juxtaposed with Juliet, and potentially dangerous when compared with the Friar, thus becomes, when isolated, the beautiful and noble young lover who chooses to die for love.

Creation of Inter-Character Assessment of Romeo

In the first acts of the play, critical audience assessment of Romeo is further encouraged by Shakespeare's establishment of other characters' assessments of the lover. This inter-character evaluation represents still another departure that Shakespeare makes from his source material. In Brooke's narrative, Shakespeare found a young hero who was such a reasonable sort, even when he was pining over unrequited love, that his friends made no skeptical judgments about his demeanor. In fact, the only kind of assessment about Romeus that the other characters in Brooke's poem make is of such a positive nature, that Brooke clearly intends to reinforce reader perception of Romeus as indisputably admirable. After Romeus kills Tybalt, for example, Brooke writes:

This Romeus was borne so much in heavens grace
Of Fortune, and of nature so beloved, that . . .
A certain charme was graved by natures secret arte
That vertue had to draw to it, the love of many a hart (1067–72).

Shakespeare, however, allows his audience to listen to Benvolio, Mercutio, and the Friar making less than glowing remarks about Romeo's behavior. While there is fondness in Benvolio's and Mercutio's judgments of their friend, they nonetheless mock his self indulgence. Even the gentle Benvolio acknowledges that "Blind is his love, and best befits the dark" (2.1.32). The Friar's assessments of Romeo, delivered to Romeo's face, are given primarily after Romeo has killed Tybalt, and the direness of the situation prompts him to make more severe judgments. Romeo's hyperbolic oaths on hearing that he has been banished prompt the Friar to exclaim over his pupil's "rude unthankfulness," (3.3.24) terming him a "fond mad man" (3.3.52). Romeo's attempt to commit suicide in the Friar's cell brings forth a stronger judgment still: "Art thou a man? thy form cries out thou art:/ Thy tears are womanish; thy wild acts denote/ The unreasonable fury of a beast:/ Unseemly woman in a seeming man!/ Or ill-beseeming beast in seeming both! Thou hast amazed me" (3.3.109.114). As the audience forms its interpretation of Romeo, Shakespeare is peppering his portrait of the young lover with views that are not always the most complimentary. Thus the audience is given the opportunity to compare their own emerging interpretation of the lover with those assessments of him made by his friends and the Friar.

Yet Shakespeare does not allow the audience to embrace these assessments as the key to interpreting Romeo. He makes acceptance of these judgments problematic by offering them in situations and from sources where credibility must be questioned. The points of reference for judging the actions of a character, such as Romeo, will simply not stay anchored for the audience. They see, for example, that each time Romeo's friends form a judgment between themselves as to why Romeo behaves so foolishly, those friends' shared judgment is based upon limited information (2.1), (2.4). Benvolio and Mercutio never do discover that Romeo has shifted his ardor for Rosaline to Juliet. But for the audience, who has watched Romeo's meeting and wooing of his new love, Benvolio's and Mercutio's justifiable mockery of Romeo carries with it elusive assessment and irony.

Nor do the Friar's pronouncements about Romeo stand inviolate. Not only does Shakespeare employ them just a little too quickly for them to be embraced as the ultimate assessment about the situation and the character, but he makes the Friar's sententious declarations themselves subject to the judgement of other characters. No sooner is the audience allowed to sense the validity of the Friar's advice to Romeo after Tybalt's death, than the Nurse (who was not present in this situation in the poem) adds her assessment of the Friar's words. This simple effusive personality applauds the Friar's judgments by gushing, "O Lord, I could have stayed here all the night/ To hear good counsel: O, what learning is!—" (3.3.159–60). Shakespeare has thus created a situation in which the foolish Nurse's praise undercuts the wisdom of the Friar's judgment.[21]

Alterations in Plot

The changes that Shakespeare makes in the plot of the story emphasize action as an extension of character attitude. One of the most notable plot changes, the compression of time in the play from several months to four days, has been acknowledged by critics, for good reason, as a change which heightens dramatic tension.[22] Yet this change has significance beyond the creation of audience anxiety. The shortened span of time also emphasizes the personality which Shakespeare shapes for Romeo, underscoring Romeo's attitude towards passion. The lover's idealism and impatience with mundane processes is such that he hastens events in a desperate attempt to create a timelessness for himself and Juliet. The brevity of time in the world of the play thus appears to reflect the attitude of the central character.

A second kind of alteration which Shakespeare makes is to limit the action which he chooses to transpose from poem to story. The change is not surprising, since a narrative poem can sweep a reader through myriad events and locations, whereas a play is usually more limited in the events and locales it can depict. Yet, the way in which Shakespeare limits the action of his source material allows us to view this limitation as more than simply theatrical necessity. While he reduces the number of incidents that the audience is allowed to view, he enriches the characters' attitudes about those incidents which remain.

Such a refocusing of attention from proliferating events to intensity of attitude and mood in deliberately restricted action occurs in Shakespeare's alteration of Romeo's life in exile. In Brooke's poem, there is a great deal of description explaining how Romeus spends his days in Mantua (1738-1780). In Shakespeare's hands, Romeo's routine is, quite naturally, minimized since the entire time in the play is compressed. Yet Shakespeare gives Romeo one lengthy speech describing the impact that Romeo's exile has had upon him. The news of Juliet's ostensible death elicits Romeo's detailed account of the shop of a poor apothecary he had seen in his wanderings about the streets of Mantua. The effect of Shakespeare's omission of all details about Romeo's exile, except for those concerning the shop at which he can buy poison, focuses attention on one element alone—Romeo's attitude and impending action in the face of what he believes to be Juliet's death. The important aspect of Romeo's life in Mantua, for Shakespeare and for the audience who watches his version of the story, is that during this brief time in a new city, Romeo has already discovered the means by which to end his life. Thus, an incident from the source is reduced and reshaped into the kind of information which highlights Romeo's characteristic intensity, his death-centered passion and the action it triggers.

In keeping with this shift from event to the attitude underlying the event, Shakespeare invents two new incidents that did not appear in Brooke's poem at all: the deaths of Mercutio and Paris. These new story elements provide the audience with instances of Romeo's behavior which add a dimension of complexity to the audience's perception of the lover.

I have previously discussed the death of Mercutio as a rhetorical strategy whereby Shakespeare removes a major foil to Romeo. But Mercutio's death also functions to change the hues of Tybalt's death from black and white in Brooke's poem to a more shadowy area in the play. Romeus's motivation for killing Brooke's Tybalt is clearly and solely self-defense. With the addition of Mercutio's death, Shakespeare provides his Romeo with a different cause for murder—a death prompted by revenge.[23] While Elizabethan audiences had been reared on plays which stressed revenge as a motive for killing and would not have become morally confused by Romeo's action, the changed rationale for Romeo's killing of Tybalt provides another piece in the emerging portrait of a character ruled by passion. The killing shows the extent to which Romeo's impulsiveness has consequences. Shakespeare provides for his audience the suggestion that Romeo's impulsiveness and passion are triggered in response to external events and the violence of other characters.

The death of Paris, however, makes Romeo's passion seem generated from within himself. Not only has Shakespeare invented this death, but he has also introduced Paris early in the story, unlike Brooke, who brings Paris on only once after Romeo has been banished. Shakespeare's early introduction of Paris serves to heighten anxiety about the impending conflict between Paris's desires and those of Romeo and Juliet. It also allows the audience time to become acquainted with Paris as a virtuous (albeit unexciting) personality.[24] With the addition of Paris's death, the audience is allowed to see that anyone who stands in the way of Romeo's attainment of his goal, even those who are innocent of wrongdoing, are destroyed by the obsessed behavior of the lover.[25] Shakespeare thus affords one last complex, disquieting perception of a passionate young man, whose intentions do not seem to be immoral, cutting down another who is virtuous. Tybalt was involved in a fight in which Mercutio died. For that provocation Tybalt's death does not appear surprising or unwarranted. Paris's sudden, senseless death, however, appears to be simply the result of Paris's attempt to restrict a powerful man whose feelings are beyond control.

Conclusion

The changes Shakespeare made from Brooke's poem appear to be more than random alterations. They create a strikingly consistent configuration which invites the audience to form a vastly different kind of understanding and perspective of the story of Romeo and Juliet.

Until the third act of the play, the changes from Brooke's narrative are used to evoke a certain sort of critical perception on the part of the viewing audience. It is at this point, moreover, that the play shifts from comedy to tragedy, a shift which some critics attribute to the sudden deaths of Mercutio and Tybalt. Certainly, the narrowing of the audience's frames of reference reinforces the change from comedy to tragedy. Shakespeare essentially returns to the sentimental core of his source material and does so by diminishing the multiple perspectives on Romeo's behavior that had earlier held audience attention. With little perspective other than that of the lovers, it is not difficult to become drawn into the bleakness and anxiety of the last two acts. This immersion in emotion is made stronger still by the absence of the impetuous Romeo for the entire fourth act during which time the audience watches only the more sympathetic half of the love duo and her pitiful problems.

Despite this shift from critical awareness to emotional involvement, from comedy to tragedy, from the experimentation with a radically different story of Romeo and Juliet to a return to the pathos of the traditional tale, Shakespeare's changes in his source actually work to make the emotional ending far more intense than Brooke's. In the last half of the play, the audience watches characters who have in some measure created the very situation which is destroying them. The emotional involvement of the audience can thus be much more intense than if they had been offered a story in which calamity struck characters without any provocation.

Although the kind of critical perception of a character that Shakespeare initially establishes is shifted to a less rational level of dramatic experience in *Romeo and Juliet,* in his mature tragedies, Shakespeare uses similar strategies with more sophistication to create more sustained perceptions of a similar kind. We have only to turn to *Antony and Cleopatra,* for example, to view in Antony a character who, like Romeo, may be perceived as both beautifully noble and dangerously foolish; like Romeo, one who evokes and eludes attempts to pin down and assess his behavior. In plays such as *King Lear* and *Othello,* we see complex connections between diction, thought, and action that Shakespeare establishes in simpler fashion in *Romeo and Juliet,* connections which once again suggest that the characters themselves have created the situations in which they struggle. As departures from the traditional saga of Romeo and Juliet, and as incipient structures for mature work, Shakespeare's changes in his source material give us access to the playwright's direction of audience perception and interpretation.

Notes

1. Among the various renditions of the tale which were popular in the Renaissance are those by Masuccio, da Porto, and Bandello in Italian, Boiastuau's French adaptation of Bandello's narrative, Brooke's English version based on Boiastuau, and Painter's translation of Boiastuau into English.
2. See, for example, Olin H. Moore, "Shakespeare's Deviations from 'Romeus and Juliet,'" *PMLA,* 52 (March, 1937), 68–74; and Arthur J. Roberts, "The Sources of *Romeo and Juliet," Modern Language Notes,* 17 (February, 1902), 82–87.
3. After examining use of characters, plot variations, and ideas emphasized in versions of the story by da Porto, Boaistuau, and Bandello, those writers whose works are occasionally mentioned as possible sources for Shakespeare's play, I agree with the consensus that attributes the source fully to Brooke's poem.
4. For discussions of these changes, see Georges A. Bonnard, *"Romeo and Juliet:* a possible significance?" *Review of English Studies,* 2 (October, 1951), 319–27; Susan Snyder, *"Romeo and Juliet:* Comedy into Tragedy," *Essays in Criticism,* 20 (October, 1970), 391–402; and Roberts, "The Sources of Romeo and Juliet."
5. For a discussion of how the rhetorical structures within a work reveal the author's means of controlling his or her audience, see Wayne C. Booth, *The Rhetoric of Fiction* (Chicago: The Univ. of Chicago Press, 1961). For an excellent analysis of how Shakespeare controls audience perception in *Julius Caesar,* see Kenneth Burke, "Antony in Behalf of the Play," in *The Philosophy of Literary Form: Studies in Symbolic Action,* 3rd ed. (Berkeley: Univ. of Calif. Press, 1973), pp. 320–43. See also E. A. J. Honigmann, *Shakespeare: Seven Tragedies: The Dramatist's Manipulation of Response* (London: Macmillan, 1976).
6. Citations from Brooke's work are from his poem found in *Narrative and Dramatic Sources of Shakespeare,* 1, ed. Geoffrey Bullough (New York: Columbia Univ. Press, 1961), p. 284.
7. This blanket sameness of style and tone between narrator and characters in Brooke's work is not to be confused with alignment of style and tone between a narrator and a character for rhetorical effect. In well crafted fiction, a writer will often emphasize the relationship between an omniscient narrator and a character by purposefully coloring the narrator's report of character thought with diction and

tones similar to that of the character. For a discussion of this narrative strategy see Booth's *The Rhetoric of Fiction.* For an investigation of how these relationships in narrative may be staged, see Robert S. Breen, *Chamber Theatre* (Englewood Cliffs, N.J.: Prentice-Hall, 1978).

8. The tenor of this prologue is often attributed to Shakespeare's reliance on the fate controlled story which he used as his source.

9. There are those critics who believe that the play illustrates only fate's interference in the lives of totally helpless victims. See, for example, Herman Harrell Horne, *Shakespeare's Philosophy of Love* (Raleigh: Edwards & Broughton, 1945); Norman Holland, *The Shakespearean Imagination* (Bloomington: Indiana Univ. Press, 1964); and Bonnard, "*Romeo and Juliet:* a possible significance?"

10. For an extensive investigation of the kinds of figures of speech which Shakespeare generally used in his plays, see Sister Miriam Joseph, *Shakespeare's Use of the Arts of Language* (1947; rpt. New York: Hafner, 1966). For a discussion of how figures of speech may be seen as models of action in ordinary language as well as in literature, see Arthur Quinn, *Figures of Speech: 60 Ways to Turn a Phrase* (Salt Lake City: Peregrine Smith, 1982).

11. All citations from *Romeo and Juliet* in this essay are from *The Complete Works of Shakespeare,* ed. Hardin Craig and David Bevington (Glenview, Ill.: Scott Foresman, 1973).

12. Romeo's recital of love's paradoxes in this speech is concluded by a *chiasmus,* a device favored by love poets and by Shakespeare himself in his sonnets. Shakespeare's use of the figure here helps to underscore the conventional nature of Romeo's utterances at this point in the play.

13. William J. Brandt, *The Rhetoric of Argumentation* (Indianapolis: Bobbs-Merrill, 1970), pp. 146–147.

14. See, for example, Holland, *The Shakespearean Imagination.*

15. While some might argue that Shakespeare created more distinctive diction from his characters than did Brooke because he was a playwright whose aim lay in fashioning dramatic personae, the explanation is not that circular nor the phenomenon that easily explained. A backward glance to the plays Shakespeare wrote before *Romeo and Juliet* reveals an absence of distinct styles of diction. When a character in them is occasionally distinguished in such a manner, the stylistic portrayal of him or her is either not conveyed with consistency, or the quality of that character's diction suggests only the most basic stereotypic thought and behavior.

    Lucentio, in *The Taming of the Shrew,* for example, is initially characterized by the hyperbole of the idealistic lover, but this individualizing style is not carried through in his characterization. Holofernes, the schoolmaster of *Love's Labour's Lost* provides an illustration of a character consistently drawn. Yet his characterization, achieved partly through the liberal use of Latin quotations, is the complete stereotype of the pedant. For a fuller discussion of the lack of distinct styles of diction for characterization in Shakespeare's early plays, see Roberta Jill Taft, "A Rhetorical Perspective of *Romeo and Juliet,*" Diss. Univ. of California, Berkeley, 1975.

16. Shakespeare's characters in earlier plays are also drawn in this manner, the content of their speeches emphasizing past and future action rather than attitude. For further discussion of this phenomena, see Taft, "A Rhetorical Perspective."

17. For a discussion of how an attitude can be considered the "first step towards an act," see Kenneth Burke, *A Grammar of Motives* (1945; rpt. Berkeley: Univ. of California Press, 1969), pp. 235–247.

18. Ernst Hans Gombrich, *Art and Illusion* (Princeton: Princeton Univ. Press, 1969), p. 40. Gombrich discusses contrast and perception in relationship to the visual arts, but his observations about the way perception and discrimination are aroused by contrasts can be applied to dramatic art as well.

19. The Juliet of the poem does not act upon her passion. She is a young girl in her father's house, less able to take the initiative in the relationship. Shakespeare transposes the proclivity for emotional behavior to a more active agent, Romeo, and in so doing creates a heightened sense of drama. The switch from the passionate Juliet of the poem to a passionate Romeo in the play more convincingly enables the audience to expect passionate action as a result of passionate attitudes.

20. While Shakespeare's Juliet does become more like her lover and consequently more like Brooke's Juliet as the play progresses, Shakespeare does not juxtapose Juliet's new passionate stance with contrasting stances. Thus, Shakespeare does not give the audience the broadened perspectives for questioning and assessing Juliet's behavior the way he does with Romeo. As Shakespeare depicts her, Juliet serves to elicit sympathy, not judgment.

21. Alfred Harbage makes a similar point in his *As They Liked It* (New York: Macmillan, 1947).

22. Snyder sums up the race against time which this compression creates when she states, "The tragic world is governed by inevitability—law is inherent; imposed by the individual's own nature. The events of tragedy acquire urgency—those in comedy move toward a conclusion that has all the time in the world" p. 347.

23. The reasoning behind Shakespeare's removal of Mercutio in the play's third act has been debated by critics for centuries. Dryden began the controversy in 1684 in his *On the Dramatique Poetry of the Last Age* ed., W. P. Ker, 2 vols, 1900, quoted in R. E. Halliday, *Shakespeare and His Critics* (New York: Schocken, 1965), p. 158, by commenting: "Shakespeare show'd the best of his skill in his Mercutio, and he said himself, that he was forc'd to kill him in the third Act, to prevent being kill'd by him. But, for my part, I cannot find he was so dangerous a person. . . ."

24. For a discussion of how Paris's diction serves as a formal language foil to Romeo's thereby making Romeo appear more life-like and engaging, see Harry Levin, "Form and Formality in *Romeo and Juliet,*" *Shakespeare Quarterly,* 11 (Winter, 1960), 1–11.

25. The addition of Paris's death baffled Roberts, who wrote of the tomb scene: "It is hard to see what artistic end the introduction of Paris subserves. His presence there is an intrusion. His death at Romeo's hands is not at all a dramatic necessity. Shakespeare has quite robbed the scene of all the pathetic dignity and appealing sense of unavailing woe which it has in the Italian original, or even in Brooke's poem" p. 86.

9

Rhetoric of Political Action

Political establishments and governments use actions and objects to reinforce the politics of normalcy. Everything from inaugural parades and police uniforms to public monuments, men's neckties, and women's skirts are instruments to indicate and maintain the status quo as normal, natural, inevitable, and proper. And insofar as the status quo governs access to property and power, all of the means used to reinforce it are political and rhetorical. Typically, the political nature of public action is invisible to us until it is resisted by speech or action.

A fundamental strategy of groups seeking political change is to reveal the taken-for-granted "normalcy" of its establishment opponents as arbitrary, to make visible the "invisibility" of its actions, to unmask the "legitimacy" of its arrangements as unjust, and to challenge the apparent "concreteness" of its technology and economy. The strategy, in other words, is to reveal the actions and institutions of the status quo as being symbolic and political, rather than natural and universal.

The two essays in this section address questions about action-as-politics. They do so by focusing on anti-establishment groups in the 1960s. Both were published in *The Quarterly Journal of Speech* in 1969, near the end of a decade of intense political action, encompassing the nonviolent direct action of the civil rights movement and riots in the black ghettos of American cities, the peaceful witness of opposition to growing war in Vietnam and angry, sometimes coercive demonstrations of growing student outrage and opposition.

The essay by Scott and Smith on "The Rhetoric of Confrontation" is wide-ranging and speculative, attempting to fathom the root psychology and the pragmatic strategy of groups committed to displacing the establishment. Andrews' essay on "Confrontation at Columbia: A Case Study in Coercive Rhetoric," examines one instance of political action and speculates about its ethical and rhetorical dimensions.

Both essays reveal ways in which the political communication of the 1960s force a reconsideration of the definition and scope of rhetoric. Scott and Smith talk "of the *rhetoric* of confrontation, not merely confrontation, because this action, as diverse as its manifestations may be, is inherently symbolic. The act carries a message. It dissolves the lines between marches, sit-ins, demonstrations, acts of physical violence, and aggressive discourse. In this way it informs us of the essential nature of discourse itself as human action." Scott and Smith seem to be seeking an inclusive definition of rhetoric, one that encompasses any action insofar as it is symbolic—which, from a rhetorical point of view, virtually any human action is.

Andrews, on the other hand, although admitting to the realm of the rhetorical "all the available means of influencing human behavior," argues for reserving a primarily ethical distinction. Unlike some scholars before him, Andrews does not exclude from rhetorical studies actions that are non-verbal, non-rational, or irrational. But within the field of rhetoric, Andrews nevertheless holds out for a distinction between *persuasion* and *coercion.* For Andrews, persuasion, whether verbal or nonverbal, rational or irrational, can occur only where the participants are capable of making a free choice. "Rhetoric," he argues, "becomes less persuasive and more coercive to the extent that it limits the viable alternatives open to the receivers of communication."

These essays raise many questions useful to the student of rhetoric. Is Andrews's distinction between coercion and persuasion inherently political, in that it seems to favor the status quo? Is the distinction an ethical one, or does it also usefully distinguish patterns of strategy and influence in practice? If there is a rhetoric of confrontation, is there also a rhetoric of accommodation, using the same range of symbolic means but to different ends? Should all human action, insofar as it is symbolic, be classed as rhetorical? If so, are there no differences, in principle or practice, between "speech" and "action"? Is "action" inherently more likely to be coercive than "speech?" Should the same principles that apply to freedom of speech be extended to freedom of action? In addition to these and other theoretical questions, the essays in this section point us to the possibility of using a rhetorical perspective to engage in close analysis of a wide range of nonverbal political actions, whether violent or nonviolent, official or marginal.

The Rhetoric of Confrontation

Robert L. Scott and Donald K. Smith

"Confront" is a simple enough verb meaning to stand or to come in front of. Like many simple words, however, it has been used in diverse contexts for varied purposes and has developed complex meanings. Among these the most interesting, and perhaps the strongest, is the sense of standing in front of as a barrier or a threat. This sense is especially apparent in the noun "confrontation."

Repeatedly in his book *Essays in the Public Philosophy,* Walter Lippmann uses the word "confrontation" in the sense of face-to-face coming together of spokesmen for disparate views. Confrontation, as he saw it then, was the guarantee of open communication and fruitful dissent. But Lippmann's book was copyrighted in 1955. Today, his phrase "because the purpose of the confrontation is to discern truth" sounds a bit archaic. If so, the remainder of his sentence, "there are rules of evidence and parliamentary procedure, there are codes of fair dealing and fair comment, by which a loyal man will consider himself bound when he exercises the right to publish opinion,"[1] seems absolutely irrelevant to the notion of "confrontation" as we live with it in marches, sit-ins, demonstrations, and discourse featuring disruption, obscenity, and threats.

Although certainly some use the word "confrontation" moderately, we shall be concerned here with the radical and revolutionary suggestion which the word carries more and more frequently. Even obviously moderate circumstances today gain some of the revolutionary overtones when the word is applied, as it might be for example, in announcing a church study group as the "confrontation of sacred and secular morality."

Acts of confrontation are currently at hand in such profusion that no one will lack evidence to prove or disprove the generalizations we make.[2]

Confrontation crackles menacingly from every issue in our country (Black Power and Student Power, as examples), and globe (Radical Nationalism everywhere). But primary to every confrontation in any setting, radical or moderate, is the impulse to confront. From what roots does that impulse spring?

From *The Quarterly Journal of Speech,* Volume 55, 1969. Reprinted with permission of the Speech Communication Association and the authors.

Radical Division

Radical confrontation reflects a dramatic sense of division. The old language of the "haves" and the "have-nots" scarcely indicates the basis of the division, nor its depth. The old language evokes the history of staid, well-controlled concern on the part of those who have, for those who have not. It suggests that remedy can come from traditional means—the use of some part of the wealth and talent of those who have to ease the burden of those who have not, and perhaps open opportunities for some of them to enter the mainstream of traditional values and institutions. It recalls the missionary spirit of the voluntary associations of those who have—the legislative charity of the New Deal, the Fair Deal, the Welfare State, and the whole spectrum of international development missions.

A benevolent tone characterizes the old rhetoric of social welfare. The tone assumes that all men seek and should increasingly have more of the available wealth, or education, or security, or culture, or opportunities. The values of those who "have" are celebrated as the goals to which all should aspire, and effective social policy becomes a series of acts to extend opportunity to share in those values. If those who have can provide for others more of their own perquisites—more of the right to vote, or to find employment, or to go to college, or to consume goods—then progress is assured.

Although the terms "have" and "have not" are still accurate enough descriptions of the conditions that divide people and groups, their evocation of a traditional past hides the depth and radical nature of current divisions. Those on the "have not" side of the division, or at least some of their theorists and leaders, no longer accept designation as an inert mass hoping to receive what they lack through action by the "haves." Neither do they accept any assumption that what they wish is membership in the institutions of those who have, or an opportunity to learn and join their value system. Rather the "have nots" picture themselves as radically divided from traditional society, questioning not simply the limitations of its benevolence but more fundamentally its purposes and modes of operation. Whether they experience deprivation as poverty, or lack of political power, or disaffection from traditional values, the "have not" leaders and theorists challenge existing institutions. This radical challenge, and its accompanying disposition toward confrontation, marks the vague attitudinal web that links revolutionaries in emerging nations to Black Power advocates in America or to students and intellectuals of the New Left. Three statements will illustrate the similar disposition of men who serve rather different causes in varied circumstances.

For Frantz Fanon, Algerian revolutionary and author of *The Wretched of the Earth,* the symbol of deprivation is the term "colonisation," and the end of confrontation is "decolonisation": "In decolonisation there is therefore the need of a complete calling in question of the colonial situation. If we wish to describe it precisely, we might find it in the well-known words 'The last shall be first and the first last.' Decolonisation is the putting into practice of this statement. That is why, if we try to describe it, all decolonisation is successful."[3]

For Black Power advocate Stokely Carmichael, the enemy is white racism, which is to be confronted, not joined: "Our concern for black power addresses itself directly to this problem, the necessity to reclaim our history and our identity from the cultural terrorism and depredation of self-justifying white guilt. To do this we shall have to struggle for the right to create our own terms through which to define ourselves and our relationship to the society, and to have these terms recognized. This is the first necessity of a free people, and the first right that any oppressor must suspend."[4]

For students in the New Left, the enemy to be confronted is simply "the establishment," or often in the United States, "technocracy." As student Frederick Richman sees the division:

> The world in which the older generation grew up, and which the political systems support, is no longer one which youth can accept. In a world of rampaging technology, racial turmoil, and poverty, they see a President whose program is constituted largely of finishing touches to the New Deal, and a Congress unwilling to accept even that. In a time when personal freedom is of increasing concern, they see a republic operated by an immense bureaucratic structure, geared more to cold war adventures than to domestic needs, stifling individual initiative along with that of states and cities. Finally, they see a political system obsessed with stability and loyalty instead of with social justice.[5]

Those have-nots who confront established power do not seek to share; they demand to supplant.

They must demand to supplant for they live in a Manichean world. Fanon, who features the term, argues that the settler (we may translate "settler" into other words, e.g., racist, establishment, or power structure) is responsible for the situation in which he must now suffer: "The colonial world is a Manichean world."[6] Those who rule and take the fruit of the system as their due create an equation that identifies themselves with the force of good (order, civilization, progress) which struggles with evil (chaos, the primitive, retrogression). In such a circumstance, established authority often crusades to eliminate the vessels of evil by direct action; but often its leaders work benignly and energetically to transform the others into worthy copies of themselves. At best, the process of transformation is slow, during which time the mass of the others must be carefully held apart to keep them from contaminating the system. Only a few can cross the great gulf to be numbered among the good. Claiming to recognize the reality of this process, which is always masked under exalted labels, black radicals in America cry that the traditional goal of integration masks and preserves racism. In an analogous posture, Students for a Democratic Society picture their educational system as a vast machine to recruit servants for a traditional society, perpetuating all of the injustices of that society.

Whether the force of "good" works energetically and directly or indirectly and somewhat benignly, those without caste must strive to supplant such holders of power. Forced to accept a Manichean struggle, they must reverse the equation, not simply to gain food, land, power, or whatever, but to survive. Reversing the equation will deny the justice of the system that has dehumanized them.

The process of supplanting will be violent for it is born of a violent system. To complete the long quotation introduced above from Fanon: "The naked truth of decolonisation evokes for us the searing bullets and bloodstained knives which emanate from it. For if the last shall be first, this will only come to pass after a murderous and decisive struggle between the two protagonists. That affirmed intention to place the last at the head of things . . . can only triumph if we use all means to turn the scale, including, of course, that of violence."[7]

As Eric Hoffer concludes in his study of mass movements, those who make revolutions are apt to see themselves as spoiled, degraded, and without hope as things exist. But they locate the genesis of their degradation in things, in others, in the world as it is organized around them.[8]

The Rite of the Kill

The enemy is obvious, and it is he who has set the scene upon which the actors must play out the roles determined by the cleavage of exploitation. The situation shrieks kill-or-be-killed. "From here on in, if we must die anyway, we will die fighting back and we will not die alone," Malcolm X wrote in his "Appeal to African Heads of State." "We intend to see that our racist oppressors also get a taste of death."[9]

Judgments like "the oppressor" cannot be made without concomitant judgments. If there are those who oppress, there are those who are oppressed. This much seems obvious, but beneath that surface is the accusation that those oppressed have been something less than men ought to be. If one stresses the cunning, tenacious brutality of the oppressor, he suggests that the oppressed has been less than wise, alert, and strong. If one feels the heritage of injustice, then he senses the ignominy of his patrimony. The blighted self must be killed in striking the enemy. By the act of overcoming his enemy, he who supplants demonstrates his own worthiness, effacing the mark, whatever it may be— immaturity, weakness, subhumanity—that his enemy has set upon his brow.

To satisfy the rite that destroys the evil self in the act of destroying the enemy that has made the self evil, the radical may work out the rite of kill symbolically.[10] Harassing, embarrassing, and disarming the enemy may suffice, especially if he is finally led to admit his impotence in the face of the superior will of the revolutionary. Symbolic destruction of some manifestation of evil is well illustrated by the outbursts on campuses across America directed toward Dow Chemical. As far as we know in every confrontation of authority centering around the presence on the campus of a recruiter from Dow Chemical, the demonstrators early announced their intention of paralyzing the process until the recruiter agrees on behalf of the company to contaminate the scene no further with his presence.

Michael Novak, a Stanford University professor, pictures student disruption as a tactic to remove the mask of respectability worn by the establishment and kept in place both by the centralized control of communication processes and the traditional canons of free speech.

> The balance of power in the formation of public opinion has been altered by the advent of television. The society of independent, rational individuals envisaged by John Stuart Mill does not exist. The fate of all is bound up with the interpretation of events given by the mass media, by the image projected, and by the political power which results. . . . In a society with respect for its political institutions, officials have only to act with decorum and energy in order to benefit by such respect and to have their views established as true until proven false. . . .
>
> What, then, does freedom of speech mean in a technological society? How can one defend oneself against McCarthyism on the one hand and official newspeak on the other? The solution of the students has been to violate the taboos of decorum and thus embrace Vice President Humphrey, the CIA, Dow Chemical, and other enemies in an ugly scene, hoping that the unpopularity of the radicals will rub off on those embraced. They want to make the heretofore bland and respectable wear that tag which most alarms American sensibilities: "controversial."[11]

Student Stephen Saltonstall of Yale University views coercive disruption as the obvious tactic by which "a small concentrated minority" group can bring society to heel and proposes use of this tactic by students to "destroy the university's capability to prop up our political institutions. By stalemating America's intellectual establishment," he continues, "we may be able to paralyze the political establishment as well." Saltonstall's specific recommendations are far-ranging: "A small, disciplined group of shock troops could pack classes, break up drills, and harass army professors. . . . Students could infiltrate the office staffs of the electronic accelerators and foreign policy institutes and hamper their efficiency. The introduction of a small quantity of LSD in only five or six government department coffee-urns might be a highly effective tactic. Students should prevent their universities from being used as forums for government apologists. Public figures like Humphrey and McNamara, when they appear, should be subject to intimidation and humiliation."[12]

Some who confront the oppressive authority seek to transform its representatives as well as themselves, working to wipe out the Manichean world. Such a stance is typical of the strongly Christian representatives of the Civil Rights Movement in this country. But those who advocate killing the enemy or degrading him symbolically act out more simply and more directly the dynamics dictated by the sense of radical division.

371

Confrontation is a Totalistic Strategy

Part of the attraction of confrontation is the strong sense of success, so strong that it may be a can't-lose strategy. After all in the Christian text Fanon cites ironically, "The last *shall be* first." The last shall be first precisely because he is last. The feeling is that one has nowhere to go but up, that he has nothing to lose, that after having suffered being down so long, he deserves to move up. Aside from the innate logic of the situation, four reasons for success seem apparent. In them we can imagine the radical voice speaking.

a. *We are already dead.* In the world as it is, we do not count. We make no difference. We are not persons. "Baby, it don't mean shit if I burn in a rebellion, because my life ain't worth shit. Dig?"[13] There is no mistaking that idiom, nor the sense behind it. Some radicals take oaths, changing their names, considering themselves as dead, without families, until the revolution succeeds. It is difficult to cow a dead orphan.

b. *We can be reborn.* Having accepted the evaluation of what is, agreeing to be the most worthless of things, we can be reborn. We have nothing to hang on to. No old identity to stop us from identifying with a new world, no matter how horrifying the prospect may seem at the outset; and a new world will certainly be born of the fire we shall create. You, the enemy, on the other hand, must cling to what is, must seek to stamp out the flames, and at best can only end sorrowing at a world that cannot remain the same. Eventually you will be consumed.

c. *We have the stomach for the fight; you don't.* Having created the Manichean world, having degraded humanity, you are overwhelmed by guilt. The sense of guilt stops your hand, for what you would kill is the world you have made. Every blow you strike is suicide and you know it. At best, you can fight only delaying actions. We can strike to kill for the old world is not ours but one in which we are already dead, in which killing injures us not, but provides us with the chance of rebirth.

d. *We are united and understand.* We are united in a sense of a past dead and a present that is valuable only to turn into a future free of your degrading domination. We have accepted our past as past by willing our future. Since you must cling to the past, you have no future and cannot even understand.

Confrontation as a Non-Totalistic Tactic

Radical and revolutionary confrontation worries and bleeds the enemy to death or it engulfs and annihilates him. The logic of the situation that calls it forth bids it be total. But undoubtedly confrontation is brought about by those who feel only division, not radical division. For these the forces of good and evil pop in and out of focus, now clearly perceived, now not; now identified with this manifestation of established power and now that. These radicals may stop short of revolution because they have motives that turn them into politicians who at some point will make practical moves rather than toss every possible compromise and accommodation into the flaming jaws that would destroy the old order.

Student activists in the New Left vacillate in their demands between calls for "destruction" of universities as they are now known and tactical discussions of ways of "getting into the system" to make it more responsive to student goals.[14]

Drift toward non-totalistic goals seems consistent with both the general affluence of this group and its position as a small minority in a large student population generally committed to establishment goals and values. It may also reflect a latent response to the embarrassment of affluent students, beneficiaries of the establishment, who claim the language and motivations of the truly deprived.[15]

Similarly, the perception of confrontation as a tactic for prying apart and thus remodeling the machines of established power seems evident in many adherents of the Black Power movement. In many ways, the power Stokely Carmichael and Charles V. Hamilton forecast in their book is quite conventional, drawing analogies from past, thoroughly American experiences.[16]

Finally, one should observe the possible use of confrontation as a tactic for achieving attention and an importance not readily attainable through decorum. In retiring temporarily from his task of writing a regular newspaper column, Howard K. Smith complained bitterly of a press which inflated Stokely Carmichael from a "nobody who . . . had achieved nothing and represented no one" into "a factor to be reckoned with."[17] But Carmichael knows, from bitter experience, the art of confrontation. Martin Luther King writes of meeting a group of small boys while touring Watts after the riot. "We won!" they shouted joyously. King says his group asked them, "How can you say you won when thirty-four Negroes are dead, your community is destroyed, and whites are using the riot as an excuse for inaction?" The reply was, "We won because we made them pay attention to us."[18]

Without doubt, for many the act of confrontation itself, the march, sit-in, or altercation with the police is enough. It is consummatory. Through it the radical acts out his drama of self-assertion and writes in smeary, wordless language all over the establishment, "We know you for what you are. And you know that we know." Justifying the sense of rightness and, perhaps, firing a sense of guilt in the other is the hopeful outcome of the many coy confrontations of some shy radicals.[19]

Confrontation and Rhetorical Theory

We have talked of the *rhetoric* of confrontation, not merely confrontation, because this action, as diverse as its manifestations may be, is inherently symbolic. The act carries a message. It dissolves the lines between marches, sitins, demonstrations, acts of physical violence, and aggressive discourse. In this way it informs us of the essential nature of discourse itself as human action.

The rhetoric of confrontation also poses new problems for rhetorical theory. Since the time of Aristotle, academic rhetorics have been for the most part instruments of established society, presupposing the "goods" of order, civility, reason, decorum, and civil or theocratic law. Challenges to the sufficiency of this theory and its presuppositions have been few, and largely proposed either by elusive theologians such as Kierkegaard or Buber, or by manifestly unsavory revolutionaries such as Hitler, whose degraded theories of discourse seemed to flow naturally from degraded values and paranoid ambitions.

But the contemporary rhetoric of confrontation is argued by theorists whose aspirations for a better world are not easily dismissed, and whose passion for action equals or exceeds their passion for theory. Even if the presuppositions of civility and rationality underlying the old rhetoric are sound, they can no longer be treated as self-evident.[20] A rhetorical theory suitable to our age must take into account the charge that civility and decorum serve as masks for the preservation of injustice, that they condemn the dispossessed to non-being, and that as transmitted in a technological society they become the instrumentalities of power for those who "have."

A broader base for rhetorical theory is also needed if only as a means of bringing up to date the traditional status of rhetoric as a theory of managing public symbolic transactions. The managerial advice implicit in current theories of debate and discussion scarcely contemplates the possibility that respectable people should confront disruption of reasonable or customary actions, obscenity, threats of violence, and the like. Yet the response mechanisms turned to by those whose presuppositions could not contemplate confrontation often seem to complete the action sought by those who confront, or to confirm their subjective sense of division from the establishment. The use of force to get students out of halls consecrated to university administration or out of holes dedicated to construction projects seems to confirm the radical analysis that the establishment serves itself rather than justice. In this sense, the confronter who prompts violence in the language or behavior of another has found his collaborator. "Show us how ugly you really are," he says, and the enemy with dogs and cattle prods, or police billies and mace, complies. How can administrators ignore the insurgency of those committed to jamming the machinery of whatever enterprise is supposed to be ongoing? Those who would confront have learned a brutal art, practiced sometimes awkwardly and sometimes skillfully, which demands response. But that art may provoke the response that confirms its presuppositions, gratifies the adherents of those presuppositions, and turns the power-enforced victory of the establishment into a symbolic victory for its opponents.

As specialists interested in communication, we who profess the field of rhetoric need to read the rhetoric of confrontation, seek understanding of its presuppositions, tactics, and purposes, and seek placement of its claim against a just accounting of the presuppositions and claims of our tradition. Often as we read and reflect we shall see only grotesque, childish posturings that vaguely act out the deeper drama rooted in radical division. But even so, we shall understand more, act more wisely, and teach more usefully if we open ourselves to the fundamental meaning of radical confrontation.

Notes

1. (New York, 1955), p. 128.
2. Readers will find our generalizations more or less in harmony with other discussions of radical rhetoric which have appeared in the *QJS* recently, e.g., Parke G. Burgess, "The Rhetoric of Black Power: A Moral Demand?" LIV (April 1968), 122–133; Leland M. Griffin, "The Rhetorical Structure of the 'New Left' Movement: Part I," L (April 1964), 113–135; and Franklyn S. Haiman, "The Rhetoric of the Streets: Some Legal and Ethical Considerations," LIII (April 1967), 99–114.

   These writers sense a corporate wholeness in the messages and methods of various men. An attempt to explain the combination of message and method which forms the wholeness gives rise in each case to a *rhetoric*. All these efforts seem to us impulses to examine the sufficiency of our traditional concepts in dealing with phenomena which are becoming characteristic of contemporary dissent. In seeing rhetoric as an amalgam of meaning and method, these writers break with a tradition that takes rhetoric to be amoral techniques of manipulating a message to fit various contexts.

   Rhetoric has always been response-oriented, that is, the rationale of practical discourse, discourse designed to gain response for specific ends. But these writers see response differently. For them, the response of audiences is an integral part of the message-method that makes the rhetoric. Thus, rhetoric is shifted from a focus of reaction to one of interaction or transaction. (See especially Burgess, 132–133; Griffin, 121; and Haiman, 113.)

   Although we believe we share the sense of *rhetoric* which permeates these essays, we claim to analyze a fundamental level of meaning which underlies them.
3. Tr. Constance Farrington (New York, 1963), p. 30.
4. "Toward Black Liberation," *Massachusetts Review,* VII (Autumn 1966), 639–640.
5. "The Disenfranchised Majority," *Students and Society,* report on a conference, Vol. 1, No. 1; an occasional paper published by the Center for the Study of Democratic Institutions (Santa Barbara, Calif., 1967), p. 4.
6. Fanon, p. 33. The book is replete with references to "Manicheanism."
7. *Ibid.,* p. 30.
8. *The True Believer* (New York, 1951), pp. 19–20 and *passim.*
9. *Malcolm X Speaks,* ed. George Brietman (New York, 1966), p. 77.
10. See Fanon, p. 73.
11. "An End of Ideology?" *Commonweal,* LXXXVII (March 8, 1968), 681–682.
12. "Toward a Strategy of Disruption," from *Students and Society,* p. 29.

13. Quoted by Jack Newfield, "The Biggest Lab in the Nation," *Life,* LXIV (March 8, 1968), 87.
14. *Students and Society.* A full reading of the conference proceedings reveals clearly this split among the most vocal and militant of New Left students.
15. For an analysis of the structure and characteristics of the student left, see Richard E. Peterson, "The Student Left in American Higher Education," *Daedalus,* XCVII (Winter 1968), 293–317.
16. *Black Power: The Politics of Liberation in America* (New York, 1967), see especially Chap. 5.
17. "Great Age of Journalism Gone?" *Minneapolis Star,* February 19, 1968, p. 5B.
18. *Where Do We Go From Here: Chaos or Community?* (New York, 1967), p. 112.
19. See Norman Mailer, "The Steps of the Pentagon," *Harper's Magaine,* CCXXXVI (March 1968), 47–142 [published in book form as *Armies of the Night* (New York, 1968)]. It may seem difficult to believe but Mailer, who calls himself a "right radical," fits our adjectives, coy and shy.
20. Herein lies a major problem for rhetorical theory. In a sense Haiman's essay (note 2) is a defense of these values accepting the responsibility implied by his analysis which shows a significant case made by the very existence of "A Rhetoric of the Streets" which demands a rebuttal. Burgess' essay (note 2) sees Black Power as a unique method of forcing conventional thought to take seriously its own criterion of rationality.

Confrontation at Columbia:
A Case Study in Coercive Rhetoric

James R. Andrews

On the broad steps leading up to Columbia University's Lowe Memorial Library, dominating College Walk, sits the placid, weather-stained figure of *alma mater.* On April 30 of last year there swirled about her feet the currents of anger, fear, puzzlement, and frustration; about her neck hung a boldly lettered sign: "Raped by the Cops."

The University had, indeed, been raped; it had been seized, immobilized, and ravished before the eyes of millions of American television viewers and newspaper readers, and word of the assault was reported throughout the world. But the attack that paralyzed the one hundred and fourteen year old institution[1] was not only an attack on Columbia University, it was the rejection of persuasive rhetoric for coercive rhetoric. To say that the "rape" was carried out "by the cops" is simplistic and propagandistic. What occurred on Morningside Heights was much more complex and has serious implications for the student of rhetoric.

The actual events of the crisis have been described exhaustively by the news media; it would be pointless to reiterate them here.[2] But the ends of a relevant rhetorical criticism may well be served by an immediate and intimate examination of the rhetorical issues posed by the upheaval at Columbia. As a member of the Columbia University community I observed much of the action firsthand, while, at the same time, as a faculty member of Teachers College I was not involved as a direct participant in the actual circumstances of the rebellion.

The Columbia incident forces the critic to face squarely the distinction between coercion and persuasion. Leland M. Griffin makes a clear distinction between these two concepts.[3] He sees a rhetorical action as being "coercive rather than persuasive" when it is "essentially non-rational," when it is "dependent on 'seat of the pants' rather than 'seat of the intellect.' "[3] Nevertheless, Professor Griffin does see even coercive actions as rhetorical, identifying, for example, a "physical rhetoric of resistance" and "body rhetoric."[5]

It seems eminently reasonable to view rhetoric as embracing all the available means of influencing human behavior and to recognize that some of these means are *persuasive* and some are not. Rhetoric, then, may be either persuasive or coercive. To make such distinctions is not merely to quibble over

From *The Quarterly Journal of Speech,* Volume 55, 1969. Reprinted with permission of the Speech Communication Association and the author.

terminology. To be able to recognize a difference in these types of rhetorical activities should serve to sharpen our analytical powers and to enhance our interpretive abilities. The political scientist Yves Simon presents an interesting delineation of the two terms. "Roughly a man is subjected to coercion when power originating outside himself causes him to act or be acted upon against his inclination," Simon wrote. "Persuasion, on the other hand, is a moral process. To persuade a man is to awaken in him a voluntary inclination toward a certain course of action. Coercion conflicts with free choice; persuasion implies the operation of free choice."[6]

Undoubtedly, such a definition has flaws. The whole question of the extent to which man ever has a completely free choice, for example, is a profound philosophical one. Further, men may act against their inclinations at the behest of powers outside themselves and are said to be "persuaded" to do so. There is, nonetheless, a continuum suggested: Rhetoric becomes less persuasive and more coercive to the extent that it limits the viable alternatives open to the receivers of communication.[7] For while persuasion aims at moving a receiver to select one of the many avenues of action open to him, coercion attempts to offer only one route by removing all other approaches from the realm of the possible. In this view "rationality" and "emotionalism" are not on opposite ends of a continuum. Such a position would call into question practically all the means of modern protest, which, as Franklyn S. Haiman has pointed out, are much different from "a Faneuil Hall rally or a Bughouse Square soapbox orator."[8] I fully agree with the implication of Professor Haiman's article, that a view of persuasion that tends to see the process as an exclusively, or even essentially, rational one is too restricting.

Accordingly, the distinction between persuasive and coercive rhetoric focuses on choice. The Columbia incident demonstrates that rhetoric ceases to be persuasive and becomes coercive as the attempt is made to restrict choice. The Columbia incident affords a case study that might point the way to a reasonable distinction between these two types of rhetoric. I propose to examine coercive tendencies as they relate to specific events in the situation: the identification and exploitation of issues; the adaptation to counterarguments; the predictive results of strategy; and the use of physical force. Further, I intend to discuss whether coercive rhetoric is justified, with particular reference to the disruption of Columbia.

Coercive Tendencies at Columbia

Identification and exploitation of issues. Two questions had long agitated the Columbia community. First, should the construction of a gymnasium in Morningside Park, city-owned land adjacent to the campus that had been leased to the University with the proviso that it be a shared facility with the Harlem community, be continued in the face of mounting hostility by community groups and growing dissatisfaction with the plan by students and faculty? And, second, should the University modify or sever its relations with the Institute for Defense Analysis? It was on these issues that the Students for a Democratic Society seized.

The use of these issues by the SDS was exploitative. The protestors clearly were not offering, nor encouraging the exploration of, real alternatives. There was no option offered to propose a variety of solutions to the IDA and gymnasium problems. Clearly the SDS was not prepared to debate issues because to them these apparent issues were not real. The aims of the radicals were larger than those that they ostensibly espoused. Mark Rudd, in a position paper drafted in October, 1967, which outlined SDS strategy for the coming year, clearly stated the organization's objectives: "(1) the 'radicalization' of students—showing people the connections in the liberal structure, showing them how our lives really are unfree in this society (and at Columbia), getting them to act in their own interest" and "(2) striking a blow at the Federal Government's war effort ('resistance')."[9] Rudd went on to describe the results of a sustained SDS campaign: Students "will become conscious of their own interests and needs and the way the university acts against them, corrupting and distorting education. . . . We will be able to present our alternative to this university and this society as we discuss the role of the university under capitalism."[10]

To the SDS far more was involved than the gym and the IDA. The University itself, and through it the society of which it was an agent, was deplored by student radicals; nothing less than an "alternative" was envisioned. The goal was destruction, not reconstruction, of the university. Radical leaders logically discerned that such goals would be unsuccessful in gaining widespread support and that they could "never force the university to submit to our demands unless we have behind us the strength of the majority of students on campus."[11] To gain such backing Rudd proposed a strategy that depended on extensive organization and the statement of *specific* goals, for "to be militant is to fight to achieve a specific goal."[12] In the halting of gym construction and the abandonment of the IDA, the SDS had found specific goals that could marshal strong campus backing.

The subsidiary nature of these issues, however, became apparent as the crisis evolved. On April 28 the Board of Trustees announced the suspension of construction of the gymnasium, purportedly at the behest of Mayor John Lindsay.[13] Further, many believed that the report of Professor Henkin's committee studying the IDA would deal the Institute the death blow on the Columbia campus. One member of the *Ad Hoc* Faculty Committee, canvassing support for the Committee's mediation efforts, stated to me and to a group of my colleagues that the IDA was a "dead issue," since students and faculty alike believed it to be "on the way out." The apparent issues might have been on the way to resolution with substantial compromises being made by the administration were it not for another issue that the protestors had injected: full amnesty for all students involved in demonstrations. (This argument will be discussed later in another context. What it demonstrates at this point is that the protestors had not focused their efforts exclusively on the apparent issues.)

In "The Rhetoric of Confrontation," Scott and Smith have suggested that student radicals generally see as their goal the destruction of universities and by so "stalemating America's intellecutal establishment," they will eventually "paralyze the political establishment as well."[14] Through their seizure of the two most burning Columbia issues, the SDS leaders had attempted to make only two choices available—support the SDS or support the administration's plan to construct the gym and stay with the IDA (for the moment, at least). But support of the SDS did not allow for a meaningful stand on the issues— it implied so much more. And the unhappy floundering of many faculty members and students during the hiatus between the seizure of the buildings and the police intervention clearly demonstrated their reluctance to accept either alternative. But the SDS would offer no other. Their exploitative manipulation of the issues was decidedly coercive in that it severely limited the kind of choices that could have been explored in a truly persuasive atmosphere.

Adaptation to counterarguments. Throughout the controversy radical leaders were at pains to prevent counterarguments or compromises from eroding their position. Their actual goal was not to answer objections or persuasively defend rejections of compromise. Their aim was to limit the choice of possibilities offered to the student audience. The answer to official statements and offers to negotiate was an unequivocal "bull shit," from Mark Rudd.[15] The choice then was between the SDS position and "bull shit"; no choice at all. Through a linguistic tactic designed not to answer arguments, but to dismiss them from the realm of the possible, Rudd and other leaders consistently vilified the administration and obscured their offers to talk. Who, for example, could consider the position of a "son-of-a-bitch" who had rejected students' demands "a million times," as Rudd pointed out in a speech at the sundial.[16]

Words are so powerful, as Ogden and Richards observed, that "by the excitement which they provoke through their emotive force, discussion is for the most part rendered sterile."[17] Certainly one of the striking rhetorical tactics employed by the radicals was to use language and description to render counterarguments beyond the pale of consideration. The University itself was repeatedly labeled as "racist," as Rudd had done when he seized the microphone to disrupt a memorial service held for Dr. King earlier in the month.[18] Black militant leaders who invaded the campus contributed their own inflammatory descriptions to the racist theme. Charles 37X Kenyatta, leader of the Mau Mau, pictured the University as the "Columbia octopus," and the Chairman of the Harlem branch of CORE, Victor Solomon, proclaimed that "this community is being raped."[19] In a speech at a teach-in at Teachers College Professor Eric Bentley, a firm supporter of the strike, strongly suggested that President Kirk was a racist who disliked the recently murdered Martin Luther

King. Whether or not the past actions of Columbia University had been in its own best interests, or in the best interests of its Harlem neighbors, or even in the best interests of the liberal, intellectual community at large is beside this particular point. Radical rhetoric offered a choice between support for the protestors or support for their "racist" enemies. Again, no choice at all, but a coercive attempt designed to eliminate real alternatives.

From the very beginning of the crisis many recognized that the police might be called in to clear the buildings. The radicals failed to come to grips with this possibility publicly before the event occurred. When it came radical rhetoric was mobilized to place, once again, the reasonable investigation of the merits and demerits of such action beyond consideration. Their hyperbolic description of the event attempted to equate its defense with defense of fascist totalitarianism. Stories of blood and beating were rife on the campus; there were many examples of rumors and exaggeration. Now it seems apparent from all accounts that some police acted viciously; some took out their frustrations, built up during days and nights of tension and taunts, on unarmed students. It is a sad and distressing sight to see any student with blood running down his face. Nevertheless, the injuries sustained were superficial and none of a serious nature resulted.[20] A press release from the Strike Steering Committee is typical of the use of language to describe this incident:

> Students have been clubbed, beaten, and carted off in police vans by the hundreds. Faculty members have been carried out on stretchers. And with that it is clear. University violence against students and faculty is an extension of its violence against black people in Columbia University owned buildings, against the community in the seizure of park land, against third world struggles in IDA weapons systems, against employees in denial of unions and decent wages. And now, in a 3 A.M. police raid, violence is used against students and faculty.
>
> The nature of the University was clearly revealed. The Trustees and administration respond only to outside interests, student and faculty demands are met with violence.[21]

To label all counterarguments as total evil, to describe hyperbolically the controversial situation, and to picture the only choice as between the SDS position and brutal racism was to limit reasonable choices coercively.

The predictive results of strategy. When rhetorical strategy is so designed that it leaves the opposition no viable persuasive alternative, it is a coercive one. Scott and Smith have forcefully pointed out that "those who would confront have learned a brutal art, practiced sometimes awkwardly and sometimes skillfully, which demands response. But that art may provoke the response that confirms its presuppositions . . . and turns the power-enforced victory of the establishment into a symbolic victory for its opponents."[22] The demand of the radicals for amnesty was indeed coercive; it left no room for maneuvering, compromise, or examination of alternatives. It forced the administration to use coercive measures itself or submit to unconditional surrender.

The demand for amnesty obviously rendered meaningful discussion and compromise impossible. Student radicals could hardly have failed to realize that the administration would view such an action as surrender. Certainly on the subject of amnesty the administration's response, and that of the Trustees who "advised the president that they wholeheartedly support the administration position that there shall be no amnesty accorded to those who have engaged in this illegal conduct," was highly predictable.[23]

While faculty groups worked arduously to achieve a compromise, the demonstrators were adamant. Even the generally sympathetic *Spectator* was moved to comment that "the most serious loss of perspective has been shown by the students negotiating on the side of the demonstrators . . . throughout the latter part of the week, the demonstrators consistently refused to accept any solutions at all that were offered them by the faculty groups."[24] As the sit-in continued, reaction began to emerge. Anti-SDS students formed a group called the Majority Coalition and blocked the entry of pro-SDS students with food and supplies into Lowe Library. One disgruntled student, addressing a faculty meeting, asserted, "Three years of the administration giving in to the SDS is a long time to restrain ourselves. . . . And in the last three days we've been sold out several times."[25] Pressure on the administration from the alumni was also building. The President of Murray Space Corporation, for example, wired the Alumni Secretary: "As an alumnus I am shocked at the handling of mob rule taking over Columbia University. These people are not supporting the University. How can law respecting alumni be expected to support a university run by hoodlums and law breakers."[26] The tide of sympathy was beginning to run against the demonstrators.

It became extremely likely that, unless a compromise were reached, the administration would feel compelled to call in the police; the demonstrators utterly refused to agree to any compromise. They undoubtedly anticipated police action—one of the students in an occupied building said that he and his compatriots would not leave until their demands were met or until "we are carried out by the cops."[27] Undoubtedly, as Scott and Smith assert, in many cases "altercation with the police is enough. It is consummatory."[28] In the Columbia case, it not only fulfilled the function of unmasking the establishment in its true brutality (as the radicals saw it), but it also served to unite campus opinion behind the SDS leaders. The violent confrontation led to a broader base of support.[29] These supporters had not been persuaded; they had clearly been coerced. By inflexibly pursuing a strategy that almost inevitably led to confrontation, the demonstrators had forced the university community to choose, not between discernible positions, but between the bloodied students, armed only with their intellect and their passion to right hypocritical wrongs, and the unseen, powerful administration moving to protect its plush offices, aided by beats with blackjacks and billy clubs. The choice of propositions, like the prose, was purple. And it was coercive.

The use of physical force. I do not propose to devote much space to this consideration. Actions like pulling down a metal fence,[30] or holding a dean captive[31] seem clearly non-persuasive in that they employ direct physical force or its threat. Likewise the burning of a professor's papers,[32] or the fears one heard expressed that the strikers would retaliate against faculty who refused to support them, would generally be held to be coercive and not persuasive rhetorical strategies. Suffice it to say that such actions were also a part of the Columbia incident.

Is Coercive Rhetoric Justified?

Not all demonstrations, as Professor Haiman observes perceptively, are coercive. He clearly differentiates between the actions of a peaceful demonstrator whose act of protest is not inherently coercive, and the hostile audience that chooses "to go forth to do battle with them."[33] Violence, in such a case, is clearly the result of hostile action by anti-demonstrators who seek a confrontation.

At Columbia, however, no choice was given those who dissented from the protest: In the occupied buildings students could not go to classes, professors could not work undisturbed in their offices, administrators could not carry out their duties. The protest was clearly not a persuasive demonstration that gave an audience a choice of responsive alternatives.

Given the distinction between persuasion and coercion that I have suggested, the student radicals at Columbia chose to employ coercive rather than persuasive rhetorical procedures. Their rhetorical strategy was one of polarization; it aimed to admit only two choices, one of which was consistently distorted. Were such procedures justified?[34]

Professor Haiman asserts that "if the channels for peaceful protest and reform become so clogged that they appear to be (and, in fact, may be) inaccessible to some segments of the population, then the Jeffersonian doctrine that 'the tree of liberty must be refreshed from time to time, with the blood of patriots and tyrants' may become more appropriate to the situation than more civilized rules of the game."[35] In the Columbia case, there were, no doubt, some clogs in the channels. The Kirk administration was accused, for example, by as relatively moderate a student as the President of the Student Council of "sitting for almost ten months on a report recommending a greater role for faculty members and students in Columbia's disciplinary machinery," and of "being inaccessible to student leaders."[36] To think, however, in this case of "patriots" and "tyrants" is to oversimplify, to make an exceedingly skewed judgment that the acts hardly seem to warrant. This is no doubt the quintessential problem, for it hangs ultimately on the extent to which one may allow himself to go when condoning rhetorical strategies used in behalf of what *he* considers to be worthy causes. If rhetorical theory in the twentieth century must take into account the change described by Scott and Smith, that "civility and decorum serve as masks for the preservation of injustice,"[37] then rhetorical criticism obviously must also provide for the examination of those cases in which civility and decorum are discarded for ends that are not obviously and unquestionably just. In the film based on Gore Vidal's *The Best Man,* the former President observed to a ruthless young politician that in politics, as in life, "there are no ends, only means." It may be that in the examination of the means of protests, and not necessarily in any inherent worthiness of their goals, that rhetorical critics can hope to make meaningful contributions. An understanding of the distinction between persuasion and coercion might provide one means whereby rhetorical critics could reach judgments concerning the essential rhetorical nature of confrontation.

Notes

1. The entire University was not immobilized. The primary unit affected was Columbia College, which is for undergraduate men. Columbia University is a loose confederation rather than a unified structure, and such units as Teachers College and Barnard College (each of which has its own President and Board of Trustees), and the School of Law, functioned with much less interruption of schedules, classes, and programs. This is not to say that all units were not deeply affected by the crisis. Significant changes in the role of students in influencing policy are underway throughout the entire University community. (See, e.g., *New York Times,* May 13, 1968, pp. 1 and 47). In my own department at Teachers College, for example, a joint student-faculty departmental meeting resulted in the institution of a committee composed of all the faculty plus an *equal* number of elected students to pass on all matters over which the department has decision-making authority.
2. The most thorough account of the events at Columbia appears in the *New York Times,* daily issues from April 24 through May 23; a good summary account is given in *Newsweek,* May 6 and May 13; *Crisis at Columbia: An Inside Report on the Rebellion at Columbia from the Pages of the Columbia Daily Spectator,* a collection of issues of the campus newspaper from April 24 through May 8, gives lively and complete coverage of the events from the students' point of view.
3. "The Rhetorical Structure of the 'New Left' Movement: Part I," *QJS,* L (April 1964), 113–135.
4. *Ibid.,* 127.
5. *Ibid.*
6. *Philosophy of Democratic Government* (Chicago, 1951), p. 109.
7. This interpretation is similar to the one expressed by Thomas Nilsen in his chapter on "Persuasion" in *Ethics of Speech Communication* (Indianapolis, 1966). Nilsen, however, seems to place great emphasis on the "openness" with which a speaker reveals his strategy (p. 55), a proposition I find very difficult to accept.
8. "The Rhetoric of the Streets: Some Legal and Ethical Considerations," *QJS,* LIII (April 1967), 99.
9. *New York Times,* May 13, 1968, p. 46.
10. *Ibid.*
11. *Ibid.*
12. *Ibid.*
13. *Ibid.,* April 28, 1968, p. 74.
14. Robert L. Scott and Donald K. Smith, "The Rhetoric of Confrontation," *supra,* p. 5.

15. "Columbia at Bay," *Newsweek,* LXXI (May 6, 1968), 43.
16. *Columbia Daily Spectator,* April 24, 1968, p. 3.
17. C. K. Ogden and I. A. Richards, *The Meaning of Meaning* (New York, 1923), p. 45.
18. *Columbia Daily Spectator,* April 12, 1968, p. 1.
19. *Newsweek,* LXXI (May 6, 1968), 44.
20. The question of what is or is not "brutal" is a difficult one. The *Columbia Daily Spectator* of April 30 reported that 135 people were treated for injuries in nearby hospitals and at a special infirmary set up at Philosophy Hall. *Newsweek* reported that 132 students, four faculty members, and twelve policemen were injured. No student or faculty member, however, was hospitalized. The Mayor's reaction was based on the reports of his aides on the spot, and is probably the most accurate assessment. Mr. Lindsay admitted that while some members of the police force "used excessive force," the majority demonstrated "great professionalism and restraint," *Newsweek,* LXXI (May 13, 1968), 59–60. To describe the police action as "beyond comprehension," as a flyer distributed by the *Ad Hoc* Teachers College Strike Committee did, is certainly to overstate the case.
21. Press statement, April 30, 9 A.M., distributed on campus.
22. Scott and Smith, *supra,* p. 8
23. *New York Times,* April 28, 1968, p. 74.
24. *Columbia Daily Spectator,* April 29, 1968, p. 4.
25. *Ibid.,* April 26, 1968, p. 3.
26. *Connection: A Magazine Supplement of the Columbia Daily Spectator,* I, 2, May 10, 1968, p. C5.
27. *Columbia Daily Spectator,* April 26, 1968, p. 3.
28. Scott and Smith, *supra,* p. 7.
29. The campus reaction is accurately described and documented in "The End of a Siege—and an Era," *Newsweek,* LXXI (May 13, 1968), 60.
30. *Columbia Daily Spectator,* April 24, 1968, p. 1.
31. *Ibid.,* and also April 25, 1968, p. 1.
32. *New York Times,* May 23, 1968, p. 51.
33. Haiman, 112.
34. I have not discussed the question of civil disobedience in the Columbia case. At Columbia the protestors were not breaking a law that was in itself deemed unjust (the laws of trespass), nor were they willing to be punished in any way for their actions. The argument that such incidents as the one at Columbia fall outside the concept of civil disobedience is ably articulated by Mr. Justice Fortas in *The New York Times Magazine,* May 12, 1968, and I could not improve on it here.
35. Haiman, 105.
36. *New York Times,* May 13, 1968, p. 47.
37. Scott and Smith, *supra,* p. 8.

10
Rhetoric of Architecture

Architecture is one of humanity's dominant symbolic forms. From the temples and ziggurats of the ancients to the skyscrapers and crystal cathedrals of today, artists working with the raw materials of stone, glass, lumber, sheet metal, brick, and mortar have attempted to express themselves through the creation of their hands. In so doing, they have taken on the role of cultural rhetoricians, often expressing the views and values of the society from which they come—occasionally reacting against those traditional views.

The making of physical structures—houses, churches, barns, bridges, display windows, schools, supermarkets, and graveyards, among others—requires that the maker engage in a conscious decision-making process: What raw materials shall be used to construct the edifice? How shall the parts of the structure be related to one another? What overt themes or motifs shall be incorporated into the design? How should the users feel or what emotions should they experience upon encountering or entering the structure? These are questions of rhetoric—of how a maker chooses to compose and structure his or her creation, and how that creation evokes a response—intellectual, moral, economic, aesthetic—from its users.

In his essay, "The Medieval Marquee: Church Portal Sculpture as Publicity," Charles F. Altman argues that a significant change occurred in the architectural design of European churches, starting in the 11th century. This change involved the design of entrances and exits, and marked a change in the rhetorical functioning of the church portal and its immediately surrounding environs.

In practice, architecture intersects with rhetoric at several levels. A structure embodies and symbolizes ideas and values. The structure, further, determines the activities of those who inhabit it, and their relations to one another, including their communicative relationships. Hence, a church is both a rhetorical artifact and the setting for the enactment of rhetorical, sacred ritual. An executive's office is both an expression of his or her position and role in an organization, and a direct influence on the human behavior of those who use the office, including especially the talk that takes place there.

According to Altman, the portal area becomes "a symbolic dissertation on the place of the door in sacred geography." By understanding the symbolic significance of portal art, one can better understand the persuasive efforts of the Church and how those efforts were carried out, in part, by architectural means. To understand the messages on and about the portal to the church was, Altman argues, to understand the place of the church in relationship to the outside world.

By examining one of the more popular portal sculptures—the story of the rich man and Lazarus—Altman is able to show how the choice of the story and the specific icons of its representation function to advertise the salvation that awaits sinners if they will but enter the door. The portal sculpture is a symbolic, visual representation to the public at large of the Church's vision of itself and its mission. As such, it is a form of visual rhetoric.

Elizabeth Walker Mechling and Jay Mechling bring the reader back to the twentieth century with a semiotic analysis of two amusement parks, Disneyland and Marriott's Great America. Starting from the Marxist-structuralist analysis of Disneyland by Louis Marin, the Mechlings bring the same perspective and procedures to bear on the "text" of Marriott's Great America. What they find is that Marriott's is a cultural enactment of the dominant trend in bourgeois society—"the transformation of quality into quantity."

To best understand the values promoted by Marriott's park, it is argued, one must recognize the dichotomous values that are presented in "an undulating, rhythmic, repetitive pattern." These values are expressed by rides and amusements which participate in one of the two dominant value clusters: BIG/ EXPENSIVE/DANGEROUS or HUMAN SCALE/INEXPENSIVE/ SAFE. The architectural layout of the park is characterized by a ceaseless repetition of these two value clusters. One enters the BIG/EXPENSIVE/ DANGEROUS world of the rides only to be returned to the HUMAN SCALE/INEXPENSIVE/SAFE world of the park, a world where one can "celebrate" having survived the danger by eating or buying or browsing among the consumer goods.

To understand the rhetoric of the amusement park, the Mechling's seem to argue, is to be inculcated with the values of the bourgeois social structure which constructed the park in the first place. By learning to read and value the architectural signs, one comes to understand the ideological implications of seemingly mundane cultural artifacts. As the medieval marquee functioned to announce the Church's values and vision to the pagan world, so the twentieth century amusement park masks the cultural values of free market capitalism.

Architectural signs are omnipresent. Yet the very obviousness of such signs, the fact that they announce their existence by occupying public space and appealing to the human senses, often results in the masking and de-politicizing of their cultural bias. To be fully aware of any given structure's ostensible, pragmatic functions is often to be unaware of the symbolic meanings which lurk just beyond the everyday-ness of its representation. By understanding that architecture is a symbol system, replete with social, cultural, economic, and moral significations, the critic takes the first step toward unmasking the hegemony that physical structures exert on the way we envision ourselves, our environment, and our relations with others.

The Medieval Marquee:
Church Portal Sculpture as Publicity

Charles F. Altman

How may we speak of popular culture in a world where transportation is inadequate, mass communications non-existent, and printing not yet invented? We meet elite culture at every turn, in the carefully turned Latin phrases of learned clerics, in the polished language of the courtly lyric and romance, in the exquisite workmanship of the goldsmith or enamelist. Folk culture is everywhere present—in the oral performance and rough syntax of the vernacular epic, in the scabrous short tale, in the pre-Lenten carnival festival. Given current definitions, however, we must conclude that popular culture as such is not a phenomenon which we may associate with the medieval period. Only by extending and reformulating the accepted definition may we arrive at an approach to popular culture less historically limited than current ones, an approach which gives primacy to functional relationships rather than technology.

Let us begin by unpacking the current notion which ties popular culture to the mass media. This simple claim in fact covers two separate principles:

1. The artifacts of popular culture achieve wide distribution among all classes of society. They are easy of access, inexpensive to consume, and made of relatively cheap materials.
2. Popular culture is by definition a mediated culture. Between the popular artist and his public stands an institution which publishes the popular text for its own ends—profit production and self-preservation. This mediatory publishing institution strongly influences the form of the popular text, making the popular artist only partially responsible for the form in which the work is disseminated. He may choose what to write, but the publisher (network, manufacturer) decides what will actually be produced.

The first of these principles has long been recognized. The second has not been adequately acknowledged, yet it lies at the heart of popular culture's special position within society. We may appreciate this more fully by comparing popular art to its elite and folk counterparts. In general, folk art is unmediated art. Not only *for* the people, it is also *of* and *by* the people. The folk artist belongs to the same class as his audience and has regular personal

Reprinted from the *Journal of Popular Culture,* Volume 14, 1980, with permission of the Popular Press, Bowling Green, OH.

contact with the members of that audience. Performers are live, thus permitting on-the-spot interaction between artist and audience; typically each performance is different because the performer reacts differently to each audience. Furthermore, the distinction between performer and audience is not permanent and irreversible; at any moment a member of the audience may take up the guitar and become a performer. According to the romantic notions which color every aspect of our sense of elite art, the elite artist is a demiurge, a seer, a *vates* who creates because he must. Art in the post-romantic world enjoys the status of religion. The elite artist thus creates his art work totally oblivious to the media which will distribute it, on the understanding that they will faithfully transmit it to the public. Any editor or producer who alters the finished product of a T. S. Eliot or an Orson Welles is immediately labeled a charlatan. For the conventions of elite art declare the art work to be the inviolate creation of a sacred individual: the inspired artist. Tampering with such a holy institution is tantamount to sacrilege.

In contrast, the popular artifact is always tainted, soiled by the spectre of monetary gain, less than immaculate conception, and the heretical hand of the artistically inept publisher, producer, or press agent. Where the elite or highbrow artist—at least in theory—writes in a vacuum and is eventually published by an organization convinced of the artistic value of his work, the popular artist is for all practical purposes the employee of a publishing institution with its own values and vested interests. Consequently, the popular text typically speaks with two voices:

1. Written for the people, the popular text panders to the people's supposed preferences, reaffirming their values, encouraging their dreams, playing to their fantasies. Indeed, the very presence of this populist voice tends to make the public unaware of another voice which it masks.
2. Distributed by an institution, the popular text serves that institution's vested interests, in particular the institution's drive for survival. The popular text thus always functions as an advertisement for the institution which produced it. This self-advertisement may take the blatant form of praise for the text's very medium (e.g. the importance of reading competence for Horatio Alger's heroes, the laudatory treatment of Hollywood in the musical). More often, however, it is the producing institution's values which are celebrated by the popular text (e.g. the Hollywood film's incessant rewarding of romantic love, boy scout virtue, and free enterprise).

How then do these general precepts about the nature of popular culture affect the study of the field in the pre-modern period? In general we may formulate the following guidelines:

1. Popular culture may be said to exist when a given text achieves wide dissemination through the efforts of a publishing institution (taken in a broad sense) with a vested interest in survival.

390

2. Therefore, use of mass media is not a necessary condition for the existence of popular culture.
3. Conversely, broad dissemination of a particular artifact does not constitute a sufficient condition for the existence of popular culture.
4. Analysis of the popular text must take into account both aspects of the text's rhetoric—the voice which advertises the publishing institution's values and services as well as the voice which appeals to the public's pre-existing tastes and self-interest.

These four principles will be kept in mind as we pursue a specific example of medieval popular culture.

II. From Altar to Portal Art: Taking the Sacred Image to the People

During the course of the 11th century in Western Europe there occurred an innovation in church decoration which was to have a profound effect on the arts in general throughout the middle ages. Prior to the romanesque period the church building regularly took on the appearance and structure of a fortress, its walls serving to separate a sacred space within from the secular space without. The outside of the edifice bore little if any witness to the activities taking place within. In contrast to the coarse exterior of wood, stone or brick, the inside was commonly aflame with the bright colors of mosaic, fresco, embroidered cloth or precious metals. Though from time to time the nave may have been decorated with hieratic or narrative compositions, church art of the first millennium was in general concentrated in the altar area. Often this art work was distributed into three separate levels: the crypt, where relics were displayed (frescoes, decorated sarcophagi, reliquaries fashioned out of precious metals, rare stones or carved ivory), the main altar, where the scripture was read and the mass celebrated (finely wrought paten and chalice, sumptuous candelabra or chandelier, embroidered altar cloths, illuminated manuscripts), and the vault above (where God's dominion over the universe is figured in mosaic or fresco). Of all the arts displayed in the altar area, most remained only marginally visible to the faithful; those which presented figures large enough to be recognized—such as the apse *Majestas*—served not so much to teach or persuade but only to illustrate the Christian message to those already familiar with it. The church art of the first millennium is thus a radically private art, limited to the believer and to the most sacred parts of his place of worship. Like the mass which the priest celebrates even when no one is present to participate, early church art exists primarily for the glory of God and not for the rhetorical effect which it might have on man.

Altar art never disappears entirely from the Christian repertory, but during the romanesque period it is rapidly replaced as the primary mode of religious art by another type of art with a radically different location and function.

Given its status as sacred fortress, the early church (baptistry, mausoleum, etc.) pays little attention to entrances and exists, unles it is to limit them and assure their impenetrability to the unfaithful.

Beginning in the 11th century, however, the churches of Western Europe begin to pay increased attention to the *Westwerk,* the western end of the church which is henceforth often endowed with twin towers and multiple portals. Now in previous churches, a door was most often just a door, an entrance or an exit with practical rather than symbolic value. With the romanesque church, however, this practical approach to the portal is radically modified. By surrounding the door itself with a sculptural program ranging from a band of ornamentation to tens of square yards of narrative sculpture, the 12th-century church turns the portal area into a symbolic dissertation on the place of the door in sacred geography. In the early church, the door—except for that fleeting instant when an individual is passing through it—constitutes part of the wall separating secular and sacred space. In the romanesque church, however, the portal must simultaneously figure both in the separation between the holy and the worldy and their potential continuity.

Not only does representational art, previously reserved for the church interior, spill over onto the jambs, tympanum, archivolt and facade of the romanesque church, but in so doing it changes character radically. If altar art is static art designed to celebrate God's glory, portal art combines that celebratory sense with a narrative impulse revealing the process by which one may pass from secular space to sacred space (a process obviously prefigured by the act of passing through the church portal itself).[3] Scenes of the Last Judgment, parables with a clear moral lesson (e.g. the Wise and Foolish Virgins), episodes from the lives of well-known saints all provide the faithful with an example to be followed as well as a counter-example to be avoided.

Furthermore, portal art is no longer private, limited access art, as was altar art. The tympanum dominates not the altar but the town square—secular space supreme. Visible at any time of the day or night, portal art becomes a part of the townspeople's daily lives, whereas altar art was a Sunday experience. Portal art is thus by its very nature *evangelical* art, and as such addressed to a far wider and more varied public than altar art could ever have been. Instead of simply expressing a truth, it seeks to communicate that truth, to convince someone of it. Portal art interfaces, as it were, the eternal repose of the church within and the hustle-and-bustle of the world without. In general the rise of representational and narrative sculpture in romanesque art may be related to this desire to evangelize, to make truths live for the masses.

At the risk of oversimplification we might summarize the preceding comments in the following way:

Early Altar Art	Romanesque Portal Art
ritual reaffirmation	evangelism
static	narrative
private	public
precious or perishable materials	stone
designed to be contemplated primarily during religious ceremony	available at any time, freed from any specific relationship with the Holy Office
part of a unified religious experience	part of an uncontrolled secular scene

In short, romanesque portal art has many of the characteristics which we associate with the popular arts. Produced in general by lay masons working in close connection with the church, romanesque portal art displays the apocalyptic subjects and narrative representational techniques which have the best chance of appealing to the people at large.[4] Relying on the familiar image rather than the written language, west facade programs typically reach a far larger percentage of the population than any previous religious art form. It remains to be seen, however, how the popular imagery of romanesque portal art manages simultaneously to fulfill the needs of its varied public as well as the requirements of the text's publisher—the Church.

III. Beggar and Rich Man at the Church Door: The Function of the Dives and Lazarus Parable in the Portal Program

Of all the subjects carved in medieval portal programs, the most common are undoubtedly apocalyptic scenes, often accompanied by episodes from the life of Christ. Indeed, so many romanesque churches display such scenes that it would be impossible in an article of this length even to begin an analysis of their form and function. Instead, I will concentrate on the fascinating and often represented parable of the rich man *(Dives)* and the poor beggar Lazarus (Luke 16:19ff).[5] Beginning in the 11th century, this parable was represented throughout Europe in every medium and location imaginable: as a nave fresco,[6] in stone capitals located in every part of the church,[7] in manuscript illustrations,[8] even in bronze and glass.[9] By far the most common location for the Dives and Lazarus parable, however, is the area directly adjacent to or above the church entrance: the tympanum,[10] in a series of porch capitals,[11] or in a sequence of reliefs.[12] Why, we may well ask, is this particular story so often chosen as part of a portal program? What function does it play in terms of the overall program? As popular narrative—in every sense of that expression—does the Dives and Lazarus story have particular appeal to the uneducated masses? Does it carry any self-advertisement for the church (the work's "publisher," though not its immediate author)?

As analyzed by medieval artists, the Dives and Lazarus story is typically divided into four segments:

1. The rich man at his table feasting, accompanied by a small number of revelers (at least one of whom is a woman), and often attended by a servant.
2. Lazarus lying at the rich man's door; he is covered with sores which are licked by a trio of dogs.
3. Lazarus is shown comfortably nestled in Abraham's bosom.
4. The rich man is licked by the fires of Hell; the common gesture of reaching out toward Lazarus is explained by the text as a request for a drink of water to relieve his parched throat.[13]

The first two segments are invariably combined in a single composition; the third and fourth segments—depending on the space available—are either combined or treated in similar but separate scenes. However these four basic segments are arranged, the parable's basic structure becomes apparent.[14] Just as Lazarus is offered not even the crumbs from the rich man's table, so the rich man is refused divine sustenance in the afterlife. The tale's operative dualities are clearly defined by the four-part division of the text: rich/poor, salvation/damnation, worldly life/eternal life.

On the surface this parable seems obviously addressed to the urban poor. Take heart, it says to them, for your condition is a sacred one. Those who wield power and enjoy the pleasures of this world are doomed to a life of eternal torture unless they share their worldly treasures. Viewed in this way Poverty takes on something of the sacred character which the mendicant orders would confer on it from the 13th century on. In fact, according to Emile Male, the Dives and Lazarus story is particularly appropriate to the area surrounding the church entrance, because it was there that the medieval poor congregated to beg alms.[15] Transfigured by the tale of poor Lazarus, the beggar might expect a more generous gift from the rich parishioner.

To this socio-historical explanation of the popularity of this parable as part of a portal program we may add a formal justification. The church portal, as we have seen, represents both the dividing line and the passageway between secular and sacred space. On one side the dealing of the marketplace, where men are judged by their pocketbook; on the other side the church—early symbol of the heavenly city—where only spiritual riches may be counted. This same duality is clearly reflected in the story of Dives and Lazarus, where the first and second segments take place in this world, while the third and fourth are projected into a realm beyond time. In other words, Dives and Lazarus in the first diptych are to the world outside the church as Dives and Lazarus in the second diptych are to the hallowed space within. This parable thus serves as a guide to the symbolic meaning of the portal itself. To enter in is to adopt certain values and leave others behind.

To the poor beggar seated at the church door, the meaning of the parable is hardly ambiguous. Radulphus Ardens sums it up well in a 12th-century sermon: "By this example the poor and the sick learn not to complain about their misfortunes, nor to condemn the rich, but to praise God and to blame their suffering on their own sins."[16] The promise of a reward in the next world serves to divert any criticism which the lower classes might be tempted to level at the moneyed classes. The Dives and Lazarus story thus serves the rich and poor alike: to the impoverished masses it is a tale which dignifies poverty and promises paradise; to the rich burgher or nobleman it is a defense against potential revolt. To the church, however, this parable might seem nothing short of an implicit condemnation: just as Lazarus lies penniless at the rich man's door, so the city's beggars sit unrewarded at the church portal. By carving the story of Lazarus at the church door, the church paradoxically places itself in the position of the rich man, the affluent institution which refuses to share its wealth with those who have none. Why then place this story in a position which underscores the church's formal correspondence to the uncharitable Dives?

To answer this question we must momentarily desert portal sculpture and consider instead a tradition too often forgotten in the interpretation of church art: the homily. Every year, on the second Sunday after Pentecost (first Sunday after Trinity), in churches all across Europe, the Gospel passage for the day was taken from Luke 16: 19ff; that is, the parable of Dives and Lazarus. Following the reading of the Holy Scripture, the priest would expose the meaning of the passage to the faithful. This homily was not, however, entirely of the priests's invention. In general, nearly every aspect of it would be borrowed from a long line of Church fathers stretching from Jerome and Augustine through Gregory and Bede to more recent glosses believed to be the work of Walafrid Strabo and Hugh of Saint-Victor. From the 4th century through the 12th, not much changes in the standard interpretation of this familiar parable. The rich man is given no name because at the final hour God will not know him; Lazarus is named because his name is written in the Book of Life.[17] The rich man represents the proud Jews, Lazarus the humble Gentiles hungry for knowledge. But the Jews refuse to share their Law with the Gentiles, so Lazarus is condemned to lie at the door where the dogs lick his sores. Now the sores of the flesh clearly figure, on the moral plane, the sins of the Gentiles, which can be opened only by confession, thus paving the way for the confessors' saving counsel (represented by the dogs curative licking).

Two aspects of this interpretation require particular attention; not surprisingly it is in regard to the dogs, the unexpected heroes of this reading, that more information is needed. Now the original intent of the parable can hardly have been to underscore the rich man's avarice by opposing it to the animals' charitable attention, for the dog as pet, as household companion and faithful friend, is a Western innovation. In the Middle East two millennia ago the dog was a scavenger, a coprophagous pest, hardly a fit hero for a tale of poverty rewarded. In the first century, then, the presence of the dogs must have evoked horror, graphically expressing the depths of Lazarus' misery and the extent of the rich man's lack of concern. The medieval church's interpretation of the parable thus differs radically from the original; whereas the oriental version reveals no agent of change, no method whereby Lazarus is transfigured from lowly beggar to heavenly vision, the medieval version treats the dogs as intercessors, as institutional intermediaries between this world and the next. But who exactly are these intercessors, these charitable figures who by opposition to the rich man's avarice seem somehow like a prefiguring of paradise? Here the commentators reveal a most interesting progression. Whereas Jerome in the 4th century identifies the dogs with teachers *(doctores),* nearly all commentators after Gregory the Great stress the role of the preacher-confessor.[18] In the 12th century the allegorical interpretation regularly likens the dogs to preachers *(praedicatores).*[19] The Victorine *Allegoriae in Novum Testamentum* (generally attributed to Hugh of Sant-Victor) sums up this approach quite succinctly: "the dogs lick the wounds of the pauper, because preachers by preaching take away sins—as if they were touching wounds they lead the sinner to salvation—thus the wounds of the flesh are cured when they are licked."[20]

Now this standard version of the parable must have been preached literally hundreds of thousands of times during the middle ages. No faithful parishioner could have remained unaware of this accepted interpretation.[21] Viewed in this light, the parable of Dives and Lazarus takes on a new function within the portal program. Far from simply extolling Poverty or criticizing Avarice, the parable now becomes an advertisement for the activities which take place within the church, an invitation to partake of the preaching which alone can guarantee the masses a passport to paradise. The Church's typological identity with the Heavenly City is thus reinforced and the portal's function as passageway from the secular to the sacred underscored. The hero of the portal program is thus the preacher; far from being implicated as an uncharitable institution by the parable carved at its door, the church is recognized as the dispensary of heavenly rewards.[22]

For the common people, the parable of Dives and Lazarus represents a call for charity from the rich and promise of ultimate reward. For the Church this parable represents the perfect publicity, a well disguised but nevertheless effective identification of salvation with the church and its preachers. Like a well planned theater marquee, which appeals to the customer's taste only in order better to attract him inside, the romanesque portal program remains constantly self-conscious of its position and function. Deploying representational carving and narrative sequences to a degree never before displayed, the romanesque portal complex provides the Western world with its first truly popular genre, replete with the institutional rhetoric which will characterize popular culture right down to the present era of mass media.

Notes

1. In an interesting paper which greatly helped to refine my own ideas, Stephen G. Nichols, Jr. has suggested that typanum art represents a projection of apse art onto the church's facade. In one sense this is clearly true, for romanesque tympanum iconography borrows heavily from Byzantine apse iconography. The narrative dimension of the romanesque portal area represents novelty, however. Nearly every west facade program combines scenes recalling Christ's first coming, usually narrative in nature, with a static vision of Christ's second coming. It is the combination of these two impulses which characterizes romanesque portal art. (Nichols' paper was delivered to the Medieval French Literature section of the 1977 meeting of the Modern Language Association in New York City.)
2. On the preference of the medieval lower classes for apocalyptic material, see Norman Cohn, *The Pursuit of the Millenium: Revolutionary Millenarians and Mystical Anarchists of the Middle Ages* (New York: Oxford Univ. Press, 1970; revised and enlarged), pp. 53ff.
3. There was a rich man, who was clothed in purple and fine linen who feasted sumptuously every day. And at his gate lay a poor man named Lazarus, full of sores, who desired to be fed with what fell from the rich man's table; moreover the dogs came and licked his sores. The poor man died and was carried by the angels to Abraham's bosom. The rich man also died and was buried; and in Hades, being in torment, he lifted up his eyes, and saw Abraham far off and Lazarus in his bosom. And he called out, 'Father Abraham, have mercy upon me, and send Lazarus to dip the end of his finger in water and cool my tongue; for I am in anguish in this flame.' But Abraham said, 'Son, remember that you in your lifetime received your good things, and Lazarus in like manner evil things; but now he is comforted here, and you are in anguish. And besides all this, between us and you a great chasm has been fixed, in order that those who would pass from here to you may not be able, and none may cross from there to us.' And he said, 'Then I beg you, father, to send him to my father's house, for I have five brothers, so that he may warn them, lest they also come to this place of torment.' But Abraham said, 'They have Moses and the prophets; let them hear them.' And he said, 'No, father Abraham; but if some one goes to them from the dead, they will repent.' He said to him, 'If they do not hear Moses and the prophets, neither will they be convinced if some one should rise from the dead'." (Revised Standard Version)
4. Frescoes—Italy: Sant-Angelo in Formis, Brindisi (Santa Maria del Casale); Spain: San Clemente de Tahus (partial); Germany: Burgfeldun; England: Hardham (Saint Botolph); France: Vicq-sur-Saint Chartier (Eglise Saint-Martin), Ponce (Eglise Saint-Julien), Saint-Junien (collegiale).
5. Capitals—nave: Vezelay (Basilique Sainte-Marie-Madeleine); aisle: Besse-en-Chandesse (Eglise Saint-Andre); exterior blind arcades: Vigeois (ancienne priorale Saint-Pierre); cloister: Moissac (ancienne abbatiale Saint-Pierre), Monreale (cathedral).
6. Manuscript illustration—*codex aureus Epternacensis,* Nuremberg, Germanisches National museum, hs.2°156142, fol. 79 recto; a copy of the above, Escorial Codex Vitrinas 17, fol. 117 verso; Herrad of Landsberg, *Hortus Deliciarum* (destroyed in the Strasbourg fire of 1870; for a copy see A. Straub and G. Keller, Herrade de Landsberg, *Hortus deliciarum,* Stransbourg: Monuments historiques d'Alsace,

1879–99; illus. 32bis); New York, Pierpont Morgan Library MS 521, recto (a leaf which may have prefaced the Eadwine Psalter); Godefridus, Abbot of Admont, *Homilies*, Library of the Abbey of Admont (Styria); *La Somme le roy, Millar MS (published in Eric George Millar, La Somme le roy,* Oxford: Roxburghe Club, 1957; fol. 188 verso).

7. Bronze—the column at Hildensheim; stained glass—Bourges (Cathedrale Saint-Etienne, choir).

8. Sympanum—Avila (San Vincente), York (now in Museum of Yorkshire Philosophical Society), and possibly Ruffic (north blind doorway of Saint-Andre).

9. Porch capitals—Toulouse (Saint-Sernin, the south door known as the Porte des Comtes), Lescure d'Albigeois (ancienne priorale Saint-Michel), Autun (Cathedrale Saint-Lazare, north door), Nevers (Saint-Sauveur, part now in Musee Lapidaire).

10. Reliefs—Moissac (ancienne abbatiale Saint-Pierre), Lagrauliere (Eglise Saint-Marcel), Argenton-Chateau (Eglise Saint-Gilles), Lincoln (Cathedral), Rouen (Cathedrale Notre-Dame, south portal known as the Portail de la Calende).

11. The popular 12th-century preacher Radulphus Ardens (Raoul Ardent) outlines six parts: "There are then six parts of the parable in question; first the worth of the rich man is set forth, second the worth of the pauper, third the reward of the pauper, fourth the punishment of the rich man, fifth the rich man prays for himself, sixth for his kin, but his prayers are not answered." Migne, *Patrologia Latina* (hereafter PL), vol. 155, col. 1962. The last two sections as outlined by Radulphus Ardens are never to my knowledge represented in medieval iconography.

12. This claim holds only for the romanesque period. Gothic treatments of the Dives and Lazarus parable tend to split the narrative into a continuous progression of minuscule segments, thus sacrificing the parable's exemplary dualism to realistic representation and cause-and-effect sequentiality. It is interesting in this respect to note Emile Male's misconceptions about the 13th-century popularity of this parable. In *The Gothic Image: Religious Art in France of the Thirteenth Century* (trans. Dora Nussey; New York: Harper, 1958, 1958; orig. 1913) Male lists the Dives and Lazarus parable as one of the four most common in 13th-century French art. In fact, of the thirty-three locations listed above, some twenty-eight are either 11th or 12th century, while only four are from the 13th century.

13. Male, *op. cit.,* p. 200; see also Raymond Rey, *La Sculpture romane languedocienne* (Paris: Didier, 1936), pp. 77ff.

14. Radulphus Ardens, PL vol. 155, col. 1963.

15. The fact that Lazarus is the only named character in any of Christ's parables gives rise to a great deal of interesting commentary on the specific genre of the Dives and Lazarus story. The 9th-century *Glossa Ordinaria* (falsely attributed to Walafrid Strabo) says that the story seems more like a narrative than a parable ("magis videtur narratio quam parabola," PL vol. 114, col. 316); Radulphus claims it is not only a parable but also a story ("non solum parabola sed etiam historia est," PL vol. 155, col. 1962); Werner of Saint-Blasus in the Black Forest points out that naming a character is more appropriate to narration than parable ("Nota cum parabolae non ponant nomina, et Dominus per humilitatis approbationem pauperis hugus nomen dicat, non parabola, sed rei gestae narratio haec est," PL vol. 157, col. 1004–05; Zacharias Chrysopolitanus gives word for word the same passage, ultimately borrowed from Ambrose and Petrus Chrysologus (PL vol. 186, col. 337).

16. Jerome, PL vol. 30, col. 594; Gregory the Great, PL vol. 76, col. 1303 *(Homiliae XL in Evangelia,* but see also *Moralia in Job,* book 25, ch. 13); Bede, *Expositio in Lucae Evangelium,* PL vol. 92, col. 533 (also his homily on the parable, PL vol. 94, col. 267); Smaragdus, PL vol. 102, col. 348.

17. Werner, PL vol. 157, col. 1007; Godefridus, PL 174, col. 387; Zacharias Chrysopolitanus, PL vol. 186, col. 337.
18. Hugh of Saint-Victor, PL vol. 175, col. 822.
19. The sermons which I have quoted are all conserved in Latin, but students of the medieval homily have repeatedly insisted that these Latin originals served as the basic text for vernacular sermons. See L. Bourgain, *La Chaire franciase au XII e siecle* (Paris: Societe generale de Librarie catholique, 1879), p. 186; more recently Michel Zink has dealt with the same problem in *La Predication en langue romane avant 1300* (Paris: Champion, 1976), pp. 85ff.
20. In the later middle ages the connection between the Dives and Lazarus parable and preaching is further reinforced by an identification of Lazarus and/or his dogs with the mendicant preaching orders, especially the Dominicans. Known by a common pun as the bloodhounds of God *(domini canes),* the members of this order mixed poverty and preaching in a manner clearly reminiscent of the Dives and Lazarus parable. It is thus not surprising to find Lazarus interpreted as a Dominican in the Bible Moralisee of the later middle ages or represented as a talented preacher in the Middle English *Dives and Pauper* (ed. Priscilla Heath Barnum; London: Oxford Univ. Press, 1976; Early English Text Society, No. 275.

The Sale of Two Cities: A Semiotic Comparison of Disneyland with Marriott's Great America

Elizabeth Walker Mechling and Jay Mechling

One of the most troubling insights coming out of mythic analysis of American popular culture materials is the realization that, like R. D. Laing's schizophrenic patients, "We are acting parts in a play that we have never read and never seen, whose plot we don't know, whose existence we can glimpse, but whose beginning and end are beyond our present imagination and conception."[1]

The point of a semiotic approach to popular culture is precisely parallel to Laing's communication systems approach to family therapy—namely, to discover the larger "stories" of which individual signs, symptoms, (i.e., transformed signs of internal states) and clusters of symptoms are a part. There is some risk in stating simply that the goal of a semiotic approach to popular culture is the search for "stories" in the data, but semiotic theory and method are worth saving from the terminological obfuscation that seems to be accompanying the spread of structuralism, semiology, and semiotics through the culture studies disciplines.[2]

C. S. Peirce established the term *semiotic* as the "formal doctrine of signs," as a scientific method for discovering from observed signs what must be the system of signs characteristic of a "thinking" system, either an individual or a group.[3] To discover the meaning of signs and symptoms is to discover the patterns of their relations, and the semiotician is interested in the relations between signs, between signs and their objects, and between signs and their "interpretants" (Peirce's term for a sign created by a sign). Stories are the vehicles by which members of a culture communicate to each other patterns of relations and transformations in their shared symbolic systems. What the semiotic approach to popular cultures does, then, is expand its view to take in all sign systems of a culture and seek in those sign systems those myths and other formula narratives that are the culture's characteristic stories.[4]

Put most simply, in this essay we intend to ask: "What are the *stories* that Disneyland and Marriott's Great America tell?" Or, more precisely, "What are the stories that the *visitor* to Disneyland or to Marriott's Great America *enacts* as she or he walks and rides through these two parks?" At issue is the degree to which the parks' stories force an interpretation upon the visitor, and the degree to which visitors exercise freedom in enacting their own stories

Reprinted from the *Journal of Popular Culture,* Volume 15, 1981, with permission of The Popular Press, Bowling Green, OH.

within each park. To the extent that the radical response to bourgeois popular culture is an accurate one, to that extent will be revealed the ways in which popular culture both teaches and evokes stories that "think themselves" in our minds.[5]

The choice of these two parks for a semiotic comparison is not happenstance. Disneyland is commonly seen as the prototypical total fantasy park in America, probably in the world. In an entirely separate category is the "themed" amusement park, of which Marriott's two Great America parks stand as the most successful cases.[6] These two categories represent different, yet both fully American, experiences. (We omit here, of course, the earlier form—the unthemed amusement park—which manages to survive in the shadow of its flashier descendants.) But recent changes in Disneyland (which are mentioned later) suggest the impending victory of the Marriott "theme" paradigm over fantasy.

The strategy of our comparison begins with Louis Marin's semiotic analysis of Disneyland.[7] Following his example of reading the map of Disneyland as a text of possible narratives to be pursued by the visitor, we shall turn to the map of Marriott's for a similar exercise. The examination of the two maps and their respective possible narratives leads us to discover contrasting clusters of signs, symptoms, and values in the two parks. This contrast, the transformation (really) of one cluster into another, sets the tone for our concluding remarks.

Disneyland

Marin's Marxist-structuralist analysis sees Disneyland as "centered space" with Main Street USA as the narrative operator that leads the visitor/performer into the center of the text (see Map 1). Main Street USA is the axis of Disneyland, leading from reality to fantasy. The passage forces the visitor/performer to see the relations and differences between these two worlds.

But, as Marin continues, Main Street USA is *also* a "district," one that "separates and links Frontierland and Adventureland on the one hand, and Tomorrowland on the other." On the left, the two districts, Frontierland and Adventureland, "represent the two distances of history and geography." And on the right, Tomorrowland represents (still in Marin's scheme) "space as time, the universe captured by science and technology." So Main Street USA is *both* a passageway from reality to fantasy *and* a mediating space between America's past history and geography and her future space/time. Main Street USA is the *center,* the central mediator, in this semantic space. Main Street USA represents, for Marin, "the *USA Today.*"

> *USA Today* appears to be the *term referred to and represented;* it is the term through which all of the contrary poles of the structure are exchanged, in the semantic and economic meaning of the term, or in other words, through which they are fictively reconciled. And by his narrative, the visitor performs, enacts reconciliation. This is the mythical aspect of Disneyland.[8]

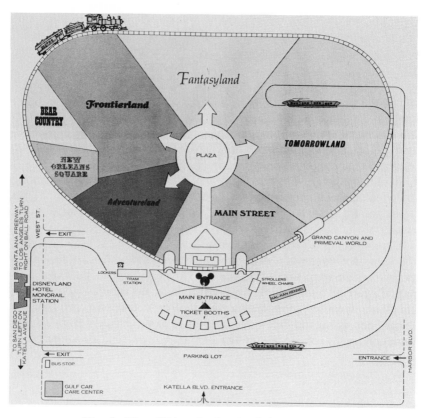

Map 1. Map of Disneyland at Anaheim, California

Marin finds the economic exchange modeled in the two "eccentric centers" on either side of Main Street USA—New Orleans Square on the left and the Carousel of Progress on the right. The economic meaning of the left eccentric center lies in the lesson of its most important narrative, the Pirates of the Caribbean ride. The juxtaposition of skulls and skeletons with treasure states the point that the feudal hoarding of treasure is a symptom of *death.* In contrast is the *alive* exchange of commodities in the shops and restaurants of Main Street USA. It is this contrast that makes the consumption of Main Street seem morally correct, a choice of life over death. Of course, Marin sees in the other eccentric center, General Electric's Carousel of Progress, simply another version of this same message—the symbolic representation of "the passive satisfaction of endlessly increasing needs."[9]

The Marriott Narrative

With Marin's analysis of Disneyland as our model and point of comparison, let us turn now to the map (See Map 2) of Marriott's Great America in Santa Clara, California, and ask what the narrative is that the visitor to Marriott's performs.

Like Disneyland, Marriott's engineers a gradual transition from the everyday world of a California suburb to the fantasy world created by the park. Visitors leave their cars for a brief walk or tram ride to the ticket booths marking the transition from real into fantasy world, and where the visitor exchanges his/her United States money for the currency of the park. Here, already, we discover an important difference between the two parks. Disneyland money consists of a book of tickets coded to specific attractions and rides. As Marin puts it,

> the Disneyland money is less a money than a language; with his real money the visitor buys the signs of the Disneyland vocabulary thanks to which he can perform his part, utter his "speech" or his individual narrative, take his tour in Disneyland.[10]

The book of Disneyland tickets, like a grammar of syntactic rules, limits the number of possible combinations of attractions (signs) into a narrative. In contrast is Marriott's policy whereby one admission price allows the visitor/performer unlimited access to the park's rides and attractions. So while there is a symbolic exchange of United States currency for the signs of a Disneyland vocabulary that narrows syntactic choices, no such exchange or narrowing occurs at Marriott's.

Once the Marriott's visitor/performer passes through the ticket booths, the first focal point of the park is confronted. This is Carousel Plaza, featuring at the end of a large reflecting pool the double-decked merry-go-round that is in many ways the Marriott's logo. From the Carousel the visitor/performer can turn left into Orleans Place or, more frequently, right into Hometown Square. Here, once more, the design of Marriott's departs from Disneyland. From the ticket booths at Disneyland, the visitor/performer passes through a tunnel under the embankment of the Santa Fe and Disneyland Railway. Beyond the embankment the visitor/performer enters fantasy space, out of eyesight and earshot of surrounding Anaheim. Marriott's consciously violates this principle. Like Disneyland, the railroad embankment more or less circles the park, creating a visual barrier between the fantasy world of the park and surrounding Santa Clara; but, unlike Disneyland, some important parts of the park are *not* within the perimeter of the railroad. Marriott's prefers not to distinguish clearly between the everyday world and Great America, emphasizing instead the continuity between the two Americas.

There are other striking contrasts between the layout of Marriott's and of Disneyland. Marriott's lacks the obvious bilateral symmetry of Disneyland, having no main artery like Main Street USA to mediate the symmetry and

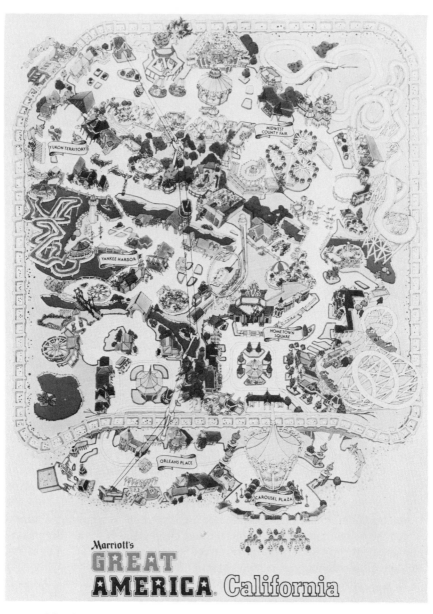

Map 2. Map of Marriott's Great America at Santa Clara, California

function as both the physical and symbolic center of the park. The centrality of the Disneyland Plaza, from which the visitor/performer can select many possible tours of Disneyland, is missing at Marriott's. Since Marriott's is designed as a huge perimeter, with an interior barrier of buildings and fences that make crossover impossible, the visitor/performer's only choice is between performing Marriott's Great America in a clockwise or counterclockwise fashion.

While there may not be a physical symmetry to Marriott's, there is a symmetry that does turn out to be the semiotic key to unpacking the narrative content of Marriott's Great America. In inspecting the Marriott's map for binary opposition or symmetry, the clearest case is the pair of carousels, one at the top of the map (in the Midwest County Fair) and the other the famous double-decker Carousel Plaza. It is the contrast between these two carousels that establishes the symbolic vocabulary for the Great America narrative. The guidebook describes "The Columbia" in these terms:

> This massive multi-colored, ornate gazebo is the center attraction to guests entering Marriott's GREAT AMERICA. The Columbia is more than just the world's finest, most expensive ($1.5 million), largest double-decked merry-go-round; it is a tribute to American craftsmanship, both past and present, and an impressive return to the days of elegance.
> Each of the figures on the Columbia is a fiberglass replica of the world's rarest carousel horses and animals.[11]

At the exact opposite side of the park from The Columbia is the one-story "Ameri-go-round, a real 1918 carousel." If we compare the two carousels, we can see the sort of symbolic, ideological transformation that is involved between the "real" carousel of 1918 and the 1976 "replica." The two carousels represent

BIG/EXPENSIVE/DANGEROUS

versus

HUMAN SCALE/INEXPENSIVE/SAFE

White the rhetoric of the guidebook suggests that a ride on The Columbia is a "return to the days of elegance," in fact Marriott's engineers have "improved" upon the 1918 version by performing the operation characteristic of bourgeois society—namely, the transformation of quality into quantity.[12] Marriott's Great America features both sets of values, and a performance of the Marriott's narrative involves moving between the two poles in an undulating, rhythmic, repetitive pattern.

Consider the vistor/performer's tour of Marriott's, now, from the point of view of this dichotomy between BIG/EXPENSIVE/DANGEROUS and HUMAN SCALE/INEXPENSIVE/SAFE, beginning at the Columbia, which represents the first set of values. The Columbia is big and expensive, as the guidebook reminds us, and although it may not be *really* dangerous, a ride on the second deck *seems* dangerous, certainly in comparison with a ride on the first deck or (later) with a ride on the Ameri-go-round.

After leaving The Columbia, the visitor/performer most often turns right into Hometown Square, a zone that may be characterized as HUMAN SCALE/INEXPENSIVE/SAFE. Hometown Square is "themed" to represent "A typical American hometown in the 1920s." The late Victorian architecture is of a decidedly human scale. Much of the "software" entertainment—i.e., musical shows and films—takes place in buildings on Hometown Square.[13] But there is another face to this relatively small-scale, safe zone. Attached to Hometown Square are two attractions representing the BIG/EXPENSIVE/ DANGEROUS cluster of values. The first is the Pictorium, a movie theatre with a huge screen and a series of filmed scenes meant to scare and disorient the viewer. The second attraction attached to Hometown Square is Willard's Whizzer. "Willard's Whizzer," explains a recent newspaper article, "features 70-foot high spiraling track with 70-degree banked turns. It reaches a top speed of 52 mph, takes one minute and 45 seconds to complete, and has had 9 1/2 million riders since the park opened in 1976."[14] As sad testimony to the *DANGEROUS* value of Willard's Whizzer, this newspaper article was describing the accident that occurred March 29, 1980, killing a thirteen-year-old boy and injuring eight others.

Willard's Whizzer, in fact, is a nice case study of the way in which Marriott's Great America *mediates* the two value clusters, linking them without opting for one or the other. For the architectural facade of Willard's Whizzer is in the same human scale, comfortable, reassuring late Victorian style that characterizes Hometown Square. The visitor/performer stands in line within that safe facade before stepping into the roller coaster car and steps back into that facade at the end of the ride. The two value clusters are thus fused in a way that seems natural. At the end of a BIG/EXPENSIVE/DANGEROUS ride the visitor/performer returns to a "safe" zone to continue his/her narrative performance.

The visitor/performer next moves through arches into the next zone, The Midwest County Fair. Again, the relatively safe zone offers rides of the opposite value cluster. It is revealing to quote from the guidebook:

> Start out on the Turn of the Century, but hold onto your hat! This is the world's largest corkscrew roller coaster . . . a real screamer that drops 95 feet and ends in two complete upside-down barrel rolls.
>
> Across the fair grounds is the Sky Whirl, the world's first triple Ferris wheel. If that's still too frightening, ride one of the Barney Oldfield cars. They reach the breakneck speed of seven miles per hour.[15]

The visitor/performer is offered BIG/DANGEROUS in the Turn of the Century and the Sky Whirl, with the HUMAN SCALE/SAFE option of automobiles that were popular when gasoline was only pennies a gallon. The

Games Gallery, Gallery arcade, "a real 1900s style circus," and the familiar Ameri-go-round complete the safe zone of the Midwest County Fair.

And so it goes. The Yukon Territory, "themed" to 1890s Yukon, is a safe zone that features performing animals in a way that links nature and culture comfortably, on a human scale. But the Yukon Territory has its own share of thrills in the Logger's Run, a log flume ride that "ends in a 60-foot drop down a waterfall to the park's lagoon." Yankee Harbor, the next safe zone in the park is "themed" as "an early 1900s New England fishing village," which should be nostalgically reassuring. But also part of Yankee Harbor are its own flume ride, with a 60-foot waterfall, and The Tidal Wave, for a time the most notoriously frightening ride at the part. The Tidal Wave features a high-speed ride through a 360-degree loop, forward and backward. "I Survived the Tidal Wave" read bumper stickers and tee-shirts available in Marriott's souvenir shops. Indeed, the notion of subjecting oneself to the DANGER of these rides and *surviving* them is an important clue to the meaning of these rides. Note, too, that the Tidal Wave is located on the physical center of Marriott's, matching its symbolic centrality in the park's BIG/EXPENSIVE/DAN-GEROUS value cluster.

The fifth and final safe zone is Orleans Place, "themed" to the Old South of 1850s. Human scale attractions abound in Orleans Square, including "software" entertainment in a live stage show and in the daily MardiGras parade. But even Orleans Place of the antebellum South includes the Orleans Orbit, a ride that spins riders at high speeds though a circle perpendicular to the ground. As we noted earlier, Orleans Place spills out under the railroad embankment, bringing the visitor/performer back to the starting point, Carousel Plaza. It becomes clear now that the apparent choice between turning left or right beyond Carousel Plaza is a meaningless one. Marriott's Great America reads the same forwards as backwards, its prime feature being the rhythmic alternation of the two value clusters, BIG/EXPENSIVE/DANGEROUS and HUMAN SCALE/INEXPENSIVE/SAFE.

Thinking of the visitor/performer's tour through Marriott's as a kind of folktale, we see immediately that it is the rhythm of placing oneself in danger and returning to safety that dominates the tale. Always returning safely, always "surviving" the Tidal Wave, is one important "point" to the story. Moreover, the survivor returns not simply to safety but to *reward* as well. The safe zones are filled with *consumer goods* available in souvenir shops, gift shops, and restaurants. One way to look at this juxtaposition of safety and consumption is to see consumption as a relief from anxiety. In most people the major rides create the adrenalin rush associated with fear. Consumer motivation research has established consumption as a palliative after a highly energized state of agitation and anxiety.[16] Another view of the safety/consumption contiguity is less physiological than symbolic. In this view consumption becomes an earned reward for risk-taking.

The link between risk-taking and entrepreneurial behavior is a complex one, to be sure, but research by McClelland and his associates indicates that those with a high "need for achievement" prefer challenges of moderate risk wherein there is objective evidence to support a general self-confidence in being able to do better than the stated odds.[17] This connection between moderate risk-taking and entrepreneurial consciousness helps explain some reactions to the fatal accident on Willard's Whizzer. According to the San Francisco *Chronicle* reporter covering the accident,

> Saturday's fatality was the first at Great America since it opened, but the screams of satisfied customers heard throughout the 100-acre park yesterday and the long waiting lines on the two other roller coaster showed customers still believe the rides were safe.
>
> "It doesn't make me nervous," said David Bentley, 17, of Hanford, who waited 1 1/2 hours to go on the Demon, the park's newest and scariest ride.
>
> "It would make anybody think twice," said Fred McKay of Temple, Maine, who rode the Demon with his 14-year-old son, and described it as like a barrell roll in an airplane. "But what I see of it looks safe."
>
> London Bishop of Oakland, who rode the Demon with his wife and two daughters, said it was very safe. "That was a freak accident. It's like taking an airplane ride. The chances are one in a million."[16]

Far from proving the rides unsafe, the fatality seems to confirm the *moderate* risk of riding Willard's Whizzer, the Demon, the Tidal Wave, and the Turn of the Century. Those with a strong achievement motive would be bored by a perfectly safe activity, just as they would avoid an activity which signaled excessive risk-taking (e.g., a string of fatal accidents). Moreover, there is a likely dialectic between the salient features of these rides and the personalities of the people who ride them. Not only are people with high "need for Achievement" attracted to these rides, but (if McClelland and others are correct) we might think of the ride as training grounds for people to acquire and enhance their "need for Achievement." As a training ground for entrepreneurial consciousness and behavior, rides like Willard's Whizzer reward moderate risk-taking and success (survival) with the opportunity to consume food and merchandise in a safe zone. Again and again, as the visitor/narrator moves from attraction to attraction, the lesson of this tale is confirmed—take a moderate risk and you shall be rewarded.

Mythic Transformations

The discovery of the two clusters of values mediated in the visitor's narrative of Marriott's prompts us to return to Disneyland in order to see if there is a similar mediation in the older park. The return to Disneyland confirms what we uneasily suspected. Marriott's has achieved a transformation of values originally established in Disneyland, and the transformations center around three values issues:

Quality into quantity. As a utopian fantasy, Disneyland is lively testimony to the achievement of an aesthetic, clean, efficient social order. The only ugliness or disorder allowed in Disneyland is intended as a counterpoint to the ideal. The ugly pirates, the ghosts of the haunted mansion, the witch in Snow White's magic cavern, the ersatz dust and cobwebs of the graveyard, are all messages that directly conflict with the purity, the grace, and elegance of the utopian order. The highly valued technology making the fantasy possible is all hidden. Doors open silently, boats glide imperceptibly on carefully controlled tracks, animatrons advance and retreat realistically as the visitor moves through the fantasy.

Throughout Disneyland the attention to detail is impressive, the pace of each ride sufficiently leisurely to allow the visitor time to appreciate the aesthetics and care taken in the creation and maintenance of each component of an overall experience. Employees are equally carefully programmed, trained in the provision of efficient and unobtrusive service. Crowd control is subtle and courteous; deviant behavior is almost unthinkable in this utopian model. Nothing is permitted to intrude upon the illusion.

The *quality* motives so consistently expressed in the Disneyland narrative myth are replaced by *quantity* motives at Marriott's. For Marriott's the measure of the Best is in superlatives: biggest, fastest, farthest, highest, scariest, and the most expensive. While Disney hides technology away to maintain the illusion of magic, Marriott's reveals the technology in all its splendor of gears and buttons, highlighting its direct contribution to intense physical sensation. In direct contrast to the compulsive cleanliness of Disneyland are Marriott's littered walkways, overflowing trashcans, and maintenance personnel who find time to chat among themselves (a sight unknown at Disneyland). Crowd control is minimal. While no alcohol is available at Disneyland, Marriott's has "beer gardens" adding one more element to the already heightening adrenalin rush as visitors shakily disembark from scarey rides. The concise shorthand for these observations is to say simply that the "theming" of Marriott's preserves only the shell of fantasy without its substantive details, a clear case of bourgeois culture's transformation of quality into quantity.

Community into individuated alienation. Recurring throughout Disneyland are episodes in which the visitor is expected to join together with other visitors in enacting the mythic script. This begins with the family's need to negotiate a collective plan for using its limited number of tickets, but the sense of collective effort is maintained as well by the structure of many Disney rides. Groups of visitors, larger than any single family, are led by Disneyland employees to take "active" roles in creating and maintaining the fantasy. The choreography of the Jungle Cruise, for example, calls for each boatload of visitors to turn and wave goodbye to those left behind on the docks, and the operators engage in "patter" designed to cement the group. The operators on this ride often ask the passengers to act in concert for the good of the members ("Quick, everyone lean right or the folks in the back will get wet"). The Davy Crockett canoe ride in Frontierland has visitors participate directly in paddling the large canoes—a cooperative effort by any standard.

While it would be difficult to see these circumstances as creating anything like genuine community, the effort at Disneyland is directed toward creating at least the illusion of cooperative Gemeinschaft. Very much in contrast to this effort and design is the individuated approach to attractions at Marriott's. The emphasis at Marriott's is upon physical sensation rather than imaginative illusion. On no ride are the visitors thrown together under the care of a chatty, friendly tour director. At Marriott's, rides happen *to,* rather than *with,* the visitor.

One other symptom of Marriott's emphasis upon the individuated experience over any collective one is the competitive experience one finds at the Games Gallery. In the egalitarian utopia of Disneyland, every visitor is guaranteed a happy and equal fantasy, but in the Marriott's Games Gallery a variety of prizes are available only for the more agile, dextrous, and just plain lucky. There are many disappointments among the children and adults leaving the Games Gallery empty-handed, perhaps another valuable lesson about the marketplace for consumers-in-training.

Nature under control versus Nature the antagonist. At Disneyland the myth calls for the benevolent control of Nature by culture. Nature is made part of the fantasy, is programmed, directed, even sculpted (hedges clipped to become topiary animals). At the same time, Disney respects and protects Nature. The lawns are clean of litter, high fences make the lawns an exhibit rather than grounds for activity, and flowers are not for picking. Only within the closely defined, limited space of Tom Sawyer's Island may visitors stray off the path onto rocks or trees. And there are no weeds anywhere, not even on Tom Sawyer's Island. In fact, plants do not die at Disneyland, where (as at other parks) gardeners change beds of colorful flowers before they have a chance to brown.[19] Fleet pooperscoopers scoop poop during the parade of horse-drawn floats.

Whereas the myth of Disneyland portrays a world in which Nature is under the benevolent control of culture, the myth of Marriott's describes a scene in which culture *defies* Nature. Litter accumulates on streets and lawns, where low fences are no barrier to children and adults who trespass upon the lawns for picnics, play, and sitting. Marriott's Nature is something to be used, consumed, and defied. This attitude is not limited to the physical setting of the park; it is incorporated into the very rides themselves. The myth of BIG/EXPENSIVE/DANGEROUS demands that culture go beyond what is natural to what is *super-natural*—higher, faster, farther. The myth asks its actors to defy gravity, wind, and water, its rewards reserved for those who meet Nature with defiance and return safely to feed upon Nature once more.

Conclusion

We said at the outset that the victory of Marriott's "theme" approach over Disney's fantasy approach to park mythic narratives in many ways explains all the value transformations we discover upon comparing the two parks.

A detailed comparison confirms this claim. The quality/quantity transformation *is* the fantasy/theme transformation, and we can find in the statements of theme park designers and executives themselves symptoms of the prevailing preference for *form over substance.* "The only purpose of theming," says Six Flags President Ned DeWitt, "is to complete the sense of an integrated, full escape. . . . Guests care less about what the theme is than they do about how fully it's carried out."[20] Walt Disney would have agreed with DeWitt's first premise; he wanted Disneyland to be a place to shuck off all the cares of the outside world. But Disney certainly would have rejected DeWitt's claim that theme form is more important than theme substance. For Disney, the fantasy escape must have a *moral content,* and he built that moral force into every Disney project. Marriott's theming has no moral content, unless it is to legitimate consumption.

The point of the claim about the transformation, of course, was that it represented a victory for the Marriott model, hence, a portent of future patterns in theme park values. Marriott's claim to victory stands on three facts. First, the thirty-some major theme parks in America are amusement parks molded in the Great American pattern rather than the Disney fantasy one. Second, among the theme parks Marriott's supremacy is financial. Even by industry standards, wherein the typical in-park spending per capita is about twelve dollars, Marriott's is a leader with fourteen dollars.[21]

But replicas and riches do not tell the whole story of the hegemony abandoning the fantasy utopia approach in favor of the attractions of amusement park "hardware." The two newest attractions at Disneyland—Space Mountain and the Big Thunder Mountain Railroad—are essentially roller-coaster rides in the style of Willard's Whizzer. True enough, the Disney people take pains to create a story frame for each ride, *but with the adoption of Marriott's speed and scale for these rides the Disney people vitiate the fantasy utopia valued elsewhere in the park.* With the possible exception of the Matterhorn bobsleds, every other ride and attraction in Disneyland takes the visitor slowly and deliberately through a fantasy exhibition experience allowing the necessary time for wonder and awe. Space Mountain creates this experience for the visitor standing in line, but once visitors get into the roller-coaster car they have a 55-mile-per-hour ride and very little time for wonder and awe. The Big Thunder Mountain Railroad, the newest Disney attraction, is perhaps the saddest example in this regard. Here the Disney people create their fantasy environment with artificial landscape and animatron creatures, but the railroad remains a roller-coaster ride. The animatron critters do their cute things, as they do in the Jungle Cruise and elsewhere in the park, but this time the visitor is traveling at 50 miles per hour rather than at a leisurely three. Many visitors simply miss the entire fantasy frame, turning their full attention to the BIG/EXPENSIVE/DANGEROUS experience that is at the core of a roller coaster ride. What was meant to be an experience marked by an external fantasy show has been transformed into an old fashioned amusement park thrill ride—the very thing Disneyland was created to replace and improve.

The semiotic comparison of the mythic narratives of Disneyland and Marriott's Great America, then, ends on this socio-political observation: Disneyland and Marriott's represent quite different value clusters, even though what the two share is a bourgeois capitalist culture. Louis Marin calls Disneyland a "degenerate utopia," which it may be, but value clusters embodied in Marriott's and the steady transformation of Disneyland into Marriott's mode impels us to seek a word more forceful than "degenerate" for describing the current trend. Walt Disney would have found the word.

Notes

1. R. D. Laing, *The Politics of the Family* (New York: Pantheon, 1971), p. 87.
2. See John G. Blair, "Structuralism and the Humanities," *American Quarterly,* 30 (Bibliography Issue, 1978), 263–81, and David Pace, "Structuralism in History and the Social Sciences," *American Quarterly,* 30 (Bibliography Issue, 1978), 282–97, two useful bibliographic essays. Terrence Hawkes's *Structuralism and Semiotics* (Berkeley: University of California Press,1977) explains the differences between structuralism, semiotics, and semiology. Consult, too, the essays in the journal *Semiotica.*
3. C. S. Peirce, "Logic as Semiotic: The Theory of Signs," in Justus Buchler, ed., *The Philosophy of Peirce: Selected Writings* (London: Routledge and Kegan Paul, 1940), pp. 98–119.
4. A good introduction to semiotics is Thomas A. Sebeok, ed., *Sight, Sound and Sense* (Bloomington: Indiana University Press, 1978), especially the essay, "For a Semiotic Anthroplogy," by Milton Singer, pp. 202–31.
5. See Elizabeth Walker Mechling, "Patricia Hearst: Myth America 1974, 1975, 1976," *Western Journal of Speech Communication,* 43(1979), 168–79, and Will Wright, *Six Guns and Society: A Structural Study of the Western* (Berkeley: University of California Press, 1975).
6. There is a growing literature on theme parks. See James C. Starbuck, *Theme Parks: A Partially Annotated Bibliography of Articles About Modern Amusement Parks* (Monticello, Illinois: Council of Planning Librarians, 1976), Exchange Bibliography No. 953. Among the more useful essays are Millicent Hall, "Theme Parks: Around the World in 80 Minutes," *Landscape,* 21(1976), 3–8; Robert Levy, "Theme Parks: The Profits in Pleasure," *Dun's Review,* (April, 1977), 88, 91, 114; Bro Uttal, "The Ride is Getting Scarier for 'Theme Park' Owners," *Fortune,* (December 1977), 167–72, 177, 181, 184; and David L. Brown, "Thinking of a Theme Park?" *Urban Land,* (February, 1980), 5–11. Brown heads the consulting firm responsible for the design, construction, and operation of Marriott's Great Americas.
7. Louis Marin, "Disneyland: A Degenerate Utopia," *Glyph,* Johns Hopkins Textual Studies No. 1 (Baltimore: Johns Hopkins Press, 1977), pp. 50–66. For the context of Marin's interest in Disneyland, see his *Utopiques: Jeux D'Espaces* (Paris: Les Editions de Minuit, 1973). There is, of course, a substantial literature on Disney,

See, for example, Robert Jewett and John Shelton Lawrence, *The American Mon-omyth* (Garden City, New York: Anchor Press/Doubleday, 1977). Relevant to our "reading" of the map of Disneyland are Peter Blake, "Walt Disney World," *Architectural Forum,* 136(June, 1972), 24–41, and Richard V. Francaviglia, "Main Street USA the Creation of a Popular Image," *Landscape,* 21(Spring-Summer, 1977), 18–22.

8. Marin, "Disneyland," p. 58.
9. *Ibid.,* pp. 63–64.
10. *Ibid.,* p. 55.
11. *Marriott's Great America* (Santa Clara, Ca.: Marriott Corporation, 1977), un-paged.
12. On the "quantification of quality" in modern bourgeois society, see Roland Barthes *Mythologies,* trans. Annette Lavers (New York: Hill and Wang, 1957 [1972]), esp. pp. 153–4; Marshall Sahlins, *Culture and Practical Reason* (Chicago: Univ. of Chicago Press, 1976); and Peter Berger, Brigitte Berger and Hansfried Kellner, *The Homeless Mind: Modernization and Consciousness* (New York: Vintage/Random House, 1973).
13. The "hardware/software" race in theme parks is discussed in Uttal, p. 184.
14. Bill Soiffer, "Brakes Suspected in Coaster Tragedy," *San Francisco Chronicle,* March 31, 1980, p. 3.
15. *Marriott's Great America,* unpaged.
16. See Ernest Dichter, *Handbook of Consumer Motivations: The Psychology of the World of Objects* (New York: McGraw Hill Book Co., 1964).
17. David C. McClelland, *The Achieving Society* (New York: Free Press, 1961), p. 222. A study that links risk-taking with child training in the entrepreneurial setting is Daniel R. Miller and Guy E. Swanson, *The Changing American Parent* (New York: John Wiley and Sons, Inc., 1958).
18. Soiffer, p. 3.
19. Uttal, p. 172, comments upon the obsessive cleanliness and landscaping: "To combat unruly Nature, some parks change their elaborate plantings two or three times yearly, thus ensuring perpetual bloom—and adding to horticultural bills that range from $100,000 to over $500,000."
20. Quoted in Uttal, p. 177. Brown, 9, discusses "theming" from the designer's point of view. An important consideration in comparing Disneyland with Marriott's Great America is the observation that in the former some employees are dressed in costumes representing Disney cartoon/comics characters and in the latter they are dressed as Warner Brothers cartoon/comics characters (e.g., Bugs Bunny, Porky Pig, Daffy Duck, Wile E. Coyote). Thus, children and adults bring to each park a "frame" learned from the narratives of those respective cartoons and comics. Compare Ariel Dorfman and Armand Mattelart, *How to Read Donald Duck: Imperialist Ideology on the Disney Comic,* trans. David Kunzel (New York: International General, 1971) and David M. Abrams and Brian Sutton-Smith, "The Development of the Trickster in Children's Narrative," *Journal of American Folklore,* 90 (1977), 29–47.
21. Levy, 88, 91, and Uttal, 171, 177, provide dollar and attendance figures on theme parks (e.g., the combined revenue from the two Marriott's Great Americas was $75 million in 1977). Says Uttal: "Marriott has managed to achieve about $200 of sales per square foot of selling space, compared with the typical park's figure of some $120. For Marriott, more and better has meant one of the highest levels of per capita spending in the industry, over $14" (184).

Bibliography

The following bibliography is a fairly comprehensive, but necessarily incomplete, introduction to the theory and practice of rhetorical criticism of a variety of media and genres other than traditional oratory. In most cases, categories in the bibliography correspond to the subjects treated in the essays in this anthology, with some exceptions. For considerations of space we have been unable to include in the anthology examples of rhetorical criticism of painting, photography, poetry, fashion, and several other categories that have been an essential part of the widening understanding of the scope of rhetorical studies in our century. Some writings on each of these subjects are listed in the bibliography. The bibliography is divided into subsections as follows:

Theory and Method
Television
Film
Radio
Visual Arts
    Painting and Prints
    Comics and Cartoons
    Photography
    Architecture
Music
Literature
    Drama and Theatre
    Fiction
    Poetry
    Biography and Autobiography
    Other Literature
Letters
Magazines, Newspapers, and Other Journalism
Political Action
Other Forms

A note on the journals: in the bibliography several frequently cited journal titles have been abbreviated, based on the most recent title of the journal. Some journals have changed their titles several times over the years, as noted here.

CE: Communication Education (*The Speech Teacher.* vols. 1–24 (1952–1975); *Communication Education,* vols. 25–   (1976–present)).

CSSJ: Central States Speech Journal
CM: Communication Monographs (Speech Monographs, vols. 1–42 (1934–1975); *Communication Monographs,* vols. 43– (1976–present)).
CQ: Communication Quarterly (Today's Speech, vols. 1–23 (1953–1975); *Communication Quarterly,* vols. 24– (1976–present)).
CI: Critical Inquiry
FQ: Film Quarterly
JOC: Journal of Communication
JPC: Journal of Popular Culture
JPFT: Journal of Popular Film and Television (Journal of Popular Film, vols. 1–6 (1973–1978); *Journal of Popular Film and Television,* vols. 7– (1979–present)).
JQ: Journalism Quarterly
LFQ: Literature/Film Quarterly
PMLA: Publications of the Modern Language Association
PR: Philosophy and Rhetoric
QJS: The Quarterly Journal of Speech (Quarterly Journal of Public Speaking, vols. 1–3 (1915–1917); *Quarterly Journal of Speech Education,* vols. 4–13 (1918–1927); *Quarterly Journal of Speech,* vols. 14– (1928–present)).
QRFS: Quarterly Review of Film Studies
SSCJ: Southern Speech Communication Journal (Southern Speech Bulletin, vols. 1–4 (1935–1939); *Southern Speech Journal,* vols. 5–36 (1939–1971); *Southern Speech Communication Journal,* vols. 37– (1971–present)).
TQ: Television Quarterly
WJSC: Western Journal of Speech Communication (Western Speech, vols. 1–38 (1937–1974); *Western Speech Communication,* vols. 39–40 (1975–1976); *Western Journal of Speech Communication,* vols. 41– (1977–present)).

RHETORIC AND THE ART OF CRITICISM

Theory and Method

Books
Abrams, M. H. *The Mirror and the Lamp: Romantic Theory and the Critical Tradition.* New York: Oxford University Press, 1953.
Andrews, James R. *A Choice of Worlds.* New York: Harper and Row, 1973.
Andrews, James R. *The Practice of Rhetorical Criticism.* New York: Macmillan, 1983.
Arnold, Carroll C. *Criticism of Oral Rhetoric.* Columbus: Merrill, 1974.
Atkins, J. W. H. *Literary Criticism in Antiquity: A Sketch of Its Development.* 2 vols. Cambridge: Cambridge University Press, 1934.
Baldwin, Charles Sears. *Ancient Rhetoric and Poetic.* New York: Macmillan, 1924.

Baldwin, Charles Sears. *Medieval Rhetoric and Poetic.* New York: Macmillan, 1928.

Barthes, Roland. *Mythologies.* Trans. Annette Lavers. New York: Hill and Wang, 1972.

Barthes, Roland. *Writing Degree Zero* and *Elements of Semiology.* Trans. Annette Lavers and Colin Smith. Boston: Beacon Press, 1970.

Benson, Thomas W., and Michael H. Prosser, eds. *Readings in Classical Rhetoric.* Bloomington: Indiana University Press, 1972.

Bercovitch, Sacvan. *The Puritan Origins of the American Self.* New Haven: Yale University Press, 1975.

Bitzer, Lloyd F., and Edwin Black, eds. *The Prospect of Rhetoric.* Englewood Cliffs: Prentice-Hall, 1971.

Black, Edwin B. *Rhetorical Criticism: A Study in Method.* New York: Macmillan, 1965.

Blankenship, Jane, and Hermann G. Stelzner, eds. *Rhetoric and Communication: Studies in the University of Illinois Tradition.* Urbana: University of Illinois Press, 1976.

Booth, Wayne. *Critical Understanding: The Powers and Limits of Pluralism.* Chicago: University of Chicago Press, 1979.

Booth, Wayne C. *Modern Dogma and the Rhetoric of Assent.* Chicago: University of Chicago Press, 1974.

Booth, Wayne C. *A Rhetoric of Irony,* Chicago: University of Chicago Press, 1974.

Brigance, William N., ed. *History and Criticism of American Public Address.* 2 vols. New York: McGraw-Hill, 1943.

Brock, Bernard L., and Robert Scott, eds. *Methods of Rhetorical Criticism: A Twentieth-Century Perspective.* 2nd ed. Detroit: Wayne State University Press, 1980.

Bryant, Donald C. *Rhetorical Dimensions in Criticism.* Baton Rouge: Louisiana State University Press, 1973.

Bryant, Donald C., ed. *Papers in Rhetoric and Poetic.* Iowa City: University of Iowa Press, 1965.

Bryant, Donald C., ed. *The Rhetorical Idiom.* Ithaca: Cornell University Press, 1958.

Burke, Kenneth. *Attitudes Toward History.* New York: Editorial Publishers, 1937.

Burke, Kenneth. *Counter-Statement.* New York: Harcourt, Brace, 1931.

Burke, Kenneth. *A Grammar of Motives.* Englewood Cliffs: Prentice-Hall, 1945.

Burke, Kenneth. *Language as Symbolic Action.* Berkeley: University of California Press, 1966.

Burke, Kenneth. *Permanence and Change.* New York: New Republic, 1935.

Burke, Kenneth. *The Philosophy of Literary Form.* Baton Rouge: Louisiana State University Press, 1941.

Burke, Kenneth. *A Rhetoric of Motives.* Englewood Cliffs: Prentice-Hall, 1950.

Burke, Kenneth. *The Rhetoric of Religion.* Boston: Beacon Press, 1961.

Campbell, Karlyn Kohrs. *Critiques of Contemporary Rhetoric.* Belmont, California: Wadsworth, 1972.

Campbell, Karlyn Kohrs. and Kathleen Hall Jamieson, eds. *Form and Genre: Shaping Rhetorical Action.* Falls Church: Speech Communication Association, 1978.

Cathcart, Robert. *Post Communication: Critical Analysis and Evaluation.* Indianapolis: Bobbs-Merrill, 1966.

Clark, Donald Lemen. *Rhetoric and Poetry in the Renaissance: A Study of Rhetorical Terms in English Renaissance Literary Criticism.* New York: Columbia University Press, 1922.

Corbett, Edward P. J. *Classical Rhetoric for the Modern Student.* New York: Oxford University Press, 1965.

Corbett, Edward P. J., ed. *Rhetorical Analyses of Literary Works.* New York: Oxford University Press, 1969.

Corti, Maria. *An Introduction to Literary Semiotics.* Trans. Margherita Bogat and Allen Mandelbaum, Bloomington: Indiana University Press, 1978.

Crane, R. S. *The Languages of Criticism and the Structure of Poetry.* Toronto: University of Toronto Press, 1953.

Crane, R. S., ed. *Critics and Criticism.* Chicago: University of Chicago Press, 1952.

Culler, Jonathan. *Structuralist Poetics: Structuralism, Linguistics, and the Study of Literature.* Ithaca: Cornell University Press, 1975.

Eco, Umberto. *The Role of the Reader.* Bloomington: Indiana University Press, 1979.

Eco, Umberto. *A Theory of Semiotics.* Bloomington: Indiana University Press, 1976.

Ehninger, Douglas, ed. *Contemporary Rhetoric: A Reader's Coursebook.* Glenview: Scott, Foresman, 1972.

Empson, William. *Seven Types of Ambiguity.* New York: New Directions, 1947.

Fish, Stanley E. *Is There a Text in This Class?* Cambridge: Harvard University Press, 1980.

Fish, Stanley E. *Self-Consuming Artifacts.* Berkeley: University of California Press, 1973.

Fisher, Walter R., ed. *Rhetoric: A Tradition in Transition.* East Lansing: Michigan State University Press, 1974.

Fogarty, Daniel. *Roots for a New Rhetoric.* New York: Teachers College Press, 1959.

Frye, Northrup. *Anatomy of Criticism: Four Essays.* Princeton: Princeton University Press, 1957.

Geiger, Don. *The Dramatic Impulse in Modern Poetics.* Baton Rouge: Louisiana State University Press, 1967.

Gomme, Andor. *Attitudes to Criticism.* Carbondale: Southern Illinois University Press, 1966.

Greene, Theodore E. *The Arts and the Art of Criticism.* 2nd ed. Princeton: Princeton University Press, 1947.

Grube, G. M. A. *The Greek and Roman Critics.* Toronto: University of Toronto Press, 1965.

Guerin, Wilfred L., Earle G. Labor, Lee Morgan, and John R. Willingham. *A Handbook of Critical Approaches to Literature.* 2nd edition. New York: Harper & Row, 1979.

Hart, Roderick P. *The Political Pulpit.* West Lafayette: Purdue University Press, 1977.

Hawkes, Terrence. *Structuralism and Semiotics.* London: Methuen, 1977.

Hillbruner, Anthony. *Critical Dimensions: The Art of Public Address Criticism.* New York: Random House, 1966.

Hirsch, E. D., Jr. *The Aims of Interpretation.* Chicago: University of Chicago Press, 1976.

Hirsch, E. D., Jr. *Validity in Interpretation.* New Haven: Yale University Press, 1967.

Howell, Wilbur Samuel. *Poetics, Rhetoric, and Logic.* Ithaca: Cornell University Press, 1975.

Howes, Raymond F., ed. *Historical Studies of Rhetoric and Rhetoricians.* Ithaca: Cornell University Press, 1961.

Jamieson, Kathleen Hall, and Karlyn Kohrs Campbell. *The Interplay of Influence: Mass Media and Their Publics in News, Advertising, and Politics.* Belmont: Wadsworth, 1983.

Johannesen, Richard L., ed. *Ethics and Persuasion: Selected Readings.* New York: Random House, 1967.

Johannesen, Richard L. *Ethics in Human Communication.* 2nd ed. Prospect Heights: Waveland Press, 1983.

Johannesen, Richard L., ed. *Contemporary Theories of Rhetoric: Selected Readings.* New York: Harper and Row, 1971.

Joyce, Robert. *The Esthetic Animal: Man, the Art-Created Art Creator.* Hicksville, N.Y.: Exposition Press, 1975.

Kennedy, George. *The Art of Persuasion in Greece.* Princeton: Princeton University Press, 1963.

Kennedy, George. *The Art of Rhetoric in the Roman World.* Princeton: Princeton University Press, 1972.

Kennedy, George. *Classical Rhetoric and Its Christian and Secular Tradition from Ancient to Modern Times.* Chapel Hill: University of North Carolina Press, 1980.

Kwant, Remy C. *Critique: Its Nature and Function.* Pittsburgh: Duquesne University Press, 1967.

Lanham, Richard A. *The Motives of Eloquence: Literary Rhetoric in the Renaissance.* New Haven: Yale University Press, 1976.

Leach, Edmund. *Culture and Communication.* Cambridge: Cambridge University Press, 1976.

Levin, Harry. *Contexts of Criticism.* Cambridge: Harvard University Press, 1957.

McKerrow, Ray E., ed. *Explorations in Rhetoric: Studies in Honor of Douglas Ehninger.* Glenview: Scott, Foresman, 1982.

McLuhan, Marshall. *The Gutenberg Galaxy.* Toronto: University of Toronto Press, 1962.

Matejka, Ladislaw, and Irwin R. Titunik, eds. *Semiotics of Art: Prague School Contributions.* Cambridge: MIT Press, 1976.

Miller, Joseph M.; Michael H. Prosser; and Thomas W. Benson, eds. *Readings in Medieval Rhetoric.* Bloomington: Indiana University Press, 1973.

Mohrmann, G. P.; Charles J. Stewart; and Donovan J. Ochs, eds. *Explorations in Rhetorical Criticism.* University Park: The Pennsylvania State University Press, 1973.

Moore, Arthur K. *Contestable Concepts of Literary Theory.* Baton Rouge: Louisiana State University Press, 1973.

Murphy, James J. *Rhetoric in the Middle Ages: A History of Rhetorical Theory from St. Augustine to the Renaissance.* Berkeley: University of California Press, 1974.

Murphy, James J., ed. *Medieval Eloquence.* Berkeley: University of California Press, 1978.

Nebergall, Roger E., ed. *Dimensions of Rhetorical Scholarship.* Norman: University of Oklahoma Press, 1963.

Nichols, Marie Hochmuth. *Rhetoric and Criticism.* Baton Rouge: Louisiana State University Press, 1963.

Nichols, Marie Hockmuth, ed. *History and Criticism of American Public Address.* vol. 3. London: Longmans, Green, 1955.

Nilsen, Thomas R. *Ethics of Speech Communication.* Indianapolis: Bobbs-Merrill, 1966.

Nilsen, Thomas R., ed. *Essays on Rhetorical Criticism.* New York: Random House, 1968.

Ohlgren, Thomas H., and Lynn M. Berk, eds. *The New Languages: A Rhetorical Approach to the Mass Media and Popular Culture.* Englewood Cliffs: Prentice-Hall, 1977.

Ong, Walter J. *Interfaces of the Word.* Ithaca: Cornell University Press, 1977.

Ong, Walter J. *Rhetoric, Romance, and Technology.* Ithaca: Cornell University Press, 1971.

Pratt, Mary Louise. *Toward a Speech Act Theory of Literary Discourse.* Bloomington: Indiana University Press, 1977.

Preminger, Alex; O. B. Hardison; and Kevin Kerrane, eds. *Classical and Medieval Literary Criticism.* New York: Frederick Ungar, 1974.

Reid, Loren, ed. *American Public Address: Essays in Honor of Albert Craig Baird.* Columbia: University of Missouri Press, 1961.

Richards, I. A. *The Philosophy of Rhetoric.* New York: Oxford University Press, 1936.

Richards, I. A. *Practical Criticism: A Study of Literary Judgment.* New York: Harcourt, Brace, 1929.

Richards, I. A. *Principles of Literary Criticism.* London: Routledge and Kegan Paul, 1924.

Richards, I. A. *Speculative Instruments.* Chicago: University of Chicago Press, 1955.

Ricoeur, Paul. *The Rule of Metaphor.* Toronto: University of Toronto Press, 1977.

Roberts, W. Rhys. *Greek Rhetoric and Literary Criticism.* 1928; rpt. New York: Cooper Square Publishers, 1963.

Rueckert, William H. *Kenneth Burke and the Drama of Human Relations.* Rev. ed. Berkeley: University of California Press, 1983.

Rueckert, William H., ed. *Critical Responses to Kenneth Burke.* Minneapolis: University of Minnesota Press, 1969.

Saintsbury, George. *History of Criticism.* 3 vols. Edinburgh: William Blackwood and Sons, 1861.

Sapir, J. David, and J. Christopher Crocker, eds. *The Social Use of Metaphor.* Philadelphia: University of Pennsylvania Press, 1977.

Schwartz, Joseph, and John A. Rycenga, eds. *The Province of Rhetoric.* New York: Ronald, 1965.

Smith, James, and Edd Winfield Parks, eds. *The Great Critics: An Anthology of Literary Criticism.* New York: W. W. Norton, 1932.

Sontag, Susan. *Against Interpretation.* New York: Farrar, Straus & Giroux, 1966.

Steinmann, Martin, Jr., ed. *New Rhetorics.* New York: Scribner's, 1966.

Suleiman, Susan, and Inge Crosman, eds. *The Reader in the Text.* Princeton: Princeton University Press, 1980.

Sutton, Walter. *Modern American Criticism.* Englewood Cliffs: Prentice-Hall, 1963.

Sutton, Walter, and Richard Foster, eds. *Modern Criticism: Theory and Practice.* New York: The Odyssey Press, 1963.

Taylor, Warren. *Tudor Figures of Rhetoric.* Whitewater, Wisconsin: The Language Press, 1972.

Thonssen, Lester: A. Craig Baird; and Waldo W. Braden. *Speech Criticism: The Development of Standards for Rhetorical Appraisal.* 2nd ed. New York: Ronald, 1970.

Wallace, Karl R. *Understanding Discourse: The Speech Act and Rhetorical Action.* Baton Rouge: Louisiana State University Press, 1970.

Weaver, Richard M. *The Ethics of Rhetoric.* Chicago: Henry Regnery, 1953.

Wellek, Rene. *Concepts of Criticism.* Edited by Stephen G. Nichols, Jr. New Haven: Yale University Press, 1963.

White, Eugene E., ed. *Rhetoric in Transition: Studies in the Nature and Uses of Rhetoric.* University Park: The Pennslvania State University Press, 1980.

Wimsatt, William K., Jr., and Cleanth Brooks. *Literary Criticism: A Short History.* New York: Vintage Books, 1957.

Winick, Charles, ed. *Deviance and Mass Media.* Beverly Hills: Sage, 1979.

Winterowd, W. Ross. *Rhetoric: A Synthesis.* New York: Holt, Rinehart, Winston, 1968.

Zitner, Sheldon P. *The Practice of Modern Literary Scholarship.* Glenview: Scott, Foresman, 1966.

Zitner, Sheldon P., James D. Kissane, and M. M. Liberman. *The Practice of Criticism.* Glenview: Scott, Foresman, 1966.

Zitner, Sheldon P., James D. Kissane, and Myron M. Liberman. *A Preface to Literary Analysis.* Glenview: Scott, Foresman, 1964.

Articles

Arnold, Carroll C. "Oral Rhetoric, Rhetoric, and Literature." *PR* 1 (1968), 191–210.

Bashford, Bruce. "The Rhetorical Method in Literary Criticism." *PR* 9 (1976), 133–146.

Benson, Thomas W. "The Senses of Rhetoric: A Topical System for Critics." *CSSJ* 29 (1978), 237–250.

Bigelow, Gordon E. "Distinguishing Rhetoric from Poetic Discourse." *SSCJ* 19 (1953), 83–97.

Black, Edwin. "A Note on Theory and Practice in Rhetorical Criticism." *WJSC* 44 (1980), 331–336.

Black, Edwin. "The Second Persona." *QJS* 56 (1970), 109–119.

Booth, Wayne C. "Metaphor as Rhetoric: The Problem of Evaluation." *CI* 5 (1978), 49–72.

Bormann, Ernest G. "Fantasy and Rhetorical Vision: The Rhetorical Criticism of Social Reality." *QJS* 58 (1972), 396–407.

Breen, Myles P. "Rhetorical Criticism and Media: The State-of-the-Art." *CSSJ* 27 (1976), 15–21.

Brockreide, Wayne. "Rhetorical Criticism as Argument." *QJS* 60 (1974), 165–174.

Bryant, Donald C. "Some Problems of Scope and Method in Rhetorical Scholarship." *QJS* 23 (1937), 182–189.

Burke, Kenneth. "The Party Line." *QJS* 62 (1976), 62–68.

Campbell, Karlyn Kohrs. "Criticism: Ephemeral and Enduring." *CE* 23 (1974), 9–14.

Campbell, Karlyn Kohrs. "The Nature of Criticism in Rhetorical and Communication Studies." *CSSJ* 30 (1979), 4–13.

Campbell, Paul N. "Language as Interpersonal and Poetic Process."*PR* 2 (1969), 200–214.

Campbell, Paul Newell. "The *Personae* of Scientific Discourse." *QJS* 61 (1975), 391–405.

Campbell, Paul N. "Poetic-Rhetorical, Philosophical, and Scientific Discourse." *PR* 6 (1973), 1–29.

Cathcart, Robert S. "Movements: Confrontation as Rhetorical Form." *SSCJ* 43 (1978), 233–247.

Chatman, Seymour. "What Novels Can Do That Films Can't (and Vice Versa)." *CI* 7 (1980), 121–140.

Chesebro, James W., and Caroline Hamsher. "Rhetorical Criticism: A Message-Centered Approach." *CE* 22 (1973), 282–290.

Croft, Albert. "The Functions of Rhetorical Criticism." *QJS* 42 (1956), 283–291.

Dyrenforth, Harald O. "Narration: The Cinderella of Radio and Film." *WJSC* 15 (1951), 46–50.

Erlich, Howard S. "The Congruence of Aristotle's *Rhetoric* and *Poetics*." *SSCJ* 38 (1973), 362–370.

Farrell, Thomas B. "Critical Models in the Analysis of Discourse." *WJSC* 44 (1980), 300–314.

Fish, Stanley E. "Normal Circumstances, Literal Language, Direct Speech Acts, the Ordinary, the Everyday, the Obvious, What Goes without Saying, and Other Special Cases." *CI* 4 (1978), 625–644.

Fisher, Walter R. "Genre: Concepts and Applications in Rhetorical Criticism." *WJSC* 44 (1980), 288–299.

Fisher, Walter R. "Method in Rhetorical Criticism." *SSCJ* 35 (1969), 101–109.

Foss, Sonya K. "Criteria for Adequacy in Rhetorical Criticism." *SSCJ* 48 (1983), 283–295.

Geiger, Don. "Poetic Realizing as Knowing." *QJS* 59 (1973), 311–318.

Griffin, Leland M. "The Rhetoric of Historical Movements." *QJS* 38 (1952), 184–188.

Gronbeck, Bruce E. "Dramaturgical Theory and Criticism: The State of the Art (or Science?)." *WJSC* 44 (1980), 315–330.

Gronbeck, Bruce E. "Rhetorical History and Rhetorical Criticism: A Distinction." *CE* 24 (1975), 309–320.

Grube, G. M. A. "Rhetoric and Literary Criticism." *QJS* 42 (1956), 339–344.

Hahn, Dan F., and Ruth M. Gonchar. "Studying Social Movements: A Rhetorical Methodology." *CE* 20 (1971), 44–52.

Hardt, Hanno. "The Dilemma of Mass Communication: An Existential Point of View." *PR* 5 (1972), 175–187.

Herrick, Marvin T. "The Place of Rhetoric in Poetic Theory." *QJS* 34 (1948), 1–22.

Hillbruner, Anthony. "The Moral Imperative of Criticism." *SSCJ* 40 (1975), 228–247.

Howell, Wilbur Samuel. "Literature as an Enterprise in Communication." *QJS* 33 (1947), 417–426.

Howell, Wilbur Samuel. "The Two-Party Line: A Reply to Kenneth Burke." *QJS* 62 (1976), 69–77.

Hudson, Hoyt H. "The Field of Rhetoric." *QJS* 9 (1923), 167–180.

Hudson, Hoyt H. "Rhetoric and Poetry." *QJS* 10 (1924), 143–154.

Karstetter, Allan B. "Toward a Theory of Rhetorical Irony." *CM* 31 (1964), 162–178.

Kaufer, David. "Irony and Rhetorical Strategy." *PR* 10 (1977), 90–110.

Kaufer, David S., and Christine M. Neuwirth. "Contrasts Between Ironic and Metaphoric Understanding: An Elaboration of Booth's Observations." *WJSC* 47 (1983), 75–83.

Leff, Michael C. "Interpretation and the Art of the Rhetorical Critic." *WJSC* 44 (1980), 337–349.

McLuhan, H. Marshall. "Poetic vs. Rhetorical Exegesis." *Sewanee Review* 52 (1944), 266–276.

Montague, Gene. "Rhetoric in Literary Criticism." *College Compositon and Communication* 14 (1963), 168–175.

Nilsen, Thomas R. "The Interpretive Function of the Critic." *WJSC* 21 (1957), 70–76.

Partee, Morriss Henry. "Plato on the Rhetoric of Poetry." *Journal of Aesthetics and Art Criticism* 33 (1974), 203–212.

Riches, Suzanne Volmer, and Malcolm O. Sillars. "The Status of Movement Criticism." *WJSC* 44 (1980), 275–287.

Rosenfield, Lawrence W. "The Anatomy of Critical Discourse." *CM* 35 (1968), 50–69.

Rosenfield, Lawrence W. "The Experience of Criticism." *QJS* 60 (1974), 489–496.

Salper, Donald E. "Some Rhetorical and Poetic Crossroads in the Interpretation of Literature." *WJSC* 37 (1973), 264–272.

Sharpam, John R., George A. Matter, and Wayne Brockriede. "The Interpretive Experience as a Rhetorical Transaction." *CSSJ* 22 (1971), 143–150.

Sillars, Malcolm O. "Defining Movements Rhetorically: Casting the Widest Net." *SSCJ* 46 (1980), 17–32.

Simons, Herbert W. "Requirements, Problems, and Strategies: A Theory of Persuasion for Social Movements." *QJS* 56 (1970), 1–11.

Staub, A. W., and Gerald P. Mohrmann. "Rhetoric and Poetic: A New Critique." *SSCJ* 28 (1962), 131–141.

Staub, August W. "Rhetoric and Poetic: The Rhetor as Poet-Plot-Maker." *SSCJ* 26 (1961), 285–290.

Swanson, David L. "The Requirements of Critical Justifications." *CM* 44 (1977), 306–320.

Winterowd, W. Ross. "The Realms of Meaning: Text-Centered Criticism." *College Composition and Communication* 23 (1972), 399–405.

Television

Books

Adams, William C., ed. *Television Coverage of the 1980 Presidential Campaign.* Norwood, New Jersey: Ablex, 1983.

Adler, Richard, ed. *Understanding Television: Essays on Television as a Social and Cultural Force.* New York: Praeger, 1981.

Altheide, David L. *Creating Reality: How TV News Distorts Events.* Beverly Hills: Sage, 1976.

Altheide, David L., and Robert P. Snow. *Media Logic.* Beverly Hills: Sage, 1979.

Arlen, Michael J. *The Camera Age: Essays on Television.* New York: Farrar, Straus and Giroux, 1981.

Arlen, Michael J. *The Living Room War.* New York: Viking, 1969.

Baggaly, Jon. *Psychology of the TV Image.* Farnborough, England: Gower Press, 1980.

Barnouw, Erik. *The Image Empire.* Vol. III of *A History of Broadcasting in the United States.* New York: Oxford University Press, 1970.

Berger, Arthur Asa. *Media Analysis Techniques.* Beverly Hills: Sage, 1982.

Berger, Arthur Asa. *The TV-Guided American.* New York: Walker, 1976.

Diamond, Edwin. *The Tin Kazoo: Politics, Television, and the News.* Cambridge: MIT Press, 1975.

Elliott, Philip. *The Making of a Television Series.* London: Constable, 1972.

Epstein, Edward Jay. *News From Nowhere.* New York: Random House, 1973.

Fiske, John, and John Hartley. *Reading Television.* London: Methuen, 1978.

Frank, Robert Shelby. *Message Dimensions of Television News.* Lexington: Lexington Books, 1973.

Gans, Herbert J. *Deciding What's News.* New York: Random House, 1979.

Geis, Michael L. *The Language of Television Advertising.* New York: Academic Press, 1982.

Gitlin, Todd. *The Whole World Is Watching.* Berkeley: University of California Press, 1980.

Goulart, Elwood. *A Critical Examination of Rhetorical Argument in Narrative Entertainment on Television: A Case Study of Selected Dramatic Programs.* Ann Arbor: UMI, 1982.

Gronbeck, Bruce E. *Television Criticism.* Chicago: Science Research Associates, 1984.

Hazard, Patrick, ed. *TV as Art: Some Essays in Criticism.* Champaign: National Council of Teachers of English, 1966.

Hunt, Albert. *The Language of Television.* London: Eyre Methuen, 1981.

Jensen, Richard J., Robert L. Schrag, and Janice E. Schuetz. *Rhetorical Perspectives on Communication and Mass Media.* 2nd ed. Dubuque: Kendall/Hunt, 1980.

Mander, Jerry. *Four Arguments for the Elimination of Television.* New York: Morrow, 1978.

Newcomb, Horace. *TV: The Most Popular Art.* Garden City: Anchor Press, 1974.

Newcomb, Horace, ed. *Television: The Critical View.* 3rd ed. New York: Oxford University Press, 1982.

Primeau, Ronald. *The Rhetoric of Television.* New York: Longman, 1979.

Schlesinger, Philip. *Putting "Reality" Together: BBC News.* London: Constable, 1978.

Schwartz, Tony. *The Responsive Chord.* New York: Anchor Press, 1974.

Shayon, Robert Lewis. *Open to Criticism.* Boston: Beacon Press, 1971.

Silverstone, Roger. *The Message of Television: Myth and Narrative in Contemporary Culture.* London: Heinemann Educational, 1981.

Smith, Robert Rutherford. *Beyond the Wasteland: The Criticism of Broadcasting.* Revised edition. Falls Church: The Speech Communication Association, 1980.

Timberg, Bernard M. *Daytime Television: Rhetoric and Ritual.* Ann Arbor: UMI, 1982.

Tracey, Michael. *The Production of Political Television.* London: Routledge and Kegan Paul, 1978.

Williams, Raymond. *Television: Technology and Cultural Form.* New York: Schocken Books, 1974.

Zettl, Herbert. *Sight, Sound, Motion: Applied Media Aesthetics.* Belmont: Wadsworth, 1973.

Articles

Averson, Richard. "*The Fugitive:* TV's Rogue-Saint." *TQ* 3:4 (1964), 57–66.

Bantz, Charles R. "The Critic and the Computer: A Multiple Technique Analysis of the *ABC Evening News.*" *CM* 46 (1979), 27–39.

Barton, Richard L., and Richard B. Gregg. "Middle East Conflict as a TV News Scenario: A Formal Analysis." *JOC* 32 (1982), 172–185.

Baughman, James L. "*See It Now* and Television's Golden Age, 1951–58." *JPC* (1981), 106–115.

Bean, Susan S. "Soap Operas: Sagas of American Kinship." In *The American Dimension: Cultural Myths and Social Realities,* edited by W. Arens and Susan P. Montague. Sherman Oaks, California: Alfred, 1976.

Benson, Thomas W. "Another Shooting in Cowtown." *QJS* 67 (1981), 347–406.

Benson, Thomas W. "Implicit Communication Theory in Campaign Coverage." In *Television Coverage of the 1980 Presidential Campaign,* edited by William C. Adams. Norwood, New Jersey, Ablex, 1983.

Benson, Thomas W. "Videology: Space and Time in Political Television." *The Pennsylvania Speech Communication Annual* 31 (1975), 23–38.

Benson, Thomas W., and Richard L. Barton. "Television as Politics: The British View." *QJS* 65 (1979), 439–445.

Berg, David M. "Rhetoric, Reality, and Mass Media." *QJS* 58 (1972), 255–263.

Berger, Asa. "Newscasts as Theatre of the Absurd (Curtain Up on the Cronkite Show)." *TQ* 13:1 (1976), 19–26.

Berquist, Goodwin F., and James L. Golden. "Media Rhetoric, Criticism, and the Public Perception of the 1980 Presidential Debates." *QJS* 67 (1981), 125–137.

Blair, Karen. " 'Star Trek' in Retrospect—A Celebration of the Alien." *TQ* 16:2 (1979), 39–47.

Booth, Philip. "*Route 66*—Television on the Road Toward People." *TQ* 2:1 (1963), 5–12.

Bormann, Ernest G. "A Fantasy Theme Analysis of the Television Coverage of the Hostage Release and the Reagan Inaugural." *QJS* 68 (1982), 133–145.

Brown, William R. "The Prime-Time Television Environment and Emerging Rhetorical Visions." *QJS* 62 (1976), 389–399.

Brown, William R. "Television and the Democratic National Convention of 1968." *QJS* 55 (1969), 237–246.

Caughie, John. "Rhetoric, Pleasure and 'Art Television'—*Dreams of Leaving.*" *Screen* 22:4 (1981), pp. 9–31.

Chapel, Gage William. "Television Criticism: A Rhetorical Perspective." *WJSC* 39 (1975), 81–91.

Charland, Maurice. "The Private Eye: From Print to Television." *JPC* 12 (1979), 210–216.

Chesebro, James W., and Caroline D. Hamsher, "Communication, Values, and Popular Television Series." *JPC* 8 (1974), 587–603.

Claus, Peter J. "A Structuralist Appreciation of 'Star Trek.' " In *The American Dimension: Cultural Myths and Social Realities*. Edited by W. Arens and Susan P. Montague. Sherman Oaks: Alfred, 1976.

Combs, James E. "Political Advertising as a Popular Mythmaking Form." *Journal of American Culture* 2 (1979), 331–340.

Cragan, John F., and Donald C. Shields. "Foreign Policy Communication Dramas: How Mediated Rhetoric Played in Peoria in Campaign '76." *QJS* 63 (1977), 274–289.

Cusella, Louis P. "Real-Fiction Versus Historical Reality: Rhetorical Purification in *Kent State*— The Docudrama." *CQ* 30 (1982), 159–164.

DeSousa, Michael A. "The Emerging Self-Portrait: The Television of Television." *JPFT* 9:3 (Fall 1981), pp. 144–148.

DeSousa, Michael A. "The Curious Evolution of the Video Family." *Television Quarterly* 16 (Winter 1979–80), 43–45.

Devlin, L. Patrick. "Contrasts in Presidential Campaign Commercials of 1976." *CSSJ* 28 (1977), 238–249.

Doll, Howard D., and Bert E. Bradley. "A Study of the Objectivity of Television News Reporting of the 1972 Presidential Campaign." *CSSJ* 25 (1974), 254–263.

Eaton, Mick. "Television Situation Comedy." *Screen* 19:4 (1978–79), 61–89.

Farrell, Thomas B., and G. Thomas Goodnight. "Accidental Rhetoric: The Root Metaphors of Three Mile Island." *CM* 48 (1981), 271–300.

Fine, Marlene G., Carolyn Anderson, and Gary Eckles. "Black English on Black Situation Comedies." *JOC* 29 (1979), 21–29.

Frank, Robert S. "The 'Grammar of Film' in Television News." *JQ* 51 (1974), 245–250.

Gilbert, Craig. "Reflections on *An American Family.*" *Studies in Visual Communication* 8:1 (Winter 1982), 24–54.

Goggin, Richard J. "Television Drama: Form and Content." *WJSC* 15 (1951), 51–53.

Gould, Christopher, Dagmar C. Stern, and Timothy Dow Adams. "TV's Distorted Vision of Poverty." *CQ* 29 (1981), 309–315.

Gregg, Richard B. "The Rhetoric of Political Newscasting." *CSSJ* 28 (1977), 231–237.

Gronbeck, Bruce E. "Narrative, Enactment, and Television Programming." *SSCJ* 48 (1983), 229–242.

Hammerback, John. "William F. Buckley, Jr., On *Firing Line:* A Case Study in Confrontational Dialogue." *CQ* 22 (Summer 1974), pp. 23–30.

Honan, William H. "TV and the 'Bloody' Classics." *QJS* 51 (1965), 145–151.

Jewett, Robert, and John S. Lawrence. " 'Star Trek, and the Bubble-Gum Fallacy." *TQ* 14:1 (1977), 5–16.

Johnson, R. E., Jr. "The Dialogue of Novelty and Repetition: Structure in *All My Children.*" *JPC* 10 (1976), 560–570.

Larson, Charles U. "Media Metaphors: Two Models for Rhetorically Criticizing the Political Television Spot Advertisement." *CSSJ* 33 (1982), 533–546.

Lawrence, John Shelton, and Bernard Timberg. "News and Mythic Selectivity: Mayaguez, Entebbe, Mogadishu." *Journal of American Culture* 2 (1979), 321–330.

Lomas, Charles W. "Television in British Political Debate." *CSSJ* 17 (1966), 97–105.

Munoz James, and Renee Munoz. *"Gidget:* A Viewer Analysis." *TQ* 6:2 (1967), 59–69.

Murray, Michael D. "Persuasive Dimensions of *See It Now's* 'Report on Senator Joseph R. McCarthy.' " *CQ* 23 (Fall, 1975), pp. 13–20.

Murray, Michael D. "To Hire a Hall: 'An Argument in Indianapolis.' " *CSSJ* 26 (1975), 12–20.

Murray, Michael D. "Wallace and the Media: The 1972 Florida Primary." *SSCJ* 40 (1975), 429–440.

Nimmo, Dan, and James E. Combs. "Fantasies and Melodramas in Television Network News: The Case of Three Mile Island." *WJSC* 46 (1982), 45–55.

Porter, Michael J. "The *Grande Syntaqmatique:* A Methodology for the Analysis of the Montage Structure of Television Narratives." *SSCJ* 47 (1982), 330–341.

Rogers, Jimmie N., and Theodore Clevenger, Jr. " 'The Selling of the Pentagon': Was CBS the Fulbright Propaganda Machine?" *QJS* 57 (1971), 266–273.

Rollins, Peter C. "*Television's Vietnam:* The Visual Language of Television News." *Journal of American Culture* 4 (1981), 114–135.

Rollins, Peter C. "*Victory at Sea:* Cold War Epic." *JPC* 6 (1973), 463–482.

Sawyer, Corrine Holt. " 'If I Could Walk That Way, I Wouldn't Need Talcum Powder': Word Play Humor in M*A*S*H." *JPFT* 11 (Spring 1983), pp. 42–52.

Scher, Saul N. "The Role of the Television Critic: Four Approaches." *CQ* 22 (Summer 1974), pp. 1–6.

Schrag, Robert L. "Teach Your Children Well: Method and Rationale in the Criticism of Adolescent Oriented Television Programming." *WJSC* 46 (1982), 98–108.

Schrag, Robert L., Richard A. Hudson, and Lawrance M. Bernabo. "Television's New Humane Collectivity." *WJSC* 45 (1981), 1–12.

Smith, Craig R. "Television News as Rhetoric." *WJSC* 41 (1977), 147–159.

Smith, Robert Rutherford. "Mythic Elements in Television News." *JOC* 29 (1979), 75–82.

Swanson, David L. "And That's the Way It Was? Television Covers the 1976 Presidential Campaign." *QJS* 63 (1977), 239–248.

Tiemens, Robert K. "Television's Portrayal of the 1976 Presidential Debates: An Analysis of Visual Content." *CM* 45 (1978), 362–370.

Tuchman, Gaye. "Television News and the Metaphor of Myth." *Studies in the Anthropology of Visual Communication* 5 (1978), 56–62.

Tyrrell, William Blake. "*Star Trek* as Myth and Television as Mythmaker." *JPC* 10 (1977), 711–719.

Wander, Philip. "Counters in the Social Drama: Some Notes on *All in the Family.*" *JPC* 8 (1974), 602–609.

Wander, Philip. "*The Waltons:* How Sweet It Was." *JOC* 26 (1976), 148–154.

Wander, Philip. "On the Meaning of 'Roots.' " *JOC* 27 (1977), 64–69.

Washburn, Frank. "The Television Panel as a Vehicle of Political Persuasion." *WJSC* 16 (1952), 245–253.

Williams, Brien R. "The Structure of Televised Football." *JOC* 27 (1977), 133–139.

Film

Books

Affron, Charles. *Cinema and Sentiment.* Chicago: University of Chicago Press, 1982.

Arnheim, Rudolf. *Film as Art.* Berkeley: University of California Press, 1957.

Barsam, Richard Meran, ed. *Nonfiction Film: Theory and Criticism.* New York: E. P. Dutton, 1976.

Bazin, Andre. *What Is Cinema?* 2 vols. Berkeley: University of California Press, 1967, 1971.

Bettetini, Gianfranco. *The Language and Technique of the Film.* The Hague: Mouton, 1973.

Bluestone, George. *Novels into Film.* Berkeley: University of California Press, 1957.

Braudy, Leo. *The World in a Frame: What We See in Films.* Garden City: Anchor Press, 1976.

Browne, Nick. *The Rhetoric of Filmic Narration.* Ann Arbor: UMI Research Press, 1982.

Carroll, John M. *Toward a Structural Psychology of Cinema.* New York: Mouton Publishers, 1980.

Cavell, Stanley. *The World Viewed: Reflections on the Ontology of Film.* Cambridge: Harvard University Press, 1979.

Durgnat, Raymond. *Films and Feelings.* Cambridge: MIT Press, 1967.

Edmonds, Robert. *The Sights and Sounds of Cinema and Television.* New York: Teachers College Press, 1982.

Eidsvik, Charles. *Cineliteracy: Film Among the Arts.* New York: Random House, 1978.

Eisenstein, Sergei. *Film Form.* Trans. Jay Leyda. New York: Harcourt, Brace, Jovanovich, 1949.

Eisenstein, Sergei. *The Film Sense.* Trans. Jay Leyda. New York: Harcourt, Brace, Jovanovich, 1947.

Fell, John L. *Film and the Narrative Tradition.* Norman: University of Oklahoma Press, 1974.

Harrington, John. *The Rhetoric of Film.* New York: Holt, Rinehart, and Winston, 1973.

Huaco, George A. *The Sociology of Film Art.* New York: Basic Books, 1965.

Insdorf, Annette. *Indelible Shadows: Film and the Holocaust.* New York: Vintage Books, 1983.

Jacobs, Lewis, ed. *The Movies as Medium.* New York: Farrar, Straus, and Giroux, 1970.

Jarvie, Ian C. *Movies as Social Criticism: Aspects of Their Social Psychology.* Metuchen, N.J.: Scarecrow Press, 1978.

Kawin, Bruce F. *Mindscreen: Bergman, Godard, and First-Person Film.* Princeton: Princeton University Press, 1978.

Kerr, Walter, *The Silent Clowns.* New York: Knopf, 1975.

Kinder, Marsha, and Beverle Houston. *Close-Up: A Critical Perspective on Film.* New York: Harcourt, Brace, Jovanovich, 1972.

Kolker, Robert P. *The Altering Eye: Contemporary International Cinema.* New York: Oxford University Press, 1983.

Kracauer, Siegfried, *From Caligari to Hitler.* Princeton: Princeton University Press, 1947.

Mast, Gerald, and Marshall Cohen, eds. *Film Theory and Criticism: Introductory Readings.* 2nd ed. New York: Oxford University Press, 1979.

Metz, Christian. *Film Language: A Semiotics of the Cinema.* Trans. Michael Taylor. New York: Oxford University Press, 1974.

Metz, Christian. *Language and Cinema.* Trans. Donna Jean Umiker-Sebeok. The Hague: Mouton, 1974.

Monaco, James. *How to Read a Film.* New York: Oxford University Press, 1981.

Montagu, Ivor. *Film World.* Baltimore: Penguin Books, 1964.

Nelson, Thomas Allen. *Kubrick: Inside a Film Artist's Maze.* Bloomington: Indiana University Press, 1982.

Nichols, Bill. *Ideology and the Image.* Bloomington: Indiana University Press, 1981.

Nichols, Bill, ed. *Movies and Methods.* Berkeley: University of California Press, 1976.

Nilsen, Vladimir. *The Cinema as a Graphic Art.* Trans. Stephen Garry. New York: Hill and Wang, 1959.

Pryluck, Calvin. *Sources of Meaning in Motion Pictures and Television.* New York: Arno Press, 1976.

Reisz, Karel, and Gavin Millar. *The Technique of Film Editing.* 2nd edition. London: Focal Press, 1981.

Richie, Donald. *The Films of Akira Kurosawa.* Berkeley: University of California Press, 1965.

Roffman, Peter, and Jim Purdy. *The Hollywood Social Problem Film: Madness, Despair, and Politics from the Depression to the Fifties.* Bloomington: Indiana University Press, 1981.

Ross, Lillian. *Picture.* Garden City: Doubleday, 1962.

Schatz, Thomas. *Hollywood Genres.* New York: Random House, 1981.

Screen Reader 1: Cinema/Ideology/Politics. London: The Society for Education in Film and Television, 1977.

Sesonske, Alexander. *Jean Renoir: The French Films, 1924–1939.* Cambridge: Harvard University Press, 1980.

Stephenson, Ralph, and J. R. Debrix. *The Cinema as Art.* Baltimore: Penquin, 1976.

Rothman, William. *Hitchcock–The Murderous Gaze.* Cambridge: Harvard University Press, 1982.

Simon, John. *Ingmar Bergman Directs.* New York: Harcourt, Brace, Jovanovich, 1972.

Stott, William. *Documentary Expression and Thirties America.* New York: Oxford University Press, 1973.

Talbot, Daniel, ed. *Film: An Anthology.* Berkeley: University of California Press, 1959.

Walker, Alexander, *Stanley Kubrick Directs.* Expanded edition. New York: Harcourt, Brace, Jovanovich, 1972.

Wright, Will. *Sixguns and Society: A Structural Study of the Western.* Berkeley: University of California Press, 1975.

Wollen, Peter. *Signs and Meaning in the Cinema.* 3rd ed. Bloomington: Indiana University Press, 1972.

Worth, Sol, and John Adair. *Through Navajo Eyes.* Bloomington: Indiana University Press, 1972.

Articles

Alley, Kenneth D. "*High Sierra*—Swan Song for an Era." *JPFT* 5 (1976), 248–262.

Andrew, Dudley. "The Gravity of *Sunrise.*" *QRFS* 2 (1977), 356–387.

Armour, Robert. "*Deliverance:* Four Variations of the American Adam." *LFQ* 1 (1973), 280–285.

Behrens, Lawrence. "The Argument in Film: Applying Rhetorical Theory to Film Criticism." *Journal of the University Film Association* 31:3 (Summer 1979), pp. 3–11.

Belton, John. "Alfred Hitchcock's *Under Capricorn:* Montage Entranced by Mise-en-Scene." *QRFS* 6 (1981), 365–383.

Benderson, Albert. "An Archetypal Reading of *Juliet of the Spirits.*" *QRFS* 4 (1979), 193–206.

Benson, Thomas W. "*Joe:* An Essay in the Rhetorical Criticism of Film." *JPC* 8 (1974), 608–618.

Benson, Thomas W. "The Rhetorical Structure of Frederick Wisemen's *High School.*" *CM* 47 (1980), 233–261.

Benson, Thomas W., and Stefan Fleischer. "Teaching the Rhetoric of Film: Access to Images." *CQ* 23 (Winter, 1975), pp. 27–37.

Biskind, Peter. "The Politics of Power in *On the Waterfront.*" *FQ* 29 (Fall 1975), pp. 25–38.

Biskind, Peter. "*Rebel Without a Cause:* Nicholas Ray in the Fifties." *FQ* 28 (Fall 1974), 32–38.

Biskind, Peter. "Vigilantes, Power and Domesticity: Images of the 50's in *Walking Tall,*" *JPFT* 3 (1974), 219–229.

Borden, Diane M. "Bergman's Style and the Facial Icon." *QRFS* 2 (1977), 42–55.

Boyd, David. "Mode and Meaning in *2001.*" *JPFT* 6 (1978), 205–215.

Breen, Myles P. "The Rhetoric of the Short Film." *Journal of the University Film Association* 30:2 (Summer 1978), pp. 3–13.

Browne, Nick. "The Spectator-in-the-Text: The Rhetoric of *Stagecoach.*" *FQ* 29 (Winter 1975–76), pp. 26–38.

Campbell, Gregg M. "Beethoven, Chopin and Tammy Wynette: Heroines and Archetypes in *Five Easy Pieces.*" *LFQ* 2 (1974), 275–283.

Campbell, Russell. "The Ideology of the Social Consciousness Movie: Three Films of Darryl F. Zanuck." *QRFS* 3 (1978), 49–71.

Caputi, Jane E. "*Jaws* as Patriarchal Myth." *JPFT* 6 (1978), 305–326.

Cardullo, Robert J. "The Space in the Distance: A Study of Altman's *Nashville.*" *LFQ* 4 (1976), 313–324.

Carpenter, Ronald H., and Robert V. Seltzer. "Nixon, *Patton,* and a Silent Majority Sentiment about the Viet Nam War: The Cinematographic Bases of a Rhetorical Stance." *CSSJ* 25 (1974), 105–110.

Carringer, Robert L. "*Citizen Kane, The Great Gatsby,* and Some Conventions of American Narrative." *CI* 2 (1975), 307–325.

Cavell, Stanley. *"North by Northwest." CI* 7 (1981), 761–776.

Cowart, David. "Cinematic Auguries of the Third Reich in *Gravity's Rainbow.*" *LFQ* 6 (1978), 364–370.

Davies, Robert A., James M. Farrell, and Steven S. Matthews. "The Dream World of Film: A Jungian Perspective on Cinematic Communication." *WJSC* 46 (1982), 326–343.

Dayan, Daniel. "The Tutor-Code of Classical Cinema." *FQ* 28 (Fall 1974), pp. 22–31.

D'Lugo, Marvin. "Signs and Meaning in *Blow-up:* From Cortazar to Antonioni." *LFQ* 3 (1975), 23–29.

Dumont, J. P., and J. Monad. "Beyond the Infinite: A Structural Analysis of *2001: A Space Odyssey.*" *QRFS* 3 (1978), 297–316.

Evans, Walter. "Monster Movies and Rites of Initiation." *JPFT* 4 (1975), 124–142.

Farber, Stephen, and Estelle Changas. *"The Graduate." FQ* (Spring 1968), pp. 37–41.

Farguhar, Judith. "An American Horror Myth: *Night of the Living Dead." Semiotica* 38 (1982), 1–15.

Fischer, Lucy. "The Image of Woman as Image: The Optical Politics of *Dames." FQ* 30 (Fall 1976), pp. 2–11.

Free, William J. "Aesthetic and Moral Value in *Bonnie and Clyde." QJS* 54 (1968), 220–225.

Frentz, Thomas S., and Thomas B. Farrell. "Conversion of America's Consciousness: The Rhetoric of *The Exorcist." QJS* 61 (1975), 40–47.

Frentz, Thomas S., and Mary E. Hale. "Inferential Model Criticism of 'The Empire Strikes Back.' " *QJS* 69 (1983), 278–289.

Frentz, Thomas S., and Janice Hocker Rushing. "The Rhetoric of 'Rocky': Part Two." *WJSC* 42 (1978), 231–240.

Giannetti, Louis D. *"Member of the Wedding." LFQ* 4 (1976), 28–38.

Gomez, Joseph A. "*The Third Man:* Capturing the Visual Essence of Literary Conception." *LFQ* 2 (1974), 332–340.

Gordon, Andrew. "*Star Wars:* A Myth for Our Time." *LFQ* 6 (1978), 314–326.

Hark, Ina Rae. "The Visual Politics of *The Adventures of Robin Hood." JPFT* 5 (1976), 3–17.

Henderson, Brian. "*The Searchers:* An American Dilemma." *FQ* 34:2 (Winter 1980–81), pp. 9–23.

Hendrix, Jerry, and James A. Wood. "The Rhetoric of Film: Toward Critical Methodology." *SSCJ* 39 (1973), 105–122.

Holdstein, Deborah H. "*Tootsie:* Mixed Messages." *Jump Cut* No. 28 (1983), p. 1.

Isenberg, Michael T. "The Mirror of Democracy: Reflections on the War Films of World War I, 1917–1919." *JPC* 9 (1976), 878–885.

Jones, Christopher John. "Bergman's *Persona* and the Artistic Dilemma of the Modern Narrative." *LFQ* 5 (1977), 75–88.

Kepley, Vance, Jr. "Griffiths's *Broken Blossoms* and the Problem of Historical Specificity." *QRFS* 3 (1978), 37–47.

Kepley, Vance, Jr. "*The Musketeers of Pig Alley* and the Well-Made Sausage." *LFQ* 6 (1978), 274–284.

Kepley, Vance, Jr. "The Scientist as Magician: Dovzhenko's *Michurin* and the Lysenko Cult." *JPFT* 8:2 (1980), 19–26.

LeGacy, Arthur. "*The Invasion of the Body Snatchers:* A Metaphor for the Fifties." *LFQ* 6 (1978), 285–292.

Litton, Glenn. "Diseased Beauty in Tony Richardson's *Hamlet.*" *LFQ* 4 (1976), 108–122.

Mast, Gerald. "Kracauer's Two Tendencies and the Early History of Film Narrative." *CI* 6 (1980), 455–476.

Mayne, Judith. "*King Kong* and the Ideology of Spectacle." *QRFS* 1 (1976), 373–387.

Medhurst, Martin J. "*Hiroshima, Mon Amour:* From Iconography to Rhetoric." *QJS* 68 (1982), 345–370.

Medhurst, Martin J. "Image and Ambiguity: A Rhetorical Approach to *The Exorcist.*" *SSCJ* 44 (1978), 73–92.

Medhurst, Martin J., and Thomas W. Benson. "*The City:* The Rhetoric of Rhythm." *CM* 48 (1981), 54–72.

Mellen, Joan. "Sexual Politics and *Last Tango in Paris.*" *FQ* 26 (Spring 1973), pp. 9–19.

Merritt, Russell L. "The Bashful Hero in American Film of the Nineteen Forties." *QJS* 61 (1975), 129–139.

Merritt, Russell. "D. W. Griffith Directs the Great War: The Making of *Hearts of the World.*" *QRFS* 6 (1981), 45–65.

Mitchell, Charles Reed. "New Message to America: James W. Gerard's *Beware* and World War I Propaganda." *JPFT* 4 (1975), 275–295.

Murphy, William Thomas. "The Method of *Why We Fight.*" *JPFT* 1 (1972), 185–196.

Naremore, James. "John Huston and *The Maltese Falcon.*" *LFQ* 1 (1973), 239–249.

Nichols, Bill. "The Voice of Documentary." *FQ* 36:3 (Spring 1983), pp. 17–29.

Palmer, R. Barton. "*Chinatown* and the Detective Story." *LFQ* 5 (1977), 112–117.

Pearson, Maisi K. "*Rosemary's Baby:* The Horns of a Dilemma." *JPC* 2 (1968), 493–502.

Perebinossoff, Phillipe R. "Theatricals in Jean Renoir's *The Rules of the Game* and *Grand Illusion.*" *LFQ* 5 (1977), 50–56.

Perry, Ted. "A Contextual Study of M. Antonioni's Film *L'Eclisse.*" *CM* 37 (1970), 79–100.

Poague, Leland A. "The Detective in Hitchcock's *Frenzy:* His Ancestors and Significance." *JPFT* 2 (1973), 47–58.

Rice, Julian C. "Transcendental Pornography and *Taxi Driver.*" *JPFT* 5 (1976), 109–123.

Rollins, Peter C. "Ideology and Film Rhetoric: Three Documentaries of the New Deal Era." *JPFT* 5 (1976), 126–145.

Rose, Bryan. "*It's a Wonderful Life:* Last Stand of the Capra Hero." *JPFT* 6 (1977), 156–166.

Ross, T. J. "Death and Deliverance in the Western: From *The Virginian* to *The Man Who Shot Liberty Valance.*" *QRFS* 2 (1977), 75–87.

Rushing, Janice Hocker, and Thomas S. Frentz. " 'The Deer Hunter': Rhetoric of the Warrior." *QJS* 66 (1980), 392–406.

Rushing, Janice Hocker, and Thomas S. Frentz. "The Rhetoric of 'Rocky': A Social Value Model of Criticism." *WJSC,* 42 (1978), 63–72.

Rutherford, Charles S. "A New Dog with an Old Trick: Archetypal Patterns in *Sounder." JPFT* 2 (1973), 155–163.

Sadkin, David. "Theme and Structure: *Last Tango* Untangled." *LFQ* 2 (1974), 162–173.

Safer, Elaine B. " 'It's the Truth Even If It Didn't Happen': Ken Kesey's *One Flew Over the Cuckoo's Nest." LFQ* 5 (1977), 132–141.

Scheurer, Timothy E. "The Aesthetics of Form and Convention in the Movie Musical." *JPF* 3 (1974), 307–324.

Schuetz, Janice. " 'The Exorcist': Images of Good and Evil." *WJSC,* 39 (1975), 92–101.

Self, Robert T. "Invention and Death: The Commodities of Media in Robert Altman's *Nashville." JPFT* 5 (1976), 273–288.

Sharrett, Christopher. "Operation Mind Control: *Apocalypse Now* and the Search for Clarity." *JPFT* 8 (1980), 34–43.

Simone, R. Thomas. "The Mythos of 'The Sickness Unto Death': Kurosawa's *Ikiru* and Tolstoy's *The Death of Ivan Ilych." LFQ* 3 (1975), 2–12.

Smith, Julian. "Orson Welles and the Great American Dummy–Or, The Rise and Fall and Regeneration of Benjamin Franklin's Model American." *LFQ* 2 (1974), 196–206.

Stewart, Garrett. "Coppola's Conrad: The Repetitions of Complicity." *CI* 7 (1981), 455–474.

Stewart, Garrett. "Modern Hard Times: Chaplin and the Cinema of Self-Reflection." *CI* 3 (1976), 295–314.

Turner, John W. "*Little Big Man,* the Novel and the Film: A Study of Narrative Structure." *LFQ* 5 (1977), 154–163.

Vogelsang, Judith. "Motifs of Image and Sound in *The Godfather." JPFT* 2 (1973), 115–135.

Waugh, Thomas. " 'Men Cannot Act in Front of the Camera in the Presence of Death': Joris Ivens' *The Spanish Earth." Cineaste* 13:3 (1983), pp. 21–29.

Williams, Alan. "Narrative Patterns in *Only Angels Have Wings." QRFS* 1 (1976), 357–372.

Williams, Linda. "Dream Rhetoric and Film Rhetoric: Metaphor and Metonymy in *Un chien andalou." Semiotica* 33 (1981), 87–103.

Williams, Linda. "*Hiroshima* and *Marienbad:* Metaphor and Metonymy." Screen 17 (1976), 34–39.

Wood, Denis. "Growing Up Among the Stars." *LFQ* 6 (1978), 327–341.

Wood, Denis. "The Stars in Our Hearts—A Critical Commentary on George Lucas' *Star Wars." JPFT* 6 (1978), 262–279.

Zambrano, Ana Laura. *"Throne of Blood:* Kurosawa's *Macbeth." LFQ* 2 (1974), 262–274.

Radio

Books

Arnheim, Rudolf. *Radio: An Art of Sound.* Trans. Margaret Ludwig and Herbert Read. New York: DaCapo Press, 1972.

Barnouw, Erik. *The Golden Web.* Vol. II of *A History of Broadcasting in the United States.* New York: Oxford University Press, 1968.

Barnouw, Erik. *A Tower in Babel.* Vol. I of *A History of Broadcasting in the United States.* New York: Oxford University Press, 1966.

Buxton, Frank, and Bill Owen. *Radio's Golden Age: The Programs and the Personalities.* New York: Easton Valley Press, 1966.

Cantril, Hadley, and Gordon W. Allport. *The Psychology of Radio.* New York: Arno Press, 1971.

Chester, Edward W. *Radio, Television, and American Politics*. New York: Sheed and Ward, 1969.

Delmer, Sefton. *Black Boomerang*. New York: Viking Press, 1962.

Fang, Irving E. *Those Radio Commentators*. Ames: Iowa State University Press, 1977.

Goffman, Erving. *Forms of Talk*. Philadelphia: University of Pennsylvania Press, 1981.

Harmon, Jim. *The Great Radio Heroes*. Garden City: Doubleday, 1967.

Fornatale, Peter, and Joshua E. Mills. *Radio in the Television Age*. Woodstock, N.Y.: Overlook Press, 1980.

Lewis, Peter, ed. *Radio Drama*. New York: Longman, 1981.

MacDonald, J. Fred. *Don't Touch That Dial!: Radio Programming in American Life, 1920–1960*. Chicago: Nelson-Hall, 1979.

Meo, Lucy D. *Japan's Radio War on Australia, 1941–1945*. Carlton, Victoria: Melbourne University Press, 1968.

Smith, Ralph Lewis. *A Study of the Professional Criticism of Broadcasting in the United States, 1920–1955*. New York: Arno Press, 1979.

Stedman, Raymond Williams. *The Serials: Suspense and Drama by Installment*. 2nd ed. Norman: University of Oklahoma Press, 1977.

Wertheim, Arthur Frank. *Radio Comedy*. New York: Oxford University Press, 1979.

Articles

Bormann, Ernest G. "This Is Huey P. Long Talking." *Journal of Broadcasting* 2 (1958), 111–122.

Breitinger, Eckhard. "The Rhetoric of American Radio Drama." *Revue des Langues Vivantes* 44 (1978), 229–246.

Chester, Giraud. "How Good Is British Radio?" *QJS* 35 (1949), 320–328.

Clements, William M. "The Rhetoric of the Radio Ministry." *Journal of American Folklore* 87 (1974), 318–327.

Cohen, Herman, and John C. Weiser. "Radio and the 1948 Presidential Campaign in the West." *WJSC* 15 (1951), 10–12.

Culbert, David H. " 'This Is London': Edward R. Murrow, Radio News and American Aid to Britain." *JPC* 10 (1976), 28–37.

Degnan, James M. "Oratorical Style and Newscasting." *WJSC* 19 (1955), 69–73.

Kagan, Norman. "*Amos 'n Andy:* Twenty Years Late, or Two Decades Early?" *JPC* 6 (1972), 70–75.

MacDonald, J. Fred. "Government Propaganda in Commercial Radio—The Case of *Treasury Star Parade, 1942–1943*." *JPC* 12 (1979), 285–304.

Medhurst, Martin J. "A Man and a Microphone: The London Broadcasts of Edward R. Murrow." *The Pennsylvania Speech Communication Annual* 36 (1980), 9–15.

Morson, Gary Saul. "The War of the Well(e)s." *JOC* 29 (1979), 10–20.

Rouse, Morleen Getz. "Daytime Radio Programming for the Homemaker, 1926–1956." *JPC* 12 (1978), 315–327.

Schroeder, Fred E. H. "Radio's Home Folks *Vic and Sade:* A Study in Aural History." *JPC* 12 (1978), 253–264.

Steele, Ralph W. "Radio in a World at War." *SSCJ* 8 (1942), 37–39.

Summers, Harrison B. "Radio in the 1948 Campaign." *QJS* 34 (1948), 432–438.

Warner, W. Lloyd, and W. E. Henry. "The Radio Day-Time Serial: A Symbolic Analysis." In *Reader in Public Opinion and Communication*. Edited by Bernard Berelson and Morris Janowitz. Glencoe, Illinois: Free Press, 1950.

Wertheim, Arthur Frank. " 'The Bad Boy of Radio': Henry Morgan and Censorship." *JPC* 12 (1978), 347–352.

Wertheim, Arthur Frank. "Relieving Social Tensions: Radio Comedy & the Great Depression." *JPC* 10 (1976), 501–519.

Willis, Edgar E. "Radio and Presidential Campaigning." *CSSJ* 20 (1969), 187–193.

VISUAL ARTS

Painting and Prints

Books

Arnheim, Rudolf. *Art and Visual Perception: The Psychology of the Creative Eye.* 2nd edition. Berkeley: University of California Press, 1974.

Arnheim, Rudolf. *Picasso's Guernica: The Genesis of a Painting.* Berkeley: University of California Press, 1962.

Arnheim, Rudolf. *The Power of the Center: A Study of Composition in the Visual Arts.* Berkeley: University of California Press, 1982.

Arnheim, Rudolf. *Toward a Psychology of Art: Selected Essays.* Berkeley: University of California Press, 1966.

Arnheim, Rudolf. *Visual Thinking.* Berkeley: University of California Press, 1969.

Berger, John. *About Looking.* New York: Pantheon, 1980.

Castleman, Craig. *Getting Up: Subway Graffiti in New York.* Cambridge: The MIT Press, 1982.

Clark, Kenneth. *The Nude: A Study in Ideal Form.* Princeton: Princeton University Press, 1956.

Gombrich, E. H. *Art and Illusion.* Princeton: Princeton University Press, 1969.

Gombrich, E. H. *The Story of Art.* 12th edition. London: Phaidon, 1972.

Gombrich, E. H., and Ernst Kris. *Caricature.* London: King Penguin, 1940.

Hollander, Anne. *Seeing Through Clothes.* New York: Viking, 1978.

Ivins, William M., Jr. *Prints and Visual Communication.* Cambridge: Harvard University Press, 1953.

Lucie-Smith, Edward. *Thinking About Art: Critical Essays.* London: Calder and Boyars, 1968.

Margolis, Joseph. *The Language of Art and Art Criticism.* Detroit: Wayne State Press, 1965.

Mauner, George. *Manet, Peintre-Philosophe: A Study of the Painter's Themes.* University Park: The Pennsylvania State University, 1975.

Mayor, A. Hyatt. *Prints & People: A Social History of Printed Pictures.* New York: The Metropolitan Museum of Art, 1971.

Mitchell, W. J. T., ed. *The Language of Images.* Chicago: University of Chicago Press, 1980.

Panofsky, Erwin. *Meaning in the Visual Arts.* Garden City: Doubleday, 1955.

Panofsky, Erwin. *Studies in Iconology.* New York: Oxford University Press, 1939.

Pepper, Stephen C. *Principles of Art Appreciation.* New York: Harcourt, Brace, 1949.

Rigby, Ida Katherine. *An alle Kunstler! War—Revolution—Weimar.* San Diego: San Diego State University Press, 1983.

Rhodes, Anthony. *Propaganda: The Art of Persuasion: World War II.* New York: Chelsea House, 1976.

Shikes, Ralph E. *The Indignant Eye: The Artist as Social Critic.* Boston: Beacon, 1969.

Articles

Agresto, John. "Art and Historical Truth: The Boston Massacre." *JOC* 29 (1979), 170–174.

Fehl, Phillip P. "Farewell to Jokes: The Last *Capricci* of Giovanni Domenico Tiepolo and the Tradition of Irony in Venetian Painting." *CI* 5 (1979), 761–791.

Fried, Michael. "Painter into Painting: On Courbet's *After Dinner at Orleans* and *Stonebreakers.*" *CI* 8 (1982), 619–649.

Gilman, Ernest B. "Word and Image in Quarles' *Emblemes.*" *CI* 6 (1980), 385–410.

Gombrich, E. H. "Visual Metaphors of Value in Art." In *Symbols and Values: An Initial Study.* Edited by Lyman Bryson, et al. New York: Harper, 1954.

Jordan, John O. "A Sum of Destructions: Violence, Paternity and Art in Picasso's 'Guernica'." *Studies in Visual Communication* 8:3 (Summer 1982), pp. 2–27.

Olsen, Lester C. "Portraits in Praise of A People: A Rhetorical Analysis of Norman Rockwell's Icons in Franklin D. Roosevelt's "Four Freedoms" Campaign." *QJS* 69 (1983), 15–24.

Roskill, Mark. " 'Public' and 'Private' Meanings: The Paintings of Van Gogh." *JOC* 29 (1970), 157–169.

Scott, Robert L. "Diego Rivera at Rockefeller Center: Fresco Painting and Rhetoric." *WJSC* 41 (1977), 70–82.

Searle, John R. "*Las Meninas* and the Paradoxes of Pictorial Representation." *CI* 6 (1980), 477–488.

Swiderski, Richard M. "The Idiom of Diagnosis." *CQ* 24 (Spring, 1976), pp. 3–11.

Comics and Cartoons

Books

Dorfman, Ariel, and Armand Mattelhart. *How to Read Donald Duck: Imperialist Ideology in the Disney Comic.* New York: International General, 1975.

Harrison, Randall P. *The Cartoon: Communication to the Quick.* Beverly Hills: Sage, 1981.

Articles

Barshay, Robert. "The Cartoon of Modern Sensibility." *JPC* 8 (1974), 523–533.

Bormann, Ernest G., Jolene Koester, and Janet Bennett, "Political Cartoons and Salient Rhetorical Fantasies: An Empirical Analysis of the '76 Presidential Campaign." *CM* 45 (1978), 317–329.

Brown, Lloyd W. "Comic-Strip Heroes: Leroi Jones and the Myth of American Innocence." *JPC* 3 (1969), 191–204.

Carl, LeRoy M. "Political Cartoons: 'Ink Blots' of the Editorial Page." *JPC* 4 (1970), 39–45.

DeSousa, Michael A., and Martin J. Medhurst. "Political Cartoons and American Culture: Significant Symbols of Campaign 1980." *Studies in Visual Communication* 8 (Winter 1982), 84–97.

Faust, Wolfgang. "Comics and How to Read Them." *JPC* 5 (1971), 194–202.

Harvey, Robert C. "The Aesthetics of the Comic Strip." *JPC* 12 (1979), 640–652.

Medhurst, Martin J., and Michael A. DeSousa. "Political Cartoons as Rhetorical Form: A Taxonomy of Graphic Discourse." *CM* 48 (1981), 197–236.

Meyer, Katherine, John Seidler, Timothy Currey, and Adrian Aveni. "Women in July Fourth Cartoons: A 100 Year Look." *JOC* 30 (1980), 21–30.

Mintz, Lawrence E. "Fantasy, Formula, Realism and Propaganda in Milton Caniff's Comic Strips." *JPC* 12 (1979), 653–680.

Morrison, Matthew C. "The Role of the Political Cartoonist in Image Making." *CSSJ* 20 (1969), 252–260.

Sagarin, Edward. "The Deviant in the Comic Strip: The Case History of Barney Google." *JPC* 5 (1971), 178–193.

Steakley, James D. "Iconography of a Scandal: Political Cartoons and the Eulenburg Affair." *Studies in Visual Communication* 9 (Spring 1983), 20–51.

Steig, Michael. "Dickens, Hablot Browne, and the Tradition of English Caricature." *Criticism* 11 (1969), 219–233.

Streicher, Lawrence H. "David Low and the Mass Press. *Journalism Quarterly* 43 (1966), 211–220.

Streicher, Lawrence H. "David Low and the Sociology of Caricature." *Comparative Studies in History and Society* 8 (1965–66), 1–23.

Turner, Kathleen J. "Comic Strips: A Rhetorical Perspective." *CSSJ* 28 (1977), 24–35.

Wechsler, Judith. "Caricature, Newspapers, and Politics—Paris in the 1830s." *Studies in Visual Communication* 7 (Fall 1981), 2–29.

Young, William H. "That Indomitable Redhead Little Orphan Annie." *JPC* 8 (1974), 309–316.

Young, William H., Jr. "The Serious Funnies: Adventure Comics During the Depression, 1929–1938." *JPC* 3 (1969), 404–427.

Photography

Books

Adams, Ansel. *Singular Images.* Dobbs Ferry: Morgan & Morgan, 1974.

Akeret, Robert U. *Photoanalysis.* New York: Peter H. Wyden, 1973.

Barthes, Roland. *Camera Lucida: Reflections on Photography.* Trans. Richard Howard. New York: Hill and Wang, 1981.

Berger, John. *Ways of Seeing.* Harmondsworth: Penquin, 1972.

Berger, John, and John Mohr. *Another Way of Telling.* New York: Pantheon, 1982.

Burgin, Victor, ed. *Thinking Photography.* London: Macmillan, 1982.

Coke, Van Deren. *The Painter and the Photograph.* Albuquerque: The University of New Mexico Press, 1972.

Coleman, A. D. *Light Readings: A Photography Critic's Writings, 1968–1978.* New York: Oxford University Press, 1979.

Frank, Robert. *The Americans.* Revised edition. New York: Museum of Modern Art, 1968.

Hicks, William. *Words and Pictures.* New York: Arno Press, 1973.

Jussim, Estelle. *Visual Communication and the Graphic Arts: Photographic Technologies in the Nineteenth Century.* New York: R. R. Bowker, 1974.

Lesy, Michael. *Bearing Witness.* New York: Pantheon, 1982.

Lesy, Michael. *Real Life: Louisville in the Twenties.* New York: Pantheon, 1976.

Lesy, Michael. *Wisconsin Death Trip.* New York: Pantheon, 1973.

Lyons, Nathan. *Photography in the Twentieth Century.* New York: Horizon, 1967.

Lyons, Nathan, ed. *Photographers on Photography: A Critical Anthology.* Englewood Cliffs: Prentice-Hall, 1966.

Newhall, Beaumont. *The History of Photography.* Rev. ed. New York: Museum of Modern Art, 1964.

Siskind, Aaron. *Aaron Siskind, Photographer.* Edited by Nathan Lyons. Rochester, New York: The George Eastman House, 1965.

Sontag, Susan. *On Photography.* New York: Farrar, Straus and Giroux, 1977.

Steichen, Edward *A Life in Photography.* Garden City: Doubleday, 1963.

Stieglitz, Alfred. *Alfred Stieglitz: Photographs & Writings.* Washington, D.C.: National Gallery of Art, 1982.

Stryker, Roy Emerson, and Nancy Wood. *In This Proud Land: America 1935–1943 as Seen in the FSA Photographs.* Boston: New York Graphic Society, 1973.

Szarkowski, John. *Looking at Photographs*. New York: Museum of Modern Art, 1973.
Szarkowski, John. *Mirrors and Windows: American Photography Since 1960*. New York: Museum of Modern Art, 1978.
Szarkowski, John. *The Photographer's Eye*. New York: Museum of Modern Art, 1966.
Thomas, Alan. *Time in a Frame: Photography and the Nineteenth-Century Mind*. New York: Schocken Books, 1977.
Wagner, Jon, ed. *Images of Information: Still Photography in the Social Sciences*. Beverly Hills: Sage, 1979.
Ward, John L. *The Criticism of Photography as Art: The Photographs of Jerry Uelsmann*. Gainesville: University of Florida Press, 1970.

Articles

Barthes, Roland. "Rhetoric of the Image." In *Classic Essays on Photography*. Edited by Alan Trachtenberg. New Haven: Leete's Island Books, 1980.
Bazin, Andre. "The Ontology of the Photographic Image." In *Classic Essays on Photography*. Edited by Alan Trachtenberg. New Haven: Leete's Island Books, 1980.
Bossen, Howard. "A Tall Tale Retold: The Influence of the Photographs of William Henry Jackson upon the Passage of the Yellowstone Park Act of 1872." *Studies in Visual Communication* 8:1 (Winter 1982), pp. 98–109.
Hardt, Hanno, and Karin B. Ohrn. "The Eyes of the Proletariat: The Worker-Photography Movement in Weimar Germany." *Studies in Visual Communication* 7:3 (Summer 1981), pp. 47–57.
Hattersley, R. "Notions on the Criticism of Visual Photography." *Aperture* 10 (1962), 91–114.
Rudisill, Richard. "On Reading Photographs." *Journal of American Culture* 5 (1982), 1–14.
Sekula, Allan. "On the Invention of Photographic Meaning." *Artforum* 13:5 (January 1975), pp. 36–45.
Smith, Henry Holmes. "Image, Obscurity and Interpretation." *Aperture* 5 (1957), 136–147.
Snyder, Joel, and Neil Walsh Allen. "Photography, Vision, and Representation." *Critical Inquiry* 2 (1975), 143–169.
White, George Abbott. "Vernacular Photography: FSA Images of Depression Leisure." *Studies in Visual Communication* 9:1 (Winter 1983), pp. 53–75.
White, Minor, and Walter Chappell. "Some Methods for Experiencing Photographs." *Aperture* 5 (1957), 156–171.

Architecture

Books

Adams, Henry. *Mont-Saint-Michel and Chartres*. 1905; rpt. Garden City: Doubleday, 1959.
Arnheim, Rudolf. *The Dynamics of Architectural Form*. Berkeley: University of California Press, 1977.
Bloomer, Kent C., and Charles W. Moore. *Body, Memory, and Architecture*. New Haven: Yale University Press, 1977.
Broadbent, Geoffrey, Richard Bunt, and Charles Jencks, eds. *Signs, Symbols, and Architecture*. New York: John Wiley and Sons, 1980.
Girouard, Mark. *Life in the English Country House*. New Haven: Yale University Press, 1978.
Oliver, Paul. *Shelter, Sign & Symbol*. Woodstock, N.Y.: The Overlook Press, 1977.
Tuan, Yi-Fu. *Topophilia*. Englewood Cliffs: Prentice-Hall, 1974.

Articles

Altman, Charles F. "The Medieval Marquee: Church Portal Sculpture as Publicity." *JPC* 14 (1980), 37–46.

Ames, Kenneth L. "Ideologies in Stone: Meanings in Victorian Gravestones." *JPC* 14 (1981), 641–656.

Eco, Umberto. "A Componential Analysis of the Architectural Sign/Column/" *Semiotica* 5 (1972), 97–117.

Hildebrandt, Walter. "Fort Battleford and the Architecture of the North-West Mounted Police." *JPC* 14 (1980), 313–325.

Kato, Hidetoshi. "The City as Communion: Changes in Urban Symbolism." *JOC* 24 (1974), 52–60.

Mechling, Elizabeth Walker, and Jay Mechling. "The Sale of Two Cities: A Semiotic Comparison of Disneyland with Marriot's Great America." *JPC* 15 (1981), 166–179.

Stuart, Charlotte L. "Architecture in Nazi Germany: A Rhetorical Perspective." *WJSC* 37 (1973), 253–263.

Wallis, Mieczyslaw. "Semantic and Symbolic Elements in Architecture: Iconology as a First Step Towards an Architectural Semiotic." *Semiotica* 8 (1973), 220–238.

Music

Books

Berry, Wallace. *Form in Music*. Englewood Cliffs: Prentice-Hall, 1966.

Cooke, Deryck. *The Language of Music*. New York: Oxford University Press, 1959.

Coker, Wilson. *Music and Meaning: A Theoretical Introduction to Musical Aesthetics*. New York: Free Press, 1972.

Copland, Aaron. *Music and Imagination*. Cambridge: Harvard University Press, 1952.

Denisoff, R. Serge. *Great Day Coming: Folk Music and the American Left*. Urbana: University of Illinois Press, 1971.

Denisoff, R. Serge. *Sing a Song of Social Significance*. Bowling Green: Bowling Green University Popular Press, 1972.

Denisoff, R. Serge, and Richard A. Peterson, eds. *The Sounds of Social Change: Studies in Popular Culture*. Chicago: Rand McNally, 1972.

Diamond, Harold J. *Music Criticism: An Annotated Guide to the Literature*. Metuchen: Scarecrow Press, 1979.

Ferguson, Donald Nivison. *The Why of Music*. Minneapolis: University of Minnesota Press, 1969.

Frye, Northrup. *Sound and Poetry*. New York: Columbia University Press, 1957.

Maranda, P., and E. K. Maranda, eds. *Structural Analysis of Oral Tradition*. Philadelphia: University of Pennsylvania Press, 1971.

Meltzer, Richard. *The Aesthetics of Rock*. New York: Something Else Press, 1970.

Meyer, Leonard B. *Emotion and Meaning in Music*. Chicago: University of Chicago Press, 1956.

Meyer, Leonard B. *Explaining Music: Essays and Explorations*. Berkeley: University of California Press, 1973.

Meyer, Leonard B. *Music, the Arts, and Ideas*. Chicago: University of Chicago Press, 1967.

Pichaske, David R. *A Generation in Motion: Popular Music and Culture in the Sixties*. New York: Schirmer Books, 1979.

Price, Kingsley, ed. *On Criticizing Music: Five Philosophical Perspectives*. Baltimore: Johns Hopkins University Press, 1981.

Reynolds, Roger. *Mind Models: New Forms of Musical Expression.* New York: Praeger, 1975.

Sizer, Sarah S. *Gospel Hymns and Social Religion: The Rhetoric of Nineteenth Century Revivalism.* Philadelphia: Temple University Press, 1978.

Tarasti, Eero. *Myth and Music: A Semiotic Approach to the Aesthetics of Myth in Music.* The Hague: Mouton, 1979.

Articles

Bloodworth, John David. "Communication in the Youth Counter Culture: Music as Expression." *CSSJ* 26 (1975), 304–309.

Booth, Mark W. "The Art of Words in Songs." *QJS* 62 (1976), 242–249.

Campbell, Gregg M. "Bob Dylan and the Pastoral Apocalypse." *JPC* 8 (1975), 696–707.

Carter, David, A. "The Industrial Workers of the World and the Rhetoric of Song." *QJS* 66 (1980), 365–374.

Cowser, R. L., Jr. "Uses of Antithesis in the Lyrics of Oscar Hammerstein II." *JPC* 12 (1978), 507–512.

Denisoff, R. Serge. " 'Take It Easy, But Take It': *The Almanac Singers.*" *Journal of American Folklore* 83 (1970), 21–32.

Donovan, Timothy P. "Oh, What a Beautiful Mornin': The Musical, *Oklahoma!* and the Popular Mind in 1943." *JPC* 8 (1974), 477–488.

Ellis, Bill. " 'The "Blind" Girl' and the Rhetoric of Sentimental Heroism." *Journal of American Folklore* 91 (1978), 657–674.

Gonzales, Alberto, and John J. Makay. "Rhetorical Ascription and the Gospel According to Dylan." *QJS* 69 (1983), 1–14.

Hall, James W. "Concepts of Liberty in American Broadside Ballads 1850–1870: A Study of the Mind of American Mass Culture." *JPC* 2 (1968), 252–275.

Hays, Peter L. "A Slightly Smudged *Pinafore.*" *JPC* 2 (1969), 665–678.

Irvine, James R., and Walter G. Kirkpatrick. "The Musical Form in Rhetorical Exchange." *QJS* 58 (1972), 272–289.

Knupp, Ralph E. "A Time for Every Purpose Under Heaven: Rhetorical Dimensions of Protest Music." *SSCJ* 46 (1981), 377–389.

Kosokoff, Stephen, and Carl W. Carmichael. "The Rhetoric of Protest: Song, Speech, and Attitude Change." *SSCJ* 35 (1970), 295–302.

Le Coat, Gerard. "The Rhetorical Element in Monteverdi's *Combattimento:* A Study in 'Harmonic Oratory.' " *WJSC* 39 (1975), 165–174.

Merriam, Alan P. "Music as Symbolic Behavior," In *The Rhetoric of Nonverbal Communication.* Edited by Haig Bosmajian. Glenview: Scott, Foresman, 1971.

Meyer, Michael. "The SA Song Literature: A Singing Ideological Posture." *JPC* 11 (1977), 568–580.

Mohrmann, G. P., and F. Eugene Scott. "Popular Music and World War II: The Rhetoric of Continuation." *QJS* 62 (1976), 145–156.

Pickens, Donald K. "The Historical Images in Republican Campaign Songs, 1860–1900." *JPC* 15 (1981), 165–174.

Roth, Lane. "Folk Songs as Communication in John Ford's Films." *SSCJ* 46 (1981), 390–396.

Smith, Stephen A. "Sounds of the South: The Rhetorical Saga of Country Music Lyrics." *SSCJ* 45 (1979), 164–172.

Stone, Michael K. "Heav'n Rescued Land: American Hymns and American Destiny." *JPC* 10 (1976), 133–141.

Thomas, Cheryl Irwin. " 'Look What They've Done to My Song, Ma': The Persuasiveness of Song." *SSCJ* 39 (1974), 260–268.

LITERATURE

Drama and Theatre

Books

Beckerman, Bernard. *Dynamics of Drama: Theory and Method of Analysis.* New York: Knopf, 1970.

Bilton, Peter. *Commentary and Control in Shakespeare's Plays.* New York: Norwegian Studies in English, 1974.

Burns, Elizabeth. *Theatricality: A Study of Convention in the Theatre and in Social Life.* New York: Harper & Row, 1972.

Burns, Elizabeth, and Tom Burns, eds. *Sociology of Literature and Drama.* Baltimore: Penguin, 1973.

Doran, Madeleine. *Endeavors of Art: A Study of Form in Elizabethan Drama.* Madison: University of Wisconsin Press, 1954.

Gassner, John. *Form and Idea in Modern Theatre.* New York: The Dryden Press, 1956.

Gorelik, Mordecai. *New Theatres for Old.* 1940; rpt. New York: Samuel French, 1955.

Granville-Barker, Harley. *Prefaces to Shakespeare.* Princeton: Princeton University Press, 1946–1947.

Harbage, Alfred. *As They Liked It: An Essay on Shakespeare and Morality.* New York: Macmillan, 1947.

Honigmann, E. A. J. *Shakespeare: Seven Tragedies: The Dramatist's Manipulation of Response.* London: Macmillan, 1976.

Joseph, Sister Miriam. *Shakespeare's Use of the Arts of Language.* 1947; rpt. New York: Hafner, 1966.

Kitto, H. D. F. *Poesis: Structure and Thought.* Berkeley: University of California Press, 1966.

McDonald, Charles Osborne. *The Rhetoric of Tragedy: Form in Stuart Drama.* Amherst: University of Massachusetts Press, 1966.

Shank, Theodore. *The Art of Dramatic Art.* Belmont: Dickenson, 1969.

Styan, J. L. *Drama, Stage, and Audience.* Cambridge: Cambridge University Press, 1975.

Styan, J. L. *The Elements of Drama.* Cambridge: Cambridge University Press, 1969.

Trousdale, Marion. *Shakespeare and the Rhetoricians.* Chapel Hill: University of North Carolina Press, 1974.

Articles

Adler, Thomas P. "The Dialogue of Incompletion: Language in Tennessee Williams' Later Plays." *QJS* 61 (1975), 48–58.

Adler, Thomas P. "*The Wesker Triology* Revisited: Games to Compensate for the Inadequacy of Words." *QJS* 65 (1979), 429–438.

Aeschbacher, Jill. "Kenneth Burke, Samuel Beckett, and Form." *CQ* 21 (Summer, 1973), pp. 43–47.

Arnold, Richard L. "A Study of Comic Techniques in the Farces of John Maddison Morton." *WJSC* 29 (1965), 19–28.

Booth, Stephen. "On the Value of *Hamlet.*" In *Reinterpretations of Elizabethan Drama.* Edited by Norman Rabkin. New York: Columbia University Press, 1969.

Booth, Stephen. "Syntax as Rhetoric in *Richard II.*" *Mosaic* 10:3 (1977), 87–103.

Cope, Jackson I. "Rhetorical Genres in Davenant's *First Day's Entertainment at Rutland House.*" *QJS* 45 (1959), 191–194.

Culp, Ralph Borden. "Drama-and-Theater in the American Revolution." *CM* 32 (1965), 79–86.

Downer, Alan S. "Macready's Production of Macbeth." *QJS* 33 (1947), 172–182.

Drummond, A. M., and Richard Moody, "Indian Treaties: The First American Dramas." *QJS* 39 (1953), 15–24.

Dukore, Bernard F. "*The Blacks*—The Rite of Revenge and the Reality of the Double Negative." *WJSC* 27 (1963), 133–141.

Durant, Jack D. "Laughter and *Hubris* in *She Stoops to Conquer:* The Role of Young Marlow." *SSCJ* 37 (1972), 269–280.

Fife, Iline. "The Confederate Theatre." *SSCJ* 20 (1955), 224–231.

Foster, Jacob Flavel. "Social Criticism in the Broadway Theatre During the Inter-War Period." *CM* 10 (1943), 13–23.

Frye, Roland Mushat. "Rhetoric and Poetry in *Julius Caesar*." *QJS* 37 (1951), 41–48.

Fuller, Marcus. "What Part of Theatre Set Design Is Communicative?" *WJSC* 15 (1951), pp. 42–45.

Gillespie, Patti P. "Feminist Theatre: A Rhetorical Phenomenon." *QJS* 64 (1978), 284–294.

Glenn, Stanley. "The Development of the Negro Character in American Comedy Before the Civil War." *SSCJ* 26 (1960), 133–148.

Goldhamer, Allen D. "*Everyman:* A Dramatization of Death." *QJS* 59 (1973), 87–98.

Gottlieb, Lois C. "The Antibusiness Theme in Late Nineteenth Century American Drama." *QJS* 64 (1978), 415–426.

Grimsted, David. "*Uncle Tom* from Page to Stage: Limitations of Nineteenth-Century Drama." *QJS* 56 (1970), 235–244.

Gross, Nicholas P. "Alcestis and the Rhetoric of Departure." *QJS* 60 (1974), 296–305.

Hansen, Bert B. " 'A Tale of the Bitter Root': Pageantry as Sociodrama." *QJS* 33 (1947), 162–166.

Harrison, Cleveland A. "*Miss Julie:* Essence and Anomaly of Naturalism." *CSSJ* 21 (1970), 87–92.

Harshbarger, Karl. " 'I Know Who I Am': The Revenge of Biff Loman." *WJSC* 42 (1978), 250–257.

Hellweg, John D., and Susan A. Hellweg. "*The Sea Gull:* A Communicative Analysis of Chekovian Drama." *CQ* 30 (1982), 150–154.

Hewitt, Barnard. "Uncle Tom and Uncle Sam: New Light from an Old Play." *QJS* 37 (1951), 63–70.

Hill, Philip G. "Dramatic Irony in *Mourning Becomes Electra*." *SSCJ* 31 (1965), 42–55.

Holtan, Orley I. " 'Machine' vs. 'Garden': Tennessee Williams and the Southern Myth." *CSSJ* 20 (1969), 14–19.

Howard, Jean E. "Figures and Grounds: Shakespeare's Control of Audience Perception and Response." *Studies in English Literature* 20 (1980), 185–199.

Hulsopple, Bill G. "Barabbas and Shylock Against a Background of Jewish History in England." *CSSJ* 12 (1960), 38–50.

Jackson, Esther Merle. "The Emergence of the Anti-Hero in the Contemporary Drama." *CSSJ* 12 (1961), 92–99.

Jones, John Bush. "Impersonation and Authenticity: The Theatre as Metaphor in Kopit's *Indians*." *QJS* 59 (1973), 443–451.

Karimi, A. M. "*Tableaux Vivants:* Their Structure, Themes, and Rhetorical Function." *SSCJ* 42 (1977), 99–113.

Kaufman, Michael W. "O'Casey's Structural Design in *Juno*." *QJS* 58 (1972), 191–198.

Kennedy, George. "Antony's Speech at Caesar's Funeral." *QJS* 54 (1968), 99–106.

Kildahl, Erling E. "Jacob Engstrand's Use of Persuasive Devices in Ibsen's *Ghosts.*" *CSSJ* 13 (1962), 106–111.

Kirk, John W. "Kenneth Burke's Dramatistic Criticism Applied to the Theatre." *SSCJ* 33 (1968), 161–177.

Knapp, Bettina. "Racine's *The Theban Brothers:* A Study in Cosmic Antagonism." *CQ* 18 (Summer, 1970), 9–14.

Knauf, David M. "The Affective Texture of Anouilh's *Becket.*" *SSCJ* 34 (1968), 135–147.

Kolin, Philip C. "Obstacles to Communication in *Cat on a Hot Tin Roof.*" *WJSC* 39 (1975), 74–80.

Lazier, Gil "A Comic View of the Sophists: Aristophanes' *Clouds.*" *WJSC* 30 (1966), 156–166.

Lewis, George L. "Elements of Medieval Horror Tragedy in *The Duchess of Malfi.*" *CSSJ* 12 (1961), 106–110.

Lippman, Monroe. "An Analysis of the Protest Play." *SSCJ* 21 (1955), 127–132.

Lippman, Monroe. "The Theatre in War." *SSCJ* 8 (1943), 114–115.

Lippman, Monroe. "Uncle Tom and His Poor Relations: American Slavery Plays." *SSCJ* 28 (1963), 183–197.

Long, Chester Clayton. "Cocteau's *Orphee:* From Myth to Drama and Film." *QJS* 51 (1965), 311–325.

McAlindon, T. "Language, Style, and Meaning in Troilus and Cressida." *PMLA* 84 (1969), 29–43.

Macksoud, S. John, and Ross Altman, "Voices in Opposition: A Burkeian Rhetoric of *Saint Joan.*" *QJS* 57 (1971), 140–146.

Maher, Mary Z. "Internal Rhetorical Analysis and the Interpretation of Drama." *CSSJ* 26 (1975), 267–273.

Martin, Sister Kathryn. "The Relationship of Theatre of Revolution and Theology of Revolution to the Black Experience." *CQ* 19 (Spring, 1971), pp. 35–41.

Matherne, Beverly M. "A Kierkegaardian Study of 'Hedda Gabler,' " *WJSC* 42 (1978), 258–269.

Matlack, Cynthia S. "Metaphor and Dramatic Structure in *The Chalk Garden.*" *QJS* 59 (1973), 304–310.

Miranda, Kathleen Bindert. "Pirandello's Parable: *Right You Are (If You Think You Are)." CSSJ* 29 (1978), 201–205.

Morrison, Kristin. "Pinter and the New Irony." *QJS* 55 (1969), 388–393.

Murphy, Robert P. "Non-Verbal Communication and the Overlooked Action in Pinter's *The Caretaker.*" *QJS* 58 (1972), 41–47.

Nassar, E. P. "Shakespeare's Games with His Audience." In *The Rape of Cinderella: Essays in Literary Continuity.* Bloomington: Indiana University Press, 1970.

Nolan, Paul T. "Marc Connelly's 'Divine Comedy': *Green Pastures* Revisited." *WJSC* 30 (1966), 216–224.

Nolan, Paul T. "The Way of the World: Congreve's Moment of Truth." *SSCJ* 25 (1959), 75–95.

Nolan, Paul T. "William's *Dante:* The Death of Nineteenth-Century Heroic Drama." *SSCJ* 25 (1960), 255–263.

Patterson, Sylvia W. "Setting as Character in Lorca." *SSCJ* 30 (1965), 215–222.

Post, Robert M. "The Outsider in the Plays of John Osborne." *SSCJ* 39 (1973), 63–74.

Powell, Vio Mae. "Dramatic Ritual as Observed in the Sun Dance." *QJS* 33 (1947), 167–171.

Powlick, Leonard. "A Phenomenological Approach to Harold Pinter's *A Slight Ache.*" *QJS* 60 (1974), 25–32.

Riach, W. A. D. " 'Telling It Like It Is': An Examination of Black Theatre as Rhetoric." *QJS* 56 (1970), 179–186.

Robinson, David. "The Brothers' Debate in Milton's *Comus*." *SSCJ* 41 (1975), 30–44.

Robinson, James E. "The Ritual and Rhetoric of *A Midsummer Night's Dream*." *PMLA* 83 (1968), 380–391.

Scanlan, Ross. "Rhetoric and the Drama." *QJS* 22 (1936), 635–642.

Schmitt, Natalie. "Impassioned Art: An Interpretation of 'Tonight We Improvise' by Luigi Pirandello." *WJSC* 33 (1969), 184–191.

Scott, Davis A. " 'Oh Thou Corrupter of Youth,': Henry Ward Beecher vs. Indianapolis Theatre." *CSSJ* 14 (1963), 17–22.

Shafer, George. "The Dramaturgy of Fact: The Testament of History in Two Anti-War Plays." *CSSJ* 29 (1978), 25–35.

Skloot, Robert. "Putting Out the Light: Staging the Theme of Pinter's *Old Times*." *QJS* 61 (1975), 265–270.

Skriletz, Dorothy. "The *Rhetoric*: An Aid in the Study of Drama." *SSCJ* 25 (1960), 217–222.

Smiley, Sam. "*Peace on Earth:* Four Anti-War Dramas of the Thirties." *CSSJ* 21 (1970), 30–39.

Smiley, Sam. "Rhetoric on Stage in Living Newspapers." *QJS* 54 (1968), 29–36.

Smiley, Sam. "Rhetorical Principles in Didactic Drama." *QJS* 57 (1971), 147–152.

Smith, Harry W. "Synge's *Playboy* and the Proximity of Violence." *QJS* 55 (1969), 381–387.

Solomon, Jerry. "Edward Albee: American Absurdist." *WJSC* 28 (1964), 230–236.

Speer, Jean Haskell. "The Rhetoric of Ibsenism: A Study of the Poet-As-Persuader." *SSCJ* 38 (1972), 13–26.

Steyers, John D. "The Long Morning: A Re-evaluation of Arthur Schnitzler's *Anatol*." *WJSC* 37 (1973), 34–46.

Taft-Kaufman, Jill. "A Rhetorical Perspective for Teaching the Solo Performance of Shakespearean Dramatic Literature." *CE* 29 (1980), 112–124.

Tornqvist, Egil. "Personal Addresses in the Plays of O'Neill." *QJS* 55 (1969), 126–130.

Waal, Carla. "Rhetoric in Action: Orators in the Plays of Henrik Ibsen." *SSCJ* 37 (1972), 249–258.

Walker, Phillip. "Arthur Miller's 'The Crucible': Tragedy or Allegory?" *WJSC* 20 (1956), 222–224.

Weisman, Martha. "Ambivalence Toward War in Anti-War Plays." *CQ* 17 (September, 1969), 9–14.

Wellwarth, George E. "Eugene Ionesco: The Absurd as Warning." *SSCJ* 28 (1962), 6–16.

West, E. J. "*Saint Joan:* A Modern Classic Reconsidered." QJS 40 (1954), 249–259.

Wiethoff, William E. "Machiavelli's *Mandragola:* Comedic Commentary on Renaissance Rhetoric." *WJSC* 44 (1980), 153–161.

Wilds, Nancy G. " 'Of Rare Fire Compact': Image and Rhetoric in *The Revenger's Tragedy.*" *Texas Studies in Literature and Language* 17 (1975), 61–74.

Willcox, Gladys D. "Shakespeare and Rhetoric." *Essays and Studies* 29 (1943), 50–61.

Wilson, Willard. "Genesis and Development of Ibsen's 'Pillars of Society.' " *QJS* 25 (1939), 43–51.

Zanger, Jules. "The Minstrel Show as Theatre of Misrule." *QJS* 60 (1974), 33–38.

Zeitlin, Froma I. "Travesties of Gender and Genre in Aristophanes' *Thesmophoriazousae*." *CI*, 8 (1981), 301–327.

Zortman, Bruce H. "The Theatre of Ideology in Nazi Germany." *QJS* 57 (1971), 153–162.

Fiction

Books

Booth, Wayne C. *The Rhetoric of Fiction*. Chicago: University of Chicago Press, 1961.

Cohn, Dorrit. *Transparent Minds: Narrative Modes for Presenting Consciousness in Fiction*. Princeton: Princeton University Press, 1978.

Doody, Terrence. *Confession and Community in the Novel*. Baton Rouge: Louisiana State University Press, 1980.

Garvin, Harry R., ed. *Literature and Ideology*. Vol. 27:1 of *The Bucknell Review*. Lewisburg, Pennsylvania: Bucknell University Press, 1982.

Girard, Rene. *Deceit, Desire, and the Novel*. Baltimore: The Johns Hopkins University Press, 1965.

Irwin, W. R. *The Game of the Impossible: A Rhetoric of Fantasy*. Urbana: University of Illinois Press, 1976.

Jameson, Fredric. *The Political Unconscious: Narrative as a Socially Symbolic Act*. Ithaca: Cornell University Press, 1981.

Lubbock, Percy. *The Craft of Fiction*. New York: The Viking Press, 1957.

McKeon, Zahava Karl. *Novels and Arguments: Inventing Rhetorical Criticism*. Chicago: University of Chicago Press, 1982.

Sacks, Sheldon. *Fiction and the Shape of Belief*. Berkeley: University of California Press, 1964.

Secor, Robert. *The Rhetoric of Shifting Perspectives: Conrad's Victory*. University Park: The Pennsylvania State University Press, 1971.

Spilka, Mark, ed. *Towards a Poetics of Fiction*. Bloomington: Indiana University Press, 1977.

Wadlington, Warwick. *The Confidence Game in American Literature*. Princeton: Princeton University Press, 1975.

Articles

Adamowski, T. H. "Being Perfect: Lawrence, Sartre, and *Women in Love*." *CI* 2 (1975), 345–368.

Anderson, Howard. "*Tristram Shandy* and the Reader's Imagination." *PMLA* 86 (1971), 966–973.

Arac, Jonathan. "Rhetoric and Realism in Nineteenth Century Fiction: Hyperbole in *The Mill on the Floss*." *English Literary History* 46 (1979), 673–692.

Bass, Jeff D. "The Romance as Rhetorical Dissociation: The Purification of Imperialism in *King Solomon's Mines*." *QJS* 67 (1981), 259–269.

Blessing, Richard. "The Moving Target: Ken Kesey's Evolving Hero." *JPC* 4 (1971), 615–627.

Blodgett, Harriet. "Necessary Presence: The Rhetoric of the Narrator in *Vanity Fair*." *Nineteenth-Century Fiction* 22 (1967), 211–223.

Booth, Wayne C. "Irony and Pity Once Again: *Thais* Revisited." *CI* 2 (1975), 327–344.

Bryant, Donald C. "Persuasive Uses of Imaginative Literature in Certain Satires of Jonathan Swift." *SSCJ* 46 (1981), 175–183.

Cansler, Ronald Lee. "*Stranger in a Strange Land:* Science Fiction as Literature of Creative Imagination, Social Criticism, and Entertainment." *JPC* 5 (1972), 944–954.

Cohn, Jan. "The Civil War in Magazine Fiction of the 1860's." *JPC* 4 (1970), 355–382.

Colvert, James B. "Style and Meaning in Stephen Crane: *The Open Boat*." *Texas Studies in English* 37 (1958), 34–45.

Consigny, Scott. "Aschenbach's 'Page and a Half of Choicest Prose': Mann's Rhetoric of Irony." *Studies in Short Fiction* 14 (1977), 359–367.

Consigny, Scott. "Rhetoric and Madness: Robert Pirsig's Inquiry into Values." *SSCJ* 43 (1977) 16–32.

Corder, Jim W. "Efficient Ethos in *Shane,* With a Proposal for Discriminating Among Kinds of Ethos." *CQ* 25 (Fall, 1977), pp. 28–31.

Crocker, Lionel. "Sinclair Lewis on Public Speaking." *QJS* 21 (1935), 232–237.

Crusius, Tim. "In Praise of Pirsig's *Zen and the Art of Motorcycle Maintenance.*" *WJSC* 40 (1976), 168–177.

deSpain, Jerry Lynn. "A Rhetorical View of J. R. R. Tolkien's *The Lord of the Rings* Triology. *WJSC* 35 (1971), 88–95.

Downey, Sharon D., and Richard A. Kallan. "*Semi*Aesthetic Detachment: The Fusing of Fictional and External Worlds in the Situational Literature of Leon Uris." *CM* 49 (1982), 194–204.

Espinola, Judith C. "The Nature, Function, and Performance of Indirect Discourse in Prose Fiction." *CM* 41 (1974), 193–204.

Friedman, Stanley. "Condon's *The Manchurian Candidate: Hamlet* Freely Adapted?" *JPC* 2 (1968), 510–512.

Geiger, Don. "The Interpreter's 'Artistic' Emphasis: Technique and Meaning in *Moby Dick.*" *SSCJ* 20 (1954), 16–27.

Geiger, Don. "Tragic Order in *Moby Dick:* The Ishmael-Queequeg Relationship." *CSSJ* 9 (1957), 32–36.

Gilbert, James B. "War of the Worlds." *JPC* 10 (1976), 326–336.

Godden, Richard. "Call Me Nigger!: Race and Speech in Faulkner's *Light in August.*" *Journal of American Studies* 14 (1980), 235–248.

Grandsen, K. W. "Graham Greene's Rhetoric." *Essays in Criticism* 31:1 (1981), 41–60.

Hanna, Mark. "College Speech and 'The Grapes of Wrath.' " *QJS* 27 (1941), 223–227.

Heston, Lilla A. "An Exploration of the Narrator in Robbe-Grillet's *Jealousy.*" *CSSJ* 24 (1973), 178–182.

Hill, Leslie. "Flaubert and the Rhetoric of Stupidity." *CI* 3 (1976), 333–344.

Holloway, John. "Narrative Structure and Text Structure: Isherwood's *A Meeting by the River,* and Muriel Spark's *The Prime of Miss Jean Brodie.*" *CI* 1 (1975), 581–604.

Houghton, Donald E. "The Failure of Speech in *The Ox-Bow Incident.*" *English Journal* 59 (1970), 1245–1251.

Houghton, Donald E. "Two Heroes in One: Reflections Upon the Popularity of *The Virginian.*" *JPC* 4 (1970), 497–506.

Ingham, Patricia. "Speech and Non-Communication in *Dombey and Son.*" *Review of English Studies* (New Series) 30 (1979), 144–153.

Jacobus, Mary. "The Question of Language: Men of Maxims and *The Mill on the Floss.*" *CI* 8 (1981), 207–222.

Jones, Daryl E. "Blood 'N Thunder: Virgins, Villains, and Violence in the Dime Novel Western." *JPC* 4 (1970), 507–517.

Kaplan, Jane P. "A Visual and Temporal Decoding of the Pragmatic Structure of *Jacques le fataliste.*" *Semiotica* 36 (1981), 273–297.

Kevelson, Roberta. " 'Figures' and Semiotic Relations: A Rhetoric of Syntax in Balzac's *Sarrasine.*" *Semiotica* 24 (1978), 113–147.

Kinney, Arthur F. "Rhetoric as Poetic: Humanist Fiction in the Renaissance." *English Literary History* 43 (1976), 413–443.

Koelb, Clayton. "Kafka's Rhetorical Movement." *PMLA* (1983), 37–46.

Lamoreaux, David. "*Stover at Yale* and the Gridiron Metaphor." *JPC* 11 (1977), 330–344.

Leverence, W. John. "*Cat's Cradle* and Traditional American Humor." *JPC* 5 (1972), 955–963.

Liedel, Donald E. "The Puffing of *Ida May:* Publishers Exploit the Antislavery Novel." *JPC* 3 (1969), 287–306.

Light, Martin. "Lewis's 'Scarlet Sign': Accomodating to the Popular Market." *JPC* 1 (1967), 106–113.

Linehan, Thomas M. "Rhetorical Technique and Moral Purpose in Dickens' *Hard Times*." *University of Toronto Quarterly* 47 (1977), 22–36.

MacDonald, J. Fred. " 'The Foreigner' in Juvenile Series Fiction, 1900–1945." *JPC* 8 (1974), 534–548.

McKeon, Richard. "*Pride and Prejudice:* Thought, Character, Argument, and Plot." *CI* 5 (1979), 511–528.

Marotta, Kenny. "*What Maisie Knew:* The Question of Our Speech." *English Literary History* 46 (1979), 495–508.

Matherne, Beverly M. "Hope in Camus' *The Misunderstanding*." *WJSC* 35 (1971), 74–87.

Marcus, Fred H. "*A Farewell to Arms:* The Impact of Irony and the Irrational." *English Journal* 51 (1962), 527–535.

Marcus, Fred H. "*Cry, the Beloved Country* and *Strange Fruit:* Exploring Man's Inhumanity to Man." *English Journal* 51 (1962), 609–616.

Mellard, James M. "Counterpoint as Technique in *The Great Gatsby*." *English Journal* 55 (1966), 853–859.

Mellard, James M. "Faulkner's Jason and the Tradition of Oral Narrative." *JPC* 2 (1968), 195–210.

Mengeling, Marvin E. "Ray Bradbury's *Dandelion Wine:* Themes, Sources, and Style." *English Journal* 60 (1971), 877–887.

Mengeling, Marvin E. "*A Separate Peace:* Meaning and Myth." *English Journal* 58 (1969), 1322–1329.

Merkle, Donald R. "The Furnace and the Tower: A New Look at the Symbols in *Native Son*." *English Journal* 60 (1971), 735–739.

Merrell, Floyd. "Communication and Paradox in Carlos Fuentes' *The Death of Artemio Cruz:* Toward a Semiotic of Character." *Semiotica* 18 (1976), 339–360.

Michaels, Walter Benn. "*Sister Carrie's* Popular Economy." *CI* 7 (1980), 373–390.

Miller, Jacqueline T. "The Imperfect Tale: Articulation, Rhetoric, and Self in *Caleb Williams*." *Criticism* 20 (1978), 366–382.

Natanson, Maurice. "The Privileged Moment: A Study in the Rhetoric of Thomas Wolfe." *QJS* 53 (1957), 143–150.

Oates, Joyce Carol. "Lawrence's Gotterdammerung: The Tragic Vision of *Women in Love*." *CI* 4 (1978), 559–578.

Ostroff, Anthony. "The Moral Vision in 'Dubliners.'" *WJSC* 20 (1956), 196–209.

Pearson, Roger L. "Gatsby: False Prophet of the American Dream." *English Journal* 59 (1970), 638–642.

Philipson, Morris. "*Mrs. Dalloway,* 'What's the Sense of Your Parties?'" *CI* 1 (1974), 123–148.

Prior, Moody E. "Mrs. Stowe's Uncle Tom." *CI* 5 (1979), 635–650.

Prosser, Michael H. "A Rhetoric of Alienation as Reflected in the Works of Nathaniel Hawthorne." *QJS* 54 (1968), 22–28.

Rackin, Donald. "Corrective Laughter: Carroll's *Alice* and Popular Children's Literature of the Nineteenth Century." *JPC* 1 (1967), 243–255.

Rank, Hugh. "The Rhetorical Effectiveness of *Black Like Me*." *English Journal* 57 (1968), 813–817.

Ross, Stephen M. " 'Voice' in Narrative Texts: The Example of *As I Lay Dying*." *PMLA* 94 (1979), 300–310.

Simrell, V. E. "John Galsworthy: The Artist as Propagandist." *QJS* 13 (1927), 225–236.

Skerrett, Joseph T., Jr. "Irony and Symbolic Action in James Weldon Johnson's *The Autobiography of an Ex-Colored Man." American Quarterly* 32 (1980), 540–558.

Smith, Jane S. "The Reader as Part of the Fiction: *Middlemarch." Texas Studies in Literature and Language* 19 (1977), 188–203.

Stephens, Robert O. "Language Magic and Reality in *For Whom the Bell Tolls." Criticism* 14 (1972), 151–164.

Spilka, Mark. "Eric Segal as Little Nell, or the Real Meaning of *Love Story." JPC* 5 (1972), 782–798.

Strine, Mary S. "*The Confessions of Nat Turner:* Styron's 'Meditation on History' as Rhetorical Act." *QJS* 64 (1978), 267–283.

Strine, Mary Susan. "Ethics and Action in Conrad's *Heart of Darkness." WJSC* 36 (1972), 103–108.

Suderman, Elmer F. "Popular American Fiction (1870–1900) Looks at the Attributes of God." *JPC* 4 (1970), 383–397.

Tanner, Bernard. "The Gospel of Gatsby." *English Journal* 54 (1965), 467–474.

Tompkins, Phillip K. "The Rhetoric of James Joyce." *QJS* 54 (1968), 107–114.

Tyson, Raymond W. "Trollope on Public Speaking." *SSCJ* 32 (1966), 146–153.

Wasson, Richard. "On the Popularity of *Steppenwolf:* A Contemporary Reading." *JPC* 3 (1969), 575–589.

Westervelt, Linda A. " 'A Place Dependent on Ourselves': The Reader as System-Builder in *Gravity's Rainbow." Texas Studies in Literature and Language* 22 (1980), 69–90.

Willy, Todd, G. "The 'Shamefully Abandoned' Kurtz: A Rhetorical Context for *Heart of Darkness." Conradiana* 10 (1978), 99–112.

Zacharias, Donald W. "Thackeray on 'This Ambulatory Quack Business.'" *WJSC* 31 (1967), 51–58.

Poetry

Books

Colie, Rosalie L. *"My Echoing Song": Andrew Marvell's Poetry of Criticism.* Princeton: Princeton University Press, 1970.

— Gage, John T. *In the Arresting Eye: The Rhetoric of Imagism.* Baton Rouge: Louisiana State University Press, 1981.

Griffin, Dustin H. *Alexander Pope: The Poet in the Poems.* Princeton: Princeton University Press, 1979

Javitch, Daniel. *Poetry and Courtliness in Renaissance England.* Princeton: Princeton University Press, 1978.

McFadden, George. *Dryden: The Public Writer, 1660–1685.* Princeton: Princeton University Press, 1978.

Patterson, Annabel M. *Marvell and the Civic Crown.* Princeton: Princeton University Press, 1978.

Sloan, Thomas O., and Raymond B. Waddington, eds. *The Rhetoric of Renaissance Poetry* Berkeley: University of California Press, 1974.

Wimsatt, W. K., Jr. *The Verbal Icon.* The University Press of Kentucky, 1954.

Articles

Balliet, Conrad A. "The History and Rhetoric of the Triplet." *PMLA* 80 (1965), 528–534.

Bates, Ronald. "A Topic in *The Wasteland:* Traditional Rhetoric and Eliot's Individual Talent." *Wisconsin Studies in Contemporary Literature* 5 (1964), 85–104.

Beale, Walter H. "On Rhetoric and Poetry: John Donne's 'The Prohibition' Revisited." *QJS* 62 (1976), 376–386.

Bennett, A. L. "The Principal Rhetorical Conventions in the Renaissance Personal Elegy." *Studies in Philology* 51 (1954), 107–126.

Bennett, Daphne Nicholson. "Auden's 'September 1, 1939': An Interpreter's Analysis." *QJS* 42 (1956), 1–13.

Berek, Peter. " 'Plain' and 'Ornate' Styles and the Structure of *Paradise Lost.*" *PMLA* 85 (1970), 237–246.

Bogel, Fredric V. "Dulnes Unbounded: Rhetoric and Pope's *Dunciad*" *PMLA* 97 (1982), 844–855.

Bouissac, Paul. "Decoding Limericks: A Structuralist Approach." *Semiotica* 19 (1977), 1–12.

Browne, Robert M. "The Shropshire Lad as Funeral Orator." *QJS* 57 (1971), 134–139.

Chayes, Irene H. "Rhetoric as Drama: An Approach to the Romantic Ode." *PMLA* 79 (1964), 67–79.

Daniels, R. Balfour. "Rhetoric in Gower's *To King Henry the Fourth, In Praise of Peace.*" *Studies in Philology* 32 (1935), 62–73.

Duhamel, P. Albert. "Sidney's *Arcadia* and Elizabethan Rhetoric." *Studies in Philology* 45 (1948), 134–150.

Dundas, Judith. "The Rhetorical Basis of Spenser's Imagery." *Studies in English Literature, 1500–1900* 8 (1968), 59–76.

Elliott, Emory B., Jr. "*Persona* and Parody in Donne's *The Anniversaries.*" *QJS* 58 (1972), 48–57.

Emperor, John. "The Rhetorical Importance of Lucan's *Pharsalia.*" *QJS* 26 (1930), 463–471.

Empson, William. "Donne and the Rhetorical Tradition." *Kenyon Review* 11 (1949), 571–587.

Evett, David. " 'Paradice's Only Map': The *Topos* of the *Locus Amoenus* and the Structure of Marvell's *Upon Appleton House.*" *PMLA* 85 (1970), 504–513.

Feder, Lillian. "John Dryden's Use of Classical Rhetoric." *PMLA* 69 (1954), 1258–1278.

Finkel, William Leo. "Robert Ingersoll's Oratory and Walt Whitman's Poetry." *CM* 16 (1949), 41–56.

Fish, Stanley E. "Interpreting the *Variorum.*" *CI* 2 (1976), 465–485.

Gallagher, Michael P. "Rhetoric, Style, and George Herbert." *English Literary History* 37 (1970), 495–516.

Galperin, William. " 'Imperfect While Unshared': The Role of the Implied Reader in Wordsworth's 'Excursion.' " *Criticism* 22 (1980), 193–213.

Geiger, Don. "Essay on a Poem's Being Meaning Something." *WJSC* 25 (1961), 242–249.

Gillespie, Patti P. "The Bells: A Re-Appraisal." *CSSJ* 25 (1974), 282–287.

Hahn, T. G. "Urian Oakes's *Elegie* on Thomas Shepard and Puritan Poetics." *American Literature* 45 (1973), 163–181.

Harrison, Benjamin S. "Medieval Rhetoric in *The Book of the Duchess.*" *PMLA* 49 (1934), 428–442.

Havelock, Eric A. "The Ancient Art of Oral Poetry." *PR* 12 (1979), 187–202.

Hill, Mary A. "Rhetorical Balance in Chaucer's Poetry." *PLMA* 42 (1927), 845–861.

Hollis, C. Carroll. "Whitman and the American Idiom." *QJS* 43 (1957), 408–420.

Hyman, Lawrence W. "The Reader's Attitude in *Paradise Regained.*" *PMLA* 85 (1970), 496–503.

Jensen, Richard J., and John C. Hammerback. " 'No Revolutions Without Poets': The Rhetoric of Rodolfo 'Corky' Gonzales." *WJSC* 46 (1982), 72–91.

447

Kaller, Katherine. "Art, Rhetoric, and Holy Dying in the *Faerie Queene* with Special Reference to the Despair Canto." *Studies in Philology* 61 (1964), 128–139.

Kokeritz, Helge. "Rhetorical Word-Play in Chaucer." *PMLA* 69 (1954), 937–952.

McCarron, William E. "The 'Persuasive Rhetoric' of *Paradise Regained.*" *Milton Quarterly* 10 (1976), 15–21.

Mason, John B. "Walt Whitman's Catalogues: Rhetorical Means for Two Journeys in 'Song of Myself.' " *American Literature* 45 (1973), 34–49.

Meyer, Sam. "Teaching the Rhetorical Approach to the Poem." In *Rhetoric: Theories for Application.* Edited by Robert M. Gorrell. Champaign: National Council of Teachers of English, 1967.

Moore, Arthur, K. "Lyric Voices and Ethical Proofs." *Journal of Aesthetics and Art Criticism* 23 (1965), 429–439.

Morgan, Gerald. "Rhetorical Perspectives in the General Prologue to the Canterbury Tales." *English Studies* 62 (1981), 411–422.

Okerlund, Arlene N. "The Rhetoric of Love: Voice in the *Amoretti* and the *Songs and Sonets.*" *QJS* 68 (1982), 37–46.

Peachy, Frederic. "Pound's 'Cantos': A Greek Approach." *WJSC* 20 (1956), 210–217.

Quintana, Ricardo. "The Deserted Village: Its Logical and Rhetorical Elements." *College English* 16 (1964), 204–214.

Sackton, Alexander H. "Architectonic Structure in *Paradise Regained.*" *Texas Studies in English* 33 (1954), 33–45.

Salper, Donald R. "The 'Sounding' of a Poem." *QJS* 57 (1971), 129–133.

Sedano, Michael Victor. "Chicanismo: A Rhetorical Analysis of Themes and Images of Selected Poetry from the Chicano Movement." *WJSC* 44 (1980), 190–201.

Shaw, W. David. "*In Memoriam* and the Rhetoric of Confession." *English Literary History* 38 (1971), 80–103.

Sklute, Larry M. "Phoebus Descending: Rhetoric and Moral Vision in Henryson's *Testament of Cresseid.*" *English Literary History* 44 (1977), 189–204.

Sloan, Thomas O. "Argument and Character in Wyatt's 'They Fle From Me.' " *WJSC* 28 (1964), 145–153.

Sloan, Thomas O. "On Prohibition and Repeal." *QJS* 62 (1976), 387–388.

Sloan, Thomas O. "The Persona As Rhetor: An Interpretation of Donne's *Satyre III.*" *QJS* 51 (1965), 14–27.

Sloan, Thomas O. "The Rhetoric in the Poetry of John Donne." *Studies in English Literature, 1500–1900* 3 (1963), 31–44.

Sloan, Thomas O. "A Rhetorical Analysis of John Donne's *The Prohibition.*" *QJS* 48 (1962), 38–45.

Smith, Charles Daniel. "Speechmaking in the Iliad and Odyssey." *CSSJ* 4 (1953), pp. 6–11.

Smith, George William, Jr. "Iterative Rhetoric in *Paradise Lost.*" *Modern Philology* 74 (1976), 1–19.

Spears, Monroe K. "The Meaning of Matthew Prior's *Alma.*" *English Literary History* 13 (1946), 266–290.

Sturdivant, Pina S. "Ode to a Nightingale: Analysis for Oral Performance." *SSCJ* 43 (1977), 162–168.

Teager, Florence E. "Chaucer's Eagle and the Rhetorical Colors." *PMLA* 47 (1932), 410–418.

Williams, Kathleen. "Vision and Rhetoric: The Poet's Voice in *The Faerie Queen.*" *English Literary History* 36 (1969), 131–144.

Wilson, Gayle E. "Genre and Rhetoric in Dryden's 'Upon the Death of Lord Hastings.' " *SSCJ* 35 (1970), 256–266.

Wilson, William S. "The Eagle's Speech in Chaucer's *House of Fame.*" *QJS* 50 (1964), 153–158.

Wimsatt, W. K., Jr. "Rhetoric and Poems: The Example of Pope." In *English Institute Essays, 1948.* Edited by D. A. Robertson, Jr. New York, 1949.

Winterowd, W. Ross. "Richard M. Weaver: Modern Poetry and the Limits of Conservative Criticism." *WJSC* 37 (1973), 129–138.

Wyler, Siegfried. "Marlowe's Technique of Communicating with an Audience as Seen in His Tamburlaine, Part I." *English Studies* 48 (1967), 306–316.

Wright, Keith. "Rhetorical Repetition in T. S. Eliot's Early Verse." *Review of English Studies* 6 (1965), 93–100.

Biography and Autobiography

Books

Olney, James, ed. *Autobiography: Essays Theoretical and Critical.* Princeton: Princeton University Press, 1980.

Pascal, Roy. *Design and Truth in Autobiography.* Cambridge, Massachusetts: Harvard University Press, 1960.

Spacks, Patricia M. *Imagining a Self: Autobiography and Novel in Eighteenth-Century England.* Cambridge, Massachusetts: Harvard University Press, 1976.

Articles

Alkon, Paul K. "Visual Rhetoric in *The Autobiography of Alice B. Toklas.*" *CI* 1 (1975), 849–882.

Bell, Robert. "Metamorphoses of Spiritual Autobiography." *English Literary History* 44 (1977), 108–126.

Benson, Thomas W. "Rhetoric and Autobiography: The Case of Malcolm X." *QJS* 60 (1974), 1–13.

Cusella, Louis P. "Biography as Rhetorical Artifact: The Affirmation of Fiorello H. LaGuardia." *QJS* 69 (1983), 302–316.

DeEulis, Marilyn Davis. "Mark Twain's Experiments in Autobiography." *American Literature* 53 (1981), 202–213.

Eakin, Paul John. "Malcolm X and the Limits of Autobiography." *Criticism* 18 (1976), 230–242.

Griffith, John. "The Rhetoric of Franklin's *Autobiography.*" *Criticism* 13 (1971), 77–94.

Johnston, Dillon. "The Recreation of Self in Wells's 'Experiment in Autobiography.'" *Criticism* 14 (1972), 345–360.

Krupat, Arnold. "The Indian Autobiography: Origins, Type, and Function." *American Literature* 53 (1981), 22–42.

Mandel, Barrett John. "The Autobiographer's Art." *Journal of Aesthetics and Art Criticism* 27 (1968), 215–226.

Mandel, Barrett John. "Bunyan and the Autobiographer's Artistic Purpose." *Criticism* 10 (1968), 225–243.

Rendall, Steven. "The Rhetoric of Montaigne's Self-Portrait: Speaker and Subject." *Studies in Philology* 73 (1976), 285–301.

Schwalm, David E. "The *Life of Johnson:* Boswell's Rhetoric and Reputation." *Texas Studies in Literature and Language* 18 (1976), 240-289.

Other Literature

Books

Fussell, Paul. *The Great War and Modern Memory.* New York: Oxford University Press, 1975.

Langer, Lawrence L. *The Holocaust and the Literary Imagination.* New Haven: Yale University Press, 1975.

Articles

Betz, Brian R. "Erich Fromm and the Rhetoric of Prophecy." *CSSJ* 26 (1975), 310–315.

Boyd, John Douglas. "T. S. Eliot as Critic and Rhetorician: The Essay on Jonson." *Criticism* 11 (1969), 167–182.

Brown, William R. "Will Rogers: Ironist as Persuader." *CM* 39 (1972), 183–192.

Bryant, Donald C. "Burke's *Present Discontents:* The Rhetorical Genesis of a Party Testament." *QJS* 42 (1956), 115–126.

Buell, Lawrence J. "Reading Emerson for the Structures: The Coherence of the Essays." *QJS* 58 (1972), 58–69.

Burdick, Norman R. "The 'Coatesville Address': Crossroads of Rhetoric and Poetry." *WJSC* 42 (1978), 73–82.

Campbell, John Angus. "Charles Darwin and the Crisis of Ecology: A Rhetorical Perspective." *QJS* 60 (1974), 442–449.

Campbell, John Angus. "Darwin and *The Origin of Species:* The Rhetorical Ancestry of an Idea." *CM* 37 (1970), 1–14.

Campbell, John Angus. "The Polemical Mr. Darwin." *QJS* 61 (1975), 375–390.

Carpenter, Ronald H. "Alfred Thayer Mahan's Style on Sea Power: A Paramessage Conducing to *Ethos.*" *CM* 42 (1975), 190–202.

Carpenter, Ronald H. "The Rhetorical Genesis of Style in the 'Frontier Hypothesis' of Frederick Jackson Turner." *SSCJ* 37 (1972), 233–248.

Carson, Herbert L. "An Eccentric Kinship: Henry David Thoreau's 'A Plea for Captain John Brown,' " *SSCJ* 27 (1961), 151–156.

Clark, Tom. "A Note on Tom Paine's 'Vulgar' Style." *CQ* 26 (Summer, 1978), pp. 31–34.

Clark, Thomas. "Rhetorical Image-Making: A Case Study of the Thomas Paine-William Smith Propaganda Debates." *SSCJ* 40 (1974), 248–261.

Cone, Carl B. "Major Factors in the Rhetoric of Historians." *QJS* 33 (1947), 437–450.

Davisson, Ora B. De Vilbis. "The Early Pamphlets of Alexander Hamilton." *QJS* 28 (1942), 168–173.

Dodds, Walter E. "The Rhetorical Style of the Collects in the Book of Common Prayer." *QJS* 28 (1942), 407–414.

England, A. B. "Private and Public Rhetoric in the *Journal to Stella.*" *Essays in Criticism* 22:1 (1972), 131–141.

Funk, Alfred A. "Henry David Thoreau's 'Slavery in Massachusetts,'" *WJSC* 36 (1972), 159–168.

Gill, John M. "Newman's Dialectic in *The Idea of a University.*" *QJS* 45 (1959), 415–418.

Gronbeck, Bruce E. "Rhetorical Invention in the Regency Crisis Pamphlets." *QJS* 58 (1972), 418–430.

Grossman, Manuel L. "The Language of Dada." *JOC* 18 (1968), 4–10.

Grossman, Manuel L. "Propaganda Techniques in Selected Essays of George Bernard Shaw." *SSCJ* 32 (1967), 225–236.

Hunt, Everett L. "Matthew Arnold: The Critic as Rhetorician." *QJS* 20 (1934), 483–507.

Hynes, Sandra Sarkela. "Dramatic Propaganda: Mercy Otis Warren's 'The Defeat,' " *CQ* 23 (Fall, 1975), pp. 21–27.

Jamieson, Kathleen. "Interpretation of Natural Law in the Conflict over *Humanae Vitae.*" *QJS* 60 (1974), 201–211.

Johnstone, Christopher L. "Thoreau and Civil Disobedience: A Rhetorical Paradox." *QJS* 60 (1974), 313–322.

Kolodny, Annette. "Turning the Lens on 'The Panther Captivity': A Feminist Exercise in Practical Criticism." *CI* 8 (1981), 329–345.

Koper, Peter T. "Samuel Johnson's Rhetorical Stance in *The Rambler.*" *Style* 12 (1978), 23–34.

Mader, Thomas F. "Agitation over Aggiornamento: William F. Buckley vs. John XXIII." *CQ* 17 (November, 1979), 4–15.

Makay, John J. "John Milton's Rhetoric." *CSSJ* 22 (1971), 186–195.

Manierre, William Reid. "Verbal Patterns in Cotton Mather's *Magnalia.*" *QJS* 47 (1961), 402–413.

McCoard, William B. "Report on the Reading of Hiroshima." *QJS* 34 (1948), 174–176.

McCracken, David. "The Development of Edmund Burke's *Reflections.*" *WJSC* 40 (1976), 157–167.

McGuire, Michael. "Mythic Rhetoric in *Mein Kampf:* A Structuralist Critique." *QJS* 63 (1977), 1–13.

McGuire, Michael D. "Rhetoric, Philosophy and the *Volk:* Johann Gottlieb Fichte's *Addresses to the German Nation.*" *QJS* 62 (1976), 135–144.

Mohrmann, G. P., and A. W. Staub. "Rhetoric and Poetic: A New Critique Applied." *SSCJ* 30 (1964), 36–45.

Moldenhauer, Joseph J. "The Rhetorical Function of Proverbs in *Walden.*" *Journal of American Folklore* 80 (1967), 151–159.

Morrisroe, Michael, Jr. "Hume's Rhetorical Strategy: A Solution to the Riddle of the *Dialogue's Concerning Natural Religion.*" *Texas Studies in Literature and Language* 11 (1969), 963–974.

Mowe, Gregory, and W. Scott Nobles. "James Baldwin's Message for White America." *QJS* 58 (1972), 142–151.

Nelson, Cary. "Soliciting Self-Knowledge: The Rhetoric of Susan Sontag's Criticism." *CI* 6 (1980), 707–726.

Parrella, Gilda. "The 'I' of the Beholder: A Rationale for Physicalization in Performance of Narratives." *CSSJ* 25 (1974), 296–302.

Rewa, Michael. "Aspects of Rhetoric in Johnson's 'Professedly Serious' *Rambler* Essays." *QJS* 56 (1970), 75–84.

Schweik, Robert C. "Rhetorical Art and Literary Form in Mill's *The Subjection of Women.*" *QJS* 61 (1975), 23–30.

Simrell, V. E. "H. L. Mencken the Rhetorician." *QJS* 13 (1927), 399–412.

Speer, Diane Parkin. "Milton's *Defensio Prima: Ethos* and Vituperation in a Polemic Engagement." *QJS* 56 (1970), 277–283.

Speer, Richard. "The Rhetoric of Burke's Select Committee Reports." *QJS* 57 (1971), 306–315.

Stuart, Charlotte L. "The Constitution as 'Summational Anecdote,' " *CSSJ* 25 (1974), 111–118.

Stuart, Charlotte L. "Mary Wollstonecraft's *A Vindication of the Rights of Men:* A Rhetorical Reassessment." *WJSC* 42 (1978), 83–92.

Volpe, Michael. "Socrates' Rhetorical Dilemma in the Apology." *WJSC* 42 (1978), 124–133.

Zacharias, Donald W. "Tom Paine: Eloquent Defender of Louis XVI." *CSSJ* 13 (1962), 183–188.

Letters

Books

Doty, William G. *Letters in Primitive Christianity.* Philadelphia: Fortress Press, 1973.
Rigaux, Beda. *Letters of St. Paul: Modern Studies.* Chicago: Franciscan Herald, 1968.

Articles

Betz, Hans Dieter. "The Literary Composition and Function of Paul's Letter to the Galatians." *New Testament Studies* 21 (1975), 353–379.
Bosmajian, Haig A. "Rhetoric of Martin Luther King's Letter from Birmingham Jail." *Midwest Quarterly* 8 (January 1967), 127–143.
Campbell, A. P. "*Ars dictaminis:* Order, Beauty, and Our Daily Bread." *Humanities Association Bulletin* (Canada) 22 (1971), 13–21.
Church, F. Forrester. "Rhetorical Structure and Design in Paul's Letter to Philemon." *Harvard Theological Review* 71 (1978), 17–33.
Faulhaber, Charles B. "The Letter-Writer's Rhetoric: The Summa dictaminis of Guido Faba." In *Medieval Eloquence: Studies in the Theory and Practice of Medieval Rhetoric.* Edited by James J. Murphy. Berkeley: University of California Press, 1978.
Fernandes, James J. "The Public Letters of Cicero." *CQ* 26 (Winter 1978), pp. 21–26.
Fulkerson, Richard P. "The Public Letter as a Rhetorical Form: Structure, Logic, and Style in King's 'Letter from Birmingham Jail.' " *QJS* 65 (1979), 121–136.
Griffin, Leland M., and Reisler, Marsha. "Persuasion through Antithesis: An Analysis of the Dominant Rhetorical Structure of Pascal's *Lettres provinciales.*" *Romanic Review* 69 (1978), 172–185.
Griffin, Leland M. "Letter to the Press: 1778." *QJS* 33 (1947), 148–150.
Hill, Sidney R., Jr. "Dictamen: That Bastard of Literature and Law." *CSSJ* 24 (1973), 117–124.
Kane, Peter E. "*Dictamen:* The Medieval Rhetoric of Letter-Writing." *CSSJ* 21 (1970), 224–230.
Marambaud, Pierre. "Dickinson's *Letters from a Farmer in Pennsylvania* as Political Discourse: Ideology, Imagery, and Rhetoric." *Early American Literature* 12 (1977), 63–72.
Murphy, James J. "Alberic of Monte Cassiono: Father of the Medieval *Ars dictaminis.*" *American Benedictine Review* 22 (1971), 129–146.
Roberts, Donald F., Linda A. Sikorsky, and William J. Paisley, "Letters in Mass Magazines as 'Outcroppings' of Public Concern." *Journalism Quarterly* 46 (1969), 743–752.
Rollins, Peter C. "The Context and the Rhetorical Strategy of Will Rogers' *Letters from a Self-Made Diplomat to His President (1926).*" *Journal of American Culture* 3 (1980), 70–79.
Whigham, Frank. "The Rhetoric of Elizabethan Suitors' Letters." *PMLA* 96 (1981), 864–882.

Magazines, Newspapers, and Other Journalism

Books

Breed, Warren. *The Newspaper, News, and Society.* New York: Arno Press, 1980.
Boyce, George, James Curran, and Pauline Wingate, eds. *Newspaper History: From the 17th Century to the Present Day.* Beverly Hills: Sage, 1978.

Brown, Lee. *The Reluctant Reformation: On Criticizing the Press in America.* New York: David McKay, 1974.

Chibnall, Steve. *Law-and-Order News: An Analysis of Crime Reporting in the British Press.* London: Tavistock, 1977.

Cohen, Stanley, and Jock Young, eds. *The Manufacture of News: A Reader.* Beverly Hills: Sage, 1973.

Epstein, Edward Jay. *Between Fact and Fiction: The Problem of Journalism.* New York: Vintage Books, 1975.

Hulteng, John L. *The Messenger's Motives . . . .: Ethical Problems of the Mass Media.* Englewood Cliffs: Prentice-Hall, 1976.

Klaits, Joseph. *Printed Propaganda under Louis XIV.* Princeton: Princeton University Press, 1977.

Knightley, Phillip. *The First Casualty.* New York: Harcourt, Brace, Jovanovich, 1975.

LeRoy, David J., and Christopher H. Sterling, eds. *Mass News: Practices, Controversies, and Alternatives.* Englewood Cliffs: Prentice-Hall, 1978.

Liebling, A. J. *The Press.* 2nd ed. New York: Ballantine, 1975.

McLuhan, Marshall. *The Mechanical Bride: Folklore of Industrial Man.* Boston: Beacon, 1967.

Merrill, John C. *Existential Journalism.* New York: Hastings House, 1977.

Merrill, John C., and Ralph D. Barney, eds. *Ethics and the Press: Readings in Mass Media Morality.* New York: Hastings House, 1975.

Rivers, William L. *The Opinionmakers.* Boston: Beacon Press, 1965.

Rivers, William L. *The Other Government: Power and the Washington Media.* New York: Universe Books, 1982.

Schiller, Dan. *Objectivity and the News: The Public and the Rise of Commercial Journalism.* Philadelphia: University of Pennsylvania Press, 1981.

Schudson, Michael. *Discovering the News: A Social History of American Newspapers.* New York: Basic Books, 1978.

Shaw, Donald L., and Maxwell E. McCombs. *The Emergence of American Political Issues: The Agenda-Setting Function of the Press.* St. Paul: West Publishers, 1977.

Smith, Anthony, ed. *Newspapers and Democracy: International Essays on a Changing Medium.* Cambridge: MIT Press, 1980.

Smith, Culver H. *The Press, Politics, and Patronage.* Athens: The University of Georgia Press, 1977.

Taft, William H. *American Magazines for the 1980s.* New York: Hastings House, 1982.

Thayer, Lee, ed. *Ethics, Morality, and the Media: Reflections on American Culture.* New York: Hastings House, 1980.

Tuchman, Gaye. *Making News: A Study in the Construction of Reality.* New York: Free Press, 1978.

Articles

Anderson, Ray Lynn. "Rhetoric and Science Journalism." *QJS* 56 (1970), 358–368.

Anderson, Ray Lynn. "The Rhetoric of the *Report from Iron Mountain.*" *CM* 37 (1970), 219–231.

Berg, Meredith W., and David M. Berg. "The Rhetoric of War Preparation: The New York Press in 1898." *Journalism Quarterly* 45 (1968), 653–660.

Berkman, Dave. "Advertising in *Ebony* and *Life:* Negro Aspirations vs. Reality." *Journalism Quarterly* 40 (1963), 53–64.

Brown, William R., and Richard E. Crable. "Industry, Mass Magazines, and the Ecology Issue." *QJS* 59 (1973), 259–272.

Casalis, Matthieu. "The Discourse of *Penthouse:* Rhetoric and Ideology." *Semiotica* 15 (1975), 355–391.

Chambers, Stephen, and G. P. Mohrmann. "Rhetoric in Some American Periodicals, 1815–1850." *CM* 37 (1970), 111–120.

Clarke, Peter, and Virginia Esposito. "A Study of Occupational Advice for Women in Magazines." *Journalism Quarterly* 43 (1966), 477–485.

Cook, Richard I. "The 'Several Ways . . . of Abusing One Another': Jonathan Swift's Political Journalism." *CM* 29 (1962), 260–273.

Corder, Jim W. "Ethical Argument and *Rambler* No. 154." *QJS* 54 (1968), 352–356.

Dasback, Anita Mallinckrodt. "U.S.-Soviet Magazine Propaganda: *America Illustrated* and *USSR.*" *Journalism Quarterly* 43 (1966), 73–84.

Elzey, Wayne. "The Most Unforgettable Magazine I've Ever Read: Religion and Social Hygiene in *The Reader's Digest.*" *JPC* 10 (1976), 181–190.

Gieber, Walter. "The 'Lovelorn' Columnist and Her Social Role." *Journalism Quarterly* 37 (1960), 499–514.

Hart, Roderick P., Kathleen J. Turner, and Ralph E. Knupp. "A Rhetorical Profile of Religious News: *Time,* 1947–1976." *JOC* 31 (1981), 58–68.

Hirsch, Paul M. "An Analysis of *Ebony:* The Magazine and Its Readers." *Journalism Quarterly* 45 (1968), 261–270.

Honey, Maureen. "Images of Women in *The Saturday Evening Post* 1931–1936." *JPC* 10 (1976), 352–358.

Kallan, Richard A. "Style and the New Journalism: A Rhetorical Analysis of Tom Wolfe." *CM* 46 (1979), 52–62.

Kallan, Richard A., and Robert D. Brooks. "The Playmate of the Month: Naked But Nice." *JPC* 8 (1974), 328–336.

Kidd, Virginia. "Happily Ever After and Other Relationship Styles: Advice on Interpersonal Relations in Popular Magazines, 1951–1973." *QJS* 61 (1975), 31–39.

Nelson, Paul E. "Norman Cousins: Editor as Persuader." *Journalism Quarterly* 48 (1971), 695–699.

Newman, Robert P. "The Weekly Fiction Magazines." *CSSJ* 17 (1966), 118–124.

Pence, James W., Jr. "Invention Gone Awry: The London 'Times' and Civil Service Reform in 1854." *WJSC* 33 (1969), 199–204.

Rosi, Eugene J. "How 50 Periodicals and the *Times* Interpreted the Test Ban Controversy." *Journalism Quarterly* 41 (1964), 545–556.

Sonenschein, David. "Love and Sex in the Romance Magazines." *JPC* 4 (1970), 398–409.

Sproule, J. Michael. "Newspapers as Political Persuaders: The Campaign against James G. Blaine." *CSSJ* 24 (1973), 310–318.

Wilson, Charles R. "Racial Reservations: Indians and Blacks in American Magazines, 1865–1900." *JPC* 10 (1976), 70–79.

The Rhetoric of Political Action

Articles

Andrews, James R. "Confrontation at Columbia: A Case Study." *QJS* 55 (1969), 9–16.

Benson, Thomas W. "Violence: Communication Breakdown?" *CQ* 18 (Winter 1970), pp. 39–47.

Benson, Thomas W., and Bonnie Johnson. "The Rhetoric of Resistance: Confrontation with the Warmakers, Washington, D.C., October, 1967" *CQ* 16 (September, 1968), pp. 35–42.

Bosmajian, Haig A. "The Persuasiveness of Nazi Marching and Der Kampf um Die Strasse." *CQ.* 16 (November, 1968), 17–22.

Burgess, Parke G. "Crisis Rhetoric: Coercion vs. Force." *QJS* 59 (1973), 61–73.

Butler, Sherry Devereaux. "Maryknollers in Guatemala: A Case Study of Violence as the Last Communication Plateau." *CQ* 19 (Fall, 1971), 51–57.

Bytwerk, Randall L. "Rhetorical Aspects of the Nazi Meeting: 1926–1933." *QJS* 61 (1975), 307–318.

Cox, J. Robert. "Perspectives on Rhetorical Criticism of Movements: Antiwar Dissent, 1964–1970." *WJSC* 38 (1974), 254–268.

Doolittle, Robert J. "Riots as Symbolic: A Criticism and Approach." *CSSJ* 27 (1976), 310–317.

Haiman, Franklyn S. "Nonverbal Communication and the First Amendment: The Rhetoric of the Streets Revisited." *QJS* 68 (1982), 371–383.

Haiman, Franklyn S. "The Rhetoric of the Streets: Some Legal and Ethical Considerations." *QJS* 53 (1967), 99–114.

Merriam, Allen H. "Symbolic Action in India: Gandhi's Nonverbal Persuasion." *QJS* 61 (1965), 290–306.

Norton, Robert Wayne. "The Propaganda of Bodies." *CQ* 18 (Spring, 1970), 39–41.

Ritchie, Gladys. "The Sit-In: A Rhetoric of Human Action." *CQ* 18 (Winter, 1970), 22–25.

Ritter, Kurt W. "Confrontation as Moral Drama: The Boston Massacre in Rhetorical Perspective." *SSCJ* 42 (1977), 114–136.

Scott, Robert L., and Donald K. Smith "The Rhetoric of Confrontation." *QJS* 55 (1969), 1–8.

Sillars, Malcolm O. "The Rhetoric of the Petition in Boots." *CM* 39 (1972), 92–104.

Other Forms

Books

Barthes, Roland. *The Fashion System.* Trans. Matthew Ward and Richard Howard. New York: Hill & Wang, 1983.

Benson, Thomas W., and Kenneth D. Frandsen. *Nonverbal Communication.* 2nd ed. Palo Alto: Science Research Associates, 1982.

Benthall, Jonathan, and Ted Polhemus, eds. *The Body as a Medium of Expression.* New York: E. P. Dutton, 1975.

Bosmajian, Haig A., ed. *The Rhetoric of Nonverbal Communication.* Glenview: Scott, Foresman, 1971.

Bouissac, Paul. *Circus and Culture: A Semiotic Approach.* Bloomington: Indiana University Press, 1976.

Hall, Edward T. *The Hidden Dimension.* Garden City: Doubleday, 1966.

Hall, Edward T. *The Silent Language.* Garden City: Doubleday, 1959.

Henley, Nancy M. *Body Politics: Power, Sex, and Nonverbal Communication.* Englewood Cliffs: Prentice-Hall, 1977.

Knapp, Mark L. *Nonverbal Communication in Human Interaction.* 2nd ed. New York: Holt, Rinehart and Winston, 1978.

Leathers, Dale. *Nonverbal Communication Systems.* Boston: Allyn and Bacon, 1976.

Mehrabian, Albert. *Silent Messages* Belmont: Wadsworth, 1971.

Molloy, John T. *Dress for Success.* New York: Warner Books, 1976.

Polhemus, Ted, ed. *Social Aspects of the Human Body.* New York: Penguin Books, 1978.

Reusch, Jurgen, and Weldon Kees. *Nonverbal Communication.* Berkeley: University of California Press, 1956.

Rupp, Leila J. *Mobilizing Women for War: German and American Propaganda, 1939–1945.* Princeton: Princeton University Press, 1978.

Scheflen, Albert E. *How Behavior Means.* New York: Gordon and Breach, 1973.

Articles

Abrahams, Roger D. "Introductory Remarks to a Rhetorical Theory of Folklore." *Journal of American Folklore* 81 (1968), 143–158.

Abrahams, Roger D. "A Rhetoric of Everyday Life: Traditional Conversational Genres." *Southern Folklore Quarterly* 32 (1968), 44–59.

Ames, Kenneth L. "Material Culture as Non Verbal Communication: A Historical Case Study." *Journal of American Culture* 3 (1980), 619–641.

Barton, Stephen Nye, and John B. O'Leary, "The Rhetoric of Rural Physician Procurement Campaigns: An Application of Tavistock." *QJS* 60 (1974), 144–154.

Black, Edwin. "A Consideration of the Rhetorical Causes of Breakdown in Discussion." *CM* 22 (1955), 15–19.

Brown, William R. "Ideology as Communication Process." *QJS* 64 (1978), 123–140.

Brummett, Barry. "Gary Gilmore, Power, and the Rhetoric of Symbolic Forms." *WJSC* 43 (1979), 3–13.

Bytwerk, Randall L. "The Rhetoric of Defeat: Nazi Propaganda in 1945." *CSSJ* 29 (1978), 44–52.

Bytwerk, Randall L. "Rhetorical Aspects of Nazi Holidays." *JPC* 13 (1979), 239–247.

Campbell, Karlyn Kohrs. "The Rhetoric of Women's Liberation: An Oxymoron." *QJS* 59 (1973), 74–86.

Carpenter, Ronald H. "America's Opinion Leader Historians on Behalf of Success." *QJS* 69 (1983), 111–126.

Cawelti, John G. "Myths of Violence in American Popular Culture." *CI* 1 (1975), 521–542.

Collins, Catherine Ann. "Kissinger's Press Conferences, 1972–1974: An Exploration of Form and Role Relationship on News Management." *CSSJ* 28 (1977), 185–193.

D'Angelo, Frank J. "Sacred Cows Make Great Hamburgers: The Rhetoric of Graffiti." *College Composition and Communication* 25 (1974), 173–179.

Devlin, L. Patrick. "The McGovern Canvass: A Study in Interpersonal Political Campaign." *CSSJ* 24 (1973), 83–90.

Fisher, Jeanne Y. "A Burkean Analysis of the Rhetorical Dimensions of a Multiple Murder and Suicide." *QJS* 60 (1974), 175–189.

Gaw, Beverly A. " 'Rhetoric and Its Alternatives as Bases for Examination of Intimate Communication': A Humanist Response." *CQ* 26 (Winter, 1978), pp. 13–20.

Goodman, Richard J., and William I. Gorden, "The Rhetoric of Desecration." *QJS* 57 (1971), 23–31.

Gravlee, G. Jack, and James R. Irvine, "Watts' Dissenting Rhetoric of Prayer." *QJS* 59 (1973), 463–473.

Hay, Robert P. "The Liberty Tree: A Symbol for American Patriots." *QJS* 55 (1969), 414–424.

Henderson, Mary C. "Food as Communication in American Culture." *CQ* 18 (Summer, 1970), 3–8.

Hill, Alette. "Hitler's Flag: A Case Study." *Semiotica* 38 (1982), 127–137.

Hoffer, Thomas William. "Nguyen Van Be As Propaganda Hero of the North and South Vietnamese Governments: A Case Study of Mass Media Conflict." *SSCJ* 40 (1974), 63–80.

Illka, Richard J. "Rhetorical Dramatization in the Development of American Communism." *QJS* 63 (1977), 413–427.

Knapp, Mark L., Roderick P. Hart, Gustav W. Friedrich, and Shulman, Gary M. "The Rhetoric of Goodbye: Verbal and Nonverbal Correlates of Human Leave-Taking." *CM* 40 (1973), 182–198.

Lomas, Charles W. "The Rhetoric of Japanese War Propaganda." *QJS* 35 (1949), 30–35.

Lydenberg, Robin. "The Rhetoric of Advertising." *Michigan Quarterly Review* 17 (1978), 65–75.

McBurney, James H. "Some Contributions of Classical Dialectic and Rhetoric to a Philosophy of Discussion." *QJS* 23 (1937), 1–13.

Mechling, Elizabeth Walker. "Patricia Hearst: MYTH AMERICA 1974, 1975, 1976." *WJSC* 43 (1979), 168–179.

Medhurst, Martin J. "American Cosmology and the Rhetoric of Inaugural Prayer." *CSSJ* 28 (1977), 272–282.

Newman, Robert P. "Communication Pathologies of Intelligence Systems." *CM* 42 (1975), 271–290.

Patton, John H. "Rhetoric at Catonsville: Daniel Berrigan, Conscience, and Image Alteration." *CQ* 23 (Winter, 1975), pp. 3–12.

Philipsen, Gerry. "Navajo World View and Culture Patterns of Speech: A Case Study in Ethnorhetoric." *CM* 39 (1972), 132–139.

Philipsen, Gerry. "Speaking 'Like a Man' in Teamsterville: Culture Patterns of Role Enactment in an Urban Neighborhood." *QJS* 61 (1975), 13–22.

Phillips, Gerald M. "Rhetoric and Its Alternatives As Bases for Examination of Intimate Communication." *CQ* 24 (Winter, 1976), pp. 11–23.

Porter, Dennis. "The Perilous Quest: Baseball as Folk Drama." *CI* 4 (1977), 143–157.

Porter, Laurinda W. "The White House Transcripts: Group Fantasy Events Concerning the Mass Media." *CSSJ* 27 (1976), 272–279.

Real, Michael R. "Super Bowl: Mythic Spectacle." *JOC* 25 (1975), 31–43.

Rosenfield, Lawrence W. "Politics and Pornography," *QJS* 59 (1973), 413–422.

Scott, Robert L. "Rhetoric and Silence." *WJSC* 36 (1972), 146–158.

Sharf, Barbara F. "A Rhetorical Analysis of Leadership Emergence in Small Groups." *CM* 45 (1978), 156–172.

Starosta, William J. "Toward the Use of Traditional Entertainment Forms to Stimulate Social Change." *QJS* 60 (1974), 306–312.

Starosta, William J. "The Village Level Worker as Rhetorician: An Adaptation of Diffusion Theory." *CSSJ* 27 (1976), 144–150.

Toch, Hans. "'I Shot an Arrow in the Air . . .': The Performing Arts as Weapons of Social Change." *JOC* 21 (1971), 115–135.

Wallenstein, Martin. "The Myth of the Self-Made Man and the Decision to Cover Up: The Illusion of Control in the Language of the Watergate Tapes." *Journal of American Culture* 2 (1979), 42–50.

Wander, Philip C. "The Rhetoric of Science." *WJSC* 40 (1976), 226–235.

Weimer, Walter B. "Science as a Rhetorical Transaction: Toward a Nonjustificational Conception of Rhetoric." *PR* 10 (1977), 1–29.

List of Contributors

Richard L. Barton (Ph.D. Oregon) is Associate Professor of Telecommunications at The Pennsylvania State University.

John G. Bayer (Ph.D. St. Louis University) is Professor of English at St. Louis Community College, Meramec.

Thomas W. Benson (Ph.D. Cornell) is Professor of Speech Communication at The Pennsylvania State University.

Lawrance M. Bernabo (M.A. New Mexico) is a doctoral candidate at the University of Iowa and a Teaching Associate in Speech Communication at the University of Illinois, Urbana.

F. Forrester Church (Ph.D. Harvard) is Senior Minister of the Unitarian Church of All Souls in New York City.

Michael A. DeSousa (M.A. Iowa) is a doctoral candidate in Speech Communication at the University of Iowa.

Thomas S. Frentz (Ph.D. Wisconsin) is Associate Professor of Speech Communication at the University of Arkansas.

Richard P. Fulkerson (Ph.D. Ohio State) is Professor of English at East Texas State University.

Richard B. Gregg (Ph.D. Pittsburgh) is Professor of Speech Communication at The Pennsylvania State University.

Bruce E. Gronbeck (Ph.D. Iowa) is Professor of Communication and Theatre Arts at the University of Iowa.

Roderick P. Hart (Ph.D. Penn State) is F. A. Liddell Professor of Communication at the University of Texas, Austin.

Alette Hill (Ph.D. University of North Carolina) is Associate Professor of Women's Studies at Metropolitan State College in Denver, Colorado.

Richard A. Hudson (M.A. New Mexico) is Assistant Professor of Speech Communication at the University of Wisconsin, Eau Claire.

Virginia Kidd (Ph.D. Minnesota) is Professor of Communication Studies at California State University, Sacramento.

Ralph E. Knupp (Ph.D. Purdue) is Vice President of Administration and Corporate Services at Chilton Company, a subsidiary of American Broadcasting Company, Inc.

J. Fred MacDonald (Ph.D. UCLA) is Professor of History at Northeastern Illinois University in Chicago.

Michael McGuire (Ph.D. Iowa) is Associate Professor of Speech Communication at the University of Georgia.

Elizabeth Walker Mechling (Ph.D. Temple) is Associate Professor and Chair of Marketing at California State University, Hayward.

Jay Mechling (Ph.D. University of Pennsylvania) is Professor and Director of American Studies at the University of California, Davis.

Martin J. Medhurst (Ph.D. Penn State) is Associate Professor of Rhetoric at the University of California, Davis.

Gary Saul Morson (Ph.D. Yale) is Associate Professor of Russian Literature and Chairman of Slavic Languages at the University of Pennsylvania.

Janice Hocker Rushing (Ph.D. University of Southern California) is Assistant Professor of Speech Communication at the University of Arkansas.

Robert L. Schrag (Ph.D. Wayne State) is Assistant Professor of Speech Communication at North Carolina State University.

Robert L. Scott (Ph.D. Illinois) is Professor of Speech Communication at the University of Minnesota.

Donald K. Smith (Ph.D. Wisconsin) is Professor Emeritus of Communication Arts at the University of Wisconsin, Madison.

Jill Taft-Kaufman (Ph.D. University of California, Berkeley) is Associate Professor of Speech Communication and Dramatic Arts at Central Michigan University.

Kathleen J. Turner (Ph.D. Purdue) is Associate Professor of Communication at Tulane University.